THE
STAGECRAFT
AESCHYLUS

THE STAGECRAFT OF AESCHYLUS

*The Dramatic Use of
Exits and Entrances in
Greek Tragedy*

BY

OLIVER TAPLIN

CLARENDON PRESS · OXFORD

Oxford University Press, Walton Street, Oxford OX2 6DP

Oxford New York Toronto
Delhi Bombay Calcutta Madras Karachi
Petaling Jaya Singapore Hong Kong Tokyo
Nairobi Dar es Salaam Cape Town
Melbourne Auckland
and associated companies in
Berlin Ibadan

Oxford is a trade mark of Oxford University Press

Published in the United States
by Oxford University Press, New York

First published 1977
First issued as a Clarendon Paperback (with corrections) 1989

British Library Cataloguing in Publication Data
Taplin, Oliver
The stagecraft of Aeschylus
1. Aeschylus—Criticism and interpretation
I. Title
882'.01   PA3829
ISBN 0-19-814486 5 (Pbk.)

Library of Congress Cataloging in Publication data
Data available

Printed in Great Britain by
Biddles Ltd, Guildford & King's Lynn

PREFACE

THIS volume is derived from an even more obese doctoral dissertation which occupied me from 1967 to 1973. I must apologize for the vestigial vices of that genre. The bibliographical references have pretensions to thoroughness, deluded of course, up until 1973; but any later references have been insinuated at random.

Along the way I have incurred many debts, and I welcome this opportunity to acknowledge them. I was an undergraduate and graduate student at Corpus Christi College, Oxford, where I was given every encouragement; then a Fellowship by Examination at Magdalen College supplied the ideal opportunity to put my shoulder to a task of this kind. In 1970–1 I spent an invaluable year as a Junior Fellow of the Center for Hellenic Studies in Washington D.C. I should also mention the indispensable aid I have had from the staffs of the Ashmolean Library and of the Oxford University Press.

Among personal debts I must put first Eduard Fraenkel. He inspired me at a decisive stage, and showed me that a deep feeling for literature and a humility before great art can be combined with scholarship and honesty. My highest hope for this book is that he would have approved of it. John Gould was a great help in my first years of research, and I suspect I owe him many fundamental ideas and methods. Hugh Lloyd-Jones has been an unfailing source of aid and encouragement. He sets a bracing ideal of vigour and rigour, and I have come to appreciate more and more his warm belief in the value of Greek culture. My examiners, Sir Kenneth Dover and T. C. W. Stinton, made many useful suggestions. I find it hard to do justice to my debt to Colin Macleod, who has stimulated and restrained my ideas at every level from my basic assumptions about humankind to the minutiae of my manuscript.

I am delighted also to name some of the friends and colleagues who have patiently suffered talking shop with me and have contributed in innumerable ways to the finished product. This selection is inevitably somewhat arbitrary: David Bain, Peter Brown, Richard Carden, Colin Hardie, Nick Fisher, Emrys Jones, Bernard Knox, Piero Pucci, Richard Tarrant, Christian Wolff. Simon Squires has been a great help with the proofs. My thanks to these and many others.

My wife, Kim, has been a true companion and collaborator as well as the focus of my home. In return for the voluntary gift of years of her freedom devoted to my benefit this fat book is thin recompense.

OLIVER TAPLIN
Old Whitehill
28 April 1977

CONTENTS

REFERENCES AND ABBREVIATIONS

BOOKS and articles which are only cited once or twice are given a bibliographical reference. Those which are quoted more often are normally cited only by the author's name, with an abbreviated title where appropriate (thus Andrieu, Wilamowitz *Kl Schr* etc.). The key and the full reference will be found in the Bibliography. I have not listed there the standard reference works, which are cited by abbreviation only (*LSJ, RE, ARV*² etc.).

Editions, commentaries, and translations of Aeschylus are quoted by the author's name only (with the addition of *ed, tr* etc. in ambiguous cases); and these are also listed in the Bibliography. I have not, however, listed the commentaries etc. cited on authors other than Aeschylus. In these cases I have abbreviated the reference by means of the scholar's name followed by the work and a page reference; as e.g. Barrett E. *Hipp ed* p. x, Handley Men. *Dysc ed* p. x etc. I hope that these will be self-explanatory. I also use the standard abbreviations for editions of fragments etc. (e.g. P[earson], K[ock]).

Internal cross-references are by simple page number, except when a whole section is referred to. Chapter I is subdivided by sections; thus, see §5 etc. The other chapters are divided by play-title and line number with subdivision by letters, and a cross-reference is marked with an asterisk: thus, cf. *Pers* 155b*, *Ag* 1372a*, etc.

In the spelling of Greek names, having decided on Aeschylus rather than Aiskhulos, I have pusillanimously latinized most others. I have, however, transliterated the titles of most plays.

I. INTRODUCTION

§1. Aims and Scope

'For Greek tragedy there exists also something like a grammar of dramatic technique.' (Ed. Fraenkel)

'No one can write an adequate commentary on a Greek play, or even edit it adequately, without producing it in his mind.' (K. J. Dover)

'... a meaning which can be *seen*' (N. Coghill, on Shakespeare)

THESE three quotations sum up the triple purpose of this book. It is at one and the same time a reference book, a commentary on certain aspects of Aeschylus' composition, and an attempt at literary criticism.

First, it is a contribution towards a 'grammar' of the dramatic technique of the Greek tragedians. It is a compilation and classification of their standard practice in matters related to the handling of exits and entrances; and in establishing the conventions it naturally gives emphasis to the variations and exceptions. By using the indexes the reader may hope to find the relevant 'facts' on any particular passage or technique (though inevitably there must be much I have missed). While I should not like to push the 'grammar' analogy too hard—the dramatists are constantly creating their usage, and a departure from the norm is not thereby 'ungrammatical'—this work does also resemble a grammar-book in that its ultimate aim is to elucidate the medium it analyses: in this case the meaning of a tragedy.

Secondly the book takes the form of a novel kind of scene-by-scene commentary on Aeschylus' surviving tragedies from the aspects of dramatic and theatrical technique. Each chapter may, therefore, be read in conjunction with the play in question. I try to apply to each entrance and exit in its context the questions 'Who? When? How? Whither and whence?' As well as fixing the coming and going of the characters, this obviously raises, and I hope elucidates, important problems of formal structure, plot construction, staging, authenticity, and text.

Lastly, and to my mind most importantly, I hope to do something towards showing what Aeschylus is about, how it is that he is a great artist, why he deserves our attention. By relating his stage action to the meaning of the play, and thus bringing out his visual meaning, I attempt to show how the precise handling of the action may throw light on the playwright's larger dramatic purposes. The stage actions are part of the dramatist's creation, and a thorough consideration of the particular way he handled their timing, manner, and context may both clarify well-known issues, and also light up new aspects and purposes in his work. I hope my material and approach may also provoke others to advance the critical interpretation of Greek tragedy.

Given its wide terms of reference this book is inevitably something of a miscellany. There are, however, some persistent underlying preoccupations. I set out primarily to explore the relation in Greek tragedy between the play on paper and the action on stage, and between the stage action and the drama as a whole. Two main theses emerge from these explorations. First, the stage action, which the playwright devised and presented as part of his creation, is to some extent recoverable. Many important features of the artist's original realization of his play in the theatre, far from being only a matter for the whim or intuition of editor, translator, or producer, can be elicited with more or less confidence from close consideration of the text and from the comparative study of recurrent or conventional dramatic methods. Secondly the scenic presentation (*mise-en-scène, Inszenierung*) is not an inessential external feature or a gross and incidental encumbrance: it is part and parcel of the playwright's handiwork, and is an inextricable element of his communication and hence of his meaning. If we wish to understand and appreciate the work of art it would not do to consider the scenic presentation without the sense and poetry of the words: conversely the full meaning of the words cannot be divorced from their enactment. The texts are all we have to work from, apart from some disparate and often perilous secondary evidence; but my claim is that all, or at least most, stage actions of significance can be worked out from what we have.

I have made no attempt to isolate and assess all kinds of stage action, but have concentrated on entrances and exits. Every character has necessarily to come into and to leave the visible sphere of the play. 'Reduced to its barest minimum what the actors do is to go into and out of the acting space ("They have their exits and their entrances"): so much in the way of "action" we can expect from the least spectacular and most static of plays.'[1] In the huge Greek theatre these were large and lengthy stage movements. Since this was a relatively static kind of drama and since exits and entrances tend to come at particularly stressed junctures—the beginnings and ends of acts, the rearrangement of the few participant characters—the dramatist often took the opportunity to create a conspicuous and significant stage event. Entrances and exits provide, no doubt, the most frequent and most complex material in the two areas I have indicated, the relation of text to action and of action to dramatic meaning; none the less the approaches and methods used here could be applied to any other kind of significant stage action.

Nor have I attempted to discuss all entrances and exits in the entire corpus of surviving tragedy, but have centred my observations on Aeschylus. The alternative would have been to cover all three tragedians in much less depth and detail. I choose Aeschylus partly because he is the earliest, partly because he has, perhaps, been comparatively neglected in the aspects under consideration, but, above all, because he is the tragedian I personally find most powerful and absorbing—not that I love the others less, but that I love him more. The *Oresteia*, to my mind the greatest creation of the Greek theatre, responds most rewardingly to this kind of approach. But I have drawn widely and often on Sophocles and Euripides for comparative material; and they are not, so far as I can see, essentially different in the respects under scrutiny. A similar kind of study could well be extended to their plays. It may be that the particularly effective use of stage action was one of the qualities which already by the time of Aristophanes' *Frogs* marked Aeschylus, Sophocles, and Euripides as the great three tragedians.

It should be evident that for my purposes each stage action must be taken in its unique dramatic context. In order to consider why the dramatist has managed any exit or entrance in the way that he has and to ask what he means by it the movement

[1] Emrys Jones *Scenic Form in Shakespeare* (Oxford 1971) 5.

must be observed in its particular place within the play. Context
is all-important. That is why the main bulk of this work is taken
up with a kind of commentary on the exits and entrances in the
plays. Each is registered in order, and the ensuing discussion
follows no fixed pattern, but pursues the issues raised by that
particular stage direction. (A few warrant no comment, and
some places are discussed where it is significant that there is *no*
exit or entry.)

Of course I discuss the staging of Greek tragedy, but that is,
for me, ancillary to literary criticism. Much valuable work has
been done on the layout of the Greek theatre, its stage machinery,
costumes, and other related *Realien*;[1] but theatre history has
almost invariably been regarded as a subject to itself, and hardly
any connection has been made with the actual interpretation of
the plays. Absorbing though these studies are, they can be of
little more than purely antiquarian interest unless they are
brought to bear on the understanding of the tragedies themselves.
Theatre history has concerned itself with what happened and
what was seen in the 'real' world of the Theatre of Dionysus,
the actors, and the μηχανοποιός: dramatic criticism, however,
considers what happens in the created world of the play in performance, and what is 'seen' by the sensibility of a captivated
audience. Theatre historians have worked on the tangible objects
which are shared by all the plays and which continued to exist
outside the plays: I shall try to observe the theatre as it is used
in each unique stage event with its own particular artistic significance. Sometimes indeed I have pursued a problem of staging
for its own sake; but usually my observations, however preliminary, are meant to point the way to a deeper appreciation of the
play as a work of art. Any clarification of theatrical or dramatic
technique—or even the pertinent formulation of a question—
may help, given a critical framework, toward constructive interpretation.

I cannot attempt to sort out in this introduction the many ways
in which entrances and exits can be put to dramatic use: that
must be left to the main commentaries. Indeed it is one of my
prime theses that stage action can only be effectively interpreted

[1] One thinks of the books of, among others, A. Müller, Haigh, Dörpfeld and
Reisch, Flickinger, Hourmouziades, Simon; and Pickard-Cambridge's volumes
have been standard works for many years.

when it is taken in its full context. But the main questions which the critic may ask when faced with any particular entrance or exit may be reduced to two groups. First, there are the objective interrogatives: who? when? how? whither and whence? And in the light of all these the more important interpretative questions may be posed: why thus? what is the significance of the action? These questions are valid for all three tragedians (and many others), and could be adapted to other kinds of stage action besides entrances and exits.

Let me take the questions one by one. 'Who?', the identity of the person entering (the question can hardly arise independently for an exit), may seem almost too basic and obvious to be asked. But it is surprising how often there is some uncertainty over precisely who is entering at any particular juncture. Usually the context makes the answer to this question amply clear; but it is not hard to see that it can on occasion be of basic critical importance. The question 'when?' may also at first sight seem rather banal. Either, it might be objected, the playwright makes the event of an entrance or exit perfectly clear, or he leaves it vague precisely because it is of no importance. But, in fact, the precise timing may be open to dispute, even in cases where it is of great importance. Some such problems are well known (e.g. the movements of Clytemnestra in A. *Ag*), but there are others to be observed which have been neglected. It is, after all, the presence or absence of a character during a certain portion of the play which is at stake. The question 'when?' has to be faced before the dramatic impact of the movement within the play can be properly considered. 'How?' may appear to pose merely the traditional problems of staging. But as well as the mechanics of stage management the question raises the entire manner and visual treatment of the movement (whether or not this was realistically represented, an issue discussed in §3). For example, Dingel (221–33) has catalogued some 200 entries in Greek tragedy where attention is drawn to props or costumes which contribute to the effect of the action. We should also consider, to give one other illustration, the pace of the movement: whether it is hurried and excited, stately and ceremonial, slow and pathetic, and so on. Finally the question of direction, 'whither and whence?', is comparatively slight, since it mainly relates to the contingent and only partially existent world off-stage.[1] All the same, the direction of the entry or exit is also towards or away from the visible focal world of the play on-stage, and can on occasion be important.

To what extent are these matters of stage technique—the identity, timing, manner, and direction of each entry and exit— within the control and discretion of the playwright? Scholars insist that the Greek tragedian was under many constraints; that many features of his composition were determined by the myth, conditions of performance, conventions, and so on. While I do not wish to underrate these factors, they are often invoked as an easy, unthinking alternative to a more positive explanation of what is, rather, a deliberate artistic choice. Thus the handling of exits and entrances, and particularly their timing and manner, are obviously to a very large extent in the hands of the play- wright. He has positively contrived each stage movement in the way he has; he might easily have done otherwise, but he has not. To recognize how far such things are at the discretion of the dramatist leads the way to the subjective question 'why thus?' Why has the artist handled the entrance or exit in the particular way he has rather than any other?

These 'objective' questions are sometimes raised in a desultory sort of way in the traditional commentaries on Greek tragedies; but they are hardly ever seen as issues which affect the meaning and understanding of the play as a whole. I shall attempt in this work not only to treat the 'objective' questions in a thorough and systematic way, but to relate them to the more important 'subjective' questions of critical interpretation. Obviously the question 'why thus?' cannot be asked until the 'objective' in- terrogatives have been answered. That is why so much of my discussion is spent on such matters. But I reiterate that the real interest of such studies lies in their extension into interpretative criticism. Seen in this light exits and entrances become a very varied collection of dramatic events. Some are inconspicuous or highly conventional, in which case their significance is likely to rest in those very qualities. Others are somehow aberrant or unconventional and this very peculiarity is likely to be a clue to their particular meaning. Some entrances and exits are simply arrivals and departures with no more far-reaching associations

[1] Yet the world off-stage has recently supplied matter enough for a long dis- sertation by Joerdën (see Bibliography, cf. also *Bauformen* 369ff.).

than the deed itself. Others, seen in their full dramatic context, become imbued with wider and deeper significance. The stage action may be only a matter of a few paces, but these paces may convey victory or defeat, death or life, a world of suffering or of joy.

What range of phenomena is being isolated under cover of the terms 'exit' and 'entry'? At first sight it might seem obvious that by 'entry' we mean the movement which brings an actor into the field of vision of the audience, and by 'exit' the movement which takes him out of it. This is certainly what we often mean by the words; but their full range is more complicated. Apart from the small but valid complaints that not all of the actor comes into view at the same moment (apparently the side-entrances at Athens sloped uphill) and that he would not enter or leave the field of vision of all the audience simultaneously (especially not in a theatre of Greek shape), there is the more substantial point that we cannot possibly know at what moment the actor crossed the line between out of sight and in sight of the audience. It must have happened several seconds before he joined the actors or chorus already on stage,[1] or after he left them. The distances involved are considerable; it was over ten yards even from the skene door to the centre of the orchestra. This leads to the larger point that, since we are not dealing with an intimate proscenium-arch stage but with a large open acting area, the moment of coming into view is not the same as that of joining the characters on stage. And so in the study of entrances and exits the stage movement which is of interest is not the momentary movement in and out of view, but the prolonged movement across to the centre of attention, and back again.

So far I have been speaking in terms of externals, of the actors and audience in the theatre. But 'entry' and 'exit' are also used of the dramatic world of the play, of the characters who exist in the heightened and enthralled awareness of the audience. In this sense the words are almost synonymous with 'arrival' and 'departure', except that they have less specific implications about the handling of place. And, paradoxically, we can be rather more precise about the isolation of entrances and exits in this sense, for, instead of being thrown back into our ignorance of the details of fifth-century staging, we are dealing with the one

[1] Phrases like 'on stage' are not to be taken literally (see pp. 441f. below).

aspect of the play which has survived virtually intact: the words. The entry of a character (as opposed to an actor) occurs, in effect, when the character newly engages in or impinges on the words and action of the play—and his exit when he withdraws or disengages from them. This may sound vague, but in practice it is usually quite a precise event.

The ways in which the event can be traced are as a rule simple. Many arrivals are clearly marked as such in the words, which will include appropriate verbs of motion. Even where they are not their occurrence is nearly always clear in the case of a major character: the character 'arrives' either when he first speaks or when he is first addressed. The exceptions to this are few and far between.[1] A minor character, if his entry is not explicitly marked, should be supposed to have entered with the superior character to whom he is attached.[2] Exceptions to these rules of thumb have been alleged by scholars here and there throughout Greek tragedy (in most cases, wrongly), but this does not affect the validity of the notion of the new engagement of a character in the play. The situation is much the same with exits. The moment of a character's disengagement from the play is usually signalled in the words which include an appropriate verb of motion. When this is not so, major characters go, as a rule, either after their last words or in the company of another with whom they are connected.[3] Minor characters must occasionally be supposed to have disengaged themselves without trace, but even they usually depart at an ascertainable moment.[4] (Of course, I should add, in all cases where we are uncertain when and

---

[1] Most uncertainties depend on difficulties of verbal or textual interpretation, see e.g. *Seven* 854c*, *Hik* 836b*, *Ag* 258b*. For serious exceptions see *Ag* 783b* (Cassandra), *Eum* 574* (Apollo). Outside Aeschylus consider Tecmessa at S. *Aj* 646ff., Adrastus at E. *Hik* 381ff., Menelaus at E. *Hel* 1369ff. (enter 1390?), Dolon at *Rh* 154ff. (when did he enter?), Agamemnon at *IA* 607ff. Problems like these, which are very much the exception and are mostly well known, require individual discussion.

[2] This leaves very few uncertain cases; e.g. the Old Man at E. *Hipp* 88ff., the Servant (?) at E. *Hel* 1627ff. (the very uncertainty favours attribution to the chorus). On the Handmaids in A. *Hik* see *Hik* 974b*.

[3] There are problems, e.g. at *Seven* 1053*, but none so serious as *Eum* 777b* (Apollo). Outside Aeschylus consider E. *Tro* 1334 (?Talthybius), E. *Phoen* 638 (?Jocasta), *Rh* 223 (?Aeneas). Again these are demonstrably exceptional problems.

[4] On the inconspicuous exit of secondary characters see *Pers* 514*. There is uncertainty at *Cho* 892b* (servant); cf. S. *Trach* 1278 (Old Man), S. *OT* 1185 (Corinthian and Shepherd), E. *Hec* 904 (maidservant) etc.

whether a character engages in or disengages from the play we are necessarily also uncertain about the actual staging of the entry or exit in the theatre.) 'Impingement' and 'disengagement' become in performance one of an infinite variety of dramatic situations which can cluster around an arrival or departure in its full context. But it is this moment which I shall be working out from in critical discussion of exits and entrances.

For a translation or a commentary which adds stage instructions (or for an edition which notes the action, like Wilamowitz *Aeschylus ed maj*), or for a commentary on dramatic technique like the present work it is a great convenience to be able to attach entrances and exits to a particular line, as I have done throughout. This is a useful convention, but it should not be taken to imply that the entry or exit took place instantaneously or only after the previous line was finished or anything of that sort. I shall use the line number of the *dramatic* entry or exit, as defined above; and I do not necessarily mean to imply anything about the moment when the actor went into or out of the view of the audience. This has, in fact, been the conventional practice of most translators and commentators.

There are still quite a few places left where it is difficult to decide just which line number to attach to the stage instruction, but in nearly every case the context or my discussion should make the situation clear. Thus, for instance, I mark entries after an entry announcement (though the actor may well have been in sight earlier), but before an address to the new arrival (see e.g. *Pers* 155a*). I always put the exit after a character's last lines (although the lines may have been said in the process of going out of sight), but before 'lines cast at a departing back' (since the character has detached himself, cf. *Hik* 951*, *Ag* 350*). In any case the mere line number is of little consequence, as long as it is clearly appreciated what is going on in dramatic and theatrical terms.

One of my purposes in this book will be to give some idea of the various methods of 'preparation', that is of the ways in which a stage action may be led up to. I use the term in a broad and general sense, perhaps in a broader sense than is usual, to cover a range of techniques and devices connected with entrances and exits. It might be roughly defined as 'anything said or done before an entry or exit which prepares for that event or has a bearing on it'. Of course whatever is said and done at the actual time of the event is of vital importance since attention is then directly concentrated on it; also what transpires after it may reflect back on it, and to some extent change its meaning in retrospect. But to a large degree the significance of an entry or exit depends on what has passed before it, on the preparation for it. It is the preparation which creates expectation and which puts the event into its dramatic context, and hence gives it work to do in the play.

In a real sense, the entire play up to the point of any particular event should be regarded as preparation for it, because everything together contributes to the complete dramatic context. None the less it is legitimate, and only practical, to pick out some features which have a more particular bearing on the future event. It would, on the other hand, be a mistake to limit 'preparation', as is usually done, to explicit forecasts that a certain person will arrive, to direct statements of intention to depart, and to commands to these effects. There are many ways in which the event itself may be foreshadowed, and this may be done with many degrees of directness or indirectness. These techniques cannot be conveniently classified, precisely because they depend on context. It would be an oversimplification, for example, necessarily to treat the occurrence of a name as preparation for that person's arrival (*contra* Webster *Preparation*): it depends on the context in which the name is used. Also many people who are named never become characters in the play, while many characters are never named before their entry.

The amount and degree of preparation can vary enormously. In *Pers*, for example, the re-entry of the Queen at 598 is prepared for by just one explicit sentence (521–4), while the entry of Darius is given a not very long but extremely intense preparation which builds up to a climax of excitement (see 681a*), and the preparation for the return of Xerxes is sustained throughout the entire play, though often it is submerged or indirect (see 909b*). Note also that personal preparation is not the only kind: an arrival may be prepared for by situation, so that it is his function rather than the character himself who is expected. Thus, for instance, the need for information about momentous off-stage events prepares for the entry of a messenger (cf. *Pers*

249a*).[1] And as well as the identity of the person who makes the entry or exit, the timing and the manner of the action may or may not be prepared for. Attention has usually been restricted to the person, but the stress on the preparation for the other two aspects, or the absence of it, may be dramatically even more important. Thus, to give one example, we know in S. *Phil* that Odysseus is a *dramatis persona*, but the timing and manner of his entry from ambush at 974 are a complete surprise (see *GRBS* 1971 pp. 27–8).

Most entrances and exits in Greek tragedy are prepared for, more or less explicitly and with more or less frequency and intensity. Movements are few and important, and preparation for them makes a considerable contribution toward the unity, economy, and direction of the play. But there are exceptions.[2] And it would be a serious and insensitive error to assume, as it often is assumed, that all such unprepared-for movements are a failure on the part of the playwright. Precisely because preparation is normally so carefully managed, special opportunities for surprise and disjunction are offered by the lack of it. (In what follows I am talking primarily about entries; most of the observations could be adapted to apply to exits also.) An entry which is totally unprepared for makes for a startling new turn of events which upsets expectations and introduces an element of the unpredictable. This is a device particularly associated with Euripides.[3] We may find his use of it objectionable or unsuccessful, but we cannot deny that it is calculated and deliberate. Artistic failure should only be invoked as an explanation if there is no perceivable point and if there is positive detriment in the lack of preparation. Even if an entry is not totally unprepared for there are still opportunities for surprise, particularly in the

---

[1] In E. *Med* Aegeus is prepared for situationally though not personally: Medea's need of refuge prepares for her protector (see lines 359ff., 387ff., 437, 441, 502ff., 603f., 642, 653ff.).

[2] I have noted a quotation from one Sidney Hickson in *Trans. New Shakespeare Soc.* for 1874: 'throughout the entire range of the plays of Shakespeare there is not a single instance of a character turning up in the unravelling of plot, whose existence was not at least implied, and whose appearance might not reasonably be looked for.' While this can hardly be true, it is interesting that the claim could be made at all.

[3] See e.g. Orestes in *Andr*, Iphis and Evadne in *Hik*, Menelaus in *Tro*, Pythia in *Ion*, Pylades in *Or* (cf. Aeneas and Paris in *Rh*). The nearest equivalent in Sophocles is Tiresias and Eurydice in *Ant*. Examples are not found in genuine Aeschylus (see *Seven* 1005a*), except for Oceanus at *Prom* 284 and Io (see *Prom* 561*)—if they are genuine Aeschylus.

handling of timing and manner. Entries which through the
withholding of certain aspects of preparation still have notable
elements of surprise are a favourite device of Sophocles;[1] for
Aeschylus see *Ag* 1577b*. But these techniques of surprise are
exceptional. Usually the Greek tragedian makes full use of the
tightening effect of forward-looking preparation. And generally
expectation, as Coleridge noted in his *Lectures on Shakespeare*, is
more powerful an emotional force than surprise.

The degree and extent to which a stage action is led towards
by means of the infinitely variable techniques of preparation
can supply an important and observable pointer to the artistic
purposes and priorities of the dramatist. Our observation of
dramatic preparation indicates what the playwright wanted his
audience to expect and how he wished it to look at the event.

§2. *Visual Meaning*

The fifth-century Attic tragedian composed to be performed at
the dramatic festivals; for him his play was not the written
libretto but the work in performance. Likewise for his audience
a tragedy was the production which they saw and heard in the
theatre, and not, as it is for us, a paper copy of the text. The
plays must be interpreted accordingly. These basic assertions are
probably acceptable to most scholars and readers of Greek
tragedy today. Their validity, though not their critical consequences, have become widely accepted over the last decades.
Yet these dogmas are not in the last resort provable. We are not
really in a position to contradict with finality someone who flatly
asserts the opposite—that the poet primarily wrote to be read.
All the same, common sense and our meagre evidence both
point in the other direction.

To consider the matter first from the angle of the playwright,
he did not in the fifth century 'write' a tragedy (γράφειν), rather
he 'created' or 'produced' it (ποιεῖν has a wide range of sense),
and he 'taught' or 'directed' it (διδάσκειν). ἐδίδασκε was evidently

---

[1] e.g. S. *Ant* 384, 823, *Trach* 531, *El* 660, 871, 1326, 1397, 1464 (far from an
exhaustive list). Webster *Preparation*, who wishes to prove the inane claim that
'the arrival of a Sophoclean character is expected, Euripidean characters arrive
unexpectedly' (123) completely misses this technique in Sophocles.

the word used in the official records of the festival, which were collected by Aristotle under the title Διδασκαλίαι (see Pfeiffer 81).

Thus the word τραγωιδογράφος supplies a late notion (Polybius and later) while the words τραγωιδοποιός and τραγωιδοδιδάσκαλος are used of Agathon without distinction at Arph. *Thesm* 30 and 88. Indeed ποιεῖν and διδάσκειν used of tragedy effectively mean the same thing, to 'produce' or 'put on', as can be seen from Arph. *Frogs* 1021 δρᾶμα ποιήσας Ἄρεως μεστόν followed five lines later by εἶτα διδάξας Πέρσας. We have no evidence of a fifth-century tragedian who did not want his plays performed: to have his work performed was the only way to realize it.[1] We have no evidence that the performance was regarded as in any way a superficial or coarse or unsatisfactory realization of the play—the performance *was* the play.

The dramatists were practical men of the theatre, they did not merely supply the script. In the early days they were actors themselves (Arle. *Rhet* 1403b22). All, so far as we know, composed the music of their lyrics, devised the accompanying choreography, and supervised the production in general. This would include the over-all direction of delivery, gesture, grouping, movement, etc., and also probably of such technical matters as props, costumes, masks, and stage machinery. No doubt he had help and advice from others, but we have no reason to think that any of these tasks was put entirely in another's hands. And this is, indeed, why he was said to διδάσκειν his play—he literally

---

[1] A diversion has been raised in this context by the misinterpretation of the stylistic term ἀναγνωστικός at Arle. *Rhet* 1413b12, where it has wrongly been taken to mean 'intended solely for reading' instead of 'suited to reading'. It was rightly explained long ago by Sandys and Crusius; there is a good discussion with bibliography in Zwierlein 128ff. Yet the mistake continues to be made (e.g. P-C *DFA*² 82, Lucas on Arle. *Poet* 1450b18, Baldry *The Greek Tragic Theatre* (London 1971) 131) and to be corrected (e.g. Pfeiffer 29).

At Athen. 270a Metagenes' Θουριοπέρσαι and Nicophon's Σειρῆνες are both called δράματα ἀδίδακτα, which presumably means that they were never performed. But this is suspicious, since it seems too much of a coincidence that two comedies which Athenaeus quotes consecutively on the same topic should both have been exceptional in this way—and how would Athenaeus know this anyway? Dover's claim (Ar. *Clouds* ed. xcviii, 270, *Ar Com* 104, cf. Wilamowitz *Hellenistische Dichtung* (Berlin 1924) I 98 n. 4) that the revision of Arph. *Clouds* was for readers only is far from compelling. We do not know how the present text of *Clouds* survived, but there is no particular reason to suppose that Aristophanes put it into circulation. The fact, if it is one, that the revision is incomplete argues for the contrary. Calder has recently speculated (*CPh* 67 (1972) 291–3) that E. *Phaethon* was never performed, but without any good reason (of his seven points nos. 2–5 are irrelevant).

taught his performers what to do.[1] That the dramatists composed their own music is universally assumed; it supplies, for instance, the point of Arph. *Frogs* 1249ff., *Birds* 749, etc.[2] Aeschylus and Phrynichus were particularly famous for their choreography.[3]

It is not so simple to illustrate the role of the playwright as production supervisor or director.[4] But, besides the very use of διδάϲκειν etc., it is surely assumed throughout Old Comedy that the play in performance and not just the words is the responsibility of the *poietes*. One only has to go through the contest in *Frogs* (where the chief emphasis is on diction) to see that Aeschylus and Euripides are holding each other responsible for the general presentation of their plays. Aeschylus is liable, for instance, for the staging of his silences (911ff.), his chariot-borne entries (961ff.), the presentation of the dirges in *Pers* (1026). Costumes are part of their province (1061ff.; cf. *Acharn, Thesm*). Staging and presentation are quite often parodied in Aristophanes, and are regarded as part of the author's work, and not as the responsibility of actor, ϲκευοποιόϲ, μηχανοποιόϲ, or someone else. Consider, for example, the parodies of *Telephus* in *Acharn* or of *Andromeda* in *Thesm*. The features of presentation which come in for parody include gestures, postures, costumes, props, stage machines, and so on.[5]

---

[1] Cf. Johannes Rhenanus writing in 1613: '. . . even the most eminent actors have to allow themselves to be instructed by the Dramatists'. For this and other evidence that the 'Elizabethan' playwright taught his plays see J. Isaacs in *Shakespeare and the Theatre* (Shakespeare Assoc. London 1927) 88ff. esp. 97f.

[2] See in general Kranz *Stas* 137–46. It is quite possible that the musical notation of the famous papyrus fragment of E. *Or* (*c*. 200 B.C., see Turner *Greek Manuscripts* etc. (Oxford 1971) 70) goes back to Euripides himself; cf. Longman *CQ* N.S. 12 (1962) 61ff. esp. 65 n. 1. Compare also Dion. Hal. *de comp. verb.* 63, who discusses Euripides' scoring of *Or* 140–2.

[3] See Chamaeleon fr. 41 Wehrli (*ap.* Athen. 21c), Arph. fr. 677, 678 K. Philocleon's performance at the end of Arph. *Wasps* may be a tribute to Phrynichus' choreography (cf. 1479, 1490, 1524); see also the beautiful couplet attributed to him ϲχήματα δ᾽ ὄρχηϲιϲ τόϲα μοι πόρεν, ὄϲϲ᾽ ἐνὶ πόντωι / κύματα ποιεῖται χείματι νὺξ ὀλοή (Plut. *Quaest. Symp.* 732f). See further Kranz *Stas* 146–8.

[4] I cannot resist quoting the anecdote in Plutarch (*de rect. rat. aud.* 46b) Εὐριπίδηϲ . . . ὡϲ ὑπολέγοντοϲ αὐτοῦ τοῖϲ χορευταῖϲ ὠιδήν τινα πεποιημένην ἐφ᾽ ἁρμονίαϲ εἰϲ ἐγέλαϲεν, 'εἰ μή τιϲ ἦϲ ἀναίϲθητοϲ' εἶπε κτλ.

[5] Aristotle in *Poetics* authorized the mistaken notion that the theatrical aspect of the play was unworthy of the artist and should be left to the mechanicals (see Appendix F), but he mentions in passing (1455a26) that Carcinus ἐξέπεϲεν because he did not take sufficient care over a detail of staging. Snell (on *TrGF* 70 F 1c) says 'nescio quo pacto ὁ διδάϲκαλοϲ haec non notaverit': if he means to imply that the διδάϲκαλοϲ was someone other than Carcinus himself, then he has missed the point.

It is possible that the lack of marginal stage directions is further evidence. Stage directions (παρεπιγραφαί) are very few and far between in our texts; and what few there are may well not go back to the dramatist.[1] There would be no need of written instructions, of course, when the playwright himself looked after rehearsals. I conclude, then, that the dramatist himself supervised the visual and aural presentation of his work in all aspects. This function, as well as the furnishing of the script, was an essential part of being a τραγωιδοδιδάσκαλος.

Consider the same issue from the side of the audience. There can be little doubt that tragedy was sometimes read in the fifth century as well as being seen in performance. Vase paintings and the increasing use of imagery of books and writing are alone clear evidence of the rise of the book during the course of the century.[2] The very fact that so much of fifth-century tragedy survived to reach Alexandria may be evidence that the text was circulated; though it is no less likely that the family of the dramatist (often also in the trade) ensured the preservation of at least one copy.[3] At the same time (despite the influential speculation of Wilamowitz to the contrary (*Einleitung* 121ff.)) there is no good reason to think that the reading of tragedy was at all widespread before the end of the century, let alone that tragedians composed with any consideration of a public of readers. It is perhaps worth noting that the very first surviving reference to

---

[1] Cf. Andrieu 183ff., 348f. This is a rather complex subject which I hope to discuss fully elsewhere. Of some fourteen examples of παρεπιγραφαί in tragedy which I have found alleged in one place or another, there are only four which may well go back to the dramatist himself (A. *Eum* 117–29, *Diktyoulkoi* fr. 474 l. 803, E. *Cycl* 487, and *trag. adesp. POxy* 2746). All the others are either certainly or probably the work of later editors, either in ancient or modern times. For myself, I doubt whether any parepigraphai at all, even those giving noises off, go back to the fifth century.

[2] See in general Turner *Athenian Books in the Fifth and Fourth Centuries* (London 1952) esp. 16ff., Pfeiffer chapter 2 esp. 25–32.

[3] It is possible that a copy of the text was deposited in some official collection, but we have no evidence of it. Not everything did survive; see in general Fraser *Ptolemaic Alexandria* (Oxford 1972) ii 486f. According to the *Life* of Euripides some dozen of his plays did not survive, and we have the tell-tale οὐ cώιζεται for the satyr play of 431 (Hypoth. *Med*) and maybe of 409, if the corrupt hypoth. *Phoen* is rightly restored by Snell *TrGF* DID C 16a. It is salutary to recall that Shakespeare, the most popular playwright of his day, did not ensure the survival of his plays. Had it not been for the collection of the First Folio by Heminge and Condell, fifteen of his plays, including *Tempest*, *Macbeth*, and *Antony and Cleopatra*, would presumably have been lost.

reading tragedy does not occur until the end of the century, at
Arph. *Frogs* 52f.; and there Dionysus is characterized as a
passionate devotee of tragedy.[1] No doubt tragedies were read
by associates of the dramatist, by those who had for some reason
failed to see the play, by tragedians, comedians, and rhetoricians
who wished to use and draw on an earlier tragedy, by tragedy
fanatics like Dionysus, and, probably above all, by those who
wished to learn by heart parts of tragedies for private singing
and recitation (see e.g. Arph. *Clouds* 1364ff., *Frogs* 151; cf. Plato
Phaedr 228). But nowhere before Aristotle is there, so far as I
know, any suggestion that the appreciation of tragedy by reading
might be fuller or more developed: the text was only a convenient abstract of the real work.

Aristophanes always refers to tragedy in terms of its effect on
a theatre audience, and never in terms of a significant reading
public.[2] For his purposes a tragedy was a production in the
theatre. Thus, for example, it is after attending a tragedy of
Euripides that husbands suspect their wives (*Thesm* 389ff.),
εὐθὺς εἰσιόντες ἀπὸ τῶν ἰκρίων . . . (395); and this happens not
wherever a text is circulated but ὅπουπερ ἔμβραχυ / εἰσὶν θεαταὶ
καὶ τραγωιδοὶ καὶ χοροί (390f., cf. *Frogs* 971 ff., especially l. 981).
It is worth noting also how the critical discussion of tragedy in
Aristophanes tends to be in terms of practical technique. This
is particularly clear in the discussion in *Frogs* 905–91, where
throughout it is the audience (θεαταί 909, 919; cf. θεώμενοι 926)
which is the object of the technique. And it is likely that fifth-
century critical theory of tragedy, like the theory of rhetoric,
was put in terms of τέχνη, the τέχνη of affecting the audience
(ψυχαγωγία, ἀπάτη, etc.), whether by the speech in the law-
court or the tragedy in the theatre.[3]

[1] See Rau 118ff. For the phrase ἀναγιγνώσκοντί μοι τὴν Ἀνδρομέδαν πρὸς ἐμαυτὸν
cf. Plato Com. fr. 173 K (a cookery book is the victim). Incidentally Eupolis fr.
304 K οὗ τὰ βυβλία ὤνια does not imply texts of *tragedy* on sale. (And might βυβλία
mean only 'stationery'?)

[2] *Frogs* 1114 βιβλίον τ᾽ ἔχων ἕκαστος μανθάνει τὰ δεξιά has, of course, been the
subject of much controversy; cf. Rossi *BICS* 18 (1971) 78. Walcot has recently
suggested (*G and R* 18 (1971) 45f.) that βιβλίον means a quotation-book, in which
the spectator would copy striking lines so that he could then learn them by heart
(μανθάνει). At least this, unlike many interpretations, accounts for the wording,
though it conjures up an incredible picture.

[3] Pohlenz *Kl Schr* II 436ff. remains a valuable collection of evidence, although
many of his conclusions are unacceptable (see Pfeiffer 47 n. 1); also cf. Rosenmeyer
235ff.

It is usually claimed in this connection that Aristophanes' parodies show that a greater or smaller part of his audience must have read tragedies closely and persistently.[1] But we must ask whether this is not a matter of scholars assuming that Aristophanes' audience must have considered his comedies in the same way as they do. Of course we like to know the wording and context of the original of every parody and to compare it word by word with Aristophanes' version: but how often is this necessary for the appreciation of the parody? In the case of the one extended parody where we have the original—the parody of E. *Hel* at *Thesm* 850ff.—a close knowledge of the text of *Hel* is clearly unnecessary: all Aristophanes requires of his audience is that they should have been present at the first production of *Hel* a year or two before. In many instances of paratragedy it is recognition of the fact of the paratragedy and not of the tragic original which is required; in many others the source is a scandalous tag or an opening line or a famous speech which many could recite by heart. And in the more extended parodies it seems to be acquaintance with a performance rather than with the text which is required of the audience. It has been rightly observed that 'again and again it is visual effects which Aristophanes recalls, knowing that for an audience a play is a thing done in their presence' (Harriott op. cit. 5). This suggests that successful plays were not performed just once at Athens for the first and only time, but that they were reperformed at later festivals. There is some evidence that Aeschylus' plays were reperformed at the City Dionysia (Arph. *Acharn* 9ff., *Frogs* 866f., Philostr. *Vit Ap* 6. 11); but if other playwrights were reperformed it must have been at the rural festivals. Here, unfortunately, our evidence is minimal; but one wonders how much truth lies behind Plato's caricature of the φιλοθεάμονες at *Rep* 475d, who περιθέουσι τοῖς Διονυσίοις, οὔτε τῶν κατὰ πόλεις οὔτε τῶν κατὰ κώμας ἀπολειπόμενοι.[2] Perhaps most theatre-goers went to more than one dramatic festival each year, and so saw the most famous plays more than once.

---

[1] The chief exception is a brief but well argued article by R. Harriott in *BICS* 9 (1962) 1ff. The study of paratragedy in Aristophanes has been greatly facilitated by the valuable collection made by Rau.

[2] On the rural festivals see P-C *DFA*² 42ff., 99f.; cf. also Calder in *Educ. Theatre Journ* 10 (1958) 237–9 (a sensible three pages called 'The Single-Performance Fallacy').

There is, then, enough evidence to indicate that the reading
of tragedy in the fifth century was a subsidiary activity, and that
it did not enter significantly into the playwright's intentions,
nor into his public's expectations. If these conclusions are
accepted, even with reservations, then there are far-reaching
consequences for the interpreter of Greek tragedy. For instance,
the play should be treated as sequential; that is to say that, since
the work was performed from start to finish in a certain time, it
must be taken in order, and we should be wary of treating the
play as 'spatial', that is as an indivisible whole in which all
parts bear on all others (a notion applied by G. Wilson Knight
to Shakespeare). We should hesitate to explain anything earlier
in the play in terms of something which is only divulged later,
though we may reinterpret the earlier feature. We should, in
general, avoid picking at random from here and there in the
play, and should treat it as an ordered succession. Further, we
should be reluctant to read between the lines. The phrase gives
itself away, since an audience does not read and so cannot read
between the lines, any more than it can turn the pages back. A
performed work should wear its meaning in view; it cannot afford
to be inexplicitly cryptic, or to hide its burden in inconspicuous
corners. The playwright's first requirement is his audience's concentrated attention. This he must capture and keep, and he must
be very careful how he disperses or diverts or distracts this
concentration. So the critic should not 'extract from the text
subtleties so tortuous that they could never reach the conscious-
ness of an audience through a medium as fast moving and un-
haltable as music'.[1]

But these are negative cautions, and one should take care in
pressing them.[2] Especially one should be careful not to dog-
matize too confidently about what an author could or could not
put into his work, for there are many levels of creative conscious-

[1] Richard David on Shakespeare in *PBA* 47 (1961) 158.
[2] There is a lesson here from Homeric studies. The discovery that Homer is
the culmination of an oral tradition led to dogmatic assumptions about the kind
of detailed artistry it is legitimate to expect from him. Some have insisted that
certain kinds of large-scale 'literary' artistry, e.g. complex structures of theme or
imagery, corresponding scenes, are out of the question for an oral poet—even
though they are clearly there in the poems. The case against this patronizing and
arbitrary circumscription of Homer's genius is well put in A. Parry's introduction
to *The Making of Homeric Verse* (Oxford 1971) esp. l–lxii and by A. Amory Parry
in *CQ* N.S. 21 (1971) 1ff. esp. 6.

ness besides clearly formulated deliberation; and similarly with what an audience could or could not register during a work in performance, for there are many degrees of apprehension besides the full and conscious recognition which it is the critic's task to formulate. My concern here is, in any case, not so much with what can *not* be expected of a play in performance but with what *is* to be expected: visual meaning.[1]

The critic of a work which is only fully realized in performance should always keep his mind's eye on the work in action. As he reads he must envisage how these lines would be bodied forth in the theatre. He must ask how the performance adds to and interprets the lines, and how the words put meaning into the action. For both are part and parcel of the work as a whole. Anyone who has read A. *Ag* must sense that Agamemnon's walking over the red cloth has some special meaning, or that in S. *OC* the action of the blind Oedipus leading those who can see is imbued with significance, or that Pentheus' Bacchant's clothing in E. *Ba* is more than an adventitious detail. These are very obvious examples of visual drama which call for interpretation; but if one looks a little closer one can see that each tragedy in performance is full of significant theatrical points which need to be recognized and appreciated. For example, there is the dramatic use of gestures, of stage groupings, of the direction of movements, of props, of tableaux. Such practical aspects of staging can in their context be given great significance. Anyone who has seen a Greek tragedy (or any other play) and thought about it knows that visual elements like these are part of the essential fabric of the work.

So when the playwright draws attention to a stage action, we should take up the invitation and consider what the significance of that action is meant to be. And if the dramatist is a great dramatist, or just a good one, then we should not be content with the answer that the action 'adds spectacle' or 'enhances verisimilitude'; we should look for something which the action conveys which could not be put in any other way. In such a brief and concentrated dramatic form as Greek tragedy the great artist is not going to squander time and attention on superfluous or superficial stage business. As Steidle (15) has put it, 'in the

[1] This phrase is the title of the excellent first chapter of N. Coghill's *Shakespeare's Professional Skills* (Cambridge 1964).

whole of ancient drama the stage actions are never there for mere effect, but rather have a meaningful function for the understanding of the work'.

There was in Greek tragedy much more stage action than is generally acknowledged. None the less it would be most misleading if the impression were given that there were notable scenic effects going on all the time or even most of the time. There are long stretches of the tragedies where there is little movement besides (presumably) the conventional gestures which accompany speech; and the stage picture, once established, would cease to be visually notable until it changed again. (Throughout the lyric portions the possible significance of the choreography is almost completely lost to us.)[1] Significant stage effects, those reflected in the words, tend to come together in groups, and are often separated by quite long static scenes. There is no denying that the tragic theatre of the fifth century was more static than most other schools of drama. But that is no reason for neglecting the visual element which is there: on the contrary, its sparing use tends to give it heightened prominence when it is brought into play.

The close study of stage action as an approach to critical interpretation is still in its early days, and has really got under way only in the last few years.[2] The whole approach has grown

[1] G. R. Kernodle 'Symbolic Action in the Greek Choral Odes' in *CJ* 53 (1957–8) 1–7 argues briefly but forcibly that the chorus actually danced out the events which it was singing about—the sacrifice of Iphigenia, the punishment of Capaneus, the death of Phaedra or Pentheus. The theory has its attractions; but, apart from the lack of corroborative evidence, it runs into difficulties. The chorus would lose its corporate identity, the responsion of strophe and antistrophe would be lost, many allusions are too brief to be danced out, some would be grotesque, and, above all perhaps, the contrast of the songs with the action—their removal in time and space, diction, and particularity—would be destroyed.

[2] There is a similar movement in Shakespearean criticism. This goes back at root to Poel or further, but it was put on a sound basis in theory and in practice by Granville Barker (there is a good programmatic statement in *Companion to Shakespeare Studies* (Cambridge 1934) 83). Its development seems, however, to have been slow and unsteady. Two recent books which apply this approach are J. Russell Brown *Shakespeare's Plays in Performance* (London 1966) and J. L. Styan *Shakespeare's Stagecraft* (Cambridge 1967), both of which offer valuable observations, though they tend to fail to distinguish between the way that Shakespeare had the work performed and the way that they themselves would do it if they were to mount a production. The whole critical approach is still in its formative stages to judge from the contribution of D. Seltzer to the *New Companion to Shakespeare Studies* (Cambridge 1971) 35ff., and from Stanley Wells's critical survey in the same book, where he says (p. 261) 'criticism based on a strong sense of the

out of a combination of the traditional study of dramatic technique combined with a greater awareness among scholars of the practical theatre and of the problems of producing the great plays of the past. (There is a brief doxographical survey on pp. 488–9.) It is not an easy field of study: one seldom deals in certainties, usually in possibilities, or, at best, probabilities. Thorough accumulation and careful discrimination of all relevant evidence is required, especially when trying to establish conventional or unconventional techniques. Complete consideration of the dramatic context of a stage action and close attention to the accompanying words are needed for an assessment of its function. But clearly there is work to be done.

But, if this approach is likely to be as productive as has been made out, why has it not been recognized and exploited earlier? I can suggest several reasons for this. One is that there are virtually no stage directions in our transmitted texts, and hence in the scholarly editions.[1] The handful that there are seem to have been preserved at random, and most of them concern noises off-stage (cf. p. 15 n. 1 above). The plain text with no explicit reminder that it is the libretto of a work to be performed has encouraged scholars to neglect the stage action. If full stage instructions from the author's own hand had been transmitted with the text then this aspect would certainly have received due attention. Another reason is that there is little on the dramatic significance of stage action in the remnants of ancient scholarship on the plays, the scholia. Scholars so regard the scholia that if some topic receives attention in them then, however

play as something that is incomplete until it is performed seems likely to grow in importance, but it is a difficult area of discussion'.

[1] There have been exceptions, above all Wilamowitz's *ed maj* of Aeschylus which has an *actio* section at the foot of each page. Van Leeuwen put Latin directions in his text of Aristophanes (often too freely). Koerte has made this the usual practice for editors of Menander (though Sandbach *OCT* has regrettably not followed the convention). Since the stage action is part of the play as a whole, it would be a good thing, in my view, if Wilamowitz's precedent were followed. ('No one can write an adequate commentary on a Greek play, or even edit it adequately, without producing it in his mind' Dover *Skene* 2.) But as long as it remains traditional for an edition to be as nearly as possible a corrected copy of the transmitted text with a catalogue of scribal errors, this practice is unlikely to be adopted. Translators do, of course, usually include stage instructions; but few have taken any trouble over them.

foolish or trivial, it is treated with respect. But in this case there
is little encouragement.[1]

Consider next a feature of theatre history which has probably
had a much deeper and more insidious influence. Each age re-
produces old plays with its own visual and theatrical conventions
and fashions. It is true that there is often some nominal allusion
to the theatre of the original production (in costume or music,
say), but generally directors and designers and actors feel free
to handle the presentation of the play entirely in their own way.
With time the lay-out of the stage and theatre changes, ideas
about costumes, lighting, and scenery change, techniques of
acting and delivery change. But it is not only in these external
trappings that the presentation of the play is no longer as its
creator meant it to be; the visual meaning of his drama, woven
into it by means of gestures, movements, tableaux, etc., this too
goes by the board or is obliterated. Yet the greatest damage is
done by the interpolation of extraneous spectacle and visual
effects. No doubt visual interpolation has always seemed easily
acceptable because, although not explicitly supported by the
text, it does not positively contradict or make nonsense of it. So
this has been regarded as perfectly legitimate practice in almost
every chapter of theatre history, and above all, perhaps, in the
latest. Modern reinterpretations depend almost entirely on visual
means, and these mainly take the form of extra action and
spectacle which are not directly founded or reflected in the text.
Of course the text itself may also be cut, added to, and rewritten
(and this was no less true of the ancient world, see Page *passim*),
but this is always comparatively inhibited, since the text is the
one aspect of the play which is laid down in black and white.
It is above all through visual presentation in all its aspects,

[1] In the scholia there are, in fact, scattered remarks on the stage action, and
even aesthetic comments on dramatic and scenic technique. These are presumably
derived from Alexandrian commentaries which may well have given considerable
weight to such matters; but too little has survived the process of selection to
embolden modern scholiasts to follow suit. See e.g. scholia on A. *Eum* 1 (see p.
368 n. 3); S. *El* 190, *OC* 1547, *Aj* 308; E. *Hipp* 569, *Tro* 99, *Or* 223. The collection,
discussion, and *index verborum* in A. Trendelenburg *Grammaticorum Graecorum de
Arte Tragica Iudiciorum Reliquiae* (Bonn 1867) is still valuable, and there are some
helpful observations in G. Malzan *De Scholiis Euripideis* etc. (Darmstadt 1908). Cf.
also Rutherford III 101ff. esp. 114 (on pp. 118–25 R. attempts a complete list of
scholia on Aristophanes which have to do with entrances, exits, scenery, dress,
attitude, movements, and gestures). Weissmann *Anweisungen* is of little value on
this topic.

inevitably including visual meaning, that actor-managers, producers, and directors have felt free to adapt, refurbish, reinterpret, and, all too often, travesty old plays.

Complete freedom in the theatrical production of old plays is nothing new and there have been few exceptions to it.[1] The ancient Greek theatre was no exception. Within a century of the death of Sophocles and Euripides there had been considerable changes to the stage, the skene, machinery, masks, buskins, etc.[2] Visual effects were confidently interpolated (see index on Page p. 221f., and §4 below), and there was not, so far as we know, any idea that the way that the fifth-century dramatists themselves produced their plays had any claims on the later theatre. No doubt the visual meaning of their plays, embodied in comparatively small details of gesture and movement, were disregarded along with the more obvious external features of staging. The tragic theatre of the fourth century was, it seems, dominated by the virtuoso actor; and he is unlikely to have restricted himself to the small (though significant) actions inherent in the original work. There do seem to have been some scholars who were interested in the dramatist's visual meaning (see p. 22 n. 1 above); but equally there were others who with no sense of the history of the theatre were happy to recount the contemporary staging as though it were the same as the original (see §4 below).

If we turn to consider the revival in the production of Greek tragedy led by Max Reinhardt early this century, then theatrically speaking the situation is little different.[3] The outward staging was quite unlike the original—proscenium arch, artificial lighting, no masks, naturalistic acting, and so on. Visually the production was dominated by huge visual effects in scenery and in crowd grouping, which were supposed to convey the grandeur of Greek tragedy. In this welter of spectacle the plain stage actions

[1] A few come to mind e.g. the traditional Japanese theatres, the Comédie-Française, the D'Oyly Carte Opera.

[2] For details see D–R 375ff., Frickenhaus 31ff., P-C *TDA* 134ff., Bieber *Hist*[2] 108ff. etc.

[3] For Greek tragedy on the modern stage in Germany see Schadewaldt *HuH*[2] ii 636ff. My random illustrations do not pretend to be a complete account of the production of Greek tragedy in recent times. The best modern productions of Greek tragedy are, in my view, those done by modern Greek companies, especially the National Theatre of Greece at Epidaurus. Many of these productions try to take serious consideration of the dramatist's scenic intentions, and yet avoid antiquarian lifelessness.

which convey the author's visual meaning, even if they were
noticed and carried out, would be inconspicuous and of little
weight. And now in the contemporary professional theatre of
ritual, cruelty, and the absurd there is no place for the scenic
techniques of the Greek tragedian.[1] Quite apart from incongruous
doctrines of the function of the theatre and of the relationship
between actor and audience, so much stage action and ritualistic
hocus-pocus is interpolated, and this so dominates the production
as a whole, that the visual meaning of the original play is
neglected and lost.

This is not the place to go into the awkward and contentions
—and extremely important—question whether it is right for the
producers of old plays to regard themselves as under no obligation to the dramatist's visual meaning, or whether on the other
hand they ought to hamper their own scenic imagination by
paying attention to it. The problem seems to be to find a tenable
position which rejects the two extremes of a lifeless and unachievable reconstruction of the first performance on the one hand, and
on the other a complete and arrogant independence which
treats the play as a mere starting-point for improvisations and
the author as no more than a fine name. My point here is that
directors and actors hardly ever have, as a matter of fact, taken
account of the dramatist's theatrical intentions, once he is no
longer around to insist on them. This must have had its effect
on scholars and critics. Either they have been so bound up with
the theatrical practices of their own day that they have failed to
see how these have fought against and obliterated an essential
aspect of the original work, or they have been so put off by the
high-handed treatment of their beloved plays that they have
turned their back on the theatrical aspect of the tragedies
altogether, and have treated them as incorporeal poems or as
mere corrupted texts.

Now to the notion which has had the most far-reaching effect:
the idea that the performance in the theatre is not the province
of the tragic poet or of the critic, and may even be unworthy of
them. This is clearly implied in Aristotle's *Poetics* and through

[1] I have in mind in particular the 'seminal' figures like Peter Brook and Jerzy
Grotowski, and the influence of the actor-lunatic Antonin Artaud and the sage
Jan Kott. The first chapter of F. Fergusson *The Idea of a Theater* (Princeton 1949)
has been influential here. Ironically the theory of a ritual theatre stems in part
from Hellenists like Frazer, Cornford, Jane Harrison, and Murray.

Poet has had untold influence. The distinction is made near the beginning at 1449a8f. where Aristotle talks of judging the development of tragedy αὐτό τε καθ' αὐτὸ . . . καὶ πρὸς τὰ θέατρα. Whatever is meant exactly by θέατρα[1] Aristotle must here be driving a wedge between the essential work and its manifestation in the theatre; and this is irreconcilable with the view I am advocating. I postpone a full discussion of what Aristotle has to say on the theatrical aspects of drama to Appendix F.

Aristotle's *Poetics* is the most influential critical work on Tragedy ever written, and with good reason. But its influence has not been wholly for good. The over-emphasis on plausibility and consistency, for example, has wasted a lot of disciples' time on insignificant trifles, the teleological framework has led to an over-emphasis on the primitive in Aeschylus, and the failure to appreciate complex plots has hindered the understanding of Euripides (see Burnett chapter I). On the particular topic of visual meaning Aristotle's failure seems to lie in his times. During the fourth century it had become possible to regard the text of a Greek tragedy as the tragedy itself and not as the libretto of a performance.[2] This attitude is not to be found in Plato, and may to some extent be a reaction to Plato's emphasis on performance. Once tragedy is treated as a text then it is all too easy to lose sight of its visual meaning. That Aristotle did, and critics ever since have turned their backs in the same direction.

All these actions for which I am claiming dramatic significance take place, of course, on stage in view of the audience. I am not concerned here with actions off-stage, those that took place before the play began, or those that take place elsewhere. Indeed I should claim that the actions which take place off-stage and outside the play, although they are generally larger and more violent, are comparatively unimportant. A Greek tragedy concentrates on a certain short sequence of events set at a particular place and within a certain brief space of time; and every action

---

[1] There has been a tendency among recent commentators to try to exculpate Aristotle from his disparagement of the theatrical aspect of tragedy. Thus, on this place Lucas, for example, glosses τὰ θέατρα as (p. 79) 'accidental factors like the requirements of dramatic festivals—as it might be by dinner and licensing hours'. But that would be πρὸς τοὺς ἀγῶνας; and θέατρα must be to do with spectators and the play in visible performance. Unfortunately Aristotle does not elaborate the distinction here (ἄλλος λόγος 9).

[2] Cf. in general the clear and informed exposition of Mehmel *Virgil und Apollonius Rhodius* (Hamburg 1940) 20–3.

outside that time and place, however huge and horrendous, only matters in so far as it is brought to bear on the focus of the play on stage. It has only as much prominence as the attention it is given. The actions on the stage, on the other hand, although usually rather slight and lacking in violence, become the object of concentrated attention and bear the visible burden of the tragedy.

It might seem obvious that in a play the things that happen before the eyes of the audience will be of crucial importance in a way that actions which are only alluded to or reported cannot be. Yet in the discussion of Greek tragedy there is a widespread and pervasive notion that the mighty deeds off-stage are somehow what the play is 'about'. One cannot but suspect that this idea owes something to the usual practice of the handbooks which both in antiquity and in modern times have given synopses of the plot. The texts of most plays are prefaced by a summary of the plot in the *hypothesis*; and the contents of each Greek tragedy have been reduced to a paragraph of paraphrase in dozens of modern handbooks. Yet a mere summary of the plot can tell us nothing of critical value about a play, nothing of its special qualities and emphases—it cannot even distinguish a mediocrity from a masterpiece.[1] Whatever the reasons behind it, there is a widespread misconception that there is little or no action in a Greek tragedy, and that all the momentous and notable actions take place off-stage. We find, for example, in *GGL* I 2 p. 121 the assertion that 'What the public actually sees with its eyes in Greek tragedy is as a rule not *action* in the physical sense'. But if one reads on (p. 122) then one finds that what Schmid allows to qualify as 'Handlung' is simply and only physical *violence*.

---

[1] Perhaps the over-emphasis on plot summary, and hence on actions which take place off-stage, is in part due once more to Aristotle *Poet*. Aristotle did not mean anything so superficial as this by μῦθος nor by πρᾶξις, but a misleading impression might easily be gained. When, for instance, he says at 1453b3ff. that pity and fear may be aroused simply by hearing τὰ πράγματα γινόμενα . . . ἅπερ ἂν πάθοι τις ἀκούων τὸν τοῦ Οἰδίπου μῦθον, the reader might well take μῦθος here to mean a summary of the plot. Even such a sensitive critic as Jones (198) can say 'the *Antigone* is about the burying of Polyneikes: this is the single distinct action which, in the Aristotelian analysis, the tragedy imitates' (cf. *hypoth* I to *Ant* τὸ δὲ κεφάλαιόν ἐστι τάφος Πολυνείκους . . .). Yet the burial does not even take place on-stage. In fairness to Aristotle the variant reading in B should probably be accepted at *Poet* 1450a16, giving μίμησις . . . πράξεων καὶ βίου (rather than πράξεως); and elsewhere in *Poet* the singular πρᾶξις may mean 'action = acts' rather than 'one single particular action'.

And yet there are many kinds of human action other than those which draw blood.[1]

There is another widespread misconception which also tends to direct attention away from the small but immediate actions on stage towards the large but distant actions beyond. The dogma is that the inherited body of myth was firmly fixed by tradition and allowed the dramatist very little freedom in his use of 'action'. Quite apart from all the evidence for variation and innovation in the handling of myth in Greek tragedy, it is not even true that the immutably fixed elements in the story put any significant constraint on the dramatist's invention. It is mistaken to claim, as is often done, that the 'story dictates' the dramatic treatment, or that 'it is the poet's initial choice of the subject of his play or trilogy that determines the details of its treatment'.[2] The three 'Electra' plays, the *Philoctetes* plays (Dio Chrys. *Or* 52) and even more clearly the three 'Seven against Thebes' plays (A. *Seven*, S. *Ant*, E. *Phoen*) are the simple refutation of this assertion. It is entirely up to the dramatist which brief sequence of events he selects from the myth, which aspects he emphasizes, which characters he concentrates on, which he neglects. The identity and role of the chorus is in his hands, so is the sequence of events and their relative emphasis, so is the selection and articulation of themes. In sum, it is up to the playwright how he makes his play.

And so it is up to the playwright to invent the stage action and to use it; the few fixed elements make no difference to this. And it is, indeed, precisely in his dramatization that his art lies; not in the story, but in *how* he turns it into a drama. For the critic the quality of the play depends on the artistic arrangement and selection, including the stage action, and not on the mere story, which is shared by good and bad dramatist alike. The compulsion of the myth may be exaggerated as a joke (as it is in Antiphanes fr. 191 K), but it is not to be taken seriously. Aristotle with his admirable emphasis on ἡ τῶν πραγμάτων cύcτacιc would no doubt have agreed with this (though it is a pity he did not

[1] I should mention that the word 'Handlung' was used in a metaphysical sense by that school of *Geistesgeschichte* which saw all great works of art as chapters in the history of ideas. Aeschylus is seen as struggling with the emergent concepts of choice, individuality, and responsibility in Snell's *Aischylos und das Handeln im Drama* (*Philol* Supp. XX, 1 (1928)) 1ff.

[2] Garvie 143 (quoted with approval in *AC* 1969 p. 493).

say it more explicitly). In conclusion, the kind of action which is under the dramatist's control and in which his stagecraft consists is the stage action, the deeds which are done before the eyes of the audience.

§3. *Text and Stage Action*

Now we must face the problem of how to discover the stage action, and how to distinguish the significant from the trivial. How in the absence of explicit stage directions are we to know what is going on? The answer is, in principle, simple: the significant stage instructions are implicit in the words. The characters of Greek tragedy say what they are doing, or are described as they act; and so the words accompany and clarify the action. Wilamowitz put the matter succinctly: 'acerrime contendo, e verbis poetarum satis certe colligi actionem . . .'.[1] With this goes the converse, which was put thus by Fraenkel (A. *Ag ed* III 642–3): 'In ancient dramatic literature it is never allowable to invent stage-directions which are not related to some definite utterance in the dialogue.'

In practice, however, the inference of the stage action from the words is not so simple (as is frequently witnessed in this work). The relation between text and action is not always straightforward and is not uniform. None the less, what is required for the moment is a rule of thumb. It would be a good start if it could be broadly accepted that the words, if we know how to use them, give the significant action, and that there was no significant action other than that indicated by the words.

There arises straight away a pair of basic difficulties. (i) How can we tell that the plays did not include all sorts of stage business which are not indicated at all by the words? (ii) How can we tell that when characters say they are doing something they are in fact translating their words into stage action?

First, how much stage action did the dramatist sanction which is not accompanied or referred to at all in the words? It has already been observed that the most important element in

---

[1] Wilamowitz *ed maj* xxxiv; cf. his vigorous earlier formulation in E. *Her ed* ii 5 n. 1 and Haupt's passing dictum (*Opusc* II 460) 'nihil autem fere fit in Graecorum tragoediis comoediisque quin fieri simul indicetur oratione'. The principle has been recently reasserted more fully by Steidle 22f., Ortkemper 18f.

theatrical revivals and reinterpretations is precisely the interpolation of significant stage business which is not authorized by
the text: perhaps, it may be claimed, in the original performance
there was a lot more going on, not only decorative details but
important stage actions which coloured and altered the entire
play—and perhaps these are not reflected at all in the text.
Why should they be? The text is, after all, only a 'libretto',
not a complete casebook of the production. If any play does
not make sense unless we have to suppose some stage action
which is not indicated by the words, then this would be the thin
end of the wedge. Zielinski[1] claimed that there are many such
places, and formulated the principle: 'If a certain passage is
logically incomprehensible or psychologically implausible without the assumption of a certain piece of accompanying stage
business, then that stage business is to be assumed.' But are there
any such places? Tycho v. Wilamowitz in an excellent passage
(140–2) argues that the interpretation of a play must proceed
from what is there, not from what is not there, and shows that
Zielinski by a *petitio principii* wishes to interpolate stage action
in order to support an interpretation which is not grounded in
the play we have. Only if a play makes indisputable nonsense
without an imagined stage action should we be willing to interpolate it.

But one might take a more arbitrary and less rigorous standpoint. Why should we suppose that the relation between words
and action was so close? As it has been put, 'we cannot demonstrate that fifth century producers did not sometimes indulge
their fancy. Greek Tragedy was not necessarily austere at all
times.'[2] There is in the last resort no refutation of this contention,
even though there is no external evidence of any such procedure.
But it becomes a most unlikely notion when considered in
practical terms. For this extra action would either have to take
place in a dumb show or it would have to be going on while
the words were being spoken. In the former case, why should
the dumb actions not be accompanied by words? In the latter,

---

[1] Zielinski *Philol* 64 (1905) 6–14, with special reference to S. *Trach.* The quotation is from p. 8.

[2] H. L. Tracy *CJ* 53 (1958) 338ff.; the quotation is from p. 345. Cf. on p. 344
'There may well have been much more free invention on the producer's part
than any surviving evidence suggests': but we have the 'producer's' invention—
the play itself.

this would be a serious distraction from the words, for if the action is sufficiently conspicuous and important, then the words, if they are not to be mere mouthings, ought to reflect it, and should not be about something else. Both these alternatives are, I suggest, sufficiently objectionable to leave us still with a fair working hypothesis that there was no important action which was not also signalled in the words.

This is not to say that every single action on the Greek stage was noticed in the words. Mute attendants play their part without any attention being paid to them (see *Pers* 155c*), conventional gestures must have been made where appropriate, and so on.[1] Sometimes there is room for uncertainty over exact movements and over the timing of exits and entrances especially of minor characters. But if an action is significant, then it does not go by unnoticed. I do not know of a single stage action in Greek tragedy which is essential to the play and yet has to be assumed without any indication from the text. It is true that not only directors in the theatre but scholars in their commentaries have alleged all sorts of other stage business, both decorative and significant, which are not sanctioned by the text: but I do not know of one single instance which is inevitable, which must be accepted for the play to work. In every case the considerations which led to the positing of the stage instruction can be otherwise explained. And, if every action which would have to be assumed in any case is, in fact, indicated in the words, then it is a fair working hypothesis, though it is not logically entailed, that there were not other important actions which are not signed in the text.[2]

Whenever circumstances are relevant to the dramatic action in its proper sense, they are rendered unambiguous and can be easily discerned without the effort of peeping into what are supposed to be

[1] For some other examples (not all right) of trivial stage instructions which are left unsigned see Andrieu 201–2.

[2] The apparent counter-example which is often cited in this context is the chariot entry of the Queen at A. *Pers* 150ff., which is not given any direct attention at the time, but is only alluded to later at 607ff. Scholars have come to hot-headed conclusions on the strength of this one place; I quote some on *Pers* 155b*. I also try to argue there that this apparent exception is explicable on its own terms, and should not be regarded as a true counter-example to my thesis. For discussion of other comparable problems in Aeschylus, which are also explicable, see *Seven* 719a* on the alleged arming scene at *Seven* 677ff., and *Eum* 574* and 777b* on the arrival and departure of Apollo at the trial scene.

hidden allusions or making complicated calculations. Where, on the other hand, facts belong only to the general background or where they are primarily connected with things that play no direct part in the evolution of the plot or the themes of the dialogue, they remain indifferent: we are not to think of them at all. (Fraenkel A. *Ag comm* II 255f.)

Greek tragedy is a concentrated and single-purposed art form; and it would be quite uncharacteristic for the actors to be doing one thing while talking about another. If actions are to be significant, which means they must be given concentrated attention, then time and words must be spent on them. If it is accepted that we cannot legitimately interpret a tragedy in terms of things which are not spoken about in the play, then we can hardly allow any importance to actions which are not even referred to in the words. So we should allow significance only to those actions which are sanctioned by the words.[1]

The negative argument—that there was *not* significant action which is *not* reflected in the words—may seem only reasonable. The positive corollary—that the action indicated in the words was translated into visible stage action—may seem more controversial. Although it is in many ways a less important point, it is hard to establish firm ground.

The generation of Wilamowitz and that of his teachers tended to assume that in stage presentation the Greek theatre aimed at realism and illusion in all possible respects. In 1886 A. Müller (110) was able to claim, for instance, 'It is indubitable that the Greeks strove for illusion, and tried to achieve this through scenic resources' (he goes on to qualify this). This assurance was based on contemporary theatrical and operatic stage practice (though it also rested, no doubt, on an entire vision of the Golden

---

[1] Generally speaking the same is true of Greek comedy also, though not so rigidly, just as the gripping of attention is less concentrated. In Aristophanes props are not always identified, for example; see Dover Arph. *Clouds ed* on 1146 (p. 232), cf. *Ekkles* 890. For actions without clear verbal accompaniment in later comedy consider e.g. Arph. *Pl* 1097ff., where Hermes evidently knocks and hides without saying anything. At Men. *Dysc* 211–14 there is some vague silent business between Sostratus and the girl, at *Misoum* 211f. the Nurse must be gesticulating or whispering etc. On the whole, however, the action is clearly indicated in Greek Old and New Comedy as well as Tragedy. Contrast the situation in Seneca, see Zwierlein 55f. The same rule of thumb also seems to be true of Shakespeare, with the special exception of dumb shows, and of stage instructions to be performed in silence: these are marked by the author. But it is possible for Styan (cited in p. 20 n. 2) 53 to say 'instructions to the actors are *always* found built into the text' (my italics).

Age in Athens). During this century it has gradually become
recognized that the words of the play may not simply report
what the audience sees, but rather may interpret what it sees,
may fill it out, and may even be in lieu of any attempt to stage
in practice what is said to be happening. Spectators whose
imaginations have not been spoiled by realistic stage management will 'see' what the dramatist tells them they are seeing
(always provided that the dramatist conjures skilfully). It may
be that, when the words are most vivid and explicit, the staging
is most rudimentary, and most is left to the imagination.[1] We
have been helped to see this by comparative work on other
theatrical traditions—the early English stage, Brechtian counter-
realism, the traditional Oriental schools—and by contemporary
stage practice, especially the production of Shakespeare in the
tradition of William Poel and Granville-Barker. Each new handbook still tends to speak as though the contemporary theatre still
commonly indulges in the realistic extravagances of Beerbohm
Tree, and still enjoys some easy polemic against the view that
the Greek theatre was realistic: but in fact there must be very
few who still retain that notion.[2]

The reaction against a position like Müller's has gone far, and
some scholars are now approaching the opposite pole. The
extremely non-naturalistic conventions of the Noh and Kabuki
dramas[3] have encouraged some to question whether even the
simplest movements and stage objects were represented in any
realistic or mimetic way. After all, we cannot say that anything
in a play 'demands' or 'necessitates' representation on the stage.

[1] A. M. Dale put the situation with characteristic clarity in the opening paragraph of her 'Seen and Unseen on the Greek Stage' (*Papers* 119) : 'Our only reliable
evidence, in detail, for the staging of fifth-century tragedy is the text of the plays
themselves. But since those texts were written for performance, not with the
idea of helping a reading public to visualise the scene, or even of helping a sub-
sequent producer to stage a correct revival, the most precise indications often
concern, somewhat paradoxically, what was invisible to the audience, or visible
in so rudimentary a form that they needed help in interpreting what they saw.
Here the text elucidates and supplements the spectacle.'

[2] There seems to be something of an informed reaction back towards high
realism in the fifth century, especially in scene painting. This is led by H. Kenner
Das Theater und der Realismus in der griechischen Kunst (Vienna 1955), and is based on
the study of the later influence of fifth-century painting. I am not competent to
judge Kenner's arguments; but they do not seem to be altogether convincing, see
Bieber *Gnomon* 28 (1956) 129–34.

[3] For comparison of Noh Theatre with Greek tragedy see Lesky *Ges Schr* 275ff.
and P. Arnott *The Theatres of Japan* (London 1969) 162ff.

'No play . . . *needs* anything except human beings with
limbs. Everything else can be mimed and imagined . . .
Skene p. 2 (Dover is only exploring the methodology; he doe.
imply that he himself believes that everything was mimed a.
imagined in the Greek theatre). Pursuing this train of argument
we find a paragraph added in the second edition of P-C *DFA²*
(p. 176):

> If we remember the undoubted fact that facial expressions such as
> weeping, which were certainly not visible on stage, are frequently
> described in the plays, we must at least reckon with the possibility
> that the descriptions of striking and vigorous movement that we meet
> in the plays are not unequivocal evidence for the occurrence of these
> same movements in a naturalistic performance by the actor. We are
> simply ignorant of the degree of stylization that prevailed, even in
> gesture.

The extreme conclusion of this approach would be that Greek
tragedy was a kind of *Rezitationsdrama* in which the actors did
little more than stand and deliver their lines, leaving all the
visualization of the play to the imagination of the audience. No
one has ever maintained this position, but it remains true that
the descriptions in the plays 'are not unequivocal evidence for
a naturalistic representation in the theatre'. Most would suppose, I imagine, that the truth lies somewhere between these
two extremes: but the difficulty lies, precisely, in drawing the
line. How much was represented on stage and how realistically,
and how much was left to the imagination? In our present state
of knowledge some of the line-drawing is bound to be arbitrary;
but there are at least some guidelines.

Neither of the extreme positions is reasonably tenable. It is
not difficult to undermine a totally illusionist position. Most of
the work on the conventionality and non-naturalism of the
Greek theatre has been devoted to formal and compositional
techniques;[1] but attention has also been paid to staging, and
this is the chief preoccupation of Arnott's book especially. One
need only point to the masks, the continuous presence of the
chorus, the 'cancelled' openings (see *Seven* 1b*) or the ekkyklema

---

[1] See *Bauformen*, especially Jens's *Einleitung*, and all the literature which lies
behind that collection.

(see pp. 442–3) to show that Greek tragedy was not completely illusionist. Clearly the Athenian spectator had a lively imagination which was ready and able to achieve considerable feats under the guidance of the dramatist. This imagination could doubtless picture many events far more vividly than any attempt, however ingenious, at realistic representation.[1] Few would claim, I imagine, that any attempt was made to represent (for example) the seismic upheavals of the palace in E. *Ba* and other plays,[2] or the beacon in A. *Ag* (see p. 277 n. 2) or the birds in E. *Ion*. But to establish that the Greek theatre was not totally naturalistic and that the audience's imagination was asked on occasion to supplement or supplant representation is not by any means to show that there was nothing realistic about the staging of the plays, or that everything visual was left to the imagination of the spectator.

The other extreme—that which claims a high degree of stylization with little or no naturalistic representation—is more difficult to modify, since it is so adaptable. One cannot say *a priori* that anything *must* have been represented. Nor can one argue from vase painting, for instance, since the painter may have translated the play into naturalistic terms; and one must beware of Aristophanic parody since there may be extra comic point in the lack of correspondence. Nevertheless there is some firm ground to be held by the representationalist. For a start, it is hard to deny that there was a skene which represented a building, and that it had a door which represented a door, and that there were eisodoi which represented ways to and from the place of action. There can be little doubt that entrances and exits were made by walking in a not unnaturalistic way.

Masks were cited in *DFA*[2] (quoted above) as sure evidence that not everything which is described was represented: but masks are also evidence for a degree of realism. The masks of the fifth-century tragic theatre were not nearly as stylized as those used in some other theatres, e.g. the featureless half-masks

---

[1] The *locus classicus* on the potentialities of the imagination in the theatre is, I suppose, the four speeches of the Chorus in Shakespeare's *Henry V*.

[2] See p. 274 below. This is not to say that earthquakes and so on are beyond the ingenuity of a classical scholar with a mechanical bent, even though he were to restrict himself to the resources of the fifth century (such a man could probably make a mask with movable expressions). But the imagination can do it better, and with much less trouble.

sometimes used in Brecht. There is evidence that the art of the προcωποποιόc was fairly lifelike; there was detailed differentiation of sex, age, status, etc. (see P-C *DFA*² 190ff.). And there is no reason to doubt that, for instance, there were snakes on the heads of the Erinyes, or that Oedipus' bloody eyes were represented, or that Dionysus was given an effeminate beauty. The chorus is another non-naturalistic convention of the Greek theatre which is also evidence for some degree of realism. We have good evidence that Greek dancing was strongly mimetic (see P-C *DFA*² 246ff.); while the choreography was no doubt highly stylized, it must also have been to some degree representational. And if the chorus is to mime in choreography, then the actors must have made some representational movement also.[1] If the chorus of A. *Pers* is to dance the ghost-raising of Darius, then the Queen must act out her pouring of libations; if the chorus of A. *Hik* is to dance frantic flight, then the Egyptian herald must represent his pursuit in movement. And when actors sang in monody or lyric dialogue, then they presumably danced mimetic actions: if they are to make representational movements when singing, then they must also surely make them when speaking. And we might expect movements accompanied by speech to be less stylized and more naturalistic than those accompanied by song.

Aristophanes is tricky evidence for a problem like this. By no means everything represented in a parody was necessarily represented in the original.[2] But he does provide evidence of a device of the tragic stage which may suggest a considerable degree of representational realism: the crane or μηχανή (see pp. 443ff.). In any highly stylized theatre it seems obvious that flying should be represented by choreography, or even simply by verbal depiction. Yet the Greek theatre went to the trouble and expense of having a special piece of machinery in order to stage literal movement through the air. Of course the *mechane* was a special spectacular

[1] Note [Arle.] *Probl.* 918b27ff. (19. 15) τὰ μὲν ἀπὸ τῆc cκηνῆc οὐκ ἀντίcτροφα, τὰ δὲ τοῦ χοροῦ ἀντίcτροφα. ὁ μὲν γὰρ ὑποκριτὴc ἀγωνιcτὴc καὶ μιμητήc, ὁ δὲ χορὸc ἧττον μιμεῖται.
[2] It would be a mistake to suppose that Dicaeopolis' chopping-block was a prop in E. *Telephos*! On the other hand, to take two examples at random, the scenes where the coal-bucket and wine-skin are threatened (*Acharn* 331, *Thesm* 688ff.) are strong evidence for sword, baby, and altar in Euripides (despite Gould *JHS* 93 (1973) 101–3); and *Wasps* 995ff. is evidence that tragic swooning was accompanied by falling to the ground.

show-piece, but it is still an indication of a certain desire for representation.

I now leave comparatively firm ground for a consideration which, although less solid, is, I suggest, important. In the case of many props, movements, and gestures, which are clearly marked in the texts of the plays and are important to them, one may fairly ask what would be the point of *not* representing them naturalistically. In the case of larger fixed props—e.g. tombs, statues, bushes—we may legitimately question whether they were realistically represented (see Arnott chapters 3, 4, 6); but with smaller portable props what is the point in *not* having them?[1] It is not difficult to think of stage properties which are so imbued with dramatic significance that it would do positive harm to the play in performance if they were not straightforwardly repre-sented: the purple cloth in A. *Ag*, the sword in S. *Aj*, the bow in S. *Phil* or E. *Her*, the image of Artemis in *IT* and many others (cf. Dingel *passim* esp. 123–95). Similarly the differentiations of costume can be so significant that there seems to be no positive gain in maintaining that costumes had no naturalistic features. There is real dramatic point in the tatters of Xerxes (see *Pers* 909b*), the squalor of Philoctetes, or the contrast between the regal finery and the servile dress of the pairs of opposed women in E. *Andr* and *El*.[2] Is there any point in *not* using costume visually as well as verbally? And the same argument holds good in the most important sphere of representation: movements and ges-tures.[3] What is the point of the actors *not* doing what they say they are doing, provided it is practicable?

Now, there are probably many who consider that there is no question but that the actors performed the things which they say they are doing, and that this whole discussion is unnecessary. But the fact remains that we are dealing with a theatre which was in many important ways stylized and non-naturalistic; and

[1] Unfortunately Dingel never faces the question of realism and illusion, but simply takes as a working hypothesis that everything in the text was represented on the stage. He is criticized for this by Collard *Gnomon* 40 (1968) 195.

[2] Cf. Dingel 195ff., P-C *DFA*² 202f. (202 n. 14 seems to doubt whether the kings in rags really did wear ragged costumes; cf. Webster *GTP* 39: but why should they not?) For Shakespearean analogies consider Hamlet's black, the contrast of Romans and Orientals in *Antony and Cleopatra*, or English and French in *Henry V*.

[3] Neither Spitzbarth nor Shisler considers the possibility that actors might not have naturalistically put their words into action; though Shisler notes the impossi-bility of weeping, trembling, and facial expression (392–3).

so nothing should be taken for granted. And the fact remains that there is a considerable range of aspects of staging where there is legitimate doubt over how much was represented and how naturalistically, and where any decision is bound to be more or less arbitrary. Consider further actions and the handling of props. It seems to me fairly safe to assume that simple 'everyday' actions were represented in a straightforward way. I include among these entrances and exits; also, holding and handing over portable objects, veiling the head, sitting and lying down, running, drawing swords, pouring libations, and so on. For the purposes of argument one might make a class of rather more involved actions which might include kneeling, supplication, embracing, fainting, striking, crawling, binding, knocking at the door, kissing.[1] All these are practicable actions, and for my part I reckon they were carried out fairly realistically. But it should be admitted, in all caution, that these actions may have been highly stylized. And there are some more difficult and out of the ordinary actions and props, such as arming (see *Seven* 719a*), carrying lighted torches (see *Eum* 1047b*), and chariot-borne entries (see *Pers* 155b*). Even here I believe there was fairly realistic representation; but I admit that this is to some extent an arbitrary opinion. It is worth recalling, however, that some attempt was made at the representation of flying.

We may always for the purposes of discussion draw a distinction between what was actually done and actually seen in the theatre, and what the playwright means his audience to envisage and to see with enthralled eyes. Once this distinction is made, the degree to which the actual stage picture and the imaginative dramatic picture coincided can remain an open question. For we can usually build up the dramatic picture from the words and their context, and can attempt to see it in the mind's eye (always provided the dramatist is doing his work well). And this is, for the purposes of dramatic criticism, by far the more important picture, since it is what is meant to be happening in the play, within the drama, which has direct bearing on the understanding

---

[1] Literal kissing was not, of course, possible, as is pointed out in P-C *DFA²* 171: but even on the modern stage there are 'stage kisses' where the actors do not actually osculate. *DFA²* 171f. lays great stress on the fact that naturalistic weeping was impossible: but not many actors *without* masks can actually weep tears on stage—most simply act out the accompanying sounds and gestures. For a list of actions to accompany weeping in Greek tragedy see Shisler 381.

and appreciation of the work of art. Having done our best to see
what we are meant to see within the play, we can then go on, if
we wish, to the secondary consideration of how closely or how
remotely this was imitated in the theatre. But the significant
dramatic action remains both more important and more accessible, since it is incorporated to a large extent in the text, and the
text is preserved for us comparatively unimpaired.

   In order to imagine how far the Greek tragic theatre was
representational, it may be useful to suggest a distinction, however indistinct, between 'active' and 'passive' aspects of staging.
By active staging I mean those aspects which comprise the basic
action of the drama, which are, in effect, those aspects handled
by the ὑποκριταί, the speaking actors: this I take to have been
fairly naturalistic. By passive staging, on the other hand, I mean
all impersonal aspects of stage management, in effect those
aspects which were the task not of the actor but of those 'behind
the scenes'. Thus it is, to say the least, open to doubt how much
realism there was in matters such as scenery, larger props, stage
machinery, crowds, and in 'happenings' such as earthquakes,
sunrises, or birds. This rough distinction does have the virtue of
drawing attention to the fact that some aspects of staging are
far more integral to the drama than others. Matters of passive
staging are part of the setting rather than of the real action of
the play; and, since they are important only in their effect and
bearing on the characters and the action, it is not of great
critical importance how realistic or unrealistic they were. But
the active staging, the stage actions and the personal stage
properties, are often at the very centre of dramatic attention. If
this kind of stage action, which includes entrances and exits, is,
as I maintain, an integral and important part of the artist's
creation, then the staging will inevitably make a difference to
our critical assessment. We cannot but consider whether a
particular stage action was completely naturalistic, fairly
naturalistic, rather stylized, highly stylized, completely non-
representational, or even not represented in action at all, even
though we may not be able to come to any confident decision
between these alternatives. Since it would be tedious every time
I mention a stage action to make the caveat that it may not
have been naturalistically represented, I shall take this as read.
I shall also persevere in my supposition that most 'active' staging

was fairly realistic, until I am made aware of good reasons for thinking otherwise.

§4. *Spectacle in Aeschylus*

Since I am stressing the importance of the visual element (ὄψις) in the Greek theatre, Aeschylus may seem the obvious choice for special attention, since, as every handbook and introduction tells us, he was particularly lavish with his spectacular effects (ὄψις). The word ὄψις may prevaricate in sense between 'what is seen' on the one hand and 'outward show' on the other; and the word 'spectacle' to some extent translates this range of meaning (cf. Appendix F). One of my chief theses is that the use of ὄψις in the superficial sense has been overplayed with reference to Aeschylus and that his use of ὄψις in the less blatant but much more important sense has been neglected.

The tragic theatre of the fifth century is not usually thought of as a particularly spectacular one compared with, say, the modern opera house or more lavish productions of Shakespeare, or even with modern productions of Greek tragedy in the style of Max Reinhardt.[1] On the other hand there clearly was an element of spectacle in the fifth-century productions, particularly in the costumes, which were one of the chief expenses for the choregus. The evidence of pottery painting suggests that while costumes may have been fairly plain earlier in the century they were elaborately decorated by the end of it (see P-C *DFA*² 198f.). But most of the other features which might have provided spectacle, in the sense in which we think of it, are in one way or another controversial—scene painting, crowds and extras, stage machinery, for example.

But one thing is generally agreed: Aeschylus was by far the most spectacular dramatist. Aeschylus is supposed to have astounded his spectators with exotic crowds and to have stunned them with huge and complex machines. Compared with this almost Wagnerian extravaganza the stage of Sophocles and Euripides is seen as simple and austere (and, it is sometimes

[1] A bizarre exception seems to be Wirsing in his drawings in Bulle–Wirsing *Szenenbilder zum gr. Theater* (Berlin 1950). Wirsing's skene building is about 40 feet high, and everything else is in the same inflated style. These pictures are an entertaining deterrent against exaggerated notions of realism in 'passive' staging.

implied, more profound). But my own observations on Aeschylus'
stagecraft have led me to conclude that the orthodox view of his
monstrously alarming spectacle is to a large extent unfounded,
and that it seriously hinders the full appreciation of Aeschylus as
an artist. The usual view would have us believe that the spectacle
is there in order to cover over weak content, and so to dazzle
the audience that it neglects the failings.[1] I maintain, on the
contrary, that the visual in Aeschylus is integrally bound up with
the content and indivisible from it, so that if one is weak then so
is the other. Moreover, I hope to show that a notable aspect of
Aeschylus' quality as a dramatic artist lies in his use of 'life-
sized' actions, like entrances and exits, which do real work
within their plays. Such smaller visual effects, while not incompatible with grand spectacle, would inevitably tend to be
lost or overlooked in the storm and dazzle, not only by scholars
but by an audience in the theatre. I do not mean to deny that
there is a strong element of the exotic and of the ceremonial in
the theatre of Aeschylus: on the contrary these are particularly
characteristic features of his tragedies, though far from absent in
the later theatre, particularly Euripides. (There is an excellent
account of outlandish elements in Greek tragedy in Kranz *Stas*
chapter III (71ff.).) But the spectacles which involve these
elements are integral to the plays and are a significant part of
them. The spectacles which I hope to obliterate from our vision
of Aeschylus' stagecraft are inessential visual effects—particularly crowds, machines, and massive 'happenings'—which are
not founded in the plays, and which are, I maintain, the additions of later producers and scholars, both ancient and modern.
They are nothing to do with the authentic Aeschylus.

I am not the first to have raised such a protest. This was one
of the bones of contention in the famous battle between Hermann
and K. O. Müller. Müller introduced extravagant spectacle into
Eum at every possible opportunity, and in this he was, it seems,
followed by some contemporary productions. Hermann attacked
this along with everything else; but he also treated the subject

---

[1] This is perhaps clearest in Page's spectacular footnote on *Eum* in Denniston–
Page *Ag ed* xxii n. 1; in particular 'but its faults might be . . . overlooked in the
brilliance of the spectacle which it provided'. The implication, by the way, that
such vacuous spectacle is in itself quite an achievement cannot be allowed. Any
hack impresario can, given sufficient funds, mount a spectacular. The 'epic' cinema
is an illustration.

separately in his still valuable *De Re Scaenica in Aeschyli Orestea*.[1]
There he applies the admirable dictum: 'naturae legem esse
constat, quod paucis fieri possit, non efficere per multa, hoc est,
ut aliis verbis dicam, nihil instituere quod non sit necessarium'
(though the crucial relative terms are in practice indefinite). On
this issue Hermann lost the battle with Müller, and since then
the astounding extravaganza has been almost universally
assumed.[2] It has in recent times been expounded elegantly and
influentially by K. Reinhardt and by Murray.[3] It is even
accepted by Arnott (107ff.), despite the fact that he argues that
(111) 'the fifth century saw a gradually increasing interest in
spectacle for its own sake', and that the Greek theatre became
more and more spectacular as the playwright himself lost control
of the presentation—a very plausible view.

What, then, is our evidence for the degree of spectacle in the
staging of Aeschylus? I must refer to Appendix B for a full discussion of the nature and evaluation of such evidence. Clearly,
however, our primary source and final criterion must be the
plays themselves. And in going through the texts I have found
that a great deal of the spectacle alleged by scholars simply is
not warranted by the plays themselves; it is either added without
any textual basis, or it is built up on quite insufficient grounds.
The plays themselves do clearly indicate a fair number of exotic
and ceremonial spectacles, and very fine they are. I need only
mention the ghost-raising of Darius and the abandoned oriental
dirges in *Pers*, the funeral procession in *Seven*, the purple cloth in
Ag, the *kommos* at Agamemnon's tomb in *Cho*, the final procession
in *Eum*, the very idea of the Erinyes as a chorus. These alone
establish Aeschylus as a dramatist who makes brilliant use of

---

[1] *Opusc* viii 158ff., first published in 1846; the essay is also printed in the edition
of 1852 vol. ii 648ff.

[2] Bethe brought valid points to bear against alleged spectacular effects in
Aeschylus, but these are tied up with his unhappy theory of a scenic revolution in
about 427 B.C. On the other hand in 1906 Bolle argued sensibly and effectively
that much of the spectacle supposed to have been indulged in by Aeschylus simply
is not justified by a consideration of the *plays* themselves. Note his conclusion (18):
'There is absolutely no justification in attributing to Aeschylus grand staging
with ingenious scenery and machines. All his plays may be produced with extremely
simple resources . . .' But Bolle's work has been overlooked.

[3] Wilamowitz 240 must have been influential. For a particularly extravagant
account of the Aeschylean stage see Denniston–Page *Ag ed*, xxix–xxxi. (The
spectacular Aeschylus is taken to really fantastic lengths by W. Barton *Schauplatz
und Bühnenvorgänge bei Aischylos* (Diss. Jena 1951).)

visual effects, and perhaps as one who does so more strikingly than Sophocles or Euripides. But 'spectacular' elements like these are all doing dramatic work within their plays; and they are far from all that has gone into the usual version of Aeschylus' spectacular stagecraft.

Archaeology is of limited value on this as on other aspects of Aeschylus' staging, since little survives of the early theatre and since early tragedy seems to have had little influence on pottery painters (cf. Appendix B p. 435). The archaeology of the later theatre does, however, contribute to a picture of a theatre which developed from comparatively plain beginnings into a spectacular showpiece. The skene and cavea at Athens were gradually built up in a more monumental and expensive way. It is in the fourth century and later that finely constructed theatres are built throughout the Greek world. And it is in the fourth century that theatrical spectacle provided such an inspiration for the showy vases of South Italy. And it is later that we begin to hear of lavish and ostentatious dramatic festivals mounted by Dionysius of Syracuse, Philip, Alexander, and Antiochus.[1] The archaeological evidence suggests that the masks, costumes, and buildings of the early theatre were comparatively plain and simple; and this makes for a presumption that other aspects of staging were so also.

Old Comedy is the only creditable secondary evidence on a matter such as this. Aristophanes does not, so far as I can see, corroborate the usual view of a spectacular Aeschylus. Aeschylus is not remarkable in Aristophanes for his extravagant spectacle but for his bombastic and monstrous language. He is also characterized by his choreography, his lyric, his silences, his expression of war and of dirge: but nowhere for crowds, stage machinery, or huge visual 'events'. There are two passages in *Frogs* which might be claimed to support the usual view. At 1060f. in explaining why tragic characters should be grandiloquent Aeschylus says κἄλλως εἰκὸς τοὺς ἡμιθέους τοῖς ῥήμασι μείζοσι χρῆcθαι· / καὶ γὰρ τοῖς ἱματίοις ἡμῶν χρῶνται πολὺ cεμνοτέροιcιν. But this is leading up to a joke on the favourite theme of Euripidean kings in rags; and in view of the archaeological evidence the other way

---

[1] The evidence is briefly surveyed by Haigh *TDG* 438–9. One might add Cicero *ad Fam* vii. 1. 2 for 600 mules and 3,000 bowls of booty in Pompey's new theatre in 55 B.C.

it cannot be used as proof that Aeschylus' costumes were out-standingly spectacular. Rather more serious evidence is 961–3: Euripides defends everyday themes, talkativeness, and rational inquisitiveness, and adds ἀλλ' οὐκ ἐκομπολάκουν / ἀπὸ τοῦ φρονεῖν ἀποσπάcαc, οὐδ' ἐξέπληττον αὐτούc, / Κύκνουc ποιῶν καὶ Μέμνοναc κωδωνοφαλαροπώλουc.¹ Even though we do not know of a play of Aeschylus which involved Cycnus (see p. 422f.), there is no doubt that Aeschylus did use chariot-borne entries. These may have been particularly associated with the early pre-skene theatre, though they are not unknown in Euripides: on all this see *Pers* 155b*. In a play which involves the fall of a great military hero an impressive, perhaps over-confident, chariot entry might well be an effective and integral piece of theatre; and we seem to have a play directly in this tradition in *Rh*.² But while Aristophanes does confirm that Aeschylus made use of spectacular chariot entries, he has nothing about the massive use of stage machinery which figures so largely in Murray's and Reinhardt's account. It is Euripides and Agathon who are associated with the ekkyklema (*Acharn*, *Thesm*), and Euripides who is associated with the mechane (*Peace*, *Thesm*). If anyone was notorious for his use of machinery it was Xenocles, son of Carcinus. At *Peace* 791 the reference to Carcinus' sons as μηχανοδίφαc is explained by the scholia (= *TrGF* 21 T 3c): Ξενοκλῆc γὰρ ὁ Καρκίνου δοκεῖ μηχανὰc καὶ τερατείαc εἰcάγειν ἐν τοῖc δράμαcι; and they go on to quote Plato's *Sophistai* for Ξενοκλῆc ὁ δωδεκαμήχανοc.³ So the dramatist who was famous for machinery comes at the end of the century not the beginning, which is what we might expect.

Aeschylus is, indeed, repeatedly characterized in Aristophanes as alarming and astonishing his audience with mass and monstrosity:

¹ I can think of two ways (neither of which I accept) of avoiding the inference that Μέμνων κωδωνοφαλαρόπωλοc was displayed on stage. One is to suppose that he was described in a report (cf. *Rh* 301ff.); the other is to regard Κύκνουc καὶ Μέμνοναc as play titles and to take κωδωνοφαλαροπώλουc as an evocative epithet of the play as a whole.

² See p. 77 and p. 472 below. If *Rh* is by Euripides then this is yet another example of a playwright in Aristophanes attacking something which he himself goes in for. On the other hand this might be a very small point against authenticity (Ritchie 99 does not see either alternative).

³ Plato Com. fr. 134 K. Xenocles is also called εὐμήχανοc in Σ on *Thesm* 440 (= *TrGF* 33 T 4b). Platnauer on Arph. *Peace* 790 thinks that all these references are to dancing and not to production; but he does not realize that Xenocles was also a playwright himself. The passage in *Peace* might refer only to dancing, but the evidence suggests that Xenocles was also enterprising mechanically.

but with the mass and monstrosity of his *words*, not of his stage production. It may well be that Aristophanes' account of his language was later transferred in theory and practice to the presentation of his plays, and that this lies behind the tradition of the super-spectacular Aeschylus (see further below). But Aristophanes does not substantiate the notion that the Greek stage developed from a spectacular circus to an austere and static theatre of ideas. And this is, in itself, an implausible notion. It is a general pattern of stage history that schools of theatre develop the other way, from strong and plain beginnings to ornate, showy, novelty-seeking decadence (cf. Arnott 111–12). It is *a priori* more likely that the Greek tragic theatre moved in this direction, and I contend that the creditable evidence (as opposed to later scholarship and biography) confirms that this was the case.

It remains to try to explain how it is that the usual view of Aeschylus' stagecraft arose in antiquity and has been perpetuated and embellished by more recent scholars. First, it should be admitted that one of the seven surviving tragedies does *prima facie* support this view—*Prometheus*. The binding of Prometheus, the flying entry of the chorus, and the final cataclysm must, *if* they were to be presented with any attempt at realism, have required unusually complex and large-scale stage machinery. But many scholars are coming round to the view that there was no attempt at realistic representation of these events, and that, while they are verbally spectacular, they were performed simply. In my discussions of these places (*Prom* 1b*, 128b*, 1093b*) I tend to the position that either they were staged simply, or the scenes are not authentic. Outside *Prom* there are no scenes which indicate massive spectacle on anything like the same scale. (The reconstructions of *Psychostasia* are based not on text but on suspect ancient scholarship, see pp. 431ff.)

Now I shall consider the ancient scholarship which, I suspect, is the true basis of these aberrations. There are two groups of words which, while they are part of the vocabulary of ancient rhetorical and poetic theory in general, became especially associated with Aeschylus: the cognates and compounds of τέρας and πλήccειν.[1] It is worth noting that these words are used of Aeschylus

---

[1] The two groups of terminology are discussed by Pohlenz *Kl Schr* ii 454–9, Kranz *Stas* 71–2, 284. (I notice that Polybius used them of tragic historians, see ii 56. 10, xvi 18. 2 etc.)

in Arph. *Frogs*, and that *Frogs* was enormously influential on later writing on tragedy (it is twice referred to directly in the *Life* of Aeschylus). When the tragedians very first enter and Aeschylus maintains a miniature Aeschylean silence Euripides says (833f.) ἀποσεμνυνεῖται πρῶτον, ἅπερ ἑκάστοτε / ἐν ταῖς τραγωιδίαισιν ἐτερατεύετο (cf. *HSCP* 1972 p. 60). And at 962 (discussed on p. 43 above) Euripides contrasting himself with Aeschylus says οὐδ' ἐξέπληττον αὐτούς. Although the noun τέρατα is not used, they are also held against Aeschylus in 923–40 where Euripides mocks his grotesque creatures 'like those in Median tapestries' (938).[1]

But in *Frogs*, except for the reference to chariots, Aeschylus is regarded as monstrous and astounding in his words not his production. Why the same epithets have become attached to his staging is an interesting question. Some scholars claim Aristotle's *Poetics* as support for the transference.[2] In the course of his disparagement of ὄψις (see Appendix F) Aristotle says (1453b8–10) οἱ δὲ μὴ τὸ φοβερὸν διὰ τῆς ὄψεως ἀλλὰ τὸ τερατῶδες μόνον παρασκευάζοντες οὐδὲν τραγωιδίαι κοινωνοῦσιν. 'It is not known to what A. is referring unless it be Aeschylus', says Lucas (*ed* p. 150), in agreement with virtually all the commentators. But it is hard to believe that Aristotle, for all his neglect of Aeschylus, would disqualify his tragedies from the title of τραγωιδία: he may well be referring to fourth-century shows in the tradition of Xenocles.[3]

[1] This refers in particular to decorated cloth, such as was used for tragic costumes; see von Lorentz *MDAI* (*Röm. Mitt.*) 52 (1937) 165ff. esp. 199ff. (and 216ff. on tragic costume). But one thinks also of the Oriental influence on the bestiaries of Greek art, especially earlier Corinthian vase painting; cf. Kranz *Stas* 284f., and more particularly Payne *Necrocorinthia* (Oxford 1931) 76–91.

[2] ἔκπληξις is a recurrent term in *Poet*, see e.g. 1454a4, 1455a17. On it as a technical term see Russell on [Longinus] 15.2.

[3] In the difficult if not incomprehensible passage (1455b32ff.) where Aristotle illustrates the fourth εἶδος of tragedy with (1456a2f.) αἵ τε Φορκίδες καὶ ὁ Προμηθεὺς καὶ ὅσα ἐν ἅιδου, it does look as though he has Aeschylus in mind. The labelling of the type is notoriously corrupt—τὸ δὲ τέταρτον οης—and scholars have seized the opportunity to substantiate the spectacular Aeschylus. Bywater's emendation ὄψις is not only a noun after three adjectives, but is contradicted by 1459b8–10. Schrader's widely followed τερατῶδες emends away the innocent τέταρτον, and also contradicts the later passage. Else Arle. *Poet comm* p. 525 also makes the point that Aristotle's fourth kind should not be based on elements which he has condemned as 'untragic'. Allen *CQ* N.s. 22 (1972) 84–6 still seems to favour τερατῶδες; Kassel *OCT* obelizes οης; but the reading which would fit best with Aristotle's other classifications would be ⟨ἡ ἁπλῆ⟩ (thus Bursian, Gudeman, see Lucas 184f.).

The most influential of all the testimonia for the super-spectacular Aeschylus is the anonymous *Life*, which, while it does not seem to depend on Aristotle himself, does probably go back to a later Peripatetic source (the only scholar named in it is Dicaearchus (§15)). §7 reads ταῖc τε γὰρ ὄψεcι καὶ τοῖc μύθοιc πρὸc ἔκπληξιν τερατώδη μᾶλλον ἢ πρὸc ἀπάτην κέχρηται. The sentence seems to imply that instead of enthralling his audience (like the best kind of dramatist) Aeschylus just horrified them out of their wits.[1] Another overtly neutral passage in the *Life* carries comparably disparaging undertones. At the very beginning among the aspects of tragedy which Aeschylus is said to have advanced are τὴν διάθεcιν τῆc cκηνῆc τήν τε λαμπρότητα τῆc χορηγίαc καὶ τὴν cκευὴν τῶν ὑποκριτῶν (the sentence goes on to quote *Frogs* 1004–5, although that is specifically about his style). It will be remembered that Aristotle says (*Poet* 1453b7–8) that the exploitation of ὄψιc is ἀτεχνότερον καὶ χορηγίαc δεόμενον (see p. 478 below).

As evidence of the spectacular Aeschylus these passages are always backed up by the quotation of §14 τὴν ὄψιν τῶν θεωμένων κατέπληξεν τῆι λαμπρότητι . . .[2] Scholars do not as a rule continue this extract to the end of the sentence: it continues γραφαῖc καὶ μηχαναῖc, βωμοῖc τε καὶ τάφοιc, cάλπιγξιν, εἰδώλοιc, Ἐρίνυcι· τούc τε ὑποκριτὰc χειρῖcι cκεπάcαc καὶ τῶι cύρματι ἐξογκώcαc μείζοcί τε τοῖc κοθόρνοιc μετεωρίcαc. Suspicion, indeed disbelief, is aroused here, not only by the loose sleeves, trailing cloaks, and high boots, which definitely have nothing to do with Aeschylus, but also by the examples of 'razzle-dazzle' which seem almost all to be drawn from *Eum*.[3] Lastly §9 tells how the entry of the chorus in *Eum* had sensational effects (note τοcοῦτον ἐκπλῆξαι τὸν δῆμον . . .).

Fortified by what they take to be the incontrovertible evidence of Aristotle and the *Life*, scholars grasp eagerly at any hint of ἔκπληξιc τερατώδηc in the scholiastic tradition. I need do no more

---

[1] Cf. Pohlenz *Kl Schr* II 452–6, Rosenmeyer 234f.

[2] It is possible that ⟨τῆc χορηγίαc⟩ should be added after λαμπρότητι, cf. *Life* §2.

[3] Podlecki *Phoenix* 28 (1969) 137 seems unaware that we can no longer share Dindorf's high opinion of the material in §14; though he may well be right that the source is Peripatetic. Maybe the same source lies behind all the references to Aeschylus' invention of the large trailing costume, cf. Horace *AP* 278, Athenaeus 21d, Philostratus *Apoll* 6. 11, *Soph* 1. 9. It may all in origin be a false elaboration of *Frogs* 1061.

than give some examples of places where I shall argue that scholars have been unjustifiably credulous. Many, for example, have believed the hypothesis to *Ag* that Agamemnon returned with chariots and spoils: see *Ag* 783b*. Most have unthinkingly believed the scholion on *Eum* 64 which says that machinery was used to reveal the scene inside the Delphic temple: see on *Eum* 140*.[1] Nearly all scholars have swallowed Pollux's account (4. 130) of the staging of *Psychostasia*, although there are strong reasons for rejecting it (see pp. 431ff.). Some have even been lured into believing Pollux (4. 110) that the chorus numbered fifty until *Eum* caused such a stir; and they quote in support the *Life* §9 which tells that this same incident caused Aeschylus to retreat to Sicily. Yet both these anecdotes bear the marks of being drawn from the worst kind of biographical tradition (see p. 438 n. 1).

But it would be unfair to imply that scholars have based their version of the function of spectacle in Aeschylus entirely on a transference to staging of what Arph. *Frogs* says about his language combined with snippets of ancient scholarship which are based on sensational anecdotes. Besides the equivocal evidence of *Prom* there is reason to think that later reproductions of Aeschylus interpolated spectacular effects, and that these have left their mark both on the ancient scholarship and on the plays themselves. The evidence of the scholion on E. *Or* 57 that actors interpolated a spectacular procession at the beginning of *Or* is well known (see p. 77 below). In my discussions of the relevant places in *Ag*, *Eum*, and *Psychostasia* cited in the previous paragraph I air the possibility that later, more spectacular productions have influenced our secondary sources.

And there are, in my opinion, places where there have been actual textual alterations or interpolations made wholly or partly in order to admit more spectacular effects. It is widely agreed, and rightly in my view, that *Eum* 405 was interpolated so that Athena could make a chariot entry (see *Eum* 397b*). There are reasons for thinking that *Cho* 713 was altered to bring on a crowd of interesting extras (see *Cho* 653*). It may be that the interpolator of the last scene of *Seven* also wished to bring on a group of silent city officials (see *Seven* 1005c*). Then there are

---

[1] Perhaps there is an echo of Aristotle in this scholion in καὶ γίνεται ὄψις τραγική. (But note, by the way, the perfectly innocuous use of τερατεύεται by the scholia on *Prom* 793c (p. 193 H) and 803a (p. 195 H).)

other much more controversial possibilities which are at least
worth consideration. For example, Bethe's theory that there are
interpolations in *Prom* in order to add grand spectacles deserves
more respect than it has received (see *Prom* 128b*, 1093b*). On
Hik 974b* I air the conjecture that *Hik* has been tampered with
in order, among other things, to introduce a supplementary
chorus of Handmaids. I also argue that there may have been
interference with our text of the trial in *Eum*; and one of the
motives for this may have been to make possible a supernatural
appearance and disappearance for Apollo: see *Eum* 574*, 777b*.

But this is speculative stuff liable to make choler run high. I am
on safer ground when I attack the many spectacular stage instructions which modern editors, translators, and producers have
introduced into Aeschylus' plays without proper justification
from the text. These are seldom made up without any support
whatsoever from the text, but they are inflated on completely
insufficient grounds simply to add substance to the picture of
Aeschylus as a spectacular showman. Some scholars are rightly
suspicious of such inventions, but many others are too tolerant
of them or simply accept them unquestioningly. Even when there
is no hint whatsoever in the text, some people seem reluctant
to abandon a chance for empty spectacle.[1]

I shall, then, maintain that Aeschylus does indeed make powerful use of the sight of his plays in performance, and that this
includes some outlandish and ceremonial spectacles; and I shall
try to show how all these sights do integral dramatic work. On
the other hand I shall argue that, with the possible exception of
Prom, there are no spectacles that are set up for their own sake;
and I think I have eliminated virtually all of the many places

[1] One example from each play should be quite enough to show the scope and
nature of the kind of unwarranted stage instructions which are under attack.
Pers 1000f. is usually taken in such a way as to bring on Xerxes in a tented waggon:
yet a much more sensible way of taking the words brings him on on foot (see
909a*). Some bring on six fully armed champions in *Seven* on the strength of little
more than two dubious deictic pronouns (371c*). *Hik* is often singled out for the
vast numbers on stage, over 200 at one point, it is claimed: but this is based on a
series of false suppositions which all collapse together—see *Hik* 234c*. It is sometimes claimed for no good reason that Hermes flies on the mechane at *Prom* 944*.
The introduction of an elaborate dumb show between *Ag* 39 and 40* is at least
an inference from the text of 83ff., although unjustified. The great crowd of
citizens often introduced in *Cho* is again without any grounding in the text (973a*);
nor is there good reason, I argue on *Eum* 566b*, for a crowd of citizens for the trial
scene.

where such a vacuous, gratuitous spectacle has been alleged by ancient or modern scholars.

§5. *Action and Formal Structure*

Virtually all European drama since the fourth century B.C. has used a formal structure of scenes or of acts and scenes. These parts are articulated by the rearrangement of the participant characters: scenes begin with the entry of characters and end with the clearing of the stage, and they are divided by a 'vacant stage' (unfortunately this phrase is a recognized technical term). This structure is recognized by playwright, audience, and reader. It is marked in texts typographically; and in performance the dividing point signalled by the vacant stage may be further reinforced by intervals, house lights, change of scenery, interlude music, etc. It is now clear that Menandrean New Comedy was based on a structure of five parts divided by choral interlude songs.[1] The meagre evidence also suggests that much of fourth-century tragedy used a similar structure.[2]

Structural divisions which supply a recognized ground-pattern are an important aspect of dramatic technique. The dramatist can both shape his individual units, and put together the units in a form which is artful and dramatically telling: and the audience will, more or less consciously, respond to this shaping and to the relation of the parts to the whole.[3]

[1] See Blanchard *REG* 83 (1970) 38f. Blanchard also makes a preliminary investigation of the interesting subdivisions which may be made within the acts of Menander. See now N. Holzberg *Menander* etc. (Nuremberg 1974) esp. 114ff.

[2] I hope to discuss this obscure subject properly elsewhere. The chief evidence of such a structure in post-classical tragedy is:

(i) The fragments of Ezechiel's *Exagoge* (*TrGF* 128); cf. Snell *Szenen* 172ff.

(ii) The high stage and *periaktoi*; cf. Sifakis *Studies in the History of Hellenistic Drama* (London 1967) 113ff., esp. 122–4, 133–5.

(iii) The Byzantine treatise on tragedy, quoted on p. 57 below.

(iv) The occurrence of χοροῦ (μέλος) in some tragic papyri, notably *PHib* 4, *PHib* 174 (= *TrGF* 60F** 1h?), and perhaps *PLit. Lond.* 77.

I would conclude from this that there were normally five acts (μέρη) divided by choral interludes. Between the acts the scene was invariably empty of actors; the scene setting might then change and time elapse. The playwright did not compose special choral songs, but simply put χοροῦ in his script and left the matter in the hands of the χοροδιδάσκαλος (in the fifth century the playwright himself: but things changed, see P-C *DFA²* 90f.). See now *LCM* 1 (1976) 47–50.

[3] For an extremely interesting study of Shakespeare's mastery of scene construction see Emrys Jones *Scenic Form in Shakespeare* (Oxford 1971).

But Greek tragedy is debarred from this kind of straight-forward structural basis by its peculiar formal continuity, which is largely due to the continuous presence of the chorus. Yet the unbroken form is still made up of an ordered series of parts. Anyone who has read a Greek tragedy must be aware that it is a structure of parts; and anyone who has seen one in performance will be even more definitely assured of it. Extraordinary though it may seem, no satisfactory analysis of the structural basis of Greek tragedy has ever been established by scholars. And since there is no analysis available which truly reflects the actual construction of the plays, most modern commentators have abandoned any thorough consideration of the formal structure of the tragedies. Observations on plot construction are, of course, to be found, and these can be most illuminating; but plot construction is not the same thing as formal construction.[1] Formal structure remains an aspect which has to be, and should be, worked out; though some extremely valuable contributions on the structural functions of lyric have been made by Kranz. I shall offer here an analysis which, I hope, goes some way to supplying that need. And during the rest of the book I attempt to show how the structural technique is used to dramatic ends.

The study of the structural technique of Greek tragedy has been disastrously inhibited by the terms and definitions which are found in the texts of Aristotle's *Poetics* as chapter 12 (1452b14–27). The authority of the source has made them the starting-point for nearly every treatment of the subject. Yet the chapter is, I contest, as good as useless for a meaningful analysis of surviving tragedy: this I argue in full in Appendix E. Clearly it has been widely felt that there is something unsatisfactory about the application of these terms and definitions, since an analysis based on them used to adorn nearly every edition of a Greek tragedy (for an early exception see Wilamowitz's E. *Her* which simply uses the two terms 'Auftritt' and 'Gesangnummer'): but now this practice has been generally abandoned, leaving only vestigial traces. Hundreds of pages have been filled in the attempts to make something useful and informative out of the traditional

---

[1] Cf. e.g. Matthiessen *Elektra* etc. (Göttingen 1964) 16ff. Remarks on plot construction turn up in many books and commentaries. There has been particularly good work on Euripides: see Strohm 165ff., Ludwig *Sapheneia* (diss. Tübingen 1954), and Burnett. Two specialized studies on formal aspects have been Detscheff 82ff. and Holzapfel *Kennt die gr. Tr. eine Akteinteilung?* (diss. Giessen 1914).

analysis; but the disuse into which it has fallen is an index of
their failure (see p. 470 n. 1). There is room to doubt the
authenticity of the chapter in *Poetics*, as is argued in Appendix E
(pp. 475f.); but even if Aristotle is responsible for it, we would
still have to reject it, because it simply does not give a proper
account of a structural basis which reflects the way that the
plays are in fact constructed. An analysis in terms of *Poet* ch. 12
is no more than an editorial imposition, like the imposition of
the five-act structure on many of Shakespeare's plays by the
editors of the First Folio,[1] and the act and scene divisions derived
from some manuscripts of Plautus and Terence.[2] If an account
of structural technique is to be of any critical value, then it must
be based on the plays themselves: it must not be imposed on
them from without. So I shall attempt a fresh start, using the
plays themselves as the first and final foundation of any theory.

First and most obviously, the alternation of speech and song
has something to do with the structural basis of Greek tragedy.
But the differentiation of the mode of delivery cannot be the
whole story, since there are many examples of lyrics, particularly
lyric dialogues, which are inextricably tied *within* the units which
also contain speech. The first refinement is to note the pre-
dominance of strophic choral lyric in an act-dividing position
(by 'choral' in this kind of context I mean 'sung by the chorus
alone without the participation of actors'). Can the structural
basis be simply the alternation of acts (consisting of both speech
and lyric) with choral strophic songs? (Cf. *Poet* 1452b20f. ἐπεισόδιον
δὲ μέρος ὅλον τραγωιδίας τὸ μεταξὺ ὅλων χορικῶν μελῶν.) This
will indeed take us part of the way to a workable structural
analysis, and is, in effect, the best that scholars have been able
to extract from *Poet* ch. 12.

But there are still many structural phenomena which this
analysis does not account for. While there is only one strophic
choral lyric which definitely does not divide two acts (A. *Hik*
418ff.), there are many examples of two acts which are divided
by something other than a choral strophic song. It is widely
acknowledged that in this act-dividing position one finds astrophic

[1] Cf. H. L. Snuggs *Shakespeare and Five Acts* (New York 1960). Snuggs's first
chapter is, in fact, a very competent survey of act-division in ancient drama.
[2] See Leo *Plautinische Forschungen*[2] (Berlin 1912) 15 n. 1, Handley *Menander and
Plautus: A Study in Comparison* (London 1968) p. 14 and 20 n. 12.

anapaests (see Kranz *Forma* 7, *Stas* 162), and astrophic dochmiac
lyrics (see Kranz *Forma* 21ff., *Stas* 117, 177, and cf. *Hik* 974a*).
One also finds epirrhematic lyric structures and irregular lyric
dialogue: these are marked in the table in Kranz *Stas* 124–5 as
'dialog(ischen Lieder)', and are discussed on *Prom* 88*. And one
even finds actor's monody (E. *Or* 960ff., *IA* 1283ff.; see Kranz
Stas 229). Those who wish to give an adequate structural account
of Greek tragedy, and are not content to distort the plays to fit
an inflexible predefined system, will readily admit that all these
other kinds of lyric structures may divide acts, and that not only
strophic choral lyrics have this function.

    These lyrics are usually covered by terms such as 'stasimi
loco', 'stasimis suppositos', 'instead of a stasimon' or 'having the
function of a stasimon' (see e.g. Kranz *Forma* 7, 24, Detscheff
chapter II, Aichele 16ff.). But what in these phrases is meant by
stasimon? 'Stasimon' is apparently assumed to be defined in
structural terms as a 'choral song which divides two acts'; and
an 'act' is defined as 'the part between two stasima'. The process
is circular, and the question of what is really taken as the basis
for the structure is never faced, but is left to intuition.

    The simple analysis in terms of the alternation of acts with
strophic choral songs is found to be further inadequate when one
observes that there is occasionally such a heavy break between
two sequences that one wants to speak in terms of two separate
acts, and yet no lyric at all, let alone a strophic choral song,
intervenes. The most obvious instance is at those places where
the chorus leaves the scene and then re-enters within the course
of a play: cf. *Eum* 231*, 235*, 276*. At such junctures the break
is, if anything, even more marked than that between acts, though
it is still less than that between the plays of a trilogy. Also there
can be heavy structural breaks in the part of the play before the
chorus enters (see *Eum* 139*): in such circumstances there can
be no choral lyric, and yet a division of structural units undeniably occurs. And there are further circumstances where
there are notable structural divisions without any strophic choral
song, especially in later tragedy. Whether on these occasions we
should speak of two separate structural units or of a heavy break
within a unit matters little, as long as the structural technique is
appreciated. Structural divisions of this kind may be marked,
for example, by isolated anapaests or astrophic lyric or by one

part of a divided strophic pair (see e.g. S. *Trach* 205, E. *Med* 358, 759, *IT* 643), or by a rapid rearrangement of the characters on stage (some examples are given in *GRBS* 1971 p. 41 n. 38), or by a new turn of events late in an act (see e.g. on *Eum* 777c*). These phenomena are without doubt structural divisions which are worthy of note in any proper analysis, yet they are less obviously marked than by a full-scale strophic choral lyric.

Clearly some other factor besides the alternation of modes of delivery must be brought into play; and clearly that factor is something to do with what is going on in the action of the play, the 'Handlung'. It is precisely in view of the structure of the *action* that scholars have intuitively recognized that astrophic lyrics can 'stand in place of a stasimon' or that a break with no lyric may be 'equivalent to a break between acts'. Kranz acknowledges this, in effect, when he says (*Forma* 23 on S. *Trach* 205ff.) that a song is not equivalent to a stasimon 'cum non distribuat actionem sed ipsum actionis pars sit'. And again at *Stas* 177 he distinguishes between songs which are 'handlunggliedernd' and 'handlungunterstützend'. But by itself this criterion is too vague: too many songs have both these functions. What we want is some independent feature of the *Handlung* which is complementary to the divisive function of the song.

The particular elements in the action which may help to articulate the structural form are, of course, entrances and exits (hence the inclusion of the topic in this work). It is by entrance and exit that the combination of actors participating in the action is altered, and this process of rearrangement is fundamental to the form of the action. But it should not be assumed that every single entry and exit marks a structural articulation (as is the case in French classical drama, on paper at least). Many entrances, particularly those soon after the beginning of an act, and many exits, particularly near the end of an act, are clearly *within* a structural unit, and in no way mark the beginning or end of one.[1] It is, rather, those entrances which inaugurate a new act and those exits which take away the characters at the end of an act which are structurally important: the movements which fill and empty the stage.

Now, the emptying of the scene before a vacant stage and the

[1] A lack of discrimination on this point mars Goodell's analysis and much of Aichele chapters 6 and 7.

INTRODUCTION

refilling after it has been the structural basis for most non-choral drama, as was noted at the very beginning of the section. Perhaps the occurrence of vacant stage also has a basic place in the structural formation of Greek tragedy? Because of the chorus a total vacant stage occurs only rarely; but the stage is quite often empty of *actors*, leaving only the chorus present.[1] And as a rule this happens precisely during those choral songs which have already been seen to be of structural importance. Is there, after all, some equivalent or precursor of the later vacant-stage construction in fifth-century tragedy?

If one now turns to the plays in the hope that the stage is always vacant of actors during any act-dividing song, one is quickly disappointed. The structure of Greek tragedy is hardly so simple. It is quite common for one actor, or even two, to stay on during an act-dividing song; in fact, as was noted above, he sometimes even takes part in the song. An actor stays on in these circumstances about once per play on average in Aeschylus, and nearly twice per play in Sophocles and Euripides (though this is not evenly distributed throughout the plays).[2] An actor may even stay on for all or most of a tragedy: cf. A. *Prom*, S. *OC*, E. *Tro*.

But this initial disappointment may be more than compensated for if we go on to observe that, even when an actor stays on during an act-dividing song, there is still almost always an exit by another actor before the song, and still a new entry after it. It is not the vacant stage, but the *sequence of exit and entry*, which provides the regular pattern. It is this rather simple observation which is the basis for my theory of the structure of Greek tragedy. Detscheff (6off.) and Aichele (19ff.) both document the phenomenon of the sequence of exit and entry, but they fail to see its larger structural significance. Kranz also makes the observation when he says (*Forma* 7) that certain songs are 'stasimi loco, id est post abitum histrionis atque ante introitum alterius'. Yet he makes nothing further of this, although he has put his finger on a working definition of a 'stasimon' (i.e. of an act-dividing song).

My theory is simply that the alternation of speech and song in

---

[1] Weissinger assumes the importance of vacant stage, yet he does not then make this simple step.

[2] Catalogues of the occurrence of this phenomenon have been compiled, independently and for various different purposes, by Dignan 39ff., Graeber 48ff., Stephenson 9ff. (Aeschylus only), Spitzbarth 73ff., Ritchie 116 (Sophocles and Euripides only).

Greek tragedy is integrally bound up with the rearrangement of the action by means of actors' exits before songs and entries after them. If the songs are considered in relation to the shaping of the acts, as marked by entrances and exits, then their structural function becomes clear: if the arrangement of actors through entrances and exits is considered in relation to the placing of songs, then the formal shape of the acts becomes clear. At once the awkward counter-examples which I raised to a simple analysis in terms of the alternation of delivery (pp. 51–3 above) all fall into place. A. *Hik* 418ff. is not associated with any exit or entrance. The non-strophic and non-choral lyrics which have an act-dividing function ('stand in place of a stasimon') are all preceded by an exit and followed by an entry. All the heavy structural breaks which are not associated with any lyric involve a notable rearrangement of participant actors with an entry following closely after an exit. All the lighter yet distinct structural divisions involve either an exit, usually just before some kind of lyric structure, or an entry, usually just after one.

As I see it, then, the formal structure of Greek tragedy is founded on a basic pattern: enter actor(s)—actors' dialogue—exeunt actor(s) / choral strophic song / enter new actor(s)—actors' dialogue . . . and so on. Beneath the many complexities of the construction of the plays there lies, I suggest, this simple form. This is not to imply that this was chronologically speaking the original form of Greek tragedy, though this is quite possible. In fact, of surviving tragedies the earlier plays of Sophocles and Euripides approach it most nearly. S. *Ant* is almost perfectly regular.[1] But the basic pattern is seldom so near the surface: there are a multitude of variations on it, and most plays provide several greater or smaller departures. Yet in every tragedy the ground-pattern also asserts itself, and thus supplies a norm for the structural variations to work upon. For some idea of the range of variations see the list of places where I discuss the Aeschylean variations in detail (p. 60 below).

This method of analysis was derived from an examination of the plays, and when it is applied to the plays it can be fairly claimed, I think, that it effectively reflects the ways that they are in fact constructed. In practice it works. Almost every

---

[1] The only exception is the heavy break without an act-dividing song which is caused by the exit of the Messenger followed by the entry of Creon at 1256–61.

departure from the norm can be honestly accounted for as a
purposeful variation, and not one need be regarded as an intract-
able counter-example.[1] The only objection to the validity of the
method would have, so far as I can see, to be based on what is,
I should counter, its great and necessary strength: flexibility.
Analysis in these terms does not produce the uniformity which is
the result of the distortion of the traditional system: on the contrary it brings out diversity. There is no *a priori* reason to suppose
that there should be some rigid structural form to Greek tragedy:
rather one should expect a flexible structural form to underlie
the genre which produced such a great variety of masterpieces
within a single century.[2]

In outline an analysis of a Greek tragedy according to *Poet*
ch. 12 would not be wildly different from an analysis by the
method offered here, though *Poet* allows far less definition of
detail. But my theory shares neither terms nor definitions with
Poet ch. 12, and, if it is along the right lines, then that chapter is
simply inadequate and misleading. Most other observations on
the formal structure of Greek tragedy which are preserved in
ancient scholarship are late, and most of them are broadly along
the same lines (and possibly from the same source) as *Poet*
ch. 12: see p. 471. But if my theory is acceptable, then the lack
of corroboration in the surviving ancient scholarship should not
matter: the tragedies themselves should be the sole test.

As it happens there are one or two hints that something more
like this theory was also current in antiquity. First, there is the
existence of the technical term ἐπεισόδιον. If the word in fact
means, as Kranz (*Stas* 14) puts it, 'das durch den Neueintritt
einer Person hervorgerufene Stück' (a part inaugurated by the
new entry of a character), then it implies one important element
in my theory: that a new act begins with an entry.[3] But against
this must be set the consideration that in the fifth century and in
Aristotle except for *Poet* ch. 12, the word seems to have a different

---

[1] I have, in fact, undertaken the rather dreary task of applying the method to
the entire corpus of surviving tragedy in an unpublished prize essay.
[2] This is partly intended as polemic against handbooks which have taken too
much notice of *Poet* ch. 12 and too little of the plays themselves; e.g. most recently
Baldry *The Greek Tragic Theatre* (London 1971) 81–4.
[3] Other suggested glosses e.g. 'the second entry of an actor' or 'a scene in
addition to the entry of the chorus' (cf. Flickinger *TAPA* 61 (1930) 91) do not
in practice make sense.

meaning, which may suggest that the structural sense was a late development: see p. 472. Further, the contribution of the prefix and the diminutive ending are unclear in this connection; one might expect simply εἴcοδος (cf. German *Auftritt*). And finally the occurrence of ἐπείcοδος in Sophocles (*OC* 730, fr. 273 P) suggests that ἐπειcόδιον was not a technical term in the fifth century.[1]

Secondly there is an intriguing paragraph in a recently published Byzantine treatise on tragedy.[2] One section (§10) reads: ἡ δὲ κορωνὶς μέρους ἐcτὶ cημεῖον, ὅταν οἱ ὑποκριταὶ ἐξελθόντες τῆc cκηνῆc μόνον τὸν χορὸν καταλείπωcι, καὶ ἐπειcέλθωcι πάλιν, ὁπόταν καὶ τὸν τόπον ἔcτιν ἀλλάξαι, καὶ τόπον καὶ χορόν, καὶ ὅλον τὸν μῦθον, ἀρχῆι δὲ ἐπειcοδίου ἢ τελευτῆι. Scholars do not seem to have seen the possible implications of this paragraph. First, some of the phenomena alluded to here do not apply to fifth-century tragedy (cf. p. 49 n. 2 above). Next, while the paragraph has features in common with Hephaestion περὶ cημείων §6 (p. 75 Consbruch), we did not before have clear evidence that the school of metricians which was led by Heliodorus and his pupil Hephaestion considered the change of delivery in tragedy to be integrally related to the coming and going of actors. The scholia on Aristophanes make it clear that they connected the two things in comedy.[3] So these ancient metricians, at least, connected entry and exit with act-dividing songs, and related this combination to the structure as a whole (μέρους ἐcτὶ cημεῖον).

It may, I should add, serve as some slight confirmation of my analysis of the structure of Greek tragedy that it can *not* be applied to satyr plays. In E. *Cycl* there is some interrelation of choral song (often astrophic) with the rearrangement of actors by means of exit and entrance, but the papyrus fragments of satyr plays by Aeschylus and Sophocles strongly suggest that *Cycl* was exceptional in this, perhaps because of its strong paratragic element. In the fragments of Aeschylus and Sophocles

---

[1] *Contra* Aichele 7. Creon's entry is a new (ἐπ-) element in the situation at Colonus. Greek tragedy does not use the technical vocabulary of the theatre, which would undermine its particular type of relationship with the audience; see further p. 133.

[2] Possibly the work of Michael Psellos. The text was first published with introduction and commentary by Browning in Γέρας. *Studies presented to G. Thomson* (Prague 1963) 67–81. Kassel *RhM* 116 (1973) 104 n. 25 makes the admirable suggestion that it should be known as the *Tractatus Baroccianus*.

[3] See in general O. Hense *Heliodoreische Untersuchungen* (Leipzig 1870) esp. 35–48, and cf. also Koster *Schol. in Ar. Plut. et Nub.* (Leiden 1927) 51–6 and tables.

choral lyrics, which are astrophic or in divided strophic pairs, are not related with any consistency to entrances and exits, and conversely the movements of actors are not grouped round the songs.[1] Compared with tragedy satyr play has a loose and un-defined structure that makes for a rambling continuity which does not really fall into parts.

The rejection of the definitions of *Poet* ch. 12 implies also the rejection of its familiar terminology. Of the seven terms and six definitions given there not one survives a sceptical scrutiny un-scathed: see Appendix E. For the application of my scheme of analysis only two words are required: one for the unit of action bounded by entry and exit, and one for the song which divides such units. In the fifth century these would have been called, I suspect, μέροc and μέλοc respectively.[2] I shall simply use the words 'act' and 'song'; but when I have to make it clear that I mean 'song' in a structural sense I shall use the term 'act-dividing song' (cf. 'epeisodientrennenden Lieder'—unfortunately I could find in English nothing better than this ugly term).

So much for theory. While the theory is, I hope, right and of interest for itself, it is the use of the structural techniques in practice which should be our real concern. How has the play-wright used the construction of his play to convey and to reflect his meaning? Why are the parts made up as they are, and what is the relationship of the parts to the whole? A complete dis-cussion of this subject involves most aspects of dramatic technique and would require a dissertation to itself. For the structural techniques of the acts one would have to consider the use of the length and brevity of parts, of the amount of coming and going, the inclusion of lyric elements, the placing of rhesis and of stichomythia and so on. For the structural techniques of the

---

[1] For Aeschylus see p. 420 on *Diktyoulkoi*, and on *Theoroi or Isthmiastai*. In S. *Ichn* there are songs at (Pearson's numbering) 58–72, 82–4, 94 etc., 170–97, 207–10, 237–44 = 285–90, 321–9 = 362–70, ?434f. etc.: but the entrances come at 1, 39, 215, before 439, and ?446 (Dr. R. Carden advises me that the trace before 446 is probably not c), and the exits at 57, 199, before 439. In S. *Inachos* (*PTeb* 692 = fr. 3 Carden) there are snatches of lyric (5–9, 16–20, 25ff.), yet they are not associated with any entrance or exit; and in *POxy* 2369 (fr. 2 Carden) it does not look as though there is an exit before the lyric at 51ff.

[2] It seems likely that μέροc rather than ἐπειcόδιον was the usual word for an act in antiquity (cf. *HSCP* 1972 p. 61 n. 12), though the only possibly relevant occurrence in the fifth century is at Arph. *Frogs* 1119f. μέλοc is used repeatedly of tragic lyric in Aristophanes, though not with a specifically structural connotation.

songs, among other features, length, strophic construction, metre, choreography, the use of apostrophe, the internal links with the acts before and after would have to be taken into account: of course, some of these tasks have already been begun, above all by Kranz. And then the connections between parts and the relation of each to the whole would have to be assessed. The only aspect which I shall be concentrating on in this work is the place of exits and entrances in structural technique. While this is only one of many aspects, it is an important one, since, as has been explained, the placing of exits and entrances in relation to the songs marks the articulation of the structure, and is an integral element in the division of the basic parts.

The ground-pattern which I have elicited from a study of the entire corpus of surviving tragedy supplies a kind of structural pattern or rhythm. The usual combination of choral song with the rearrangement of actors creates an assumption and an expectation which can then be dramatically used. Conformity to the normal pattern is to be expected; and so any departure from it becomes a device in the hands of the playwright which he can exploit for his special purposes.

We can never know for sure whether the dramatists consciously formulated the structural basis of their works, or whether this was part of their intuitive art. But it is quite likely that they were aware theoretically of the basic structural pattern: the Greeks thought of art in terms of τέχνη.[1] The application to tragedy of metaphors of shipbuilding at Arph. *Thesm* 52ff. and of anatomy and carpentry at *Frogs* 862, 799ff. are some indication that the techniques of construction were a concern of literary theory in the fifth century. Whether some or most of the audience were also consciously aware of the structural basis of tragedy is of little consequence, for an unconscious expectation is all that the artist requires to work upon. As long as the audience has a sense of the normal pattern, the dramatist can exploit this sense for his artistic ends.

While a sustained adherence to the norm might be put to dramatic ends to give some sense of orderliness or of inevitability, it is as a rule in the departures and variations that we may detect

---

[1] At this point it would be traditional to point out that Sophocles wrote a theoretical treatise περὶ τοῦ χοροῦ, as *Suda* attests. But this is surely a fiction, as is argued by Crusius *Philol* 80 (1925) 178. On the notion of unwritten laws for early poetry see Rossi *BICS* 18 (1971) 69ff., esp. 75–80.

artistic purposes. And so I shall not be noting all the places where the playwright sticks to the usual pattern, but only those places where he varies it in one way or another. And it is the exception which proves the rule, the variation which confirms the norm: for it is here that we can see the positive dramatic use of structural techniques. Whenever the pattern is departed from we should try to discover the purpose of the variation; for we should, on principle, always expect there to be a good reason. When one is completely unable to account for a structural phenomenon, then short of concluding that the whole theory of structural analysis is mistaken, the most obvious explanation is that one has failed to perceive what the dramatist is trying to do. In the face of a natural reluctance to resort to either of these explanations there are two other alternatives: either the original text has been so tampered with as to disturb the original structure, or the dramatist is technically incompetent. Classical scholars have generally been as reluctant to accept the former possibility as they have been only too ready to fall back on or embrace the latter. (In my view the former explanation which I consider on *Seven* 854b*, 1005a*, *Hik* 974a*, and *Eum* 777b* usually deserves more serious consideration than the latter, which I raise on *Prom* 88*, 436*, and 944*.) In any case, we should always search for *some* explanation of any unusual structural technique.

I hope to show that the whole subject of the formal structure of Greek tragedy is worth reviving from its state of moribund stagnation; and to do something towards showing how this kind of analysis is a way of approaching the artistic shaping and formation of a tragedy, and hence its critical interpretation.[1]

---

[1] I append a catalogue of the main discussions of structural technique. First, there are those places where there is no exit before an act-dividing song (*Pers* 622*, *Prom* 88*, 436*), where there is no entry after an act-dividing song (*Hik* 710*, *Prom* 88*, 436*), and where there is or may be an entrance or exit during the course of an act-dividing song (*Seven* 854b*, c*, *Ag* 258a*, b*). In all these places an actor must be on-stage during all or part of the song. I also consider those places where there is not a strophic choral song between two acts: that is, where there are astropha or anapaests (*Hik* 974a*, *Ag* 1372a*, *Cho* 732a*, 892a*) or a lyric dialogue involving an actor (*Prom* 88*), or where there is nothing at all (e.g. *Eum* 139*). The exit and re-entry of the chorus inevitably disrupts the structure (see *Eum* 231*, 276*); but in Aeschylus the secondary choruses are structurally inconspicuous (see *Hik* 974b*, *Eum* 1047a*). There are also some heavy structural breaks where there is neither a sequence of consecutive exit and entry nor a strophic choral song (see e.g. *Seven* 1005a*, *Ag* 1577a*, *Eum* 777c*).

II. PERSAI

1 enter chorus

(*a*) προλογίζει χορὸς πρεσβυτῶν

P<small>ERSAI</small> is the earliest tragedy we have. We have now learned to
live with the fact that *Hik*, far from being one of Aeschylus'
earliest works, is one of his latest (the date is discussed on *Hik*
1c*). There is an obvious temptation to look in *Pers* for signs of
primitive and undeveloped artistry, for dramaturgy which is
'naiv' or 'kunstlos' as Wilamowitz liked to put it. Yet it should
be remembered that in 472 Attic tragedy had already for more
than half a century been a distinct art form, distinguishable
from ritual folk mumming, and that Aeschylus himself had been
active in the theatre for some 25 years and had probably produced by then over half of his dramatic output. While there are
many things in *Pers* which seem simple and unsophisticated when
compared with later Aeschylus, let alone with Sophocles and
Euripides, none the less tragedy is already a fully fledged art
form, and this tragedy shows a strength and assurance in its
dramatic technique which rebuts the patronizing of those who
detect in it naïve or undeveloped artistry.

By opening the play with the long first song of the chorus,
instead of a spoken prologue by an actor, Aeschylus is able to
build up in a way that could not be otherwise achieved a sense
of the communal dread and of the vulnerability of national
prosperity which is to be the keynote of much of the play. *Pers*
is about the impact of the defeat and return of Xerxes on Persia
as a whole, and the choral 'prologue' firmly and vividly establishes this.

When *Hik* was taken to be early then a choral opening was
supposed to be archaic; and 'archaic' tended to bring with it
notions of crudity and lack of art, which distracted attention
from positive interpretation and appreciation. But now we are
not sure whether in 472 a choral prologue was any more archaic
than a spoken one. Walter Nestle was wise before the event of

the redating of *Hik*, and many others have been wise after it.[1]
From Themistius' well-known sentence on innovations in tragedy
(*Or* 26, 316d — *TrGF* 1T6) τὸ μὲν πρῶτον ὁ χορὸς εἰcιὼν ᾖδεν
εἰc τοὺc θεούc is now relatively disregarded, and much play is
made with the antithesis Θέcπιc δὲ πρόλογόν τε καὶ ῥῆcιν ἐξεῦρεν.
In any case, it seems that none of Thespis' scripts survived, and
both these claims are, as likely as not, mere speculation.[2] The
best evidence that the spoken prologue as well as the choral
prologue-parodos was in general use by the time of *Pers* is to be
found in the plays and fragments of Aeschylus and his contemporaries.

First, although the prologues[3] of *Ag* and *Cho* are simple, that
of *Seven* is not: it has three distinct parts and involves two speaking actors. And the prologue of *Eum* is one of the most remarkable
in all surviving tragedy, falling into three—or rather four—parts
which give different views of the dramatic situation—see further
Eum 139*. The prologue of *Prom* is not only made up largely of
dialogue (see *Prom* 1a*) but also includes a link-scene where a
solo character sings (see *Prom* 88*). The complexity of these
three openings suggests that the non-choral prologue had been
in development for many years. Among the lost plays we know
that *Phryges*, which may have been an early play,[4] began with a
prologue scene with Hermes which also included some dialogue
with Achilles (fr. 243a M). Fr. 169 M (*POxy* 2256) shows that

---

[1] Nestle 13–19 (Schmidt *Bauformen* 1ff. adds little of consequence); cf. Lesky
*TDH*² 40–2, Garvie 120ff.

[2] It is true that Themistius cites Aristotle as his authority, and that he had
studied him professionally. But other details in the same sentence make this
appeal to authority suspect: notably Αἰcχύλος δὲ τρίτον ὑποκριτὴν καὶ ὀκρίβαντας
(ὑποκριτὴν Ψυ, ὑποκριτὰς ΑΛΣ, the text and apparatus of Downey and Norman
(Leipzig 1970)). This not only uses a late word from the antiquarian controversy
over the πρῶτος εὑρετής of the high-soled buskin (cf. P-C *DFA*² 205 and n. 3),
but also apparently comes down in the dispute over the introduction of the third
actor on the opposite side from the *Poetics* (see p. 457 n. 4); cf. on these points
E. Hiller *RhM* 39 (1884) 330–6 and Smith *HSCP* 16 (1905) 123ff. esp. 155. For
bibliography on the Themistius passage see Garvie 104 n. 1 and Lesky *TDH*³
53 n. 14.

[3] I am using 'prologue' here to designate all the play which comes before the
entry-song of the chorus, as in Arle. *Poetics* ch. 12 and in modern discussions. In
fact the meaning of πρόλογος in the fifth century was probably more limited—
see p. 471.

[4] For probable illustrations of the Achilles trilogy on vase paintings from *c*. 490
onwards see Döhle 95ff., 136ff. (Leo was, by the way, almost certainly mistaken
to claim fr. 404 M as the first line of A. *Philoctetes*.)

Laios began with a prologue spoken by Laios himself;[1] fr. 223 M is almost certainly the opening lines of a spoken prologue (play unknown, see *HSCP* 1972 p. 65 n. 25). Last but not least, we know that the play of Phrynichus on which *Pers* is said to have been modelled began with a speech spoken by a eunuch (*TrGF* 3 F 8).[2] So we can see that actors' prologue speeches were no rarity even earlier than *Pers*.

Turning to plays with a choral opening there is, besides *Pers* and *Hik*, *Prom. Lyomenos* (see p. 424); and in view of Arph. *Frogs* 911ff. there can be little doubt about *Niobe* also. *Myrmidones* is attested by two sources besides *Frogs*, and was probably, like *Phryges*, an early play.[3] We have no particular reason to suppose that in the late 470s a choral opening had any archaic associations or was regarded as anything other than a perfectly acceptable alternative to an actor's prologue. It is true that later in the century the spoken prologue became the rule, and that the use of a choral prologue might have produced a distinctly strange and archaic effect. As it is, the only play not by Aeschylus which we know had a choral opening is *Rh*. But that is nothing like the Aeschylean openings, and rather than evoking the archaic it is directed at novelty and excitement.[4] Choral openings

---

[1] Mette's combination of fr. 4 with frr. 1 and 2 is attractive: in that case the hypothesis tells us that the chorus consisted of old citizens and that the opening words were spoken by Laius. The only objection to Mette's combination is that the ζ of προλογίζων is on fr. 1, and yet there seem to be traces in fr. 4 also. Assuming the Didot papyrus (fr. 145 M = 99 N² = pp. 599ff. Ll-J) to come from *Kares or Europe*, we can safely say that this expository rhesis comes from early in the play, as like as not the prologue.

[2] There is a growing and justifiable suspicion that the play in question was not, as we are told, Phrynichus' *Phoinissai*, cf. *HSCP* 76 (1972) 68 n. 36. Lloyd-Jones (*Cuadernos de la Fundación Pastor* 13 (1966) 23f.) suggests that *Phoinissai* may have been the first play of a trilogy which included the more likely model Δίκαιοι ἢ Πέρσαι ἢ Σύνθωκοι (*TrGF* 3 F 4a). Arnott 70 approves of the foolish theory that the Eunuch was never on-stage and implies that Phrynichus' play began with choral anapaests: but the source itself (Hypoth. *Pers*) directly contradicts this. (For sitting on-stage, which Arnott takes exception to, see A. *Eum* 629 and cf. the councillors on the name-painting of the Darius painter (*Illustrations* p. 112).)

[3] For *Niobe* see *HSCP* 76 (1972) 61; for *Myrmidones* ibid. 65.

[4] The opening of *Rh* forwards two of the dramatist's main aims: to set a drama on the field of war, and to give the chorus a realistically integrated role. Cf. Strohm *Hermes* 87 (1959) 272f. The writer of the hypoth. to *Rh* knew of two spoken prologues to *Rh*, and Ritchie 101–13 argues that one belonged to the original play (which he argues is the work of Euripides). But his points are, in my view, far from convincing. He contends that the play must have once had a prologue since, if it did not, it would be unlike any other surviving tragedy: but if it is not Euripidean then that would not be so surprising. One of his detailed arguments

evidently went out of use some time in the middle of the century, but that does not mean that they were necessarily an archaic feature, and it certainly does not mean that Aeschylus might not put them to a positive—even novel—use, and thus produce dramatic situations which could not be created in any other way.

Pers, *Hik*, *Prom Lyom*, and *Myrm* all began with marching anapaests. In *Pers* and *Hik*, at least, there are long systems of anapaests before the strophic part of the first song begins; and there are comparably long stretches in *Ag* and in S. *Aj*. The chorus also enters to anapaests of different kinds in some other plays (e.g. E. *Hec*, *Alc*, *Med*). It is an obvious inference that the chorus actually made its entrance stepping to these anapaests, and continued its marching movements until it began on the choreography of the strophic lyrics. But how, then, did it enter when there are no preliminary anapaests? In some plays it may have entered during the final words of the preceding speech (e.g. see *Prom* 128a* or *Cho* 22*), but in many plays this is out of the question, e.g. in S. *Ant*, *OT*; E. *Hipp*, *El*. In such circumstances it might be argued, as it is e.g. by P-C *DFA*² 243, that the chorus entered in silence and did not sing until it was in position for the first strophe. But, against this, we should expect some words to cover the movement instead of an empty and awkward silence. Also there are two plays of Euripides where this arrangement seems to be impossible. In *Hel* Helen sings the first strophe (167ff.) and the chorus first joins in with the antistrophe (179ff.); there is no sign that it entered before 179, and a pause for entry between strophe and antistrophe is hardly likely. Also in *Hyps* the chorus apparently enters after the beginning of the strophic song at fr. I col. ii 15 (p. 26 Bond); here a long pause would be even less acceptable.¹ So it seems probable that when there was no anapaestic prelude the chorus entered with the opening words of the first strophe. In what respects, if any, the choreography of the antistrophe responded to the entry we cannot say. It may seem strange that a choral entry should be

(106–7) is that there is a lack of forewarning for the contributions of the various characters. But Rhesus is well prepared for, and the entries of Odysseus, Diomedes, and Athena are all deliberately surprising.

¹ Bond 61–2 in his discussion of the structure of the song does not see the peculiarity of the *entry* of the chorus during the course of the strophic structure. *Hel* is the nearest parallel, but *Hyps* is still unique in that the chorus enters to the second section of the strophe and not to the first antistrophe.

made to a lyric metre, but it is presumably not impossible. It is likely that the technical term 'parodos', as opposed to 'stasimon', referred to the choreography of the entrance song: it is the lyric in which 'the chorus is "coming on"', and has to move on to and across the orchestra to take its place in the middle' (A. M. Dale, see further p. 473). In *Pers*, however, there are marching anapaests to accompany the entrance of the chorus.

(b) motivation of entries

The chorus identifies itself immediately (1–7); but it does not divulge where it is, nor therefore why it is there. This is only revealed after the song in the lines which return to the main action (140ff.), and then only indirectly. The exhortation to sit down in 'this ancient building' shows, though casually, that they are supposed to be thought of as inside a council chamber— see p. 454—a very reasonable place for the elders to be. It is quite possible that there were seats for the councillors (as there were in Phrynichus' earlier 'Persians' play, see p. 63 n. 2 above). It may be, as is often claimed, that the audience would assume that the scene-setting was the same as in the earlier play: but Aeschylus cannot have meant his audience to rely on complex comparative references—a playwright with an obvious model tends, in any case, to diverge no less than he coincides. Many scholars have taken it upon themselves to point out that the motivation of the entry of the chorus is not explicitly and immediately made clear;[1] some have labelled this as primitive, and have found fault with Aeschylus for his hamfistedness. I agree with those who find the critics hamfisted.[2]

The general topic of the motivation of entries has received more than its fair share of attention (the motivation of exits, though less studied, is liable to the same reservations). When Aichele writes (72 n. 1) 'there is abundant literature on the introduction of characters' entrances in Greek tragedy' he is evidently referring to this particular aspect.[3] As a rule these

---

[1] There is a considerable bibliography in Garvie 122 n. 7, to which may be added Groeneboom ii p. 5, Korzeniewski 553–6.

[2] Good sense in Riemschneider *Hermes* 73 (1938) 348 n. 2, Pohlenz *Die griechische Tragödie*[2] (Göttingen 1954) ii pp. 26f., Richter 135f.

[3] Far the best treatment I know is that of Deckinger. Other literature includes Harms, Flickinger 229ff., Schadewaldt *Monolog* 8 n. 4, G. F. Davidson *HSCP* 43 (1932) 170–3 (summary of a Harvard dissertation), Webster *Preparation* 117ff. I

writers, with the notable exception of Deckinger, have taken
'motivation' in its usual, but superficial, sense: the explicit
explanations offered for the entry (or exit), the reasons actually
spelt out why that person enters. Such explanations may be
divulged by the play in various ways, but the most obvious and
commonplace is in the lines immediately after an entry or
immediately before an exit. This kind of short-term motivation
is easily extracted from its context and collected on a card index;
and this may be one reason why the topic has been favoured
(this is particularly obvious in Webster's article). But more
influential, no doubt, is Aristotle's insistent stress in *Poetics* on
plot construction, on the importance of εἰκός (over twenty times
in *Poet*) and on the undesirability of ἄλογα. Indeed when Aristotle
complains at 1461b20 that Euripides has made unnecessary use
of ἄλογον in the case of Aegeus, it is generally supposed that he is
complaining about the strained motivation of Aegeus' entry at
E. *Med* 666 (see below).

But surely this kind of motivation is a relatively trivial matter.
Any hack can, if he gives the matter priority, supply a plausible
motive for each exit and entry:[1] a good playwright, particularly
in a conventional and unrealistic theatre, might well feel that he
has better things on which to employ his skill, and so regard
short-term motivation as a secondary or dispensable consideration. In a theatre which had no pretence of presenting a realistic
slice of life the audience will not expect to hear about the
detailed motivation of arrivals and departures, except in unusual
circumstances (e.g. the arrival of a stranger in a foreign city).
Ask no questions, and you will be given no unconvincing answers.
Much more important than such petty circumstantial details is
the way that an entry or exit is fitted into the dramatic con-

---

have not been able to see P. E. Lindemann *De Introductione* etc. (Diss. Marburg
1922). On comedy, besides Harms and Davidson, there is K. S. Bennett *Motivation of Exits* etc. (Michigan 1932), Gomme *Essays in Gk. History and Literature*
(Oxford 1937) 254–61—Gomme has the virtue of seeing that realistic motivation
is not essential. I have not seen W. Koch *De Personarum Comicarum Introductione*
(Breslau 1914) nor M. Johnston *Entrances and Exits in Roman Comedy* (Geneva N.Y.
1933). There is still further bibliography in Andrieu p. 183 n. 1.

[1] Neophron, for example, in his *Medea* gave Aegeus a more plausible motivation
for arriving than Euripides did, see schol. on E. *Med* 666. On 'hack' elements in
the Neophron fragments see Page E. *Med ed* xxxiv–xxxvi. On the priority of
Euripides see Séchan 592–4. (Yet the other view is still maintained by e.g. Thompson
CQ 38 (1944) 10ff., Snell *Szenen* 199ff.)

struction as a whole, the way it is worked in, and so the way it works. In a good play each entrance and exit does not happen at random; it is put into a dramatic context in order to further artistic purposes which could not be served in any other way. Obviously the dramatic integration of entrances and exits is much more important than short-term motivation, and is largely independent of it. (Aristotle himself would, no doubt, agree.) Yet there is a sense in which this also may be called 'motivation', for in a much more important sense it *explains why* the entrance or exit is as it is. If this kind of motivation is well handled then the entrance or exit can have a rightness and carry conviction in despite of trivial and suppressed implausibilities. Only Deckinger has clearly made this distinction between circumstantial and dramatic motivation, which he calls 'äussere' and 'innere Motivation' respectively (*Einleitung* 1–7 and *passim*).

In view of this it can be seen why I, for one, might be tempted to concur with Wilamowitz when he says (E. *Her ed* ii 160) 'In keeping with the style of Greek drama, the motivation of trivial matters is disdained . . .' Yet this is not altogether true. The Attic tragedians often, though by no means always, do go to some trouble to give entries (and to a less extent exits) a plausible short-term motivation. Repeatedly, and particularly in later tragedy, an entrance or exit is accompanied by some quite explicit explanation of why it has occurred in the way it has (time, place, and manner). Evidently this adds a degree of verisimilitude to the action which is presumably put there to induce the audience to involve itself more intimately in the play.[1] It was said above that an audience would not ask awkward questions provided that those questions were not allowed to obtrude themselves. But since answers are quite often supplied to circumstantial questions about entrances and exits, it may be that the later fifth-century audience did come to expect some sort of gesture at realistic motivation. Note how at Arph. *Frogs* 971ff. Euripides boasts that he taught people to ask questions— πῶς τοῦτ' ἔχει; ποῦ μοι τοδί; τίς τοῦτ' ἔλαβε; Observation of dramatic methods may underlie Aristophanes' joke here. Most

---

[1] Tragedy still contrasts, however, with the realism of New Comedy; consider e.g. the intricately realistic motivations in Men. *Dysc*, see Handley *ed* index on 'Motivation, late or casual'. Yet Gomme (op. cit.) rightly makes the point that, when it does not suit him, Menander pays no attention to motivation.

such short-term motivation is brief and discreet. On those occasions when it is positively prolonged or laboured we may suspect some further artistic motive. For example, some choruses whose presence on the scene is particularly unrealistic give elaborate lyric motivation to their entry (see further below). Far from adding verisimilitude these motivations seem to remove the chorus from the grasp of a realism which would be unachievable and to give their presence a poetic justification. The motivation of actors may also be laboured on occasion. Aegeus in E. *Med* is an example: it seems that Euripides is trying to convey that for both Aegeus and Medea the other is just the person who is needed at this juncture.

However, I can see no comparably laboured motivation in Aeschylus. In Aeschylus the problem is, rather, at the opposite end of the scale. Is there any special significance—or is there artistic failure—in a total *lack* of explicit motivation? While the absence of motivation might on occasion imbue a character with mysteriousness or with a sense of fated destiny, this is clearly not the usual explanation. On the other hand the explanation of primitive incompetence, which is often invoked, is surely not justified. The dramatist could easily have supplied an adequate motivation, had he wished to: he has chosen rather to give some other artistic consideration priority, as I shall argue is the case here in *Pers*. The audience has better things to occupy its attention than asking trivial questions which are not put to it. This is true at any rate of Aeschylus; though it may be that later in the century the habit of asking for a short-term motivation was formed in the audience by dramatists, especially Euripides, who saw more value in the evocation of circumstantial details.

To return to *Pers*: if in 472 a chorus of elders entered at the beginning of a play no member of the audience would carp that the entry had not been precisely motivated. The chorus enters because it is the chorus. Had Aeschylus thought it desirable he could easily have supplied some explicit motivation; it is ridiculous to imply that such a 'sophisticated' touch was beyond his powers. He has preferred to hold back an indirect motivation until the end of the first song because he wants the chorus, as soon as it has established its identity and status, to turn to the crucial theme of the return of the King (see 909b*), and so on to the departure of his expedition. It is a matter of artistic priorities.

The handling of the chorus in *Ag* is quite closely comparable:
a chorus of old men, left at home, is concerned about the return
of the King, and sense that his departure was not wholly pro-
pitious. In *Ag* the elders turn back to the departure immediately
on entry (40ff.), and do not even identify themselves until 72ff.
The motive for their presence is then obliquely revealed—
curiosity—in the questions at 83ff.: see *Ag* 40*. So in *Ag* the
matter of motivation is even more subordinate to other priorities.
Yet scholars have not so readily called *Ag* primitive. This is,
I suspect, because, like the writer of the hypothesis to *Ag*, they
think that l. 258 supplies an explicit circumstantial motivation:
on *Ag* 40* I shall argue that they are mistaken in this. But even
if they were right, 258 would be a mere paper motivation: in
performance Aeschylus has suppressed questions (and answers)
which he regards as insignificant, and has concentrated on other
deeper matters.

   None the less we might particularly approve of choral entries
which, unlike those of *Pers* and *Ag*, are integrally concerned with
the action of the play, so that the entry is thus self-explanatory.
The plays of Aeschylus are, in fact, the place to look. The entrance
of the chorus in *Hik* and *Eum* is part of the development of the
action, and so its motivation is all part of its essential role. In
Seven and in *Cho* the presence of the chorus is closely integrated
through the advance of the besiegers and through Clytemnestra's
dream, and so its motivation is quickly and easily made evident.
But the kind of integral participation of the chorus found in
Hik and *Eum* did not become accepted. Only in *Rh* among
post-Aeschylean tragedies is there any serious attempt to make
the chorus realistic in mundane terms. To put it bluntly, people
do not normally go around merged anonymously in groups of
fifteen. It is true that Sophocles and Euripides do usually try to
give a plausible motivation for the presence of their choruses,[1]
and sometimes manage to connect the inevitable arrival with
the action of the play, as e.g. in S. *OC*; E. *Hik*, *Tro*, *Ba*. But there
is often some hint of self-consciousness over the unrealistic presence of the chorus, such as is scarcely found in Aeschylus,
except in *Prom*. It seems to be a characteristically Euripidean
technique to give the chorus an elaborate and self-contained
motivation soon after entry, e.g. *Hipp* 121ff., *El* 167ff., *Phoen*

   [1] On this see Flickinger 150–2, *GGL* i 2 p. 130, Kannicht E. *Hel ed* ii p. 71.

202ff., *IA* 164ff. Although these motivations tend to include οἰκεῖα πράγματα they are far from realistic; if anything they are anti-realistic. They are rather illustrations of that 'curious self-consciousness [which] seems to obsess dramatic poets and force them to call the hearer's attention to the very difficulty that they are striving to avoid' (Flickinger 141). The contrived, poetic motivation of the chorus has a single Aeschylean precedent or analogy. The chorus in *Prom*, which has by far the least significance in its play, also has the most elaborate and self-contained arrival-motivation: see *Prom* 128a*.

If a chorus is not so closely bound up with the action of the play that the reason for its arrival is self-evident, then one simple way of avoiding unwanted distraction over its motivation is to neglect the matter, or only to touch on it later and indirectly. If the question is not raised by the dramatist then the audience will not ask it; it will accept the arrival of the chorus as something given. In *Pers* and *Ag* Aeschylus has, I conclude, used this traditional acquiescence to avoid circumstantial details and to go straight to more pressing themes and preoccupations. In the later theatre it may be that such questions of detail become unavoidable; and so time and trouble are usually expended on supplying pretexts, sometimes at the expense of directness and of concentration of dramatic impact. Dio Chrys. seems to have noted this very contrast when he compared the entries of the chorus in the *Philoctetes* plays of Aeschylus and Euripides: (*Or* 52, §7) ἀλλ᾽ ὁ μὲν Εὐριπίδης εὐθὺς ἀπολογουμένους πεποίηκε περὶ τῆς πρότερον ἀμελείας . . . ὁ δ᾽ Αἰσχύλος ἁπλῶς εἰσήγαγε τὸν χορόν, ὃ τῶι παντὶ τραγικώτερον καὶ ἁπλούστερον, τὸ δ᾽ ἕτερον πολιτικώτερον καὶ ἀκριβέστερον.

155 enter the Queen (on a chariot, with attendants)

(a) announcement and greeting

The anapaests 150–4 announce the approach of the Queen, and end by saying that the chorus should greet her properly προσφθόγγοις . . . μύθοισι. A four-line greeting then follows in trochaic tetrameters, which are to be the metre of the following scene. We cannot, of course, say at precisely what moment the Queen first came into the sight of the audience, but the change of metre and the change from third-person report to second-person address marks the moment of her actual engagement in the play (on this notion see pp. 8f.). It would, therefore, be more helpful for the stage instruction to go by 155 rather than by 150 (where many have put it).[1]

There are some distinctions to be drawn between the extremely common entrance announcement and the rather rare entrance greeting or address. I use 'announcement'[2] synonymously with 'introduction', and both in distinction from 'preparation' (see pp. 9ff.). A working definition might be 'anything said about the approach of a character after that approach has first been seen (or otherwise perceived)[3] by someone already on stage'. Entrance announcements are, of course, common in Greek tragedy. It would be a mistake, however, to suppose that they are almost invariably used: in fact only just under half of all entries are announced. In Aeschylus the announcement is usually delivered by the coryphaeus (see *Prom* 944*), but in later tragedy about half are spoken by actors. Most announcements simply take the form of between one and four spoken iambic lines. Some, however, are longer; we find up to twenty lines (see further *Ag* 503b*), and occasionally (in which case the classification is no longer really appropriate) they are even longer (see *Hik* 234a*). Announcements are found in other metres, in particular in anapaests (see further below), but also rarely in trochaic tetrameters and even sung in lyric metres (see *Seven* 854c*). The language of entrance announcements is often rather colourless, even formulaic in later tragedy; but sometimes the language can be vivid and unusual, particularly in Aeschylus (see *Seven* 371a*).

Entrance announcements are a phenomenon of the open stage; they are rare, though not unknown, in the proscenium-arch

---

[1] Including Hermann, Sidgwick, Wecklein, Smyth, Groeneboom, Rose, and trs. of 'Droysen', Vellacott, Werner.

[2] Besides scattered remarks in commentaries (often inaccurate) I have noted special studies on announcements in Wilamowitz *Analecta* 199ff. (identification), Bodensteiner 705–21 (all announcements are collected in the *Anhang* on 725ff.), Graeber ch. III (19ff.), Deckinger *passim* especially 53ff., 142ff., *GGL* i 2 p. 75 n. 9, 288 n. 3, 484, Andrieu 196f., Hourmouziades Appendix I (137ff.).

[3] Sound and smell at *Prom* 114ff. (see 128a*). In later tragedy approaches from the house are sometimes heard, e.g. E. *Hel* 858ff., *Or* 1366, *Ba* 638, and perhaps *Hyps* fr. 34/35 (p. 36 Bond; this is my own tentative suggestion). This became common in New Comedy—see Dedoussi *Hellenika* 18 (1964) 6ff., Petersmann *WSt* N.F. 5 (1971) 91ff.

theatre.[1] Since considerable distances had to be traversed by
characters joining or leaving the play, the lines of announcement
doubtless helped to cover and accompany these long movements.
Thus almost all processional entries (funereal or ceremonial
entries, for example) are given longer announcements, often in
anapaests. But this observation by no means accounts exclusively
for the convention. Many entries from the skene door, which
would not take so long, are nevertheless announced, while many
entrances from the side eisodoi are not announced at all. Often
there is no apparent reason in terms of staging why one entry
should be announced while another is not.[2] There are, in fact,
other functions which an announcement may fulfil. Obviously it
may identify a new character (see especially Wilamowitz *Analecta* 199ff.)—or it may betray an exciting ignorance of his
identity. It may draw attention to interesting visual features of
the person approaching (see Dingel 221ff.). There are ways in
which an announcement may build up expectation or anxiety
or curiosity about what a new entry may have in store for the
play. It may, for instance, speculate or ask questions about the
significance of the approaching character. The reason for a
longer than usual announcement may sometimes be that the
dramatist wishes to build up tension over the entry (see *Ag*
503b*). The announcement may also inform us about the person
who makes it; it may show how he responds and prepares himself for the imminent arrival. In general, the convention allows
the playwright a useful opportunity to guide his audience in its
response to a new turn of events.

There are fair grounds for regarding an announcement as
marking the approach rather than the arrival of a character,
both in dramatic and literal terms. Although an announcement
might easily be made to provide a starting topic for the new
scene, this is hardly ever done: examples are *Prom* 128a*; S. *Ant*
387; E. *Alc* 141; *Rh* 890. Usually, however, the words following
the arrival are completely independent of the announcement,
and there is no suggestion that the approaching person might

[1] Entrance announcements in Shakespeare are discussed by W. D. Smith in
Shakespeare Quarterly 4 (1953) 405ff. He documents the decline in frequency in
the later proscenium-arch theatre.

[2] For an attempt to relate entrance announcements to staging see Hourmouziades
137ff., who argues that whether it is the chorus or an actor who makes the announcement depends on their relative positions in the theatre at that moment.

have heard it. Further, there are quite a few announcements which are so extended that it is impossible to suppose that the new character was near by right from the beginning of the announcement; cf. *Hik* 234a*, *Ag* 503b*.[1] In some of these places the announcement and the reaction it provokes must positively *not* be heard by the approaching character, e.g. at S. *El* 1429ff.; E. *El* 962ff., *Her* 1153ff., *Or* 456ff., 1313ff.

But, while it is fair to say that in dramatic terms an arrival normally happens after an announcement, it does not follow that the new arrival was never in sight of the audience before the end of the announcement; in all probability he usually came into sight during the course of it. In particular all slower entries, those in some way processional or ceremonial, must have used the time taken up by the announcement to make the long entrance movement. It is worth noting that many such slower entries are accompanied, like this one in *Pers*, by an anapaestic announcement. While the iambic trimeter is by far the most common metre, we have in surviving tragedy thirty or so ana-paestic announcements, recited by the chorus or coryphaeus. In nearly every case there is some obvious way in which the entry is slow or stately.[2] Thus, anapaests tend to be used to announce funereal processions (e.g. *Seven* 871; S. *Ant* 1257; E. *Hik* 794, *Tro* 1118, *Phoen* 1480); the entry of those condemned to death (e.g. S. *Ant* 801;[3] E. *Andr* 494, *Her* 442, *IT* 456, *Or* 1013); and grand or pompous entries (e.g. S. *Ant* 155; E. *Or* 348, *Phrixos POxy* 2685 fr. i ll. 10ff.).[4]

[1] There is a useful catalogue of longer entrance announcements in Bodensteiner 710–25. Unfortunately he seems to think that characters were visible to the audience right from the start of the announcement (704f., 710ff.; similarly J. Hampel *Was lehrt A. Orestie für d. Theaterfrage?* (Prague 1899) 25). B. was taken to task for this by Haigh (*CR* 8 (1894) 176ff., *AT*³ 192f.)—rightly in this instance, but see p. 450 n. 1.

[2] Sophoclean exceptions are *Ant* 376, 526, 626 (curiously all six anapaestic announcements from Sophocles are in *Ant*). Two apparent exceptions in Euripides are Talthybius at *Tro* 230 and Amphiaraus at *Hyps* fr. I iv 10 (p. 29 Bond). Both announce key characters at the key juncture after the first song.

[3] That these anapaests clearly are an entry announcement (see also ἀνύτουσαν 805) is the chief refutation of Ziobro *AJP* 92 (1971) 81–5, who argues that Antigone was already on stage before 781ff. He claims that she embodies the lyric about Eros and Aphrodite: but Antigone herself has singularly little to do with that god.

[4] Ino is making some sort of defiant stand by having her maids carry out her rich dowry, cf. E. *Andr*. 147ff. Webster is certainly right that the lines are an entry announcement, despite the caution of the *ed pr* (*POxy*. vol. 34 pp. 9, 13). Also the emendation to καὶ μήν in l. 10 is inevitable.

A πρόϲφθογγοϲ μῦθοϲ such as we have here in 155–8 is a more
unusual and attention-catching device. Since the new character
is addressed in the second person there is a presumption that he
has by now arrived and is fully engaged in the play. In some
instances the character actually takes up the words of the greeting, as the Queen does here with ταῦτα δὴ λιποῦϲα κτλ. (159);
cf. e.g. A. *Ag* 266, 830; E. *Tro* 577; *IA* 607. Of course, one actor
may address another before he speaks on arrival and, so to speak,
'usurp' his first word; for a discussion see pp. 397f. But that
device is used in different circumstances and with different
dramatic purposes from the phenomenon under consideration
here, which is the 'usurpation of first word' by the chorus.
Several of the other instances are, like this one, honorific greetings. There are two in A. *Ag*: 258ff. (trimeters, see 258b*) and
783ff. (anapaests, chariot entry, see 783a*), both without any
preceding announcement.[1] There are, besides, three other
chariot-borne entries which are met by honorific greetings, all
in anapaests: E. *El* 988ff.; *Rh* 379ff.; *IA* 590ff., 599ff.[2] There is
one particularly grand entry, that of Menelaus at E. *Or* 352
which, though apparently on foot (ϲτείχει 348), has both
announcement (348ff.) and greeting (352ff.), all in anapaests.

Otherwise, choral greetings tend to occur in situations of high
pathos, usually those with a spectacular element where some time
is needed to react to a visual tableau. In *Seven* the two sisters are
addressed at 871–4 after they have been announced: these
anapaests in Aeschylean style probably date from the later fifth
century, see *Seven* 871a*.[3] In Sophocles, Oedipus is addressed on
first revelation at *OT* 1297ff. And I would suggest that *Ant*
379–83 might be regarded as an address on arrival to Antigone
rather than as part of the announcement begun at 376. This
would draw attention to her defiantly silent pose which is maintained until 443. In Euripides there is a choral anapaestic
address to greet the chariot-borne entry of Andromache and

---

[1] Fr. 16 M (*POxy.* 2250) (which is not from *Isthmiastai*, see p. 420) begins like
Ag 783 (ἄ]γε δή, βαϲιλεῦ . . .), and may be another honorific greeting.

[2] Probably neither of these greetings in *IA* is Euripidean, see p. 77 n. 1 below.

[3] Pötscher *Eranos* 56 (1958) 146f. and 57 (1959) 91 makes much of detailed
resemblances between *Pers* 140ff. and *Seven* 861ff., and claims that these prove
the authenticity of the latter. But the common features are not particularly
Aeschylean and are to be found throughout Greek tragedy: the slight resemblances
are far outweighed by the larger differences.

Astyanax at *Tro* 572;[1] but this chariot entry is ironically different from the others, since she is being conveyed as a chattel to the ships of Neoptolemus. One might also compare the choral comment, though without second-person address, after the revelation of Alcestis at *Alc* 238 (anapaests) and of Amphitryon and the carnage at *Her* 1028 (trimeters and lyric).[2]

(b) ὀχήματα χλιδή τε: *an unsigned stage-direction?*

The reader of *Pers* does not discover until lines 607ff.—

> τοιγὰρ κέλευθον τήνδ᾿ ἄνευ τ᾿ ὀχημάτων
> χλιδῆc τε τῆc πάροιθεν ἐκ δόμων πάλιν
> ἔcτειλα κτλ.

—that the first entry of the Queen was made ceremonially in a vehicle: in performance the audience would know at once. Obviously there were a great many things which the audience could see which are not given any attention in the words of the play; mute attendants (see 155c* below) are an example, colour of hair, and decorative props are others. But it was argued in §3 that all *significant* visual aspects of stage management are singled out for attention in the words. If there were all sorts of significant visual effects which are given no notice at all in the words then work on theatrical technique loses much of its point.

The chariot at *Pers* 155ff. seems to be a counter-example to my thesis. Much has been inferred on the strength of it. Harmon,[3] for example, asserts that 'it is not his [A.'s] way to write into his lines unnecessary exposition or stage business'—though that 'unnecessary' is crucially vague. Dingel[4] concluded simply from this instance that the visual aspects of Greek tragedy are 'wort-unabhängig', although, if true, this would undermine his entire work, which tries to demonstrate the significance of stage

---

[1] Kirchhoff, who is followed by most editors, was surely right to attribute 572ff. to the chorus, despite the MS. attribution to Hecuba. For anapaests which turn from announcement to address see the places cited in *Seven*, E. *Or*, S. *Ant*.

[2] The choral couplets addressed to a new character at *Cho* 732f. and S. *Aj* 1316 are quite different: see *Cho* 732b*.

[3] Harmon *TAPA* 63 (1932) 18; cf. Anderson *G and R* 19 (1972) 171 n. 2 '—proof, if any were needed, that Aeschylus does not always reinforce significant use of spectacle with explicit verbal reference'.

[4] *Bauformen* 359–60. Dingel also cites the colour of Menelaus' hair in E. *Or*, which is not verbally noted until l. 1532. But every character's mask had hair of a certain colour; yet this was never important enough to be given verbal attention, unless there was some special point to be made—as at *Or* 1532, cf. e.g. E. *Ba* 235.

properties. Steidle[1] claims that Aeschylus, unlike Sophocles and Euripides, composed with no thought of a reading public, and so implies that much more important stage business may be lost. But, again, this is the only evidence he can cite. No one, so far as I know, has been able to point to a single comparably important stage instruction which is not properly highlighted by the words. So if some explanation can be found for this apparent counter-example then my basic premise may still hold good.

First, the case must be made that chariot-borne entries were a commonplace in the early theatre. This requires a survey of all places in surviving tragedy where a chariot is indicated on stage.[2] Agamemnon and Cassandra enter on a chariot at *Ag* 783b*, though no explicit reference is made to it for another 120 lines. I argue against a wheeled entry at *Pers* 909a*; but that it is probable that Pelasgus is on a vehicle at *Hik* 234b*. Aristophanes evidently regarded such entries as characteristic of Aeschylus, since at *Frogs* 962ff. he has Euripides say that, unlike Aeschylus, he did not alarm his audience 'with Memnons with bells on the horses' harness' (cf. p. 43 and p. 422). Further, I argue in Appendix C that the *skene* background was introduced only in Aeschylus' last years; and, once there, it would obviously tend to represent a palace, and royal characters would use its door for the majority of their exits and entrances. But during most of Aeschylus' career Kings and Queens had perforce to come on by the *eisodoi*, and their arrivals may well have been made more regal by the use of chariots.

If this is right, then we should expect to find little use of chariots in Sophocles or Euripides. We read that in Euripides' plays 'royal personages frequently enter in chariots' (Arnott 116); but I would recognize only two instances in Euripides and none in Sophocles. In E. *El* Clytemnestra, who brings the corrupt riches of the palace to the yeoman's cot, enters on a chariot at 988, as is made clear in 966 and 998ff. And at *Tro* 572 Andromache and Astyanax are brought on in a chariot with the rest of Neoptolemus' spoils; this is clearly marked in 569 and 572ff. (cf. 614, 626).

---

[1] Steidle 11. Cf. Bodensteiner 661 'Äschylos ist mit Andeutungen über szenische Vorgänge sparsamer als jeder der späteren Dichter'. But I have not found this to be the case.

[2] Cf. Bodensteiner 707–8, Dingel 65f. I use 'chariot' to mean any beast-drawn vehicle.

However, chariot-borne entries seem to have become popular again in the fourth century. Clytemnestra and Iphigeneia enter on a chariot at *IA* 590, as is not only repeatedly indicated by Clytemnestra's first speech (607ff.) but also by the second choral greeting (598ff.): however, it is very doubtful whether this scene is the work of Euripides.[1] There is, on the other hand, no explicit indication that Rhesus enters on his chariot at *Rh* 380; but the Shepherd lavishly described him approaching on a chariot (301–8), and he is greeted with choral anapaests such as tend to accompany chariot entries, see 155a* above. Moreover, Rhesus has bells on his armour (384f., κωδωνοκρότους), and the Shepherd tells of bells on his horses' trappings (306–8, πολλοῖσι σὺν κώδωσιν): this seems to be directly in the tradition of the fated Aeschylean heroes who came to help Troy κωδωνοφαλαροπώλους. Next, there is the important scholion on E. *Or* 57, which tells us that actors interpolated a spectacular procession at the beginning of that play;[2] since this included spoils, it is likely that there were chariots (cf. *Ag* 783b*). Further, processions of prisoners and spoils are found in Menander, e.g. in *Sik* and *Aspis*. And, finally, on *Eum* 397b* I support the view that *Eum* 405 was interpolated so that Athena could make a chariot-borne entry to suit post-classical tastes.

Taken together this evidence supports the description 'das alte prächtige Bild' which Kranz (*Stas.* 233) applies to chariots in his discussion of Euripides' archaizing. Aeschylus' uses (*Pers, Ag, ?Hik*) are not stressed, and this casual treatment suggests that the device was commonplace. The two later fifth-century uses (E. *El, Tro*), by contrast, serve conscious and stressed dramatic purposes. The fourth-century revival was mainly, one presumes, for spectacular effect (cf. p. 47); though *Rh*, at least, shows signs of archaizing. So the burden of this first part of the

---

[1] Lines 590–7 not only contain a metrical anomaly unknown in Euripides (see Barrett E. *Hipp ed* 368 n. 1), but also suspicious similarities to E. *El* 988ff. (see Page 160). But, above all, the inappropriate ἐμήν in 592 cannot be explained away. Unless one is willing to believe Webster *The Tragedies of Euripides* (London 1967) 260 'Euripides forgot that they were not an ordinary chorus of confidantes', it is best to regard the lines as hurriedly composed pastiche. As for the alternative stanza of anapaests (599–606), see Page 160–1. On 607ff., also under the influence of Euripides and indivisible from one or other set of anapaests, see Page 161–9.

[2] Cf. Wilamowitz *Einl.* 153 n. 62, Page 41f., Burnett 198. Malzan *De Scholiis Euripideis* etc. (diss. Darmstadt 1908) 18f. makes the interesting suggestion that rather than merely add a dumb-show the actors also added an extra prologue which was then expunged by Alexandrian editors.

argument is that the fact that the entry at *Pers* 155 is made in a chariot is *not* significant. The chariot entries of royalty, particularly of oriental royalty, were in the early pre-*skene* theatre so much a matter of course as to call for no particular comment.

The second stage of the argument is to see that by the time of lines 607ff. the use of the chariot back at 155ff. has become significant and worthy of notice: that is why it is alluded to. Aeschylus has taken something which is so usual as to call for no comment and, through the development of the play, has turned it into something which becomes *retrospectively* important and demonstrative. At 155 the chariot is no more than a conventional sign of the great prosperity of the royal house: but by 598 the Queen has learned that wealth *per se* without judgement or divine favour is superficial and vulnerable—see further 598a*. When this realization is reached the chariot, which was a matter of course, has become the symbol of a moral attitude.

There is another way in which the chariot comes gradually within the play to represent wealth without judgement. This is the persistent use of the imagery of yoking and chariot-driving: words formed around -ζυγ- abound in *Pers*, in both literal and figurative contexts.[1] In the first song the Elders sing without moral bias how Xerxes set off in his chariot (84) with other chariot-borne commanders (29, 46) to put the yoke on Hellas (50); and how to achieve this he yoked the sea in the Hellespont (72, 130). But as the play progresses it becomes clear that these two yokings, of Greece and of the Sea, were the manifestations of Xerxes' disastrous misjudgement. That of Greece is made memorably explicit in the Queen's dream (181ff.): that of the Hellespont is especially condemned by Darius (722ff., 745ff.). Ill-judged confidence in wealth led to ill-judged yoking: that is what the Queen learns by the time of her second entry. This seems to be what she forebodes soon after her first entry in the difficult line 163: μὴ μέγας πλοῦτος κονίσας οὖδας ἀντρέψηι ποδὶ / ὄλβον. Acceptable ὄλβος tries to yoke the chariot of μέγας (excessive) πλοῦτος, and comes to grief by being thrown out[2]—like Xerxes in the dream.

[1] Cf. Fowler *C et M* 28 (1970) 3–10, Anderson (op. cit. p. 75 n. 3) 167f. Fowler evidently regards the yoke as the chief image in the play, to the neglect of the *sea*, cf. Anderson 171f.

[2] For this interpretation see Wilamowitz *ed maj* ad loc., Groeneboom ii pp. 46f., Korzeniewski 577f. Broadhead 261f., set on offering a conjecture, fails to show any-

So I contend that the chariot in *Pers* does not show that important visual effects in Greek tragedy could be 'wortunabhängig', and so that there were not, in fact, many such effects which we cannot know about. Aeschylus has used the imaginative and unusual technique of making some stage business, apparently unremarkable, significant in retrospect. Attention is, therefore, drawn to the visual meaning of the event not at the time of its occurrence, but only later.

(c) *mutes and extras*

The Queen has attendants with her. There is no direct indication of their presence in the text; yet we can say with confidence that all characters of high social status were accompanied by appropriate attendants, unless there is some positive reason why they should not be. Again and again in Greek tragedy there are places where, although late in a scene and although there has been no previous reference to them, a character turns to his or her servants with some command. No particular attention is paid to the servants until there is some purpose in doing so. Many such places were collected by G. Richter.[1] It is so common that we must assume that all appropriate characters had servants with them, even when no positive use is made of them at all. The Queen's royalty and the wealth and pomp of her position are stressed in *Pers*, and this entry was surely accompanied by handmaidens, although they remain purely 'extra'.

It is not difficult to illustrate these points from Aeschylus alone. Some places where servants, who have been paid no previous attention, are addressed: *Seven* 675f. (to an attendant who presumably entered at 375, see *Seven* 652*), *Ag* 909 (entered 855), 1650 (see 1577b*), *Cho* 712 (entered 668). Some characters whom we should suppose to have some suitable attendants with them, although no mention is made of them, are: Eteocles at *Seven* 1, the Egyptian Herald at *Hik* 836 (see 836b*), Clytemnestra throughout *Ag*, Agamemnon at *Ag* 783 (see 783b*). But the most interesting class is those characters who, although of high social

---

thing wrong with this. Coxon *CQ* N.s. 8 (1958) 47 compares *Il* 14. 145 κονίουϲιν πεδίον, and claims that the chariot must be raising dust in *flight*. But κονίοντεϲ πεδίοιο is twice used of the chariots in the race in *Il* 23 (372 and 449), and so the Homeric phrase conveys headlong *speed*, not necessarily in flight.

[1] *De Mutis Personis* etc. (diss. Halle 1934) *passim*; cf. also Bethe 336f., Spitzbarth 59ff., Hunger *RhM* 95 (1952) 370 n. 2, Andrieu 203f.

standing, have *no* attendants. For such a person to be without
servants makes a positive visual impression. Examples in Aeschylus
are: Xerxes at the end of *Pers* (see 909b*), probably the Queen
on her second entry (598a*), Orestes and Pylades in *Cho* (see
Cho 653*), and Aegisthus at *Cho* 838.

We cannot tell how many attendants there were in *Pers*, or
anywhere else. No doubt the number varied; and some choregoi
will have had deeper pockets than others.[1] There are often commands in the plural, and two is the minimum for most occasions.
We cannot give a maximum figure, though I should be surprised
if there were ever more than eight or so, since a larger group
would tend to detract visually from the chorus. Even *Eum*, which
demands a larger number of extras than any other surviving
tragedy, might be played with some twenty players in addition
to the speaking actors and the chorus (see *Eum* 566b*, 1047b*).

In English these silent attendants tend to be called 'mutes' or
'extras', or, more precisely, 'handmaidens', 'bodyguards', etc.
For a Greek term scholars tend to use κωφὰ πρόcωπα (found in
Cicero, Plutarch, and later writers). However, this term is also
used more often to refer to another class of 'mutes', those named
independent characters who none the less have non-speaking
parts (see *Cho* 1b*). In order to avoid this confusion I shall
reserve κωφὸν πρόcωπον for those characters—Bia, Pylades, etc.
If one wants a Greek term for 'attendants' then παρειcαγόμενα
πρόcωπα might do.[2] In the modern theatre a slightly derogatory
term for non-speaking extras is 'spear-carriers': it is agreeable to
find that δορυφορήματα is used in the same way.[3]

249 enter advance Messenger

(a) ἄγγελοc and dramatic function

The uncertainty and disquiet of the chorus and the Queen must
be resolved; the anxious questions must have an answer (cf.
Jens p. 247). So, although the messenger is not personally prepared for, his role is given 'situational' preparation (cf. p. 10).

---

[1] Consider the anecdote in Plutarch *Vit. Phocion* 19 about a vain actor who was
playing a queen and was refused an excessive number of attendants by his choregos.
[2] See the Hippocratic *Nomos* §1 (the whole context is pleasant).
[3] For lexicography see G. Richter op. cit. p. 9 n. 3. The rare word παραχορήγημα
('something furnished in addition'?) is used widely and indiscriminately by
modern scholars, and is best avoided. For discussion see Rees *CPh* 2 (1907) 387ff.
P-C *DFA*² 137.

There is even some sort of direct preparation when the chorus chants near the beginning of the play (14f.) κοὔτε τιϲ ἄγγελοϲ οὔτε τιϲ ἱππεὺϲ / ἄϲτυ τὸ Περϲῶν ἀφικνεῖται.[1] No news has come yet, but anxiety now reaches such a pitch that it must be relieved—even though by bad news.

The manuscripts, and hence the editors, call this new character ἄγγελοϲ. It is not unlikely that Aeschylus would have used this term himself: the noun is used in l. 14 (see above) and the verb by the messenger himself in 253. None the less the points should be made that a variety of characters with widely differing functions are covered in the manuscripts and editions by this single label, and that this particular *angelos* is not one of the most common type.[2] Our main notions of the messenger speech in Greek tragedy are based on the long, vivid set-piece narratives of terrible events which are delivered by an anonymous eye-witness and which tend to occur about three-quarters of the way through the tragedies of Sophocles and Euripides. These speeches and their introductory dialogues collected many conventional features which were sufficiently stereotyped to supply material for Aristophanes and later comedy.[3] But despite this basic stock scene it is on closer consideration hard to isolate more precisely the *angelos* elements in Greek tragedy.

Not every scene with any sort of narrative element will pass as a messenger scene. Rather, there are three elements involved: anonymous eye-witness, set-piece narrative speech, and over-all dramatic function. When all three elements are combined then

---

[1] Rose p. 89 seems to have missed the point when he says that ll. 14f. 'heightens the dramatic surprise of the news when it does come': the lines accentuate the suspense of waiting for the news, but, when it does come, it comes as no surprise.

[2] There is a considerable body of learned literature on messengers, from which I select what I have found most instructive. Two useful dissertations appeared simultaneously in 1910: the better is by J. Fischl in *Diss. Philol. Vindobonenses* 10, the other by E. Henning (diss. Göttingen). More recent contributions include *GGL* i 2 pp. 118f., 3 pp. 777f., W. Ludwig *Sapheneia* (diss. Tübingen 1954) 11ff., H. Strohm *Hermes* 87 (1959) 266ff., R. Lattimore *The Poetry of Greek Tragedy* (Baltimore 1958) 32 n. 5, Dingel 106ff., L. di Gregorio (which I reviewed in *JEA* 57 (1971) 235–6—in p. 235 n. 1 I list no fewer than five post-war dissertations on messengers which I have not been able to consult).

[3] There is a very useful survey of Aristophanic parodies in Rau 162–8 (with 46f.). For adaptations of classical tragic messengers in later comedy see J. Wagner *De Nuntiis Comicis* (diss. Wroclaw 1913), E. Fraenkel *De Media et Nova Comoedia* (diss. Göttingen 1912) 5–53. Recent papyri of Menander have added, above all, *Dysc* 666ff. (see Handley *comm* p. 243), *Sik* 169ff. (see Handley *BICS* 12 (1965) 61 n. 10, Lloyd-Jones *GRBS* 7 (1966) 140f.), *Aspis* 23ff. (see Austin *comm* ad loc.).

we have an unmistakable ἀγγελία; if one or two are absent then we have a scene with affinities or analogies to a messenger scene. The usual *angelos* is, like this in *Pers*, a lower-status character who has no other part in the play. However, it would be wrong to imply that he is in no way individualized: he usually has an occupational identity, a reason for being involved, and some personal reaction to the events he reports.[1] None the less a narrative scene takes on a different tone if the narrator is a major named character, or has some more personal role in the play as a whole.[2] We should distinguish also scenes which, although they have an ἀγγελία function, are cast in some form other than the long speech.[3] In *Pers*, however, the Messenger does deliver set speeches in iambic trimeters, even though before and after his longest speech (353–432) his narrative is split into shorter speeches by dialogue with the Queen. Compare the more symmetrical divisions of the *sieben Redepaare* in *Seven*.[4]

The way in which the messenger scene in *Pers* most diverges from the later norm is in its dramatic function within the structure of the play. The usual kind of *angelos* comes at the transitional juncture between the departure of the major character(s) to some crucial off-stage event and the return of the survivors or remnants of that event. After the departure to battle, murder, suicide, trial, or whatever there is usually a choral song, and

[1] One way in which scholars have tended to depersonalize messengers is by assuming that they wore a uniform messenger-costume. But there is no evidence for this. The messenger in *Pers* presumably wore Persian costume, but without any particular features: *contra* Kranz 83, Broadhead 94f. For protest against this alleged messenger-uniform see Fischl 25–6, di Gregorio 8f.

[2] As e.g. Danaus in *Hik* (605ff.), Clytemnestra in *Ag* (1380ff.); Tecmessa in S. *Aj* (284ff.), Oedipus in *OT* (771ff.), the Guard in *Ant* (249ff., 407ff.); Polymestor in E. *Hec* (1132ff.), Talthybios in *Tro* (1123ff.); the Charioteer in *Rh* (756ff.); cf. the Queen's narrative in the *Gyges* fragment (*POxy* 2382).

[3] The most obvious instance is the Phrygian's aria at E. *Or* 1369ff.; but consider also, e.g., the Cassandra scene in *Ag* (see p. 324), the battle chorus in S. *OC* (1044ff.), the dialogue and Creousa's monody at E. *Ion* 752ff., the half-lyric *teichoskopia* in *Phoen* (103ff.), the lyric catalogue of ships at *IA* 164ff., and, perhaps, a narrative divulged in stichomythia in E. *Alexandros* fr. 18 Snell. Note also the narrative element in the parody of Euripidean monody at Arph. *Frogs* 1331ff. The tendency to diversify the narrative elements, especially by means of lyric, may be a feature of later Euripides. *Rh* also shows this tendency; and in the strange post-classical fragment *POxy* 2746 the battle narrative seems to be couched in the form of semi-lyrical clairvoyance by Cassandra (cf. A. *Ag*).

[4] The ἀγγελία in S. *Eurypylos* (*POxy* 1175 fr. 5 = fr. I5 Carden) is split up in an unparalleled way by a piece of lyric dialogue between Astyoche and the chorus (30–48). This may be an isolated astropha or one half of a divided strophic pair.

sometimes an entire intervening act before the messenger arrives to tell what happened. After him there is usually a shorter interval before the re-entry of the chief character(s) fresh from the catastrophic event, or of the mourning survivors or of the corpses (see further *Seven* 854b*). This kind of *angelos*, who might be called an 'aftermath' messenger, figures in nearly every surviving tragedy of Euripides.[1] But the only one of this sort in Aeschylus is that in *Seven*.

The next most common structural function for an *angelos* is that of the herald or advance messenger; and this one in *Pers* is a variant of this type. He usually leads up towards the arrival of a central character, and hence towards the catastrophe. As a rule he is closely followed by the major character in question, as e.g. in A. *Ag*; S. *Aj*; E. *El*, *IT*; *Rh*. But here in *Pers* a major event—the Darius scene—intervenes between the Herald and Xerxes; cf. *mutatis mutandis* S. *Tr*, E. *IA*. Also, the events reported by most advance messengers arise out of the course of the play, and are to be supposed to have been happening simultaneously with the earlier scenes. Often, indeed, there is an exit to the events in question (as there is later in the play an exit to the events to be reported by the aftermath messenger). In *Pers*, however, the events are set some while in the past: in this respect the most closely comparable report is that of the Herald in *Ag*.[2]

These observations direct attention to two particular features of the construction of *Pers*. The first is that the events recounted in the vivid narrative speeches occurred in the past before the play began. The past looms large in *Pers*: the more distant past in the opening choral song, the nearer past in the messenger scene (nearly 300 lines long) and in the following song, the future through the past in the Darius scene and in the song which follows it. And, at last, the present brings all these elements together in the final Xerxes scene. By telling of the journey home

[1] There are also traces of many others among the fragments. The exceptions among the surviving plays are *Alc*, *Hec*, *Tro*, *El*, and *IA* (lost or never written?).

[2] Of course, this brief survey of the two main types of messenger scene has left several exceptional scenes unaccounted for. For example the Paidagogos at S. *El* 680ff. reports fictitious events from a fictitious past and leads up to the arrival of the fictitious remains of Orestes. Comparably, the false merchant at *Phil* 603ff. reports half-truths which pretend to lead up to the arrival of Odysseus. The messenger from the hills at E. *Ba* 66off. is exceptional in that his report leads up to no arrival. In another sense he proves the arrival of Dionysus at Thebes: his function is to confront Pentheus with this proof, though he fails to accept it.

(296–301, 468–515) the Messenger helps to lead up towards the
return of Xerxes (see 909b*); but the main burden of his narrative
is set, so to speak, *before* the play. The narratives of the Herald
in *Ag* are comparable in many respects, though they do not so
dominate the first half of the play. Secondly, the entry which
the Herald in *Pers* foreruns does not materialize halfway through
the play, but at the opening of the last act; and it does not precede the crucial catastrophe, it is—or rather it stands for—the
catastrophe itself (see 909b*). In this S. *Tr.* supplies the closest
analogy. Hyllus functions as a herald-messenger (though he has
in turn been preceded by Lichas and the Old Man): all leads
up to the return of Heracles, and the long final scene is, like that
of *Pers*, the focus and conclusion of the tragedy.

Thus, several qualifications have to be made before the
ἄγγελος of *Pers* can be included in the category of tragic ἄγγελοι.
Moreover, it may have been apparent that the chief features have
rarely been illustrated from Aeschylus. The truth is that Aeschylus
uses messengers in the usual sense least of the great three; he
tends to incorporate his narrative elements in other ways. In
Seven, whatever the function of the *sieben Redepaare* (see *Seven*
371d*), it is a far cry from a normal messenger scene: while it
has vivid narrative parts, it is divergent in all other respects. The
'ἄγγελος' at *Seven* 792* is the one character in Aeschylus with a
true aftermath-messenger function, but he has no proper set-
piece ἀγγελία. In *Hik* there are narrative elements in the opening
choral song and in some speeches of Danaus, but there is no
set-piece report of off-stage events. Prometheus' long narratives
have totally different functions from those of a messenger scene;
though Io's story at *Prom* 640ff. is slightly closer. The Herald in
Ag is a fairly normal advance messenger (see above); but the
report of the death of Agamemnon is woven into the scene of
Cassandra before the event and Clytemnestra after. There is
little narrative of off-stage events in *Cho* and *Eum*, and what there
is is incorporated in various ways, but never in a set speech by
an anonymous character. So there is strikingly little in the way
of messenger scenes in Aeschylus.[1] They are characteristic of

[1] It might be claimed that it is coincidental that Aeschylus does not have proper
messenger speeches in the seven plays to survive. But the fragments yield few
traces of ἀγγελίαι either. The best policy may be a complete survey. First, it
looks as though *Glaukos Potnieus* fr. 445–6 must come from a full-scale ἀγγελία of
the kind familiar from Euripides. Several of the fragments of *POxy* 2160 (443–4,

Sophocles and, above all, of Euripides, but not, it seems, of earlier tragedy. Aeschylus expends his skill on diversifying his narrative elements, and there is no clear sign of any prototype for the familiar scenes of later tragedy.

Thus the internal evidence of the plays themselves weighs heavily against any secondary evidence or *a priori* speculation which may encourage the notion, first spelt out by Hermann, that the messenger scene was the original 'core' of Greek tragedy.[1] The discussion of Fischl (cited above, p. 81 n. 2) 5ff., 62f. still holds good in my view, and his conclusion puts the matter well (p. 63): 'nullum igitur apud Aeschylum invenimus nuntium, qui aliquo iure Euripideis et Sophocleis nuntiis exaequari possit. Quod ipsum quoque vehementer nos admonet, ne quid in illa forma antiquitus traditum atque excultum quaeramus.'

(b) the 'epirrhematic' opening

In his opening lines (249–55) the messenger, like a Euripidean ἄγγελος, gives the burden of his message in brief (cf. also *Seven* 792ff.). He addresses first Asia (249), then Persia (250), and then comes down to the chorus as representative of the Persian people

447–9 M) may well also come from this speech. The change of metre marked by eisthesis in fr. 8 (448 M) probably indicates the end of the messenger scene and the beginning of the following choral lyric. No doubt the mangled corpse of Glaucus was brought on stage and lamented in a θρῆνος. Next, the scholion on S. *Aj* 815 (= 292a) expressly tells us that Aeschylus had Ajax's death reported δι' ἀγγέλου ἀπαγγείλας in his *Threissai*. If this is strictly accurate then this must have been an 'aftermath' messenger of the type we do not happen to have in the surviving plays. No doubt the words quoted in fr. 292b come from his speech. Fr. 172 evidently comes from the report of the surviving servant of Laius who tells of the fatal meeting with Oedipus, though we do not know if it was a messenger-speech in the usual sense of the word. (I take it that this fragment came from *Oidipous* not *Laios*, *contra* Mette.) *Toxotides* fr. 422 may be from a set-piece ἀγγελία (followed by the corpse of Actaeon?). Finally we may have evidence of another advance-messenger: *Glaukos Pontios* fr. 55 (*POxy* 2159 = 273 Ll-J) probably comes from early in the play (a satyr play), and precedes the eventual entry of the transformed Glaucus. This is briefly but well argued by Winnington-Ingram *BICS* 6 (1959) 58f. On the other hand it remains possible that Glaucus also took a part in the play before his transformation, in which case the report would have an 'aftermath' function rather than a preparatory one. (*POxy* 2369, by the way, also seems to be a description connected with a metamorphosis, in this case from Sophocles' satyr play *Inachos* (fr. 2 Carden); there also Io was probably seen after her transformation.)

[1] Yet the elaboration of this insupportable theory was the chief burden of di Gregorio, whose book was, on the whole, favourably received. I objected in my review (op. cit.), and so did Imhof *Gnomon* 41 (1969) 204f.

(255).[1] This provokes from the Elders a series of threnetic lyric
stanzas which are individually separated by a couplet spoken
by the messenger, so as to form what is now generally known as
an 'epirrhematic' structure.[2] Symmetrical dialogues of lyric and
speech in this manner are found particularly in Aeschylus,
where they always occur within acts. But the tight structures of
Pers, *Seven*, and *Hik* are relaxed in the *Oresteia* to admit longer
speech elements (e.g. *Ag* 1407ff., *Eum* 777ff.), and in the Cassandra scene the lyric and speech roles are first reversed and
then progressively blended and exchanged to produce a unique
and highly effective adaptation. Epirrhematic structures occur
occasionally in Sophocles and Euripides; but the lyric part is
not always choral, and the structures are also found in act-
dividing positions (cf. on *Prom* 88*). There are, then, sound,
though limited, reasons for regarding epirrhematic lyric structures as particularly characteristic of early tragedy.[3]

Another feature of this entry scene which it may be fair to
regard as early is the way that the Messenger addresses himself
to the chorus, to the neglect of the Queen who remains a by-
stander. It is usual in Aeschylus for a newly entered character to
address the chorus rather than another actor; although we do
not have to look far for exceptions, even in the earlier plays,
e.g. *Seven* 375, *Hik* 911, and repeatedly in *Prom*.[4] On the other
hand, it is distinctly rare in Sophocles or Euripides for this to
happen even though there may be another actor present. As a
rule the chorus is addressed first only when the other actor is for
some reason inconspicuous, as e.g. *Hec* 484, *Or* 375.[5]

[1] It should go without saying that the messenger's entry is not accompanied by
a pointless crowd of miscellaneous other Persians (*contra* Jurenka *WSt* 23 (1901)
216f., taken too seriously by Broadhead *Pers ed* 95 n. 1).

[2] This application of the term is a coinage of modern scholarship. Among the
several uses of ἐπίρρημα found in ancient scholarship is its application to certain
spoken parts of the comic parabasis. Zielinski extended this to cover all alternating
spoken and lyric structures in comedy. The transference to tragedy was established
by Kranz (esp. 14ff.) and Peretti. Epirrhematic structures have been recently
surveyed by H. Popp in *Bauformen* 222ff. esp. 222–3, 230–2, 239–42.

[3] This is not to say that they were the original 'Keimzelle' of Greek tragedy.
See Peretti *contra* Kranz; further bibliography in Garvie 118 n. 1.

[4] Graeber ch. I tries to make a 'lex' of this phenomenon, and to use this as proof
that *Prom* is not authentic. It is true that *Prom* is out of step in this and many other
aspects of the handling of the chorus (cf. pp. 462f. below), but, even if there were
not counter-examples, Graeber's method is too rigid.

[5] For the Aeschylean mode in Euripides consider E. *Hik* 634ff., which may be
consciously archaizing. Compare the way that in Aeschylus (apart from *Prom*)

Two technical explanations present themselves for this kind of attention to the chorus at the expense of the actors. Both have some plausibility, but both call for some qualification. One is that the second actor was still a recent innovation at the time of *Pers*, and that Aeschylus therefore tends to stick to the techniques of one-actor tragedy.[1] While it is likely that force of habit had some weight, Aeschylus seems on the whole to have made imaginative and integral use of innovations. In *Oresteia* his use of the *third* actor is remarkable (see e.g. *Cho* 892a*), and so is his use of the new skene (see Appendix C). And he shows no lack of control in his use of two actors at *Hik* 911ff., nor, come to that, at *Pers* 703ff. Secondly, we may detect the influence, perhaps already waning, of the central function of the chorus in early tragedy. If the chorus had been not long before a protagonist (so to speak),[2] then its part must have been more extensive in the acts as well as in the songs. The way, for example, that the dialogues of earlier Aeschylus usually involve the chorus, even when a second actor is present, may be a reflection of early techniques. And yet, now that *Hik* has been redated, the notion is becoming accepted that *Hik* and *Eum*, far from illustrating the protagonist chorus of early tragedy, were experiments in the dramatic integration of the chorus, and that the early chorus was, like the later one, an essentially non-active group, and that its contribution was greater only in quantitative terms. Attractive though this view is, a consideration of Aeschylean dramatic techniques for handling the fuller participation of the chorus (such as this one in *Pers*) and a certain reluctance (not shared by many scholars) to write off Phrynichus and earlier Aeschylus as composers of primitive cantatas may give us pause. All this is discussed more fully on *Hik* 503b*.

In any case, the technique is put to excellent dramatic use. The Queen's silence conveys both her aloofness and her even greater suffering.

---

most stichomythias are between chorus and actor, even when a second actor is present, see pp. 462f., *Hik* 503b*, *Cho* 930* : in Sophocles and Euripides it is the other way round.

[1] Another pointer in the same direction may be the way in which the Queen is brought back into the dialogue at 290ff. (cf. 703ff.). (This is not a proper 'Aeschylean silence' as is claimed by, e.g. Jurenka *WSt* 23 (1901) 219f., Groeneboom ii p. 73, Rau 123, Korzeniewski 27 n. 135: see *HSCP* 76 (1972) 80.)

[2] On Arle. *Poet* 1449a17f. in the light of the new date for *Hik* see *Hik* 503b*.

514 exit Messenger

the departure of minor characters

Nearly all those who have taken the trouble to send off the messenger at all have rightly sent him off after the last line of his last speech (514): but there have been a few who have kept him on until the end of the act (531).[1] That the earlier exit is preferable is a trivial matter; but since the arguments involved apply to many other minor characters, and since in a few places rather more depends on the timing of the exit of a messenger, I shall briefly put the case.

Most of the major named characters of Greek tragedy are given an existence off-stage (though it may be claimed that this existence only matters in so far as attention is drawn to it, see pp. 25–6). So when they go off they generally motivate their exit and say where they are going, and the exit becomes a proper departure from the place where the play is set. On the other hand, the majority of unnamed lower-status characters, which includes most messengers, have little or no existence beyond their role on stage. Their exit is therefore, in effect, the end of their existence. So they are given no proper departure: when their part is played, they simply go away. Sometimes, it is true, they may be dismissed or may expressly say that they are going, but this is only done if there is some positive point to it; attention is not distractingly drawn to the departure of a minor character for its own sake.[2]

This is not to say that we cannot be fairly confident (without, of course, being certain) when minor characters did, in fact, leave the stage; cf. p. 8. It is fair to suppose, if there is no clear sign to the contrary, that when a character drops out of the play he made his exit after his last spoken line. Usually his last lines are, in fact, in some way final, and so they give a certain appropriateness to his exit at that point. I can detect no intrinsic difference between the final lines which go with an exit and the closing codas often found at the end of a rhesis or section of a rhesis;[3] none the less some words of rounding off are obviously

---

[1] I have noted Bodensteiner 727 ('514 or 526'), Wecklein, Goodell 76.

[2] Cf. Graeber 40, Andrieu 200. Fischl (op. cit. p. 81 n. 2) 24f. and di Gregorio 6ff. seem to be overconcerned at the lack of motivation of the arrivals and departures of messengers. It is sufficient motivation for the exit that his part is played.

[3] Compare the pairs of rhymed lines in many Elizabethan and Jacobean plays,

appropriate even to a minor exit. Thus here the messenger has the final couplet (513f.) ταῦτ ἔστ' ἀληθῆ. πολλὰ δ' ἐκλείπω λέγων / κακῶν ἃ Πέρcαιc ἐγκατέcκηψεν θεόc. These lines are not very different from those which concluded his earlier speeches (329f., 431f., 470f.), though the asseveration of truthfulness may be particularly associated with the departure of messengers.[1] But since this is the end of his last speech, these are fitting also as his last lines on stage.

Most messengers go similarly at the end of their speeches; but there are exceptions. At S. *Ant* 1244ff., for example, the messenger, alarmed at Eurydice's silent exit, follows her inside, and presumably he returns as the (so-called) *exangelos* of 1278ff. This brings home the sequence of family disasters befalling Creon. In E. *Hik* the messenger finishes conclusively enough at 730, but evidently he does not leave, since Adrastus engages him in dialogue at 750ff. This adds to the range of responses elicited by Theseus' different qualities. But other apparent exceptions involve characters who, while they have a messenger function, are exceptional in other ways and have a role in the play which goes beyond that of supplying narrative. Thus, for instance, the Old Man in S. *Tr*, who brings news of the approach of Lichas (though in short speeches, not in a proper ἀγγελία), does not go at 199, but lurks in the background until 335 when he makes his fatal intervention. It may be that Sophocles meant his audience to assume that he had no further part to play after 199.[2] Even more peculiar in some ways is the charioteer in *Rh*, who brings news of the death of Rhesus. He is badly wounded and begins in anapaests (729ff.); his speech proper (756ff.) is nearing a close at 798, when pain overtakes him again. However, Hector returns, and there is a fierce and inconsequential dispute before he is eventually taken off for treatment at 878. Another irregular messenger who does not go at the end of his narrative is the Phrygian in E. *Or* (1503ff.).[3]

which, while they occur at many points of articulation, do particularly accompany exits.

[1] Hermann p. 217 (on l. 508 in his numeration) gives other examples.
[2] Cf. *GRBS* 12 (1971) 30. The fact that his last line (199) comes just before a song would further reinforce the assumption that his part was played. P. Easterling (*CR* n.s. 22 (1972) 21) rightly criticizes the notion (*contra* e.g. Webster *Introduction to Sophocles*² (London 1969) 91f., 168) that the Old Man has been making frantic gestures throughout the intervening time. His intervention at 335 must be a surprise.
[3] The entire little farce of 1506–36 was deleted by Grüninger; cf. more recently

There are some places where the timing of the exit of a
messenger has a bearing on the attribution of parts or some other
controversy; and in such places the tendency for the messenger
to go after the last line of his rhesis may be a factor to be taken
into account. One such instance is discussed on *Seven* 652*; and
I give here three from later tragedy. At E. *Hel* 1627ff. someone
intervenes to prevent Theoclymenus from venting his wrath on
Theonoe, and it has been suggested that this was the messenger
of 1512ff.[1] But his closing lines (1617ff.) are very final, and it
would be preferable even to produce a servant out of the background (cf. *Hipp* 88): in any case, the lines are probably best
attributed to the coryphaeus.[2] Next, the best arrangement of
speakers at E. *Phoen* 1270ff. has Jocasta say 1279 to an attendant;
and it is suggested that he was the messenger of 1067ff.[3] But his
last lines (1259–61) are particularly final (see Fraenkel *Phoen*
65–7), and he should go after them: 1279 can be addressed
simply to an attendant servant (see 155c* above). Finally, the
Shepherd in *Rh* concludes with 314–16, and should go then.
Editors keep him on and attribute to him an isolated line (335)
solely in order to make sense of l. 339.[4]

I add one final observation on the dramatic technique of
entrances and exits, which also serves to confirm that the
messenger went at 514. When, as was often the case, the tragedian
had to bring on *two* characters at the beginning of a new act, or
to take *two* off at the end, he tended to move them consecutively
rather than simultaneously, unless there was some specific point
to their making the stage movement at the same moment. (I
discuss this point with reference to entries on *Seven* 371a* and
Prom 1a*.) Most simultaneous exits are made by two characters
together, and there is almost always some clear and positive

B. Gredley *GRBS* 9 (1968) 409ff., M. Reeve *GRBS* 13 (1972) 264, Arnott *G and R*
20 (1973) 58 n. 1. For an inspired rationale see Burnett 217–20.

   [1] e.g. Wecklein (*ed* 1907), A. Y. Campbell *ed* ad loc., Hourmouziades 167 n. 1.
   [2] See Dale *ed* 165–6, Kannicht *ed* 422–4. It is, perhaps, an objection to this
attribution that, after such pious bravery, the chorus should not win a mention
in the final dispensation of the Dioscuri.
   [3] Thus Kassel *RhM* 97 (1954) 96, Jackson 174, approved by Fraenkel *Phoen*
50, 85 n. 4.
   [4] Also for the sake of this line editors follow Nauck and transpose 334–5 to
after 338, although 334 follows well on 333, and not very well after 336–8. Rather
than all this, we should suspect some textual trouble, or even author's incompetence, in lines 333–41, especially 339–41.

reason why they are together. Thus Clytemnestra and Aegisthus go together at the end of *Ag* (1673a*), and Clytemnestra and Orestes go off together for very different purposes at *Cho* 930*. A few later examples, which carry particular point, are Orestes and Hermione at E. *Andr* 1008, Theseus and Heracles at *Her* 1426, Oedipus, his daughters, and Theseus at S. *OC* 1555. Simultaneous exit together is not uncommon: it is much rarer for two characters to go at the same time in *different* directions. This provides a striking visual presentation of separation, and nearly all instances have positive dramatic significance. The only clear instances in Aeschylus are at *Seven* 1078*, where, although the exits may not be quite simultaneous, the separation is very clear, and at *Eum* 93*, where Apollo relinquishes Orestes to the world of men. An example from Sophocles is *OT* 462, where Oedipus' silent departure into the palace, while Tiresias makes his way off, shows Oedipus' complete failure to read the riddles of 449ff.[1] From Euripides, consider the separations which happen at the ends of several tragedies;[2] see on *Seven* 1078*.

This is not to say that minor characters never slip off at the end of an act in such a way that their exit is simultaneous with another and yet is to be neglected. In S. *Tr* the Old Man should go unobtrusively at 496, just as he stayed unobtrusively at 199; and at *OT* 1185 the Corinthian and the old Shepherd go unnoticed in the high pathos of Oedipus' discovery. None the less, it is much more usual for exits to be kept separate, even when one of them is relatively insignificant. One does not have to look far in earlier Aeschylus to find examples of two exits separated by a few lines, e.g. *Pers* 843/851, *Seven* 68/77, *Hik* 503/523, 951/?976, *Prom* 81/87; and the phenomenon is even more common in later tragedy, when there are more characters.

---

[1] Sheppard's theory, taken up by Carrière *AFLT* v 3 (1956, *Pallas* iv) 5ff., that Oedipus has gone at 446 and that Tiresias' speech is made to thin air, destroys this tense moment. The audience find the riddles easy to solve, but Oedipus does not—καὶ ταῦτ' ἰὼν / εἴcω λογίζου (460f.).

[2] I had also thought in this context of the separation of Andromache from Astyanax (and Talthybius) at *Tro* 789. But on further consideration I find the accepted text suspect. Andromache should have some final words before her exit (and she can hardly go at 778, as some claim, in view of 782f.). Perhaps the transmitted ὑμετέραc in 788 should be kept, and then 782–9 can be attributed to Andromache. The lines are even more moving in her mouth. Talthybius would then go in silence, as he did earlier at 461 (cf. also Odysseus at *Hec* 437).

528 (or 531?) exit the Queen

lines 529–31: false preparation?

After the Messenger has gone the act is closed by a short speech
from the Queen before her departure. Her last three lines present
a well-known problem which calls either for a drastic textual
solution or for an explanation in terms of unusual dramatic
technique. She first outlines her own course of action (521–6),
and thereby motivates her departure and her eventual return
(fulfilled at 598). She then gives a couplet (527–8) of instructions
to the chorus about taking counsel.[1] It is common, almost
formulaic, for departure lines to contain a recommendation of
action to the chorus and then a statement of intention by the
actor, or, as here, vice versa: see, in earlier Aeschylus alone, *Pers*
839ff., *Seven* 280ff., *Hik* 520ff., 772ff. (cf. *Seven* 65ff., 649ff.). So
line 528 would make an eminently satisfactory ending to the act.

There are, however, the three further lines (529–31):

> καὶ παῖδ᾽, ἐάν περ δεῦρ᾽ ἐμοῦ πρόσθεν μόληι,
> παρηγορεῖτε καὶ προπέμπετ᾽ ἐς δόμους,
> μὴ καί τι πρὸς κακοῖσι προσθῆται κακόν.

The lines are a counterfactual conditional: the Queen's pro-
visions are not fulfilled, and she duly returns as she predicted
in 524. Assuming, for the present, that the lines are in the place
in the text where Aeschylus meant them to be, then we may
justifiably look for a good reason why they are there. It is in
this case particularly idle and implausible to fall back on carelessness or primitive incompetence.[2] The scene would be quite
satisfactory without the lines: Aeschylus has positively added
them. The words are explicit, and are put in a particularly
conspicuous and stressed position as the final lines of the act.
Dawe (28) says 'if he mentions the topic, he must have a purpose': Aeschylus not only mentions it, he draws attention to it.
Yet I know of only two purposes which have been proposed.
One does not bear serious consideration, and the other is not
entirely satisfactory.

---

[1] It is no matter that they, in fact, embark on a lament; cf. the chorus' response
to Eteocles' instructions at *Seven* 280ff. In 528, if the transmitted πιστοῖσι is not
accepted (see Broadhead ad loc.), the best emendation seems to be πιστούς γε
(Hermann) or τά (Hartung).

[2] Dignan is always eager to find primitive botching in Aeschylus, and seizes
his opportunity (p. 31). Stephenson, who usually defends Aeschylus, here concedes
that he is 'guilty of poor motivation' (p. 18).

One explanation is that the chief purpose of the lines is to characterize the Queen. Thus Broadhead (p. xxxvii) says that the lines 'reveal her practical nature and maternal solicitude', and on p. 143 (with a glance at the alternative explanation) that 'we expect there to be some personal reason for the Queen's charge, not that it should be merely a sign-post for the spectators'. By 'we' Broadhead evidently means the contemporary Western reader complete with the expectations made a matter of habit by the novel and by modern psychology: he never questions his assumption that the precise delineation of personality was also an autonomous priority for Aeschylus. But many students of Greek tragedy in this century have come to doubt that characterization *for its own sake* concerned the Attic tragedians, and to think that, in so far as it is attended to, it is always subordinate to the action and to other overriding concerns.[1] This is still a confused and controversial topic, and is likely to remain so; but one does not need to take up any extreme position to reject categorically the notion that these three lines in *Pers*, in their conspicuous setting, can possibly be there solely or primarily to fill out the details of a personality study of the Queen—something which could in any case have been done less awkwardly and more effectively. Characterization can be allowed, at most, an incidental function in these lines. No less objectionable is Broadhead's phrase 'merely a sign-post to the spectators'. There is a by no means trivial sense in which Greek tragedy is entirely a complex of sign-posts to the spectator; certainly this is the function of all forward-looking preparation. There is no theoretical objection to seeing these lines as a sign-post: the trouble is that it points down a dead-end.

So to the more acceptable explanation (always provided that the text is sound): that the lines 'keep up the expectation of the return of the defeated and disgraced Xerxes'.[2] The preparation for the return of Xerxes runs right through the play, and makes

[1] The question seems to be in what ways and to what degree a residue of ἦθος remains once other overriding factors have been given due weight. This is not the place (fortunately) for a full discussion. The works in English which I have found most clear and most helpful are Dale E. *Alc ed* introd. §4, *Papers* ch. 24, Garton *JHS* 77 (1957) 247ff., Jones *passim*, Easterling. I have not been able to consult G. J. M. S. Te Riele *Les Femmes chez Éschyle* (Groningen 1955), who apparently champions detailed character studies.

[2] Sidgwick 66; also see particularly Wilamowitz 44, Dawe 27f.

his eventual entry a kind of focal point (see 909b*). Lines 529–31, it is argued, lead the audience to expect his entry sooner than it in fact occurs, and so keep the imminence of his return vividly in mind. We have, in other words, an instance of the device of false preparation.

The consistent use of preparation to arouse anticipation in his audience gives the dramatist the opportunity to arouse and then thwart expectations: this might be called 'counter-preparation'. This device may have a double function, since it not only brings about a surprise when the prepared-for event fails to materialize, it also builds up tension towards and derives vicarious dramatic power from an event which never happens. But this difficult device is not often used in Greek tragedy. The playwright has to be confident of his effect, and be confident that his audience will not feel cheated or will not suppose his false preparation to be careless lack of control. It may have been the danger of going astray and the unpredictability of the effect of the technique which led to its virtual disuse.

This is a possible explanation of these lines; indeed, if the text is sound, it is the best explanation. But before it is accepted too complacently, some weaknesses should be pointed out. First, the return of Xerxes, envisaged by the Queen, does later happen: the counter-preparation does not evoke, as in the most effective uses (see below), a scene which never in fact takes place. Moreover, the Queen does say that she will return, and only puts the possibility of Xerxes' arrival before her in a conditional clause: so there is little effect of surprise or frustration when she does return first. And it cannot be claimed that this is the only way or the best way in which Aeschylus could raise the expectation of Xerxes' imminent return. Only a few lines earlier the messenger has said that those who survived have now reached Persia (508–11), and he said earlier that Xerxes survived (299). The point is taken up in the following song at 564–7.

The comparative triviality and inconsequence of this example of counter-preparation may be brought out by a rapid survey of some other examples of the device from Greek tragedy.[1] The

---

[1] This does not pretend to be a complete catalogue: it does not consider, for example, the false preparation in some Euripidean prologues. In general on Euripides' defeat of expectation see Arnott *G and R* 20 (1973) 49ff. For some examples of false preparation in Roman Comedy, where some may be deliberate and some the result of contamination and adaptation, see Duckworth *The Nature*

clearest illustration from Aeschylus is in *Cho*: at 554ff. Orestes
looks forward to going straight into the palace and instantly
dispatching Aegisthus. In fact, Aeschylus will arrange Orestes'
entry to the palace quite differently, see *Cho* 668*, 718*; but the
counter-preparation heightens the suspense, and captures some
of the excitement of a scene which never happens. At E. *Hipp*
661f. Hippolytus looks forward to witnessing the return of
Theseus and his confrontation with the Nurse and Phaedra. We
are thus given a foretaste of a highly emotional event which
never happens: on the contrary, Hippolytus himself has to face
Theseus in the presence of the corpse of Phaedra. In E. *Andr* we
are constantly led to expect the return of Neoptolemus from
Delphi. But it is his corpse which is eventually brought on stage
(1172ff.). On a smaller scale in both *Med* (1293ff.) and *Or*
(1554ff.) the audience is led to expect a hand-to-hand encounter;
but in both cases the weaker party gains the upper hand by
appearing above the palace. In the prologue of S. *Phil* (48) a
man is sent off to guard against Philoctetes' catching Odysseus
unawares. Nothing comes of this, but the counter-preparation
keeps the audience expecting the arrival of Philoctetes, as well
as preparing for the tenor of the later confrontations of Odysseus
and Philoctetes. So it may be seen that a great variety of theatrical
techniques are employed for a variety of ends in these different
examples of counter-preparation. But all of them, it should be
clear, have a more precise and more effective dramatic purpose
than the alleged example in *Pers*. The resultant surprise or the
emotional hint of a scene which never happens are two clear
dramatic gains which are both missing in *Pers*.

   I have kept till last a problematical piece of false preparation,
which is perhaps most like the one in *Pers*, though I have not
seen it cited in this context. In the last lines of the second act
of *Seven* (282-6) Eteocles says that he will post seven champions,
including himself, at the seven gates, before urgent dispatches
arrive. Now in the next act Eteocles is (despite those who claim
otherwise) doing just that—posting the seven champions, see
further *Seven* 374d*. And yet this is *after* the messenger has
arrived. Thus, again, as in *Pers*, Aeschylus has used the final
lines of an act to outline explicitly a development of the action

which is not fulfilled. Again the dramatic gain is slight, and again it might easily have been achieved in a less confusing way. I discuss this problem on *Seven* 286*, where I favour other explanations. Still, those who wish to defend the usual explanation of *Pers* 529–31 had best refer to *Seven* 282–6 for a similar phenomenon. At the same time they can hardly deny that in both cases Aeschylus has used a confusing and inconsequential counter-preparation for meagre dramatic ends. In fact, they can scarcely defend Aeschylus from the charge of uncharacteristically incompetent dramatic technique.

Many scholars are for some perverse reason glad to reach this sort of conclusion: others, I trust, are not. I hope to have raised sufficient reservations and criticisms to justify at least considering some sort of textual emendation. For there is a highly ingenious and attractive conjecture which disposes both of this problem and of another later in the play, and which has not been given a fair run.

But first it is necessary to consider the final lines spoken by the Queen on her second and last exit. In 845–51, after lamenting the news of Xerxes' rags, she closes (849–51)

ἀλλ' εἶμι καὶ λαβοῦϲα κόϲμον ἐκ δόμων
ὑπαντιάζειν παιδί πωϲ¹ πειράϲομαι·
οὐ γὰρ τὰ φίλτατ' ἐν κακοῖϲ προδώϲομεν.

She does not meet him, however, and Xerxes does appear in rags, see 909a*. Aeschylus has to take the Queen off the scene, for he has overriding reasons why she should not take part in the final act, see further 851*. So, it seems, he takes this further opportunity to lay stress on the significance of Xerxes' rags. He has put himself in a difficult position by his determination to keep the Queen out of Xerxes' act, but he clearly yet unobtrusively prepares for this by πειράϲομαι in 850.² Wilamowitz (p. 46) calls this 'ein Wink an die Zuschauer', and, granted the text, this is the only plausible explanation. While accepting this, one may not disagree with Broadhead (p. 211) that it is 'a rather clumsy expedient'.³ But once Aeschylus has rejected the alterna-

¹ παιδὶ πωϲ (Rogers, Wilamowitz 46 n. 1) has the advantage of stressing the uncertainty. Most editors read παιδί μου (Burges); MSS. transmit παιδὶ ἐμῶι, ἐμῶι παιδὶ vel sim.

² Broadhead's emendation (p. 280) to πορεύϲομαι merely aggravates the problem.

³ Dawe (28, approved by Lesky *TDH*³ 86) is much more clever. He says, with a reference to 529–32, 'the audience have heard words very similar to this once

tive—'I shall await Xerxes at the palace'—then it is hard to see how some such expedient is to be avoided. However, the awkwardness would be considerably alleviated, if not eliminated, if the Queen were to add 'if Xerxes arrives first, then bring him to the palace'. One might compare the way that Euripides prepares for the absence of Xuthus in the final scenes of *Ion* by having the messenger report his instructions (1130f.) that, if he is delayed, the feast should go ahead without him.

Nikitine was the first to see that the final lines at the Queen's first exit are more appropriate to her second exit. He suggested that 527–31 should be transposed to follow 851, and his view was championed by Weil.[1] However, Sidgwick (pp. 65f.) strongly rejected the transposition, and since then, while nearly all commentators mention the conjecture, they do so only to reject it. Sidgwick was certainly right to reject the transposition of 527–8 which are perfectly acceptable where they stand; see above (p. 92).[2] But the way that the transposition of 529–31 both cures the earlier problem and alleviates the later one is remarkable, and the arguments against it may, I suggest, have been too easily accepted. Sidgwick objects that l. 851 looks like a closing line: but many lines might do well as closing lines and yet are not, compare e.g. 512, 526, 838. A more weighty point, which has been regarded as decisive (e.g. by Page p. 80), is that καὶ παῖδα in 529 does not fit after παιδί in 850. This is true, but easily mended. Suppose that Aeschylus himself did have 529–31 after 851, then in making the transition from the Queen's declaration of intent to her instructions to the chorus he probably used the standard ὑμεῖς δέ (see *Pers* 840, *Hik* 772 etc.). Once the lines had been displaced to their present position the transition had

---

before, and they were deceived'. This time, Dawe argues, the audience is prepared for deception, and so Aeschylus double-bluffs them by fulfilling the prediction. Apart from the fact that there is no similarity whatsoever between the wording of the two passages this is all much too bookish.

[1] Journal of *Ministerstva Narodnago Prosvêstcheniia* 1876 (in Russian); Weil *Ann. des Ét. Gr.* 17 (1883) 75ff., and edition of 1884. Conradt (*ed* Berlin 1888 p. 119) deleted 527–30 and Girard *RPh* 20 (1896) 1ff. deleted 527–31 (neither in Dawe's *Repertory*): neither contributes anything positive. Bodensteiner 727 accepts Nikitine's conjecture without comment; so does Flickinger 175.

[2] 527–8 (without 529–31) still make a kind of 'ring' with the opening of the act; cf. Holtsmark *SO* 45 (1970) 15. However, the vitiating faults of Holtsmark's article are typified by his claim (p. 19) that lines 843–51 'ring' with 598–680: there is no significant connection whatsoever between these two disparate sections.

already been made by ὑμᾶς δέ in 527, and the topic of Xerxes had not yet been introduced: so ὑμεῖς δέ was changed to καὶ παῖδα. It has also been objected that κακόν in 531 refers to political trouble, and so goes best before the song at 532ff.[1] But in either context the word would be deliberately inexplicit. Moreover μὴ καί τι πρὸς κακοῖσι προσθῆται κακόν goes much better after ἐν κακοῖς in 851, and then reiterates the sequence of thought suggested by Darius in 832–8: 'meet Xerxes with new clothes, and soothe him in case he makes things even worse'.

What is so attractive about this bold emendation is the way that it kills two birds with one stone: it not only removes the insignificant and confusing counter-preparation from the earlier exit, it also alleviates the problem of the Queen's failure to return after her second exit. With the lines in their new place she says that she will try to meet Xerxes and then adds that, if he should come first, the Elders should console him and escort him to the palace. προπέμπετ' ἐς δόμους in 530 fits the end of the play exactly, see 1077*. Of course, it is impossible to account for the transposition: but that does not mean that it could not have happened. For example, if the original autograph was written on sheets or tablets rather than on a roll,[2] then the last lines of an act may have been copied out at the end of another act.

So I suggest that this emendation—viz. the transposition of 529–31 to after 851 and the change of καὶ παῖδ' in 529 to ὑμεῖς δ'—deserves more serious consideration. I would draw two lessons from this discussion. First, I think it shows that questions of dramatic technique may be sufficient to be the chief— or even sole—grounds for textual emendation. Secondly, it may defend Aeschylus from two accusations (one slight, one more serious) of incompetent or clumsy dramaturgy. And it is one of my aims to show that Aeschylus was a sure and steady master of his craft.

598 the Queen returns

(a) ἄνευ τ' ὀχημάτων χλιδῆς τε τῆς πάροιθεν

I have already argued on 155b* that it is only at this stage of

---

[1] Dawe 29, cf. Wilamowitz 44.

[2] Admittedly the poet is shown with a papyrus roll on the Pronomos vase and on ARV² 1215 no. 1 (Illustrations 117): but in real rehearsal a roll would have been rather impractical.

the play that the audience is meant to realize that the pomp of the Queen's first entry was not merely decorative spectacle. The alteration in her mode of entry embodies her change of attitude to wealth and good fortune, as is made quite clear in 607–8, where it is tied to her opening moralizing by τοιγάρ. I shall argue that this is an example of a 'mirror scene', a device which I shall discuss more generally in 598b* below.

The most obvious difference between the two entries is the chariot, but there are several other features covered by χλιδή which would be immediately apparent in performance.[1] The Queen's costume on her first entry was, no doubt, splendid: this time it is likely that she is in black. Her former entry was accompanied by several attendants also in fine costume (see 155c*): now she is probably by herself. Most commentators, following Wilamowitz (p. 45, first in *Perser* p. 385), say that she is accompanied by several servants, but there is no sign of them in the text. In 610ff. she is carrying the offerings herself: she could easily have some tray or basket. Earlier she may well have held some ornate oriental symbol of her power; but this time she carries the plain and pure offerings. The poetry of 611–18 is not gratuitous: these simple, universal gifts of nature contrast with the earlier artificial luxury. On her earlier entry there was an honorific announcement and greeting (see 155a*), accompanied by extravagant prostration: now her entry is made without formal accompaniment. The first scene was spoken in the rather lively trochaic tetrameter: this is made more sober by the iambic trimeter.[2]

The dramatic and moral explanation, which the Queen explicitly attaches to her different mode of entry, is her appreciation of the divine control over changes of fortune and prosperity (598–606). The material embodiment of her new insight is able to convey its ramifications in a way more direct and immediate than any amount of purely verbal moralizing. The Queen appreciates that material wealth is the mere outward manifestation of the prosperity which follows from divine favour, and

[1] Riemschneider *Hermes* 73 (1938) 351f. greatly oversimplifies when he regards the chief point of the chariot as being the high platform which it affords the Queen.

[2] This point is seen by Drew-Bear *AJP* 89 (1968) 388. The dramatic uses of the trochaic tetrameter are also considered by Imhof *MH* 13 (1956) 125ff., Mannsperger *Bauformen* 164–7.

that a thoughtless over-confidence in these externals leads to
their destruction. Darius will spell the matter out in these terms
(824–6): μηδέ τις / ὑπερφρονήϲαϲ τὸν παρόντα δαίμονα / ἄλλων
ἐραϲθεὶϲ ὄλβον ἐκχέῃ μέγαν. If ὄλβοϲ tries to put the yoke on too
much, whether riches or the sea or Greece, then it will come to
grief (cf. p. 78 above). The Queen's discarding of her chariot
shows that she has learned this lesson.

The complex visual meaning of the Queen's second entry
illustrates my chief theme: that Aeschylus did not use the presentation of his plays for mere eye-catching spectacle, but as an
integral part of the total fabric. The sight embodies and interprets the words, it is indivisible from them, and without the
sight the words cannot be fully appreciated. It also illustrates
the point that one of the most common and effective ways of
presenting visual meaning is by the creation of paired scenes,
which use some similarity in order to bring out contrast.

(b) mirror scenes

The repetition or reflection of an incident or scene in such a
striking way as to recall the earlier event is a basic device for the
playwright and is to be found in most kinds of drama. In Greek
tragedy this technique is used with particular force and discrimination, and is facilitated by the comparatively brief and
spare form of the drama. Such a repetition may be aural ('echo'
scene), repeating verbally or by other means, e.g. music, or
visual ('mirror' scene[1]), or, as often, both. The repetition should,
of course, be pointing to some similarity in the two situations:
but nearly always the similarity is there in order to bring out the
contrast between them. As Greek tragedy tends to centre on or at
least contain—as Aristotle stressed—a reversal in people's fortune,
the mirror scenes often come on either side of the περιπέτεια.

I am by no means the first to have noticed the use of these
techniques of repetition and contrast in Greek tragedy, though
they have been generally overlooked along with all the other
dramatic uses of the visible action.[2] But 'this is a dangerous

[1] I used this term in my article in GRBS 12 (1971). It has been current for
some time in Shakespeare studies e.g. H. T. Price in J. Q. Adams Memorial Studies
(Washington D.C. 1948) 101ff. (who uses it in a different sense), M. Mack in
Stratford-upon-Avon Studies 1 (1960) 11ff. esp. 28ff. on the mirroring of 'the
emblematic entrance and exit'.

[2] Reinhardt was alive to this formative dramatic technique in Aeschylus, as is

subject; it is too easy to chase out subtle symmetries . . .', as Webster warns.[1] If the critic is to carry conviction, then he must clearly establish the correspondence: the doublet must be striking enough to catch the attention of an audience, albeit an attentive audience alive to the technique.

Some brief cautionary observations. The alluring symmetries and patterns which can easily be made tend to lead the critic away from the play as a work for the theatre. The most elementary point is that in any doublet the audience can only become aware of the contrivance on the performance of the second element. During the presentation of the earlier element it cannot know that this particular scene is going to be reworked later in the play, and so this unknown factor cannot throw light on the scene at that stage. While the earlier scene may to some extent be reinterpreted and seen in a new light, the chief significance of the device is bound to lie in the way it bears on the later scene.

This precaution should be extended further to the detection of complex 'symmetrical' patterns in Greek tragedy. This entertaining game has been encouraged by the emphasis given to 'underlying patterns' by some schools of literary criticism, and no doubt also by the widespread recognition of 'ring-composition' as a structural technique in Greek lyric poetry.[2] As a result diagrammatic representations of the 'structure' ('the word is overworn') adorn many recent essays on all kinds of ancient poetry, including Greek tragedy. In a simpler form this kind of symmetrical analysis goes well back (see e.g. the quotation from Wilamowitz on p. 165 below); but more recently the alleged patterns of 'Chinese boxes' have become far more complex. And it is in the very complexity and the typographical attraction of

particularly clear in his account of Agamemnon and Cassandra (90ff. cf. 124, and see *Ag* 1330b*). Strohm and Burnett have made good use of their detection of this device in Euripides. In Strohm see the places listed in the index under 'Responsion von Handlungselementen'; Burnett has no comparable entry, but I have noted observations of this kind on pp. 37, 42, 61f., 98, 146, 163 n. 9, 169. Dingel, under the heading 'Korrespondierende Bilder' (192–5) perceptively isolates several important instances, but for some reason he goes through them very briefly, and offers hardly any interpretative comment. Finally, Steidle makes use of this approach, and gives on pp. 15–17 a good survey of its possibilities as he sees them.

[1] *The Tragedies of Euripides* (London 1967) 282. He himself is prey to the danger of treating patterns in isolation from any possible dramatic significance, as he immediately goes on to show.

[2] For a brief survey of work on this see D. C. Young *Three Odes of Pindar* (Leiden 1968) 122 n. 1.

the exercise that its shallowness is betrayed. First, the elements that are balanced against each other are often not commensurable. Sometimes the correspondence lies in trivialities, while there is no comparison in any important respect, and all too often the correspondence is virtually a fabrication of the critic.[1] And even if we allow (as we should) a generous range for the perceptiveness of the audience and for the levels at which they may register a pattern, all too many of these elaborate schematisms remain meaningful only on paper.[2] And, finally, the concentric rings of symmetry are often given no critical application and often cannot sustain one. What is the point of all that trouble on the part of the poet if the result does nothing for the play? A pattern is only acceptable if we appreciate the drama the better for recognizing the correspondence when the second element materializes. Unless there is some point to the shaping it remains a mere game on paper played for its own sake. While this is possible as an end in itself in some particularly artificial schools of lyric poetry, it cannot work in a play.[3]

Finally after this display of caution it may be necessary to defend looking for mirror scenes at all against the accusation that it is too subtle and merely a fantasy of over-ingenious modern critics. Not only are many so manifestly there that their existence cannot be denied; the dramatists occasionally draw explicit attention to them. This is the case here in *Pers*. Most commentators have given the matter scant attention, regarding ll. 607–9 as mere filling, or concealing them from serious attention with the blanket term 'visual effect'. But, if Aeschylus takes the trouble to draw attention to the visual contrast with the Queen's first entry, then he should surely mean something by it. In this particular case the visual resemblance between the two scenes goes no further than the movement of the entry of the Queen, otherwise they are visually in complete contrast; and that is probably why Aeschylus felt it necessary to draw attention

[1] An early but atrocious example is Stoessl's parallelization of A. *Ag* and *Cho* in *Die Trilogie des Aischylos* (Vienna 1937) 23–42. Meanwhile several important parallels which *are* there go by neglected.

[2] For example the fashionable stress on stichometric 'symmetries' seems meaningless in the context of the theatre. The length of a scene in performance is something subjective and cannot be measured in terms of the number of lines.

[3] When, for example, Holtsmark on A. *Pers* (*SO* 45 (1970) 22) claims that 'to a large extent the ring structure *is* the play', I cannot imagine what he means in theory let alone what this might mean in performance.

verbally to the correspondence. In most mirror scenes there is far more visual similarity which in performance would be so evident that it is not necessary for the playwright to point it out. In *Cho*, for example, the visual similarity of the scene of carnage to that in *Agam* is so detailed and striking that many scholars have been unable to overlook it: see *Cho* 973b*. These two examples can hardly be denied: their significance may be subtle, but the actual contrivance of them is obvious. And if some examples are once admitted, then the critic cannot object to the detection of the technique in principle: on the contrary he should look for more.

(c) scene setting

There has been controversy over whether the scene shifts during *Pers*. Before considering this particular issue, I shall go into the whole question of 'unity of place' in Greek Tragedy.

All the surviving plays of Sophocles and Euripides, except S. *Aj*, are set in one place. And this is not simply a matter of the scene's not expressly changing; the play is positively set at a certain place. This may be seen from the handling of exits and entrances. Most, especially those of major characters, are not simply a matter of slipping in and out of the action; an entry is an arrival, a positive journey to the place where the play is set, and an exit is a positive departure from that place. This contrasts with Shakespearean tragedy where frequent changes of scene and vague scene settings (despite the misguided attempts of editors to be precise) often make entries and exits a matter of simply joining in and withdrawing from the action. This is not to say that the scene setting of Greek tragedy is of uniformly prominent importance in each play and throughout each play. In most the scene is set near the beginning, and this setting, while sometimes brought into prominence, is more often a matter of latent background. In a few plays the precise setting is of very little significance (e.g. E. *Hik*, *Hkld*, see Zuntz *The Political Plays of Euripides* (Manchester, 1955), 97ff.); but in others the exact setting and even the details of its topography are of great importance (e.g. S. *Phil*, *OC*; *Rh*). So in Sophocles and Euripides the scene can only be changed if the chorus is taken off and then brought back on at the new location. This happens in

S. *Aj* (see *Eum* 235*), but it was evidently a rarely used resource. On the other hand, in post-classical tragedy, where the chorus was detached from the play, changes of scene between the acts were probably common (cf. p. 49 n. 2).

There can be no doubt that four of the seven plays of Aeschylus (*Seven, Hik, Prom, Ag*) are similarly set at one place. There has been great controversy over whether or not there is unity of place in the other three; but it seems to me an inevitable conclusion that there is not. I discuss the details below and on *Cho* 584* and *Eum* 566a*. In each case the chorus does not leave the stage, and in *Eum* it seems that an actor also stays on across the change of scene. Also some complicated puzzles are raised by a fragment of a hypothesis which speaks of several changes of scene within a single play (*Aitnaiai?*): see pp. 416f.

Much of the controversy over these scene changes has arisen from inappropriately rigid conceptions of what is involved in a 'change of scene' in a play. It used to be assumed, no doubt under the influence of contemporary practice, that the scene must be changed at one particular moment, and that it should be accompanied by a visual change of background scenery. The decline of realism in the presentation of Renaissance drama and a fluid handling of place in some modern drama (e.g. in Brecht) have no doubt helped scholars to see that neither of these assumptions is necessarily true. A scene which is set in the imagination of the audience, and not by means of scenery, may simply go out of focus, and when it is 'refocused', that is when it is brought back into sharp definition, it is somewhere else.[1] The action is not tied to one particular place; rather the place refocuses to suit the action. The change does not occur at one definable moment, but the words and action make it clear that the play is no longer set at the same place as it was earlier. Yet the chorus has not moved from the orchestra. It is generally recognized that this is much the way that Aristophanes handles place in his comedies.[2]

Why, when this flexible and useful convention was exploited

---

[1] I take the suggestive term 'refocus' from the brief and clear discussion of this phenomenon in Dale *Papers* 119; cf. 'fluid or adjustable scene' (ibid. 120). The basic idea is not new; see Wilamowitz *Kl Schr* i 157ff. (1886); cf. also Goodell *Athenian Tragedy* (New Haven 1920) 86ff., De Falco[2] 9ff.

[2] See e.g. Niejahr *Quaestiones Aristophaneae Scaenicae* (diss. Greifswald 1877) 12ff., Bodensteiner 655–8, D–R 213f.

in the early theatre, did it not persist later in the century? First, the point should be made that we have no particular reason to think it was ever widely used; it may have been an experiment which was judged to be unsuccessful (certainly it has offended many modern critics). Then perhaps, if it is true that the skene building was first introduced toward the end of Aeschylus' life (see Appendix B), this permanent background may have worked against a flexible handling of place by providing a local focus. On the other hand, two of the three plays with a shifting scene were played before the skene (*Cho, Eum*); and it made no difference for Aristophanes (nor for Shakespeare). It may be that the fluidity of scene in comedy contributed to its rejection in tragedy, and the device may have become especially associated with comedy (cf. Dale *Papers* 120). Note that in Old Comedy the house in the background seldom has a sustained and integral place in the play, as it has in Tragedy and, indeed, in New Comedy.

The only part of *Pers* itself where the setting is stressed and where it really matters is the Darius scene, which is, of course, set at his tomb. It is this, no doubt, which accounts for ἔϲτιν ἡ μὲν ϲκηνὴ τοῦ δράματος παρὰ τῶι τάφωι Δαρείου in the hypothesis. But later scholars would expect a unity of place, and should be allowed no final authority on this point.[1] The very first mention of the tomb of Darius comes at l. 647, and it is not until 659 that it is quite clear that it is the setting of the ghost-raising. Indeed it is not until 619–22 that it is suddenly made clear that there is going to be a ψυχαγωγία at all. There have been many places earlier where Aeschylus might have prepared for it, but he has positively eschewed them. Associated ideas are introduced earlier, but not the fact that it will be acted out on stage. At 219ff. the chorus advise the Queen to pray to the Gods and then to pour libations to Earth and the dead, and to entreat Darius' help. She agrees that she will do all this when she goes back to the palace (229–30). At the end of the act there is a slight but important change of plan: she will pray to the Gods at the palace, but then she will return with offerings for Earth and the

[1] I argue on pp. 416ff. that there may possibly have been a similar misunderstanding over *Aitnaiai*. Trendelenberg (see p. 22 n. 1) 21 makes the interesting observation that the most authentic Aristophanean hypotheses are more explicit and name the city at which the play is set. He suggests, therefore, that this detail in hypoth. *Pers* does not go back to Aristophanes of Byzantium himself.

dead (521–4). When she does return she says only that she has brought soothing offerings for Darius (609–10). Throughout all this there is no mention of ghost-raising nor of the tomb. Broadhead (p. xxxvi) assumes that Aeschylus missed these opportunities because of primitive clumsiness, and thus failed to manage 'satisfactory preparation'. But it makes better sense and does more justice to Aeschylus to recognize that he has deliberately not brought any direct preparation for the ghost-raising into the earlier scenes. Since the ghost-raising is the most exotic and exciting event in the play it could easily come to dominate the whole work. Aeschylus wishes to avoid this, and to give the disaster of the Persian army and of Xerxes full play.

The stage property which is to represent the tomb of Darius was presumably in full view from the very beginning (on staging, see 681b*). It can hardly have been identified as such,[1] however, and it cannot be clear until the ghost-raising gets under way that the property has this particular function. Throughout the earlier scenes of the play little attention is paid to location. I take it (see p. 454) that 140ff. show that the elders are to be imagined as inside a council-chamber. But that is the only explicit indication, though the Queen's instructions about counsels (528) may be a slight resumptive reminder. After Darius has returned to the dead, there is no more mention of his tomb, and presumably it goes out of focus once more. The tomb could easily have been alluded to in the final act had Aeschylus wished it, but he prefers that the setting should be vague: it is simply a place where the returning Xerxes might be met. Even Wilamowitz's location (p. 48)—'somewhere outside the city . . . on the highway'—is too specific.

That, in brief, is the case for a fluid scene setting in *Pers*. Yet the idea that some early tragedies did not observe a unity of place offends some scholars; possibly because they associate this with the indignities of Aristophanes, possibly because of the influence of the neo-Aristotelian 'laws' of unity. In this case I shall single out two particularly spirited attempts to show that *Pers* is all set at one place. Harmon (*TAPA* 63 (1932) 7ff.) argues

[1] It is true that the settings of vase paintings are sometimes written in, e.g. the tomb on *ARV²* 1301 no. 5 (c. 440, *Cho?* see *Illustrations* p. 41) is inscribed *ΑΓΑΜΕΜ* (and on a puzzling white-ground lekythos (Achilles painter?) Akrisios sits on a tomb inscribed *ΠΕΡΣΕΩΣ*; see I. Jucker *AntK* Beiheft 7 (1970) 47–9 and plate 26). But any equivalent inscription on stage is highly unlikely.

that the play is set at the city gates. This is a good place to meet
Xerxes (true), for the tomb of Darius (true?), and, Harmon
argues from Old Testament evidence and Herodotus, it was the
usual place in an oriental city for an open-air council. A small
objection is that this fails to account for ϲτέγοϲ ἀρχαῖον in 141,
but the fatal weakness is that there is no trace whatsoever in the
text of the play of the city gates (cf. Broadhead xlvi). Harmon
argues (18) that 'a bit of scenery and a soldier or two on guard
ought to mark it plainly enough'. But, even supposing that the
Aeschylean theatre had representational scenery, which is unlikely, it is hard to see how the city gates might be represented.
Korzeniewski (548–53) argues, on the other hand, that the skene
represented the royal palace, and that the tomb and council
were set before its doors. He claims that the dramatic impact of
the chariot entry by the Queen overrides the realistic consideration that she should enter from the door. Even if we could swallow
this, there is still the objection that her second entry must be
made from the same place as her first (see ll. 607ff. and 598a*
above). Korzeniewski points out that it is repeatedly implied
that the palace is nearby; but he is wrong to think that it is as
near as the skene would be, for the Queen foresees that she may
not meet Xerxes in time. And Xerxes does not simply enter the
palace, he is escorted to it (530 etc., see 1077*).

While we should grant that the scene in *Pers* is not fixed at
one place, it would be a mistake to suppose that the scene
changes are made at any particular juncture or that they were
marked by any moving of scenery or the like. There are even
suggestions in the text of a kind of continuity, which counteracts
any notion of abrupt change. When the Queen says she will
return (524) this implies that she will come to the same place;
and when she does return at 598ff. she is making the same
journey as before (κέλευθον τήνδε 607), though in a very different
manner. On her final exit she says that she will try to meet her
son (849f.) and, supposing that 529–31 should go after 851 (see
528*), she adds that if he comes first to this place (δεῦρο 529)
he should be escorted to the palace. These slight hints of continuity of scene do not, in my view, affect the larger evidence of
a fluid scene setting; but they do show clearly that the changes
of setting are imprecise, and are not tied to any particular
moment or stage rearrangement.

622 (the Queen stays)

act-ending without exit

We come here to the first divergence from the basic structural pattern of Greek tragedy propounded in §5. I shall attempt now to account for this divergence and to accommodate it to my scheme; and I hope also to resolve the troubles of some scholars who have thought that this part of *Pers* may not be susceptible to an analysis in terms which also apply to later tragedy. I argued that the construction of Greek tragedy is based on the alternation of speech and song combined with the rearrangement of actors by exits before the songs and entries after them; and that the basic ground pattern, which always reasserts itself though often departed from, is that the stage is cleared of actors before each strophic choral song and refilled again after it. So *Pers* departs in two respects here: there is no exit at 622 before the strophic choral song, and there is an actor, the Queen, on during the song. After the Queen's re-entry and before the song there is simply her single short rhesis (598–622), which closes with instructions to the chorus to call up Darius while she pours libations. Her instructions are taken up by the transitional anapaests (623ff.),[1] and the strophic song then follows (633ff.).

Aeschylus has a tendency to brief acts which involve only one actor and which consist solely or mainly of a rhesis by that actor. It may be that these acts preserve some of the formal techniques of early tragedy, when there was only one actor; but it should not be forgotten that in all likelihood the second actor had been introduced many years before *Pers*. Some of these short acts, like this one in *Pers*, approach Wilamowitz's description (p. 67) of 'merely a link element between two odes of the χορὸϲ πρωτ-αγωνιϲτήϲ', but others are nothing of the sort. Three examples of short one-actor acts are *Seven* 792ff., *Cho* 732ff. and 838ff.[2] In all three, unlike *Pers*, there is an exit at the end of the act, and the stage is clear for the following choral song. Outside Aeschylus

---

[1] Anapaests like these are found only in Aeschylus, and may well be an archaic feature. See Kranz *Forma* 48, *Stas* 135, Peretti 269ff., Fraenkel *Ag comm* ii 184.

[2] For the techniques employed in the exciting short scenes in *Cho* see *Cho* 854* and 892a*. *Prom* 436ff. may be meant to have analogies with these one-actor acts, but is aberrant in several ways—see *Prom* 436*.

the only clear examples are E. *Alc* 935ff. and the two great speeches of Ajax at S. *Aj* 646ff. and 815ff.[1]

There are, however, two other places in Aeschylus which resemble *Pers* more closely than any quoted so far. In *Eum*, after the astrophic re-entry song of the chorus, Orestes speaks a short rhesis (276–98); the chorus replies (299–306), and then without any exit or other break goes into the anapaestic prelude to the 'binding hymn' (see further *Eum* 276*). Even more like *Pers* is *Hik* 600ff. Danaus returns after the choral song, his brief rhesis (605–24) inspires the great song in praise of Argos (630ff.), which is preceded by an anapaestic transition (625–9); there is no exit. In fact, the similarities of formal structure between *Pers* and *Hik* go further than this: they cover the entire first two-thirds of each play.[2] The structural parallels may be summarized (though the precise stichometric analogies are not, of course, significant): (*a*) long prologue-parodos with anapaestic prelude (*Pers* 1–149, *Hik* 1–175); (*b*) entry (*Pers*) or intervention (*Hik* 176*) of chief 'resident' character—rhesis followed by sticho-mythia (*Pers* 150–245, *Hik* 176–233); (*c*) entry of a character from 'outside' who is decisive for the well-being of the chorus and 'chief resident'—long scene follows (*Pers* 249–514, *Hik* 234–479), including an epirrhematic structure; (*d*) the 'outsider' leaves, and the 'resident' goes on a mission (*Pers* 515–28, *Hik* 480–523); (*e*) choral song of disquiet (*Pers* 532–97, *Hik* 524–99); (*f*) the 'resident' returns (*Pers* 598, *Hik* 600), and there follows the structural sequence under discussion here. This considerable formal similarity is undeniably there. It suggests a certain continuity and care in Aeschylus' control of his structural techniques.

Returning now to the ways in which *Pers* departs from the proposed structural ground-form, let us consider first the way that there is no exit before the strophic choral song. Although this phenomenon is commoner than the lack of an entry after an act-dividing song (see *Prom* 436*), and although it is rather less rare in Aeschylus than in the other two dramatists, anyone may quickly check for himself that it is exceptional: there is an

[1] The remarkable way in which these two speeches are isolated and thrust into prominence by the structural technique alone indicates their importance. The whole play is made round this pair of speeches. Short one-actor scenes are common in New Comedy—*Misoum* 259–69, *Perik* 354–60 etc.—but there is to all intents and purposes no chorus.

[2] Jens, despite his title, pays no attention to this.

exit in about nine cases out of ten. Moreover most of the exceptions fall into distinguishable and explicable categories. For example, there are 'Euripidean parodoi'. In many plays Euripides blurs the transition from prologue to first choral song by having no exit immediately before the song; outside Euripides this is found only in S. *El* and in *Prom*, see *Prom* 88*. Then, in many apparent exceptions there has been an exit not long before the end of the act, and one actor has been left on for lament or comment or some other sort of tailpiece before the song. In most cases the exit is less than 20 lines before the song (e.g. S. *OT* 1072, *El* 803; E. *Tro* 789); but occasionally in Euripides the tailpiece is longer and forms a kind of independent scene, notably at *Med* 357ff. (52 lines before the song), 764ff. (59), *Tro* 462ff. (48), *IT* 344ff. (56).[1]

Once these two groups of places are left out of account there are (as far as I can see) only seven places left in all surviving tragedy where there is no exit before an act-dividing song.[2] In two of these seven there is some rearrangement of the actors which is virtually equivalent to an exit: at S. *Phil* 820 Philoctetes falls into a faint, and at *Tr* 199 the Old Man goes into the background in such a way that he might be assumed to have dropped out of the play (cf. p. 89 above). Two others are bound up with the structural disruptions which result from an 'epiparodos': *Eum* 306 (see above) and the similar E. *Alc* 961. This leaves *Prom* 525 (see *Prom* 436*), *Hik* 624, and *Pers* 622. This should serve to demonstrate that we are faced with something genuinely exceptional here and at the analogous juncture in *Hik*.

Secondly, an actor stays on during the act-dividing lyric. This is a much more common divergence than the absence of an exit (for when one actor stays on there is still normally an exit

[1] I do not see any good reason for sending Iphigenia off at *IT* 391; certainly none for sending her into the temple, and then bringing her back with the prisoners, as Platnauer supposes in *IT comm* on 391 and 456–66 (cf. Arle. *Poet* 1455a26ff. on the treatment of Carcinus!).

[2] At the risk of some slight circularity I leave out of consideration one or two controversial places where I take it that there was an exit before the act-dividing song (and where the structural factor is one argument in favour of the disputed exit): see notably *Ag* 350* and *Hik* 974a* (esp. pp. 224–7). If the last part of E. *IA* were to be performed with the text we have, then Iphigenia should exit at 1508 before the astrophic act-dividing lyric 1509–31, which is surely not the work of Euripides, see Page 191f. However, Page's remarks (p. 192) on the action are somewhat confused: he seems to regard performance as something wilfully independent of authorship.

by another); in fact it cannot be called exceptional. At a rough estimate an actor remains during one in three of all act-dividing songs; though this is not equally distributed among the plays, and is rather less usual in Aeschylus than in the other two.[1] It may be that back in the days of one-actor tragedy it was the rule that the actor always went off during act-dividing songs, but this is far from the case in surviving tragedy; and clearly the audience readily acquiesced in his presence (even though some modern scholars have been less comfortable). Often the actor is given some function or pose to take up during the song (as here, see below); often he is directly referred to, and not infrequently he is apostrophized (see Kranz *Stas* 163f., 204–7). Sometimes in later tragedy the actor may actually take part in the act-dividing song (for the only instance in Aeschylus see on *Prom* 88*), and may dominate the lyric dialogue or even sing a monody and thus supplant the chorus in its structural function: see p. 52. There are, on the other hand, some occasions when the actor has no direct relevance to the song, and no notice is taken of his presence.[2] The audience must be fully concentrated on the song, and the dramatist means them to pay no attention to the actor (just as, conversely, the chorus is often completely neglected during the acts).

I shall now quickly survey all the other occasions in Aeschylus where an actor is on-stage during an act-dividing song, partly in order to consider how the presence of the actor is justified or neglected, and partly in order to show the extent of Groeneboom's error when he says (p. 138) that *Pers* 623ff. is the only place in Aeschylus, apart from *Prom*, where an actor remains on during a choral song. (It hardly excuses the usually careful Groeneboom that he takes the error *verbatim* from Conradt p. 13 n. 23.)

There is a tendency in all three dramatists for an actor to be on during the first song (parodos). In *Hik* and *Cho* an actor enters with the chorus, but both remain inconspicuous during

---

[1] For a bibliography of those who consider the matter see p. 54 n. 2.

[2] The instances of this in Sophocles and Euripides are collected by Ritchie p. 116 n. 6. However, S. *OC* 1211ff. should not be there (see 1239ff.) nor should *Aj* 1185ff. (Tecmessa and the child are specially posed in a tableau.) To Ritchie's list may be transferred from his note 4 E. *Hel* 1107ff. (Menelaus' presence is to be neglected), and from n. 5 S. *Ant* 944ff. (Antigone is addressed, but it is Creon who is present).

the song (cf. *Hik* 1b*, *Cho* 22*).[1] In *Prom*, on the other hand, Prometheus is on stage before the entry of the chorus; the song is centred on him, and he contributes to it in a kind of epirrhematic structure—see *Prom* 88*. Now to songs other than the first (parodos). Danaus is on during *Hik* 630ff. (see above): he is at his lookout (see *Hik* 710*), and no attention is paid to him; he does, however, stand in a particularly close relationship to the chorus.[2] Cassandra is on during *Ag* 975ff.: attention is drawn to her before and after the song, but no notice at all is taken of her during it. It seems that she is meant to be the object of an unformulated disquiet (cf. pp. 317–8).[3] In *Eum* Orestes is on-stage during the astrophic 'epiparodos' (254ff.) and during 321ff. The latter is sung round him, while he clings to the image of Athena; and perhaps nowhere else in Greek tragedy is an actor more literally the 'object' of a choral song (cf. *Eum* 276*). Orestes is probably also present during *Eum* 490ff.; but, although the song takes its starting-point from him, it moves away to other, larger issues (see further *Eum* 566a*). Lastly, in *Prom* Prometheus himself is, perforce, on-stage during all the act-dividing songs. The first song was considered above, the second (397ff.) is a lament on his behalf, the third (527ff.) turns to him in the second strophic pair; only the last (887ff.)—a mere trifle by Aeschylean standards—has no bearing on him, and draws no attention to his presence.[4]

So it may be seen that there is a great variety in the dramatic technique of the places in Aeschylus where an actor remains on-stage during an act-dividing song. The function of the song in the play varies, and the relation of the actor to the chorus varies. And so the treatment of the actor varies: he may be all but neglected (e.g. *Prom* 887ff., *Hik* 630ff.) or he may have a central

---

[1] I argue on *Seven* 77* that Eteocles was not on during the first song of *Seven*; similarly for Clytemnestra in *Ag* on *Ag* 258a*.

[2] On the apparent presence of Pelasgus during *Hik* 966ff., according to the text as we have it, see *Hik* 974a*. This would be completely different from the phenomena under consideration here.

[3] I argue that Clytemnestra was not on-stage during *Ag* 367ff. (see 350*), nor 681ff. (see 614*), nor 975ff. (see p. 310 n. 1).

[4] It may be added that, among the lost plays, Achilles must have been on-stage during several of the choral lyrics of *Myrmidones* and Niobe during *Niobe* (see *HSCP* 1972 pp. 6off.). In both cases the silent, seated figure was the object, probably the centre, of attention. In *Prom Lyom* Prometheus must have been on during most of the songs; he was the centre of attention for the opening song, at least.

role (e.g. *Prom* 127ff., *Eum* 321ff.). During *Pers* 633ff. the Queen, who has called for the song, gives herself the task of pouring libations (621f.), and this is remarked on in the introductory anapaests (623ff.). She is not, however, given any attention during the strophic song itself, which is concentrated solely and vividly on Darius.[1] It is hard to say how conspicuous Aeschylus meant her to be; but the calling-up of Darius is purely choral, and the silent Queen should not 'upstage' the dancing singers.

In the light of all this let us return to the structural technique. Scholars who have worked within the scheme supplied by *Poetics* ch. 12 (on which see Appendix E) have run into difficulties over this part of *Pers* and the parallel sequence in *Hik*. Wilamowitz simply argued that the traditional analysis was inapplicable to early tragedy.[2] Others, less bold (e.g. Goodell 77, 90, Lucas on Arle. *Poet* 1452b20), have said that *Pers* 598–851 and *Hik* 600–775 each form one single 'epeisodion', which includes the strophic choral song within it. The situation is, however, made clearer once the more adaptable scheme which I have proposed is applied. In terms of the alternation of speech and choral song *Pers* 598–622 and *Hik* 600–29 both form brief individual acts: it is in terms of the sequence of entry and exit that there is a peculiarity. While the first of the two choral songs is bounded in the usual way by exit and entry, the second is followed by an entry or its equivalent (*Pers* 681, *Hik* 710*), but is *not* preceded by an exit. The absence of an exit lessens the structural break made by the change of delivery, and this is further lessened in both plays by the way in which the last spoken words give instructions for the song which are taken up in the introductory anapaests. The two determinant structural features, instead of coinciding as usual, clash, and so produce a lightly marked transition and a degree of continuity. It makes good sense to speak of *Pers* 598–622 as a separate act in view of the clearly marked sequence of song, speech, and song: on the other hand, the end of the act is made to run into the following song without an unequivocal structural division.

Why, finally, does Aeschylus depart from the usual structural

---

[1] I see no justification, however, for Dignan's grudging dismissal of the libations (p. 18): 'here a special device does away with the awkwardness' (note the same word also in Ritchie p. 116 with n. 6). There is no awkwardness.

[2] Wilamowitz 1–4 (cf. *Kl Schr* i p. 310 n. 1); cf. Lesky *Ges Schr* 91, *TDH*[3] 84.

pattern at this juncture? First, note that we are quite likely
dealing here with elements of archaic technique, and if we had
more early tragedy, this might well prove less exceptional. In
several other places we have brief one-actor acts, and *Hik* 600ff.
and *Eum*. 276ff. are structurally similar (see above p. 109). Only
in *Pers*, however, does the choral song (viz. 633ff.) lead directly
towards the entry which inaugurates the following act. It thus
provides an obvious forward-looking continuity with the preceding act, which has also led towards the same event. Two
dramatic factors seem to be at work here. One is Aeschylus'
decision that the chorus itself should call up the ghost of Darius,
a decision which gives it a song more directly integrated into
the action than is usual in later tragedy.[1] Since he also wishes
the Queen to be present and to supply (following from her
dream) the impetus for the ψυχαγωγία, he will have seen the
advantage of merging her instructions with the ghost-raising
song. Secondly, Aeschylus does not allow the ghost-raising to
encroach on the first half of the play, where it would be an
intriguing distraction (cf. p. 106 above): on the other hand, he
wishes to make the most of the dramatic and theatrical possibilities of an outstanding scene (see Arph. *Frogs* 1028f.!). So,
having once made effective use of the re-entry of the Queen (see
598a*), he then builds up to the entry of Darius in a single
intense sequence, uninterrupted by any heavy structural break.
So, whether or not it was archaic, we may see that Aeschylus
put the structural technique to positive and effective use.

681 enter Darius

(a) ὕμνος κλητικός

The audience cannot, so far as I can see, realize before ll. 619ff.
that Darius is going to be called up on stage before their eyes,
since preparation for this has been positively withheld up until
then. However, as was pointed out on pp. 105–6 above, associated ideas have been introduced earlier. Moreover, Darius has
been repeatedly named in the first half of the play, and called

---

[1] The question of the role of the chorus in early tragedy has already been
broached on p. 87, where I react against the view that its contribution was greater
only in terms of quantity. I would add the evidence of the ghost-raising of Darius
against the notion that *Hik* and *Eum* were novel experiments in their use of the
chorus.

to mind as the one among the dead who may be particularly
relevant to the present.[1] Above all, the Queen saw him in her
dream (197ff., cf. 220ff.).

Once the Queen has instructed the chorus to call up Darius
his entry is led up to in an exotic and colourful song, no doubt
accompanied by the lively choreography for which Aeschylus
was famous. The anapaestic programme (628–32) introduces a
prayer to the gods of the underworld, and this is carried out in
the first two strophic pairs (633–57). In the third pair (658–72),
however, Darius is called directly in the second person, and the
song takes on some of the characteristics of a ὕμνος κλητικός.[2] In
this case the conventional imperatives are especially conspicuous,
and lead in an urgent and vivid way towards Darius' entry:
ἴθι, ἱκοῦ, ἔλθ' . . . (658f.), βάσκε (663 = 671), and, above all,
φάνηθι (666).

One reason why the allusions to the hymnic form are particularly effective here is that they are actually followed by the
appearance of the 'god' (cf. Athena's arrival at *Eum* 397* in
response to Orestes' call at 287ff.). Further, the use of hymn
forms helps to establish Darius in the play as superhuman and
godlike. The Persians' view of Darius as divine cannot be regarded as barbarous blasphemy or as mere oriental colour, since
the audience also is obliged to accept it. The kletic hymn
succeeds; and when Darius says that he is a great power in the
underworld (691) there is no room to disbelieve him. All this
gives his prophecies and his moral judgement the requisite
authority. Two further advantages of the hymn are that it can
set the scene at the tomb (see p. 106), and that it can use the
conventional topoi of dwelling on the manner of the epiphany
and on the physical appearance of the 'god'.[3] This serves as
vivid and precise preparation for the entry itself.

---

[1] Darius is also named as the father of Xerxes (6, 145), the husband of the
Queen (156, 160), the accumulator of Persia's wealth (164), the sender of the
earlier invasion of Athens (244), and as a blameless ruler (554ff.). It would,
however, be a mistake to regard the naming of a character as, *per se*, preparation
for his entry—see p. 10 above.

[2] This is not noticed in any of the commentaries. But there are valuable observations on the use of this hymn form in tragedy in Kranz *Stas* 185–7 (with some
bibliography on 305–6). Also cf. V. Citti *Il linguaggio religioso* etc. (*Stud. pub.
dall'Ist. di Fil. Class. Bologna* X, 1962) 42–3. (I have not been able to see R.
Knoke *De Hymnis Tragicis* etc. (diss. Göttingen 1924).)

[3] On this see e.g. Fraenkel *Horace* (Oxford 1957) 204 n. 4.

(b) staging

The precise stage management of the entry (and exit) of Darius has been the subject of much disagreement, and we have not the evidence to resolve it with any confidence. It would be as well to settle first what the 'dramatic picture' is meant to be; that is to say, what the audience is to suppose is happening within the play, whether or not there was any attempt to represent this realistically (cf. §3). The text is not as informative as usual, but it does say that the Queen is supposed to be near the tomb (πέλας 684), and so is the chorus (ἐγγύς 686).[1] They call on Darius to come to the *top* of his tomb (659), and when he goes Darius says he is going *below* (839).[2] This implies that Darius' movements are to be thought of as vertical, so to speak (as opposed to horizontal); and this is reinforced by his account of how he has managed to get out of the underworld (688–92). Now, the 'dramatic picture' need not necessarily have been reflected in the staging; Darius *may*, for example, have simply

[1] Cf. Bodensteiner 683. The fact that Darius addresses the chorus before the Queen is nothing to do with staging, but rather with the development of dramatic technique—see 249b* above. Broadhead 173 says 'as soon as Darius appeared at the top of the tomb, he would catch sight of the chorus first, since the Queen was closer to the tomb and would not be seen till he dropped his eyes in her direction'. Such naturalistic details are totally inappropriate. Characters in a play see what the playwright has them see, regardless of the realities of optics. Compare Calder *CPh* 60 (1965) 115, who argues in favour of having Athena on the theologeion during the prologue of S. *Aj*, and argues that her invisibility (l. 15) is then explained, since if Odysseus 'is close to the *scaenae frons*, he would have difficulty in seeing her'. But a character on the ground can see a god above if the dramatist so chooses, regardless of realistic considerations. (In my view Athena is on the ground like other gods in prologues, and ll. 14–17 say that Odysseus knows Athena so well that he can recognize her by her voice alone even when she is not visible—unlike the present occasion.) In a rather similar situation, Barrett on E. *Hipp* 1283 and 1391–3 claims that Hippolytus senses Artemis' presence rather than seeing her because 'she is simply outside his field of vision'. But the point is, rather, that he who knows her voice so well (see 86f.) recognizes her without even looking for her. Compare Philoctetes who in S. *Phil* still recognizes Odysseus by his voice alone after ten years of solitary resentment (976 and 1295f.): Odysseus is not out of sight.

[2] Anderson (*G and R* 19 (1972) 174) has suggested that Darius did not go at this point, but stayed as 'a silent, brooding presence throughout the final scene'; and he refers to the way that Darius watched and pitied Xerxes in the Queen's dream (197–8). But Greek tragedy does not work with brooding yet unnoticed presences, and in the dream Xerxes sees Darius, which cannot be so in the final scene. But there are also more specific objections. At the beginning of the scene Darius implied that he could only stay a short time (691–2), and at the end he does not only say χαίρετε (as Anderson suggests) he also says in the line before (839) ἐγὼ δ' ἄπειμι γῆς ὑπὸ ζόφον κάτω. Aeschylus could hardly be more explicit.

walked on up an eisodos. But the reaction against realism in the Greek theatre may be taken too far (see §3), and if Aeschylus could devise a way of having Darius make a vertical entry and exit, then he would, I suppose, have used it. So we may consider any reasonable way of concealing steps to a height of several feet (say four, at least).

In Appendix C I argue that there was no background skene for *Pers* nor for another decade or so after it. If this is true, then this necessarily rules out any staging which uses the skene; and one of the most widely held views is that Darius emerged on to the roof of the skene building.[1] Without a skene Webster's theory that the tomb was represented by painted screens on the ekkyklema is also ruled out.[2] There have been those who suppose that a stage altar represented the tomb of Darius (e.g. Murray 55, Arnott 58f.). There is no objection in theatrical theory to an altar representing a tomb, but there are practical difficulties. It is doubtful whether the altar would have been large enough for a convincing vertical entry to be made from behind it ('it was small', Arnott 59). Secondly, the actor who has played the Messenger has somehow got to get into position without being seen (and perhaps get off again to play Xerxes, see 851*). At least the most widely held theory avoids these difficulties. According to this, Darius ascended from behind some considerable mound or other construction ('Bau' or 'podium').[3] Some such mound is favoured by the occasional indications of a higher level in early tragedy, and especially by the recurrence of a πάγος. κόρυμβον ὄχθου in 659 may be quoted in favour of some sort of conical mound (though it should be noted that ὄχθος is also used of the tomb at *Cho* 4, when there was a skene and the proposed πάγος may no longer have been there). However, Wilamowitz was surely wrong to suppose that the mound was in the middle of the orchestra, where it would have been an intolerable obstruction: it must have been somewhere at the edge, if anywhere.[4]

[1] e.g. Bethe 97, Groeneboom i 18f., Spitzbarth 46, Dale *Papers* 119, 261. Also would not the skene be too large an edifice to stand for a tomb?

[2] *GTP* 17, 165f. cf. *Staging* 499f. Further, we have no evidence for the use of the ekkyklema as a trolley for awkward stage furniture: see pp. 442ff.

[3] e.g. Wilamowitz 10, earlier in *Kl Schr* i 155ff. (1886), *Perser* 313; D–R 196f., P-C *TDA* 35, Frickenhaus 84f., Lesky *TDH*³ 85.

[4] A vertical entry from behind a mound might be facilitated if Darius came up

So several of these theories are at least possible. On the other hand, if there was an underground passage, as I have argued there may have been on p. 447, then, obviously, that was used. There would simply be a portable stage property representing the tomb in front of the opening, and Darius would come up behind it. Two possible advantages might follow from this arrangement. A slight one is that, if the passage was simply a 'fossa' covered by boards (see p. 448), then the chorus may have stamped or beaten on this as part of the ghost raising. This might help to explain the difficult line 683. A more substantial point is that Darius would be able to rise somewhere within the orchestra, instead of at the edge, and so the choreography could be arranged around the tomb (and the Queen standing by it).[1] Inevitably the discussion remains inconclusive, though some theories are definitely less acceptable than others.

Finally, it is worth considering one other intriguing piece of evidence, even though it probably has no bearing on *Pers*. In 1955 Beazley published five fragments of an Attic red-figure hydria from Corinth, which he dated to 480–450.[2] A Greek αὐλητής, whose presence shows that the subject is tragic, accompanies a scene where several similarly dressed orientals are concerned over a calm oriental 'king' whose top half shows above a flaming pyre built of logs. Beazley (319) considers Darius in *Pers* as a possible subject, but rejects him because the painting clearly shows a burning pyre. Webster has none the less championed Darius; he explains the pyre as either the painter's 'way

---

from behind the back terrace-wall (cf. Bieber *Hist*[2] 57), particularly if in the early theatre the terrace-wall also formed the edge of the orchestra circle (cf. pp. 456–7). Yet another possibility is the outcrop of natural rock which Hammond has argued stood at one side of the orchestra (see Hammond 409ff. and p. 448 below).

[1] A possible argument in favour of this may be extracted from Dionysus' reminiscence of *Pers* at Arph. *Frogs* 1028, which the MSS. transmit in the corrupt form ἐχάρην γοῦν ἡνίκ' ἤκουσα περὶ Δαρείου τεθνεῶτος. Whatever the right emendation there is no good reason to emend περί, which might mean either 'about' of subject-matter or 'round about' of place. Most editors assume the former sense, but in view of Aristophanes' way of referring to scenes in tragedy visually rather than contextually (cf. e.g. *Frogs* 1139f.) the latter sense deserves consideration. Aristophanes could not, of course, have seen the original production, but this line may suggest that in a revival (either in the Theatre of Dionysus or elsewhere) Darius' tomb was in a central position.

[2] *Hesperia* 24 (1955) 305ff.; *Corinth* vol. xiii no. X—265 and pl. 98 = *ARV*[2] p. 571 no. 74 = *MTS*[2] AV 13. The most accessible description and photograph are in P-C *DFA*[2] 182f. and fig. 36.

of saying that the king was well and truly buried' or as the producer's 'shorthand for a tomb'.[1] This special pleading is most
unconvincing. Beazley also rejects Croesus because the king's
costume is Persian. Page may be right that this is being more
meticulous than Aeschylus or the costume-maker would be.[2] It
has also been objected against Croesus (P-C *DFA*[2] 183 n. 1) that
the king is rising from the pyre; but, so far as I can see, we cannot
say that he is rising rather than sinking, and so Page may be
right that he 'had already sunk through the platform' (or could
he be half consumed?). But there is another point which has not
been raised in the discussions. It would be out of the question
to light a pyre in the theatre; and so the flames would have to
be left to the imagination of the audience. So too, if he was not
rescued, would the king's immolation, or, if he was rescued, the
extinction of the flames. The alternative, that the painting shows
off-stage events which were reported, must at least be entertained. The attempt of Amphitryon to burn Alcmene on a pyre
in E. *Alcmene*, which is illustrated on later South Italian vases
(see *Illustrations* pp. 76–7), is assumed to have been reported and
not staged. On the other hand, the *auletes,* and the identical
costumes of the chorus suggest that the 'Croesus' pyre may have
been on stage.

842 Darius redescends (see p. 116 n. 2)

851 the Queen goes

why is the Queen discarded?

Once Aeschylus had made the basic artistic decision that the
entire final act of the play should take the form of a long threnetic
lyric dialogue (kommos) between Xerxes and the chorus, then
he had to send the Queen off at this juncture for the last time.
He might simply have sent her to await Xerxes at the palace,

[1] *Staging* 499f., *MTS*[2] p. 3, *Chorus* 25, 115. Yet Webster did not include the vase
in *Illustrations*. Hammond 430f. also favours *Pers*; but he has to claim that the
flames are flames of incense and that the king rises 'from burial mound behind
pyre'.
[2] PCPhS n.s. 8 (1962) 47ff. cf. Snell *ZPE* 12 (1973) 203f. Page has, of course,
a vested interest in early tragedies about the house of Gyges: see *A New Chapter
in the History of Greek Tragedy* (Cambridge 1951). I will say no more than that the
kind of tragedy which Page envisages would be post-classical.

but he preferred to use her exit motivation as part of the preparation for Xerxes' rags (cf. p. 96 above and 909a* below). So he
gives Darius the instructions of 832–8, which the Queen takes
up in 849f., adding the precautionary πειράσομαι. On 528* I
have tried to show the advantages of transposing 529–31 to after
851 : in that case the Queen's instructions precisely foreshadow
the actual event. There is still no denying a slight awkwardness
in the elimination of the Queen even with her precautionary
conditional clause; all the same it is very slight, scarcely noticeable surely, in the distressful forward movement of the play in
performance.

The reasons for Aeschylus' initial decision to make Xerxes the
only actor at the end of the play are, it seems to me, straightforward. A consideration of the last act *as it is* makes them
immediately clear. Wilamowitz put this point briefly, and it has
been generally taken.[1] The indulgent, almost luxurious, lament
has no place for spoken dialogue and no place for a second actor.
Throughout the play the Queen receives misfortune with dignity
and wisdom, as befits the wife of Darius: this role could not
possibly be maintained in a final scene which resembles that
which we have. Xerxes' humiliation is complete, and were the
Queen there she too would be humiliated (cf. Stephenson p. 20).
Also Xerxes stands for the entire Persian host, cf. 909b*; and
the final lament concerns the whole of Persia. The Queen would
inevitably introduce an unwanted personal element.

Several scholars have produced a more mundane technical
consideration, which is for some of them the chief reason for the
elimination of the Queen. They argue that Aeschylus wanted
the same actor (presumably his best one, perhaps himself) to
play both the Queen and Xerxes.[2] No such technical consideration would excuse an artistic fault, though it might help explain
it. In this case the argument is weak, since there is no reason to

---

[1] Wilamowitz *Perser* 386f. cf. *Interpretationen* 46. Recently the case has been well
restated at greater length by Alexanderson *Eranos* 65 (1967) 6–9.

[2] See e.g. P. Richter 100, Flickinger 175, Kaffenberger 31, *GGL* i 2 p. 69 n. 4,
P-C *DFA²* 138, Croiset 98 n. 1. Bieber *History²* pp. 21f. actually goes so far as to
say that in 472 Aeschylus' control of two actors 'was so awkward and unskilful
that Xerxes, the Persian king, and his mother Atossa never meet'. But this cannot
be the explanation when the two actors are perfectly satisfactorily handled,
including in dialogue, earlier in the play. (Bieber's simplistic view of Aeschylus'
fumbling development leads her to imply on p. 21 that there was only one actor
in *Hik.*)

doubt the ability of the other actor who has played the Messenger and Darius. In terms of mere quantity the actor of the Queen has spoken about 170 lines, while the other has spoken about 300. It is conceivable that Aeschylus wanted the actor of the Queen for the part of Xerxes, but that is by no means a sufficient explanation, nor is it any excuse for what is in any case a negligible infelicity.

909 enter Xerxes

(a) visual presentation

Xerxes was, in my view, in tattered finery, on foot, and by himself. The chief argument for this presentation is its visual significance in the play as a whole: this is discussed in 909b* below. First, however, I shall attempt to establish the visual picture on independent grounds.

Nearly everyone has accepted the rags—or, rather, the torn finery.[1] What else is the point of the repeated references to Xerxes' clothes during the play? First, in the Queen's dream he rends his clothes (199), and then, in reality, after Salamis (469f.). One might naturally assume that Xerxes would have replaced his rent robes, but that Darius almost at the end of his scene (832–6) draws special attention to the fact that Xerxes is still in the finery which he tore with grief. As has been seen (p. 120 above) a further reference is combined with the Queen's exit motivation (845–50). Darius and his widow are especially upset at Xerxes' rags, which symbolize for them his degradation (ἀτιμία 847). Then, after he has arrived, Xerxes explicitly laments in 1017 ὁρᾶις τὸ λοιπὸν τόδε τᾶς ἐμᾶς στολᾶς; While there is a possible ambiguity in that the στολή might be his army (thus scholia and several editors), his clothes make a better primary sense (see Groeneboom, Broadhead), especially as he goes on to his quiver. It would be grotesque to imply more than figuratively that he has the entire surviving army with him on stage (see further below). Finally, at 1030, recalling Salamis, he tells how he rent his clothes. This takes up all the preparation earlier in the play, and stresses the connection between Xerxes' robes and the whole state of Persia.

---

[1] I leave out of consideration the idea that Xerxes was in full tragic costume and was only to be imagined as in tatters; see p. 36 above.

Yet there have been those, including Hermann, who have not accepted a Xerxes in rags.[1] They cannot argue merely that it is unrealistic that he should still be wearing the tatters of Salamis, since Darius clearly says he is: they claim, rather, that such ludicrous bathos is unworthy of Aeschylus. Their case rests entirely on a notion of the decorum of Aeschylus which is derived from Aristophanes. In Aristophanes kings in rags are the speciality of Euripides, and in *Frogs* (1061–8) an explicit contrast is made between his costumes and those of Aeschylus. But the comedian who claimed that he himself never made jokes about phalluses or the hungry Heracles can hardly be taken at literal face value on the relative decorum of two tragedians. It would be a mistake to infer from *Frogs* that Aeschylus never introduced a murderous adulteress or a talkative nurse or that Euripides never used chariots (see 155b*) or dramatic silences (see *HSCP* 1972, 95–6). Aeschylus' Philoctetes was surely in rags and in *Semele* he had Hera transformed to a begging priestess. Hermann has to suppose that the Queen did, in fact, successfully, intercept Xerxes with his new clothes. But that is to suppose an independent world off-stage which goes beyond the direct allusions to it, and that is totally uncharacteristic of Greek tragedy.

It is generally agreed that Xerxes is by himself without attendants. The text is not incontrovertibly clear, but γυμνός εἰμι προπομπῶν (1036) may in these circumstances be taken literally: at the end of the play the old men of the chorus will have to act as escort. The first part of the kommos dwells on the many who set out with Xerxes. The chorus ask where they are, and Xerxes confesses that they have all been left behind (see 955ff.). It would be ridiculous and obtrusively unrealistic if Xerxes had a few attendants and if cτολάc in 1017 (see above) referred literally to his army, since it would imply that they were all that were left. Xerxes is not the only survivor, but he represents the fragment which returns.

[1] Hermann n. on 886 ('non enim squalidum et lacerum producere Aeschyleum est'). I have also noted Weil, Paley, Sidgwick, Graeber 41f., Murray *tr* 89. For an early refutation of Hermann see Volckman *Philologus* 9 (1854) 689f. I am reluctant even in a footnote to mention the suggestion of Avery (*AJP* 85 (1964) 179ff.) that the Queen brings on new clothes for Xerxes at 1002. Not only is there no indication of the stage action in the text, but Avery assumes without question that there must be a 'psychological' explanation for the change of structure and tone in the lament. That the change is due to conventional forms is clear from a comparison with *Seven* (854b*).

So I share the usual view when I suppose that Xerxes is in tattered robes and is alone. On the other hand, it is almost universally agreed that Xerxes is not on foot, but rides in a tented wagon. Yet on entry Xerxes chants (913) λέλυται γὰρ ἐμοὶ γυίων ῥώμη: and he may go literally on his knees and so embody the elders' lament (929–31) that Asia has been brought to her knees. Despite this, the covered wagon is conjured entirely and solely from 1000–1: ἔταφον ἔταφον οὐκ ἀμφὶ cκηναῖc / τροχηλάτοιcιν ὄπιθεν ἑπομένουc.[1] These are the last words of the first part of the dirge, which then becomes antiphonal, and they thus conclude the great catalogue of those who set out with Xerxes, and have not returned. The point is that all these fine warriors with their fine names set out accompanying Xerxes in his splendid and outlandish wagon; they have not returned, nor has the wagon. The contrast is, as throughout, between what set out, and what has returned. This seems obvious, yet hardly any scholar has been able to abandon the cκηναὶ τροχήλατοι.[2] I suspect that the reason why most have been so eager to have the wagon is because it would fit with the traditional view of Aeschylus as a showman. I have criticized in §4 the usual view that Aeschylus introduced gratuitous spectacle on to the stage for its own sake. Here the tented wagon would not only be pointless, it would positively detract and distract from the stylized visual presentation of the fall of Persia, and would spoil Xerxes' entry (see 909b* below). Broadhead, who does at least try to give the spectacle some point, captures the contradiction (p. 223 n. 2): 'the gorgeous affair would here only serve to enhance the wretchedness of the King's appearance'. But it would ruin the total effect. Aeschylus has made positive use of fine spectacle in the play, especially for the Queen's first entry and for Darius: but the final scene positively contrasts with these.

(b) preparation and significance: βαιά γ' ὡc ἀπὸ πολλῶν

The entry of Xerxes is far more than a stage direction. Seen in its full dramatic context one man embodies the ruin of a nation, his few paces the disaster of retreat. It should be clear to any

[1] The text is uncertain, but there can be little doubt about the run of the sense. (The paradosis is senseless, as is shown by Young's defence of it in *GRBS* 13 (1972) 17.)

[2] Wilamowitz *ed maj* seems *ex silentio* to have rejected it. I have noted more explicit rejections in P. Richter 106, Haigh *AT*³ 201 n. 1, Rose 158.

reader, let alone spectator, that Xerxes puts the defeat in visible
and immediate terms. Perhaps it is because the point is so obvious
that so few scholars have actually made it.[1] What are the dramatic
and theatrical techniques through which Aeschylus aspires to
such an ambitious effect?

The immediate impact and significance of Xerxes' entry are
made clear by the visual presentation. But this only works because
of the way it fits into the larger dramatic context, and that is
largely a product of the *preparation* for the entry (cf. Dingel
112f.). First, *Pers* is an example of a form or pattern of plot
which is recurrent in Greek drama: it is what might be called
a 'νόϲτοϲ' play. In such plays a 'hero' returns from some mission
or expedition; he may return safely to some catastrophe at
home, or may (as here) return from a catastrophe. His first
entry is bound to be a central event, and so tends to be the object
of considerable dramatic preparation and attention. If we adapt
Lattimore's term 'story pattern', then we may speak of story
pattern entries (or exits), which are bound to be an important
stage element in the dramatization of recurrent plot forms.[2] In
this case the most influential archetype seems to have been, not
so much the epic Νόϲτοι,[3] but (as with ἀναγνώριϲιϲ and μηχάνημα)
the *Odyssey*. We cannot be sure that there had been any *nostos*
plays before *Pers*, though it is more than likely that there had
been;[4] in any case the formative pattern is made amply clear
in *Pers*, even without a precedent. The most straightforward
examples among other surviving tragedies are A. *Ag*, S. *Tr*, and
E. *Her*. There are also elements of the plot pattern in the plays
of return and revenge (notably A. *Cho*, S. *El*, E. *El*); and we may
detect a diluted version of the returning hero and his entry in
the Euripidean 'tyrants', who are away on a mission and expected
back.[5]

[1] Notably Wecklein 72, Lesky *TDH*[2] 62, Jens 248.
[2] Story pattern entrances and exits are given some attention in Strohm and
Burnett on Euripides; cf. also Aichele ch. 4 (42ff., not made explicit in the summary in *Bauformen* 47ff.).
[3] Pearson *Soph. Fragments* i p. xxxi lists eleven plays of Sophocles derived from
the Νόϲτοι, but few if any of them seem to have centred on the actual arrival home.
[4] The obvious precedent is the '*Persai*' play of Phrynichus (cf. p. 63 n. 2 above);
also possibly A. *Salaminiai*.
[5] e.g. Theseus in *Hipp*, the local tyrant in *Hel* and *IT*; cf. also Teucer in S. *Aj*
and Polyphemus in E. *Cycl*. In E. *Andr* Neoptolemus is constantly expected back,
but returns only as a corpse. It is possible that the tyrant Lycurgus returned in

The *nostos* pattern and the preparation for the return of Xerxes are established at the very beginning, as soon as the chorus has identified itself: (8–11) ἀμφὶ δὲ νόστωι τῶι βασιλείωι / καὶ πολυ-χρύcου cτρατιᾶc ἤδη / κακόμαντιc ἄγαν ὀρcολοπεῖται / θυμὸc ἔcωθεν. Disquiet over the fortunes of the absent hero (and army) point towards his return (cf. S. *Tr*, E. *Her*). Although the first song goes on to elaborate the distress of those at home, it is chiefly concerned with the departure of Xerxes and the Persian host. As in *Ag* the departure implies the return, and the audience should sense that the return will come within the play and will somehow complement the setting-out. The next scene (150ff.) begins with a dialogue between the chorus and the Queen, who are concerned about those who are absent; and after that there arrives an advance messenger with news (see 249a*). There is precisely the same structure in *Ag* (see *Ag* 783a*) and in S. *Tr* (in E. *Her* the return must remain a kind of surprise). While the Herald in *Pers* is chiefly concerned with events which occurred some time before, none the less he also traces the journey of Xerxes from these events back to Asia. First we learn that he survived (299), then that he fled (465ff.), and in his last rhesis (480ff., cf. *Ag* 636ff.) the Messenger covers the journey home, and concludes, without naming Xerxes, that a remnant has reached the homeland (510f.). Were lines 529–31 in their right place then they would serve to make the audience think that the entry of Xerxes is even more imminent than it is in fact; but see 528*.[1]

In the following song (532ff.), which is mainly concerned with the past and the dead, the chorus make the connection implied by the Messenger when they sing (564–7) that even the King has only just escaped. One of the features which distinguish the advance messenger and the entry he heralds in *Pers* is the major act and plot development which intervenes between the two (cf.

E. *Hyps*, see Bond *ed* 16f., 19. But it is hard to see what part there is for him to play. He should not be introduced after fr. 65 l. 111, since there is no room in an already over-long play, and there are already three speaking actors (cf. Burnett *CPh* 1965 p. 130). The heavy father of New Comedy, who is absent for the first acts of the play, seems in turn to be a descendant of these tragic prototypes; e.g. in Men. *Sam*, *Dysc*; Pl. *Most*, Ter. *Phormio*.

[1] Broadhead displays characteristic literal-mindedness when he says in connection with 529–31 (p. xxxvii) 'up to this point nothing has been said about Xerxes' possible arrival'.

249a*). In the Darius scene, the preparation for the entry of Xerxes is lightly but carefully handled. In the introductory dialogue Darius learns (734–8) that Xerxes has survived and reached Asia; but his arrival still seems remote. As the scene progresses Darius' ignorance is replaced by a virtual omniscience, factual and moral, about both the past and the future. So when at the end (832ff.) he tells the Queen to meet Xerxes with new clothes, he is unquestionably right that Xerxes is near enough home to be met. This is reinforced by the Queen's speech of obedience (845ff.), particularly if 529–31 are transposed to follow 851: Xerxes is so near that the Queen may not be in time to meet him.

Aeschylus makes the contrast between Darius and Xerxes very striking. The father is stately, wise, resigned to the justice of the gods: the son is abandoned to lachrymose and indiscriminate lament, his despair is total and immediate, without moral or theological depth, and in appearance he is wretched and degraded. Darius was secure and successful: Xerxes rash and disastrous. The transition is made and the antithesis pointed by the intervening song (852ff.). While the main body of it dwells on the extent and security of Darius' empire, it is framed by the bitter contrast of 861–3 νόστοι δ' ἐκ πολέμων ἀπόνους ἀπαθεῖς / ⟨αὖθις ἐς⟩ εὖ πράσσοντας ἆγον οἴκους (text uncertain, sense clear) and by the final sentence 904–8, introduced by νῦν δέ.[1] The emphasis of the song is put on the foil, the past, because the present reversal is about to be put before our very eyes.

With the entry of Xerxes much of the play up to this point takes on a new sense and direction; or, rather, much that has been heard again and again is seen to have a direct bearing on the King, once he is actually before our eyes. His robes are in tatters. So the wealth and ceremony of the Queen's first entry are shattered;[2] and the dignity and decorum of her second entry and of Darius are lost. The authority and the prosperity of the monarchy and of Persia are irreparably impaired. All this is conveyed by his robes. Then Xerxes is alone. The many-citied empire of Darius (fourth song) supplied the huge host which set

[1] For this transitional formula see Kranz 164ff. (cf. 204ff., 251); see also *Seven* 854c*.
[2] Note the recurrence of the rare word πρόσφθογγος (153) in 935 πρόσφθογγόν coι νόστου κτλ.

out (first song), and it has been left behind at the scene of carnage (302ff. and second song). Xerxes has emptied his cities and
lost his army. And he is on foot. This contrasts with all the horses
and chariots of the first song, and shows how he has been thrown
to the ground after trying to yoke excessive wealth, the sea, and
the continent of Europe (see p. 78 above). At the same time
Xerxes' steps bring to mind the terrible retreat reported in
480ff. and remembered at 564ff., 734ff., and, by contrast, 861ff.
The paces which Xerxes makes on entry are the final paces of
that retreat; the retreat, all in the same tatters, leads back to
the carnage at Salamis.

It may be clear now why I was at pains to establish the visual
picture. In its full dramatic context the appearance of Xerxes is
not ridiculous or squalid; it is the embodiment of the disaster
which has struck Persia. And because it is so charged with
meaning it is genuinely moving. Even the empty quiver of 1020ff.
is not in its context a cheap laugh; it symbolizes the way that
Persia has been emptied, it is βαιά γ᾽ ὡς ἀπὸ πολλῶν (1023, cf.
Dingel 112, 177). The many significances of the initial presentation of Xerxes now supply the subject-matter of the extended
laments which close the play. The laments are extravagant and
indulgent, but the audience is not meant to stand outside them
with an attitude of smirking and self-righteous scorn. Aeschylus
has surely, made the uninhibited pathos irresistibly powerful.[1]
The audience should feel for and experience the well-deserved
but none the less terrible and moving fall of Persia.

1077 exeunt Xerxes and chorus

processional ending

Some sort of procession makes an obvious close to a drama with
a chorus. This device is used in four of Aeschylus' plays, several
of Sophocles' and Euripides', and almost always in Aristophanes
(cf. Spitzbarth 51f.). In many cases, as here, the chorus escorts
an actor from the stage; see further *Eum* 1047c*. Xerxes evidently goes at the front of the procession (though it may be that
the *auletes* preceded him).[2]

---

[1] For a long-winded and heavy-handed, but none the less effective, rebuttal of
the view that *Pers* is mere jingoism dressed up as poetry see Kitto *Poiesis* (Berkeley
1966) 74–106.

[2] A scholion on Ar. *Wasps* 582 says that after a tragedy the chorus usually

The procession is going to the δόμοι (1038, 1069). These might be the houses of the Elders or the royal palace; but in view of the constant indications of the proximity of the palace and particularly because of προπέμπετ' ἐc δόμουc in 530 (after 851?, see 528*) I take it that we are meant to think of the royal palace. This is not, of course, represented by a visible building, see pp. 107, 454; it is off down one of the eisodoi, as is further indicated by κατ' ἄcτυ in 1071. This was duly noted by Bodensteiner and the others who first established that actors and chorus were not rigidly segregated in the fifth-century theatre. It was also used, with justification, as an argument against any raised stage; see pp. 441f. Even if there was a raised area for *Pers*, Xerxes would surely not have mounted it: the choreography of the antiphonal dirges and of the procession should be arranged around the actor. The first preparation for the final formation comes back at 1038, but otherwise it comes together in the final epode (1066ff.); and it looks as though the processional movement was begun at or soon after 1066.

This procession, unlike those e.g. at *Hik* 1073* or *Eum* 1047*, is not grand and honorific. Rather, Xerxes' total involvement in the procession, as in the lament, shows him as a shattered man, sharing the humiliation and despair of his citizens. He has none of the authority and aloofness of his parents. The procession also suggests, perhaps, the final exhaustion of the lamentation: even in defeat life at home must go on.

followed the αὐλητής—ὥcτε αὐλοῦντα προπέμπειν. Whatever the meaning of the final lines of *Wasps* (1335–7), they cannot be saying that it is unprecedented for the chorus to go off dancing (as the scholia and some editors, including MacDowell, take it). It is, rather, something to do with the extraordinary dancing of the actors; see further Vaio *GRBS* 12 (1971) 348–51.

III. SEVEN AGAINST THEBES

1 enter citizens

enter Eteocles (attended)

(a) *the citizens and 'audience participation'*[1]

THIS is one of a fairly small group of places in Greek tragedy where a 'crowd' of silent citizens is brought into play to supplicate or witness, to be addressed, told to go, etc. There is a growing tendency to suppose that groups of this kind were not actually represented by mute extras, but that the audience was supposed to identify itself with the crowd within the play. This is part of a larger attempt to find 'audience participation' in Greek tragedy, and is without doubt tied up with the movement to audience participation in the modern theatre, where this is part of larger notions about the nature and function of the theatre as a social activity. Since the Greek theatre was a social activity in a much broader way than the present-day theatre, it is inevitable that critics who follow the fashion should detect traces of audience participation in it. I shall try below to assess this trend in general, but shall first consider this particular instance.

It is alleged that it is the audience which Eteocles addresses as Κάδμου πολῖται in the opening speech of the play. Calder, who argues from the similar opening of S. *OT*, does invoke the methods of the modern theatre; Rose, however, does not use this argument, but says simply that he knows of 'no evidence that a choregus was put to such expense for παραχορηγήματα as this [a crowd of extras] would involve'.[2] But there are silent extras all over the place in Greek tragedy, as was pointed out on *Pers* 155c*. At

[1] I have at the last minute added references to David Bain's excellent article 'Audience Address in Greek Tragedy', *CQ* 25 (1975) 13–25.

[2] Calder *Phoenix* 13 (1959) 121ff. esp. 125, Rose p. 162; followed by Arnott *tr* 83, Dawson *tr* 29, Petre *Stud. Clas.* 13 (1971) 16 n. 5. I find, however, that the suggestion is already in Stephenson 50 n. 84, 54; and that Murray wrote in the margin of p. 60 of his copy of Wilamowitz *Interpretationen* (in the Ashmolean Museum Library) 'the audience?' Cf. Bain p. 22 n. 1.

least four will be needed later in this very play to carry the corpses of the brothers, and Eteocles should be attended throughout (cf. p. 156 below). Are we to suppose that the bodyguard sent with Danaus at *Hik* 503 or the henchmen of Aegisthus at *Ag* 1649ff. were represented by the audience because the choregus could not afford the extras? Rose presumably supposes that any crowd would have to be realistically numerous, as they are sometimes in modern opera houses or national theatres: but, in fact, few theatres have ever supplied more than a representative handful for crowd scenes, and I would guess that there were something between three and a maximum of twelve extras here.[1]

And there is a positive objection to audience address here: Eteocles dispatches the citizens to the ramparts at 30ff. It would be difficult enough for the spectators to equate themselves so abruptly with the Cadmeans on the point of battle. Even if they were to succeed in this, what are they to do at 30ff.? Sit there helpless? Comparably, what are the audience-suppliants to do at S. *OT* 142ff., when they are told to arise and depart? Besides, *Seven* has much to do with Eteocles' role as leader and with the relation of the fate of the city to the fate of the royal family; and so the male fighting citizens should be visibly represented, and their dependence on Eteocles' command should be seen in deed.

So I hope to have shown that there is no specific reason to suppose audience address here, and positive arguments against it. Any such suggestion must, then, rest on a wider theory about audience participation in the theatre. I shall contend briefly that the notion is as alien to Greek tragedy as it is essential to Old Comedy. We must start from a couple of theoretical points. First, there is, of course, a real sense in which the audience does participate, in that the play is addressed to it. Every word is meant for the ears of the audience, it is all for their benefit; and the audience must contribute its attention, sympathy, understanding, and appreciation, for if it does not participate in that sense the whole business is a waste of time. But all this is quite different from what is under consideration here, which is whether

---

[1] The Elizabethan theatre similarly made do with token crowds. Cf. e.g. Sidney *An Apology for Poetry* (*Elizabethan Critical Essays* ed. G. G. Smith (Oxford 1950) p. 197) esp. 'while in the meantime two Armies flye in, represented with foure swords and bucklers, and then what harde heart will not receive it for a pitched fielde?'

Greek tragedy ever *explicitly* refers to or recognizes the existence of the world of the audience. Secondly, the question of who is being addressed in a play is a matter of dramatic technique and not of mundane realism. In real life who is being spoken to is a matter of the speaker's intention (who hears is a matter of acoustics) : on stage the speaker's unexpressed intention is necessarily inaccessible, and the addressee must be picked out by a vocative or a gesture or by the run of the words and action.[1]

If this is right, then, if the audience is to be directly (as opposed to implicitly) addressed, there should be a vocative or at least a clear gesture in its direction. So it is important that there is not one single instance in Greek tragedy of a vocative to the audience, θεαταί, ἄνδρες, or the like.[2] Without a vocative, a definite gesture towards the auditorium would be required in those places where audience address is alleged ; and since on any account such places are not common, a gesture of this kind would be very striking, and should be expected only in crucially significant contexts. But in the most widely accepted claims the context is comparatively unexceptional and the second-person verb, if there is one, is distinctly casual.[3] In fact I have not encountered one single case where we must suppose that the audience is directly addressed ; and every alleged instance I know of seems to be easily explicable as a paraenetic second person or simple colloquial idiom.[4] Now, to claim that there are hardly any instances of a device is not to prove that there are none: a very rare device may still be used for special effect. None the less, if there is, as it happens, not one single instance in surviving tragedy, then that does suggest that the whole concept was alien to fifth-century tragedy.

[1] As to who hears, it must be assumed that everyone on stage hears, unless there is some clear indication to the contrary, as e.g. at E. *Hec* 736ff. Obscurity is still hard to avoid in such circumstances as e.g. S. *Phil* 573ff.

[2] The most plausible claim for audience address is at A. *Eum* 681ff. (not mentioned by Bain) ; and there the citizens addressed are at least Athenian, unlike in *Seven*. But even that instance is unacceptable, see pp. 394–5.

[3] I have in mind, for example, A. *Ag* 39 (see Fraenkel ad loc., Bain 18), E. *Tro* 36 (already in *Σ*, cf. Schadewaldt *Monolog* 10 n. 1, Bain 19), *Andr* 622f. (in *Σ*, but cf. Schadewaldt 129 n. 1, Stevens *ed* ad loc.), *Or* 128 (in *Σ*, but see Fraenkel, cited in next note, and Bain 19–21).

[4] e.g. S. *Aj* 1028 (see Bain 18–19), *Tro* 1079f. ; E. *Hec* 549, *Phoen* 1676, *Andr* 950, *Or* 804. For more detailed discussion Leo 31f., Schadewaldt 129 n. 1, Fraenkel *Phoen* 111–12, Bain *passim*. Some unnecessary complication has been made by the rigid application of the question 'who is this addressed to?' ; for in many theatrical contexts, most notably in prologues and choral songs, the question does

The situation in tragedy is brought out by the contrast with Old Comedy, where it was perfectly in order to refer to the audience and to address it directly. Usually there is a vocative; otherwise a clear second-person or deictic pronoun, which was no doubt accompanied by appropriate gesture and movement.[1] While there is a sense in which one can speak of 'dramatic illusion' in comedy it is worlds apart from that of tragedy.[2] One of the fundamental features of Old Comedy is the flexible relationship which is set up between the fantasy world of the comedy and the contemporary world of the spectators. Constantly in different ways and in different degrees the barrier between the two worlds is touched, breached, or swept aside; and in the parabasis the comic world fully invades the world of the audience. In tragedy, on the other hand, the audience is never addressed or alluded to, the world of the play never makes direct or specific contact with the world of the auditorium, the barrier is never broken.

Finally I shall very briefly touch on two important topics which are closely allied with that of audience address. Nowhere

not really arise. This misleading rigour led Leo 8 n. 1 to the concept of 'gedachte Hörer', taken up by Fraenkel in *Mus. Helv.* 24 (1967) 190ff. But who imagines the hearers? If the audience does, then, as Schadewaldt points out (*Monolog* 10 n. 2), it must suppose itself to be the hearers: but the question does not arise in the first place.

[1] For illustration see e.g. *GGL* i 4 p. 47 n. 2, Sifakis *Parabasis and Animal Choruses* (London 1971) 11f. with notes. (Incidentally Dover is, one suspects, anachronistic on Ar. *Clouds* 1104: 'Right . . . bounds out of the orchestra into the audience'.) In New Comedy audience address is also regular, though less common; cf. Dedoussi on Men. *Sam* 54 (old numeration), Handley on *Dysc* 1, 194, Gomme–Sandbach p. 14. There does not seem to be audience address in fifth-century satyr play, but I have noted a possible fourth-century example in Astydamas' *Heracles TrGF* 60 F 4, if Athenaeus' attribution is right; but one cannot but suspect that the line comes from an old comedy, cf. Bain 23–5.

[2] See in general Görler *A and A* 18 (1973) 41ff. (with relevant literature cited there). The first chapter of Sifakis's book (see previous note) is very disappointing on this aspect. Sifakis not only wishes to break down any distinction in audience relationship between the parabasis and the rest of the comedy, thus monotonizing an always varying tension, but he absurdly denies any difference between comedy and tragedy with regard to 'dramatic illusion'. The root of his error is that he equates 'dramatic illusion' with long-outmoded notions of 'realistic illusionism' which are so obviously inappropriate to Greek tragedy and comedy alike as to be irrelevant. The twentieth-century theatre has brought everyone (except it seems some classical scholars) into contact with many other kinds of 'dramatic illusion' besides the photographic realism of the late nineteenth century. (Cf. along the same lines Rau *Gnomon* 42 (1970) 91f., Bain 13 n. 1.)

in Greek tragedy are there, in my view, specific references to the theatre. This makes a telling contrast with nearly all other dramatic traditions, where the literal and figurative use of the language and associations of the theatre provides a curious and often very effective means of exploiting the frailty of dramatic illusion; this includes Old Comedy where theatrical terminology and allusions are ubiquitous.[1] A kind of exception in Greek tragedy must be made for the places where tragedians, particularly Euripides, allude implicitly to an earlier dramatization, usually in order to diverge from it. But these allusions are, on the whole, unobtrusive and well worked into their contexts, and the audience (as opposed to scholars) was not allowed to dwell on them.[2] The chorus does frequently refer to its own singing and dancing (cf. Kranz 137ff., 182ff., Kaimio 102), but, given the entire convention of the chorus, I do not see that that should put the audience in mind of the 'fact' that the chorus members are their own fellow citizens dressed up.[3] Nor can I see any 'anachronism' in Greek tragedy which is meant to be noted explicitly as an anachronism. Of course there are manifold contemporary elements in Greek tragedies, but they are all incorporated into the dramatic world of the play. They are there because the play is meant for a contemporary audience (not a Bronze Age audience). But they do not impair the unbroken division between the world of the play and that of the audience.

Secondly, this should have some bearing on the old controversy about allusions to contemporary politics and current

---

[1] Even more so in Shakespeare whose plays are full of theatrical allusion; see A. Righter *Shakespeare and the Idea of the Play* (London 1962). (She is wrong, however, to claim on pp. 44f. that this aspect of Aristophanes' practice differed between earlier and later plays.)

[2] Some of these are well discussed by Winnington-Ingram *Arethusa* 2 (1969) 129ff., cf. Bain 14 n. 1. I am doubtful about E. *Hel* 1056 παλαιότης γὰρ κτλ: is Helen's plan corny? I tend to favour Hermann's emendation ἀπαιόλη γὰρ . . . Incidentally I do not regard words like κομμός (A. *Cho* 423) or ἐπείσοδος (S. *OC* 730) as evoking technical connotations, any more than, say, σκηνή used in a military context; cf. Bain 13 n. 4.

[3] It is often claimed, for example, that S. *OT* 896 (τί δεῖ με χορεύειν;) is a theatrical reference; but χορεύειν carries the general association of observing religious ritual—cf. Lloyd-Jones *Zeus* 110. Likewise it is claimed, e.g. by Wilamowitz E. *Her ed* ii p. 149, Kranz 184, that at E. *Her* 637ff. the chorus is referring to itself as performers in the theatre: yet they themselves sing that they are old men singing before the doors of Heracles' palace (cf. Kaimio 102f., who also shows that the first person singular cannot be identified with the poet, as it can in comedy). Bain is good on this topic: p. 16 esp. n. 2.

affairs. For, if on a more formal level no direct acknowledgement is made of the existence of the audience, then we should be wary of hunting out any sort of *direct* reference to contemporary affairs. Of course the intellectual and political issues raised in the tragedies are topical, but that is far from allowing any kind of direct correspondence or anything with a direct bearing on one specific issue or personality. The search for topical allusions in Greek tragedy depends on the initial assumption by the critic or historian that the audience was predisposed to expect and look for such things. If, unlike comedy, tragedy contains no examples of audience address and no theatrical references, then we might well expect that in tragedy, unlike comedy, the audience did not look for any kind of specific political content.

(b) the 'cancelled entry' of the citizens

The play begins with a kind of tableau: Eteocles exhorts a gathering of Theban defenders. Probably the citizens were gathered before Eteocles entered, just as in the strikingly similar opening to S. *OT* the suppliants were probably in position before Oedipus entered. The stage directions in most commentaries and translations speak as though the tableau somehow miraculously materializes all ready arranged.[1] In practical terms, however, the citizens must have walked on and arranged themselves at some stage of the proceedings. Since the stage management of 'tableau' openings is a recurrent problem it may as well be faced here.

Most scholars, as I say, imply that the tableau simply materialized. In their more mundane moments they tend to suggest that it was already in position long before the play began, or even before the audience arrived (thus expressly Bieber *Entrances* 278 on S. *OT*). But not every play with a tableau opening can have been the first of the day: *Seven* was not, E. *Tro* almost certainly was not (see didaskalia), and some comedies also use the device. More sensibly, we might suppose simply that the tableau took up position quite a long time before the play began (say ten minutes?).[2] This is possible, but since in some cases the characters

[1] e.g. Wilamowitz *ed maj actio* on l. 1, Murray *tr* p. 27, Werner *tr* p. 341, Untersteiner *tr* p. 13.

[2] Thus, notably, Wilamowitz 56ff. It may be true that 'Die stumme Handlung macht Stimmung'; but how long is needed for this?

in the tableau are to be supposed to have been in position long before the play began, hours or even days, there seems no point in holding the tableau for minutes rather than seconds before the play began.

Some have been unable to accept that a character who is supposed to have been in position for a long time should be seen to enter; and they have to fall back on some sort of revelation, most commonly a curtain.[1] But, as most admit, there is no evidence for a curtain until much later—and we might have expected some evidence, particularly from comedy. There is not even anything to hang the curtain from or between. Occasionally recourse has been had, rather, to the ekkyklema.[2] But this cannot have been used in all instances, not e.g. in *Ag*, E. *Or*, or Ar. *Wasps*; and if it is once admitted that the convention of the 'cancelled' entry was used in some cases, then there is no ground for denying that it was used in all. In any case the ekkyklema was normally used for revelations (see p. 442); at the beginning of a play there is no revelation, only a presentation.

Once it is acknowledged that we are not dealing with a naturalistic conventional theatre, the tangles of these alternatives are simply cut through. The convention was that the playwright might make it clear that the first entry did not take place within the play, and should be erased, so to speak. Alternatively it might transpire that the entry did represent an arrival *within* the play. Thus, we have the positive evidence of Aristophanes that Aeschylus' Niobe came on and sat down, although she was to be thought of as having already sat there for two days. Even without this corroboration, the convention has been widely recognized, though with some uneasiness.[3]

I have already discussed the Aeschylean examples of the convention in my article in *HSCP* 76 (1972).[4] In S. *OT* the situation

---

[1] e.g. D–R 251ff., Bethe 186ff., Weissmann *Aufführung* 33ff., Rees *CPh* 10 (1915) 132ff. (Rees's whole theory is refuted at length by P-C *TDA* 75ff.).

[2] e.g. Séchan 587, Dale *Papers* 114, 121. Wilamowitz 56 n. 1 seems to envisage an interior scene descried through the open doors in E. *Tro, Or*, Ar. *Wasps*; but this is impracticable as well as unnecessary.

[3] The most straightforward discussion is that of Spitzbarth 40ff. (she coins the phrase 'inoffizielles Auftreten'). But the topic is already discussed back in A. Müller 166–70; cf. Haigh *AT*³ 219f. (leaves question open), Flickinger 243f. (reluctant, only mentions *Or, Clouds*), P-C *TDA* 80, 128ff. (shows discomfort), Arnott 129f. (only *OT, Or, Clouds, Wasps*), Hourmouziades *Ἑλληνικά* 1968 p. 264.

[4] *Niobe* (61ff.), *Myrm* (64–9), *Ag* (62 and n. 15), and *Prom Lyom* (62 n. 16).

is similar to *Seven*, except that the 'citizens' are suppliants, and they sit (2, 15); it is left vague how long they have been there. This is not unlike the favourite Euripidean opening which 'discovers' characters in a suppliant tableau at an altar, usually sitting; in Euripides too it is left vague how long the supplication had been in progress before the play began. The technique of 'cancelled' first entry is used in this way in *Hkld* (Iolaus and the boys), *Andr*, *Her* (Megara, Amphitryon, and the sons), *Hel*, and *Hik* (not only the grandchildren, Adrastus, and Aethra but also the silent chorus of mothers—a unique variation). In *Tro* Hecuba must have 'entered' and taken up her position of prostrate grief; in *Or* Orestes is supposed to have been lying sick for five days while Electra watches over him (34ff. esp. 39), yet before the play proper began Electra would have walked on, and Orestes too unless he was wheeled on.[1] Aristophanes seems to have used exactly the same convention. In *Ach*, *Lys*, and *Ekkl* a character has been waiting some time for others to arrive. In *Clouds* Strepsiades and Phidippides are in bed, nearing the end of a bad night; they may have been wheeled on, or may have pushed on their own beds. In *Wasps* the two slaves are before the house, and Bdelycleon asleep on the roof; all must have 'entered', yet they are supposed to have been on guard all night.

To return finally to *Seven*, the citizens are not presumably to be supposed to have been waiting long for Eteocles. However, there is no positive pointer to their arrival, and the audience would, in the absence of any indication otherwise, have regarded their entry as 'cancelled', and have supposed that the gathering was 'discovered' as a tableau at the beginning of the play.

35 exeunt citizens

timing

Eteocles gives his actual instructions to the citizens in 30ff., and finishes in 35 with εὖ τελεῖ θεός. He then turns away from them to his own strategic concerns with σκοποὺς δὲ κἀγώ κτλ. It is com-

[1] E. *Andromeda*, like A. *Prom Lyom* (see p. 425), poses a special problem, since the character is not only 'discovered' in position, but is bound there. It may be that Andromeda was bound ready in position before the eyes of the spectators, who were then required to cancel the binding. (Neither of the two prologues of *IA* seems to call for this convention *contra* Willink *CQ* N.S. 21 (1971) 347 and n. 4.) Men. *Synaristosai* may have opened with the tableau of the three women at the dining table (cf. *Entr. Hardt* xvi (1969) 35ff. esp. 39).

mon, not surprisingly, for one character after the exit of some
other character(s) to turn to new affairs with a δέ, often preceded with a first- or second-person pronoun.[1] It seems clear, as
Wilamowitz (p. 60) pointed out, that the citizens' part is over at
l. 35, and that they should immediately set about going off. Yet
most commentators do not put the stage instruction here, but
after 38,[2] or—much worse—after 77.[3] It may be that they feel
that 36–8 must be addressed to someone, hence to the citizens;
but in such contexts we need not ask who the lines are addressed
to (cf. p. 131 n. 4). It is rather similar at *Eum* 232–4 when, after
the exit lines of the chorus, Apollo has three lines beginning ἐγὼ
δ' ἀρήξω, which do not allow the question to arise. With stage
directions like this one in *Seven* most commentators have simply
followed their predecessors without thought. But when dealing
with a playwright who produced and acted his own plays and
who took no less trouble over stage action than over his words
some thought should be given to such details.

39 enter Scout

'lupus in fabula'

After the dispatch of the citizens Eteocles has the three lines
ϲκοποὺϲ δὲ κἀγὼ καὶ κατοπτῆραϲ ϲτρατοῦ / ἔπεμψα, τοὺϲ πέποιθα μὴ
ματᾶν ὁδῶι· / καὶ τῶνδ' ἀκούϲαϲ οὔ τι μὴ ληφθῶ δόλωι (36–8). Then
without further ado a ϲκοπόϲ-κατοπτήρ enters. There is no sign
like a deictic pronoun to show that Eteocles is supposed to have
seen the Scout before he enters; and so this is a kind of preparation
rather than an announcement.[4] In drama people often turn up
just as thoughts turn to them. The device provides preparation,
saves awkward explanations, and suggests that there is a certain
rightness and appropriateness in the way that events are falling
out. Joerden 90 speaks in this context of 'der dramatischen
Zuspitzung der Handlung'. So here we feel that affairs are firmly
in Eteocles' control. Although it is not the case here, playwrights

[1] Cf. in Aeschylus alone *Hik* 505, *Ag* 352 (see 350*), 1069, *Eum* 232; *Hik* 954,
Ag 617 (probably not however *Cho* 716, see 718*).

[2] e.g. Bodensteiner 728, Sidgwick 3, Wilamowitz *ed maj* 80 (inconsistent with
Interpretationen), Groeneboom 88, Tucker 17, Murray *tr*, 'Droysen' *tr*, Werner *tr*.

[3] e.g. Sidgwick xvi, p. 1 (inconsistent with p. 3), Smyth 329, Mazon 113,
Verrall 148, Vellacott *tr* 90, Schadewaldt *tr* 53.

[4] We might agree with Wilamowitz (p. 60) that the speech 'klappt doch etwas
nach' but not that it is an 'Ankündigung'.

often show some self-consciousness over this simple but useful device: often in Greek tragedy and comedy there is a phrase which draws attention to the opportuneness of the entry—see 371a* below.[1]

There is a distinction to be made among these 'talk of the devil' entries. In the more common variety the subject of a certain person or class of persons is brought up without any particular suggestion of an imminent arrival; the character then enters. This is too common to need illustration. Here in *Seven* we have the rarer and comparatively plain device by which a certain character is actually expected and then duly turns up. The only other instance in Aeschylus seems to be Danaus' entry at *Hik* 980. He has just been mentioned (968ff., 979), yet his entry is apparently independent of this (but on the problems of this part of the play see *Hik* 974a*). There are two strikingly similar places in S. *OT*: at 68ff. Creon turns up when expected, and so does Tiresias at 284ff.[2] But the device is not common elsewhere in tragedy (there are examples of a sort at E. *El* 758ff., *Ba* 1211ff., *IA* 1098ff.). It belongs more to the sphere of comedy, where wishes come true and where there is more room for deliberate play on the coincidences of fiction.[3] Here in *Seven*, however, while the technique is simple, I do not see that it is in any way laughable or clumsy. Indeed the precision of the military discipline and Eteocles' control over it are rather well conveyed by means of this device.

The Scout's contribution is of the greatest simplicity. He has a single rhesis bounded by his entry and his exit, and there is no dialogue of any sort. He gives his news and returns to his post without delay. Other examples of the rare phenomenon of single-rhesis appearances, possibly an archaic technique, are discussed

[1] There is some amusing play at Ter. *Ad* 537 where Ctesiphon and Syrus are talking about Demea: '*Syr*: . . . em tibi autem. *Ct*: quid namst? *Syr*: lupus in fabula. *Ct*: pater est? *Syr*: ipsest (the precise reference of 'lupus in fabula' is obscure, see Dziatzko-Kauer ad loc. and Jocelyn *Mnem* (1971) 24 pp. 90f.). Cf. Shakespeare *Lear* I. ii. 140ff. 'Edgar—and pat he comes, like the catastrophe of the old comedy.'

[2] The prologue of *OT* may be directly influenced by *Seven*, see above; for further similarities and differences see Kopperschmidt in *Bauformen* 344f. The entries of Creon and Tiresias in *OT* may be deliberately similar. In both cases the keenness and thoroughness of Oedipus' search is shown: but while he is pleased with the clear and impersonal oracle from Delphi, he is less happy with the more enigmatic and less impersonal contribution of Tiresias.

[3] A few examples: Ar. *Birds* 1121, 1269, *Knights* 146, *Frogs* 170; Men. *Dysc* 78. Some examples from Roman comedy are collected by Harms 30-2.

on *Ag* 614*. Here the Scout's function is to give Eteocles the strategic situation. He does this in large and vivid language which finely conveys the threat of the attackers. But it is not his part to respond to the news; that is for Eteocles, and then the chorus. Although the abruptness of the Scout's part makes this a simply structured prologue, it is by no means the simplest possible. Prologues were already quite highly developed in the tragedy of this time (see *Pers* 1a*).

68 exit Scout

77 exit Eteocles

does Eteocles go ?

Nearly everyone sends Eteocles off during the first song (parodos, 78–180), rightly. However, he speaks the last line before the song and the first line after it, and there is no explicit indication (a verb of motion for example) to prove that he went off. There have been those who have supposed that Eteocles remained silent and unnoticed throughout the song.[1] While most exits and entrances in Greek tragedy are clearly marked and left in no doubt, there are still many places where there is room for uncertainty. These problems particularly tend to occur when a character is on stage before and after a choral song, and it is unclear whether he stays on or goes off and returns. In such cases one has to weigh all the implicit evidence in the text and bring to bear any relevant conventions. The case is seldom evenly balanced, though certainty (for what it is worth) is rarely attainable. In this case there is, however, in my view little room for doubt that Eteocles did go off and re-enter.

Apart from the lack of explicit indication, which is not significant, I have seen only one positive argument for keeping Eteocles on. Dignan (p. 20) points out that Eteocles goes avowedly to post defenders at the gates at 286, and that this was what the Scout advised at 57f. So he claims that Eteocles cannot have been off-stage between 57f. and 286. This raises the whole problem of the relation of lines 282–6 to the great central scene,

---

[1] Dignan 20, Graeber 42, Flickinger 230, Spitzbarth 76, Schmidt *Bauformen* 11 n. 45; *ex silentio* Headlam *tr*, Grene *tr*.

on which see 286* and 371d*; but on a more general level
Dignan's argument neglects the way that in *Seven* strategical and
chronological considerations are distorted beyond any realism.[1]
The sequence of the battle off-stage is compressed and stretched
at will to suit the intensification and relaxation of the tension on-
stage. The Argive host is advancing at 59ff., its approach and
arrival are vividly evoked in the first song, the storming of the
walls is in progress at 245ff. and is taken up in the second song:
yet Eteocles does not go off to battle until 719. The Argive
champions are casting lots at 55f., and have been assigned gates
by 123ff.; Eteocles is told to post Theban champions at 57f., he
says he is about to do so at 282ff., and he does so in the great
central scene. He finally goes to his own post at 719. All this cannot be sorted out in realistic terms; it must be seen in dramatic
terms. The play is conceived around the central scene of the
seven pairs of speeches and its aftermath. Before that Aeschylus
wants, among other things, to evoke the violent threat of the
battle and to prepare for the sending of the seven Thebans to face
the seven Argives. So in his exit lines at 69–77 Eteocles does not
say precisely what he is going off to do; it is still too soon to
resume the preparation of the Scout in 57f.

The implicit evidence of the text points to an exit and re-entry.
The prologue is directed towards action, and its tone throughout
has been urgent (note e.g. 31, 59, 65). The General has ex-
horted and dispatched the citizens and his Scout has reported
urgently and efficiently; he cannot now do nothing himself.
Moreover, Aeschylus builds up a contrast between the calm
control of the warrior Eteocles and the thoughtless panic of
the fearful women of the chorus. This contrast is not helped if
Eteocles stands idly by during the first song. Of course actors do
on occasion stand by silent and unnoticed during choral songs,
see *Pers* 622*; but here there is nothing to be gained and much to
be lost.[2] The juxtaposition of Eteocles' exit with the entry of the
chorus is effective (see 78*); and similarly his return at 181
contrasts with the end of the song. This leads to the final point

[1] Dignan is not the first to be too literal-minded to appreciate Aeschylus'
techniques: see E. *Phoen* 751f. In fact, Euripides is the forerunner of all the carping
pedantry which criticizes Aeschylus for 'naïve dramaturgy'.

[2] This would not discountenance Dignan, whose thesis is that Aeschylus was
unable to handle the 'idle' actor. He seems to choose the disparaging alternative
here precisely because it is disparaging.

that the reproaches of the man of action in 181ff. lose much of their sense if Eteocles has not been busy off-stage. And his report of the demoralization of the citizens in 191f. (καὶ νῦν . . .) implies that he has been where he could see for himself the bad effects of the women's panic.[1]

Finally the conventions of structural technique may have some bearing. If Eteocles were to stay on, there would be no exit before the song, though admittedly the Scout went off shortly before; and there would be no new entry after it. According to the theory outlined in §5 there is normally an exit before each act-dividing song and an entry after it. Now, this 'rule' applies less to the entry song (parodos) than to other songs; and there is a tendency, especially in Euripides, to merge the parodos with the surrounding acts. None the less it is distinctly rare for there to be neither an exit nor an entry, as is alleged here. The exceptions (*Prom*, S. *El*, E. *Hel*, *Or*, and *Rh*) are discussed on *Prom* 88*, where it is argued that all have a certain pattern in common, which serves to bring out the isolation of the 'hero' and his friendly chorus. There is no such point in keeping Eteocles on here, and no good reason for disrupting the normal structure.

78ff. enter chorus

cποράδην?

In most tragedies, it may be assumed, the chorus entered in a regular formation. This would be true whether it stepped to anapaests or danced to a lyric metre, see p. 64 above. This very regularity provides the playwright with an opportunity to achieve a special dramatic point by an irregular or disordered choral entry. We should be bound to guess that a disordered entry was exploited in *Seven* and *Eum*, at least, even without any hint from secondary sources. As it is, the adverb cποράδην is used in the ancient *Life* §9 in connection with the entry of the chorus in *Eum* (see *Eum* 140ff.*); this seems to show at least that a scattered entry was used at some point in the history of the production of Aeschylus.[2]

The internal case for a scattered entry in *Seven* is simply that

---

[1] Eteocles' exit and re-entry were, of course, down an eisodos, and not, as Schadewaldt *tr* p. 53 says, into the (non-existent) palace.

[2] Cf. Pollux 4. 109 who says that the chorus sometimes entered καθ᾽ ἕνα. On cποράδην entry see Hermann *Opuscula* ii 134ff. (Croiset 110 n. 1 is wrong to say that a scholion on *Seven* alludes to such an entry.)

the wild opening dochmiac lyrics are astrophic as far as 108 and possibly to 149, and that the astrophica are divided into many short asyndetic sections. It would be easy and effective to distribute these outbursts to single choreuts or to small groups, perhaps gradually increasing the number who participate. This is well argued by Mesk,[1] who also acutely observes that the alternation of visual and aural evocations of the siege give a guide to the distribution of parts. One could never prove on such grounds that the chorus entered out of formation, but there is no denying that it is an attractive hypothesis which provides for some highly effective choreography and musical arrangement. The most serious opponent, Hermann (*ed* pp. 273f.), objects to such an entry that 'ea tamen nimia parumque decora virginibus perturbatio esset': but the whole context makes it clear that the perturbation should be made as extreme as possible.

A scattered entry by the chorus would make a striking end of the prologue, the disorganized terror of the women in contrast to the silent bravery and discipline of the citizens at the beginning. In particular, Eteocles' calm exit after a solemn prayer would be directly juxtaposed with the wild flight of the women away from the scene of danger. Eteocles does not perceive the women, nor they him: his resolute stride is simply put beside their panic-stricken rush.

181 re-enter Eteocles

286 exit Eteocles

the problem of lines 282–6

Eteocles' final five lines on departure (282–6) read:

> ἐγὼ δ’ ἐπ’ ἄνδρας ἓξ ἐμοὶ cὺν ἑβδόμωι
> ἀντηρέτας ἐχθροῖcι τὸν μέγαν τρόπον
> εἰc ἑπτατειχεῖc ἐξόδους τάξω μολών,
> πρὶν ἀγγέλους cπερχνούς τε καὶ ταχυρρόθους
> λόγους ἱκέcθαι καὶ φλέγειν χρείαc ὕπο.[2]

---

[1] Mesk *Philol* 89 (1934) 454ff., cf. Robert *Hermes* 57 (1922) 161ff. Wilamowitz 69f. is against splitting up the astrophics, and this view has recently been supported by Kaimio 79, 115f. But all that Kaimio shows is that the evidence does not *force* us to split the song up: that does not mean it was not. (Rode in *Bauformen* 93 tries to associate astrophica with lively action, as in satyr plays. But the distinction does not really hold good; for there are too many lively strophic dances.)

[2] Thus most MSS. I would be inclined to accept three slight and old emendations—ἐγὼ δέ γ’ in 282, ἑπτὰ τείχους in 284 and ἀγγέλου in 285 (see Page *app. crit.*).

This declaration of intention was the object of little attention
before E. Wolff made it a key passage in the vigorous debate over
whether Eteocles has any choice about meeting Polynices, or
whether he acts entirely under the compulsion of the curse.
Wolff[1] argued that these lines show unequivocally that the
Theban defenders have been posted before the *sieben Redepaare*
ever begin, and hence that in the following act the champions
are not being chosen but only described or accounted for, so that
Eteocles really has no choice over the defender of the seventh
gate. In my view such a crucial issue cannot possibly be settled
on the strength of five lines spoken 350 lines earlier and not even
in the same act; it must depend on the full context. I shall argue
on 371d* that Eteocles *is* choosing the defenders, including himself. I shall assume for now that this is right, in which case these
five lines must be otherwise accounted for.

The lines, as they stand, are simply inconsistent, indeed contradictory, with the event. Eteocles says that he will go and post the
Thebans before messengers arrive: in fact he returns and does
so *after* the messenger has arrived. The lines might lead us to
expect the return of Eteocles and the arrival of a messenger, but
after the posting of the champions. It is true that the words have a
certain grand vagueness, but taken in their context I do not see
how the audience could take them other than in their 'wrong'
sense. In purely lexicographical terms it may be argued that
τάξω might mean 'arrange' or 'pick' rather than 'post' or
'station': but in view of the urgency of the context, especially
with the expectation built up by 39ff. and 57f., the audience
could not be expected to make this distinction. Nor, it seems, did
Euripides when he evidently echoed the lines at *Phoen* 748f.: . . .
ἐλθὼν ἑπτάπυργον ἐς πόλιν[2] / τάξω λοχαγοὺς πρὸς πύλαισιν . . . Or
again, Verrall claims that μολών is equivalent to δεῦρο πάλιν
μολών; but that should have to be made clear by the context,
which it is not. Then some commentators, e.g. Tucker, have
claimed that Eteocles is saying that he will do the posting before

---

[1] *HSCP* 63 (1958) 91ff., followed by, among others, Patzer ibid. 97ff., Erbse
1ff., Cameron *Studies on the Seven against Thebes* (The Hague 1971) 34ff., Burnett
GRBS 14 (1973) 347–8. On these lines and the *sieben Redepaare* see now K. Wilkens
Tragödienstruktur u. Theologie bei A. (Munich 1974).

[2] Jackson 117f. emends πόλιν, which he attacks with good point, to ϲτόμα; but
why not the less high-flown κύκλον (Musgrave) or perhaps ὁδόν (cf. ἐξόδουϲ in
Seven)?

the inflammatory messengers reach the soldiery at the gates, not himself. Again this is a less obvious sense; and in any case Eteocles still says that he will do the posting off-stage and not on-stage.

The easiest and bluntest way out of the difficulty is to admit the inconsistency and simply to claim that this is 'false' preparation.[1] The spectators in the theatre (it is said) are not such sticklers for accuracy as scholars, and by the time that the *sieben Redepaare* get under way they will have disregarded this false lead. In 282–6 Aeschylus wishes both to continue the preparation, begun in 57f., for the pairing of the seven champions, and also to prepare for the arrival of urgent messengers. By joining the two things together with πρίν the preparation becomes, as it happens, inconsistent with the event; but, it is claimed, this is a trivial matter which the audience would overlook. I certainly agree with von Fritz that the whole *sieben Redepaare* should not be distorted merely to fit these five lines, but I do not think that his solution should be accepted too complacently and without some question. The objections are much the same as those raised on *Pers* 528* to the alleged false preparation at *Pers* 529–31. The lines are in a stressed position at the end of the act, and if they are meant to be misleading then there should be some positive dramatic point to the false direction. Here, as in *Pers*, there is no clear gain. Aeschylus could easily have left the lines out altogether, or could have given Eteocles lines to the effect 'I shall go and encourage the soldiers, and then return here to hear the latest reports and choose seven defenders accordingly.' There should be some good reason why Aeschylus said not this but something actually inconsistent with it. Von Fritz is, in effect, saying, like those who defend *Pers* 529–31, that Aeschylus is careless and confusing, but that it does not matter. But since Aeschylus is not normally incompetent in his dramatic technique—on the contrary he is careful and forceful—and since he could easily have avoided the confusion, we should at least explore some alternative explanations before reluctantly admitting mere incompetence.[2]

---

[1] Thus von Fritz 199ff., followed by, among others, Lloyd-Jones *Gnomon* 34 (1962) 741, Kirkwood 12. This line was already taken by Stephenson 21f.

[2] I should, however, dissociate myself from the way that Erbse 2f. rejects von Fritz. He pontificates that (3) 'Every word of the poet is relevant: on the other hand the greater or lesser attentiveness of an imaginary audience is irrelevant.' If he means that presumptions about the attentiveness of the audience should never

It is only recently that the lines have been seen as highly problematical, and scholars have not been inclined to offer drastic explanations in the nineteenth-century manner. I can, however, offer a few solutions which are perhaps conceivable, though none is free from considerable objections. It might be argued, for example, that at 369ff. the location of the scene has shifted from the sacred precinct of the earlier scenes to some place near the walls; and that Eteocles arrives at 374 to complete the mission on which he departed at 286. I argued on *Pers* 598c* that the scene can refocus without the chorus leaving the stage. In this case, however, I can see nothing in the words of the next act which points to a change of locale, and I do not see how the audience could realize that Eteocles is arriving to his mission rather than returning from it.

Or could it be that lines 282-6 have been interpolated or transposed?[1] 281 would make a better closing line than 286, and would be tellingly echoed and altered in Eteocles' very last line at 719. The five lines are expressed in heavy and somewhat loose language, and τὸν μέγαν τρόπον in 283 (obelized by Page) is particularly vacuous. On the other hand, there is nothing in the language of the lines which is impossibly unlike Aeschylus, and if they were interpolated they were successfully forged in the Aeschylean vein. Alternatively just 285-6 may be interpolated. Without them Eteocles' declared intention is more vague and scarcely inconsistent with the event of the next act. But 284 would make a poor last line.

A simple emendation which apparently removes the problem would be the change of τάξω in 284 to ἄξω.[2] In that case Eteocles would be saying that he is going to *fetch* the other six champions, and he should return with them at the beginning of the next act. It has indeed been suggested by some scholars that Eteocles brings on the other six Thebans, and this textual conjecture

suppress the asking of the question why each word is there, then that is clearly right: if he implies, however, that every word must be taken at face value and rigidly followed through, and that everything must be twisted to be made consistent regardless of dramatic considerations, then that is to treat a work of art for performance as though it were a reasoned monograph.

[1] Transposed, for instance, from after l. 675, where the text may have been interfered with, as I argue on p. 161 below.

[2] This does not seem to have been suggested before. If it were right, εἰς in 284 would not go with μολών but with ἀντηρέτας: 'champions for the seven gates'. For the sense cf. ἥξω λαβών at *Hik* 726.

would support the suggestion. But the rest of the evidence does not, on the whole, support the theory (see 374c*). Another objection is that Euripides apparently copied the reading τάξω in *Phoen* 748f. (quoted above). But these considerations may not be fatal.

So I suggest that 282–6 may be interpolated or displaced.[1] In the present scholarly climate of textual conservatism and of patronizing disparagement of Aeschylus' dramatic technique it is more fashionable to suppose the dramatist incompetent rather than to diagnose corruption, let alone interpolation. My own attitude should be apparent.

371 enter Scout

374 enter Eteocles (attended)

(a) the symmetrical announcements

Three trimeters (369–71) announcing the Scout are followed by another three (372–4) for Eteocles. These seem to be the only two spoken entry announcements in Greek tragedy which are consecutive without any break between them. They are plainly symmetrical, and Kranz (129) even detects a kind of verbal response between them. However, he is surely misleading when he implies that this is only one example of a frequent phenomenon. As a symmetrical pair of entrance announcements this is unique.

The formal balance of the announcements is further brought out if the majority of editors are right to read εἰς ἀρτίκολλον in 373, and to treat it as an Aeschylean equivalent of phrases like εἰς καιρόν or εἰς δέον.[2] Phrases like these are common when a playwright uses the dramatic convenience of an entry at just the right moment (for one class of the device see 39* above). They naturally tend to occur when two separate entries are made

---

[1] Colin Macleod suggests that if 282–6 are interpolated they might have been added in order to shorten the play (cf. the similar suggestion on *Hik* 966ff. in p. 229 n. 3 below). With these lines all of the seven pairs of speeches except the last could be cut. He compares the motive for the interpolation of S. *Aj* 68–70 (see Fraenkel *Kl B* i 413), and suggests that E. *Ion* 1004–5 might have been added to replace 1006–17. I find this suggestion very attractive.

[2] Some examples are listed in *GGL* i 2 p. 75 n. 9, Ritchie 252. εἰς καλόν is illustrated by Austin on Men. *Sam* 280. (*Sam* 639f. also has εἰς δέοντά μοι πάνυ καιρόν.)

simultaneously or near simultaneously: thus e.g. S. *Ant* 386f., E. *Her* 701; see further 371b* below. Fraenkel has argued, however, against this reading that the manuscript evidence is in favour of ϵἰϲ', and that the verb is needed for the sense.[1] But the manuscripts can be allowed no authority on matters of punctuation and accentuation; and the ellipse of the verb seems easy within the context of an entry announcement, cf. e.g. S. *Ant* 626ff. where ὅδϵ μήν supplies in the context the idea of Haemon's approach.

There are here several other features of entrance announcements which, whether or not they were already common in 467, were typical in later tragedy. All of them are particularly appropriate to this situation. The chorus remarks, for example, that the Scout and Eteocles are in haste: this fosters a sense of urgency and heightens excitement. Verrall observed (p. xxxviii) that all the entries and exits in the first part of *Seven* are made in haste; this contributes to the pressing sense of the situation of siege. The device is particularly common in the announcement of messengers, and this is even parodied at Ar. *Birds* 1121ff.[2] Further, the chorus conjectures (369f.) that the Scout is bringing news. This simple device stimulates anticipation, and is used throughout Greek tragedy (and in most other dramatic traditions).[3] Finally, the announcement of Eteocles begins in 372 with καὶ μὴν ἄναξ ὅδϵ. Now καὶ μήν is an extremely common formula for introducing entrance announcements in later tragedy. This is, however, its only surviving occurrence in Aeschylus, and the ordinary connective force is very clear, as it is not always in later formulaic

---

[1] Fraenkel *Kl B* 276. He also emends to ἀρτίκολλος (first Paley, also Page *OCT*). MS. Q has ἐϲ, and M^ac had ϵἰϲ without elision in the opinion of Dawe *Collation etc.* (Cambridge 1964) 263.

[2] Rau 164 compares A. *Pers* 247, E. *Hipp* 1154, *Hec* 216f.; add *Med* 1118f., *Tro* 232, *Ion* 1109f. Cf. Shakespeare *Macb* I ii 47f. 'What a haste looks through his eyes! So should he look / That seems to speak things strange.' For tragic entries and exits in haste see also A. Müller 197 n. 2, Spitzbarth 49, Steidle 12 n. 13. K. Smith *HSCP* 16 (1905) 136f. adds several less clear possibilities. Smith, who is arguing against the high-soled buskin in the fifth century, assumes that entries which are said to be made at a run were in fact made more hastily than others at walking pace. I see no reason to disagree with him.

[3] Cf. e.g. *Prom* 943, *Ag* 489ff. (see 503b*); E. *Med* 1116f., *Hec* 216f., *IT* 236f. Ritchie 251 claims that the typical contents and phrasing of *Rh* 85–6 count in favour of Euripidean authorship. But the trouble is that this is the only example of an announcement with a phrase like νέον τι πρᾶγμ' ἔχων where the character does *not* in fact have news to give: Aeneas has no news, he has come to find out the news from Hector. In view of this it is more than possible that this couplet is modelled on *Hec* 216f.

uses.[1] Similarly ἀλλ' (εἰςορῶ) γὰρ (τόνδε) occurs only once in
Aeschylus at *Prom* 941 (see 944*).[2] Aeschylus has fewer entries
and fewer announcements than Sophocles and Euripides, but
this may not by itself account for the rarity of these formulas.
Aeschylus' entry announcements are not reduced to colourless
formulae as they tend to be in later tragedy. Thus these two
announcements in *Seven*, although they contain these recurrent
elements, are expressed in curious and lively language.[3]

(b) symmetrical entries

Since the two announcements are consecutive, the Scout and
Eteocles probably did not come into the audience's view at the
same moment (as many commentators have implied by putting a
double stage direction by 374). But they may well have arrived
at a central point simultaneously, and, whatever the details, their
arrival is simultaneous to all intents and purposes. It is likely,
moreover, that they entered one from each side by the two
opposite eisodoi (on the eisodoi in the early theatre see pp. 449–
51). It is true that there is no distinction of the off-stage spheres
from which they have come, but the visual advantage of the
symmetry is so evident that it is hard to believe that Aeschylus
had them come on both by the same route.

The simultaneous or very closely consecutive entries of two or
more speaking characters were never a common occurrence in
Greek tragedy. It happens on average about once per play. The
Attic tragedian is dealing with few characters, and he usually
prefers to give each a separate entry which can receive independent attention. In most simultaneous entries two characters
enter who are in each other's company and are closely connected
in some way—friends, guard and prisoner, protector and ward,
etc. The Aeschylean instances are collected on *Prom* 1a*. It is

[1] Cf. Denniston *GP*[2] §6 on p. 356 and 586 (addenda); also Webster *Preparation* 119f. and di Benedetto *Hermes* 89 (1961) 306 n. 2.

[2] ἀλλὰ γάρ unseparated occurs at *Seven* 861. On ἀλλά . . . γάρ in later tragedy see Denniston *GP*[2] iii §4 on pp. 103f.; also Wilamowitz on E. *Her* 138, Webster op. cit. On ἀλλ' εἰςορῶ γὰρ τόνδε see di Benedetto on *Or* 725; and note Milman Parry (*The Making of Homeric Verse* (Oxford 1971) 292): 'One case I am very nearly tempted to class as a true formula . . .'

[3] Cf. p. 296 n. 2 below. Graeber 23 considers it notable that these are the only second (or third) entries of a character in Aeschylus which are given an announce-ment. But this is mere coincidence; there are only a few second entries in Aeschylus, and the others simply do not call for any announcement. (By no means all first entries are announced, see pp. 286–7 below.)

much more rare to have simultaneous yet separate entries: even
including disputed places (e.g. S. *Tr* 971, on which see p. 177)
fewer than a dozen examples survive, and there are no others
in Aeschylus (unless you count *Eum* 566, but see *Eum* 574*).
None of the other examples is handled with the same formal
symmetry as here. The way in which other occurrences are
treated more informally and naturalistically should be made
clear by the comparison of three undisputed examples: Teucer
and Agamemnon at S. *Aj* 1223ff., the guard with Antigone and
Creon at S. *Ant* 384ff., Amphitryon and Lycus at E. *Her* 701. It
seems that the kind of direct use of simultaneous yet separate
entry which we have here was too formal, too unrealistic to
become a common device in Greek tragedy.[1]

In view of these observations we may look to find the meaning
of this technique in formal and dramaturgic terms, and expect it
to reflect on the form and purpose of the great scene which
follows. Thus Verrall is characteristically over-rational when he
claims (p. xiii) that the timing of the entries is a stroke of 'Destiny'.
Wilamowitz (61) rightly insists that we should not ask awkward
realistic questions nor think in terms of coincidence. However, he
goes on to use the word 'naiv' of the technique.[2] This does not
seem to be the right word for the firmness with which Aeschylus
establishes immediately and clearly the symmetry that is to hold
together the next 300 lines. The visual handling of the entries
sets the pattern for the seven pairs of speeches, each reply of
Eteocles meeting perfectly each challenge set up by the Scout.
But to say even this involves one in the raging controversies over
what is supposed to be happening in the *sieben Redepaare*, and an
incursion into this field is unavoidable.

(c) *deictic pronouns and the other six champions*

There have been those who have supposed that Eteocles brought
on with him the six other Thebans, and that they were sent off
one by one at appropriate moments during the course of the

[1] It was exploited for comic effect in Old Comedy, particularly at *Ach* 1190ff.
and *Lys* 1072ff. Shakespeare with more characters and above all with a symmetrical
pair of doors used the device often. For a full account of all relevant preserved
stage instructions see T. J. King *Shakespearean Staging, 1599–1642* (Cambridge,
Mass. 1971).

[2] And this has had a bad influence, see Italie *ed* ad loc., Rose on l. 369.

scene.[1] If this were true then there could be little room for dispute about what is happening, since the spectators would see it with their own eyes: the seven Thebans, already selected, are being sent one by one to their gates. As well as clarifying the action this stage arrangement would have the advantage of adding a spectacular interest and visual dimension to what is undeniably a huge mass of words. And the spectacle would not be mere empty show, since as they depart one by one we should see the impending isolation of Eteocles, who is finally left alone to decide who is to defend the seventh gate. Some slight support for the theory might also be derived from Ar. *Frogs* 1013ff. where Aeschylus, after dwelling on the armour in his plays, describes *Seven* as a 'drama full of Ares' which would inspire the spectator to bellicosity. This might have more point if the audience actually saw the brave and virtuous defenders departing to battle. On the other hand, the line is subservient to Aristophanes' concern (not altogether earnest) with the social and moral effect of tragedy, and also to Dionysus' joke about the Thebans (1023f.).

But whatever advantages there may be to this staging, the six defenders come up against the simple and very substantial objection that there is insufficient sign of their presence in the text. Surely such a bold and deliberate piece of stage action should be clearly marked in the words; yet, as Fraenkel (*Kl B* 276f.) has recently reiterated, there is no announcement of their entry, no clear recognition of their presence, and no explicit reference to their departures. Even if one were to read ἄξω in 284 (see pp. 145f. above), this would hardly be enough to counteract the absence of any clear indication at the time when the champions are supposed to be actually on stage. All that the supporters of the six can point to in reply are two little deictic pronouns in ll. 408 and 472f. But before considering these, I shall have to discuss the whole matter of deictic pronouns and physical presence in Greek drama.

It has sometimes been implied that for ὅδε to be used the person referred to has actually to be present in sight of the audience or at least to be imagined as within sight of the speaker. But, while this is usually the case, there are literally dozens of places in

---

[1] Including Butler, Blomfield, Tucker, Verrall, Sidgwick, Bodensteiner (729), Rose (192 'possibly'); translations of Smyth, Murray, Vellacott, Schadewaldt (64ff.).

Greek tragedy and comedy where the deictic pronoun is used to refer to someone who is definitely not in view. In such cases the person is, rather, 'vividly present to the speaker's thought'.[1] This has long been recognized, but sometimes seems to be forgotten. On the other hand, some scholars have tended to speak as though ὅδε had negligible deictic force,[2] and this is to go too far the other way. The balance is redressed by A. M. Dale[3] who protests '. . . but the pronoun is deictic, evolved by a people used to talking with their hands, and there must be some reason for a gesture of immediacy. The vast majority of exceptions refer to people "in the skene here" . . .' This puts the matter well, though it should still be emphasized that there are many places where a gesture of immediacy elicits a ὅδε even though the person is neither present nor just inside the skene.

This can be illustrated by going no further afield than *Seven* itself. Just after the choral entry we have (80) ῥεῖ πολὺς ὅδε λεὼς κτλ used of the enemy advance. And the Scout repeatedly uses deictic pronouns of the enemy champions during the course of his seven speeches: see 395, 424, 470, 544, 631.[4] His descriptions are so vivid and threatening that the deictic is perfectly appropriate. Returning now to l. 408 it may be seen that τόνδε does not necessarily imply Tydeus' presence. Eteocles must evoke his defenders as vividly as the attackers: so τίν' ἀντιτάξεις τῶιδε; in 395 is met with τόνδ' ἀντιτάξω προστάτην (and the old emendation τῶνδ' is unnecessary). Similarly at 472 Eteocles meets the τῶιδε of 470 with his τόνδε. The man is vividly present to his mind, and is referred to with a deictic word even before he is named: Wilamowitz (76f.) aptly compares 631f. Thus the line does not entail the presence of Megareus, even if it is not interpolated.[5]

---

[1] This is the phrase used by Lloyd-Jones *CR* N.S. 15 (1965) 242, who draws particular attention to τῆςδε used of the dead Iphigenia at S. *El* 540; cf. Hunger *WSt* 65 (1950) 19ff., Newiger *RhM* 108 (1965) 237 n. 26.

[2] e.g. Platnauer on E. *IT* 558, Denniston–Page on A. *Ag* 57, Bond (p. 56) on E. *Hyps* fr. 61 l. 4.

[3] *JHS* 84 (1964) 166; cf. Stevens on E. *Andr* 735, Gomme–Sandbach on Men. *Dysc* 125.

[4] Also τῶιδε by Eteocles in 553. Other pronouns (τοῦτον, cφε etc.) are also used throughout the scene. On the untenable theory that the scene is a kind of teichoskopia see p. 155 below.

[5] For interpolation of 472 see Fraenkel *Kl B* 298–300 (followed by Page *OCT*, who also eliminates τόνδ' in 631): for counter-arguments see Erbse 9f., and for counter-argument against Erbse see Reeve *GRBS* 13 (1972) 469.

It is with some reluctance that I agree to banish the six Theban champions from the stage, for, if they had been there, this visual realization would greatly clarify the dramatic situation. Without them we must work from other more complex indications, mainly verbal, whose difficulty may be gauged from the scholarly controversies over them. None the less it is very hard to believe that Aeschylus brought on these spectacular figures and yet paid so little attention to them in the words. I shall now consider the scene on the assumption that they were not present.

(d) tenses and action

On the interpretation of the central scene inevitably depends a large part of the interpretation of the entire play, whether this is put in terms of Eteocles' free will or of the relation of the city and the cursed family or anything else.[1] And the disagreement of scholars over the more abstract issues is reflected in their disagreement over the more precise question: what is supposed to be *happening* during the *sieben Redepaare*? The dispute has tended to centre on the notorious variations in the tenses of the verbs which Eteocles uses when placing the seven defenders—three futures, one present, one aorist, and two perfects (for details see any of the articles cited below on p. 153). But the issue cannot rest on these alone: on the contrary the tenses must be explained in accordance with a balanced view of the scene as a whole.

Before examining the various theories which have been offered, a few simple observations are called for. The entire construction is symmetrical;[2] and this formality is made clear right from the beginning by the pair of entries—see 371b* above. Seven times the Scout makes a speech and seven times Eteocles replies, and after each pair except the last the chorus sings a brief strophe. So the form firmly establishes the assumption or expectation that it is the *same* thing which is going on in each pair, and that seven times the same kind of action is happening. It would need something very striking to overturn this impression; and yet there is no kind of clear disruption, except perhaps in the final speech of

---

[1] The heat of the recent controversy may be seen from the ten articles published during 1958–64 and conveniently listed by Kirkwood 9 n. 1.

[2] Cf. Peretti 154ff. The scene is symmetrical in over-all impression, not, of course, in precise stichometric responsion between each pair of speeches, as some scholars, following Ritschl, have tried to manage by means of wholesale textual fiddling.

Eteocles. And the content bears out this formal symmetry up to
and including the last pair of speeches. Each time the Scout sets
up the challenge of an aggressor, and invites Eteocles to meet it;
and each time Eteocles produces a suitable match. Six times
Eteocles can cap and so outdo the enemy, and the seventh time he
can at least equal him. Scholarly attention has been directed
towards Eteocles' replies, and particularly the tenses of his
verbs, but consideration should also be given to the Scout. For it
is important that each time he puts the challenge in similar
terms, and invites the same response from Eteocles. The relevant
passages are 395f., 435f., 470f., 499, 595f., 650.[1] They show that
each time the Scout speaks as though Eteocles is to pick a defender and to send him to the gate—πέμπειν recurs regularly. And
if this is what the Scout takes to be happening, the audience is
not in a position to think otherwise.

The question of what is happening during this scene in terms of
action on-stage or off-stage is not as a rule directly faced in the
scholarly controversies. However, the implied answers may be
sorted into five (or four) groups. If this is at all a helpful way to
approach the scene then these groups seem to exhaust the possibilities, and one of the accounts in one form or another must be
right. Roughly, the alternatives are these:

(i) All the champions have been assigned to their gates before
the scene begins, and so it simply makes known something already
fixed. Thus Wolff and followers, see p. 143 n. 1.

(ii) Each of the champions is assigned to his gate during the
course of the scene. Most of those who think this would bring the
six champions on stage, see 371c* above and p. 150 n. 1; but
there are other possibilities—see below.[2]

---

[1] The Scout invites Eteocles' response in all but his fifth speech. The final line
of this set poses problems: 650 σὺ δ' αὐτὸς ἤδη γνῶθι τίνα πέμπειν δοκεῖ. The line
is usually deleted as an interpolation (first Paley, but not Page OCT), because it
interrupts the concluding sequence 649, 651-2 (see 652*), and because the first
half of the line is repeated in 652. I would concede that the line is probably
corrupt under the influence of 652, and that it is probably out of place—it would
be in place before 649 (thus Prien Beiträge zur Kritik von Aischylos S. v. T (Lübeck
1856) 13-14). I am reluctant, however, finally to reject the line as an interpolation,
since it fits so well with the other passages listed here. (The corruption and displacement had already happened by the second century A.D. (POxy 2333 fr. b).
Wartelle Histoire du Texte d' Eschyle (Paris 1971) 315 is absurdly jubilant at the
presence of the line in a papyrus—as though that proved it genuine and un-
corrupted.)

[2] Another variation is proposed by a friend of Dawe (see Dawe 36 n. 1), who

(iii) While the warriors are selected during the scene, the actual posting, if it is to be thought of at all, takes place after the end of the scene. Thus von Fritz and followers, see p. 144 n. 1.

(iv) A permutation of i–iii: i.e. some are posted before the scene begins, but Eteocles has not had time to complete the task, and some others are posted during and/or after the scene. Thus Wilamowitz and others.[1]

(v) Dawe (33ff.) cuts through the problem by arguing that the audience is not meant to reach a single answer. In effect, this is solution iv, but put in terms of drama rather than of logistics. Dawe supposes that as a result of Aeschylus' systematic inconsistency the audience gains an impression that i and ii and/or iii is the case, despite their strict inconsistency.

Now, if the observations on form and context made above are acceptable, then three of these five solutions can be ruled out. i is incompatible with the way in which the Scout sets up a challenge which has to be met, matched not by a preselected fate but by the choice and good sense of Eteocles—hence the verbs of sending. And there is no way of twisting all of Eteocles' verbs, still less the verbs of the Scout, to fit a situation already fixed. Next, solutions iv and v are scholastic and oversubtle, because the entire shape and disposition of the structure make the audience assume that the same thing is happening each time. The Scout makes the same challenge calling for the same kind of response; and the tenses of Eteocles' verbs alone will not make the audience think that he is meeting the challenges in different ways—now by a *fait accompli*, now by a command, now by a memorandum. Solution iii remains possible but not very attractive, since the Scout's challenges call for an immediate and not a postponed defence, and since it puts a great strain on Eteocles' past tenses to suppose that the actions have been taken in intention but not in deed. Also the impression would be given that the vital postings will happen at the end of the scene, but by that time the whole subject has been superseded by other concerns.

Some form of solution ii should be sought for, because the whole pattern of challenge and response strongly suggests that

suggested that, rather than the champions themselves, a series of minor messengers are sent off during the scene. But there is no trace of them whatsoever in the text.

[1] Wilamowitz 76; similarly e.g. Groeneboom 150, Lesky *Ges Schr* 264ff. (though on p. 267 Lesky hints at solution v).

each time the action to meet the situation is actually taken. This is a great advantage for those who bring on the six champions, for with each reply of Eteocles one can be dispatched. Further, the variation in his tenses can be accounted for by the precise timing of each departure (they would go, that is, at 416, 450, 472, 504, 553, and 625). But however convenient this would be, it still runs up against the lack of proper indication of their presence, see 371c* above. An ingenious variation on this solution is hinted at by A. M. Dale, who implies that the scene is a kind of τειχοσκοπία (cf. E. *Phoen*).[1] In that case Eteocles could by means of gestures communicate his orders to his forces who are to be imagined as in the distance. This would also account for all the deictic pronouns (see p. 151 above). But the theory is unacceptable, because it is absolutely clear that the field of battle is being described and not witnessed. Consider how the Scout opens and closes with verbs of speaking (375f., 651), and how Eteocles instructs him to continue with his *narrative* at 451, 480 (cf. 400, 457f., 489f., 526). The whole series of confrontations is verbal and mental.[2]

There is a final suggestion which may rescue solution ii in a rarefied form. This is that Eteocles' selections and assignations are to be thought of as having effect off-stage, even though no actual physical sign is made or messenger sent. In realistic terms this would be to give Eteocles supernatural powers, but in dramatic terms it seems quite possible. The Scout vividly conjures up the aggressors (hence his deictics): when Eteocles matches each he not only talks about the conquering qualities of the defender, but by assigning him verbally he puts the move into action. The words of Eteocles' replies stand for actions off-stage. They also foreshadow the outcome of the contests: six times Eteocles is victorious, at the seventh gate there is deadlock. This may account for the variation of tenses, for things are, in effect, happening off-stage to the accompaniment of his words. I am not suggesting that Eteocles' words are magical, but simply that in their vivid dramatic context his words are *as good as* action,

[1] Dale *JHS* 84 (1964) 166: 'The Messenger on the citadel is pointing down to each gate in turn as a way of actualising the scene for an audience deprived of "scenery".' (For panoramic views in the pre-skene theatre see p. 200.)

[2] Cf. Cameron *TAPA* 101 (1970) 95ff. esp. 101–8 (with relevant literature cited there). It seems, however, oversimplified and over-intellectual to make out that the battle is, in effect, a purely verbal one.

and that for the audience they are supposed to be translated into action off-stage.

652 exit Scout

the continuity of Eteocles' seventh speech

In all probability the Scout departed after his last line, as most commentators have supposed. The arguments for this are much the same as those brought to bear on the Messenger in *Pers* at *Pers* 514*. When he has no further part to play a character should go after his last lines, particularly if his last lines were final. The Scout's last three lines 649, 651–2[1] have every sign of being conclusive exit lines. τοιαῦτα is the usual summing-up word (cf. p. 290 below): the Scout has used it at the end of earlier speeches (435, 499, 547), but here he covers all the enemy with ἐκείνων.[2] The assertion of reliability in 651f. is typical of the opening and conclusion of a messenger's part; cf. 40f., 64ff., 375 and p. 89 above). And finally with cὺ δέ in 652 he recommends some action on the part of the person he leaves on-stage; cf. p. 97 for parallels.

Such considerations could not prove beyond doubt that the Scout went off at this point—he might conceivably have stepped into the background. But they do show that his part is played; and attempts to involve him further in the play are unconvincing. Tucker, for example, attributes 677–85 to the Scout whom he sends off after 685. But his arguments against the attribution of the lines to the chorus do not deserve to be exhumed; and 685 is a completely pointless moment for the Scout's departure. Some, including recently Erbse (19), claim it is the Scout who is given Eteocles' command at 675f., and that he departs in obedience. But the Scout's part is to tell of the enemy champions, not to be a personal servant. As was shown on *Pers* 155c*, all major characters in Greek tragedy have attendants, unless there is some good reason why they should not; and one of the functions of such attendants is to be sent on missions, for example to fetch things.[3]

---

[1] On 650 see p. 153 n. 1 above. Dawson *tr* has recently revived Verrall's psychological defence of the line, that it is a 'stammering apology'. But the Scout is cool to the last; he shows no more sign of disquiet in his seventh speech than in the others.

[2] Pauw's conjecture ἐκείνωι γ' is admittedly tempting. But this cannot save the padding cὺ δ' αὐτὸc ἤδη γνῶθι in the next line (see previous note).

[3] See Fraenkel *MH* 24 (1967) 82–3, cf. Spitzbarth 60.

Now, assuming that the Scout does go at 652, does this make a difference to the interpretation of Eteocles' final speech (653ff.)? It has been claimed that the speech would be a kind of monologue, instead of a dialogue reply, and that this serves to put Eteocles' choice in internal rather than external terms.[1] But while each speech of Eteocles is formally a reply to the Scout, none is in any important sense addressed *to* him. Two contain no second-person verb at all, two merely tell him in the last line to continue (451, 480), and the other two have only an unemphasized λέγεις (400, 553). The dichotomy of 'monologue' and 'dialogue' is not appropriate here. I would agree that Eteocles' seventh speech is different from the others, and that its difference is enhanced by its position within the great symmetrical structure. But the difference does not lie in the matter of who is being addressed. Nor is it, in my view, in the psychology of Eteocles, as is often supposed. He does not suddenly become mad or incoherent or possessed. After the three lines (653–5) in which Eteocles recognizes in suitably distressful terms the working out of his father's curse, he goes on to pick himself as the seventh defender in a way quite as calm and well argued as the previous six—a point which is clearly made by Kirkwood (esp. 14f.). The great change at 653 lies, surely, in the introduction of the curse of Oedipus: that is, it lies not in psychology but in thematic emphasis.

The curse, which must have been formulated in the previous play, was invoked by Eteocles at l. 70, but since then it has been deliberately suppressed and put aside by Aeschylus, so that it may be released with shocking force at this moment (on this point I prefer the approach of Dawe 32 to that of Kirkwood 16f.). Here we suffer particularly from the loss of the rest of the trilogy, since it seems there is something, perhaps in the last speech of the Scout, which makes Eteocles and the chorus suddenly realize that the curse applies to this precise situation, and that it means that the brothers must shed each other's blood.[2] Yet Eteocles is not a man possessed: he is fully conscious of what he is doing, and he chooses, against advice, to do it. When faced with the classical Greek combination of determinism

[1] See Fraenkel *Kl B* 323f. and *MH* 24 (1967) 82f. (where he speaks of 'Quasimonolog').
[2] Cf. along similar lines Burnett *GRBS* 14 (1973) 351ff.

and free will in a kind of 'double motivation', we tend to say that the Greeks simply did not see the inherent contradiction. But here Aeschylus is fully alive to the doubleness of the motivation, and he terrifyingly exploits it. For any sensitive audience of this scene there can be no contradiction: we see the fulfilment of the curse, *and* we see Eteocles' fully deliberate decision to fulfil it.

719 exit Eteocles

(a) an arming scene at 677ff.?

When Eteocles goes at 719 he goes to his death. For the audience the stage act of his exit comes to stand for his slaughter and for the fulfilment of the curse (see 719c* below). For the exit to have its dramatic effect Eteocles should be in full armour when he goes. Since, it seems, he first calls for his armour at 675f., some scholars have supposed that he must have armed on stage during his final disputes with the chorus at 677–719. Not long ago this was fully argued by Schadewaldt, and his proposals have been widely accepted.[1]

At 675f. Eteocles calls for his greaves: φέρ' ὡς τάχος / κνημῖδας, αἰχμῆς καὶ πέτρων προβλήματα. Schadewaldt (359f.) rightly rules out Wilamowitz's idea (p. 77, n. 1, widely followed) that Eteocles is already fully armed except for his greaves: the fixed Homeric sequence, which is corroborated by vase paintings, makes it clear that greaves are the first, not the last, item to be put on. He goes on to argue that one or more lines calling for the rest of the panoply have dropped out after 676. This textual suggestion is questionable, since the first item, the greaves, might be taken to allude to the entire panoply (particularly if Eteocles was on the point of going off, see 719b* below).[2] Whatever the merits of the lacuna, Schadewaldt's more important suggestion (362ff.) is that

---

[1] *HuH*[2] i 357ff. (first published in 1961); accepted by Von der Mühll *MH* 21 (1964) 226, Lesky *TDH*[2] 231 (toned down in *TDH*[3] 97), Dingel 30, 142, 153f., Rivier *MH* 28 (1971) 127, Dawson *tr* 89. The arming of Eteocles was already to be found, without detailed argument, in E. Petersen *Attische Tragödie* (Bonn 1915) 372, Murray *tr* 58, 61, Rose 217f.

[2] Or, perhaps better, one might follow the hints in some MSS., and change the wording of 675 to take in more items of armour: e.g. κνημῖδας, αἰχμήν, καὶ πτερῶν προβλήματα (or πέτρων προβλήματα—either way a periphrasis for the shield). See Hermann ad loc., and cf. E. *Phoen* 779 ἐκφέρετε τεύχη πάνοπλά τ' ἀμφιβλήματα. (Neither Schadewaldt's lacuna nor the similar suggestion of Petersen (cited in previous note) 645 find their way into Dawe's *Repertory*.)

Eteocles' armour was brought and that he put it all on before his exit. He works out a scheme of stage instructions so that Eteocles dons each of six items at regular points during the following epirrhematic scene and finally takes his spear at 719. Thus, Schadewaldt claims, a 'Poesie des Dinglichen' accompanies the 'Poesie des Wortes': as the chorus tries to crack Eteocles' resolution, so his resolve is made more and more concrete as he nears the completion of his arming.

For all its attractions Schadewaldt's proposal runs up against a formidable objection. The action would not in any proper sense be accompanied by the words; there is no simultaneous indication whatsoever that all this is going on. In §3 I proposed the hypothesis that in Greek tragedy all important stage action is given by the words, and is the object of full attention, and that it does not go on regardless while the words are concentrated on something else. Some scholars (though they would not, I think, include Schadewaldt) might be happy to suppose that there was all manner of significant stage action in the Greek theatre without any simultaneous indication in the words, and hence irrecoverable by us. But they would be hard put to make a good case for any single instance. The weakness of Schadewaldt's position is made plain by his comparison (366) with *Prom* 52ff. for a scene punctuated by important stage action: the point is that the fettering of Prometheus *is* given a running commentary in the words. Further, Schadewaldt's staging would mean that the audience's attention was torn between the action and the highly demanding words of the scene. A competing distraction of this kind would surely be uncharacteristic of Greek tragedy. Rose (p. 217) unwittingly makes this clear when he praises 'the contrast between Eteocles' matter-of-fact occupation with his equipment and the chorus's impassioned appeals'. But are Eteocles' *words* matter-of-fact, and could such powerful words be accompanied by action independent of them? The putting on of armour or of any costume is a difficult thing to manage on stage; Dingel (142) notes that there are no other instances in Greek tragedy.[1] It is very hard to believe that Eteocles armed during this scene without any verbal accompaniment.

---

[1] Dingel gives a few examples of the discarding of costume, which is somewhat easier to manage. On the problems of the purple cloaks at *Eum* 1028 see pp. 412f. below. Even Shakespeare, who does incorporate arming scenes naturalistically

It may be worth considering other possible or potential arming scenes to see if they throw any light on the acceptability or practicability of such a procedure on the Greek tragic stage.[1] There are no other possible examples in the surviving plays of Aeschylus or Sophocles. Vase paintings indicate that in A. *Nereides* the armour made by Hephaestus was brought to Achilles (see Döhle 125ff. with plates 6–8): but if Achilles donned it on stage then this is likely to have been an important event fully reflected in the words. At E. *Hkld* 698f. the ancient Iolaus sends the Servant into the temple to bring him the ancient armour hanging there. When it is brought, however, at 720ff. Iolaus accepts the suggestion that it should be carried for him to the battlefield, and he takes only the spear. So Euripides studiously avoids the arming scene. But this whole sequence in *Hkld* is most peculiar; more to the point is *Phoen* 779ff. which comes at the end of a speech by Eteocles which contains several echoes of *Seven*. There Eteocles calls for his panoply, and four lines later (783) he goes off to battle. It is impossible that he should have armed in that time, and so he must be telling his attendants to follow him with his arms. At *Rh* 84 Hector apparently issues a call for arms (cf. more clearly Achaeus *TrGF* 20F37), and departure to the field seems imminent (though it never happens). At 99 Aeneas asks him cὺ δ' ὡc τί δράcων πρὸc τάδ' ὁπλίζηι χέραc; If these words are to be taken literally then this would be an arming scene without a running commentary. But in that case Hector would presumably have left his arming half completed; and so the line is more likely figurative.[2]

into his dialogue, does not normally pay no verbal attention to the stage action; for some illustrations see Seltzer (in *New Companion etc.* (cited 20 n. 2 above) 39–40.

[1] Cf. Dingel 153ff. The double arming at Ar. *Acharn* 1097ff. can owe nothing to tragic staging, although Lamachus has the odd paratragic line e.g. 1124.

[2] Arming scenes may, none the less, have been a fourth-century fashion, since we have from Astydamas' *Hektor* (*TrGF* 60F2) δέξαι κυνῆν μοι πρόcπολ' †εμονδε / ⟨μὴ⟩ καὶ φοβηθῆι παῖc. If this suggests that Hector's arming was a large set-piece scene, then this militates against attributing *PAmh* 10 to the same play—Snell's numeration reflects his doubt; 60F**11? In this fragment it seems that a messenger or Scout finishes his report in 2–4, rather as in *Seven*. The 'King' (Hector?) begins his reply (5) χώρει πρὸc οἴκουc ὅπλα τ' ε[(Blass's supplement ἐ[κκόμιζέ μοι is generally accepted, but there are other possibilities e.g. ἔκφερ' ὡc τάχοc, cf. *Seven* 675). So, like Eteocles, he called for his arms. But three lines later (8) we have ἀλλ' ἐκποδών μοι cτῆθι, μὴ[, and at 14, with no change of speaker, ἐλθὼν δε[. So it looks as though the 'King' intended to have his arms carried by a servant and to don them off-stage, and that someone (Andromache?) stood in his way.

So these comparisons do not support Schadewaldt's theory; indeed they count against it, and confirm the argument that stage actions of this kind should be reflected verbally. But if Eteocles did not arm on stage at *Seven* 677ff., then it seems that he would have to make his exit at 719 still unarmed. No doubt he would have been followed by an attendant carrying his panoply, as though he were about to put it on elsewhere; but we might well still feel that this would detract from the impact of his exit to death. Eteocles' death would surely be brought much closer to the audience's awareness if he were fully armed and all ready for battle (cf. Schadewaldt 362 with n. 8). Those who are unwilling to consider any serious interference with our text will simply have to live with this serious diminution in the dramatic power of Eteocles' fatal departure. I can, however, offer a textual escape from this, which the less conservative may think worth consideration.

Were it not for 675f. we might well have supposed that Eteocles was in his panoply right from the beginning of the play. In the prologue he is the vigorous military leader ready for any attack; and at 30ff. he sends the citizens to their posts ςὺν παντευχίαι, which may mean that they were already armed on stage. At 59 we hear that the enemy host is πάνοπλος; and the enemy armour is dwelt on by the chorus. In the *sieben Redepaare* the enemy champions are all described in full battle gear, and the six Thebans who Eteocles sends are likewise supposed to be equipped for the fight. And yet is Eteocles himself unarmed all this time? If we cut out the last two lines of his speech (i.e. 675–6), then there would be no reason to suppose that he was not armed from the start.[1] Once this simple solution is reached, it seems commendable on further grounds. Line 674 ἄρχοντί τ᾽ ἄρχων καὶ κασιγνήτωι κάσις makes a culmination to the speech which gives the terrible rightness of Eteocles' choice its full force. After that ἐχθρὸς ςὺν ἐχθρῶι στήσομαι is a weakening dilution, and the call for greaves is a further anti-climax.

---

[1] Prien (cited above p. 153 n. 1) 4–5 cut the two lines. (Dindorf and Paley excluded 674–6.) The excision of 675–6 would mean, of course, that τίς . . . ἐνδικώτερος; in 673 would be a question in parenthesis. Perhaps the interpolator did not realize this. Alternatively some later actors may have wanted to have an arming scene like the one which Schadewaldt envisages. It looks as though the interpolator modelled the lines on E. *Phoen* 779 rather than vice versa.

(b) *delayed exit at 676?*

Whether it ended originally with 674 or 676, Eteocles' last speech builds up towards his departure to battle. His actual declaration of intention is held back until 672, and then is put plainly . . . εἶμι καὶ ξυστήσομαι / αὐτός (if 675–6 were added later, then these are the verbs of his concluding sentence). Yet Eteocles does not go at the end of the speech, and he does not go until 719: he stays to argue the rights and wrongs of his position. Since Eteocles' intention is so immediate and decisive and yet the chorus manages to delay him so long, we may conjecture that Eteocles may actually have begun the movement of departure at 674 (or 676), and then have stopped at the words of the chorus. The physical movement, begun and then postponed, would in performance make more clear and powerful the issue at stake: see further 719c* below.

A further consideration which points in the same direction is the possibility that the restraint of a hero from battle may have been a recurrent scene. This would, of course, have the *Iliad* as its archetype. In tragedy, first the Servant then Alcmene try to restrain Iolaus at E. *Hkld* 68off., 709ff. In *Rh* Aeneas restrains Hector (104ff.), and then Hector restrains Rhesus (467ff.).[1] In *PAmh* 10 (cited fully in p. 160 n. 2 above) someone tries to hold the hero back from battle, presumably unsuccessfully. Finally, Murray and Pearson supposed that in S. *Eurypylos* fr. I3 (Carden = 208P) Eurypylos is keen for battle while Astyoche discourages him.[2] These amount to too little to claim with any confidence that we have a pattern; but, if we have, then *Seven* would fit it.

Delayed exit—by which I mean an exit movement which is begun and then stopped—is a simple device which occurs in most kinds of drama and in a great variety of dramatic circumstances. In Greek tragedy the most persistent and effective use is made of delayed exit in S. *Phil* where again and again characters, above

---

[1] These are different, however, in that the restraint is successful and the hero never does depart to battle (but cf. *Rh* 900f. for the parent who tries to dissuade her son from battle).

[2] But Grenfell and Hunt are right that (*POxy* vol. ix p. 118) 'the remains are really too slight to give any clear clue to the situation' (cf. Carden *ed* p. 5). It is possible that in A. *Memnon* and/or S. *Aithiopes* Eos tried to keep back her son Memnon. In *Glaukos Potnieus* the departure of Glaukos to the fatal games was probably a central event in the play, like the departure of Eteocles. Fr. 440 (37N) looks as though it may come from a stichomythia dispute over whether or not Glaukos should go, cf. *Seven* 712ff.

all Philoctetes himself, are on the point of leaving when they are prevented in one way or another (see *GRBS* 12 (1971) 26–7, 29–31, 33–9, cf. Steidle 186f.). In Aeschylus the only indubitable instances occur in the *Oresteia*, where it is most effectively exploited at *Ag* 855*, and again in the Cassandra scene—see 1330*. However, there is a probable use in *Hik*, which is not unlike this place in *Seven*: at *Hik* 733 Danaus is about to go and fetch help, but his terrified daughters involve him in an epirrhematic scene, and he does not finally go until 775*. As in *Seven* it is not absolutely clear whether Danaus actually began the physical movement of his departure.[1] In *Seven* this is not essential: what must be appreciated is that at the end of his seventh speech Eteocles' final exit is imminent. Throughout the following scene his departure is held back by a thread.

(c) exit to death

Many Greek tragedies are concerned with death, and in many a character who is alive at the start of the play meets his end before it is over. Almost always he dies off-stage, and that means that at some point he has to go off for the last time, and to leave the sight of the audience never to return, unless as a corpse. Usually the exit begins a fixed sequence: soon a messenger arrives to tell of the death (cf. pp. 171–2 below), and after him the corpse is brought back (see 854b*). Although the exit to death may occur in widely different circumstances—it may be, for instance, to self-sacrifice, to battle, to murder, to divine punishment—the exit itself, since it is the last the audience shall see of the character, always tends to be made an important, even a focal, event. But, of course, the particular impact of each exit to death and the dramatic emphasis it bears will depend on the way it is led up to and on its full context.

The last exit of Eteocles in *Seven* is the culmination of his role both as defender of the city and as the cursed son of Oedipus. It is in some ways the centre point of the play, for the first two-thirds lead up to it and the last part follows from it. However, it would be misleading to imply that the preparation for the exit is steady

---

[1] It looks as though there was an uproarious delayed exit of the chorus near the end of *Diktyoulkoi* (see p. 419). The device was, of course, common in comedy e.g. Ar. *Frogs* 174, *Ekkles* 872; for some examples from Menander cf. *GRBS* 12 (1971) 31 n. 14; for Roman Comedy see K. Bennett, *The Motivation of Exits in Greek and Latin Comedy* (Ann Arbor 1932) 16ff., Hough *CPh* 35 (1940) 39ff.

and sustained; in fact it is built up late and then with increasing
concentration. The exit is not prepared for from the first;[1] the
opening scenes convey the advance of attackers and the response
of Thebes; and, while it is never hinted that Eteocles will not
fight himself, all the emphasis is laid on his role as leader and
planner. It is first in the troublesome lines 282–6 that Eteocles
explicitly designates himself as one of the combatants. Assuming
the lines to be genuine and in the right place, then, although
they are inconsistent with the entire situation of the *sieben Redepaare* (see 286*, 371d*), they may none the less cast over that
scene an awareness that Eteocles will be one of the champions,
and hence that he will finally depart to battle. During the first
six pairs it is the battles of others which are at issue, and Eteocles'
own battle is not directly brought to mind. The repeated structure must, however, create a sense that his own crisis is inevitably
approaching (this is so with or without 282–6). In his final
speech Eteocles is, as in all the others, deciding on the merits of
the case who should defend the gate in question (or so it has been
argued on pp. 157–8 above). The new element is the curse of
Oedipus, which suddenly in some way fits into place, and which
requires exactly the same decision. So when Eteocles declares his
decision he is saying both that he will go to the seventh gate and
that he will go and fulfil the curse which means his own destruction. He is now the fighter as well as the strategist, and he is
the doomed man as well.

Eteocles may, as was argued in 719b* above, have made an
actual movement towards departure at the end of the speech; in
any case his fatal exit remains imminent throughout the following

---

[1] It is possible that an acute member of the audience would have been able to
foresee, even before the play began, that this exit would be a central point; particularly if (as I doubt) he could see the precise sense of Oedipus' riddling curses
in the preceding play.

It is very doubtful, however, whether the audience was given any advance clue
to a tragedy's contents by a knowledge of its *title*. We simply do not know whether
titles were announced at the Proagon; for the evidence see P-C *DFA*[2] 67f. We
cannot even be sure that all the titles preserved in the *didaskaliai* were given by
the dramatist himself. Ἑπτὰ ἐπὶ Θήβας is a case in point, for, although the title
is used at Ar. *Frogs* 1021, it is very unusual to have a collective plural title which
does not derive from the identity of the chorus; see Haigh *TDG* 396f. Also Καδμεῖοι
etc. are invariably used of the Thebans in this play and never Θηβαῖοι etc., cf.
Verrall *ed* xvi, xxxiii. (Dawson *tr* p. 1 n. 1 suggests that Ἐτεοκλῆς may have been
the original title.) For myself I suspect that the title was merely a convenience for
the official records, and that it was not regarded as significant by playwright or
audience. See further my note in *JHS* 95 (1975) 185.

scene. The dispute in lines 677–719 is this: should Eteocles deliberately go to fulfil the curse? If he makes an exit, then that exit will mean that he has done so and that the chorus has failed to dissuade him. So the dispute becomes, in effect, a dispute whether he should leave the stage. In the epirrhematic structure (686–711) this is implicit in the verbs of impulse and action (687, 692f., 698); and in the following brief stichomythia the chorus puts it plainly at 714: μὴ ἔλθηις ὁδοὺς cὺ τάcδ' ἐφ' ἑβδόμαιc πύλαιc.[1] When an exit from the stage will lead to certain consequences, then a dispute over whether the exit should be made at all serves to explore the dramatic situation and at the same time puts it in concrete terms on the stage. This simple and strong dramatic technique recurs throughout Greek tragedy; and it is put to particularly powerful use in the *Oresteia*, see *Ag* 974b*, 1330*, *Cho* 930*.[2] Everything that is at stake in *Seven* 677–719 will be decided by a stage action, Eteocles' exit. The act itself is held up and examined; then in the end, Eteocles breaks the suspense: (719) θεῶν διδόντων οὐκ ἂν ἐκφύγοιc κακά.[3] He goes; and in his going he fulfils the curse. For the audience, he is dead.[4]

(d) the exit within the thematic structure

The exit of Eteocles marks the end of the great central act, and a full-scale song ensues, the first for some 350 lines. In the final paragraph of his long section on 'Aufbau' Wilamowitz (69) says that the central act is surrounded on either side 'so that in the event a nice symmetry is outwardly achieved'. Before and after there is a song of fear, on either side of that a short transitional episode, framed at the beginning by the wild first song and at the end by the great θρῆνοc. Now the fashion for finding complex ring-structures was discussed with some suspicion on *Pers* 598b*;

---

[1] Cf. Seidensticker in *Bauformen* 196, who classifies the stichomythia as 'handlungsretardierend'.

[2] Deckinger 61 says that in Aeschylus an exit after a long debate occurs very rarely; yet he himself gives four examples and does not include the three instances cited from *Oresteia*. He gives Sophoclean examples on p. 151.

[3] M²sscr has ἐκφύγοι, which Dawe *Collation* 115 tends to favour (cf. Paley ad loc.). But this would naturally be taken to refer only to Polynices rather than all men in general, which would be much weaker.

[4] It seems particularly reprehensible that Grene *tr* has failed to put a stage instruction for the exit of Eteocles. This kind of neglect of the essential action has also led to 'not one thing happens in the course of the action' (Fowler *SO* 45 (1970) 24).

and even in Wilamowitz's simple scheme it is hardly legitimate to claim that two scenes 'correspond' to each other simply because they are both transitional. On the other hand it is true that the first song of the play looks forward emotionally to disaster, while the final threnos laments the completion of terrible events; and so they do enclose the core of the play. Compare the way that the first song of *Pers* expresses fear for the future, and looks forward to the return by dwelling on the departure, while the final laments confirm the completion of the disaster, and dwell on the contrast with the departure—cf. *Pers* 909b*.

More importantly, in *Seven* the two songs on either side of the *Redepaare* (287ff., 720ff.) are both dominated by fear and apprehension. This keynote is so striking that it seems plausible that the audience was meant to recognize them, more or less consciously, as a pair. If so, then the point lies, as usual, in the differences: the shift in choral emphasis reflects the thematic shift of the whole play. The fear in the earlier song, as in the parodos, was for the city and for the women themselves: in the later song, foreshadowing the dirges, the fear is for the brothers and the race of Laius. While the fate of the family is not totally absent from the first two-thirds of the play and while the fate of the city is not neglected in the last third, the emphasis moves from the city on to the royal family. And this change is not gradual but is marked exactly by Eteocles' recognition of the direction of the curse at 653ff. With this the chorus of Theban women terrified for their survival become instead mourners for the royal house and its terrible history.[1] The difference between Eteocles' seventh speech and those before is accentuated by its place within the formal structure; the same thematic change is brought out by the differences of preoccupation between the two songs which frame the central act.

But while we may accept Wilamowitz's 'Symmetrie' in broad terms, there are other structural patterns also. Thus, there is another rather more detailed correspondence between the two

[1] Cf. Wilamowitz 67–9. He is oversimplifying, however, to put the change in the role of the chorus as one from 'Mädchen' to 'das Volk von Theben'. (Yet surely Wilamowitz did not mean to imply, as Solmsen *TAPA* 68 (1937) 201 seems to think, that the chorus literally changed, i.e. went off and returned with a different identity.) For the change in Eteocles put in terms of a tension between a contemporary political outlook and an archaic mythical one see Vernant *Mythe et tragédie* etc. (Paris 1972) 28–30.

sequences at 203–86 and 677–719.[1] In both places there is an epirrhematic structure in which the choral dochmiacs alternate with sets of three trimeters from Eteocles. In both this is followed by a stichomythia, then by the exit of Eteocles, then by the songs of fear discussed above. While epirrhematic structures are rather frequent in earlier Aeschylus (see *Pers* 249b*), the similarities here are so close that an audience should recognize a parallelism. In the first sequence the dispute is about the fate of the city and its inhabitants, and Eteocles has to restrain the chorus: in the second it is the fate of the family which is at stake, and it is the chorus which tries to restrain Eteocles (see 719b* and c* above). Eteocles has changed from the responsible leader to the doomed fighter, the chorus has changed from panic-stricken women to earnest advisers of the king. To this extent the commonplace observation that Eteocles and the chorus 'change roles' is acceptable: but it would be a mistake to infer that they exchange roles. Just as there are vital similarities as well as differences between Eteocles' seventh speech and the other six, so here there are continuities as well as changes. Eteocles is still cool and the chorus still openly emotional, as the epirrhematic structure stresses. Eteocles is still bravely unflinching, the chorus still alarmed and looking for escape. And Eteocles still wants to do the right thing by the gods: but what the gods intend for the city and for the family of Laius are crucially different.

792 enter Messenger

the brevity of the scene

This Messenger is the only one in Aeschylus who has the later standard 'aftermath' function. But, as was pointed out in the discussion of Aeschylean messengers on *Pers* 249a*, he is not like the typical messenger of later tragedy because he has no long, vivid narrative ἀγγελία. Instead, his first short speech (792–802) puts his news of the salvation of the city in terms of the familiar ship imagery; its final hint about the brothers leads into a stichomythia (803–11) which forces him to tell plainly of their fate, and his final lines (812–19) then put this in terms of Oedipus' curse.

---

[1] Cf. e.g. Wolff *HSCP* 63 (1958) 89f., Cameron (cited above, p. 143 n. 1) 46, Petre *Stud. Class.* 13 (1971) 23 n. 85; for the two stichomythias see Seidensticker *Bauformen* 193.

In neither little rhesis is there any detailed narrative, and the whole scene is only some 30 lines long. It is, in fact, one of those Aeschylean brief one-actor scenes which were collected on pp. 108f. above.

There is undoubtedly some textual disruption in this scene; and it has even been suggested by Von der Mühll (*MH* 21 (1964) 225–7) that there is a major lacuna and that we have lost a long messenger speech. But his detailed arguments for this can be met by less drastic emendation,[1] and it may be claimed that we positively do not want a long messenger speech. The *sieben Redepaare* contain much martial detail, and there is a dramatic sense in which those speeches evoke and settle the contests at the gates (see above, esp. p. 155); and so it would be otiose to have a battle narrative here. Compare and contrast E. *Phoen* where the long messenger speech (1090–1199, followed by 1217–63) covers much of the ground settled in *Seven* by the *Redepaare*. By dealing with the battles before they happen Aeschylus is able to pre-empt a narrative and to concentrate on the fratricide as a fact and on its ramifications. Comparably in *Ag* Cassandra's previsions of the murder make a long aftermath narrative unnecessary and enable Aeschylus to explore the situation in a more concentrated and dramatic way. In both cases the catastrophic deed is woven into the scenes both before and after it so that it is combined with other thematic and poetic factors.

A final word on the identity of the Messenger. The list of *dramatis personae* in M does not distinguish this character from the

---

[1] Some comparatively slight textual patching is still required; and scholars have offered a great many different solutions, some worse than others. (Some recent discussions are Page 31f., Erbse 19ff. (who in 19 n. 2 counts seventeen previous arrangements), Willink *CQ* N.S. 18 (1968) 4ff., Young *GRBS* 13 (1972) 27–30 (who stubbornly preserves the paradosis), Reeve ibid. 473.) Many have adopted Weil's plausible transposition of 805 to after 810 and his consequent attribution of 810 to the chorus. One motive for this transposition is that it would make sense of 804. 804 is virtually duplicated at the end of the messenger's part (820), and many editors have followed Butler in athetizing 820–1. But, while it seems likely that 820 is an inserted duplicate, 821 is a good line and may only be displaced (from before 812?, thus Weil). 818–19 would certainly make a strong final couplet for the messenger and would set the theme for the following lyrics. Note also that, if the messenger closed with 819, then this would emphasize the theme of the burial of the brothers and of the identity of their lots. Wilamowitz (88 and *ed maj* ad loc.) may be right to attribute the interpolation (and/or displacement) of 820–1 to the same hand as that which added the final scene. For while the curse seems to demand a shared grave for the brothers, the author of the final scene evidently wished to separate them (see p. 182 and 1078* below).

ἄγγελος κατάϲκοποϲ, and a scholion in M on 792 explicitly identifies them. Some have believed this.[1] It could be that Aeschylus put this character in recognizably the same costume and mask as the Scout; but we have no reason to suppose that the scholiast had any authentic information on matters like this, and we are free to reject it. There was a point in making the Scout of the prologue and of the central scene the same man in view of 66f. and of the relationship between the two scenes. But his part was played at 652*. There is no point in bringing him back in another role with a completely different dramatic function.

819 (or 821) exit Messenger

854 the two corpses are borne on

(a) problems of authenticity

All discussion of the last parts of *Seven* is bedevilled by the suspicion that our transmitted text includes some large-scale alteration and addition. For myself, I may as well declare at once that I have little doubt that the sisters, the introductory anapaests (861–74), and the entire scene from 1005 to the end have been added, presumably by actors, to Aeschylus' original play, though not necessarily all by the same hand. And I suspect that there has been some other slight alteration and cutting in order to accommodate the interpolations (see, for example, previous page on 820–1). This is a huge controversy, and I shall only discuss it in so far as it is germane to my subject.

In this century most scholars, though by no means all, have accepted that 861–74 and 1005 ad fin. are later additions. In this they follow the basic discussions of Wilamowitz.[2] The defence against Wilamowitz was desultory until Lloyd-Jones undertook it (*End* 8off.). Since then some scholars have regarded the authenticity of the disputed parts as proven (which Lloyd-Jones did not claim to have shown); but most, I have the impression, have remained unconvinced.[3] Lloyd-Jones set out to show that

---

[1] e.g. Tucker, Murray *tr*, Kirkwood 21, Page *OCT*: see *contra* Wilamowitz 85.

[2] Wilamowitz *SBAW* 1903 pp. 436ff. and *Interpretationen* 88ff. Page *OCT* seems to have reverted to the position of Bergk who also condemned 961–1004. Without seeing detailed arguments against Wilamowitz's defence of these lines I cannot fairly consider this.

[3] Most of the significant contributions since 1959 are referred to in the following pages. P. Nicolaus *Die Frage nach der Echtheit der Schlussszene von Aischylos' Sieben* (diss. Tübingen 1967) is mediocre, but does include a full bibliography.

not one of Wilamowitz's arguments was conclusive, and that, while some were wholly unfounded, each one was at least open to a shadow of doubt. If he has succeeded in this then he has shown that the interpolation is not absolutely proven; but it does not follow from this that it is refuted. Conclusive proof is not possible in a question like this, for there is no evidence which would allow of absolute certainty. In fact, Wilamowitz's cumulative case remains extremely strong; and there are other points to be added to it, some of which are touched on below. In my view we can be reasonably confident of the case against authenticity; and that is the most that can be expected.

(b) the structural sequence 822–1004

There are no spoken iambics all the way from the exit of the Messenger at 819 up to the intrusion of the Herald at 1005. But this is not a single continuous lyric sequence: it falls into definite parts. If the structural technique can be analysed then this may help with the two questions which face us here: the question of when the corpses were first seen (854c* below), and that of whether the introduction of the sisters is acceptable or suspect (871a*). I shall approach the structural sequence from two related angles, first in the formal terms of acts and act-dividing songs (see §5), and secondly in terms of the sequence of messenger followed by corpses and mourners, a sequence often found in the concluding parts of a Greek tragedy.

It will be best to consider first the formal structure of the last part of *Pers*, which is similar to *Seven* and more easily analysable.[1]

(α) 853–908: choral act-dividing song (three strophic pairs and epode). This dwells on the past, but leads up to the entry of Xerxes (see p. 126).

(β) 909: enter Xerxes, who thus inaugurates the final act.

(γ) 909–1001: lyric dialogue lament, each strophe divided between Xerxes and the chorus (three strophic pairs). This sets Xerxes' disaster in a larger context.

(δ) 1002–1076: more indulgent antiphonal lament (four strophic pairs and epode).

The sequence in *Seven* is closely analogous, though in order to accommodate the text as it is transmitted some subdivision is

[1] Jens 249 tries to bring out similarities of structural function between the Darius scene in *Pers* and the brief messenger scene in *Seven*; but these do not go far.

necessary. (I should make it clear that I do not accept the text as it is transmitted, and I give a revised structural analysis below on p. 175.)

(α) 822–60: choral act-dividing song (anapaestic prelude, one strophic pair, and epode).[1] This dwells on Oedipus and Laius, and then turns to the introduction of the brothers.

(β1) 861?: the corpses are borne on. The timing of this is discussed in 854c*.

(β2) 861–74: anapaests introducing the entry of the sisters. See 871a*.

(γ) 875–960: lament for the brothers, each strophe apparently divided between two parts (four strophic pairs). This puts their death in the fuller context of the curse and the extinction of the family.

(δ) 961–1004: a more brief and particular antiphonal dirge (one strophic pair with ephymnia (966–88), preceded by a prelude and followed by an epode).

This pair of schemes makes it clear how in *Pers* the act-dividing song is framed by an exit (Darius) and an entry (β), and how the long final act of lament is divided into longer strophic pairs (γ) and the concluding antiphonal dirge (δ). *Seven* is similar except that the entry sequence (β1; β2) which closes the act-dividing song (α) and inaugurates the laments (γ, δ) is more complex and confused. Not only are the sisters brought on with an anapaestic introduction (β2), but we have to fit in the bearing on of the corpses (β1), either at the end of the act-dividing song or earlier.

Although there are these technical similarities to *Pers* the plot pattern in *Seven* is very different, since the final parts of the play are consequential on an exit to death or glory—see 719c*. Such an exit is usually, as in *Seven*, followed after an interval by the arrival of the 'aftermath' messenger.[2] The messenger makes the transition to the return of the 'debris' of the catastrophe—be it

---

[1] Or two strophic pairs? Several editors, following Hermann, are willing to emend sufficiently to make 848–60 a responding strophic pair. But this means splitting the opening of the invitation to lament (854ff.) between strophe and antistrophe; and in 854c* I give further reasons for regarding this 'epode' as two separate elements. (Page *OCT* suspects the anapaestic prelude 822–31.)

[2] There are exceptions; for *Ag* e.g. see p. 324. In E. *Hkld* it has been widely held that a messenger speech reporting the death of Macaria has been lost; but more probably she is deliberately forgotten so that the play may move on to new preoccupations—see Zuntz *CQ* 41 (1947) 46ff.

the dying, the dead, the mourners, the victors. That is to say that first we hear by report of what has happened, and then we see and hear the human consequences (cf. Dingel 106ff. and *Bauformen* 361). On occasion this transition from word to deed, from narrative to tangible remains, is made explicit, as in *Seven* 848: τάδ' αὐτόδηλα· προῦπτος ἀγγέλου λόγος, cf. e.g. S. *Trach* 223, E. *Phoen* 1480f. Sometimes the interval between the messenger and the 'survivors' is covered, as here, by a full-scale strophic act-dividing song,[1] but often the interval is shorter: an astrophic lyric (e.g. E. *Her* 1016ff., *Ion* 1229ff., *Ba* 1153ff.—cf. p. 226 below), or a few anapaests (e.g. S. *Ant* 1257ff., *OT* 1297ff.; E. *Andr* 1166ff., *Phoen* 1480ff.), or even at S. *OC* 1669/70 by no interval at all. The lyric announcement or introduction at *Seven* 848ff. may show this tendency to shorten the interval: see further 854c* below.

When the messenger has reported a death then he is usually followed by the corpse. If he is not, then there is some special reason, as e.g. in S. *OC* where Oedipus has gone to a secret end, or in E. *Or* where the 'corpse' has vanished (also the corpses of human sacrifice are not normally seen, e.g. E. *Hkld, Hec, Phoen*). When there is a corpse there should be a lament; a lament means mourners, and naturally the mourners are usually close relatives. So the dramatist has the task of getting both the mourners and the corpse on to the stage. Sometimes the relative is already on stage before the corpse is brought on, as e.g. in S. *El* (urn), E. *Hipp* (dying man), *Andr, Tro*; sometimes the mourner accompanies the body on to the stage, e.g. in S. *Ant*, E. *Alc, Phoen, Rh*; and occasionally one mourner is already on stage while another accompanies the corpse, e.g. in E. *Hik, Ba*, and probably S. *Eurypylos*. In *Seven* none of these occurs. If the sisters belong to Aeschylus' play then the mourners are brought on *after* the corpses; and, if they are added, then in the original the sole mourner was the chorus itself. These alternatives are discussed in 871a*.

(c) when are the corpses seen?

The opening words of the epode (848 quoted above) clearly mark

[1] E. *Hipp* is unusual in that, although there is only an astrophic lyric (1268ff.), it is not the 'survivor' Hippolytus, but Artemis, who enters after it. This is because Theseus must first know the truth. On S. *Trach* and on 'advance' messengers see *Pers* 249a*.

the moment at which the chorus first sees the bodies and their bearers approaching. As the scholion in M rather quaintly puts it, ὁρᾶι ὁ χορὸς τὰ cώματα βαcταζόμενα. Many commentators have supposed that this is the time when the audience also sees the procession; that is, they take the words to accompany the entry.[1] But this is not necessarily so, for 848ff. might be a lyric entrance announcement, in which case the corpses would not be seen until the end of the lyric structure at 861.[2] Indeed, *if* the text as we have it has not been interfered with and the structural analysis obtained on p. 171 above is right, then the entry of the corpses (β^1) should not happen until the end of the act-dividing song (a). The 'stasimon' should be *followed* by the new entry which marks the beginning of an act.

Still assuming that our text is sound, it may be worth a digression to consider the topic of entry announcement, or indeed entry itself, *during* rather than *after* an act-dividing lyric. Kranz (164ff., cf. 204ff., 251) has illustrated how Aeschylus tends in the last sentence or two of a 'stasimon' to turn, often with νῦν, to some sort of transitional preparation for the next entry and act. This has already been noted at *Pers* 904ff. (see p. 126 above), and similar techniques may be observed at *Seven* 790f., *Hik* 598f., *Cho* 649ff.; 726ff. But in none of these places should it be suggested that the entry happens during the act-dividing lyric, viz. before or during the transitional words, for this would destroy the whole effect of the allusive imagery through which the transition is made. Such places are not entry announcements but a subtle form of preparation. Three rather different and more awkward places in Aeschylus remain to be considered. *Hik* 825ff. is severely corrupt, but it seems that the Herald was given a lyric entry announcement; however, this evidently stood after and outside the strophic act-dividing song 776–824—see *Hik* 838b*. Later at *Hik* 977 it looks as though the Handmaidens

---

[1] Thus e.g. Tucker, Wecklein, Bodensteiner 729, Bolle 12, Mazon, Italie, Rose, Headlam *tr*, Schadewaldt *tr*, Dawson *tr*, Murray *tr*. Grene (120) brings on both the corpses *and* the sisters at 848, which looks like plain negligence.

[2] Thus e.g. Wilamowitz *ed maj*, 'Droysen' *tr*, Vellacott *tr*, Untersteiner *tr* However 'Droysen' (cf. Murray *tr* 67) brings on the sisters as well as the corpses at 861; but the sisters' entry should come later at 871 (see 871a*). Verrall and Arnott *tr* bring on the corpses and sisters together at 871 (Werner at 874); but there is no good reason to delay the corpses so long. (Paley for some reason brings on the corpses at 875 and the sisters at 961!)

were brought on without any introduction during the course of a
brief astrophic set of anapaests with act-dividing function: but I
am extremely reluctant to allow this—see *Hik* 974b*. Finally, it
is sometimes claimed that the last words of the first song of *Ag*
(255–7) refer to Clytemnestra, so that she entered just before the
end of the antistrophe. This difficult question is weighed on *Ag*
258b*: while I should not rule out an entry during the lyric, I
favour a reference to the chorus in these words and a new entry
after the song at 258.

Once we look outside Aeschylus there are some unequivocal
examples of entry announcement within an act-dividing song.
Consider S. *Trach* 222ff., where the last few words of an astrophic
'stasimon'[1] refer to an approaching entry, and *Trach* 962ff. where
the entire last antistrophe of a proper strophic song announces
the approach of the dying Heracles, and *Phil* 201ff. where the
last strophic pair of three in the first song (parodos) announces
Philoctetes, who is heard off-stage and is first seen at the end
(219).[2] Wilamowitz (*Analecta* 203) implies that there are no lyric
entrance announcements in Euripides; but at *Alc* 233ff. the
chorus announces the approach of Alcestis just before the end of
the last antistrophe, and similarly the last few words of the
'parodos' of *Ion* (236) introduce Creusa and those of *Phoen*
(258–60) Polynices. All those lyric entrance announcements have
some analogy with *Seven* 848ff., and they all confirm that,
although the announcement comes within the song, the entry
itself should come at the end of it. It is true that there are also
occasional places in Sophocles and Euripides where an entry
occurs *within* a lyric structure which is to a greater or lesser
extent an act-dividing lyric, but none of these exceptional pieces
of technique is remotely like the place under consideration in
Seven.[3]

---

[1] This astrophic is a kind of act-dividing lyric, although weak, since there is
an entry after it and the equivalent of an exit before it when the old man retreats
into the background (cf. p. 89 above). The scholion on 216 which explicitly
says τὸ μελιδάριον οὐκ ἔστι στάσιμον labours under a mistaken idea of what a
stasimon is, as is shown by Dale *Papers* 38–40 (*contra* Kranz 177, *Forma* 23).

[2] Robinson (*CQ* N.S. 19 (1969) 39), among others, argues that Philoctetes
entered before the end of the song.

[3] I list all such entries that I know of: S. *Aj* 895, *El* 1423 (see *GRBS* 1971 p. 41;
not *Phil* 719, see ibid. 33 n. 18), *OC* 138; E. *Hik* 798, *Cycl* 503 (or 511?). Perhaps
the controversial E. *Andr* 1041 is another instance; see, recently, Steidle 119ff.,
Stevens *Andr ed* 218f., 249.

So, if we keep the transmitted text, the epode 848–60 is apparently an entrance announcement within the act-dividing lyric (α), and the corpses were probably brought on (β¹) at the end of the song, i.e. at 861. But all of this section as well as the formal structural analysis on p. 171 has proceeded on the assumption that our transmitted text is much as Aeschylus composed it. Yet many students of Aeschylus, myself included, hold that the anapaests 861–74 have been interpolated in order to bring on two added *dramatis personae*—Antigone and Ismene. Yet, it seems, not one of the scholars who agree on this has considered what difference the elimination of the anapaests makes to the handling of the entry of the corpses.[1] Once the entry of the sisters (β²) is omitted, it is no longer necessary to regard l. 860 as the end of the act-dividing song (α); and, once the anapaests are out of the way, then what I have been calling the epode (848–60) becomes simply the lines which lie between the antistrophe which ends at 847 and the beginning of the first strophe of the great threnody at 875. In that case 848–60 need no longer be regarded as a unit, since it is no longer squashed in between the sighting of the corpses and the announcement of the sisters. Then the lines evidently fall into two sections, 848–53 and 854–60; and the masterly lyric iambics of 854–60 (beginning ἀλλὰ γόων, ὦ φίλαι) may now be taken with the following lament (875ff.). It is best, I suggest, to see these lines as an astrophic prelude to the main lament (astrophic, assuming there has been no cutting by the interpolator). Then only 848–53 (τάδ᾽ αὐτόδηλα . . . ἐφέστιοι;) remain as the entrance announcement of the brothers (the lines are so corrupt that it is even possible that the announcement was originally in iambic trimeters). This leaves as the act-dividing song just one strophic pair and a (suspect) prelude (822–47). This is just the right context for an unusually brief lyric, see p. 172 above.

If all this is along the right lines then the structural analysis on p. 171 above will have to be revised and simplified. We now have

(α) 822–47: act-dividing song (one strophic pair with prelude).
(β) 848–53: the corpses are borne on with a brief announcement.
(γ) as before, with the addition of a prelude (854–60).
(δ) as before.

---

[1] Though Kranz 126 n. 7 does, at least, raise the point that there may have been some cutting as well as interpolation.

This is, of course, much more like *Pers*, and it is altogether simpler and more powerful.

In conclusion, the timing of the bearing on of the corpses is bound up with a decision about the authenticity of the sisters and of the anapaests at 861ff. If they are kept, then the entry of the bodies should be held back until 861. But without them it can be brought forward to the time of the announcement in 848–53; and the haunting imagery and choreography of the rowing of the ship of death in 854ff. may be taken with the main lament.

871 [enter Antigone and Ismene]

(a) *the anapaests and the introduction of the sisters*

Once again I shall assume first that the anapaests are authentic, and I shall consider the consequences of that assumption before going on to the situation without them.

861–70 take the form of an entrance announcement, while 871–4 are a second-person address. This uncommon but well-established combination was discussed on *Pers* 155a*.[1] In the light of that discussion we should regard *Seven* 871, rather than 861, as the point of entry, as most editors have rightly supposed. It was also pointed out that, while the greeting in *Pers* is honorific, such entry addresses are also found at junctures of high pathos; and that anapaests tend to accompany slow entries which establish a tableau situation, particularly in a funeral context, as is the case here. In all these respects the anapaests are perfectly acceptable.

Although some have wanted to bring on the sisters together with the corpses (see p. 173 n. 2), it seems clear that our text means their entries to be separate. The corpses should be borne on at 861, if not earlier: see 854c*. And there is no hint of the corpses being with the sisters in 861ff.: on the contrary the wording of 861 suggests that the sisters are coming to join the corpses. There is no encouragement for the idea that the two pairs of entries are simultaneous, whether from the same direction or from separate directions (a rare technique, see 374b* above). It is simply the usual technique of slightly separated entries which has been employed. Even so, this is still peculiar,

---

[1] See p. 74 n. 3 for Pötscher's claim that the similarity of the anapaests in *Pers* and *Seven* shows the authenticity of those in *Seven*.

since there is nowhere else in surviving tragedy where one entry at the end of an act-dividing song is immediately followed by the full announcement of another. It is hard to find anything closer than S. *Aj* 1223–5, which is still very different. This peculiarity results from the need to bring on both the corpses and the mourners before the lament. As was seen on p. 172 above, the mourner is usually already on-stage or accompanies the corpses: but here the mourners enter after the corpses. However, we might compare E. *Hec* 658ff. where the corpse is brought on at 658 and Hecuba enters at 667, or the bolder technique at S. *Trach* 971 where Hyllus emerges from the palace to meet the procession which brings the dying Heracles.[1]

It could be claimed that, were it not for the objections which have been raised against the final scene of the play, no one would ever have suspected the anapaests or the introduction of the sisters for the lament alone. But since they have been suspected, it should be made clear that the suspicions are not without substance. The unique way that the lyric entrance announcement is followed immediately by a second announcement does seem confused and over-elaborate. While these techniques are hardly a serious point against authenticity, they certainly do not count in favour of it. Also there is the lack of any personal element for the sisters in the lament; surely if they were meant to take part there should be elements suited uniquely to them.[2] And there is

[1] This is a very blunt simultaneous and yet separate entry. Many editors insist on the hint in 901–3, and claim that Hyllus is with Heracles, although he has never to our knowledge left the house. But the death of Deianeira has distracted Hyllus as well as the audience since 901–3. There is a good discussion by Winnington-Ingram *BICS* 16 (1969) 44–7 (who does not, however, note the rarity of simultaneous yet separate entry and does not take seriously enough the suggestion (see T. von Wilamowitz 157ff.) that 901–3 (or just 901–2) are interpolated). *Trach* 962ff. is one of those places where an entry is announced within an act-dividing song (see p. 174 above); so had Hyllus been given an entry announcement, which he is *not*, *Trach* would be closely similar to the double announcement in *Seven* (as we have it).

[2] Page *OCT* on 875–960 accepts this: 'vix credibile videtur, si 875–960 sororibus tribuendi sint, nihil inesse quod sororibus unice conveniat'. On the other hand on 961–1004 he says '961–1004 sororibus tribuendos esse demonstravit Lloyd-Jones l.c. 107seqq.; his enim unice congrui sunt 996–7'. This refers to these two dochmiac metra: πρὸ πάντων δ' ἐμοί – καὶ τὸ πρόςω γ' ἐμοί. On the strength of this alone Lloyd-Jones (*End* 104 cf. 107f.) claims that it is 'certain that whoever wrote 961–1004 meant the amoebean parts of this passage for the two sisters'; and on p. 108 he calls the deletion of one or both of these phrases 'arbitrary'. Yet why should we assume that the interpolator was so crude that he could not interweave the odd connection in the genuine parts? Those who think there is good over-all

the silence of the sisters during the main part of the lament, which the anapaests seem to condone: see 871b* below. Finally, there are also some peculiarities in the language of the anapaests. Lloyd-Jones[1] has attempted a detailed defence against Wilamowitz's strictures, but he is not altogether successful. In particular his attempt to emend away πρότερον φήμης in 866 (followed by Page *OCT*) should not be accepted, see 871b* below.[2]

Finally, let us consider the situation if we once accept that the anapaests and the sisters have been added. The handling of the introduction of the corpses and of the opening of the lament is much more powerful and straightforward: see 854c*. But, without the sisters, the chorus alone sings the lament, and there is no speaking actor in the play after the Messenger. This would be the only instance in surviving tragedy of a corpse which is mourned solely by the chorus. This could be explained by the date of *Seven*. In early tragedy, when the chorus had a larger part to play, it was in all likelihood quite common for the chorus alone to sing the lyric *threnos*. In all of the plays of Sophocles and Euripides to survive, the chorus has already undergone a substantial restriction of its scope, and the only other corpses in surviving plays of Aeschylus are in *Ag* and *Cho*, where none is given a proper *threnos* at the time of death (though at *Ag* 1373ff. the chorus would lament Agamemnon if it could). But even among the papyrus fragments of Aeschylus we have one (fr. 496M) from a lyric lament, and the few lines we have are purely choral.[3] No

reason to reject the sisters should have little compunction over these two trivial phrases. Fraenkel *Schluss* 6of. also points out that πρόcω is not used in tragedy of degree without any notion of time or space. Professor Lloyd-Jones refers me to S. *El* 213 φράζου μὴ πόρcω φωνεῖν (cf. A. *Hik* 272); but is there not an association of time there?

[1] Lloyd-Jones *End* 100–4. On p. 100 he calls the lines 'the anapaests of the sisters', and 104 n. 3 furthers the misimpression that the anapaests are actually to be delivered by the sisters.

[2] The voluptuous epithets in 864f. are incongruous *Kitsch*. Wilamowitz *SBAW* 1903 p. 448 talks of 'Geschmacklosigkeit'. This is brought out, however unintentionally, by Tucker (p. 176): 'the adjectives set the soft charms of the tender breasts in contrast with the bitter sighs which rend them'. And the peculiarity of the paraphrase for women in 871–2 (again involving breasts) is not lessened by the long discussion in which Lloyd-Jones (102–4) fails to find a parallel. Fraenkel *Schluss* 58 claims that the phrase is inspired by 927f. If the interpolation is once accepted on other grounds then this is a very likely explanation, though it can hardly be allowed as a point in itself against authenticity.

[3] *POxy* 2251 = 280 Ll-J. (The attribution of this fragment to *Aigyptioi* is discussed and rightly doubted by Garvie 200–2. While it has some attractions,

one can seriously maintain that, if the lament in *Seven* was originally purely choral, then it was likely to have been the only
instance among Aeschylus' plays.

But there is also dramatic point to the technique. We have
already noticed (719d*) how the chorus has turned from a role
which was chiefly concerned with the city to one which is concentrated on the family and on the two sons of Oedipus. This
prepares the way for the long choral lament. Moreover, the
family is extinct: this is clearly, though not explicitly, implied at
several points (see pp. 181–2 below). If no members of the family
survive, then there can be no family mourners. The end of the
race would be effectively conveyed by the absence of any actors
from the last part of the play. The lament, the function of the
closest living relatives, has to be left to the chorus. The threat to
the city is chiefly conveyed by choral means; and so is the lamentable end of the royal house.

(b)   the silence of the sisters

In my view one of the strongest arguments against the authenticity of the sisters, a point not usually raised, is their silence
during the main part of the lament, 874–960. I have discussed
this in *HSCP* 76 (1972) 84–9. The crux of the argument is that
most scholars, including Lloyd-Jones, give the sisters no part in
the lament until 961; and that this inexplicable silence is totally
unlike an Aeschylean silence, and is so pointless and awkward
that it should not be foisted on him. Most recent scholars who
have wished to defend the sisters have given them parts to sing in
the main body of the lament.[1] But this cannot be allowed because
the words of the anapaests themselves explicitly say that the
sisters will sing *after* the chorus: that is what 866–70 declares,
despite its unpoetic πρότερον φήμης. The interpolator wished to
bring the sisters on before the beginning of the lament, and yet he
was not prepared to create a role for them in the main part of it.
The result is that they are left in vacant silence for nearly 100

Cunningham's case simply is not sufficient. A weighty objection which Garvie
neglects is the prima facie equation of the title and the identity of the chorus.)
Lost plays where the lament may have been wholly or chiefly choral include
Argeiai, Heliades, Threissai.

[1] In addition to Bergk (see op. cit. 87 n. 90) I have noted Weil, Sidgwick,
Murray *OCT* (but not *tr*), Webster *Chorus* 121, 'Droysen' *tr*, Grene *tr*.

lines after their entry. When he composed his anapaests the interpolator claimed that this was δίκη (866) : but to accept his word would not do justice to Aeschylus.

1005 [enter Herald (accompanied by Theban officials ?)]

(a) the 'false ending'

In the last part of the antiphonal lament it seems that the play is drawing to its conclusion. Then there is a sudden new turn of events with the entry of the Herald, and the play is unexpectedly prolonged. This is only too obvious to those who think that the final scene has been added : the reason why the lines leading up to 1004 look like an end is that they *were* the end, or almost the end. Those who defend the final scene do not usually pay any attention to this 'false ending' : but they should, for, if they are right, then the way that Aeschylus draws the play to a conclusion, which he then turns away from and supersedes, must be of significance for the interpretation of the play. It demands an explanation. To make this clear I shall examine the ways in which the impression is given that the end is approaching, and the ways in which the new turn is unexpected.

The close correspondence of the formal structure of 822–1004 with the final scenes of *Pers* was traced on 854b*. But in *Pers* the tragedy ended with the antiphonal lament (δ) ; the Elders formed a προπομπή for Xerxes, and escorted him off at 1077*. In *Seven* the chorus has already sung at 916 that its lament προπέμπει the brothers; and towards the end there are further hints of an impending procession, particularly in the last three lines we have, 1002–4. A few more lines, including verbs of motion and perhaps some more explicit reference to the joint burial, and the play would be at an end.[1] The single analogy with *Pers* does not show that the play originally ended at this juncture, but it does indicate that the audience would be expecting it to draw to a close. Similarly, Fraenkel (*Kl B* 268–71) has pointed out that the metrical form of 998, 1002 (and the catalectic form in 1001, 1004) is particularly associated with the closing lines of plays. This too

---

[1] The interpolator 'exitum genuinum chori Aeschylei truncavit' Wilamowitz *ed maj actio* on 1005. It is possible that the cutting and alteration of Aeschylus' original was complicated (consider e.g. the probable interpolation of 997–8, see p. 177 n. 2) : on the other hand the play seems almost complete at 1004.

does not necessarily show that this was the end, rather than that it was meant to be taken to be the end. Moreover, the lament is not an act-dividing song, it is itself a lyric act following on a song (α) and inaugurated by entries (β). It might be expected either to end the play, as in *Pers*, or to be followed by another act-dividing song: what could not be expected is a further entry giving the act an entirely new turn. And an audience in 467 B.C. would probably expect the final parts of the tragedy to be largely choral; cf. *Pers*, *Hik*. Even if the sisters were to dominate the antiphonal part of the lament (δ) this would still sound like the final largely choral act. But if, as some editors suppose (see p. 179 n. 1), the sisters also dominated the main body of the lament (γ), then the chorus would have very little part to play after 874; and if, further, 1005ff. is accepted as genuine then the chorus would be positively eclipsed in the last part of the play. In an earlier play of Aeschylus, this is suspicious. If, on the other hand, the sisters were added, then the Aeschylean original was purely choral from 822 to the end (see pp. 178–9 above). The desire to give the actors more to do may have been one of the interpolator's motives.

These formal and technical considerations would all give the audience the impression that the play is near its end in the antiphonal epode. In thematic and dramatic terms the same impression is fostered (cf. Wilamowitz 88f.). The brothers are about to be borne off in procession to be buried together in the earth by the side of their father. This completes the curse which had without doubt been heard in the *Oidipous*, and which is repeatedly alluded to in the last third of *Seven*. We cannot do more than guess at its precise wording, but it is clear that it concerned the 'equal distribution' of the brothers' inheritance by 'the iron foreigner'.[1] This means, of course, that they would kill each other and be possessed of 'six feet' of the earth of their fatherland. It is also implied that the race is utterly destroyed. There is nothing about children or ἐπίγονοι;[2] there is not even, indeed, any hint of sisters, except in the suspected anapaests at 861ff. In sum, there is no suggestion of an aftermath: the twin burial should end the

[1] For the main likely allusions to the contents of the curse see 727ff., 786ff., 816ff., 941ff., 947ff.; cf. E. *Phoen* 68 θηκτῶι cιδήρωι δῶμα διαλαχεῖν τόδε. See also Cameron *GRBS* 9 (1968) 247f., Burnett *GRBS* 14 (1973) 355ff., esp. 358f.

[2] Lloyd-Jones's case (*End* 87ff.) for forward-looking references to the Epigonoi is untenable. He has been effectively attacked (independently, it seems) by Dawe *CQ* N.S. 17 (1967) 19–20, Kirkwood 23–5, Cameron op. cit. 251, Dawson *tr* 24–5.

saga. But according to our text it seems in the end that the brothers are to be disposed of separately instead of together, see
1078*. And it is far from clear that Polynices will obtain an equal
share of his fatherland by being properly buried, let alone in-
humed, for 1038–41 strongly imply a rudimentary symbolic
burial as in S. *Ant.*[1] All this would contradict the main lament
(e.g. 914 and 947ff.). But these are details: the main question
facing those who defend the final scene is why Aeschylus should
create a false ending, why he should stop the curtain even as it
descends.

The Herald's intervention is a surprise, not only because the
threnody had seemed to be the ending of the play, but also because
it is given no clear preparation. Advance preparation is one of
the characteristic ways in which Greek tragedy achieves its
close-knit unity of plot and action—see, in general, pp. 9–12.
Yet in *Seven* there is nothing to lead the audience to look forward
to an intervention from the city or to an issue over claims to
burial or to the defiance of Antigone. This is, of course, one of the
main weapons of those who question the authenticity of the final
scene. Those who defend the scene stress the importance of the
city and the contrast between the two leaders in the first two-
thirds of the play, and they point out that the city, although
subordinated to the family, is not forgotten in the last third. But
this does not amount to preparation; there is nothing to suggest
that these themes will be revived and that they will close the
play. It is as though after *Eum* 1047 the ghost of Clytemnestra
suddenly reappeared and complained of the acquittal of Orestes,
and as though half of the Erinyes then set off in pursuit of
Orestes and half stayed at Athens (cf. E. *IT* 968ff.!). If this were
the case, one could not say that such a new turn of events had no
roots in the earlier parts of the play; but it could not be claimed
that it had been prepared for or that it would be anything other
than a totally unexpected departure. Similarly, those who defend
Seven 1005ff. had best admit that it is a completely unprepared-

---

[1] Lloyd-Jones's idea (*End* 97–9) that Antigone intends to cremate Polynices
hardly relieves this difficulty. Also his suggestion that κόλπωι φέρουcα (1039)
means 'dragging in my arms' is simply refuted by the rest of the line—βυccίνου
πεπλώματοc. Dawe *CQ* N.S. 17 (1967) 23–4 is so intent on his own facetious in-
vective that he does not clearly make this point. (Another indication that Dawe
is more interested in polemic than in Aeschylus is that he writes ἐν κόλπωι for
κόλπωι throughout.)

for extension of the play, and should try to justify it on those terms. They would not, however, be well advised to compare the deliberately episodic and unprepared-for scenes which are found in Euripides, in *Rh*, and in *Prom* (Io—see *Prom* 561*). For those scenes all happen in the middle of plays and not at the end, and their integration is made not through plot but through thematic links.

One particular element in the surprise effect is the absence of preparation for the entry of the Herald himself. While one would not expect an anonymous minor character to be prepared for personally, there should normally be some 'situational' preparation for his role (see pp. 10f.). So if this scene is by Aeschylus, then the Herald's entry must be a deliberate surprise.[1] Why? Although I have not seen it cited in this context, there is one comparably late and unexpected entry in Aeschylus: Aegisthus at *Ag* 1577. Although there is more premonition of Aegisthus' entry than of that of the Herald in *Seven*, *Ag* similarly leads towards a 'false conclusion' which is abruptly and unexpectedly interrupted. In *Ag* there certainly is a positive dramatic point for this—see *Ag* 1577a* and b*. Whether or not there is any comparable point in *Seven*, there is a crucial difference. The late entry of Aegisthus acts as a transition to the next play in the trilogy, and is thus integral to the dramatic structure as a whole. Contrast the finality of the end of *Eum*, where there is no such scene as that hypothetically fabricated above.[2]

These, then, are some of the ways in which *Seven* seems to be approaching completion, when it suddenly embarks on a fresh complication. Those who defend the transmitted play must make some attempt to explain these extraordinary and obviously noticeable effects. The onus is on the defence to explain what their Aeschylus is trying to do by these deliberately deviant means. I know of no serious attempt to account for them.

---

[1] Wilamowitz *Analecta* 201 considers it significant that, unlike all other anonymous characters in Aeschylus, the Herald is given no announcement or description. But this may all be part of the abruptness of his intervention. Graeber 1ff. makes much of his claim that every other character in Aeschylus addresses himself first to the chorus (cf. on *Pers* 249b*). He has a point, although he is not strictly accurate (see *Cho* 668). If one wishes to defend the Herald, this should be seen as yet another way in which his entry is made surprising and abrupt.

[2] This is why the publication of the hypothesis to *Seven* was the starting-point in the history of the authenticity question (though the truth of the matter would be the same if the scene had been first suspected yesterday—or never).

Tucker (p. 194, on 996ff. in his numeration) does at least recognize the position: 'the dramatic situation is made effective by the sudden prohibition just as the procession is moving off'. But this 'effect', while it is enough to account for many a delayed exit (see 719b*), is not significant enough to account for the entire shaping of the last part of the play. Some much larger purpose is required to account for this elaborate 'false ending': I can see none.

It would, I should add, be misleading to imply that this is the only 'false ending' in Greek tragedy (though the term is admittedly so vague that its application must be somewhat arbitrary). A brief survey of some other instances may help to highlight the particular problems of *Seven*. In a sense false endings became a kind of cliché in later tragedy. For the *deus ex machina* of Euripides (and S. *Phil*) almost always prevents a train of action which is led up to but is not allowed to be carried through. Often, however, the gesture at the alternative is little more than perfunctory. It has already been noted that *Ag* is heading for some sort of conclusion when this movement is broken by the entry of Aegisthus at 1577*. It might be argued that S. *OT* has by l. 1415 come close to an ending which would tie up the thematic threads of the play: Oedipus will go off into exile under the terms of the oracle and of his own edict, with a stick (456), and away to Cithaeron, his fatherland and nurse (1090ff. etc.). Yet with the entry of Creon the play turns to another, less powerful, conclusion. No critic has, so far as I know, explained this satisfactorily, and I hope to discuss the problem elsewhere. In S. *Phil* I have argued that there is a false ending at 1218 (see *GRBS* 1971, pp. 35–6, 39–41): this ending is the one which Neoptolemus' sense of truthfulness and loyalty must supersede. E. *Alc* reaches a tragic ending at 746; if it were a tragedy with an unhappy ending it would finish at that point. E. *Her* reaches a bleak and suicidal ending at 1152 before the entry of Theseus. Although there is to be little relief, this 'nihilistic' ending is rejected. These, then, are some other false endings against which the last scene of *Seven* may be compared.[1] In each case one ending is explored only to be rejected and superseded. Can some such point be found to justify the form and technique of *Seven*?

[1] These related techniques might prove to be a large and interesting field of study. There are possible analogies also in S. *Aj*; E. *Hkld, Phoen.*

(*b*) *the third actor*

Up until the entry of the Herald *Seven* can be played by two
speaking actors, even allowing for Antigone and Ismene. Yet,
even though Ismene has nothing to say or sing after 1005ff., the
Herald's part calls for a third actor. The *Oresteia* uses three actors,
but *Pers* and *Hik* need only two. It seems that there was in antiquity a controversy over whether Aeschylus or Sophocles (first
production in 468) was the πρῶτος εὑρετής of the third actor.[1]
But now that *Hik* has been dated to some time in the decade
after *Seven* we need not take sides in this dispute (which was
probably based on antiquarian speculation rather than authori-
tative evidence) in order to say with some confidence that *Seven*
was produced earlier than the official introduction of the third
actor.

Yet there is no acceptable way to avoid the use of a third actor
here. Lloyd-Jones (*End* 95f.)[2] claims as 'not impossible' the theory
that the actor of Ismene went off at 1004 and returned as the
Herald at 1005. But what happens on stage while the actor
changes his outfit? Antigone and the chorus are left in silence
without any cover for the unexplained exit of Ismene. This is
impossible. Flickinger's suggestion (p. 175) that Ismene was
played by a mute and that her part was sung by the second actor
concealed off-stage is almost as implausible, especially if there
was no skene to conceal the actor. He would have to sing l. 1004
from off-stage, and then walk on to interrupt himself with 1005.

Lloyd-Jones (loc. cit.) seems to derive some comfort from
pointing to other problems in the distribution of parts, e.g. in S.
OC: but that does nothing to solve this problem. Those who wish
to defend the final scene had best admit that a third actor is used
here and try to explain it. The situation is rather similar in
Prom where the prologue is the only scene in the play which
requires three actors, and where, as here, one of the three is
silent. Also in *Ag* Cassandra is silent throughout the only scene

[1] For sources see *Life Aesch.* §15 and Wilamowitz *ed maj* p. 12 §37. For the text
of Themistius see p. 62 n. 2; for Aristotle *Poet* see pp. 457 n. 4.
[2] He attributes the theory to Wundt *Philol* 65 (1906) 362: Wundt does not
suggest this, but merely that Ismene is an extra. (Hammond 432 with n. 83 claims
evidence from a vase (*ARV*[2] p. 495) for three actors in the original; but this is
recklessly speculative.) A dramatic impossibility mars Ceadel's ingenious distribution of parts in S. *OC* (*CQ* 35 (1941) 146f.). He wants the actor of Antigone to slip
off some time between 509 and 707 and to be replaced by a mute extra.

which calls for all three actors (855–974). Further, Ismene is the lesser partner of a fixed pair, like Pylades or Bia, and it may be that such characters were regarded as less than a proper part (indeed it looks as though Pylades in *Cho* was, strictly, a fourth actor, see *Cho* 892b*). It seems likely that the third actor was sanctioned officially in response to a demand established by the playwrights. It may be that before the 'regulations' were changed a third actor with a small part was occasionally allowed to a dramatist on special request. The prologue of *Prom* and the last scene of *Seven* might be examples of such extra actors, and may illustrate the kind of demand which led to the full admission of a third actor. So, if the need for a third actor were the one and only reason to suspect the authenticity of *Seven* 1005ff., it could easily be explained away. But since there are many other more substantial grounds for suspicion, it may be added as yet one more point.

(*c*) πρόβουλοι?

Along with the Herald, Wilamowitz brought on the officials of the Cadmeans as a group of mute extras.[1] He did this on the strength of the deictic pronoun in 1025 τοιαῦτ᾽ ἔδοξε τῶιδε Καδμείων τέλει, and he also emended τῆσδε in 1006 to read δήμου προβούλοις τοῖσδε Καδμείας πόλεως. Wilamowitz does not actually say that this mute junta would tell against authenticity, but surely it would. The *probouloi* are not properly introduced, and their presence on stage would add little point; indeed it would merely accentuate how useless the representatives of the *polis* are. Their silent and helpless standing by during Antigone's defiance would be bad enough; it would be even more ridiculous when they abjectly slope off with the ruffled Herald at 1053.[2] Lloyd-Jones (*End* 94f.) seems prepared to try to defend these idle politicians, and points to the Handmaidens in *Hik* and the προπομποί in *Eum*. But both of these groups are supposed to sing as a secondary chorus, both have a function within their plays, and both leave the stage in a properly managed way. If the

---

[1] Wilamowitz 89 n. 1; followed by e.g. Groeneboom 245, *GGL* i 2 p. 217 n. 1, Untersteiner *tr* 109.

[2] Alternatively Wilamowitz 90, *ed maj actio* on 1066, Groeneboom 256 send them off with the corpse of Eteocles at the end. This makes them no less ineffectual and pointless.

probouloi are accepted on stage, they are surely yet another incompetent peculiarity to count against authenticity.

Defenders of the final scene might avoid bringing them on at all. Wilamowitz's emendation of 1006 is arbitrary, and τῶιδε in 1025 might, at a pinch, be explained as not indicating actual presence but as vividly evoking their authority (cf. 374c* above; thus e.g. Rose, Italie). But it would be better to emend τῶιδε away; and there have been many suggestions.[1] Better still would be to emend τέλει, for not even Lloyd-Jones (109) is able to defend plain τέλος as meaning 'government'. A simple emendation, which does not seem to have been suggested, is τῆιδε Καδμείων πόλει (τέλει from πτόλει?), which would make a close, if crude, ring with l. 1006 at the beginning of the edict. This would, I suggest, be the best course for a defender. For myself I do not believe it, because τῶιδε τέλει is typical of the distorted tragic diction of the author of these lines (cf. Page *OCT* '1005–78 in vv. Aeschylo indignis vitia non nulla relinquenda esse censeo'). And I should not be surprised if he did intend the pointless and ineffectual *probouloi* to come on stage. For later tastes *Seven* may well have seemed to lack stage spectacle and movement. The interpolator might even have thought that a silent group of extras was in the Aeschylean manner; though he would have been wrong. This may not be the only place where some extra, but hollow, spectacle has been interpolated into Aeschylus' plays: see §4.

1053 [exit Herald (and Theban officials?)]

the Herald and Sophocles' Ismene

Editors are presumably right to send the Herald off after his last line in the stichomythia which closes the *agon* with Antigone. His feeble part is played, and he must slink off defeated. This *agon* shows in brief the ground-form—rhesis/rhesis/stichomythia— which was to be standard in Sophocles and Euripides.[2] There are other Aeschylean instances of a kind at *Ag* 855–957, *Prom*

---

[1] Several emendations have claimed the support of MS. variants though none are recorded in Dawe's *Collation* or Page *OCT*. These include ἐν τῶιδε Laubmann (M is reported to read ἔδοξεν), τῶνδε (in 'G^ac' according to Hermann), τῶι γε Blomfield (claimed as in 'F'). Other suggestions include τώδε Verrall, ἐς τόνδε Halm, ἐς τώδε Weil. M has τε**λει.

[2] Four times, e.g., in S. *Ant*, five in E. *Med*; see, in general, Duchemin, esp. 107, 132, 156ff.

298–393 and 944–1006. One reason for their rarity is the tendency in Aeschylus, outside *Prom*, for stichomythia to involve the chorus as one of the speakers (cf. p. 86 n. 5). But the *agon* in *Seven*, like later tragedy, excludes the chorus.

So the last line of the authority of the *polis* is (1053) ἀλλ' αὐτόβουλος ἴσθ'· ἀπεννέπω δ' ἐγώ. This is transmitted as the last line of the stichomythia, and is preceded by a couplet from Antigone (1052f.). To restore regularity Paley transposed 1053 to before 1052. If right, this would make the exit of the Herald even more weak and futile, since he would not even have the last word, but would move off to the accompaniment of Antigone's successful defiance. One reason why the exit of the Herald seems so abrupt and inconclusive is that he goes off at the end of a stichomythia. Though unusual, this is not unparalleled in Aeschylus: the same kind of abruptness is achieved, though with very different and much more powerful effect, at *Seven* 719, *Cho* 930.

But what has attracted criticism from those who attack the scene is, rather, the entire tone and attitude of the wretched Herald.[1] For the official representative of the City he is too puny and personal. Why, for instance, does he say ἴσθι if his job is to stop Antigone, and why ἀπεννέπω δ' ἐγώ if he is the official mouthpiece of the authority of the *polis*? I suggest that the explanation of the defensive and personal tone of the Herald lies in his inspiration in S. *Ant*. Although his function approximates to that of Creon, his relationship to Antigone is that of Ismene. His ineffectual protests in the stichomythia are modelled on Ismene in the prologue of *Ant*; and this is especially clear in his last line, which should be compared with her at *Ant* 98 ἀλλ', εἰ δοκεῖ σοι, στεῖχε (for a similar ἴσθι cf. *Ant* 71). It is not his exact words but his spirit which is derived from Ismene. And it is just the same with this autocratic Antigone, whose self-confidence and contemptuousness is modelled on the heroine of Sophocles' prologue (compare especially S. *Ant* 32, 48, 71f., 80f., 95f. with *Seven* 1026ff., 1037f., 1040, 1043, 1052). It may be impossible to show indisputably that there is anything in *Seven* 1005ff. which is modelled on S. *Ant*; but once the scene is considered in this light, there are many features which are elucidated.[2] This is, in my

---

[1] See esp. Fraenkel *Schluß* 63f., who compares Creon's exit at [E.] *Phoen* 1682.
[2] I give just one instructive example which I have noted. The antithesis θανόντι

view, the explanation of the tenor of the Herald's part and of the hurried weakness of his exit.

1071 [exeunt Antigone and one hemichorus with the corpse of Polynices]

1078 [exeunt Ismene and other hemichorus with the corpse of Eteocles]

final separations

There is no denying that the final anapaests (1054–78) after the exit of the Herald are well expressed and are perhaps not unworthy of Aeschylus. Particularly powerful are the opening invocation (1054–6) which, interestingly enough, speaks of the family of Oedipus as though there were no survivors—not even daughters—and the last lines of all (1074–8) which revive the image of the ship of state and the hostile sea of invaders. Yet these anapaests are inextricably tied up with the sisters and the Herald scene.[1] Those who hold to the interpolation of the sisters and Herald should not shrink from the possibility that more than one later hand is at work. There is no reason why the additions should not have been a co-operative venture between more than one person. The author of the final anapaests, unlike the author of 861–74 and of 1005–53, studied the rest of the play and was a competent poet. It is also possible that he incorporated material from an original ending which was cut.

The anapaests also involve a bold and effective stage action. The distribution of 1054–65 is open to dispute, but it is likely that 1066–71 is sung by one hemichorus, and 1072–8 by the other (cf. Lloyd-Jones *End* 111f.); and the division of parts must also be underlined by a division in choreography as the two hemichoruses form into two separate processions. Each side stresses

ζῷα in *Seven* 1034 is derived from the memorable expressions of the unnatural sentence of burial alive in Sophocles, especially *Ant* 920 ζῶc' εἰc θανόντων κτλ. (cf. *Ant* 774, 871, 1068f.). But in *Seven* this brings in its train the virtually meaningless antithesis of 1033—θέλουc' ἄκοντι. For some other Sophoclean features which have been pointed out recently see Fraenkel *Schluß* 62f., Kirkwood 25 n. 26.

[1] Schadewaldt *tr* rejects the sisters and the Herald, yet tries to keep a doctored version of the final anapaests, sung by the chorus. But if there is Aeschylean material in these anapaests it is inextricable. Dawson *tr* distinguishes the anapaests from the interpolated parts by means of typography; but he admits (p. 25) that they are of 'dubious authenticity'.

that it is accompanying one corpse, see 1068f., 1072. It is also very likely that one sister goes with each procession (Antigone with Polynices, of course). We cannot be absolutely certain about the stage management. It remains possible that both halves went off in one procession,[1] or that they went off consecutively in the same direction; but these are weak stagings which do not do justice to the clear implications of word and situation. What is called for is the separate departure of the two processions by the two eisodoi. It seems likely that each procession should move off, or at least get in formation, to the accompaniment of its own anapaests; and so the procession with Polynices may have moved off slightly earlier. The two processions moving off by opposite eisodoi have been accepted by most editors and translators, and are already implied by the scholion in M on 1054. This is not merely 'the most symmetrical arrangement' (Lloyd-Jones *End* 96), it is the only theatrical way to embody and convey the dramatic situation.

There are several Euripidean tragedies which end with separations or estrangements, which are put into stage terms by the simultaneous yet separate exits of two characters. Consider Orestes and Electra in *El*, Cadmus and Agave in *Ba* (cf. *Med*, *Her*, [E.] *IA*). In no other surviving tragedy, however, is the parting of the ways reinforced by the separation of two halves of the *chorus*. In fact the division of the chorus for the purposes of the action is quite a rare occurrence in Greek tragedy.[2] The outstanding instances are S. *Aj* 805ff. where the chorus is sent off in two halves to search for Ajax, and re-enters at 866ff. from two directions, and E. *Or* 1246ff. where each half patrols one eisodos looking out for the approach of Hermione. But nowhere else is there such an effective and purposeful division as here at the end of *Seven*. One half stands for the family, one for the city: the dilemma posed by the edict is brought out by the division of even the chorus.

---

[1] Thus e.g. Tucker 207, Smyth 419. Garvie (192) says that it is 'possible' that there was an additional secondary chorus at this juncture. I know of no one who has argued for this, and, unless he has in mind the *probouloi* (see 1005c*), I cannot see what he means.

[2] See P-C *DFA²* 245, Conradt in *RE* viii 233ff. The much-cited dissertation by Lammers (*Die Doppel- u. Halbchöre* etc. (Münster 1931)) is virtually useless. (For a new divided chorus from comedy see Lobel on *POxy* 2741 fr. 1 B col. ii 18ff. = fr. 95. 98ff. Austin (Eupolis *Marikas*).)

If the processions did go off in separate directions, then, in the context, one cannot avoid the implication that they are going to two separate funerals. That which goes with Eteocles is going to an official inhumation 'with full military honours': Polynices is going to be covered in some rudimentary way, as was asserted by Antigone (1035ff.). It is not clear how it will be done, but παρέcται μηχανὴ δραcτήριοc (1041). In the great laments before the final scene, however, it was clearly implied that the brothers will receive an equal share of earth and that they will be buried together by the side of Oedipus. This may even have been inherent in his curse; cf. p. 181 above. This outcome is clearest in l. 914 and in the last line 1004 πῆμα πατρὶ πάρευνον, which is the reply to ποῦ cφε θήcομεν χθονόc; (1002). So the ending of the play, as we have it, especially its unusual and striking stage arrangement, goes counter to important earlier indications. This is another serious difficulty for those who wish to defend the end. Lloyd-Jones (*End* 96) is aware of the threat, and attempts to play it down: '. . . I cannot feel sure we would be safe in inferring that they are taking the bodies to different places. It has been stated earlier that both the brothers are to be buried in the tomb of Oedipus (914), and the text as the manuscripts present it contains nothing to prevent us from supposing that they are.' But action can have meaning as well as words; and the two separate processions, as opposed to the usual united *exodos*, make absolutely clear whatever is left inexplicit by the words. The audience in the theatre can be in no doubt.

IV. HIKETIDES

1 enter chorus with Danaus[1]

(a) the arrival of the suppliants

THERE are many scenes in Greek tragedy, particularly in Euripides, where a character takes asylum at an altar or sacred place in the face of some threat against his security, usually his life. In several cases this amounts to only one incident in the play, and then the aggressor is usually the resident authority and the rescue comes from outside.[2] There are, however, five surviving plays—A. *Hik, Eum*; S. *OC*; E. *Hkld, Hik*—which are largely constructed around the reception of fugitive suppliants by a virtuous city or ruler and the repulse of their aggressive pursuers. Though this recurrent plot is given many variations it is sufficiently fixed in its main elements to be regarded as a kind of 'story pattern'.[3] The story pattern tends to bring with it recurrent roles and situations, and hence also recurrent types of exit and entry: the entry of the fugitives, of the protector, of the pursuer, the re-entry of the protector to the rescue, and the final departure to safety. There is no reason to think that A. *Hik* was the first tragedy ever to use this story pattern; but it is the earliest we have, and, as it happens, it presents these constituents in a particularly clear and archetypal form.

Four of the five suppliant plays begin with the suppliants themselves; and the exception is *Eum*, which makes a kind of

[1] Some commentators have supposed that a band of attendant handmaids also entered at the start of the play. This is discussed on 974b*.
[2] See e.g. Strohm 17ff., Kopperschmidt in *Bauformen* 321ff. (based on a much fuller dissertation, *Die Hikesie als dramatische Form* (Tübingen 1966), which completely supersedes F. Schmidt *De Supplicum* etc. (diss. Königsberg 1911)), Gould *JHS* 93 (1973) 74ff. esp. 85ff.
[3] See Lattimore *Story Patterns in Greek Tragedy* (London 1964) esp. 46f.; also Reinhardt *Sophokles* (3rd edn. Frankfurt 1947) 205, Aichele 44, Kopperschmidt *Bauformen* esp. 324–8. Lost plays which may have followed the same pattern include A. *Eleusinioi*, which seems to have had the same basic situation as E. *Hik*; and, possibly, A. *Herakleidai*?

second start with the arrival of Orestes at Athens. In A. *Hik* not only does the play open with them but the suppliants are the chorus itself. Yet, curiously, this is not the only play where this is so, for Euripides does the same in his *Hik*. It is probably a deliberate archaism, quite possibly under the direct influence of Aeschylus,[1] that Euripides has his suppliant chorus on stage at the very beginning of the play, even though it has to remain silent for some forty lines of prologue. But a notable difference between Euripides' *Hik* (cf. *Hkld*) and Aeschylus' is that it opens not with the arrival of the suppliants but with a tableau after a 'cancelled' entry (cf. *Seven* 1b*). In A. *Hik, Eum,* and S. *OC* the entry of the suppliant is also his arrival at a particular holy place, and his approach on to the sacred ground is itself the beginning of the supplication. Thus the opening anapaests of A. *Hik* cover first the flight from Egypt and the approach to Argos (1–14, note Ζεὺς μὲν ἀφίκτωρ (1) and λιποῦσαι . . . φεύγομεν (4f.)); and then they go on to the arrival and hope of protection (15–39, note esp. 19–22; cf. Gould op. cit. 89f.). The very first stage movement of the play represents the Danaids' arrival, the rest of the play will be about the circumstances in which they will leave the sacred place, and the very last movement of the play is their departure to the city (1073*). It is quite untrue to say 'in the opening scene the action is completely stagnant' (Schmidt, *Bauformen* 23). Not only is the opening entry a crucial action, but the choreography will have reflected the Danaids' flight and their hopes of security, both in the anapaests and in the great strophic song which follows.

(b) Danaus

Danaus does not speak until the end of the first song (176), and during all that time there has been only one bare reference to him. This is at 11ff. where the daughters say that it was Danaus, their πατὴρ καὶ βούλαρχος καὶ στασίαρχος, who told them to flee to Argos. There is no deictic pronoun and no other clear indication of his presence on stage. None the less it is best to suppose

---

[1] Other possible influences include the mid-act lyric at E. *Hik* 271ff. cf. A. *Hik* 418ff., the relationship of Adrastus to the chorus and his long silence at E. *Hik* 263ff., which are both like Danaus (see further 503a* below); cf. also Kranz 176, Zuntz *The Political Plays of Euripides* (Manchester 1955) 11f. Some possible, but very slight, verbal echoes are collected by Krause *De Euripide Aeschyli Instauratore* (diss. Jena 1905) 75f., Kopperschmidt diss. op. cit. 134 n. 3. The title *Hiketides* itself might be an acknowledgement of Euripides' debt; cf. in E. *Phoen* the echoes of phrase (though not subject) from Phrynichus' *Phoinissai* (*TrGF* 3 F 9–10).

that he did enter at the start with the chorus in view of his very close relationship with his daughters.[1] Lines 11ff. both introduce his inextricable place in their fortunes and the way that he will play a secondary role to the chorus throughout the play. It has been suggested, on the other hand, that he entered at some point during the song or even at the end of it.[2] But his late entry would be a pointless distraction: it would suggest a misleading separation from the chorus, when he should immediately from the start assume the position of guardian, which he will put into words when the time comes for him to speak.

One may compare in some respects the handling of Electra in *Cho*, who enters with the chorus at 22, but remains silent throughout the first choral song and eventually speaks at 84 (see *Cho* 22*). In Euripides (cf. A. *Prom* and S. *El*) it is quite usual for a character, who is closely allied to the chorus, to be brought on *before* the parodos, and for her (or him) to have a solo aria before the first choral song (see further *Prom* 88*). In the early days of tragedy, when actors' monodies were rare or unknown and the choral element was larger, it is not surprising that characters should have entered with the chorus and have remained silent throughout the first song. Danaus and Electra are, as it happens, the only examples to survive,[3] but had we more of Aeschylus there would no doubt be others. The characters are closely associated with their chorus, and once they have been briefly introduced they are simply neglected until their time comes.[4]

(c) date and trilogy

When *Hik* was assumed to be a very early play then the prologue–parodos of the chorus was seen as just one manifestation of the archaic choral dominance of the play. Now that we know better it is not difficult to argue that the reasons for using a choral

---

[1] This is argued more fully by Capps 22f., Pickard 199, Dignan 15.

[2] e.g. Tucker xvii, Mazon 19, Vellacott *tr* 59, Arnott 22. Bodensteiner 725 and Deckinger 16 remain in doubt.

[3] Most editors suppose that Iphigenia entered at the same time as the chorus at E. *IT* 123 and remained silent until 142. I would tentatively suggest that Iphigenia, as priestess, should sing the opening phrases 123–5 (though the MS. attribution to her is of no weight). For such an address to the chorus on entry cf. E. *Or* 140–2 and *Hipp* 58–60. It is also possible that Helen re-entered with the chorus at E. *Hel* 514 and was silent until 528; but probably she did not come on until the end of the little re-entry song.

[4] Cf. *HSCP* 76 (1972) 81 *contra* e.g. Dignan 15, Flickinger 230, who criticize the resultant silences.

opening were dramatic rather than merely chronological: see
Pers 1a*. None the less it may be that by the late 460s a choral
prologue–parodos was a positively old-fashioned technique. If so,
the beginning of *Hik* would not be the only piece of archaizing in
Greek tragedy; and in my view there is a considerable archaizing
element in this very play, which I shall draw attention to now
and then, especially on 503b*. The scholars who used to date
Hik early were not building their case on nothing, and the arguments which used to be put forward for a later date, while not
negligible, were not conclusive. Were it not for the papyrus
didaskalia a sober man might well put the play in the 470s rather
than the 490s, but he could not in all fairness be expected to
plump for the 460s.

Still, there is no honest and easy way to deny the evidence of
the papyrus (*POxy* 2256 fr. 3). This was already generally accepted before Garvie (ch. I) discussed the issue with exhaustive
thoroughness, and showed the implausibility of all alternatives.
However, the fragment is usually restored too fully and the date of
463 accepted too readily. It is a good thing, therefore, that Snell
has authoritatively edited the fragment with minimal restoration,
and has insisted that it dates the Danaid tetralogy no more
precisely than 467–456: see *TrGF* DID C 6.[1]

The least negligible weakness in the case for this dating of *Hik*
lies in the assumption that *Danaides* and *Hiketides* belonged together in a connected tetralogy (cf. Garvie 13f.). The *didaskalia*
certainly dates *Danaides* and *Amymone*; but how sure can we be
that *Hik* was produced in the same year? An Aeschylean satyr
play might be closely connected with the tragic trilogy (like
Sphinx) or it might be loosely connected (like *Proteus*) or it might
not be connected at all (like *Prom Pyrkaeus* in 472). It is conceivable that *Amymone* was connected with one of the three tragedies
(viz. *Danaides*) but not with the other two. It is true that for a long
time scholars have almost universally put *Danaides* and *Amymone*
in the same tetralogy as *Hik* and *Aigyptioi*; but the confirmation
of the connection of two of the four plays does not quite prove the
connection with the other two. A favourite pastime of Aeschylean

---

[1] 458 may be excluded, of course, and 457–6 are highly unlikely. The final
trace in l. 1 of the papyrus (ἐπὶ α.[) is minute, and might be several letters besides
ρ. There is no reason, *contra* Garvie 1f., to prefer ἐπὶ Ἀρχιδημίδου to ἐπὶ ἄρχοντος—
see Snell ad loc. However, the really important point is the *terminus post quem*
supplied by Sophocles.

scholars has been the tabulation of the titles of his lost plays into tetralogies, trilogies, and dilogies: but most of this has been self-indulgent speculation.[1] We know for certain of only three connected tetralogies;[2] and we know that in 472 there was little or no connection between the four plays. We have no secure grounds for arranging all the other plays in sets of three or four, except for the fact that the *Oresteia* is a masterpiece of trilogy construction. For all we know the great majority of Aeschylus' 'tetralogies' were unconnected, like that of 472. If more than one lost tragedy is drawn from the same group of myths this does not prove a trilogy. Other dramatists returned to the same myths in different years, and there is no reason why Aeschylus should not have done so.

It is also claimed that the wording of Strabo v. 221 (= fr. 127 M)—Αἰcχύλοc δ᾽ ἐκ τοῦ περὶ Μυκήναc Ἄργουc φηcὶν ἐν ῾Ικετίcιν ἢ Δαναΐcι τὸ γένοc αὐτῶν—shows that the two plays came from the same trilogy: 'the connection . . . is definitely established in Strabo's mind' (Garvie 14—'or the mind of his source' one may add). But the linking need not have arisen because both plays were in the same trilogy, but simply because the identity of the chorus was the same in both, i.e. the Danaids. In fact, this identity deserves comment, since, so far as I know, there is no other trilogy, proven or alleged, connected or unconnected, with the same chorus in two plays. Indeed, there seems to be a positive tendency to a marked variety and contrast among the three choruses. This is no significant argument against the orthodox trilogy, since Aeschylus may well have had a special artistic

[1] Among the many tabulations are Wecklein *SBAW* 1891 368ff. esp. 384–5, *GGL* i 2 p. 188 n. 8, Smyth ii 378f., Mette *Fr.* viif. It may be noted that *Diktyoulkoi* always used to be listed as a tragedy in the same trilogy as *Polydektes* and *Phorkides*: this is now quietly suppressed. For reservations see P. Wiesmann *Das Problem der tragischen Tetralogie* (diss. Zurich 1929).

[2] i.e. *Oresteia, Lykourgeia,* and the *Oedipus* plays of 467: for the evidence see P-C *DFA*² 8of. esp. 80 n. 5, *HSCP* 76 (1972) 62 n. 17. On the *Prometheus* plays see Appendix D p. 463. The case for an *Achilles* trilogy based on the *Iliad* (*Myrmidones, Nereides, Phryges*) is particularly strong; and I reckon to have added some further points in the article cited above, esp. 75–6. I should also have mentioned there the calyx-crater by Polygnotus in Vienna (*ARV*² 1030 no. 33, see *Illustrations* 54f.). Kenner (*JÖAI* 33 (1941) 1ff. esp. 9ff.) claims that this vase shows scenes from all three plays, and so is evidence of the connected trilogy. But while there are scenes which appear to be influenced by *Nereides* and *Phryges* it is far from clear that her fr. 5 (p. 5 = *Illustrations* fr. 9) shows a scene from *Myrm.* Talthybius may not have figured in *Myrm* after all, see p. 423; and if there is the bier of Patroclus in the picture, this is more likely to be from *Nereides*.

point in bringing back the same chorus, contrary to convention. But if the two plays do belong to a trilogy the observation is no less worth making.

A weak link in the orthodox trilogy is the middle play, Aἰγύπτιοι. If the title is accepted,[1] then we must suppose that the chorus consisted of the sons of Aegyptus (or conceivably of their servants?). But in that case it is hard to see how they could be treated after *Hik*; and it is out of the question that the chorus should be murdered during the play, or that its murder should be planned at all openly (cf. Hermann *ed.* i 332f., *Opusc.* viii 180–4). In the face of these objections there is only one good point in favour of *Aigyptioi*: the citation of the play in ancient lexica for a quotation which, it is claimed, comes in fact from *Hik* 156–8.[2] The quotation does indeed share the far from ordinary words τὸν πολυξενώτατον Ζῆνα [τὸν Δία in *Et Gud*] τῶν κεκμηκότων. However, in the previous line the paradosis of the play is τόνταιον which is glossed τὸν καταχθόνιον Ἅιδην in the scholia and which is usually emended to τὸν γάιον.[3] But the citation is given in illustration of Ζαγρεύς and says that Aeschylus ἐν Αἰγύπτωι (see footnote 1) οὕτως αὐτὸν τὸν Πλούτωνα καλεῖ ʽτὸν ἀγραῖον κτλ'. So far as I can see this only makes sense if ἀγραῖον is emended to Ζαγρέα or something similar, as de Stefani suggested.[4] But in that case the quotation in the lexica is not from *Hik* as we have it, and the similar wording is coincidental (cf. Garvie 189). On the other hand if Blomfield's emendation Ζαγρέα is read in *Hik* 156 instead of γάιον, then it is indeed *Hik* which is quoted. I conclude, then, that only if Ζαγρέα *vel sim.* is read both in *Et Gud* and in *Hik*, and if, preferably, the title of the middle play is Αἴγυπτος rather than Αἰγύπτιοι, can a good case then be made for Αἴγυπτ-(ος?)

---

[1] The title Αἰγύπτιοι is listed in the Medicean catalogue and is cited in *Anecd. Oxon.* (ed. Cramer) ii 443. The same quotation is given in *Et Gud* as ἐν Αἰγύπτωι (see below). If the play's title was, in fact, Αἴγυπτος, then the chorus need not have consisted of his sons: it might even have been a chorus of Danaids for the third time.

[2] For details see Wilamowitz *ed maj* 379, Garvie 188f., Johansen *ed* 64.

[3] Wellauer. But γάιος is not used elsewhere to mean (κατα)χθόνιος. (Incidentally the lemma to the scholion in Johansen *ed* 156 is supplied by the editor, O. Smith.)

[4] In his edition of *Et Gud* (Leipzig 1909) 578; alternatively Ζαγραῖον, though this is only attested elsewhere as an epithet of Dionysus (cf. Fauth *RE* ix. A. 2 col. 2232, Zuntz *Persephone* (Oxford 1971) 80f.). Johansen *ed* 64 simply gives up with 'locus severe corruptus': but if one leaves it at that then the passage should not be used as evidence for the trilogy.

as the middle play which completed the trilogy with *Hik* and *Danaides*.

So it may not be certain that there was a Danaid tetralogy, and hence that *Hik* was performed in the same year as *Danaides*; none the less, the balance is still heavily in favour of the tetralogy. Until some weighty argument is produced to the contrary, I see no sufficient reason for departing from the new orthodoxy that *Hik* is a relatively late play dating from between 466 and 459 (inclusive).

176 (no entry)

Danaus' intervention

Although when Danaus speaks this is the first time that attention is directly turned on him, there is every reason to think that he entered with the chorus—see 1b*. In that case there is no entry after the first choral song (parodos). It is much less exceptional for there to be no entry after the first song than after one of the later ones (stasima); nevertheless there is still a tendency for an entry at this point: see *Prom* 88*. However, the intervention of Danaus may be regarded as virtually equivalent to an entry. The structural break at this point is marked not only by a change from song to speech but also by a new turn of events which could normally only be achieved by an entry (cf. also 710*). Moreover, 176ff. is in a sense a very long entrance announcement for Pelasgus: see 234a*.

It transpires that Danaus has been on the look-out. In a similar context at 710ff. he says he has been watching ἱκεταδόκου τῆcδ' ἀπὸ cκοπῆc (713). This is likely to have been the same hillock or platform as the πάγοc of l. 189, and, although it is possible that this raised place and others like it elsewhere in Aeschylus were left to the imagination of the audience, it is likely that there was some permanent mound of some sort, probably outside the circle of the orchestra; see in general pp. 448–9.

234 enter Pelasgus with armed men (and chariots?)

(a) preparation and extended announcement

In a suppliant play (see 1a*) the arrival of the protector-host tends to be the object of anxious expectation, since the fate of the suppliants depends on him. In two of the other plays (S. *OC*,

E. *Hik*) the protector arrives, as here, before the pursuer. But whether he arrives before or after, his entry is always given extended and emotional preparation.

During the long first song the train of thought persistently approaches the unknown factor of the local inhabitants, though it does not face this directly. In the anapaests at 23ff. the Danaids call on the gods of the city and the land to receive them, and above all Zeus Soter, οἰκοφύλαξ ὁσίων ἀνδρῶν (26f.). At the beginning of the second strophe of the song proper (57ff.) they introduce the analogy of Tereus and the nightingale with the words εἰ δὲ κυρεῖ τις πέλας οἰωνοπόλων ἔγγαιος: so they too lament in foreign surroundings, anxious εἴ τις ἐςτὶ κηδεμών (76).[1] Throughout, when they invoke the various gods and the surrounding country, there is an awareness that it is the local inhabitants who must be the agents of the gods' will. But these are all indirect allusions couched in lyric terms: when Danaus speaks it is solid facts that he offers. He sights dust, hears axles, sees an armed host approaching (176–83); and he then speculates that they are probably local leaders coming to see the new arrivals (184f.). In the rest of his speech and the following dialogue (186–221) he prepares the chorus at the altars and images, ready to receive the inhabitants. The entire scene is conducted under the pressure of the approach of those who will decide their fate. In his final speech (222–33) Danaus reminds his daughters of the righteousness of their cause, and in his concluding couplet addresses them to the new situation.[2] Then Pelasgus enters.

As Danaus has actually seen the approach of the Argives the entire scene from 176 to 233 is strictly speaking an entrance announcement, according to the definition on p. 71, rather than simply preparation. However, since one normally uses 'announcement' to refer to the familiar brief introductions devoted exclusively to the immediate arrival, and since most of this scene is spent, rather, on the response of the Danaids, the term is only loosely appropriate. All the same, there are some places in tragedy where an approach is first sighted longer than usual before the

[1] Earlier in l. 55 Hermann introduced the attractive conjecture γαιονόμοιςι. But Johansen *ed* claims it is improperly formed (cf. Page *OCT* 'γαιαν- exspectasses'). On the nightingale comparison see Neuhausen *Hermes* 97 (1969) 167ff.
[2] However I do not think Wecklein is right that ςκοπεῖτε in l. 232 refers directly to the arrival of Pelasgus; it simply sums up. Against the suggestion that a brief entrance announcement has been lost between 233 and 234 see below p. 201 n. 3.

entry itself and where the intervening time is taken up with the tense expectation of those who are waiting on-stage. These 'extended announcements' are used where the entry is one of great dramatic importance for those already on-stage; see further *Ag* 503b*. Bodensteiner (710–15) has compiled a useful list of long announcements in Greek tragedy and comedy; and some thirteen of these are tragic announcements of ten lines or more.[1] But none of these other extended announcements is comparable in length to *Hik* 176ff. with one significant exception: that exception comes later in this same play where the Egyptian Herald enters some 125 lines after Danaus has first sighted him at l. 710. There the announcement provokes a powerful series of reactions in the Danaids, including a choral song. The similarities between the two places do not stop at the long announcements, and they provide a pointer to the form and articulation of the whole play: see 710*.

The double use of an extended entry announcement in *Hik* has, I shall argue, a particular purpose; at the same time it is quite possible that such longer announcements were not unusual in early tragedy. If there was no skene and all entrances had to be made by the eisodoi, then the illusion of a panoramic view of the surrounding country from the far side of the orchestra could have been a useful convention. There is, as it happens, no other instance in the earlier plays;[2] but in *Ag* the Watchman sees the distant beacon, and at 489ff. there is an exceptionally long announcement (see 503b*). Like chariots (see *Pers* 155b*), extended entry announcements may have been a feature of the early pre-skene theatre.

(b) armed men and chariots

Pelasgus has men-at-arms with him. Even if this is not guaranteed

---

[1] Bodensteiner does not, however, include *Hik* 176ff. and 710ff. (see p. 712 §15), because of his notion that the person announced must already be in sight of the audience—see pp. 73 n. 1 above. Also he is wrong to include E. *El* 107ff. (§27), which he counts as 115 lines, since that presents an entirely different phenomenon. Hourmouziades 145 notes the occurrence of longer entrance announcements in Euripides; but his term 'delayed' entrance is inaccurate and misleading.

[2] The look-out scenes in *Hik* are picked out by Spitzbarth 27 as 'archaisch-sta⟨t⟩uarische Technik'. The suggestion of a panorama scene in *Seven* was ruled out on p. 155 above. Dingel 113 n. 1 inaccurately but understandably refers to *Hik* 710ff. as a 'Teichoscopie'. (There seem, incidentally, to be some scenes in satyr plays where a character is seen well before his actual entry—see p. 429.)

by Danaus' description of the approaching host (180ff.), it is
certified at the end of the act when Danaus asks to be accompanied by ὀπάονας φραστοράς τ' ἐγχωρίων (492), and Pelasgus
agrees by dispatching some or all of them with the command
στείχοιτ' ἄν, ἄνδρες (500). This virtually rules out Rose's suspicion
(p. 31) that the troops were supposed to have been left out of
sight of the audience.[1] We cannot say how numerous they were;
but since there can have been no attempt to present the whole
Argive army realistically, there were probably no more than a
dozen as a token representation—cf. p. 80 and further 234c*
below. But this is not all: Danaus spoke at 181 and 183 of horses
and chariots. On the strength of this most commentators have
brought Pelasgus on in a chariot;[2] though, as Wilamowitz (7)
acknowledges, the words indicate several chariots. It might be
objected that what is described in 180ff. need not necessarily be
brought on stage—indeed the words may be a substitute for any
attempt at staging; and there are no introductory lines to cover
the entry of the chariots,[3] and no further reference to them. On
the other hand, chariots were probably quite usual in early pre-
skene tragedy, so common they did not necessarily call for
comment: see *Pers* 155b*. So I would not rule out the possibility
that there were three or four chariots at this entry.

The armed men, and the chariots if any, are no mere spectacle
for its own sake, as is usually implied. The Argives have to have a
strong force at their command in order to afford effective security
to the suppliants. Their protection is no good if it cannot be
backed up by strength. That is why words are spent on the army
at 180ff. and on the extent of Pelasgus' rule at 250ff. Respect for
the suppliants involves the commitment of the Argive army (see
342, 356ff., 398ff., 439f., 474ff., 609ff., 739ff., 942ff., etc.). But the
presence of armed men during this scene also has a significance

[1] When Podlecki (*The Political Background of Aeschylean Tragedy* (Ann Arbor
1966)) 46 says that Pelasgus was unattended, this seems to be mere error.

[2] Few have positively doubted or rejected this; but see Haigh *AT*³ 201 n. 1,
Bodensteiner 707. If there were chariots they were probably soon removed.
Pelasgus' verbs on departure give little clue: ἐλεύσομαι in 522 and the corrupt
πιετω in 518 (despite Johansen's despair, πατῶ (Wecklein), στείχω (Weil), or
σπεύσω (Martin) all seem possible).

[3] Hermann and Paley have suggested that an entry announcement has been
lost after 231. But since part of the tension of the situation arises from the Danaids'
uncertainty over who they are to be faced with (see 246–8), it is hard to see what
they might have said in either an announcement or a greeting.

through contrast: all the power at Pelasgus' command is no help to him in his vital decision over the treatment of the suppliants (cf. Kopperschmidt, *Bauformen* 325). When he first enters he is powerful, regal, and decisive: but this posture is almost immediately shaken by the Danaids' extraordinary pedigree (274ff.), and as the act progresses Pelasgus is inexorably driven to his terrible choice between two disasters. Faced with a moral and religious dilemma, force is no help, and he has to rely on φροντίς (see 407ff.). He sees (see 468ff.) that he must choose between a bloody war and a μίασμα οὐχ ὑπερτοξεύσιμον (473). The force which he has with him on stage is of no help with this decision; and yet it is bound up with its consequences either way.[1]

(c) *crowds and spectacle in* Hiketides

I have just accepted that there were armed men with Pelasgus, and possibly chariots also. But most commentators are not content with a token handful of Argives; they insist on a real host. Wilamowitz (7) asserts '. . . of course he has brought with him a fine troop of warriors, not just a couple of tedious spear-carriers, such as accompany later tragic kings'. Murray (49 cf. *tr* 45) claims 'at least fifty'. This kind of grand spectacle undeniably pays respect to the letter of 180ff.; but it is at root based not on the text so much as on an entire conception of what sort of a play this is. The vision of *Hik* as a poem of multitudes has been almost universal. Tucker (xvi) put the matter boldly and frankly: 'The scene is eminently spectacular, and is therein suited both to Aeschylus' natural taste for pomp and also to the comparatively inartistic character of the early drama . . . The "Menschengewimmel" of which Oberdick complains would really be no drawback, but the contrary. There is no thrilling action in the piece, and, despite its admirable poetry, it would have fallen flat as a drama if only twelve or fifteen Danaids had provided the spectacle.'

---

[1] Note how once his decision is made he can (without his men) command and even move the stubborn Danaids by means of trust alone (505ff.). Stephenson (25f.) rightly protests against the usual disparaging comment that 505ff. are 'but a transparent dramatic device for getting the chorus into position for the next stasimon' (thus Tucker 105, praised by Arnott 22f.). The stage movement from off the holy place demonstrates how the chorus trusts Pelasgus' word.

This inflation of the spectacle in *Hik*, and the typical attitude of Tucker which goes with it, run counter to my major thesis that Aeschylus used the theatre as an integral part of his plays and to my minor thesis that the spectacular Aeschylus is an unjustified invention by scholars. I suggest that the usual view of the stage presentation of *Hik* is based on a series of presuppositions which must stand or fall together. Put briefly these may be reduced to five: (i) Aeschylus indulged in pomp and spectacle for its own sake. (ii) *Hik* is a plain play devoid of frills and complications, and so it must have been swelled out by spectacle. (iii) Confrontations of force must be presented realistically in order to be convincing. (iv) In the early days Aeschylus had a chorus of fifty. (v) *Hik* is an early play. If these assumptions are accepted, then they bring with them a 'Gewimmel' indeed—with never less than 100 figures on stage and sometimes over 200.[1]

Point (v) was discussed in 1c*. Point (iv), although widely accepted, is very poorly attested; it has, I suspect, found more favour than it deserves precisely because it fits with the traditional view of *Hik* as a 'crowd ballet'.[2] Point (iii) has dissolved now that hardly anyone imagines any longer that the Greek theatre was naturalistic: which of two groups on stage has the upper hand is simply a matter of presentation not of numbers. There is no need for more Argives than Egyptians or more Egyptians than Danaids.[3] Points (i) and (ii) go together. I have made my general attack on (i) in §4; and the vacuous multitudes in *Hik* are one of many traditional showpieces which I hope to discredit. So, finally, point (ii): is it true that *Hik* would 'have fallen flat as drama' unless a whole lot of extraneous spectacle was added to it? I hope to hint in this chapter how Aeschylus makes effective and integral use of the visual theatre within the play, and to point to some of its dramatic tensions and movements. *Hik* is a plain play; but that is one of its strengths.

---

[1] For some extravagant evocation of milling multitudes in *Hik* see e.g. Tucker loc. cit., Wilamowitz 4ff. esp. 8, Murray 49ff., Denniston and Page *Ag ed* xxx.

[2] For the number of the chorus, and against fifty, see e.g. Peretti 85f., P-C *DFA*² 234f. esp. 234 n. 6, Lloyd-Jones *Supplices* 365ff. For early attacks on fifty see Hermann *Opusc* ii 129ff., Weil *Hik ed* on l. 1; further bibliography in Garvie 207 n. 9. (On the separate question of whether the Aeschylean chorus numbered 12 or 15 see p. 323 n. 3 below.)

[3] Cf. e.g. Fitton-Brown *CR* n.s. 7 (1957) 2f., Lloyd-Jones *Supplices* 367, Hammond 420.

503 exit Danaus (with Argive bodyguard)

(a) the neglect of Danaus

The handling of Danaus in the part of the play between the entry of Pelasgus at 234 and his exit at 503 has been roughly criticized. Danaus is silent and almost completely neglected throughout the scene until the very end, when he is drawn into it only in order to be sent off. The alleged incompetence has until recently been used as an argument for an early date.[1] Now that we know better about the date of the play can we duly find a defence against these charges of primitive clumsiness? First, even if we grant incompetence, such things are not necessarily any guide to date (this criterion would play havoc with the chronology of Euripides!). Secondly, it can be seen, I think, that the dramatic technique is calculated, and is not due to carelessness or forgetfulness. Aeschylus shows that he is perfectly aware of the problem of Danaus by putting him in the background and paying no attention to him. While they wait for the arrival of the Argives all of Danaus' instructions to his daughters are about how they should speak and how they should behave (see esp. 191ff., 232f.); there is no suggestion that he might take the initiative. Then, during the entire scene from 234 to 479 Danaus is only mentioned once at 319–21, when he could not possibly be omitted from the genealogy. He would surely have received more attention had he *not* been there. Yet, once Pelasgus' crucial decision in principle is made, Danaus is easily brought back into the dialogue once more (480ff.).

Once it is recognized that the technique is calculated, we can begin to ask why Aeschylus has managed things in this way.[2] And the answer must be that he is determined that the chorus should make its own case, and that the suppliants alone with all the dramatic devices within their choral range should confront Pelasgus. As a result the rising tension of the long scene, as Pelasgus' dilemma is screwed tight, can be conveyed with an epirrhematic structure and with a strophic song as well as spoken dialogue (see further below). Brief reflection on the dramatic

---

[1] For bibliography see Garvie 88 n. 1 and 126ff.; add Graeber 2f., Dignan 15, 31. On the handling of Danaus later in the play see 775*, 974a*.

[2] See especially Lloyd-Jones *Supplices* 363ff., Dale *Papers* 211f., and at greater length Garvie 126ff.

alternatives should show that any attempt to include Danaus in this scene would have diluted its power.

There is a feature of the handling of Danaus' exit which indicates how his role is deliberately made secondary and un-enterprising in this part of the play. He last speaks at 499, yet he actually goes after 503: that is to say, Pelasgus and not Danaus himself speaks immediately before his departure. Now, charac-ters normally have the last word on exit. Dramatic attention is on the departing person, and it is a time for him to speak unless there is some reason why he should not. In three exits out of four (at a rough count) the departing character has the last word; and many of the exceptions occur at places where two go together and one necessarily cannot have the last word (though even then this may have some dramatic significance, see *Ag* 974a*, *Cho* 718*, 930*). Of the individual exits without last word many are merely the dismissal of a servant or some minor figure; and, after these are excluded, most of the instances still left carry some positive dramatic point. The silence may, for instance, hide an over-whelming emotion, or it may betoken the defeat or repression of the departing character.[1] No great significance can be read into the submissive exit of Danaus here, but the lack of an exit line helps to keep him placed as a secondary and passive character.

E. *Hik* supplies a pertinent and instructive parallel to the handling of Danaus here. In Euripides' play Adrastus is the same kind of appended patron to the chorus; and there is, I suspect, a conscious reminiscence of Aeschylus in the way that Adrastus is present yet silent in the background all the way from 263 to 734 with only one promptly suppressed half line at 513. At the same time, there are important differences in the dramaturgic circum-stances of the two silences. During all the episodes in Euripides there are nearly always *three* actors present as well as the chorus; and, since only two parties normally take part in any dialogue,[2] two of the four parties present must remain silent—and they are Adrastus and the chorus. Adrastus speaks one half line, and

---

[1] For example the silent exits to suicide at S. *Ant* 1243 and *Trach* 812, the humiliating flight of Odysseus at *Phil* 1302 (see *GRBS* 1971 p. 37); at E. *Med* 975 Jason is outwitted by Medea, and so is Clytemnestra at E. *El* 1140. There are two problematic instances in Aeschylus which may be due to textual disruption: see *Hik* 974a* (Pelasgus) and *Eum* 777b* (Apollo).

[2] On the rarity of *Dreigespräch* see K. Listmann (diss. Darmstadt 1910), Flick-inger 170.

besides the act-dividing songs the chorus has only the odd couplet. After the speech and dactylic lyric at the beginning of the supplication (263–85) the chorus' case is taken up first by Aethra and then by Theseus. It is, of course, normal in later Greek tragedy for the chorus to be pushed into the background during the dialogue acts. This also happens occasionally in Aeschylus: there is a kind of apology for the technique in *Pers* (see *Pers* 249b*), but it is used with no awkwardness at *Hik* 911–53, and the chorus is put in the background for some 70 lines in *Ag*, 170 in *Cho*, and 450 in *Prom*. On the other hand, Aeschylus, as opposed to the later tragedians, quite often wants the *chorus* to be one of the parties to the dialogue, even when there are two actors present: this means that one of the *actors* must be put into the background. The suppression of Danaus in favour of the chorus at *Hik* 234–479 is by far the longest example of this; but compare, for example, *Pers* 249–89, 681–702, *Ag* 1035–68, 1577–1653, *Eum* 582–608, 619–73. In most of these cases, since the background silence is brief, Aeschylus is able to make some dramatic use of the silence (see *HSCP* 1972 pp. 78, 80): but in *Hik*, on the other hand, the silence is so prolonged that Aeschylus carefully directs all attention away from it, and only brings Danaus back into the play at the instigation of Pelasgus at 480ff.

I hope to have shown that the way that Danaus is treated is directed to a purposeful dramatic end. But this does not automatically free the dramatic technique from censure. By making the chorus rather than an actor the pleader for protection Aeschylus has taken a calculated risk, and critics are free to judge that it does not succeed. Most have, in fact, been bluntly censorious, though they have usually pleaded the patronizing excuse of an early date (but see recently e.g. Knox 107 n. 9). But surely the carping is not justified. All attention is on the confrontation between the chorus and Pelasgus: a good audience whose concentration has been captured will not even notice Danaus, let alone be distressed by his silent presence. Aeschylus has ensured that when the actor is not required he is forgotten: in return he has achieved a magnificent scene of individual dilemma set against choral emotion.

(b) archaic technique

I turn to the question whether there are archaic or archaizing techniques in this scene. We may now consider this topic without the distraction of simplistic equations between early and clumsy or late and polished.

It used to be supposed that early in the fifth century the chorus was a kind of 'protagonist', and that its role was always an active and central one, as in *Hik* and *Eum* (for bibliography see Garvie 107 n. 5). But now that *Hik* is redated, and the comparatively 'detached' choruses of *Pers* and *Seven* are our earliest, the view is catching on that even in early tragedy the chorus was always fairly 'anonymous and colourless' (Garvie 106), and that its central and active role in *Hik* and *Eum* was a bold experimental innovation. This view has been argued most thoroughly by Garvie 106–20.[1] He argues, with justification, that the famous sentence of Aristotle (*Poet* 1449a17f.) τὰ τοῦ χοροῦ ἠλάττωσε καὶ τὸν λόγον πρωταγωνιστεῖν παρεσκεύασεν does not say that the chorus was previously 'protagonist'; and he goes on to argue that this is simply a matter of 'the relative extent of the dialogue and lyrics'. But this leads on to a picture of archaic tragedy (which it is easy to disparage since we do not have any) as merely long choral songs interspersed with brief messenger speeches, as 'reminiscent rather of a cantata or an oratorio' or 'little more than a prolonged threnos' (Garvie 115). But it must be objected against this that the distinctive point about the handling of the chorus in Aeschylus—and not only in *Hik* and *Eum*—is that it not only has longer songs but it is also more consistently and more extensively integrated into the dialogue acts (epeisodia). This must have been even more so in the days of one-actor tragedy. *Pers* and the other surviving plays do nothing to support the unwarranted assumption that the dialogue acts of archaic tragedy were brief or that the chorus played little part in them. There is no reason, besides an unwillingness to allow that Phrynichus and early Aeschylus might have been every bit as good as the tragedy which we possess, to suppose that archaic tragedy was static and undramatic.

It is worth considering at this point the ways in which the early chorus is given a larger part in the dialogue acts in Aeschylus, and, it may be inferred, in archaic tragedy. In Sophocles

[1] Cf., in other forms, Dale *Papers* 210f., Kitto *Greek Tragedy* (3rd edn., London 1961) 25, Else *The Origin and Early Form of Greek Tragedy* (Harvard 1965) 92–6. Garvie is cogently attacked for going too far by Burnett in *CPh* 66 (1971) 57–8.

and Euripides (and in *Prom*) the only two techniques which are
used for the participation of the chorus are stichomythia and
lyric dialogue. Lyric dialogue is also common, of course, in
Aeschylus; and actor–chorus stichomythia is for him, as opposed
to later tragedy, the norm (see p. 86 n. 5). His most obvious
additional technique is the epirrhematic dialogue structure; but
the way that the actor normally addresses the chorus on entry is
another symptom of the greater part of the chorus in the acts (for
both these see *Pers* 249b*).

There are two other ways in which the chorus may have been
given a larger part in the dialogue acts of early tragedy (though
inevitably the evidence on such matters is thin). In later tragedy
the chorus (or coryphaeus) is not normally allowed more than
two or three continuous spoken lines: but earlier it may have had
longer speeches. Longer 'choral' speeches are particularly found
in Aeschylus,[1] though there are also three instances in Euripides,
one in the supplication scene of E. *Hik*.[2] Secondly the chorus of
early tragedy may have sung astrophic or even strophic songs
within the acts. The only mid-act strophic choral song is at A.
Hik 418ff. (see below). Astrophic choral lyric is found in mid-act
at two places in Aeschylus (*Cho* 152–63, *Prom* 687–95). There are
also three instances in Euripides, but two of these are in his *Hik*,
one of them again in the supplication scene.[3]

In the light of this let us now turn to the dramatic techniques
used for the participation of the chorus in A. *Hik* 234–479. On
entry Pelasgus addresses himself to the chorus (249ff.). After his
opening rheses the dialogue progresses by a lengthy actor–chorus
stichomythia (291–347); at one point, however, there is a speech
of five lines by the chorus (328–32). Then there is an epirrhematic dialogue structure (348–406), followed by the King's short
speech of indecision (407–17). The chorus then presses home its
case with a song of two short strophic pairs (418–37). This is the
only mid-act, as opposed to act-dividing, choral strophic song in
surviving tragedy; but I conjectured above that such songs may

---

[1] Notably *Pers* 215–25, *Ag* 489–502 (see 503b*), *Eum* 244–53; cf. Gross *Die
Stichomythie* etc. (diss. Berlin 1905) 42, who also considers this archaic, Garvie
120 n. 3.

[2] E. *Hik* 263–70 (plus lacuna?), *Her* 252–74, *Hel* 317–29.

[3] E. *Hik* 271–86, 918–24, *El* 585–95 (*Phoen* 291–300 goes with the following
monody). Mid-act anapaests are found at E. *Med* 357–63, 759–63, *Hkld* 288–96,
702–8. (Cf. De Falco[2] 89ff., which is, however, very confused.)

not have been uncommon in archaic tragedy.[1] The song is framed by another speech of indecision by Pelasgus (438–54); and then a brief actor–chorus stichomythia (455–67) drives him to the first stage of his decision. The final part of the act follows from there. I conclude that this scene, more than any other in surviving tragedy, gives us an idea of the ways in which the chorus was handled in archaic one-actor tragedy (cf. Kranz 20–1, who thought, of course, that the play was very early).

Once Aeschylus had decided to have the chorus and not Danaus make its own case, then he would naturally turn to the old techniques for integrating the chorus in the acts. This does not necessarily mean that the play is early, but it does mean that Aeschylus is using archaizing techniques. This conclusion may offer some excuse for those who used to assume that the play was early; and, perhaps more important, it runs counter to the usual easy notion that archaic tragedy was a kind of eventless oratorio.

523 exit Pelasgus

600 Danaus returns

624 (no exit) see *Pers* 622*

710 (no entry)

the pair of look-out scenes

In *Pers* Darius enters at the end of the song which is devoted to calling him up (*Pers* 681a*). At the equivalent point in *Hik*, on the other hand, there is no entry at all: instead Danaus describes for a second time what he sees in the distance. So not only is there no exit before the song 625–709, there is no entry after it. The exceptions to the basic structural association of entry with the end of the act-dividing song are very few. In fact, if one once excepts the first song (parodos) which often has less of an act-dividing function (see *Prom* 88*),[2] then there are, so far as I know,

---

[1] But I do not accept Kranz's conjecture (21f.) that 'stasima' arose out of such mid-act songs as this. The point about an act-dividing song is that the strophic choral lyric is synchronized with the rearrangement of actors by exit and entry (see §5). This song, on the contrary, is centred on an actor and is very much bound within the act. Kranz claims that it fills a pause in the *Handlung*: but, in fact, it is very much part of it.

[2] Choral re-entry songs (*epiparodoi*) also, not surprisingly, behave differently in structural terms: see *Eum* 276*.

only five or four other clear instances of this phenomenon.[1] The
two most blatant and least explicable occur at *Prom* 436* and
907 (see 944*). The instances from Sophocles and Euripides all
have some explanation. Thus, at S. *Phil* 864 Philoctetes reawakes
from his coma (just as he had fallen into it at the beginning of the
song at 827). The remarkable lyric dialogue at E. *Hipp* 565ff.
should not be regarded as part of the act-dividing song, since it
supplies the transition to the entry of Hippolytus and the Nurse
at 601, which is the beginning proper of the new act. And,
thirdly, the little song at *IT* 642–57 can scarcely be treated as
act-dividing, although it is preceded by the exit of Iphigenia—
it has, rather, a divisive function within the very long act by
underlining an important juncture.[2] The lack of entry at A. *Hik*
710 does not have any such explanation as these three places.
None the less one can see a new dramatic alignment at this point,
which has analogies with a new entry. Danaus intervenes from
the same separated place as he intervened from at 176* and to
which he went at 624. Also, as at 176ff., he announces the
approach of an impending arrival, and thus brings a new character into the play, although not on to the stage. The technique is
exceptional, but it is not incomprehensible.

Nevertheless we may look for some more positive dramatic
reason for the unusual lack of an entry. It may be, simply, that
Danaus, because of his special relationship to the chorus, must
not go as soon as 624, and yet he must go before the Egyptian
arrives (see 775*). But rather, I suggest, Aeschylus does this in
order to set up the parallel or 'mirror scene' (see *Pers* 598b*)
between this place and 176ff. For a second time there is no entry
after the song, and instead Danaus speaks from his vantage
point. For a second time he describes the host which he can see in
the distance, and advises that the girls should move to the altar.[3]

[1] Other exceptions may be brought about by a (wrong) decision in some controversial issue—in such problems the structural 'rule' is a factor to be taken into
account. For example, even if Ziobro's theory (*AJP* 92 (1971) 81–5) that Antigone
did not enter at S. *Ant* 806 were not suspect on other grounds (see p. 73 n. 3), it
would be so because there would then be no entry after the act-dividing song.
[2] Kranz 124–5 includes *IT* 642ff. among the act-dividing songs (stasima); but
in function it is more like the divided strophes at S. *OC* 833ff. = 876ff., or E. *Hipp*
669ff., or even the anapaests following an exit in E. *Med* and *Hkld* (listed in p. 208
n. 3 above).
[3] Cf., with some detailed verbal correspondences, Kopperschmidt's dissertation
(cited above, p. 192 n. 2), 55f.

In both cases this leads into a long and agitated scene before the eventual arrival (see 234a*, 836a*). There are also differences: the approach from the city aroused apprehension and anxiety about behaviour, while the approach from the sea arouses a fear of violence, and there is little hope of any respect or restraint; in keeping with this 176ff. is followed by a stichomythia, while 710ff. excites an epirrhematic exchange.

Yet in this case the mirror scene is set up to play off the similarities of the two situations as much as the differences. In *Hik* the suppliants at the altar have to face two confrontations; and these two scenes—with Pelasgus and with the Egyptian—are the twin poles of the play. So the play is articulated in two main parts. After the confrontation with Pelasgus there is still uncertainty until his decision is confirmed; and then the chorus sings its benedictions on Argos (630ff.) as a kind of ratification of their arrival and acceptance, rather as the 'Colonus Ode' at S. *OC* 668ff. confirms Oedipus' reception at Colonus. At this point (as in *OC*) a new start is made on the second part of the play. Now that the Argive protection has been granted, it must be put to the test. And here, again, the contrasts begin to come out. For in the matter of supplication the chorus of Danaids was calm, proficient and, in effect, in control of the situation; but now, faced with the threat of brute force, they are helpless and full of wild fear.

775 exit Danaus

the suppression of Danaus

The handling of Danaus in this part of the play has been criticized no less than his inactivity earlier (see 503a*). He is slow to go for help, and then he does not return in time; by the time that he fails to come to the rescue with Pelasgus at 911 his daughters are in serious trouble. After the danger is past he blithely returns at 980 with a personal bodyguard and ready with prudish sentiments. It is, it cannot be denied, somewhat awkward that Danaus should not be there for his daughters' greatest ordeal. The complaint is not, as Garvie (127) claims, 'based on a misplaced feeling for natural probability rather than dramatic considerations': it is, precisely, a dramatic consideration. None the less Aeschylus succeeds, I shall argue, in making the awkwardness all but negligible.

First, it should be established (as before on 503a*) that Aeschylus is perfectly aware of the difficulty, and sets about minimizing it by deliberate technique. Even before Danaus goes Aeschylus draws attention away from his mission and diverts it on to the danger and fear of the Danaids in such a way as to make us forget about him. At the beginning of the scene attention is given to the mission. In his first speech, after describing the distant boarding party, Danaus tells the girls to wait, ἐγὼ δ' ἀρωγοὺς ξυνδίκους θ' ἥξω λαβών. He even foresees the possibility that he may be late in bringing help (730f.). With a final couplet of god-fearing reassurance (732f.) Danaus has said all that needs to be said before action is taken, and it may even be that he began to go when he was stopped by the terror of his daughters.[1] This would be similar in technique to the probable 'delayed exit' at *Seven* 676 (see 719b*); but while in *Seven* the pressure of Eteocles' imminent departure pervades the following exchange, in *Hik* the urgency becomes dissipated once this opportunity is past. At the beginning of the epirrhematic exchange the chorus urges that there is no time to spare (735); but, as it progresses, they concentrate rather on the physical threat of force, while Danaus reiterates his trust in Argive strength. Attention is so diverted that at 748 the chorus actually says μόνην δὲ [or με Blaydes] μὴ πρόλειπε, λίccομαι, πάτερ. Once the initial urgency of Danaus' mission is let slip it is never recaptured; and in his final rhesis (764ff.) he says, on the contrary, that there is no call for hurry, and all but three lines are spent on the difficulties of disembarkation. In his final three lines he simply tells his daughters not to neglect the gods, and says that the city will find him eloquent, though old.[2]

---

[1] Cf. Tucker (xix) 'As he descends and is about to leave the stage . . .', Wilamowitz *ed maj actio* 'Danaus de clivo descendit . . .'

[2] There is, however, a textual complication since πράξας ἀρωγήν in 774 makes no sense as it stands. The usual solution (Hartung) is to suppose that a line has dropped out before 774 to the effect 'but I shall return' (Wecklein and Paley even offer doggerel stop-gaps). But do we want attention to be drawn at this point to Danaus' return, when he is going to fail to return? Apart from this objection it is doubtful whether ἀρωγή is a distinct enough achievement to be the object of πράccειν (like e.g. κλέος or εἰρήνη). It would be better to keep Danaus' mission vague and not too urgent so as to direct attention away from his failure to return. This could be done by emendation without recourse to a lacuna: I suggest, for instance, πέμψω δ' ἀρωγήν, cf. *Cho* 477, *Eum* 598. (For a possible example of this corruption in reverse see *Eum* 203.)

Once Danaus has gone there is probably no further mention of him before 966ff., except, without reference to his mission, at 786. Unfortunately this part of the play is exceedingly corrupt, and so we can say nothing with confidence. But the 'father' of 811 and 885 is probably Zeus, and the γέρον of 860, if not corrupt, can hardly be Danaus. Above all, at the height of their crisis in 903ff. it is not their father that the Danaids call on for help, but Pelasgus. When he arrives at 911 he is without Danaus, and he makes no reference to him at all. It is only when the danger is past in the anapaests at 966ff. (on which see 974a*) that Danaus is brought back into the play again. We may gauge how completely Aeschylus reckons he has suppressed the memory of Danaus' original motive for departure by the way the chorus asks Pelasgus to send Danaus to them to advise on their lodgings—as though he were away in blissful ignorance of their danger on some irreproachable business. When he does return there is no hint of any failure or omission on his part; his words give the impression that while away he has been doing everything that might be expected of him. Thus, at 983ff. he recounts how he told the Argives of τὰ πραχθέντα, and they, incensed, gave him a bodyguard. Yet these events must be those of 825–951, and when we last saw Danaus at 764ff. he claimed that there was no immediate danger. Again, at 1009ff. he knows about the alternative offers of lodgings: did Pelasgus tell him about this between 976 and 980? These are questions and objections which should not be taken seriously. Aeschylus simply makes us think, regardless of inconsistencies, that Danaus has made himself useful off-stage, that he has guards to show for it, and that he is in complete command of the situation. In conclusion, Aeschylus shows himself fully aware of the potential awkwardness of Danaus' absence, and he has done all he can to turn attention away from these problems as unobtrusively as possible. It is fair to say, I think, that he has succeeded.

Why, then, is the playwright at such pains to have Danaus out of the way for this vital part of the play? His motive must be the same as earlier (see 503a*): he is determined that the Danaids themselves should undergo their trials, and that no one else should do it for them. So they must face the Egyptians without an intermediary. The prize is the remarkable lyric dialogue, 825–902, which, for all its disfiguring corruption, still conveys a vivid and startling impression. The outlandish language, interjections, and bestial imagery create a scene of violent yet colourful, alarming yet almost lewd, boldness, which it is hard to match in surviving tragedy, unless in *Eum.*[1] After that, it is the resident saviour, Pelasgus, who must rescue the newly arrived suppliants: there is no place for Danaus in the tough, direct confrontation of 911ff.[2] Danaus is best away.

These considerations seem, to me at least, to clear Aeschylus of any charge of dramatic incompetence or of youthful blundering.[3] But even taking this as agreed, it would not necessarily absolve Aeschylus from the criticism that he should not have created in the first place a Danaus who is an essential counsellor for some parts of the play and an otiose encumbrance for others. Taking it for granted that Aeschylus cannot have the Danaids without Danaus,[4] then a hostile critic who is sufficiently offended by the way he is managed would have to argue either that Aeschylus should have given up the 'protagonist' role of the chorus, or that he should not have dramatized a *mythos* with this inherent problem in the first place (ἐξ ἀρχῆς γὰρ οὐ δεῖ cυνίcταcθαι τοιούτουc, Aristotle *Poet* 1460a33f.). Once this point of view is spelt out it is obvious how unacceptable it is. First Danaus' silence and then his absence are skilfully played down, and both are made negligible for a theatre audience. A reader who is so very offended

[1] It seems to me that Garvie (56f.) is too quick to dismiss the idea that *Hik* shows signs of that λέξιc γελοία and cατυρικόν which according to Aristotle *Poet* 1449a19ff. characterized early tragedy. This would still not have any serious bearing on the question of the date of *Hik*, for as in several other ways *Hik* is most like *Eum.* (On beast imagery in *Hik* see Fowler *C et M* 28 (1967) 14f.)

[2] *Contra* e.g. Flickinger 173, Schlesinger *CPh* 28 (1933) 176, and, by implication, those listed below in p. 215 n. 1.

[3] Not that the quality of the dramatic technique would necessarily be a criterion of chronology in any case. Garvie 127ff. well points out the inconsistency of the theories that Danaus is an awkward vestige of an ἐξάρχων/first actor and at the same time an incompletely handled second actor. There is no difficulty with the second actor at 911ff.

[4] See Garvie 135–8. Interestingly, Garvie's case for the indispensability of Danaus is not altogether convincing. If his absence from this play were somehow or other excused, that would satisfy his fixture in the myth and in the rest of the trilogy (assuming there was one). His other functions in the *plot* are not essential. Garvie's main argument is that Danaus supplies some of the quieter, deeper qualities normally supplied by a chorus. But these are relatively lacking in *Eum*, and Aeschylus makes effective dramatic capital out of it. It seems to me that Aeschylus must have attached great importance to the actual content of Danaus' verbal contributions, especially towards the end. Above all he is needed to bring out the sexual and sacred issues clearly.

by them is simply employing inappropriate—and naggingly trivial—criteria.

Finally, it is commonly pointed out that there is another reason why Danaus should be absent during the scene with the Egyptian. Assuming that there were only two actors available at the time of this production (see on *Seven* 1005b*), then the actor of Danaus is needed to double the part of the Herald. He would have time to change costume and mask during 775–835 and 951–80. But to say, as several scholars have,[1] that Danaus is absent *because* the actor has to play the other part would be a mistake. Danaus is absent because there is no place for him. Even if Aeschylus had a third actor at his disposal, he would not want Danaus present during this scene.

836 enter Egyptian Herald (with attendants)

(a) preparation for the pursuer

In a suppliant play the arrival of the pursuer is bound to be an important and alarming event. Here, as in S. *OC* and E. *Hik*, his arrival comes after the 'reception' scene, and thus fairly late in the play; so there is scope for anticipation of the feared moment. The preparation is so intense and persistent that the entry becomes one of the focal points of the drama. The arrival of the enemy comes to represent for the Danaids the threat of all that they fear and hate.

At the very beginning in the opening anapaests the pursuers are introduced and dwelt on (4–10, 29–39): the chorus prays that the sons of Aegyptus may be tempest-driven and drowned πρὶν πόδα χέρcωι τῆιδ᾽ ἐν ἀcώδει / θεῖναι (31f.). In the scene with Pelasgus they explain their flight and need for protection, and it is constantly kept in mind that the cousins will come and will try to abduct them. The arrival of the pursuers is vividly foreshadowed in the mid-act strophic song: μή τι τλᾶιc τὰν ἱκέτιν εἰcιδεῖν / ἀπὸ βρετέων βίαι δίκαc ἀγομέναν / ἱππαδὸν ἀμπύκων, / πολυμίτων πέπλων τ᾽ ἐπιλαβὰc ἐμῶν (428–32). The direct preparation begins with Danaus' report at 710ff. which is the start of what is, in a sense, the longest 'entry announcement' in

---

[1] e.g. Graeber 39, Kaffenberger 30f., *GGL* i 2 p. 69 n. 4, 198, Croiset 63, Lesky *TDH*² 68, cf. *TDH*³ 102.

Greek tragedy (see 234a*). Danaus sees the first ship approach the shore (722f.), and he accurately predicts its purpose—ἴϲωϲ γὰρ ἂν κῆρύξ τιϲ ἢ πρέϲβη μόλοι / ἄγειν θέλοντεϲ, ῥυϲίων ἐφάπτορεϲ (727f.). Although from 734 onwards attention is turned away from Danaus' mission to fetch help (see 775*), the advancing threat of the arrival of the Egyptians is kept to the fore: indeed it is the centre of attention. The vivid expression of fear and the virulent use of wild-beast imagery in the epirrhematic structure (736ff.) is carried on and intensified in the act-dividing choral song 776–824. The language of escape, revulsion, supplication, and ravishment leads up to the entry itself so powerfully that the Herald, when he enters, is imbued with all the menace of the cousins themselves. The entry, which has been foreseen throughout the play and directly expected for over 100 lines, comes, then, as an embodiment of all that is cruel, beastly, and rapacious.

(b) who and when?

The Egyptians have a leader, and it is he who does the talking. His patron is Hermes (920)—he is a κῆρυξ (931). This is precisely what Danaus prepared for at 727f. (quoted above). It is assumed that he has other Egyptians with him; and it is usually assumed that he has a great many of them, fifteen, fifty, or even more. There is no evidence for this in the text; it is based on the unfounded presuppositions which I called in question on 234c*. The assumption that confrontations of force must be realistic at all costs has been especially influential here. It has often been supposed, moreover, that physical force was applied in this scene, and that some or all of the chorus (and perhaps their maids too) were actually caught and held captive.[1] But the text does not indicate that the physical action ever gets beyond threats: contrast, for example, S. *OC* 826–47. Throughout the lyric dialogue (836–902) the use of force is put in terms of threat and intended action; and at 903f. the Herald is still threatening force *if* the Danaids do not submit. His last words before Pelasgus' intervention imply that he is still only on the point of using force.[2] If,

---

[1] e.g. Wilamowitz *ed maj actio* on 881 ('iam singuli singulas puellas persecuntur attrectant capiunt'), Tucker xix, Mazon 45 n. 3, Murray 52, *tr* 79f., Vellacott *tr* 81.

[2] Wilamowitz (*ed maj*) rightly argues that ll. 909–10 should be the last words before the entry of Pelasgus, and I should adopt his exchange of lines 905 and

then, there was no actual bodily violence, then there is no need
for as many Egyptians as Danaids, only for enough to inspire
them with convincing terror. Lloyd-Jones (*Supplices* 367) has
even claimed that the Herald entirely by himself could do this.
While this is not impossible, it is none the less a fact (see *Pers*
155c*) that many characters in Greek tragedy have attendants,
and it seems likely that the Herald will have had a few henchmen
with him.

All this is a blow against the extraordinary theory that the
Herald had with him a secondary chorus of Egyptians who sang
their side of the lyrics in 836–65.[1] But there is no trace whatsoever of this in the text;[2] the speculation rests on false assumptions
about theatrical realism and on empty guesswork about the
origins and early form of tragedy. Maas (*Greek Metre* (transl.
Lloyd-Jones, Oxford 1962) 53f.) tried to add the more solid
observation that minor characters of low degree do not sing in
Greek tragedy. But there is at least one exception to this 'rule'
(E. *Or*), and in any case *kerykes* were, surely, of highly respectable
social status. Moreover, the only reason why low-status characters
do not normally sing is, presumably, that they are not sufficiently
important dramatically to warrant it (except for messengers who
by convention always spoke). The Egyptian Herald, on the
contrary, is important. Garvie (194) concedes too much when he
concludes 'certainly one cannot prove that there was no chorus of
Egyptians': there is absolutely no good reason to think that there
was one, and in such a case that is the nearest to proof that can be
hoped for. (Contrast the cases of well-authenticated secondary
choruses, see pp. 236–7 below.)

Finally there is the question of when the Herald and his men
entered. Although we may still recapture a vivid impression of
the lyric scene 825–902 despite its textual state, it is impossible to
work out with any confidence the techniques which were used for

908. Heath's exchange of 906–7 and 909–10 (followed by Johansen) produces a
much weaker climax.

[1] For bibliography see Garvie 193 n. 1. Add Johansen *C et M* 27 (1966) 60,
who, however, recedes in his edition to uncertainty in the wake of Garvie's discussion (Page *OCT* is also undecided). Very few have accepted Murray's fancy
that the *dramatis personae* of *Hik* consisted simply of three choruses each with an
ἐξάρχων.

[2] This was strongly asserted by Nestle *DLZ* 1931 col. 2271; cf. Peretti 90–9,
Lloyd-Jones *Supplices* 366f.

the entry of the Egyptians. However, it seems possible that the act-dividing choral strophic song ends at 824,[1] that the strophic lyric dialogue proper, which becomes a kind of epirrhematic structure, begins at 843, and that the Herald first sings at 836. If so, then I should be inclined, along with the scholiast and with most editors,[2] to regard 825–35 as an entrance announcement sung by the Danaids (cf. ὅδε μάρπτις 826, τάδε φροίμια 830). In that case 825–35 is one of the very few examples of a lyric entry announcement: cf. *Seven* 854c*. As in *Seven* (provided we were right about the interpolation of the anapaests) the lyric announcement comes in between the end of an act-dividing song and the beginning of the ensuing lyric scene. The unusual lyric announcement keeps up the high emotional pitch.

911 enter Pelasgus (with attendants)

βοηδρομία

When an entry (or exit) is thoroughly integrated into the play, as this one is, the question of motivation simply will not arise: the event is self-evidently and unquestionably in place. But if we look further into the theatrical technique, then it can be seen that the reason for Pelasgus' arrival here is that the Danaids have cried for help and they have been heard.[3] Their call of ἄναξ προτάccου (835) is perhaps to Zeus rather than to Pelasgus.[4] But they call expressly on Pelasgus and the citizens of Argos when the threat of violence comes to a head: 908 διωλόμεcθ᾽· ἄεπτ᾽, ἄναξ, πάcχομεν = 905 ἰὼ πόλεωc ἀγοὶ πρόμοι, δάμναμαι. This cry for help is a βοή and Pelasgus' rescue βοήθεια. This social and legal procedure and its terminology was documented with a wealth of

---

[1] A few, e.g. Schroder (*Aeschyli Cantica* (Leipzig 1907) 15f.), following Hermann, make 825–35 into a strophic pair; but 836–42 would still have to be astrophic (cf. Peretti 123ff.). Page *OCT*, by reproducing M, makes the textual problem only too clear.

[2] Σ on 825: . . . ἀναβοῶcιν ἐξ ἀπόπτου τοὺc Αἰγυπτιάδαc ἰδοῦcαι (the scholiast may have had a better text, though Αἰγυπτιάδαc does not inspire confidence). Several editors have brought on the Egyptians at 825, e.g. Wilamowitz *Analecta* 201 (but not *ed maj*), Tucker 216, Rose 69, Johansen 121, Headlam *tr*, Murray *tr*, Benardete *tr*.

[3] It is not surely that Danaus has fetched him, as is implied by Garvie 136: Danaus has been forgotten—see 775*.

[4] Cf. the calls to Zeus at 811f., 892 etc. However, the scholiast says that 835 is a call to Pelasgus, and most editors emend accordingly; in that case one might compare the apostrophe at S. *OC* 831, over fifty lines before the eventual rescue (see below).

illustration from several societies by Schulze, who remarked how it was adopted and adapted by the Attic tragedians.¹ Over fifty years have added little to his masterly treatment of the subject (cf. Fraenkel *Ag ed* p. 614).

In drama the *boe* makes for an exciting rise in tension (and in the volume of the sound), and it provides a convincing and integral entry motivation. I shall quickly illustrate some of its uses (drawing largely on Schulze). Four of the five surviving suppliant plays have a *boe* which is answered by the resident protector (indeed in A. *Hik* and S. *OC* he has to be sent off somewhat unnecessarily so that he may be recalled). Orestes' appeal to Athena at *Eum* 287ff. (called a βοή in 397), since it is addressed to a god, also contains elements of a kletic invocation, see *Eum* 397a*. (Kopperschmidt *Bauformen* 327 n. 29 notes the analogy between βοή-βοήθεια and kletic call-epiphany.) At S. *OC* 887 Theseus answers the call of 884–6, first raised right back at 833. At E. *Hkld* 69ff. Iolaus' call is immediately answered by the chorus. In his *Hik* Euripides does not have a *boe*; though Theseus enters at 87 because he has heard mourning. The device, or variations on it, is also used by Euripides in other plays where he has a threatened suppliant at the altar; see e.g. *Andr* 507ff., *Her* 490ff.

But the use of the *boe* in tragedy is by no means limited to threatened suppliants. Anyone who is suffering an injustice should call out for witnesses; see e.g. A. *Ag* 1315, S. *Ant* 940ff., E. *Hec* 1091ff., *Hipp* 884,² etc. Anyone in an emergency may call out for help, as e.g. E. *Hipp* 770, *Or* 1296, *Hyps* fr. 60 13ff. (p. 40 Bond). A character who has no one else to call on may, like Prometheus, turn to the elements (*Prom* 88ff., 1091ff.), or, like Philoctetes, to the rocks and wild life (S. *Phil* 936ff., 987ff.). Two further extensions of the use of the *boe* in drama which may likewise supply the motivation of entries are the call to arms, best illustrated by the paratragic sequence at Ar. *Acharn* 566ff.,³ and

---

¹ W. Schulze *Kleine Schriften* (Göttingen 1934) 160ff. esp. 179ff. (first in *SBBerl* 1918 pp. 481ff.).

² It seems to me that Barrett *Hipp ed* 435–6 is mistaken to think that some citizens may answer this *boe*: the only response which matters is the entry of Hippolytus at 902. (On the derivative scene in Seneca's *Phaedra* see Zintzen *Senecas Phaedra* (Meisenheim 1960) 86f.)

³ Cf. Telekleides fr. 35K; see Fraenkel *Ag ed* 29, Rau 40–2 (but S. *OC* 884ff. is not really comparable, see above). For calls to arms in tragedy see p. 160 above.

the call for help with some task which cannot be achieved without aid, a motif which seems to have been common in satyr plays.[1] The use of the *boe* in tragedy seems to have been influential, as Schulze (op. cit. 173–9) shows in his discussion of the device in Roman comedy (*Rudens* 615ff. is surely paratragic). We have recently gained a good paratragic example in Menander: when at *Samia* 325 Demeas has found out half the truth about Moschion's child he cries out ὦ πόλισμα Κεκροπίας χθονός, / ὦ ταναὸς αἰθήρ, ὦ . . . , but he then restrains himself with τί, Δημέα, βοᾶις; and reflects (328) οὐδὲν γὰρ ἀδικεῖ Μοσχίων σε (cf. also *Sam* 580).

The dramatic device of an entry following on a *boe* is possible because the Greek theatre made free use of the convention that the noise of cries made on-stage may be heard by others off-stage.[2] Sometimes we are implicitly asked to suppose that the cries have been heard from some distance away, as here for example and in S. *OC*.[3] A *boe* is not the only kind of noise which may bring on another character to investigate it. He may, for instance, simply be called for, as e.g. S. *Phil* 1261ff., E. *Hec* 171ff., *Phoen* 296ff., *Ba* 55ff.; or he may come on because he has heard cries of grief or distress, as e.g. *Seven* 181, E. *Hkld* 474ff., *Hik* 87, *Hipp* 790ff., or sounds of anger or confusion, as e.g. S. *OT* 634ff., *Ichn* 215ff., or indeed sounds of joy, as e.g. S. *El* 1326, E. *Cycl* 624.

Pelasgus' opening lines, breaking in abruptly with a series of indignant questions, are similar to those found in other comparable contexts; see e.g. S. *OC* 887ff., E. *Hkld* 73ff., *Andr* 548ff. The opening vocative οὗτος is found elsewhere on an abrupt entry, e.g. S. *OT* 532, E. *Alc* 773, *Or* 1567. No doubt it was drawn from colloquial usage—though it is an oversimplification to say (Garvie 56 n. 4) that 'it clearly belongs to comedy', which S. *OC* 1627 is enough to refute.[4]

There can be little doubt that Pelasgus has some soldiers with him, as at his earlier entry: see 234b*. Great stress has been laid

[1] See p. 419 on *Diktyoulkoi*. Comparable in tragedy, perhaps, is S. *OC* 1491ff., on which see *GRBS* 12 (1971) 31.
[2] Conversely, of course, noises off-stage can on occasion be heard by those on-stage, and by the audience. Such noises are usually from inside the skene; for some examples see Joerden *Bauformen* 406 n. 37.
[3] Gods, naturally, can hear over very long distances, see e.g. *Prom* 132ff., *Eum* 397ff. They can also shout great distances—e.g. E. *IT* 1446ff., *Ba* 973ff.
[4] Distinguish between οὗτος, οὗτος σύ, ὦ οὗτος. See Wendel *Die Gesprächsanrede* etc. (Stuttgart 1929) 115f., Dale on E. *Alc* 773, Di Benedetto on E. *Or* 1567, Jebb on S. *OC* 1627.

on Argos' military strength and on its ability to protect the suppliants (see p. 201 above). But here, as elsewhere, I would not accept the hordes of extras that many scholars have foisted on the play.

951 exit Herald (and his men)

lines cast at a departing back

Pelasgus' final defiance (938ff.) ends with a blunt command: 949 κομίζου δ' ὡς τάχιϲτ' ἐξ ὀμμάτων. To this the Egyptian has just two lines of riposte: a threat ϲοὶ μὲν τόδ' ἡδὺ πόλεμον ἀρεῖϲθαι νέον,[1] and a prayer εἴη δὲ νίκη καὶ κράτοϲ τοῖϲ ἄρϲεϲιν. These are typical exit lines: for a threat in this sort of context compare e.g. S. *OC* 1036f., E. *Hik* 580; and for a brief prayer, particularly a prayer for victory, see p. 306 below. The couplet is meant, then, to be the Herald's parting shot. But Pelasgus, before he turns to the chorus (ὑμεῖϲ δέ 954), caps the couplet by defiantly taking up the taunt—ἀλλ' ἄρϲενάϲ τοι τῆϲδε γῆϲ οἰκήτοραϲ / εὑρήϲετ', οὐ πίνονταϲ ἐκ κριθῶν μέθυ. We cannot tell at precisely what moment the Herald went out of the sight of the audience; but he must, surely, have turned and begun to go after his last line, so that 952f. will have been cast at his departing back. He can hardly have stood still after 950f. and waited to be insulted before belatedly setting off after 953. Perhaps it is because it is so obvious that, whenever he actually disappeared, he began to go after 951 that scarcely any commentator makes the point.[2]

We have plenty of examples in Greek tragedy (and comedy) of lines cast after a departing back (cf. *GRBS* 1971 p. 42 n. 39). In no case can we say with absolute certainty that the departing person did not wait for the lines and then go after them; but a moment's examination of any of the instances makes the situation clear. Insults, threats, and taunts provide the most common use of the device. In similar circumstances to those in A. *Hik* compare E. *Hkld* 284ff., *Hik* 581ff.; in other contexts a sample is

[1] At the beginning of the line I have accepted Hermann's emendation of the MS. ἴϲθι μὲν τάδ' ἤδη (Hermann suggested alternatively εἴ ϲοι τόδ' ἡδύ). I share Johansen's surprise at the almost universal acceptance of Cobet's ἔοιγμεν ἤδη, though he is excessively defeatist to obelize the entire line rather than just the first half.

[2] The only exceptions I have noted are Richter 121, Wecklein *ed* 109 (though whether or not the Herald 'heard' 952f. is an insoluble irrelevance), Deckinger 16, 65 (but he does not distinguish second-person address from third-person comment), Untersteiner *tr* 103.

S. *Aj* 1161f., *Phil* 1259f., E. *Alc* 734ff., *Med* 623ff., *Phoen* 636f., *Or*
630f., 717ff. The device tends to lack dignity, and is often used to
lower the tragic or heroic tone. It is also, not surprisingly, found
in comedy; e.g. Ar. *Wasps* 1335ff., *Clouds* 1256ff., 1301f., *Birds*
1261f., Men. *Epitr* 376. However, the kind of call to a departing
back which is most characteristic of Old Comedy is good wishes
to speed someone on his way (often not in iambics): see *Acharn*
1143ff., *Kn* 498ff. etc.[1] Good wishes of this kind are found more
rarely in tragedy; but see e.g. *Cho* 1063f. (see p. 361), S. *OC*
1042f., E. *Med* 759ff., *El* 1340f. (these last two are rather like
comedy).

974 exit Pelasgus

?977 enter handmaids?

980 enter Danaus, with bodyguard (as a supplementary chorus?)

(a) the function of the anapaests 966–79

For a study of the dramatic techniques of exit and entry these
lines present the thorniest problem in *Hik* and one of the thorniest in all Aeschylus. Between lines 974 and 980 Pelasgus is
hustled off-stage, Danaus is suddenly produced, and between the
two a chorus of maids is found from nowhere. I shall maintain
that the structural and theatrical techniques used here, taking
the text as we have it, are unparalleled and inexplicable. Yet this
passage has received hardly any attention in the scholarly
literature: I can only suggest that this is because it has never been
considered from the angle I am observing.[2]

It should be said, before plunging in, that there is nothing
objectionable about uniqueness, and that we should not expect

---

[1] For a list see Rau 188. Rau is probably right to suspect the scholion which
says that *Kn* 498ff. is based on Sophocles. There is a possible Aeschylean example:
Glaukos Potnieus fr. 36 N², particularly if it is correctly identified with *PSI* 1210a
l. 5f. (= 441 M), looks like anapaestic good wishes after the departing back of
Glaucus.

[2] An honourable exception is Richter 121–2 who is very critical of the last part
of *Hik* before the final lyrics which he calls 'dispensable and merely patchwork'
('entbehrlich und lediglich Flickwerk'). His complaints arise in part from those
peculiarities which I shall discuss. The defence against Richter by Stephenson in
terms of 'character, lifelikeness' etc. is not at all convincing.

to find parallels for every dramatic technique. We have only a few plays out of many; and, in any case, there is no reason why a phenomenon unique among surviving tragedies should not have been unique in the entire corpus. In a conventional school of drama like Greek tragedy most features will recur often: but it is then the unusual which captures attention, especially if it is novel (though, of course, something which is both novel and effective tends to be repeated and imitated, and so become conventional). Indeed, we should expect unusual (even inimitable) things in a great dramatist. At the same time, when dealing with a good playwright, let alone a great one, we should be able to see *why* he has resorted to unusual technique. We are to assume that his craft is within his control; and we should write something off as pointless or incompetent only when at a complete loss for any more positive explanation (and even then we are likely to be wrong).

I defer consideration of the maids to 974b*: first Pelasgus and Danaus. The text of the anapaests given in M makes a kind of sense with only the slightest emendation. Thus Murray *OCT*, for instance, gives

ἀλλ' ἀντ' ἀγαθῶν ἀγαθοῖcι βρύοιc,
δῖε Πελαcγῶν.
πέμψον δὲ πρόφρων δεῦρ' ἡμέτερον
πατέρ' εὐθαρcῆ Δαναόν, πρόνοον
970 καὶ βούλαρχον. τοῦ γὰρ προτέρα
μῆτιc, ὅπου χρὴ δώματα ναίειν
καὶ τόποc εὔφρων. πᾶc τιc ἐπειπεῖν
ψόγον ἀλλοθρόοιc
εὔτυκοc. εἴη δὲ τὰ λῶιcτα.
975 ξύν τ' εὐκλείαι καὶ ἀμηνίτωι
βάξει λαῶν ἐγχώρων
τάccεcθε, φίλαι δμωίδεc, οὕτωc
ὡc ἐφ' ἑκάcτηι διεκλήρωcεν
Δαναὸc θεραποντίδα φερνήν.[1]

Accepting this text—for the time being only—Pelasgus must go

---

[1] In l. 966 M has ἀγαθοῖc and in 974 εὔτυκτοc. For M's ἐν χώρωι in 976 Hermann suggested τῶν ἐγχώρων, Tucker ἐγχώρων, and Headlam ἐν χώραι. The asyndeton at 975 seems tolerable, though it could easily be removed by cύν δ' εὐκλείαι (H. Voss). (The attribution in some old editions of 975ff. to Pelasgus has no MS. authority: there is a readily accessible photo of the relevant page of M in *GRBS* 9 (1968) plate 7, opposite p. 375.)

at some point during these anapaests. His last line (965) is not an
exit line, and he is directly addressed in 966–70. He might have
been meant to go at 970;[1] but since the next clause (970–1)
explains the previous one, and the next expatiates on that, and
since then εἴη δὲ τὰ λῷστα appears to round off the first part of
the anapaests, it seems preferable to send him off after 974, and
this is what has been done by most commentators.[2] So much for
Pelasgus. Danaus was evidently meant to enter with his first
speech at 980. What is said about him in 977–9 implies he is not
present; it does, however, act as preparation for his re-entry,
since it brings his role back into prominence, when he has been
so long forgotten (see 775*).

So what objection can there be to that? What troubles me is
the hurried handling of the transition from the scene with
Pelasgus to that with Danaus. This is a question of constructional
technique, not merely of stage time. It is no matter that there is
no time for Pelasgus to fetch Danaus, as instructed in 967ff., and
little time for the actor of the Herald to change to Danaus (951–
980).[3] Nor would it be any extenuation to plead that the arrangement of the handmaids would take a long time (thus Tucker xix,
183, who imagines an elaborate dumb-show, see p. 234 n. 2). The
difficulty lies deeper in the formal and constructional technique.

First it must be clear that 825ff. and 980ff. are two separate
acts (epeisodia). This is one of those many places which show the
insufficiencies of the traditional analysis based on Poetics Ch. 12
(see §5 and Appendix E). In those terms the entire play from 825
to the end forms a single unit, the 'exodos'; but this is an obvious
nonsense which in no way reflects the actual construction.[4] It is

---

[1] Thus e.g. Wilamowitz ed maj 373, Deckinger 16. Rose 78 cannot be right that
in 966ff. 'the chorus sing them [the Argives] off the stage': contrast E. Med 759ff.,
Ar. Kn 489ff. etc. (see p. 222 above).
[2] Some, e.g. Tucker, Rose, take cύν τ' εὐκλείαι κτλ. (975f.) with what precedes
and punctuate after ἐγχώρων, in which case Pelasgus would exit after 976 (cf.
Johansen 135). But l. 974 has the ring of finality.
[3] There are other changes at least as quick as this, e.g. S. Trach 946–71, E. Or
1352–69: see further P-C TDA² 138ff., Joerden 56, Ritchie 127f. (However,
Ritchie has picked some dubious examples: Alc is probably to be played with
three actors not two (see P-C DFA² 145); in Med there is no reason why the Nurse
and Medea have to be played by the same actor; in Phoen it all depends on how
seriously one takes the scholion on l. 93.) Practical experience shows that with
practice a costume change may be made very quickly, and a mask is much easier
to change than make-up.
[4] Yet it is blindly followed by even Detscheff 68, Aichele Bauformen 51, 68.

little better to look in isolation to the change from speech to song and so regard 1017/18 as the point of transition from episode (825–1017) to exodos.[1] We must take into account the structure of the action. And once this is done it is immediately evident that the threat of the Herald, his repulse, and Pelasgus' assurances make up one unit or act, and that Danaus' advice and the ensuing final song another. And this is corroborated by the formal criterion of the rearrangement of actors by exit and entry: the penultimate act is begun by the entry of the Herald and finished by the exit of Pelasgus; and the final act is begun by the entry of Danaus and closed by the 'exeunt omnes'. So it looks as though the anapaests mark the break between the two acts.

So can the anapaests be regarded as an act-dividing song; or, to put the question in a more familiar form, do the anapaests take the place of a stasimon? That is indeed the view of no less an authority than Kranz (p. 162). I quote in full: 'towards the end of the play, when tension or exhaustion tend to make a strophic ode no longer appropriate for filling any pause that occurs, even early drama uses a brief anapaestic recitative, delivered by the whole chorus as at *Cho* 723ff., 855ff., *Ag* 1331ff., or by the chorus leader as at *Hik* 966ff. This takes over the function of a stasimon, and also contains appropriate reflections (. . . die Funktion eines Stasimons übernimmt, auch entsprechende Gedanken enthält).' Yet if one turns to Kranz's fuller discussions of astrophic lyrics 'in place of a stasimon' in his dissertation of 21 years earlier (*Forma* 7f., 24f.) *Hik* 966ff. is not included. To explain this contradiction it will be necessary to look more closely at these other places. At *Ag* 1330 Cassandra goes to her death, and the anapaests (1331–42) on prosperity and retribution intervene before the death cries and the helpless choral couplets which lead up to the entry of Clytemnestra: see *Ag* 1372a*. At *Cho* 718 Clytemnestra goes in, the anapaests (719–29) pray for Orestes' success, and the nurse Kilissa enters at 732 (see 732a*). And *Cho* 855–68 is similar to *Ag*: Aegisthus goes at 854, in the anapaests the chorus is in such suspense that it cannot pray, and the next act begins with the Servant at 875.[2] These three places in Aeschylus are quite closely

---

[1] Thus e.g. Tucker xxxvif., Wecklein 98, 115, Vürtheim 154, 160; cf. Wilamowitz p. 1.

[2] On this whole sequence see *Cho* 892a*. The anapaests at E. *Med* 1081ff. are also act-dividing, but they are rather different—see Kranz *Forma* 8.

comparable with the brief astrophic dochmiac lyrics which occur at six places in Euripides with an act-dividing function. These are excellently discussed by Kranz (*Forma* 21–4 cf. *Stasimon* 117, 177 —he rightly compares also the structural function of the divided strophic pair at *Or* 1353ff. = 1537ff.). He observes that each is preceded by an exit and followed by an entry, and that each comes at a tense juncture of the play where Euripides wished to separate two acts and to rearrange his characters and yet did not want to delay the action with a full-scale strophic song. Thus Kranz shows that act-dividing anapaests or astrophic lyrics are an uncommon but clearly recognizable structural phenomenon with a useful and definable purpose.

But Kranz was, surely, right in his dissertation to exclude, and wrong in his book to include, *Hik* 966ff. as an instance. There are at least three clear and vital differences between these anapaests and the others. First, this is not a tense juncture where excitement would make a full stasimon out of place (*contra* Garvie 136 n. 4, citing Kranz): in fact there is no obvious dramatic reason why there should not be a strophic song at this point. The danger and suspense in A. *Hik* are over by 953, and from then on the play draws to a relatively relaxed conclusion. Secondly the contents of these anapaests are not like the others which are comparable to those of a stasimon though in brief ('sententiis stasimi simillimum' Kranz *Forma* 7). The words do not reflect on the action with 'entsprechende Gedanken': rather they are part of it. The dispatch of Pelasgus and arrangement of the maids are quite unlike the more general and abstract reflections in the other places. Thirdly, although it is true that Danaus enters after the anapaests, Pelasgus does not make his exit *before* them but during them, probably more than half-way through (see above). Also the handmaids may enter during them (see 974b* below).

Normally an act is ended by an exit before the act-dividing song, and the new act begins with an entry after it. But in this case would it not be true to say that the act 825ff. ends with the exit of Pelasgus who is an integral part of it, and that the final act begins with the entry or introduction of the maids who belong to that act (if anywhere)? In other words, the penultimate act ends at 974 and the last begins at 975, and there is no interval whatsoever between them except a momentary vacant stage (vacant, that is, of all but the chorus). This is hardly altered if we suppose that the maids were on from the start, or even if we eliminate them altogether, since the vacant stage is then merely extended from 975 to 980. It is very rare in Greek tragedy to have a stage vacant of actors except during act-dividing songs. I have listed all the exceptions I know of in *GRBS* 12 (1971) 41 n. 38; and none is remotely similar to this place. I can think of no other act-division in Aeschylus or all Greek tragedy whose technique resembles *Hik* 974–80 (or 974/5). The nearest is perhaps *Eum* 777/8 (see 777c*): but the differences far outweigh the similarities.

I hope, then, to have established that the construction is unique; and that it is not trivially unique, since elsewhere the structural technique of Greek tragedy follows a consistent basic pattern which admits recognizable adaptations. This juncture in *Hik* simply cannot fit the fundamental framework. Now, as I said at the start, there is no reason why the technique should not be unparalleled: but we must ask why it is unique, what is gained by it. There is no close dramatic connection between the two acts, no particular continuity: on the contrary, there is asyndeton, plain juxtaposition.[1] So is there some point to this juxtaposition, some reason why Aeschylus did not use a normal strophic song, some detectable dramatic gain in the rapid, stark transition? I can see none (though others may).

And the inexplicably abrupt transition has positive drawbacks. The run of the play is temporarily confused and obscured by hurry and bustle. Not only is Pelasgus hustled off and Danaus suddenly produced, but we are also asked to believe that an entire secondary chorus is brought on and arranged with virtually no explanation (see 974b* below). This is not like Greek tragedy, where movements are few and well separated and the sequence of events is deliberate and well marked. A rapid succession of scenes may be used for a special purpose only; notably for fast and exciting action (see e.g. on *Cho* 892a*) or for a striking and contrasting sequence (see e.g. on *Eum* 139*). Neither is the case here: the haste is merely mechanical and not dramatic. And the uncomfortable hurry is further aggravated by

[1] Pelasgus' mission to fetch Danaus is discarded. The abruptness of the join is accentuated as long as we accept the transmitted syntactical asyndeton at 974/5 (but see p. 223 n. 1 above). The whole problem is aggravated in the translation by Benardete (p. 39), who for some reason cuts out lines 975–9, and so has 'exit King, enter Danaus' in a single stage instruction.

the handling of the exit of Pelasgus. As noted on p. 205 above the characters of Greek tragedy normally speak on departure except for those who are in the company of another and for the servants who are summarily dismissed. Otherwise the silent exit is usually of some significance. But the only significance here is that the Danaids treat Pelasgus as though he were a servant. They briefly thank him for rescuing them (966f., contrast 625ff.), and then they bundle him off without a word to fetch their father.

These difficulties seem to me sufficient to justify suspicion of the text as we have it. The anapaests are not, in fact, secure. It is true that Murray's text, given above on p. 223, makes a kind of sense, but a tenuous and strained sense. In particular καὶ τόπος εὔφρων in 972 is hard to construe, and the dragging phrase ςύν τ' εὐκλείαι κτλ. in 975f. is awkward if taken with the following τάccεcθε and even worse with what precedes. Many editors have, therefore, posited a lacuna in one place or another;[1] Wilamowitz's text has a transposition and two lacunae. This might encourage one (cf. Deckinger 16f.) to suppose that the lacuna was a long one, and that during it Pelasgus had a suitable exit speech, and that a reasonable time elapsed for him to fetch Danaus. But this is not convincing, for either the King's speech has to be in anapaests or he has to speak in iambics between two sets of choral anapaests, and either way one is introducing unparalleled formal techniques by conjecture. And this would not really solve the problems of structural technique raised above. In any case, the linguistic difficulties are not so severe that they could not be cured by one or two lacunae of just a few words.

So far as I can see any really efficacious textual cure will have to be much more drastic. For example, we might conjecture that the anapaests 966–79 are an interpolation, and that they replace both (i) some spoken lines after 965 in which Pelasgus departed with a proper exit speech and (ii) a full strophic act-dividing song (stasimon). I offer this emendation not because I am committed to it but in order to bring out the critical dilemma here. The textual criticism of Greek tragedy is traditionally based above all on linguistic and palaeographic considerations, and rests on the assumption that the transmitted texts are (with a few

---

[1] For various suggestions see Wecklein *Appendix* 39, Freericks *De Aeschyli Supplicum Choro* (diss. Duderstadt 1883) 69ff. Page *OCT* has added a new one—a brief lacuna after 971.

well-known exceptions) close to the author's own except for detailed verbal corruption. My conjecture, on the other hand, is based almost entirely on grounds of dramatic technique, and implies that our texts may have been tampered with on a larger scale than we like, however credulously, to believe.

But there are at least two obvious and weighty objections to the theory that the anapaests have been interpolated in order to replace the last lines of an act and an entire choral song. First, we can hardly fault the anapaests for language or expression. The wording is peculiar, perhaps clumsy, but there is nothing which is impossibly unlike Aeschylus.[1] Secondly there is no obvious motive for the interpolation or for the cutting of a substantial piece of the original. It is not hard to think of possible motives, but they are not very strong. For instance, if the play was re-performed later in the fifth century[2] without the rest of the trilogy, then it may be that the section included references which were pointless without the other plays and so were cut. But, against that, each play of the *Oresteia* could be, and has been, performed singly without any intolerable incongruity. Or it may be that the choral element in *Hik* was too much and too strenuous for a later *chorodidaskalos* and his chorus, and so he cut a relatively dispensible lyric and replaced it with a few anapaests.[3] But then why cut the end of the previous scene as well? Another possible motive is the desire to add the supplementary chorus of maids: see p. 238 below. But that could have been done less violently by means of simple interpolation without cutting.

In the climate of textual scholarship in this century at least, this conjecture will seem like wanton violence, a major operation to remove a wart. But the point I am trying to make is that the transition as we have it is not just a minor blemish but is a grave malformation inside the body of the play. It is not only technically irregular, it also results in a hurried, fumbled, and clumsy

[1] Vürtheim 212 n. 1 rightly points out that 972–4, which is not particularly appropriate where it stands, could easily have been composed out of 994, which is in place. This duplication is positively suspect. I cannot resist the observation that lines 977–9 would go very well in a play about the wedding night of the Danaids. Might they have been lifted from later in the trilogy?

[2] This may be supported by the influence on E. *Hik*, and by the crack at the expense of A. *Hik* 276 in Ar. *Clouds* 372, if it is one.

[3] Colin Macleod again suggests abbreviation (cf. p. 146 n. 1 above): 966–79 may be added to replace lines 980–1017 as well as a stasimon, and thus circumvent the 'loose ends' in 983ff. and 1009ff.

transition. To those accustomed to criticize Aeschylus for hamfisted primitiveness in every sphere this will seem nothing
exceptionable. But to those of us who reckon that most of such
carping is the patronizing arrogance of scholars who have misunderstood a great artist, some way out of this difficulty must be
sought for. Let the matter rest there, until the maids have been
considered.

(b) a supplementary chorus of maids?

Lines 977–9, if they stand in our text as Aeschylus composed
them, evidently show that he meant a band of δμωίδες to be on
stage at this point, and that they were to be equal in number to
the chorus.[1] We cannot come to an opinion on the question when
they entered (if at all) without first considering the larger question of what part they play. For the stage management may well
depend on whether they sang or remained silent. Nearly all
scholars this century have given the maids an important part in
the final song of the play: on the other hand many in the last
century supposed that they remained purely decorative extras,
and there has recently been a return to this view.[2]

There have been two main arguments in favour of a singing
supplementary chorus: the wording of 1022f., and the claim that
the second chorus is 'essential to bring out the issues at stake'
(Barrett E. *Hipp ed* 368). First, then, the words ὑποδέξαςθε δ'
ὀπαδοὶ μέλος,[3] which occur in the middle of the first strophe
which is in praise of Argos. The usual interpretation has been
along the lines of Smyth's 'And do you handmaidens take up
the strain.' But it has been objected that it is doubtful whether
ὑποδέχομαι can bear this meaning (which requires διαδέχομαι),
and that in this context the word should mean 'hear and accept'.[4]

---

[1] ἐφ' ἑκάστηι contradicts Fitton-Brown's suggestion (*CR* 1957 p. 3) that they
were 'no more than a token group'.

[2] A list of eleven scholars who have rejected a singing part for the maids is
given by Garvie 195; add e.g. Weil, Dindorf, Wecklein, Tucker. The case against
the maids was made by Freericks (cited above, p. 228 n. 1) 72ff., and well argued
by van der Graaf *Mnem* 10 (1942) 281–5. Garvie remains undecided ('probably
the question must remain open' [*sic*] p. 195). But a singing part has recently been
rejected by Johansen *C et M* 27 (1966) pp. 61–4 and *ed*, Webster *Chorus* 124f.,
Whittle *CR* N.S. 20 (1970) 298f., Ferrari *Maia* N.S. 24 (1972) 353ff. These discussions will be cited simply by author's name.

[3] ⟨δ'⟩ add. Heath, μένος MS. corr. Legrand. Ferrari 355 has suggested ἀποδεί-
ξαςθε δ' ὀπαδοὶ μένος; but this does not make good sense in the context.

[4] See LSJ i 3, citing Hes. and Hdt; cf. van der Graaf 283, Garvie 194f. (Powell
Lexicon Hdt glosses 'embrace').

Moreover, since ὀπαδός is used of either sex and ranges in meaning from 'follower' to 'companion' the injunction might equally
well be addressed by one hemichorus to the other hemichorus
(thus Hermann, Paley). But better than either of these is the
Argive bodyguard, just called ὀπαδοί in 985.[1] The Danaids are
here praising Argos, and it is more appropriate for the bodyguard to hear and accept the song than for the maids or for half
the Danaids. So 1022f. is no evidence that the maids sang a part
in the final song; it is not even evidence for their existence.

Does the song itself demand that the maids take part in it?
Certainly the third strophic pair (1052–61) is an altercation
requiring two sides; and all the other pairs except the last would
lend themselves to division between two parts, though I cannot
see anything which absolutely demands it. All recent editors,
until Johansen, have given parts of the second and third strophic
pairs to the maids as a supplementary chorus; most have followed
the arrangement of Kirchhoff.[2] But what is this θεραποντὶς φερνή
that it should suddenly become so important? Who are these odd
handmaidens to correct their mistresses and to preach in this
way? It seems to me that the only reason for introducing them
into this song is the mention of them in 977–9.

There are no fewer than three rivals to the maids for a part in
the song; and all of them have as good, if not better, claims.
First, is there anything impossible in the old arrangement
(Hermann, among others, revived by van der Graaf) which
distributed the song between two hemichoruses? It is usually
argued that some of the views expressed on sex and marriage are
irreconcilably inconsistent with the violent revulsion expressed
elsewhere by the chorus. But an Aeschylean chorus has no rigidly
uniform outlook; it will change its attitudes to suit the context
and to further the dramatist's larger purposes (cf. p. 271 below).
It may be that here Aeschylus wishes to bring out within the
chorus issues which will loom large later in the trilogy (bearing in
mind, of course, the fragment of *Danaides*), or that, now that the
immediate danger is over, he wants to redress the earlier revulsion and bring the play to a more balanced close. I find this

---

[1] Cf. van der Graaf 282, Johansen, Webster, Whittle; also Page *OCT* on 1018—
but in the *app. crit.* on 1034–52 he uses 1022 as evidence for attribution to the maids.

[2] For fourteen other arrangements see Wecklein *Appendix* 42f. (Owen *The
Harmony of Aeschylus* (Toronto 1952) 17f. seems to think the song is all sung by an
undivided chorus.)

'inconsistent' split within the chorus easier to accept than the upstart maids. But if it is felt that a second independent party is needed to bring out the conflict of issues, then a secondary chorus of Argive bodyguards would probably be preferable to the maids (thus Johansen, Webster, Whittle). They are clearly introduced in 985ff., and are addressed in 1022f. (see above): unlike the maids they would accord with the handling of supplementary choruses elsewhere (see p. 237 below). As citizens of the pious protecting city they are in a good position dramatically to oppose a new and god-fearing attitude to the Danaids' fanaticism.[1] And there is even a third possibility which does not seem to have been considered: that the moderate voice in the final songs might be none other than Danaus (van der Graaf 284 notes that the advice would suit him). Compare *Pers* for the division of the final song between actor and chorus. Danaus is less open to complaints of inconsistency than a hemichorus, since he has been opposed to sexual lust and to marriage with the cousins rather than to sex and marriage in general. Danaus, more than maids or body-guards, has the weight and authority to deliver this sententious advice. As with all the alternatives the precise distribution of parts remains open to dispute, but there does not seem to be any insuperable difficulty.[2]

Although I look kindly on the attribution of the other voice to Danaus (since it is my own idea), the most likely of these four claimants is probably the Argive bodyguard. The traditional attribution to the maids seems to me by far the least likely. If the maids did not sing then they are not a secondary chorus, they are purely ornamental. The only explanation we are given is that they are some sort of 'dowry' (979). In that case they are simply comparable to other attendant extras who accompany characters of standing in Greek tragedy (see *Pers* 155c*); and so they should prima facie enter at line 1 along with those they attend on.

---

[1] Johansen 62, following Wecklein, also argues that the masculine γανάοντες in 1019 shows that the singers of the final songs are not all feminine. This is a point; but the text is uncertain, and it may be that masculine participles are occasionally applied to females (see Fraenkel *Ag ed* 283–5 and *contra* Barrett E. *Hipp ed* 366–8).

[2] Danaus would, for instance, fit an adaptation of Hermann's distribution among hemichoruses, thus: Cho. 1018–21, Da. 1022–5, Cho. 1026–9, Da. 1030–3; Cho. 1034–7, Da. 1038–42, Cho. 1043–6, Da. 1047–51; Cho. 1052–3, Da. 1054, Cho. 1055, Da. 1056, Cho. 1057–8, Da. 1059, Cho. 1060, Da. 1061; Cho. 1062 to end. For a different division of 1052–61 see Page *CQ* 31 (1937) 97 and *OCT*.

There is no point to a later independent entry which would only draw unwanted attention to them. Many interpreters have, in fact, brought on the maids at the very beginning;[1] and some have even faced the stage consequences of this: that they will have to keep out of the way for the next nine-tenths of the play.[2]

But it is, surely, impossible for a group of extras the same size as the chorus to remain inconspicuously out of the way for 975 lines (nor would this be in any way palliated if they were first mentioned a few minutes earlier in line 954).[3] Things would be little better if the maids had been identified and their superfluous presence explained in the first few lines of the play (as could easily have been done). As it is, they are unexplained as well as being a distracting and meaningless encumbrance to the scenic picture. And consider this in practical terms. Twelve actors, let alone fifty, cannot simply retire inconspicuously and sit or stand still 'conveniently grouped' for the best part of the play.[4] Did they not even move during the scene with the Egyptian? And if, as has been argued, they did not even take part in the final song, then what on earth are they there for at all? It is incredible that a chorus of desperate fugitive exiles should be the only chorus in all of surviving Greek tragedy to trail around a crowd of permanent attendants. The only function of the maids seems to be to

[1] Including Bodensteiner 725, Mazon, Wecklein 13, Rose 17, Hammond 420 n. 60, 'Droysen' *tr*, Werner *tr*, Untersteiner *tr* (Smyth, Vürtheim, Kraus, and others forgivably forget to give any stage direction for their entry). Rose 77f. thinks that there may have been some eunuchs as well!

[2] See e.g. Wilamowitz *ed maj actio* on 1 'comitantur eas ancillae mox recessurae'; Tucker xvf. 'they must be either grouped at the entrance or inconspicuously seated in the part of the orchestra nearest to it'; P-C *DFA*² 236 'they had doubtless been present all the time, distinguished from the Danaids by the costume and conveniently grouped in or around the orchestra'.

[3] The entire speech 954ff. is about the new Argive security which protects the Danaids, and so cùν φίλοιc ὁπάοcιν in 954 must be a reference to a bodyguard. It will mean 'with a friendly bodyguard' (cf. *Eum* 1034); and so it prepares for the armed citizens who arrive with Danaus (and who may sing as a supplementary chorus). These arguments alone are conclusive against Schütz's generally accepted emendation to φίλαιc (accepted by Page *OCT*, and strangely defended by Johansen, although he believes that the bodyguard, not the maids, form the supplementary chorus). A further point is that ὁπάων (unlike ὁπαδόc) is always masculine in tragedy, and means a bodyguard at *Hik* 492 (cf. *Cho* 769). In fact the one and only feminine use is at *h Cer* 440 (see Richardson *comm ad loc.*; van der Graaf 282 n. 2 is a mistake: the word at S. *OC* 1092 is ὁπαδόc). Schütz's emendation was rightly rejected by van der Graaf 282f. who is half followed by Garvie 195.

[4] In a Greek National Theatre production at Epidaurus in 1964 the producer, faced with this impossible practical problem, simply had the maids take part in the singing and dancing of all the choral songs, as though they were Danaids.

provide meaningless crowd scenes and spectacle. That is why all those who have taken the play to be a primitive extravaganza, which shows 'the comparatively inartistic character of the early drama' (Tucker xvi), have not hesitated to accept this vacuous and inconvenient band of extras. But I have argued throughout that the view of Aeschylus as an impresario of empty spectacle is mistaken; and I have attacked this view of *Hik* in particular on 234c*. If Aeschylus had any stagecraft at all, he cannot have had the maids of lines 977–9 on stage throughout the entire play.

This, then, is the kind of trouble we encounter if we suppose the maids entered at line 1; and it suggests that we might do better to look for an entry point for them later in the play, even though that would run counter to the convention that silent attendants always accompany their masters unless told otherwise. The maids are first mentioned at 977–9 (on 954 see p. 233 n. 3); and some scholars have, indeed, supposed that they first entered at about this point.[1] But τάccεcθε, φίλαι δμωίδεc are strange words with which to introduce the entry of a whole group of people whose existence has never even been hinted at. The context hardly justifies the statement that the maids are 'explicitly introduced' (Lloyd-Jones), 'announced' (Barrett), or 'summoned' (Garvie). Moreover, if the preceding words in 975–6 are taken with τάccεcθε, as by most editors, then this makes an even more peculiar introduction, since the Danaids would begin to speak to the maids, who are still presumably off-stage, before they have ever called them or addressed them with a vocative.

The truth is that there is no announcement or introduction of the entry: the subject of these few anapaests is not the entry but the formation of the procession. If the maids were supposed to enter at this point, we can only suppose that the entry was meant to be as informal and inconspicuous as possible, so that inappropriate questions or explanations need not be raised.[2] This

---

[1] Including Paley 81, Murray 51, *tr* 84 (where he omits the awkward 975–6), Johansen 134, Barrett E. *Hipp ed* 368, Lloyd-Jones *Supplices* 366, Garvie 194f. Although most editors have supposed that the maids were first mentioned in 954, only Vellacott *tr* 82 has taken the obvious step of bringing them on at that point.

[2] Contrast Tucker 183: 'The arrangement performed with proper grace and scenic effect would take a considerable time, during which verbal accompaniment could be dispensed with.' This not only prolongs and accentuates a meaningless triviality, it calls for a dumb-show which is, I maintain, contrary to the scenic technique of Greek tragedy.

might be just tolerable were it not for the dramatic context of this inexplicit stage movement. I have already laboriously complained (974a* above) about the hasty and unclear transition from the Pelasgus scene to the Danaus scene. If the few syllables which do intervene between the exit of one and the entry of the other are taken up with the hurried and unexplained entry of all these maids, then it becomes far worse. The result is a confused mêlée quite unlike anything in Greek tragedy as we know it (even including E. *Or* and *Rh*). While rush and confusion might in special circumstances be given dramatic point, here there seems to be none.

A modern reader might complain that I am overstating my case against this alleged confusion at 974–80; he might claim that there is nothing objectionable in a deft rearrangement of the characters, and that it could be managed in practice without too much confusion. But we are used to plays with many acts and scenes and with many movements to and fro so that the handling of exits and entrances is often necessarily hurried and inexplicit. The close observation of the corpus of surviving Attic tragedy shows that there the realignment of characters is carefully arranged round the act-dividing songs, that the exits and entrances of major characters are kept distinct and measured, and that each is given due space and attention. The consequence of this must be that the expectations of the Athenian audience would have been different, and that it would have been much more sensitive to hurried or inexplicit stage movements. It would expect them to have a clear and special dramatic purpose, and it would be offended if they did not. So, unless there is some dramatic purpose here which has not yet been discerned, there is either something wrong, or Aeschylus is guilty of bad and highly uncharacteristic dramatic technique. Faced with a choice between an entry for the maids at line 1, which clutters the scene for the entire play, or an entry at about line 977, which further confuses a hurried transition, one can only accept the lesser of two evils—or look for a third still lesser evil.

But first, since nearly all scholars of the last eighty years have supposed that the maids took part in the final song, I had better add a digression on what would be the consequences for this problem if they were in fact a supplementary chorus. This calls for a quick survey of the dramatic techniques used elsewhere for

the entries of secondary choruses in tragedy. We have sound
evidence for six of these, though there were no doubt others.[1]
Four of the six accompany an actor and are closely associated
with him.[2] Of these the only example we have in full is the chorus
of huntsmen with Hippolytus which is announced clearly by
Artemis (E. *Hipp* 54–6, sent off at 108ff.). In E. *Phaethon* there is a
chorus of girls which accompanies Merops and sings a wedding
song; they are seen approaching by Clymene at 216ff. (and sent
off at 245ff.). The scholion on E. *Hipp* 58 tells of a second chorus
of shepherds in E. *Alexandros*, and we now know that they
brought on Alexandros,[3] and of a chorus in *Antiope* accompanying Dirce. Different from these other Euripidean examples is the
chorus of children in E. *Hik*.[4] They are on-stage with the main
chorus at the start of the play, but take no part until they go with
Theseus at 954. They return with the ashes at 1123, and sing a
lament in dialogue with the main chorus (1123–64), thus assuming the function of the mourner who accompanies the mortal
remains of a dead relative. They are then disregarded again. It is
true that, like the maids in A. *Hik* (if they entered at the beginning), they are unused and unnoticed for most of the play; but
they are at least clearly identified at 107ff. and 1123ff. and self-
evidently by sight. This analogy might seem to favour an entry
at line 1 for the maids in Aeschylus, but the children in Euripides
have a function which is much more relevant to the play and
which to some extent justifies their inactive presence. (They are,
none the less, one of the many weaknesses in E. *Hik*, a play with

---

[1] The standard reference is to the dissertation of Lammers (cited above, p. 190
n. 2), but he is so speculative as to be virtually useless: see the excellent review by
Nestle *DLZ* 1931 cols. 2269ff. (cf. Kranz 273). (Nestle also disposes of Lammers's
theory, favoured by Kranz, that double choruses were somehow connected with
Ur-tragödie.) For a couple of unwarranted supplementary choruses see p. 217
above and Barrett E. *Hipp ed* 368.

[2] Cf. *GGL* i 2 p. 71 n. 5, Barrett E. *Hipp ed* 167, Zwierlein 82–3, Lanza *SIFC*
35 (1962) 237ff. The parody of a lyric dialogue by Agathon at Ar. *Thesm* 101ff.
might have one of these personal secondary choruses behind it, as Agathon
apparently takes the parts both of the actor and the chorus.

[3] See R. A. Coles 'The Hypothesis of Euripides' *Alexandros*', *BICS* Supp.
32 (1974) p. 19 on l. 15 and p. 24. His equation of the secondary chorus
with the shepherds who are hostile to Alexandros is likely, though not I think
certain.

[4] Garvie 192ff. omits this example of a secondary chorus (just as he neglects
all other analogies between A. *Hik* and E. *Hik*). As a result he implies (194) that
the maids in A. *Hik* would be the only second chorus to hold a lyric dialogue with
the main chorus.

none of the intensity or scenic and dramatic economy of A. *Hik*.)[1]
Lastly there is the chorus of προπομποί who sing the final stanzas
of A. *Eum* (1132–47), first referred to and given a function by
Athena at 1005f. If, as most editors suppose, they entered at this
point, then this would favour and to some extent parallel the late
and inexplicit entry of the maids at A. *Hik* 977. However on *Eum*
1047a* I support the old suggestion that the jurors of the trial
become the escort at the end of the play. If this is right, then the
change of role has no analogy in *Hik*, and the inexplicit entry is
eliminated.

To sum up, all these other supplementary choruses are clearly
identified and explained, and have a clearly defined function. All
but E. *Hik* and A. *Eum* are given a clear entry announcement,
and all but E. *Hik* and perhaps A. *Eum* enter shortly before they
sing. This would tend to favour an entry at 977 rather than 1 for
the maids in A. *Hik*, *if* they sang. But this, if anything, aggravates
the hurried transition criticized earlier in 974a*; and it should
be clear that the comparison with other supplementary choruses
only serves to bring out the strange pointlessness of the alleged
chorus in *Hik*. Finally it should be noted, on the other hand, that,
if it was the Argive bodyguards who sang in the final song (see
above, p. 232), then they fit the analogues well, since they
accompany an actor, are clearly introduced (985ff.), and enter
shortly before they sing.

[1] There is even a theory that there was a *third* supplementary chorus in E. *Hik*.
This is highly improbable: see the discussion of Arnoldt *Die chorische Technik des
Eur.* (Halle 1878) 71–6, cf. Wilamowitz *Gr Trag* i 220. I would omit it but that,
if it were right, it would have a bearing on the problem of the maids in Aeschylus.
Some editors, unable to conceive that a chorus of fifteen could represent seven
mothers, have seized on 71–86 esp. 72 ἀχοῦϲιν προπόλων χέρεϲ, and have argued
that the strophe is sung by a hemichorus of maids who constituted half of the
chorus. Kranz (127 n. 19, 176) among others has claimed that these maids are
a direct 'Nachbildung' of those in A. *Hik*. But the words in question are explicable
as self-reference, and these alleged maids are nowhere else identified, explained,
or commented on. Now that we are less insistent on naturalistic treatment of
numbers a whole chorus representing seven seems acceptable (cf. e.g. Grube
The Drama of Euripides (London 1941) 240–2, Kaimio 76 n. 1). (Or is it conceivable
that the chorus of E. *Hik* did consist of seven not fifteen? See Norwood *Essays on
Euripidean Drama* (Toronto 1954) 112–17.) Moreover, many of the songs of E.
Hik must be sung by the mothers only, which, if there were maids, would mean
only half the chorus (*contra* Smith *HSCP* 71 (1966) 156f.); and the chorus is
repeatedly addressed as μητέρεϲ, γεραιαί etc. (see Arnoldt 71f.). In other words
half the chorus would be idle for most of the play. If the maids in E. *Hik* were to
be accepted, then they would provide a significant analogy to A. *Hik*, since they
would be similarly unidentified, neglected, otiose, pointless, and functionless.

I have tried to show that the maids are not referred to at 1022f.
(nor 954), that they did not take part in the final song, and that
it is highly unsatisfactory to bring them on stage at 977 and no
less unsatisfactory at line 1. If I am right, then the one and only
piece of evidence for their existence is 977–9; and anyone who
has followed this far will want to see if they cannot somehow be
eliminated from the play altogether. But there can be no simple
emendation, since the maids are entrenched both in δμωΐδες
(977) and θεραποντίδα φερνήν (979). Even if we detach 975–6 from
τάccεcθε and suppose a lacuna, as many editors have done, it is
still hard to eliminate the maids from the stage, let alone from
the play. Something like '⟨when we have safely reached the city,
then⟩ τάccεcθε, φίλαι, δμωΐδας, οὕτως ὡς κτλ.'?[1] This would at
least remove the maids from the stage, though the reference to
them still remains unexplained and irrelevant. And there is still
the structural malformation.

So I return to the desperate remedy that the anapaests 966–79
might have been interpolated to replace a strophic act-dividing
song: see pp. 228–30 above. If that were right, then, of course, the
maids would be interpolated also. This would add some further
motivation for the interpolator. The last part of the play might
have seemed too dominated by choral lyric and too bare of
action and spectacle for later tastes (later fifth-century, I presume). The alteration would at once remove some choral lyric,
and add some pretty, though gratuitous, spectacle (an aspect of
the maids which many, like Tucker, have thought Aeschylean).
However, the theory is still liable to the objections raised in the
earlier discussion. I put forward this conjecture of cutting and
interpolation with the utmost diffidence, in the hope that such
a theory may eventually provoke a valid explanation of the unusual technical phenomena which I have isolated but failed to
account for.

1073 exeunt omnes (chorus, Danaus, Argive body-guard, ?maids)

the suppliants find safety

The tragedy ends with a procession off to Argos (cf. on *Pers*
1077*). Even without inessential multitudes (see 234c*), even

---

[1] The emendation δμωΐδας goes back to Geel and Hermann. φίλαι will then be
self-apostrophe (or the coryphaeus to the others).

maybe without the maids (see 974b*), it makes a fine conclusion—
a united, dignified, and organized stage movement after the wild
turbulence of the previous scenes. Stress has been laid on the
security and safe conclusion of this journey both by Pelasgus
(954ff.) and Danaus (980ff.) ; and the bodyguard provides visible
proof of the Argive strength and good will.

We cannot say when the procession began to form in choreographic terms, nor when it actually began to move off. The
change to a trochaic metre at 1062 may have some stage significance; but the opening of the song (ἴτε 1018) suggests that the
procession began to form early on, perhaps with Danaus and the
Argives leading off first.[1] By the very end at 1073 it is perhaps
more likely that the end of the procession was just disappearing
from view than that the front of it was just moving off (thus Rose
82)—but we cannot tell.

The final clearing of the stage is not merely an unavoidable
and mechanical stage movement. The willing and unmolested
departure of the chorus from the sanctuary represents in visual
stage terms the achievement and ratification of its safety. This
significance would be greatly helped by the use of the two
eisodoi (see p. 451 and Joerden *Bauformen* 394f.). One leads to and
from the sea coast, and so from danger: the other leads to and
from Argos, and so to security. The contrast and meaning of the
off-stage directions is brought out in the opening anapaests of the
play where the Danaids tell of their flight and arrival (1–22), and
pray that they may be received and the sons of Aegyptus rejected
(22–39, cf. δέξασθε 27, πέμψατε 33). The opposites are further
used by Danaus' pair of extended entrance announcements,
where the first sees an approach from the city by land, the second
from the sea (see 710*). And this sense of direction will have been
particularly telling in the grouping and choreography of the
scene with the Egyptian Herald: the abductor comes from and
pulls towards the shore, the rescuer comes from and invites
towards the city. So the entire play is framed by an arrival from
one direction (see 1a*) and a departure in the other. And the
play itself shows how the Danaids make their way from the
arrival to the departure through a series of moral, political,
emotional, and poetic vicissitudes.

---

[1] Mazon 50 and Untersteiner 109 send Danaus off right back at 1017, but it seems
pointless to separate him in this way: he arrived with them, he goes with them.

V. PROMETHEUS

Note on authenticity

SOMETIMES during this chapter I shall isolate dramatic techniques which I find inexplicably unlike Aeschylus as we know him from the other plays; and I shall voice some doubts whether *Prom* as we have it can be his work. So I had better make clear at the outset my position on the notoriously emotional controversy over authenticity. I do not believe that the play we have is the work of Aeschylus. It may be entirely by a follower and admirer; but it is my suspicion that the play was left unfinished, perhaps less than half finished, at Aeschylus' death, and that it was completed later on the model of the celebrated *Prom Lyomenos*. But this suspicion is based mainly on grounds of dramatic technique, and, since I feel that a great deal more work on other aspects of the play would be needed to arrive at any firm conclusion one way or the other, I shall throughout maintain an open, unassuming position, and I shall usually, as I have elsewhere, call the author 'Aeschylus'. The case against the play is far from proven (what in the state of our evidence would constitute 'proof'?); but it is also far from negligible. Some of the issues raised by the question of authenticity, and particularly the inadequacies of some of the traditional defences, are discussed in Appendix D.

1 enter Hephaestus, Kratos, and Bia, with Prometheus

(a) unusual dramatic techniques

This entry of four named characters all together seems to be unique in surviving tragedy. Admittedly one of the four, presumably Bia,[1] remains silent, but that is inevitable with the

---

[1] We cannot know for certain that it was not Kratos who was silent; they may have been indistinguishable in any case. But Bia is named second, and we have no reason to disagree with the scholion in the margin of M above l. 12 (12c, p 71H.) ἐν παραχορηγήματι αὐτῶι εἰδωλοποιηθεῖςα Βία. Note that Bia, like most mute named characters, is the lesser of a fixed pair (cf. *Cho* 1b*); they are paired in Hes. *Theog* 385.

limitation to three speaking actors. But it is doubtful whether
three characters, let alone four, enter together anywhere else in
Aeschylus; on *Eum* 64* I reject the only possible instance by
arguing that Hermes (as a mute) is not with Orestes and Apollo.
Indeed it is rare in Aeschylus even for *two* characters to enter
simultaneously.[1] Even in Sophocles and Euripides, when the
third actor is firmly established, it is distinctly rare to find the
simultaneous entry of all three actors together. In nearly every
case there is some qualifying factor, for example that one of the
actors is a child or has some of the characteristics of a mute or
that one actor of the three enters from a different direction.
Examples I have noted are S. *Trach* 971, *Ant* 384, *OC* 1099;
E. *Alc* 244, *Tro* 1, ?*Cycl* 503. I can find only one unequivocal
example of a triple entry, and in this case it is made highly
formal and special attention is drawn to it. After the first song
of E. *Phaethon* Merops, Phaethon, and a Herald enter together,
and in the anapaestic entrance announcement (102ff.) the chorus
chants ἀλλ’ ὅδε γὰρ δὴ βασιλεὺς πρὸ δόμων / κῆρύξ θ’ ἱερὸς καὶ παῖς
Φαέθων / βαίνουσι τριπλοῦν ζεῦγος . . .[2]

Although the technique is so unusual, it is fairly easily explicable. It follows from the dramatist's initial decision that the play
should begin with the binding (or rather fixing) of Prometheus.
Thus Prometheus' ordeals begin with the opening of the play,
and for its entire length he is fixed unmoving. This decision dictates the entry of Prometheus with his jailors and torturers.
Kratos and Bia alone would suffice for this task, but we can see
the point of bringing on Hephaestus also: it is not so much that
he is the divine smith as that through his reluctance for his task
and his pity for Prometheus the harshness of Kratos and Bia is
accentuated. Right from the beginning we are guided to sympathize with Prometheus through Hephaestus and to hate and

---

[1] There is the uniquely formal pair of entries in *Seven* (374b*), and the probably
interpolated entry of the pair of sisters (*Seven* 871a*); then in the *Oresteia* there are
Agamemnon and Cassandra (long silent) (*Ag* 783b*), the three entries of Orestes
and Pylades at *Cho* 1 (1b*), 653, and 892 (892b*), and Apollo and Orestes at
Eum 64* (Apollo was probably not with Athena at *Eum* 566, see 574*).

[2] Diggle *Phaethon ed.* 116 does not do justice to the curiosity of τριπλοῦν ζεῦγος.
Ar. fr. 576 K is actually a parody of odd phrases like this and the ζεῦγος τριπάρθενον
of E. *Erechtheus* fr. 47 A. (see Hesych. ζ 125 Latte). Further, as Kannicht E. *Hel ed*
p. 113 points out, such phrases usually occur when the three or four members of
the ζεῦγος are very closely linked. Euripides in *Phaethon* is drawing special attention
to the highly unusual triple entry.

resent Zeus through Kratos and Bia. His two faithful proxies are callous and brutal (see esp. 42, 79f.), just as Zeus is harsh, unrelenting, and tyrannical (cf. 10, 34f., 40f., 50, 53, 62, 67f.). The third party also makes possible Prometheus' silence throughout the prologue, which shows (indirectly) his resilience and defiance, and makes his eventual outburst the more effective (though this silence is not as well used as it might have been, as I have argued in *HSCP* 76 (1972) 78–9). So there are clear dramatic advantages to be gained from the quadruple entry, and these are probably sufficient to explain the unparalleled dramatic technique. This could not be used in itself as more than a very minor point against authenticity, though it may point to a later date.

Another point of technique unparalleled in surviving Aeschylus is the dialogue prologue. The opening speeches of Kratos and Hephaestus (1–35) are addressed to each other,[1] to Prometheus, and to the world in general; but then from 36 to 81 they settle down to a rigid 2/1 'stichomythia'.[2] The general technique is, as has often been noted, typical of Sophocles, who uses variations of it in all seven surviving prologues. The closest thing we have from Aeschylus seems to be *Phryges*, which according to the *Life* of Aeschylus began with ὀλίγα ἀμοιβαῖα between Hermes and Achilles. There are dialogues in the opening scenes of *Seven* and *Eum*, but neither are in stichomythia or at the very beginning. While the prologue of *Prom* is not so complex as that of *Eum* (see *Eum* 139*), it gives the impression of being the most 'modern', mainly because of the curious long stichomythia.[3]

[1] This is not, however, an entry 'im Gespräch' as it is called by Hunger *RhM* 95 (1952) 371 n. 4; it is an entry *to* a conversation not in conversation: see further *Eum* 64*.

[2] Stichomythia is defined by Pollux (4. 113): στιχομυθεῖν δ' ἔλεγον τὸ παρ' ἐν ἰαμβεῖον ἀντιλέγειν, καὶ τὸ πρᾶγμα στιχομυθίαν. (This is in fact the only occurrence of the word in Greek, besides an inappropriate use at Σ on P. *Pyth* 4. 100.) Term has by convention been extended to include dialogues conducted in pairs of lines or in half-lines; and it seems harmless to use it of any dialogue conducted in short speeches (cf. Stevens *CR* n.s. 6 (1956) 213f., Seidensticker *Die Gesprächs-verdichtung in den Trag. Senecas* (Heidelberg 1969) 20). But it is hard to draw the line: what, to take an example at random, of E. *Med* 49–95, where the speeches vary from one line to seven lines in length? For a laborious survey of the scholarship on stichomythia see Schwinge *Die Verwendung der Stichomythie in den Dramen des Eur.* (Heidelberg 1968) 12–32.

[3] On the prologue as a whole see Nestle 108–20, who takes it to be genuine (though he later changed his mind), Schmidt *Bauformen* 26f., who rather over-confidently dates it to after 431 (Stoessl *RE* xxiii 2315f. does not question authenticity). On the stichomythia in particular Jens *Die Stichomythie* etc. (Munich 1955)

It seems to me that this stylized technique can hardly be used as an argument against authenticity provided that it is put to good dramatic effect—as long as it really is, as Herington *Author* 49 claims, 'extraordinarily effective'. But Schmid (32f.) seems nearer the mark when he speaks of the prologue as 'outwardly so eventful, yet internally so lacking in drama', as a comparison with the prologues of *Seven* or *Eum* makes only too clear. The action in *Prom* is violent and is integral to the play, and so it should be vivid and striking; yet it is laboriously handled. The stichomythia is heavy and repetitive; most people would, I imagine, agree that the most impressive part of the prologue is, in fact, the most static, namely Hephaestus' 'purple passage' in 18–35. This and not the action–stichomythia itself has the power which one associates with true Aeschylus. In the main part of the prologue there is not that close interaction of word and action which is so effective in other scenes which are potentially no more impressive, e.g. *Pers* 664–702, *Seven* 677–719, *Hik* 885–915, *Ag* 910–57, *Cho* 875–930, *Eum* 235–60, 711–53. By comparison *Prom* wilts before the brilliance of these scenes.

(b) the 'dummy' theory

It is impossible to avoid a mention of the weird theory that throughout the play Prometheus' body was represented by a giant dummy (at least ten feet high, it seems), whence an actor concealed inside spoke his part. This theory has been favoured by nearly all the great authorities.[1] Yet the comment of Sikes and Willson (xliv) still holds good: 'One might have thought that only some very cogent reasons would have produced this grotesque theory. But the arguments advanced . . . would scarcely be strong enough to commend a view that was in itself unobjectionable.'

It is not worth going over all the points again. Most of them, for example the strain on the actor, the requirement of realism

---

29f. claims that it is un-Aeschylean, though he gives little argument (cf. similarly Graeber 9f.): it has recently been defended by Herington *Author* 49f., Seidensticker *Bauformen* 185 n. 5, 188, 195.

[1] Including Hermann 55f., Wecklein 19f., Robert 561ff., Kaffenberger 27f., Wilamowitz 114ff., Koerte *NJb* 44 (1920) 206, Flickinger 166f., Groeneboom 72, Murray 39, Reinhardt 11, 77. The strongest refutation is made by Focke 278ff., the longest by Joerden 125ff.; see, also, e.g. Bethe 180 n. 30, Bolle 6f., Mazon 151 n. 2, Lesky *TDH*[2] 79, *TDH*[3] 146, Dodds *Progress* 37, Herington *Author* 88f.

with the adamantine wedge, have little or no substance. Would a dummy be more realistic than an actor (even if, as Dingel *Bauformen* 364 n. 12 claims without good reason, there was blood)? Two of the arguments are more substantial. First, only two actors will be needed. But there is reason to think that *Prom*, if it is by Aeschylus, belongs to his last years (see Herington *Author* and Appendix D pp. 465–6); and, in any case, the presence of a third actor who remains silent as long as both the others are on stage is similar to the handling of Cassandra in *Ag*, and, if it is genuine, to that of Ismene in *Seven*—see further *Seven* 1005b*. If *Prom* is not late then this may be seen as the tentative beginning of the use of a third actor: if it is late (or post-Aeschylean) then it is the *lack* of exploitation of the third actor which is notable. Secondly, there is line 74, where Kratos tells Hephaestus χώρει κάτω, cκέλη δὲ κίρκωcον βίαι, on which the scholiast in M (74a, p. 82H) comments διὰ τὸ 'χώρει κάτω' τὸ μέγαθος ἐνέφηνε τοῦ δεcμευομένου θεοῦ. But we have no reason to think that the scholiast knew any more about the original production than we do, or that this is anything but conjecture: the words need mean no more than 'move on down' i.e. down his body (cf. Weissmann *Anweisungen* 21, Focke 274). And if Hephaestus (crippled?) were clambering around at various heights then how long a piece of silent, laboured action would there have to be between lines 74 and 75? If there was a dummy and some climbing about, then I am inclined to say that this laborious near-absurd staging would be even more unworthy of Aeschylus than it is already without it.

A couple of the arguments against the dummy theory are relevant to my subject. Assuming that this play was followed in a trilogy by *Prom Lyom*, then how did Prometheus leave his binding place? This forces Wilamowitz and Reinhardt (see p. 243 n. 1 above) to deny that Prometheus was actually released in *Prom Lyom*, which is a desperate measure. It would be even worse, however, if Prometheus were to be of different sizes in different plays. Secondly, Prometheus must be brought on at the start of the play. Are Kratos and Bia to enter each carrying one end of a rigid, giant dummy? Faced with this Reinhardt had recourse to the ekkyklema.[1] But this machine was used for the

---

[1] Reinhardt 77; cf. Rose 10, Havelock *Prometheus* (Seattle 1968) 114, 117, Froning *Gnomon* 45 (1973) 82f.

245

revelation of interior scenes (see pp. 442–3); and, in any case, was the door high enough to let out a giant framework? Besides, Kratos' opening words clearly imply a positive movement of arrival: ἥκομεν.[1]

87 exeunt Hephaestus, Kratos, and Bia

Hephaestus' subjection

Most commentators have sent Hephaestus off after his last words at 81, which would be normal; but a minority have kept him on a few lines more to depart with the other two at 87 (e.g. Mazon, 'Droysen' *tr*, Headlam *tr*, Murray *tr*). There is something to be said for this. If Hephaestus had to wait uncomfortably and to go in silence, then this might help to convey his unwilling subjection to the tyranny of force (cf. pp. 241–2 above). Also his last line (81) does not have the finality of an exit line. The question must remain open, but I tend to favour the slight dramatic effect to be gained from keeping him on. Arnott *tr* 55 sends both Hephaestus and Bia off at 81. This at least may be ruled out. Fixed pairs like Kratos and Bia are inseparable.

88 (no entry)

127 (no exit)

193 (no entry)

the non-coincidence of structure and action

The constructional techniques of *Prom* are irregular and idiosyncratic. While some features are unique (see e.g. 436*), others, like those associated with the first choral song (parodos) may be compared with later tragedy. A traditional structural analysis along the lines laid down in *Poetics* ch. 12 (see Appendix E) encounters no difficulty: 1–127 is the prologue, 128–92 the parodos, and 193–396 the first episode. It should be obvious that this does not do justice to the real structural peculiarity and

---

[1] Have we, in fact, any evidence that dummies (lay-figures) were ever used in the Greek tragic theatre? (Dingel 42ff. does not ask this.) Commentators assume that dummies were used to represent corpses; but a 'live' extra would be more practical. Probably babies, like Orestes in *IA*, were dummies: but that would be a very different task for the stage-manager from making a titanic Prometheus.

complexity of this part of the play. If one introduces the sequence of exits and entrances also, then a different form begins to emerge. Thus it is clear that the break at 192/3 is counteracted by a strong element of continuity, while there is a heavy structural break at 284 with the entry of Oceanus. Also, although the chorus enters at 128 and thus marks a structural juncture, the prologue proper must, surely, end at 87 with the exit of those who speak it. And so the scene 88–127 with Prometheus by himself (often called his 'monologue', see Leo 7, Schadewaldt *Monolog* 51f.) should be analysed as a separate scene which makes a transition from the prologue to the first song, though it goes rather more closely with the latter. The song itself, which is not divided from what precedes by an exit nor from what follows by an entry, takes the form of a lyric dialogue in which the stanzas of the chorus alternate with anapaests from Prometheus. If we consider the formal structure in terms of spoken acts and act-dividing songs, then 128–92 is an act-dividing song: if, on the other hand, we look at the structure of the action, the lyric dialogue is all part of a larger unit from 88 to 283. The two structural principles, instead of coinciding as usual, are superimposed one on the other and counteract each other. This is what produces the peculiarities of construction.

There are, then, four phenomena which may be studied in comparison with the techniques of Aeschylus and of later tragedy: the solo scene in between the end of the prologue and the entry of the chorus, the lack of entry before the first song, the lyric dialogue, and the lack of entry after the song.

In the four plays of Aeschylus with prologues an actor goes off immediately before the entry of the chorus (on *Seven* see *Seven* 77*, in *Cho* (21*) it is a matter of going into hiding). This is also normally the case in Sophocles;[1] but there is an exception in *El* where he uses a quite different structural technique. Between the exit of Orestes and his associates at 85 and the entry of the chorus at 121 Electra sings a monody in lyric anapaests. It is generally supposed that Sophocles is here under the influence of Euripides, who often puts an actor's monody, usually sung by the heroine, in between the end of the prologue proper and the

[1] In S. *OC* Oedipus and Antigone hide. In *Trach* it is more likely than not that Deianeira stayed on during the parodos, cf. the apostrophe in 137. In *OT* Oedipus probably went off with Creon.

entry of the chorus, and thus presents her pathos in isolation.[1]
One can see a similar technique and dramatic function in *Prom*
88–127, where there is even a gesture in the direction of monody
in the anapaests at 93–100 and the strange polymetric entrance
announcement at 114–27 (see 128a*). Assuming that *Prom* is the
work of Aeschylus, then Prometheus' monologue provides a precedent for the structural and dramatic technique which became
a favourite, almost characteristic, device of Euripides. But some
have seen this as a sign that the play was composed twenty-five
years or more after Aeschylus' death; the case is put strongly
though inflexibly by Schmidt *Bauformen* 40ff.

Next we come to the lyric dialogue 128–92, which, despite
the lack of exit before it or entry after it, is clearly the entrance
song or parodos. A lyric dialogue parodos is again unique in
Aeschylus, but widely paralleled in later tragedy. In as much as
regular systems of non-lyric metre (anapaests) alternate with
choral strophes, the form of the lyric has analogies with the
epirrhematic structures which are characteristic of Aeschylus;[2]
but its structural function is totally different, since all Aeschylean
epirrhematic lyrics come *within* the acts, whereas this entrance
song stands in what is normally an act-dividing position. It was
a bold step to put a lyric dialogue in a position where there
would normally be a purely choral song, a step which is obviously
connected with the decline in the role of the chorus. In the main
body of a tragedy this structural variation remains rare even in
late-fifth-century tragedy;[3] it is, however, found earlier and
more commonly in the parodos, indeed it looks as if the device
spread from the parodos to the other songs. The parodos takes
the form of a lyric dialogue in three plays of Sophocles (*El, Phil,
OC*) and in some eight of Euripides (first *Med*) and in *Rh*.[4] Once
again *Prom* either sets a precedent for later tragic practice—or
it is itself a later tragedy.

The lack of an exit before the song at 127 was seen to be quite

[1] See E. *Andr, Hec, Tro, Ion, Hel, Hyps,* cf. *Med, El.* More fully, Nestle 74–7,
Matthiessen *Elektra* etc. (Göttingen 1964) 20f., Barner *Bauformen* 309, Popp ibid.
268–70, Schmidt ibid. 40ff. (on 26f. Schmidt points out some particular similarities
between *Prom* and E. *Tro*).

[2] Cf. Wilamowitz 159f., Nestle 114ff., Peretti 163ff.

[3] Some clear examples are S. *El* 823ff., *Phil* 828ff., 1081ff., *OC* 510ff., 1448ff.;
E. *El* 859ff., *Or* 1246ff. (cf. *IT* 644ff., *IA* 1475ff.). See p. 52.

[4] These are considered in Detscheff 45ff., Aichele 20f., Schmidt *Bauformen*
14f.; cf. Nestle 77–82.

a common feature in the structural technique of later tragedy.
But the lack of entry after it at 193 rather interestingly narrows
the range of analogies. The end of the parodos is often the place
for a highly stressed and important entry, see pp. 283f. below; it
is a rarer and more notable device to have no entry. The plays
where there is no entry after the parodos are few enough to
allow a quick survey.[1] From Aeschylus there are *Hik* and *Cho*:
in both there follows a rhesis spoken by a character who has
entered with the chorus and who has not yet spoken. They are
also different from *Prom* in that the scene between the end of the
song and the next entry leads up towards that entry (cf. Aichele
Bauformen 66): in *Hik* there is in effect an extended entry
announcement for Pelasgus (see 234a*); and *Cho* 165ff., while
Orestes is in hiding, looks forward to his entry at 212. It is worth
noting that there was probably no entry after the parodos-
prologue of *Prom Lyom* (see pp. 425f.); there, like Danaus and
Electra, Prometheus has not spoken before this point. In S.
Trach there is an exit before the parodos, but probably Deianeira
stayed on, and so there is no exit before her rhesis, which is
followed by the arrival of the Old Man: this is structurally
different from *Prom*. So is S. *OC* where, after hiding before the
parodos at 116, Oedipus and Antigone make a premature re-
entry at 138; but after the dialogue parodos and before the
approach of Ismene there is an exposition scene (254–309) which
is comparable to *Prom* 194–283. Closer still, however, is S. *El*
where there is not only a 'Euripidean' monody and a lyric
dialogue parodos (see above), but after the song there is a scene
(251–323) in which Electra explains herself to the chorus before
the unprepared-for entry of Chrysothemis. E. *Hel* is also comparable: Helen, like Prometheus, has been on since the beginning of the play, she sings at the end of the prologue,[2] the parodos
is a lyric dialogue, and there is no entry at the end of it. However,
there is then no entry at all during the following act (253–385),

---

[1] I am assuming that there was an entry at *Seven* 181 (see 77*) and at *Ag* 258
(see 258a*); also at S. *OT* 216 (see p. 246 n. 1 above). In E. *El* the entry of Orestes
from hiding is equivalent to an entry in structural terms; and so in *Or* is Orestes'
awakening at 211.

[2] Helen's song 164–78 is part of the strophic structure of the parodos. One
cannot be sure whether the chorus entered before it, or after it with their opening
lyric at 179ff. (cf. p. 64 above). Kannicht E. *Hel ed* 59, 71 rightly suggests that
the chorus' entry motive (179ff.) favours the latter.

which ends with the exit inside of Helen and the chorus before Menelaus' 'epiprologue': this highly unusual technique accentuates Helen's isolation and her despair of any hope of rescue. Finally, in *Rh* Hector enters or wakes up during the anapaestic proem (11) and contributes to the parodos; there is then no entry at the end of the song (52), but Aeneas enters at 87: this is not like *Prom*, nor like any other tragedy we have. In sum, the construction of this part of *Prom* cannot be paralleled at all in Aeschylus, but can be in various respects by various later tragedies, and is most closely comparable with S. *El* and E. *Hel*.

As for the lack of any entry at *Prom* 193: why, when there has already been considerable exposition, unlike *Hik* and *Cho*, is there no new entry at the usual place, and why is the scene with the chorus (193–283) so totally unconnected with the following Oceanus scene? An answer to the first question seems to be that which is already in the scholia (193b, p. 103H cf. Groeneboom 131): the female curiosity of the chorus makes a good excuse for Prometheus' exposition—-Oceanus, for example, could not have questioned so simply nor listened so patiently. It is also, of course, difficult to bring new characters to such a remote setting, and the lack of an entry may contribute something to the impression of Prometheus' helplessness and isolation. These points go some way towards explaining the disruption of the normal structural technique: but, on the debit side, the lack of entry contributes to the disjointed and episodic nature of the play (see further below).

The second question poses a more serious problem. There is no connection whatsoever between the scene with the chorus (193–283) and that with Oceanus (284ff.). And yet, as has often been remarked, it would have been easy to make a link, so easy that the lack of any is positively peculiar. The chorus consists of the daughters of Oceanus, they refer to him (130f.), and yet they supply no preparation for his entry. When Oceanus arrives he takes no notice of his daughters, makes no reference to them even, and they take no part in the entire scene. This problem is considered further on pp. 257–9. This lack of connection where it is to be expected only aggravates the structural peculiarity of the new entry in mid-act instead of at the end of the song. As a result the structural pattern of exit and entry runs counter to that of song and speech, as was noted at the beginning (pp. 245–6).

It is hard to see what the dramatist hoped to achieve by this effect. Whether or not it is deliberate, it has the effect of making this act disjointedly episodic (cf. Wilamowitz *Perser* 390 'we cannot save his *Prometheus* from the charge of being ἐπειϲοδιῶδεϲ'). It may be observed that if Aeschylus left his play unfinished then this kind of phenomenon might be accounted for by the process of filling out and patching together (cf. pp. 258–9 below).

before 128 enter chorus

(a) emotional announcement and artificial motivation

Lines 114–27 make an unusually long entrance announcement for a chorus;[1] but compare *Cho* 10–21. The length is explicable since Prometheus is in an isolated and elevated spot, and since he has, presumably, supernatural powers of perception (including smell). What is much more curious about the lines is that they are in a variety of lyric and recitative metres.[2] While entrance announcements are found in anapaests or trochaic tetrameters, this is more like the rare lyric examples discussed on pp. 173–4 above. But in all those places the announcements came at the end of an act-dividing song, usually within the strophic structure, and they were all sung by the chorus; in this case the announcement is sung by an actor, and it comes before the choral entrance song. These unique lines are part of the scene (88ff.) which serves as a transition from the prologue to the entrance of the chorus, and which was compared (pp. 246f.) with the actors' monodies characteristic of Euripides.

The length and metrical excitement of the announcement are hardly justified, it turns out, by the chorus itself, which could hardly be more innocuous. The technique is evidently meant to convey the anxiety and vulnerability of Prometheus. A further reason which has occasionally been put forward is that Prometheus expects Zeus' eagle.[3] But the eagle was not alluded to in

---

[1] Some phrases similar to those in *Prom* turn up in the long paratragic build-up to Iris' flying entry in Ar. *Birds* 1170–99; see Rau 165, 177. Note especially *Birds* 1182f., 1197f. (= Tr. Adesp. fr. 47 N²); but Rau is not justified in talking of 'Reminiszenz'.

[2] The metrical technique has been called a 'Potpourri' (Bethe 163), 'herrlich' (Wilamowitz *Perser* 386 n. 1), 'curious' (Murray 45), 'odd patchwork' (Dodds *Progress* 38).

[3] Most recently by Tracy *HSCP* 75 (1971) 59ff.; his weak case is rather weakly overturned by Donovan *HSCP* 77 (1973) 125–7.

18ff. and has not yet been mentioned in the play (it is not introduced until 1021ff.): the audience should not expect, and cannot be asked to expect, what they have no reason to expect. The language is not sufficiently explicit to insinuate a totally new factor of this sort. Moreover, the opening questions (115–18) are inappropriate to the eagle, and would, so to speak, put the audience off the scent.[1]

The first words of the chorus (μηδὲν φοβηθῆιc 128) pick up the last words of Prometheus' announcement (φοβερόν 127). It is rare for a newly entered character to have heard some of the announcement of his own entry; see pp. 72–3 above. The device implies that the character is present before the end of the announcement, and it suggests in practical terms that the entry takes some time, and hence that it is in progress during the announcement. Here, then, it is likely that the Oceanids made their entry during the announcement, or at least during the last part of it. (On the problems of staging see 128b* below.)

The topic of the motivation of the chorus' entrance was discussed in general on *Pers* 1b*. The motivation here in *Prom* is isolated in the second part of the first strophe (132–5).[2] It is explicit and rather picturesque. Perhaps a rather laboured motivation is called for by the unlikely setting of the play and the unpredictable identity of the chorus; but it is even more farfetched than it need be, since the alarming clang should have petrified the timorous nymphs instead of attracting them. Studied choral motivations like this seem to be characteristic of later tragedy, particularly Euripides, when there was no attempt to integrate the chorus realistically.[3] The chorus of *Prom* is far less integrated into the play than those of Aeschylus' other tragedies; and it also has the most self-contained and artificial entrance

---

[1] Tracy 61 is wrong to give ὀδμά unpleasant connotations: see E. *Hipp* 1391 and other references collected by Donovan 126.

[2] ἔπεμψαν (132) is always taken as equivalent to προ-έπεμψαν 'escorted, sent on my way'. But since it is explained by the following clause (κτύπου γὰρ κτλ.) it would make better sense if it could be taken to mean 'sent for, fetched': but it is doubtful whether the active verb could carry this sense, though the middle can.

[3] Later theorists actually defined πάροδος or παροδικά as the part of a tragedy in which the chorus motivated its entry: see the references collected in Appendix E (p. 471). Steffen *Eos* 55 (1965) 41 is not justified in regarding *Prom* as unparalleled, let alone in claiming the influence of satyr play. It is interesting to note that earlier Old Comedy tended to labour the arrival of the chorus; cf. Cratinus frr. 144, 169, 235K and the fragments of *Ploutoi* (see p. 425).

motivation. If the play is authentic, then it foreruns later tragedy in both these respects.

While one may be reluctant to attribute these tendencies to the *chorodidaskalos* of the *Oresteia*, it would be rash to press this motivation too hard as a point against authenticity. The chorus of Titans in *Prom Lyom*, who admittedly have a better claim to come and see Prometheus, seem to have had an elaborate entry motivation: see p. 424. Phrynichus' *Phoinissai* seems to have had a comparable arrival song (*TrGF* 3F9–10). A. *Nereides* fr. 237M may well come from an entrance motivation, and the Nereids may also, as in *Prom*, have heard a noise (Achilles' laments) from afar; yet Thetis and the precedent of Homer make their arrival much less far-fetched. Although there are these possible analogies in early tragedy for a laboured and self-contained entrance motivation, it remains true that *Prom* 132–5 is particularly artificial and obtrusive in a way reminiscent of Euripides (especially *Hipp*, *El*, *Phoen*, *IA*).

(b) ways of staging and their consequences

Although there has been much discussion of the staging of the chorus' entry the matter is far from settled.[1] Since my main interest lies in the critical consequences of any method of staging, I shall try to survey the problems briefly. First, I suggest (cf. §3), we should decide what is in the word-tableau; that is, what the audience is to imagine it sees, regardless of what it actually saw. Even here there is a complication since the imaginary situation is divulged in two separate places: the first choral strophe (128–35) and the dialogue at the end of the following scene (271–83). The picture conjured up includes wings (125f., 129f., 135), one or more vehicles ($\ddot{o}\chi o c$ 135, cf. $\theta \hat{a}\kappa o\nu$ 279), a journey through the air (125f., 129f., 135, cf. 280), and, it transpires, a resting place above the ground (272, 278–81). Two points of detail call for some clarification. First, $\pi\tau\epsilon\rho\acute{v}\gamma\omega\nu$ $\theta o a\hat{\iota} c$ $\acute{a}\mu\acute{\iota}\lambda\lambda a\iota c$ (129f.) implies, as Fraenkel has emphasized, an element of competition, which would mean that each Oceanid is to be imagined as in an individual vehicle: while the phrase need not imply a race, some notion of eager striving must be present;[2]

---

[1] I have found the most helpful discussions those of Bodensteiner 665f., Bethe 167ff., D–R 216ff., Thomson *ed* 142–4 (cf. *CQ* 23 (1929) 160f.), P–C *TDA* 39f., Fraenkel *Kl B* 389ff.

[2] See Kannicht E. *Hel ed* p. 155, Lloyd-Jones *YCS* 22 (1972) 270.

and in the context it seems natural to infer that the Oceanids have been competing against each other. Secondly, the wording of 279f.—κραιπνόςυτον θᾶκον προλιποῦς' / αἰθέρα θ' ἁγνὸν πόρον οἰωνῶν—strongly implies that up to this point the chorus is to be thought of as hovering in mid-air. So the word-tableau, if left to itself, emerges: the Oceanids enter each in a winged vehicle, flying, and they come to rest hovering in the air.

The staging in actual practice is another matter. Here we are hampered by two important unknown quantities. First, we scarcely know how realistic or unrealistic the Greek theatre was (see §3). While we may be confident that some things were left to the imagination stimulated by words alone, we do not know how much Aeschylus felt able to evoke without any visual correspondence. Secondly we do not know (at least I do not) what was and was not practicable in the early theatre and what engineering resources were available or allowed to the μηχανο-ποιός.

On the first point I propose to apply a working hypothesis. There seems little point in half measures: either there should be a proper attempt at spectacular illusion, or it may as well be entirely left to the words. It is implausible, for example, to bring on the 'flying' Oceanids in wheeled vehicle(s) running on a solid surface.[1] Trundling on wheels only contradicts the illusion of flying, and rather than this the vehicle(s) should be abandoned. Nor is it plausible to split the chorus up, and have a representative two or three flown on while the rest enter on foot; for if the entry is acceptable with some on foot then it is acceptable with all on foot. If any attempt is to be made at illusion, then surely the whole chorus should actually travel through the air. The crane, μηχανή, is discussed in pp. 443 ff., and its most likely use in the Aeschylean theatre is for Oceanus (see *Prom* 284*). If it was available at the time of *Prom* then the chorus might have been hoisted on in one large container, a widely accepted theory;[2] or, as the wording of 129f. implies, each in a separate harness, i.e. twelve or fifteen Oceanids suspended from twelve or fifteen

---

[1] Be it along a ledge of rock (e.g. D–R 216f., Croiset 140 n. 5), out of an opening in the skene (e.g. Frickenhaus 11), directly into the orchestra (e.g. Sikes–Willson xlvi, Hammond 424), or, as many suppose, on the roof of the skene (thus e.g. Focke 282f., P-C *TDA* 39, Webster *GTP* 12, Arnott 76f., Dale *Papers* 263f.).

[2] e.g. Wilamowitz 115f., Murray 40f.; for others see Fraenkel *Kl B* 389 n. 1.

ropes.[1] One of these alternatives seems to be envisaged by the scholion in M (128a cf. 128b, pp. 93f.H.) ταῦτα δέ φαϲιν διὰ μηχανῆϲ ἀεροδονούμεναι. But we should hesitate to use this as evidence for fifth-century practice (see pp. 435ff. below) ; and the following explanation—ἄτοπον γὰρ κάτωθεν διαλέγεϲθαι τῶι ἐφ᾽ ὕψουϲ—does not suggest that the note is based on real theatrical considerations.

The purely practical problems of stage management are obvious. It is doubtful whether even the compromise solutions which I have disparaged would be feasible. Could the roof of the wooden skene building support the weight of a whole chorus, let alone of a vehicle whose weight would be concentrated on four points? A property rock is likely to be even less solid. Or if the Oceanids were to be in a single container on a flying machine, a weight estimated at well over a ton, then was there a foundation sufficient to take the footing?[2] Individual winged chairs are, if anything, even more difficult. What do these twelve or fifteen ropes hang from, and how are they manoeuvred in a theatre without the concealed flies of a proscenium arch? I cannot understand how Fraenkel (Kl B 395) thinks that this would be easier to manage than hoisting a single actor and a property horse (like Perseus and Pegasus). I do not claim that these things could not have been done, but it seems fair to say—with understatement—that this entry and the final cataclysm (see Prom 1093b*) present problems of stage management on quite a different scale from any posed in the rest of surviving Attic tragedy. In the absence of any comparable displays it is the availability of resources no less than practicability which is in doubt.

Is there, then, any way to cut through this mechanical tangle? A promising line leads from Bodensteiner's dictum (p. 666) 'the poet's words are powerful enough to supplant the illusion, if necessary'. This is taken to its logical conclusion by Thomson,[3]

---

[1] Thus Fraenkel; for others before him see Fraenkel Kl B 390 n. 3. His staging has since been widely accepted; e.g. Rose 254, Schadewaldt HuH[2] i 357f., Tracy HSCP 75 (1971) 62 n. 10, Unterberger Der gefesselte Prom. des Aischylos (Stuttgart 1968) 38f. cf. 11.

[2] The stone platform (T in Dörpfeld's plan) is tied in date to the brecchia foundations (H–H), which, whatever their date, are post-Aeschylean: see p. 452 n. 3.

[3] Thomson ed 142–4, apparently accepted by Grene tr 144. (However, Grene is mistaken to say that the chorus is 'birdlike', the Oceanids are not winged themselves. This may be the origin of Lowell's mawkish fancy (tr 5ff.) that the chorus should be seagulls.)

who maintains that all that is needed is an appropriate mimetic dance. Thomson weakens his case with two dispensable arguments. He argues from iconographic analogies that the chorus is to be imagined as flying on sea horses: but while sea horses are a handy means of transport in the Oceanids' own element, there is no reason to think them fitted for flying over dry land. Secondly, he wants the dance to have a recognizably conventional choreography, and so he produces the easily mocked sentence 'the Chorus performed a dance conventionally associated with the flight of sea-nymphs on their winged sea-horses'. But there is no need for the dance in question ever to have been danced or dreamt of before this performance, provided that the words make its significance clear. Shorn of these distractions Thomson's theory deserves consideration. But it still runs into difficulties. For, while it is fair enough to dance on the ground to represent flying without artificial aid (cf. *Swan Lake*), how do you dance to represent flying in a seated position on some sort of vehicle? And even if this is acceptable, how do you represent at 278ff. the descent from the imaginary seat in the air down on to the solid ground? Thomson (149) claims that 'since the end of the πάροδος, they have been clustered around the θυμέλη . . . and now they descend to earth—that is to say, they take up their positions for the first stasimon'. But this does not account for the wording of 271–83, nor does it appreciate that the θᾶκον of 279 is clearly the same as the ὄχοc of 135. This seems to be an insurmountable objection to Thomson's theory as it stands.

Although Thomson's attractive theory founders on 271–83, it should not be too hastily forgotten, since it avoids two serious and highly objectionable consequences of all the more widely accepted theories of staging. First, none of them have the entrance song, 128ff., danced in the normal way. It may be that the first choral song of a tragedy had a different choreographical basis from the other songs (stasima), which gave it the name 'parodos' (see p. 473); but every other parodos without exception was, so far as we know, accompanied by dancing, and was sung and danced in the orchestra. Yet all the orthodox theories of the staging of the choral entry in *Prom* have the parodos sung from some place other than the orchestra, whether wheeled vehicle or flying chair; and they have it sung without any dance, presumably from a sitting position. We cannot assert that

Aeschylus would never do this, but we must ask what on earth would be the point of this abnormal scenic technique. The chorus of *Prom* has little enough dancing in any case, for it must not be forgotten that the extreme brevity of the choral songs and the absence of lyric dialogue or epirrhematic lyrics contracts the amount of dancing as well as of singing.[1] Why should it be deprived of its entrance dance also? The only answer seems to be that it is in order that the Oceanids may have a spectacular flying entry and a long period of hovering.

The second undesirable consequence of all the orthodox stagings is the descent of the chorus after 277ff. It is supposed that the Oceanids have come to rest in their vehicle(s) on the skene roof or on a high ledge of rock, and that they disembark or have disembarked already on to one of these high places.[2] It is then assumed that they descend from there by means of some steps *out of sight of the audience*, and that they reappear in the orchestra during the Oceanus scene or at the end of it, ready for the choral song at 397ff.[3] In other words, the chorus makes an exit after 283 and a re-entry before 397; they go out of the sight of the spectators for a while, and then reappear.

I have not seen the stage consequences put so plainly as that, but that is what is involved.[4] But the characters of Greek tragedy,

[1] Against Focke's ingenious idea (296f.) that the Sicilian choreuts were inexperienced dancers see Appendix D p. 463. Robert (564f.) goes to the extreme of claiming that there was no dancing throughout the whole play, and that the chorus remained high up among the rocky places near the giant Prometheus' head! This is founded on an over-literal interpretation of l. 281, which is surely a verbal description to help the audience to imagine that the orchestra is a rocky terrain, and does not show that it really was strewn with boulders.

[2] For bibliography see above. Arnott (*tr* 90), who has the chorus dance the parodos on the roof, is also liable to this objection. It is special pleading to claim (see Fraenkel *Kl B* 395f.) that a rock can represent the air since it is midway between earth and heaven. A rock is a rock: air is air. It has been claimed (e.g. Wilamowitz 116f., P-C *TDA* 39, Hammond 423f.) that the chorus must be above and behind Prometheus because he cannot see it during 114–27 (contrast Hermes whom he sees at once at 941ff.). But it is unclear when during the announcement the chorus entered (see 128a* above), and this is slim evidence for staging.

[3] Some specious support is given by the scholia in M, particularly 128a (p. 93H), cf. 284b (p. 115H), 397b (p. 132H cf. A-scholia on p. 131). But apart from the lack of clarity over just what is envisaged by the scholiast, there is no reason to allow him any particular authority on such matters.

[4] Wilamowitz is fairly plain: *ed maj actio* on 287 'currus alatus in interiora scaenae vehitur, ubi Occanides descendere credendae sunt' and on 396 'incedit chorus'. See also Webster *GTP* 12 'the only certainty [*sic*] is that the chorus do not, when they enter, take their normal place in the orchestra; they only appear here after the departure of Oceanus'.

let alone the choruses, do not just slip in and out of view, they make proper arrivals and departures.[1] I do not think that the adherents of the usual view can have thought about the matter in terms of the theatre. After line 283 the audience sees the chorus disappear from view—where to? Later it reappears without any comment—where from? If it comes out of the skene door then what does this hole or cave represent? Or if from an eisodos then where is that in terms of the setting, and how did they get there? It is a rare device in Greek tragedy for the chorus to leave the stage and return in mid-play: see *Eum* 231* and 244a*. The other known examples are completely different from the instance which is tacitly assumed in *Prom*. In every case the chorus has a properly motivated mission, and it does not simply disappear and reappear, as here. Elsewhere the departure and return disrupts the formal structure (see *Eum* 276*); whereas here there is no disturbance. A quick comparison with any of the other places immediately shows how the removal of the chorus is treated quite differently from the casual manœuvring supposed in *Prom*. The orthodox staging would be an insult to the chorus and a source of bewilderment to the audience.

In the face of these objections to the chorus' going off after 283 it might be thought better to take the obvious escape and have the Oceanids alight directly from their vehicle(s) into the orchestra at 278ff. This is simplest if they were in a flying machine or machines.[2] In that case the Oceanids will be present in the orchestra throughout the Oceanus scene. This may seem a small price to pay; but one of the reasons why scholars have so easily, even gladly, accepted the disappearance and re-entry of the chorus is that it would help to explain the total lack of any contact between Oceanus and his daughters during the entire scene 284–396. Without some such excuse this fact is highly surprising and suspicious—see p. 249 above. Elsewhere in Aeschylus a character not only makes himself known to the chorus, he usually addresses it first before the other actors: see

[1] Comedy is more free, but an exception there proves the rule. Sometimes, e.g. in *Wasps* and *Ekkles* characters go out of sight upstairs and then appear downstairs; but this is done within the scenic framework of a house. This convention is quite unlike going up and down inside a mountain.
[2] Perseus and Bellerophon presumably dismounted from Pegasus; cf. Strepsiades to Socrates at Ar. *Clouds* 237. Sikes–Willson (71) have the chorus in a wheeled vehicle in the orchestra, which would also be possible.

Pers 249b*. Here, on the contrary, the chorus does not even contribute at points where it might have been expected to make a comment in Sophocles or Euripides, e.g. after 329 or 376. If the chorus is present throughout the scene then the way in which it is totally disregarded is hard to explain other than as incompetence or as the work of someone other than Aeschylus or both (cf. Schmid 7–8). But if it is not present then its absence must face the objections raised above. There is no way of avoiding both difficulties.

So, if we accept the text as we have it and the staging which has been derived from it, then we are faced with two problems which, I hope to have shown, are not inconsiderable. First, the parodos must be delivered without any dance, and secondly either the chorus is present and conspicuously neglected during the Oceanus scene or it is absent in a way unlike anything in Aeschylus or the rest of Greek tragedy (including *Rh*). At this point it is fair to consider whether there may be any textual or bibliographical solution to these problems. The former difficulty could be cauterized by adapting the theory of Bethe (167–74) that parts of *Prom* have been added to an originally simple and archaic play in order to turn it into a spectacular showpiece: cut 271–83 as one such interpolation. Without these lines there is no hovering, and the chorus may then enter on foot; either it may be imagined that the Oceanids have disembarked just off-stage,[1] or, better, Thomson's theory of the mimetic 'flying' dance may be reinstated. But this still does nothing to relieve the second problem since the chorus is now firmly in the orchestra through-out the Oceanus scene.

Once one has begun cutting pieces out of the play, whether as later interpolations or as the results of the completion of an un-finished play, then the whole Oceanus scene may as well go also. The scene comes in for fierce and far from ineffective criticism from Schmid (5–15, who unnecessarily weakens his case by claiming that it is an interpolation in an unauthentic play).

---

[1] Thus Bethe, cf. D–R 218, Weise 14, Bolle 6f. Bethe's theory is that the spectacular effects were added after 427 B.C., the year in which, he argues, the Theatre of Dionysus was reconstructed. A strong objection to this is that we have little reason to think that spectacular mechanical shows, like those in *Prom*, were more in vogue after 427 than before. However, there may be some pointers in this direction— see pp. 42–3.

With the exception of the Typhon digression (351–72), which may possibly be the only genuine part, since it shows signs of having been separate (see Focke 288f., who argues that the digression was interpolated by Aeschylus himself), with that exception the scene is turgid, wordy, and bathetic. Its chief purpose, the elaboration of Prometheus' unyielding defiance, could have been achieved in any number of better ways. It would be hard to deny, I think, that if the scene could be shown to be spurious, this would do the name of Aeschylus nothing but credit. I would personally incline to the view that, if any of *Prom* is the work of Aeschylus, then the genuine parts do not include 272–350 and 373–96. This wholesale dismemberment removes both the problems under consideration. An even more extreme remedy for the difficulties consequent on the staging of the entry of the chorus is Schmid's theory[1] that *Prom* was a *Lesedrama*, a play meant for reading or recitation (this could apply whether or not it is authentic). But it would be, as Schmid admits, the earliest known example; and it is far from clear that such a thing would even have been conceivable in the fifth century (see §2 and the excellent chapter in Zwierlein (127ff.)).

Radical theories like that of Bethe, let alone of Schmid, have not found favour. The great majority of critics believe that all of the play as we have it is genuine, and they would accept a staging of the entry of the chorus along the lines indicated by Wilamowitz or Pickard-Cambridge or Fraenkel. Most would accept, that is, a mechanical showpiece (a wheeled vehicle on the roof or a flying machine for twelve), and would accept that the first song was not danced and was not sung from the orchestra, and would probably accept that the chorus went off after 283 and re-entered later. So, finally, it should be inquired what, supposing the orthodox version to be right, Aeschylus hoped to achieve by all this. Why should he cause his choregos such expense, his *mechanopoios* such trouble, and why should he go against some basic conventions and techniques of Greek tragedy? Evidently the answer has to be that he wanted above all else to present a 'flying' entry for the chorus and to show it in mid-air for 150 lines.

[1] Schmid 104f., *GGL* i 3 p. 298, 306. (Grene's translation, which has hardly any stage instructions, gives the impression of being a *Lesedrama*.)

Why, then, should he attach such importance to this stage effect? It might be claimed that the Oceanids have come a long way in a very short time and so their entry must be made supernatural. But this could surely have been managed without all the complications of vehicle(s), of hovering in mid-air, and of laborious descents. Athena in *Eum* simply arrives on the ground and explains that she has travelled at supernatural speed (this is controversial, see *Eum* 397b*). The Titans in *Prom Lyom* simply arrive. A dancing entry like that advocated by Thomson would surely have been sufficient without all this extra paraphernalia and disruption. It is hard to suppress the suspicion that there was a cruder and less creditable motive for this staging: in such an uneventful and wordy play the dramatist felt that some extraordinary and outlandish 'happening' was needed to enliven the scene. Throughout this book I maintain that gratuitous spectacle is the resort of a poor playwright who is at a loss for true dramatic material, and that Aeschylus, as a great theatrical artist, integrates the visual aspects of the drama into the work as a whole. This is not the case, it seems, in *Prom* as we have it. The truth is, I fear, well put by Mullins (*G&R* 7 (1939) 167), though he did not intend any disparagement: 'in a severely static play like this Aeschylus had to win the attention of the uneducated majority by mechanical sensations.' This is, I suggest, a solemn way of saying that some of *Prom* is bad theatre and unworthy of Aeschylus.

284 enter Oceanus

the staging and its point

Oceanus also, it seems, makes a flying entry. The internal evidence in this case is straightforward. It is contained in the anapaests with which Oceanus introduces himself on entry (284–7), and at the end of the scene (there are no corresponding anapaests) by his final lines (394–6). The wings (286, 394), the pathway of the air (393), and the οἰωνός (286, 395) all clearly imply either that Oceanus flew through the air, or that he was to be imagined as doing so.[1]

The use of the crane (μηχανή) in the fifth-century theatre is

---

[1] cf. D–R 218, Bethe 172f. etc. This point has recently been neglected by Hammond 424.

briefly discussed in pp. 443–7. A comparison of Oceanus with
the evidence collected there shows that he is a very strong
claimant for its use—in fact the strongest in surviving tragedy,
except perhaps for the Muse at *Rh* 890. In particular, Oceanus
has a flying animal;[1] and he accompanies his entry with anapaests (cf. Ar. *Peace* 82ff., *Thesm* 1098ff.). On the other hand, as
argued on p. 446, there is some doubt whether the *mechane* was
available in the Aeschylean theatre, since there is no other likely
instance of its use. A strong case has been made, particularly by
Bodensteiner (664ff.) and Flickinger (289ff.), against the existence
of the *mechane* in Aeschylus' time. But it is virtually impossible
for them to explain away Oceanus. Flickinger concludes 'there
is nothing here which requires or implies flight through the air
within sight of the audience'. We may have to allow 'requires'
since strictly the words require nothing; but they do, on the
other hand, strongly imply that the audience saw Oceanus fly
through the air. If we reject the use of the *mechane* here then we
have to resort to some unsatisfactory compromise: that Oceanus
landed just off-stage and walked the last few yards (towing the
'bird'?), or that he mimed flying—but how then did he mime
the 'quadrupedal bird'? Since the use of the *mechane* elsewhere in
Aeschylus cannot be finally ruled out, its evident exploitation
here cannot be used as a substantial point against authenticity;
on the other hand it certainly cannot be invoked, as it sometimes
has been, as a point in favour of authenticity.

Finally we must ask yet again what Aeschylus hoped to achieve
by this scenic effect. Assuming that the crane was used, this is
likely to have been an early instance, before the device became
a theatrical cliché (though if the chorus had already used a
twelvefold crane its novelty would be utterly undermined!). It
might be claimed simply that Oceanus has come a long way,
and that, like his daughters, he needs supernatural transport.
But nearly all gods in Greek tragedy, including Kratos,
Hephaestus, and Hermes, simply arrive; their supernatural
travel is taken for granted, as in Homer. It might be added that
this elemental god (the γένεсιс of the gods and of everything)[2]

---

[1] τόνδε 286; cf. τοῦδε of Pegasus in E. *Stheneboia* fr. 665a N²–Snell.

[2] *Iliad* 14. 201, 246. At *Iliad* 20. 7 Oceanus alone is absent from the great
gathering of the gods: as the scholiast in M remarks (284b, p. 115H, cf. 393b) it is
hyperbolic to bring Oceanus on stage at all. On Oceanus see further West on

merits a particularly impressive and miraculous entry and exit. But the trouble is that Oceanus in this play is far from impressive; he seems a dull, foolish, and ineffectual old man. Such a marvellous staging would not merely be pointless, it would be wasteful and misleading. However, Bethe's elimination of the spectacular staging as the work of a *Bearbeiter* is a weak compromise, since it is the whole scene, not just the staging, which is vulnerable: see pp. 258–9 above. The incongruity and bathos of the staging are merely one element in the vacuity of the whole scene. Two other elements are the neglect of the chorus and the scene's lack of integral function within the play. Thus, there is no preparation for it (and yet what is the point of a surprise?), and no reference whatsoever to the scene once it is over. It is ironic that the same critics who have criticized Euripides for episodic technique have praised the primeval power and vision of this play. Yet Euripides' use of isolated scenes is at least part of a deliberate thematic technique: Oceanus seems frivolous by comparison.

396 exit Oceanus

436 (no entry)

static structural technique

No one would deny, I think, that 397ff. and 526ff. are act-dividing songs (or stasima), and hence that 436–525 is an act (or epeisodion). Yet it would be the only full act in all of surviving Greek tragedy to contain not a single entry or exit. There are several acts which do not end with an exit and a few which do not begin with an entry (see references in p. 60 n. 1); but here there is neither, nor is there any sort of rearrangement which might be regarded as structurally equivalent to an entry or exit. It seems almost as though in this play the dramatist is trying to break away from the normal interconnection of song and act with exit and entry. As well as this act, there are the structural techniques around the first song (see 88*) and there is no entry at the end of the song at 906 (see 944*). Hardly anyone has even noticed these structural peculiarities, let alone tried to

Hes. *Theog* 133. (I would wager, by the way, that Ge did not fly on stage in *Prom Lyom*.)

parallel or explain them.[1] I have noted just two exceptions who comment on the lack of entry or exit in 436–525. Groeneboom (174) compares S. *Trach* 141ff. But while it is true that Deianeira probably stays on during the first song and that the Old Man does not actually go off before the astrophic lyric at 205ff., there is none the less an entry during the act at 180, and the virtual equivalent of an exit at 199 (p. 89 above). Detscheff (60) has a better analogy in E. *Hel* 252–385. There is no entry after the first song, and then no exit or entry before Helen and the chorus leave the stage at 385. But lack of entry after the parodos is comparatively common (see pp. 248–9 above), and the departure of the chorus always produces structural disruption, see *Eum* 231*. *Prom* 436–525 remains the only straightforward instance of an act without entry or exit.

In the face of such an anomaly one might look for technical explanations or dramatic justifications or both. The most pressing technical consideration seems obvious: the central character is fixed permanently on stage, the setting is remote, and it is awkward to bring too many characters to the end of the earth. Though considerable, this is hardly a compelling reason for the lack of a new entry, since Oceanus and Io give only the vaguest reasons for a visit, while the motivation of the chorus is highly artificial. A realistic explanation for an entry is not required. Another technical consideration might be an attempt to give an archaic touch; though in most ways *Prom* is distinctly 'late' in its techniques. There are in early tragedy some examples of acts which involve only one actor, see *Pers* 622*; if, as happens nowhere else, the actor were to stay on during the preceding and following songs then there will necessarily be no entry or exit during the act. Indeed, if the actor ever stayed on during two consecutive songs back in the days of one-actor tragedy, then the situation would be inevitable (though I would hazard a guess that this never happened). So this might be an archaizing technique. On the other hand, if this scene is not the work of Aeschylus, then the one-actor act would appear to be a conscious

---

[1] Wilamowitz E. *Her ed* ii p. 160 does not take this into account when he says: 'Euripides' dramaturgy is completely free: Aeschylus binds himself to ἐπεισόδια, to the rule that a new character must enter, and he could not have composed like this.' Dignan (22) writes that *Prom* has 'the early episodical character, each scene beginning with the entrance of a new character and ending with his departure': this is true, in a sense, of some 'scenes', but not of the epeisodia.

piece of archaizing by an imitator who did not appreciate that in the process he had, because of the immovable actor, gone against the normal, basic structural technique.[1]

But a more dramatic and less abstruse reason may be offered for the lack of any entry or exit: it may be claimed that it emphasizes Prometheus' isolation, the isolation which was established in the prologue (1ff., 18ff., 93ff.). Prometheus, like Helen (see above), is exiled, forlorn, and without hope of salvation. However since the prologue this picture has been somewhat belied and neglected. The chorus and Oceanus have both come to visit Prometheus in sympathy and friendship, and he has even seen fit to rebuff Oceanus. Moreover the chorus has just this moment sung how they and the whole earth—Asians, Colchians, Scythians, and Arabians, the sea, Hades, and the rivers—all lament in sympathy for Prometheus. So is this the moment to use a unique structural device to emphasize Prometheus' isolation?

Yet, supposing that we allow some weight to each of these points—the avoidance of unwanted new characters, the archaizing, and Prometheus' isolation—is this enough to account for the unparalleled structural technique? To be balanced against any gain is the undeniable slowness and monotony which results from the rejection of new incident. The play has already settled into a series of rambling speeches, and now there is another whole act of this kind without even an arrival or departure to change the stage picture and to supply some variation. This static, purely verbal, sequence would be in danger of losing the audience's attention; and the lack of a new entry would, I suggest, be more noticeable for an ancient audience, which was accustomed by familiar practice to the arrival of a character after each act-dividing song. In mitigation one might claim with

---

[1] The entire sequence is, in my view, suspect. Prometheus' two catalogues 447–68 and 476–506, which comprise over half of the act, while they are, of course, of great interest to historians of ideas, contain nothing which could not be the work of a moderately talented follower of Aeschylus, particularly if he had *Prom Lyom* as a model (see fr. 336 M). The geographic lament 397–435 is (but for the desperately corrupt 425–9, see Wilamowitz 160–2) a touching lyric; but it lacks any of the strength and shock of image and phrase which characterize the songs of the *Oresteia*. And any such complaint applies with much more force to the platitudes of 526–60. Kranz's case (*Stasimon* 226ff.) against the authenticity of this lightweight ditty on the grounds of choric technique seems particularly strong.

Aichele (*Bauformen* 67—he does not notice the uniqueness of the structural technique) that the act as a whole supplies a 'dramatic interval of calm before the storm of the Io act'. But it is doubtful whether the audience would appreciate in advance this excuse for the uneventful monotony. This static act contributes a great deal, in my opinion, to the 'stagnation' of which Nestle complains.[1]

525 (no exit)—see 436*

561 enter Io
a play within a play?

The Io scene lasts over 300 lines (561–886), and so makes up nearly one-third of the play. In length it is comparable to the *sieben Redepaare* in *Seven*, the scene of Pelasgus' decision in *Hik*, or the scene at Agamemnon's tomb in *Cho*: has it some comparably central function within *Prom*? Certainly Io is, as is already pointed out in scholia (561 a, c, p. 158H), the progenitor of Heracles, the eventual deliverer of Prometheus; and she is, like Prometheus, the victim of Zeus' tyrannical behaviour. But these connections seem tangential rather than central: the kinship to Heracles is not crucial like the kinship of the Danaids in *Hik* and the range of Zeus' tyranny may be conveyed in so many ways that a single instance hardly calls for a scene of this length. Perhaps an examination of Io's entry may help with the problem of her relevance, since it is the most striking and memorable incident in the central part of the play, in fact the most vivid piece of theatre between the binding at the beginning and the cataclysm at the end.[2]

Immediately on entry Io sings her 'monody'; though it is not strictly a monody since it is not uninterrupted. The precise structure is this: after some opening anapaests (561–5), she sings in an outburst of frenzy astrophic iambics (566–73); she then sings

[1] In 'Droysen' *tr* p. 352, quoted on p. 467 below; cf. Schmid 13f., 20f. I have discussed the puzzling silence which Prometheus refers to in 436f. in *HSCP* 76 (1972) 83–4. All I have to add is the note that there have been some who actually think that the silence in question is the actor's silence during the choral song; thus e.g. Wecklein 23, Sikes–Willson 103, Rose 276.
[2] Peretti (170) goes so far as to compare Io's lyric with Cassandra's in *Ag*, and to speak of 'la parte centrale . . . l'acme tragica'; for justified criticism of this see Popp *Bauformen* 248.

a strophic pair in iambic-dochmiac lyric (574–88 = 593–607), where each strophe is followed by four lines of spoken reply by Prometheus (589–92 = 609–12).[1] At first glance this seems like an Aeschylean epirrhematic structure since lyric strophes alternate with spoken lines: but it is in fact totally different, and its effect in performance would be totally different, since no part is taken by the chorus and both the lyric and spoken elements are supplied by the actors. There are parallels to this in Euripides.[2] This is also the nearest that Aeschylus comes to actors' monody (except perhaps for the extraordinary lyric hexameters in *Semele* fr. 355, see p. 427). This foreshadows another formal technique which became much used in later tragedy, particularly in later Euripides. Euripides also used monodies for emotional entries like this.[3] Elsewhere in Aeschylus when actors sing it is always in lyric dialogue with the chorus. This is not the only place in *Prom* where the chorus is discarded in a context where it might have been expected to take part.

The entry lyrics of Io were no doubt accompanied by appropriate choreography. It is likely that her anapaests on departure (877–86) were also danced. While we know nothing of the details of such choreography, it is clear that this was an opportunity for a virtuoso piece of solo dancing. For the use of lyric and dance on entry to portray frenzy compare e.g. Cassandra at E. *Tro* 307ff. or Agave at *Ba* 1168ff. The entry of Io is a theatrically sensational moment. Without any warning we are suddenly confronted with the wild dancing and singing of a cow-horned girl. She acts out her wild rushings in front of the immobile figure of Prometheus (cf. Duchemin *Dioniso* 41 (1967) 212f.). This visual effect is imbued with dramatic meaning, and so (unlike some in this play) is characteristic of Aeschylus' use of his theatre. Both Prometheus and Io suffer under the boundless tyranny of Zeus.

---

[1] Page *OCT* on 588, 608 notes that the MSS. attribute 588 to the chorus, and wonders whether this might be the right attribution of this line and the corresponding 608. But there seems to be no point to these isolated contributions from the chorus; the two lines in question conclude Io's stanzas and lead into Prometheus' replies.

[2] e.g. E. *Alc* 244ff., 393ff., cf. Popp *Bauformen* 236, Herington *Author* 92.

[3] e.g. E. *Hec* 1056ff., *Tro* 308ff. See the brief but useful discussion by Barner (*Bauformen* 287–90) on the relationship between monody and stage action. Barner also illustrates (298) how repeated questions like those of Io at *Prom* 561ff. tend to occur in such contexts. (It is curious to note that the Σ in M [574a, p. 161 H] says of Argus Σοφοκλῆς ἐν Ἰνάχωι καὶ ἄιδοντα αὐτὸν εἰcάγει (= S. fr. 281 P); cf. Pfeiffer *SBAW* 1938 pp. 28f.)

But while Io's plight takes the form of a far-ranging never-resting journey, which is captured in miniature by her dance in the theatre, Prometheus' punishment takes the contrary form of total immobility, and forms the visual background of Io's motion. One has fetters on his limbs and is fixed by a rivet through his breast: the other has horns and is driven on by a tiny gadfly. We see in vivid terms the variety and macabre ingenuity of Zeus' cruelty.

So the entry of Io does set the main theme of this long act: the lengths to which Zeus' tyranny can go. This hardly supplies, it may be objected, a dramatic justification for the main bulk of the act, Prometheus' long catalogues of geography. None the less Io's journeys do move towards a conclusion which brings for both of them an eventual release from their miseries, Io through the birth of Epaphus, and Prometheus through his descendant Heracles. The act has direction and coherence, even though the geographical lists seem too long for the purpose they serve.

So it is strange that the Io act is so little integrated into the play as a whole. Her entry is given no preparation; it comes as a complete surprise (Dingel 114 compares Iris and Lyssa in E. *Her*). An unprepared surprise entry can be an effective dramatic device, though Aeschylus uses it rarely (see *Seven* 1005a*): but there seems here to be no special dramatic point beyond the sheer surprise of Io's entry. The price of this small gain is that the act as a whole is not fitted into the play; it is not led up to and it in no way follows from what precedes. Even more inexplicably it is never referred to again after it is over. The Io act with its highly theatrical beginning and its forward-looking internal coherence makes a kind of play within a play; yet it lacks any significant connection with what goes before and after it.

Something of the same effect of shock is achieved at the end of the act as at the beginning. Suddenly without warning at 877 Io cries out in anapaests, and with a brief vivid account of her frenzy she is gone. There are no farewells, no dwelling on her coming wanderings which have been so lengthily treated in the preceding speeches.[1] The exclusively verbal play within a play ends as abruptly and as theatrically as it began.

---

[1] Contrast Orestes at the end of *Cho*. I imagine that more was made of Heracles' exit to his further labours in *Prom Lyom* (see p. 426). (In Lowell's version (p. 48) Io's exit is even more abrupt.)

886 exit Io

944 enter Hermes

technical anomalies

Prom departs more than any other play of Aeschylus, and perhaps
more than any other surviving tragedy, from the regular association of exit and entry with act-dividing songs: see 88*, 436*.
Here too an entry was to be expected after the choral song at
907; but Hermes does not arrive until 37 lines later. It must be
stressed once more that this is extremely unusual and would not
pass unnoticed by an Athenian audience. It might be claimed
that in this case the brief scene 908–40 is preparatory for the
entry of Hermes and is almost a kind of entry announcement. It
is true that the purpose of these lines is to show Prometheus'
open defiance and flaunting of his secret, through which he provokes from Zeus the threat of further punishment. But there is
nothing in the lines which specifically looks forward to Hermes
or to any entry at all (contrast e.g. *Hik* 176ff., 710ff.). And the
fact remains that this is one of the very few places in surviving
tragedy, other than after the first song (parodos), where there
is no entry after an act-dividing song—see *Hik* 710*. It is, moreover, the only final act which is not begun by an entry.[1] This is
not 'dictated by the plot' or anything of that sort—it might easily
have been arranged otherwise: it is simply a wilful departure
from the normal structural pattern.

The entry announcement of Hermes calls for some comment,
particularly as it has several features which are more characteristic of later tragedy than of Aeschylus. After his climactic
four lines of defiance (937–40) Prometheus himself sees and
announces the approach of Hermes (941–3). Graeber (22–31;
cf. *GGL* i 3 p. 302 n. 7) contends that this announcement is a
clear sign of the spuriousness of *Prom*, or at least of 'retractatio'.
His arguments are that this is the only announcement in Aeschylus
made by one actor of another actor,[2] and the only one tacked
on to a preceding speech, whereas both of these are common

[1] Cf. Detscheff 67. This point is neglected by Kremer *Bauformen* 128. (A. *Eum*
is a special case, see *Eum* 777c*.)

[2] It is conceivable that the announcement should be attributed to the chorus
rather than to Prometheus; but the contemptuous language is in favour of the
MSS., which have no paragraphos.

phenomena in Euripides and Aristophanes (as may be clearly seen from the catalogue in Bodensteiner 718f.). Graeber claims further that this is the only trimeter announcement in Aeschylus which does not follow immediately on a stasimon, and that it is the only announcement of the first entry of a named character which does not contain a proper name. It should be added that it is the only occurrence in Aeschylus (or Sophocles) of ἀλλ' εἰcορῶ γὰρ τόνδε . . ., which is so common in Euripides that it is virtually a formula, see p. 148 n. 2 ; and that the announcement as a whole is rather simple and formulaic in the manner of later tragedy.

But, while these points are not negligible, they are not as significant as Graeber claims. We do not have enough of Aeschylus to pontificate on such details ; and in any case some of the alleged peculiarities are perfectly acceptable. The substitution of a periphrasis for a proper name is innocuous. The fact that *Pers* 247–9 is in trochaic tetrameters does not disqualify it as another announcement in mid-act; and Orestes' announcement of Electra and the chorus at *Cho* 10–21 was almost certainly tacked on to the end of his prologue speech. The formulaic tone of the announcement is more interesting, though καὶ μήν in *Seven* 372 is the only example of that formula in an Aeschylean entrance announcement (see pp. 147–8). In conclusion, if *Prom* were held on other grounds to be unauthentic, then these lines would certainly be symptomatic : but they can hardly be used as an argument *per se*.

Some scholars have maintained that Hermes entered on the flying machine; it would be for them the third use of the *mechane* in this one play.[1] But there is no sign of this whatsoever in the text (cf. Bodensteiner 666 '. . . kein Anhaltspunkt . . .'). There are no anapaests, no references to the 'pathway of the air', and in general no more reason for having Hermes fly than in the prologue of E. *Ion*.

1079 exit Hermes

timing

It is generally supposed that Hermes departs after his final

---

[1] e.g. Wecklein *ed* 110, Robert565,Murray 42f., Mazon 194, Rose 313.

threat. Wilamowitz, however, prefers him to stay on and to disappear during the cataclysm, safely outside its range (*ed maj* p. 66 *actio*, cf. *Interpr* 118). But I can see no point in keeping Hermes on as a distracting outsider during the final lines. The cataclysm is not his work, but Zeus' (1016ff.; cf. 1089). It is, in effect, the entry of Zeus in person into the play.

1093 exeunt chorus and Prometheus

(a) *what is the fate of Prometheus and of the chorus?*

Before considering the staging of the end of *Prom* (1093b* below), we must be clear on the far more important question of what is supposed to be happening, for there is not even agreement over what picture is to be imagined by the audience. First, there is blunt disagreement over the fate of the chorus: while most scholars believe that the Oceanids stay with Prometheus to the bitter end,[1] there are those who hold that they desert him at the last moment.[2] Wilamowitz insisted that the text leaves no real room for doubt that they stayed with Prometheus, and it seems to me that he was right. When at 1058–62 Hermes tells the Oceanids to withdraw lest the thunder derange them, they tell him to change his tone (1063–5), and continue πῶc με κελεύειc κακότητ' ἀcκεῖν; / μετὰ τοῦδ' ὅ τι χρὴ πάcχειν ἐθέλω—for they hate treachery (1066–71). Hermes gives a final warning that they have been given an opportunity to avoid ἄτη (1071–9); and then Prometheus tells how the catastrophe is actually happening (1080–93). There is no sign that the chorus deserts him, and the implication is that it stays to the end.[3]

The only honest way to avoid this conclusion is to reject the text as we have it. Bethe argued that the anapaests 1040–93 are a later addition, and that in the original the chorus did desert Prometheus.[4] He claims that the change of metre to anapaests for the last fifty lines is quite unlike the few metra at the end of

---

[1] Including Wilamowitz 117f., cf. *Kl Schr* i p. 161, Capps 19f., Bodensteiner 674f., Wecklein *ed* 119, Arnott 123ff., Dodds *Progress* 34.

[2] Including Todt *Philol.* N.F. 2 (1889) 524f. (into the ravines!), Sikes–Willson xlvif., Mazon 198 n. 1, Thomson 173f., Vellacott *tr* 52, 'Droysen' *tr* 393.

[3] Mr. Stinton points out that, accepting that the chorus does not desert Prometheus, there is nothing to force us to the conclusion that they share his fate. This is true; but I still doubt that the author intended this compromise.

[4] Bethe 175ff., followed by Weise 12, 15; cf. D–R 198f.

Cho (1065ff.) or even those in the suspected final scene of *Seven* (1054ff.), and that they are closely comparable to the change of pace often found at the ends of later tragedies (S. *Phil*, *OC*; E. *Med*, *El* etc.). This is scarcely by itself a sign of authorship, since it may be simply one of the many ways in which Aeschylus foreshadows later tragedy. Bethe's other point is more considerable: the change in the chorus' stance between lines 1036–9 and 1063ff. In the last iambics they say that Hermes has spoken to the point, they advise Prometheus to give way, and imply that it would be wrong not to do so: yet less than 30 lines later they aggressively reject Hermes and say that his advice is intolerable. Now, it may be claimed that an Aeschylean chorus should not be expected to show a consistent character, and is liable to express an attitude dictated solely by dramatic context; compare the change in *Seven* (see p. 166), or between *Ag* 351 and 475ff. or *Ag* 1348ff. and 1649 (cf. e.g. Dawe 43ff., *HSCP* 76 (1972) 91f.). But this inconsistency here is particularly blatant, not only because it is so abrupt, but also because there is no relevant change in dramatic circumstances. Nothing has happened between 1036 and 1063 to account for the change.[1] The Oceanids' defiant courage is quite unprepared for, particularly since they have been so judicious and retiring throughout the play. Their last-minute loyalty might be superficially quite effective: it shows the affection which the dour Prometheus may inspire, and it illustrates the indiscriminate cruelty of Zeus which does not care for innocence. Nevertheless in larger terms this touching surprise is detrimental. It is Prometheus who defies the tyrant, Prometheus who suffers by himself. Prometheus stands alone: all the others are either against him, or are sympathetic but helpless bystanders.[2] On the other hand it should be recognized, against Bethe, that it is doubtful whether the sort of spectacular mechanics implied by the end of *Prom* were any more acceptable in the last quarter of the fifth century than in the second (cf.

---

[1] It is no help to plead that there is no strict logical inconsistency, as is laboriously pointed out by Zum Felde *De Aeschyli Prometheo* (Diss. Göttingen 1914) 8ff. (Lowell in his version (p. 66) has the chorus go off with Hermes; this may make more sense than the original).

[2] Wilamowitz 126f. was evidently unhappy with the change in the disposition of the chorus. He evades the issue with: 'Theatrical pressure applies here too, and the force of the physical management of the final scene suppresses all rational considerations.'

p. 258 n. 1). And, more important, the final anapaests of *Prom*
are powerful dramatic poetry not unworthy of Aeschylus; in fact
they are considerably more characteristic than the iambics before
1040.[1] Piecemeal trimming of Bethe's sort, based on dubious
grounds of theatre history, is surely insufficient to solve the
problems of *Prometheus*.

I shall assume, then, for the moment that the final anapaests
are genuine, and that the chorus suffers the same fate as Prometheus in the final catastrophe. What is this fate? It seems
universally agreed that Prometheus is swallowed down into
Tartarus. But the text does not actually authorize that.[2] When
Hermes gives the official account of Prometheus' punishment in
1016–19 he says nothing about Tartarus. It is true that Tartarus
is invoked in his taunt at 1026–9. But in its context this is not
really a prediction; the audience would take it simply as an
ἀδύνατον.[3] It is Prometheus, not Hermes, who suggests that he
will go to Tartarus, when he replies . . . ἔς τε κελαινὸν | Τάρταρον
ἄρδην ῥίψειε δέμας | τοὐμὸν ἀνάγκης στερραῖς δίναις· | πάντως ἐμέ
γ' οὐ θανατώσει (1050–3). He is not saying what Zeus will do, but
is defying him by saying '*let* him do what he will, he cannot kill
me.' Finally Prometheus describes the cataclysm (1080ff.), but
he does not say what is actually happening to him. It may be
that the mentions of Tartarus in 1029 and 1051 would make the
audience think automatically that Prometheus would be buried
there in the traditional dungeon of Kronos and his allies.[4] But
since there is no explicit prediction that that is where Prometheus
is to go, it may well be that the audience would simply accept
Hermes' version—namely that the entire crag will be shattered
and that Prometheus, still fixed to his rock, will be buried in the
debris. This, to conclude, is the picture presented to the imagination: Prometheus and the chorus with him are buried by the
violent collapse of the mountain.

[1] For some interesting poetical connections with the frenzy of Io see Dawson
CPh 46 (1951) 237f.

[2] Though it has no particular authority I note that the hypothesis has simply
καὶ τέλος βροντῆς γενομένης ἀφανὴς γίνεται ὁ Προμηθεύς. Nor have the scholia
anything about Tartarus in this connection.

[3] On the assumption that *Prom* belongs to a connected trilogy, 1026–9 are
generally taken to be a reference to the story about Cheiron recorded in Apollo-
dorus ii 5. 4 and ii 5. 11; see Lloyd-Jones *Zeus* 96f.

[4] Cf. *Prom* 219 and, earlier, *Iliad* 8. 477ff., Hes. *Theog* 720ff., 851 etc.; cf. West
Theog ed pp. 358f.

(b) mechanical cataclysm—or just words?

The cataclysm is so vividly put into words, both in anticipation and then in description (992–4, 1014–19, 1043–52, 1061–2, 1080–93), that this strongly suggests that my earlier working hypothesis should be invoked again: either a proper attempt was made to present a convincing illusory spectacle, or everything was left to the words. Prometheus' ἔργωι κοὐκέτι μύθωι (1080) also seems to call for all or nothing in terms of stage presentation. When there is such extravagant verbal evocation a half-measure seems worse than nothing. Yet the most widely accepted version of the staging is in danger of being just such a half-measure: this is that Prometheus and the chorus were withdrawn on the ekkyklema.[1] But this means that instead of being buried by shattered massifs (and even of plunging down to Tartarus, if that is what is supposed to happen) Prometheus merely slides horizontally into the 'mountain'. There are further objections. It is argued on pp. 443–7 that it is doubtful if this machine was available during Aeschylus' time, and that its purpose was to extrude or reveal interior tableaux, not to remove awkward objects. Even if it was available it is very doubtful whether it can have been large enough to carry Prometheus and his rock and the chorus. But apart from such technical points there is the objection that a compromise of this sort would be worse than nothing.

It was argued on 1093a* that in a fully illusionist staging it would not be necessary for Prometheus to plunge downwards in order to do justice to the words; it would be sufficient if the mountain collapsed on top of him, his rock, and the chorus. Yet it is very hard to see how even this could possibly be staged realistically. It would, in fact, be scarcely any more practicable than the usual version which is that Prometheus and his rock

---

[1] Thus e.g. Frickenhaus 12, Focke 284f., Thomson *ed* 174, Reinhardt 77f., Webster *GTP* 18, Dale *Papers* 270. Simon 32f. claims that this theory is confirmed by a fourth-century Apulean calyx-crater (first published by Trendall in *J Berl M* 12 (1970) 168ff. (= *Illustrations* iii. 1. 27); see *Illustrations* p. 61), which shows Prometheus (in *Prom Lyom*) bound across the mouth of a rocky cave. But even supposing that Prometheus was staged this way at the first performance, would such a stage property cave-mouth be on the ekkyklema rather than fixed around the skene door? Simon claims that it represents the gate of Tartarus; but there is no mention in *Prom Desm* of such a gateway—and are we to suppose that another such doorway also happened to be at the setting of *Prom Lyom* (which was elsewhere, see p. 425)?

and the chorus somehow or other 'sank' out of sight.[1] It is difficult enough even in a modern theatre to take only two actors down a trap door, and in the Greek theatre there was, so far as we know, no 'cellarage' large enough for this monumental tableau (the possible underground passage discussed on pp. 447–8 would be too small). Some scholars, on the assumption that *Prom* was played in the early pre-skene theatre, have turned to the drop of several feet made by the terrace wall which held up the early orchestra from the sanctuary of Dionysus below. If a platform were built out beyond the terrace then the whole thing could somehow 'collapse' behind it.[2] But even supposing this were practicable, would all this apparatus be set up just for the sake of a single scene? And why is the chorus deliberately drawn into the catastrophe also, thus making everything much more difficult?[3]

These problems drive one to the alternative extreme, that the final cataclysm was left entirely to the words working on the imagination of the audience.[4] Other seismic upheavals are generally supposed to have been left to the imagination of the audience (viz A. fr. 76, E. *Her* 904ff., *Ba* 591ff., *Erechtheus* fr. 65 l. 45ff. Austin); so why not this one which would be by far the hardest to manage illusionistically? This way out would mean in practical terms that the chorus would group round Prometheus at about line 1067, that during 1080ff. they would either huddle closer or move violently, and then at the end, after a slight pause, all would simply walk off.[5] The economy of this simple solution has obvious attractions. On the other hand it should be noted that this staging would be unparalleled in the stage technique of Greek tragedy since it would be the only exit or entry which is actually left to the imagination. Arnott (129f.) compares those plays which begin with entries which are not part of the play and

---

[1] See e.g. Wilamowitz 117f., Murray 38, 40, Rose 321, Schadewaldt *HuH*[2] i 358, Werner *tr* 477.

[2] For theories along these lines see e.g. Pickard 204, Flickinger 228, Bieber *Hist*[2] p. 57.

[3] Recently Joerden *Diss* 125 (cf. *Bauformen* 408, Jobst 144) has set Prometheus on the skene roof so that he and his rock may collapse down into the skene. But, while difficult enough to manage with Prometheus alone, the chorus rules this theory out.

[4] I am leaving out of account Schmid's theory of a *Lesedrama*, see p. 259 above.

[5] For this solution see Haigh *AT*[3] 218, P-C *TDA* 38, Arnott 123ff. (Arnott seems to think he is the first to have made the suggestion.)

have to be 'cancelled' (see *Seven* 1b*). But the difference is that
in such cases the actors enter and then the audience must imagine
that they have *not* done so; whereas here it is claimed that the
actors do not go off and yet the audience must suppose that they
have done so. The dramatists usually take trouble over clearing
the stage at the end of the play, and there is no other trace of
a convention comparable to that of 'cancelled' entries. On the
other hand it may be countered that it would be perfectly clear
in performance what was supposed to have happened.

   I have contended in §4 and throughout that the traditional
view of Aeschylus as a showman of huge mechanical stage effects
is mistaken, and that if such displays were attempted at all in
the fifth century, it was by later and lesser men like Xenocles.
So far as internal evidence is concerned this picture of Aeschylus
stands or falls, I maintain, with three scenes. I argue on pp.
431–3 that the usual view of *Psychostasia*, based on Pollux, has
nothing to do with Aeschylus. On *Prom* 128b* I discuss the staging
of the entry of the Oceanids, and I raise doubts as to whether
the empty spectacle indicated by the transmitted text is the work
of Aeschylus. The third place is this final cataclysm of *Prom.* If
it is accepted that the mighty mountain-rending detonation was
left entirely to the imagination, then this is not incompatible
with the view of Aeschylus which I have maintained. If, on
the other hand, it is insisted that ἔργωι κοὐκέτι μύθωι must be
taken literally and the overwhelming upheaval must have been
staged realistically, then either my entire view of Aeschylus as an
artist of the theatre is jeopardized, or this part of the play is not
his work.

VI. AGAMEMNON

1 enter Watchman

on the roof?

'*AGAMEMNON* begins. We look, and nobody is on the scene; there is a palace, but nobody comes out of it. The voice comes from the roof, of all places; and the speaker is not even standing up.' This is Page's[1] vivid way of putting the traditional stage direction at the beginning of *Ag*: 'a watchman is lying on the roof' or words to that effect. But, strictly speaking, the watchman must have 'entered'; that is to say, the actor must have taken up his position. It is always possible that he got there in the darkness before the audience arrived, it is always possible that the skene had a kind of battlement, and he could have crawled into position without being seen, but since there was a recognized convention by which the first entry of a play might be 'cancelled', and treated as though it had never happened, this seems to be the obvious solution here—see in general on *Seven* 1b*. Here the Watchman says straight away that he has kept watch for a year at the house of Atreidai. This does not mean we must not suppose he has moved an inch from his post for a whole year (no more than Aegisthus' watchman at *Odyssey* 4. 526); but it does imply that he has been on watch before the play begins. So the audience will easily acquiesce in the illusion that the Watchman did not enter, but has been long at his post. (Compare the opening of *Hamlet*, where Francisco reaches the end of his watch as the play opens.)

Did the Watchman really deliver the prologue lying on the roof? The traditional case for this rests on the wording of line 3 κοιμώμενος / cτέγαιc Ἀτρειδῶν ἄγκαθεν, κυνὸc δίκην. But first,

---

[1] D–P xxxi. Two cavils: how do we know that the play has begun, before the Watchman speaks? And how do we know that the skene represents a palace, before we are told so?

cτέγαιc cannot mean 'on the roof' but rather 'in or at the house' (see Fraenkel ii 3; cf. Verrall 184). And secondly ἄγκαθεν cannot be a contraction of the non-existent ἀνάκαθεν and mean 'above', and so it must mean something like 'on my elbows'.[1] So the internal evidence collapses. It would, indeed, be legitimate, so far as the words are concerned, to put the Watchman on the ground, as has been suggested by Arnott (118f.). On the other hand these points certainly do not refute the idea that the Watchman is on the roof; and maybe they are overruled by the simple fact that the roof is the best place for the Watchman to keep his look out. After all, he is not there simply to deliver the prologue (as Arnott implies), he is on watch, and soon he does indeed see the beacon burning in the distance.[2] As Fraenkel points out, if he was on the roof then he would hardly need to say so. This staging would immediately introduce the place that the house is to have in the drama as a physical entity: cf. p. 459. And this is reinforced by the ominous hint in 37f. οἶκοc δ᾽ αὐτόc, εἰ φθογγὴν λάβοι . . . (cf. Reinhardt 84). It would also add an extra literal dimension to the final stage of Clytemnestra's account of the beacons: (310) κἄπειτ᾽ Ἀτρειδῶν ἐc τόδε cκήπτει cτέγοc. So the balance still tips in favour of having the Watchman on the roof—the more vivid staging to capture interest, and a highly imaginative use of the new skene.[3]

But, even assuming he is on the roof, is he lying down? He lies and has lain as he watches for the beacon (2, 12ff.); but that need not mean he actually delivers the first half of the prologue in this position. It is difficult to deliver lines clearly from a lying position in any theatre, let alone in one the size of the Theatre of Dionysus. This must remain an open question.

---

[1] See Fraenkel ii 4; the alternative, upheld by D–P 66, seems to have been conclusively ruled out by Renehan *CR* n.s. 20 (1970) 125–7; Professor Lloyd-Jones suggests still 'in the arms of the house', i.e. 'on the house'.

[2] It is absurd to say, as nearly everyone has, that there was a realistic attempt to represent the beacon: obviously it was left to the much more effective resources of the imagination. (Schmidt *Bauformen* 39 even suggests that the sunrise might have represented the beacon. But would the audience accept a natural phenomenon outside the theatre as representing an artificial phenomenon within the play?)

[3] For the new skene see Appendix C, for the roof p. 440. It is worth noting that Arph. *Wasps* begins with a 'watchman' scene which is to be imagined as having lasted all night before the play began. And one of the guards (Bdelycleon) sleeps on the roof. However, there does not seem to be any direct allusion to *Ag*.

39 exit Watchman

40 enter chorus

inexplicit motivation

We do not know whether there was customarily an appreciable pause between the end of the prologue and the entry of the chorus for the first song (parodos). There is no particular reason to think there was, and sometimes the entry of the chorus is announced by actors, which suggests continuity (cf. p. 335, also p. 64). Yet Wilamowitz, among others, supposes a 'longior pausa' (*ed maj actio* on 39). In *ed maj* he adds no other stage instruction (not even the entry of the chorus!), but in *Interpr* 163 he divulges that during this interval he supposes that maids come out and perform various rituals before the house. Other commentators have interpolated still more action, turning this pause into a humming scene of activity. 'The rousing of the palace, the sending out of the messengers, the kindling of fires . . . and the rejoicing of the household were typically represented in action with music' asserts Verrall liii, cf. Murray 209, Campbell 2. All this dumb-show is conjectured without any simultaneous words to leave a trace in the text.

In §3 I have claimed that in the whole of Greek tragedy there is no single indubitable case of significant stage action which is not indicated at the same time in the words, still less for actions totally unaccompanied by any words. What, then, is the evidence for this extravagant dumb-show? The inference is made almost exclusively on the strength of the chorus's anapaestic address to Clytemnestra in 83ff., especially 85–91 (on these lines see further 258a*). The first smaller point to be made is that θυοcκεῖc (87) clearly means 'you are having sacrifices performed', and need not imply that Clytemnestra is there herself performing one at that moment; and the same goes for θυηπολεῖc in 262 which resumes the issue. The larger point is that the theatre is not presenting a detailed realistic world, and so there is no reason why the audience should see messengers dispatched and maids scurrying around. The action of the play selects the few vital actions it is concerned with from the many details of a 'real life' world.[1]

---

[1] Similarly lines 28 and 587 do not justify the interpolation of the sound of a cry from within between 39 and 40, as is claimed by e.g. Thomson[2] i 20.

There is another specious argument for the pause, based on an analysis of off-stage events. If the chorus knows about the messengers and sacrifices throughout the city, then, it is claimed, there must have been time for these to get under way after the beacon and yet before the chorus' arrival. But slight technical incongruities of time are of no concern to the Greek tragedian.[1] Another more complex argument is, however, connected with this. It is widely held that the motivation of the chorus' entry is that they have been summoned by Clytemnestra; and so some time must have elapsed for the elders to be gathered together. Indeed this is to be found in the hypothesis; αὐτὴ δὲ τῶν πρεσβυτῶν ὄχλον μεταπέμπεται. This might seem to be supported by line 258 ἥκω cεβίζων cόν, Κλυταιμήcτρα, κράτοc: but κράτοc must mean 'authority' not 'command' (see Fraenkel ii 10),[2] and the line fits best with what follows if it is translated simply 'I come as one who reveres your authority'. So there is no reason in the text to suppose that Clytemnestra sent for the chorus. It will not do to compare S. *OT*, *Ant*, or *OC* (*contra* Webster *Preparation* 118), because in those cases it is clearly indicated in the prologue that the chorus has been sent for. This false inference is a typical result of the search for precise classifiable motivation of entries. It is not the trivial details of motivation that matter, but the way that the entry fits into the play as a whole: see *Pers* 1b*.

We may now consider the motivation of the entry of the chorus, as it would actually appear to the audience of the play in performance. On entry the Old Men go straight into an account of the past; they do not motivate their entry, they do not even identify themselves until later at 72ff. They have more important things to communicate. But when later at 83ff. they put all their questions to Clytemnestra, then a motive is implicitly supplied: curiosity.[3] They want to know what is going on, and the Queen is the one who knows. This accords with a common pattern of exposition which incorporates the entry of the chorus: (i) the audience learns something important in the prologue; (ii) the

---

[1] Even Fraenkel ii 52 (cf. 26) says on 83ff. 'it now becomes clear that we must imagine some time to have elapsed between the end of the prologue and the beginning of the parodos'. Members of an audience who think of things like this cannot be concentrating properly on the play itself.

[2] The hypothesis also apparently misunderstood κράτει in l. 10 to arrive at the unfounded claim cκοπὸν ἐκάθιcεν ἐπὶ μιcθῶι Κλυταιμήcτρα.

[3] Cf. Richter 134f., Harms 58f., Kranz *Studien* 264 n. 3.

chorus, which has gathered that something is afoot, comes on to the scene to find out more; (iii) in the following act it is told about it. *Prom* has something in common with this framework; in Sophocles and Euripides it is frequent, cf. S. *Aj*, *OC*, E. *Alc*, *Hipp*, *IT* (variations in S. *El*, E. *Med*, *Hkld*, *Tro*, *Hel*, *Or*). By the time that the chorus's motivation unobtrusively fits into place at 83ff. the audience will have completely forgotten that in realistic terms there was not enough time before 40 for it to have observed all the things it recounts in the questions to Clytemnestra.

258 enter Clytemnestra

(a) before or after the first song?

The movements of Clytemnestra in *Ag* are notoriously problematical. For some reason Aeschylus leaves it unclear when and whether she comes on and off. Perhaps he thought it unnecessary to clarify entrances and exits from the new skene door, a much shorter route than by way of an eisodos (cf. Dignan 25f.); though in that case he was not followed in this by Sophocles and Euripides. I have already discussed Clytemnestra's entrances and exits with special reference to Aeschylean silences in *HSCP* 76 (1972) 89–94 (hereafter *Silences*). But many other aspects of dramatic technique are also involved, and I shall take on the problems again, but with particular attention to the aspects not discussed there.

Whether Clytemnestra was present throughout the first song (parodos) of *Ag* or whether she only entered at the end of it must be one of the most disputed stage directions in Greek tragedy. First I shall review the arguments, as I see them, in favour of an early entry, and then in favour of a later entry. My own position will soon emerge.

Of those who bring Clytemnestra on early a few scholars have her enter at line 40 at the same time as the chorus;[1] but the majority bring her on at 83 or shortly before.[2] The case for this

[1] Murray 209, Campbell *ed* 2, D–P xxxii, 75f., 117, Arnott 46 cf. 55.

[2] They include Hermann 371, 651, Keck 55, Capps 23, Bodensteiner 731, Detscheff 44 n. 101, 50, Sidgwick 9, Wilamowitz *tr* 54, Deckinger 33, Lattimore *tr* 37, Rose 11, Schmidt *Bauformen* 22ff., Hammond 435. Thomson² ii 14 brings Clytemnestra on at the word 'Ερινύν in 59, although in the context it is quite inappropriate; the same goes for Winnington-Ingram *Clyt* 130 n. 6 who picks on ὄναρ in 82. For those who favour the entry at the end of the song see p. 282 n. 1 below.

early entry relies almost entirely on one argument, the argument
that the questions and requests addressed to Clytemnestra in
lines 83–103 'strongly and immediately suggest that she is
present' (D–P 75). Is this true? It is well known that in Greek
tragedy the chorus can in their lyrics apostrophize characters
who are off-stage.[1] Two places are particularly relevant in this
context: the parodoi of S. *Aj* (134ff.) and of E. *Hipp* (141ff.).[2]
It is true that there are differences between each of the three
places, but the differences do not affect the important similarity:
the chorus which is ignorant of important information puts
questions to someone who is off-stage. The similarities of dramatic
function go further. In each case the questions show the ignorance
and curiosity of the chorus (see 40* above), and they build up
tension towards the eventual appearance of the person questioned—in *Ag* because she has vital information, in *Aj* and *Hipp*
because there is anxiety about their well-being. I conclude for
the moment that the questions in *Ag* 83ff. do not tell us one way
or the other whether Clytemnestra is present, and that the issue
must therefore be decided on other grounds.

I can only see two other small points which might be claimed
to favour an early entry.[3] The prologue might suggest that
Clytemnestra is to enter soon, particularly if one were to read
cημανῶ in line 26.[4] This call might be seen as a forerunner of the
device of calling someone outside, which is common in later
tragedy (and comedy).[5] But since the Watchman does not call
Clytemnestra outside, but calls her from her bed to raise the
cry of triumph, this is of little weight. Secondly D–P (76) claim
that ἥκω in 258 should be said by the later of two arrivals, and

[1] This is illustrated and discussed for Sophocles and Euripides by Kranz *Stas*
205–7; cf. e.g. Graeber 48, Stevens E. *Andr ed* 157.
[2] See *Silences* 90–1, and cf. especially Wecklein *ed* 38, Kranz *Forma* 63ff.,
Schadewaldt *Monolog* 42 n. 3, Fraenkel ii 51f., Lloyd-Jones *tr* 20.
[3] I argue in *Silences* 89–90 against the claim that Clytemnestra's silent presence
would be 'dramatically effective' (D–P 96); and against Maas's suggestion (see
D–P 117) that Euripides' Medea may be a relevant analogy—she belongs to a
time where the relative functions of actor and chorus were completely different.
I hope I may take it as read that the allegedly effective silence of Clytemnestra
cannot be supported by a reference to the 'Aeschylean silences' made famous by
Arph. *Frogs* 911ff.
[4] But cημαίνω, the reading of M, is preferable: see Fraenkel ii 18.
[5] Catalogues of examples may be found in Graeber 21 n. 3, Mooney *The
House-door* etc. (Diss. Baltimore 1914) 19 n. 12 (incomplete, add e.g. *Rh* 6ff.,
642ff.).

hence implies that Clytemnestra was on-stage before the chorus. But the only reason why the verb is normally used by the later arrival is that when anyone arrives in Greek tragedy there is almost invariably someone else already there, if only the chorus. But ἥκω may still be used when there is no one already there, see A. *Prom* 1, *Cho* 3, E. *Hec* 1, *Tro* 1, *Ion* 5, *Hel* 426, *Ba* 1.

So it should be clear that I am far from convinced by the arguments offered for the early entry of Clytemnestra. I shall now raise some points against this, most of which positively favour the later entry at the end of the first song.[1] First, the early entry means that Clytemnestra would be on during the song, which clashes with the normal technique in several ways. It is true that there is nothing exceptional about an actor being on during the parodos of a Greek tragedy; nevertheless there is still a basic tendency to clear the stage of actors during choral songs (*Pers* 622*, *Prom* 88*); and when an actor stays on in Aeschylus he is usually given some excuse for being on, something better than Clytemnestra's interminable sacrifices and agonies of prayer. In such cases Sophocles and Euripides nearly always turn the parodos into the form of a lyric dialogue and thus involve the actor. Elsewhere in Aeschylus Danaus and Electra in *Hik* and *Cho* come on with their chorus and are closely associated with it (see *Hik* 1b*). Prometheus, on the other hand, is immovable, and is given a dialogue part in the parodos (see *Prom* 88*).

Furthermore, in nearly every other case where an actor is on-stage during the parodos, he has already been on before the chorus entered. This cannot be the case here. If we want Clytemnestra to enter at 40, then we might claim as parallels A. *Hik* and *Cho* again; but in both cases the actor is *with* the chorus and not independent of it. And it is no easier to find parallels for an entry at l. 83 which means an entry *during* the parodos, albeit the anapaestic part. In *Rh* during the anapaests (1–22) which precede the strophic song the chorus rouses Hector who first responds at line 11 (though this may not actually be an entry, see p. 455 below). But Hector speaks immediately, and he takes part in the parodos, and in general the differences far

[1] Among those in favour of a late entry I select Kranz *Forma* 63, Wilamowitz 163f., *ed maj actio* 192, Verrall 11, Hense 13, 177f., Wecklein 38, Dignan 26, Groeneboom 134, Mazon 19, Schadewaldt *Monolog* 42 n. 3; translations of Platt, Smyth, MacNeice, Lloyd-Jones.

outweigh any similarities. In S. *OC* Oedipus and Antigone enter after the first strophe at 137; but they have only been in hiding, and they take part in the parodos. In E. *IT*, which has an astrophic lyric anapaestic parodos (123ff.), some have thought that Iphigenia entered during the song at 136 or 143. But I have suggested (p. 194 n. 3) that she enters at the beginning of the song at 123, and that, as she is the presiding priestess, she sings 123–5. In any case Iphigenia is very different from Clytemnestra in that she is closely connected with the chorus, and she takes part in the parodos.[1] So there is no truly comparable instance of an actor who enters after the prologue and then stays on during the first song.

Another exceptional consequence of having Clytemnestra on during the parodos is that there would then be no entry at the end of the song. On *Prom* 88* I have collected the seven or eight plays in which this happens; and there are at least two relevant ways in which the others are unlike *Ag*. In most of them the character who stays on during the parodos and the ensuing act was already on during the prologue, and is thus properly established in the play. The exceptions are A. *Hik* and *Cho* where Danaus and Electra are closely associated with the chorus, and *Rh* whose peculiarities are obvious. Another point is that in all but two, E. *Hel* and *Or*, there is an entry during the ensuing act and in most cases the act leads up to that entry. In *Or* Orestes' awakening is equivalent to an entry; and in *Hel* there is dramatic point to the lack of entry (see pp. 248–9), such as is hard to make out for *Ag*.

Two related points of structural technique conspire to push Clytemnestra's entry to the end of the song. As pointed out on 40*, it is common for the chorus to arrive in ignorance and have the situation explained later. In some instances of this pattern the character who explains the situation is already on-stage (e.g. A. *Prom*, S. *El*, E. *Hkld*, *Hel*); otherwise he enters at the end of the parodos (e.g. S. *Aj*, E. *Alc*, *Hipp*, *Med*). For the special exceptions, S. *OC* and E. *IT*, see the previous paragraph. The second point is that the end of the parodos is often exploited for the first entry of a dominant, often 'resident', character, and the

---

[1] Some have thought that in E. *Ion* Ion re-enters during the parodos at 219 (e.g. Detscheff 50, Verrall *Ion ed* 19, 21, Owen *ed* 82): but there is no good reason for ever sending him off.

following scene tends to be a kind of showpiece for him. Examples
are A. *Pers* (no prologue), S. *Ant, Phil,* E. *Med, Hipp, Hik, Andr,
Her* (cf. *Ion, Hyps*). Of course this is not invariable; sometimes
such a character, if there is one, is encountered in the prologue
(e.g. A. *Seven*, S. *OT*), sometimes his first entry is delayed even
further (e.g. S. *Aj*, E. *Alc, Ba*). Nevertheless this is a simple and
common structural procedure, and one might expect *Ag* to fit it.

Together these points against the early entry are considerable.
The case becomes irresistible, I suggest, when the silence which
would result from the early entry is considered in its full dramatic
context. The main points were made in *Silences* 90: that Clytemnestra's silence after 103 would be unexplained and inexplicable;
and that 258–63 at the end would be impossibly incongruous.
Moreover there would be no other character in Greek tragedy
who enters by himself and yet remains silent for a fraction of
the length of time that Clytemnestra is supposed to be 'busy
with the sacrifices'. When characters enter they speak unless
there is some good dramatic reason why they should not.[1]

There is, finally, a variation on the early entry which eludes
some of the objections which have been raised. Hermann (*ed* 373)
supposed that Clytemnestra entered at 83, and then at the end
of the anapaests (103) departed to supervise matters in the city,
to return at the end of the song.[2] This would mean that she was
not on-stage throughout the strophic song proper, and that there
would be an entry at the end. But then we have an extraordinary
unexplained silent appearance during 83–103. Very occasionally
a major character in Greek tragedy will make a completely
silent appearance, e.g. Tecmessa at S. *Aj* 1168ff., Alcestis at E.
Alc 1008ff., Orestes and Pylades at *IT* 1222–8; but all these are
clearly indicated and explained in the text. Hermann's alternative still runs up against most of the objections raised above.
And the problem of the lack of reply at 103 is further aggravated.

The second part of my argument has tried to show that

[1] There are a couple of other more dubious points. It could be claimed (e.g.
Dignan 26, Groeneboom 134 n. 8) that the subject-matter of the song would be
'in bad taste' if sung in the presence of the Queen; but I doubt whether this notion
would emerge in performance. It might also be objected that, if she entered early,
Clytemnestra would not be introduced or identified. But after the prologue,
especially 25ff., there is no need of any identification, and the questions in 83ff.
would make things clear enough.

[2] Similar compromises in e.g. Keck 25 n. 7, 55, 57, Richter 137, Sidgwick 10,
Murray 209, Winnington-Ingram 130, Rose 12, Hammond 435.

Clytemnestra's entry should come at the end of the song unless there is some very pressing and effective justification for her entry earlier. The first part set out to show that the considerations offered in favour of an entry at 40 or 83 are far from sufficient to admit such extraordinary dramatic technique. The price is too high for such little advantage. I can hardly hope to have said the last word on such a gnarled old problem, but I hold that the case for entry at the end of the song is all but conclusive.

(b) introduction and timing

I shall now take it as settled that Clytemnestra first entered at the end of the song. Her entry is then prepared for both by the references to her in the prologue and by the questions and demands of 83ff. It is *her* entry that is to be expected since she is the person who has the important information and she is the dominant 'resident' (see pp. 283 f. above). In fact, if anyone but Clytemnestra were to have entered at this point it would have been an extremely surprising turn.

But there is still disagreement over the exact timing of her entry. It hangs on whether the phrase τόδ' ἄγχιστον Ἀπίας γαίας μονόφρουρον ἕρκος in 256f. should be taken as referring to Clytemnestra or to the chorus, a decision which also faces those who have brought her on early.[1] In performance, no doubt a gesture would have settled the matter, but we have to weigh the considerations of meaning and of dramatic technique.

First, verbal considerations. The most important word is ἄγχιστον. The literal spatial sense is out of favour, yet this is quite possible and would presumably favour Clytemnestra (cf. Kranz *Studien* 272 n. 21, *LSJ*). Alternatively she is also ἄγχιστον to the King in her relationship, and she is also μονόφρουρον because she is without her husband. How, on the other hand, could the word be construed with reference to the chorus? 'Closest to the throne'? Some have referred to the chorus of *Pers*: but the chorus of *Ag* is not apparently of elder statesmen,

[1] The majority of scholars favour a reference to Clytemnestra and include Hermann 388, Wecklein 50, Headlam *ed* 63, 110, Hense 32, 177f., Groeneboom 168, Kranz 165 cf. *Studien* 271f., Fraenkel ii 144f., Peradotto *AJP* 90 (1969) 2, 13: in favour of self-reference by the chorus see the scholiast in M, and e.g. Conington 31, Paley 367, D–P 92f., Lloyd-Jones *tr* 30, Kaimio 45, Hammond 436 n. 89.

but simply of old citizens.[1] D–P 93 argue for the sense 'a very present help', and refer to Pindar *P* 9. 64. But there at the climax of his eulogy of Aristaeus Chiron says he will be held as ἀνδράϲι χάρμα φίλοιϲ / ἄγχιϲτον ὀπάονα μήλων: whether ἄγχιϲτον is taken with ὀπάονα or with χάρμα, it is clearly an epithet particularly suitable to a supernatural presence. It would perhaps be too extravagant for the Old Men to use the word of themselves. Moreover it is incongruous for them to call themselves a μονόφρουρον ἕρκοϲ after their own account of their impotent senility in 72–82; and the use of μονόφρουρον might imply a condemnation of Clytemnestra which would be inappropriate at this stage of the play.

D–P (92f.) argue, on the other hand, that the chorus knows all about Clytemnestra, and that it would therefore be contradictory for it to hope that things will turn out as *she* wishes. But we cannot extrapolate from later in the play a body of knowledge which can then be attributed to the chorus earlier. It is very doubtful whether it makes sense to think of the chorus as having a body of knowledge. D–P refer to ll. 154f. as showing that they 'are aware that Agamemnon is in danger of death at her hands on his return'. But how can one possibly give the lyric quotation of a cryptic prophecy some epistemological status for the chorus? If this is 'knowledge' for the Old Men, then it must be for Agamemnon, since he too heard Calchas. There is at this stage of the play no verbal or dramatic objection to taking 255–7 as a rather heavy courtesy to Clytemnestra in much the same strain as 258ff. But, while the sense of the words favour her, we cannot finally exclude a self-reference by the chorus; and if, as a plain fact of stage performance, Clytemnestra had not yet entered and there was no gesture in her direction, then the words might perhaps make sense as an extravagant expression of loyalty.

Secondly, we should consider the issue from the angle of dramatic technique. In favour of a reference to Clytemnestra Headlam (*ed* 190, endorsed by Fraenkel ii 144) says 'it was the almost invariable practice of the Greek stage for a character on the first appearance to be announced and described'. But this simply is not true. In Aeschylus, in fact, more entries are not

---

[1] Contrast the formal vocatives at *Pers* 171, 681f. with *Ag* 855, 1393, 1657. Paley (367) talks of members of Agamemnon's βουλή but there is nothing more to justify this than the phrase πρέϲβοϲ Ἀργείων (855, 1393).

announced than are announced, and in Sophocles and Euripides it was by no means invariable. Later in this play Agamemnon, Cassandra, and Aegisthus are not announced; nor are Xerxes, Oceanus, Io, or Athena, for example. In any case, this periphrasis can hardly be said to 'announce and describe' Clytemnestra: the τόδε would be a very casual and untypical announcement of arrival.[1] Kranz (165 cf. *Studien* 271f.) also favours an entry announcement: he finds the transition by means of δ' οὖν characteristic of Aeschylus. But it could be countered that the particular and rather fulsome courtesy would follow incongruously on the lyric breadth of the preceding lines.

On the other side, in favour of a self-reference by the chorus Lloyd-Jones (*tr* 30) comments 'there is no instance of a chorus introducing an actor who enters the stage before the singing of the ode is finished'. This also may be an overstatement: some lyric entrance announcements are collected on *Seven* 854c*. But the device is rare, and it is doubtful whether there is another instance in Aeschylus. Moreover it is common for the chorus to refer to itself (though usually in the first person) at the end of a song, as is illustrated by Kranz himself (121f. cf. Kaimio 45ff.). So while the argument from dramatic technique is also inconclusive, it weighs against an announcement of Clytemnestra and in favour of a self-reference by the chorus.

At present I see no way of deciding with any confidence whether Clytemnestra entered at 255 or 258. But I have a slight preference for 258, since, if it is once granted that in performance the words of 255–7 could be made to refer to either Clytemnestra or the chorus, then considerations of dramatic technique favour the latter.

Lines 258–63 are addressed to Clytemnestra after she has entered, and are thus what I have called a 'greeting' as opposed to an announcement (see *Pers* 155a*). Honorific addresses of this kind usually only occur where the character has entered on a chariot, and may derive from that situation. The only other exception seems to be E. *Or* 352–5, where Menelaus' entry was a highly ornate progress (349). Perhaps in the case of Clytemnestra the honorific address indicates not so much pomp and splendour as extreme deference (thus cεβίζων in 258 is nearly

---

[1] Murray with justification wrote in the margin of his copy of Headlam (in the Ashmolean Museum Library) 'but not in a riddling paraphrase'.

always used of divine honour). The greeting conveys the awe in which Clytemnestra is held in Argos. If 255-7 are not an announcement of her entry, then the address in 258ff. comes abruptly without any introduction. This is unusual; but there is no announcement before the greeting of Agamemnon (at 783a*) nor for the chariot entry of Rhesus at *Rh* 380.[1] But these entries are from an eisodos, while Clytemnestra only has to appear in the skene doorway. A sudden entry in the doorway might prepare the way for her later dramatic appearances (see 587*, 855*, and 1372a*). Indeed the characteristic abruptness of her entry might be rather more striking if 255-7 is not an announcement. Further, 258-63 repeat in speech what has been excitedly chanted at 83ff., and it could be argued that, if Clytemnestra has been on-stage throughout the song, then these lines would make a strange beginning to the new act (contrast *Hik* and *Cho* where Danaus and Electra are the first to speak). They make better sense as a greeting to the new entry. For if she had been on throughout 83ff., the act could well have started with line 264; while if she has just entered for the first time the lines have more point. On the other hand 83ff. is by now so long past that either way the thread has to be taken up again.

350 exit Clytemnestra

does Clytemnestra go at 350 or 354 ?

Very nearly everyone sends Clytemnestra off at 354 before the choral song; but there has been the odd exception.[2] There is no unequivocal indication that she goes, but there should be a very good reason for departing from the normal pattern of an exit before the act-dividing song and an empty stage during it. I collected on *Pers* 622* all the places in Aeschylus where an actor stays on during an act-dividing song, and, while they amount to 8 instances out of a possible 22 (or 5 out of 19 if you leave *Prom* out of account), we can none the less see in each case why it is divergent from the normal pattern, and how either the actor

---

[1] In quite a different context the unannounced arrival of Odysseus is greeted at S. *Aj* 1316f. (*Eum* 574f. is often taken in this way, but I argue on *Eum* 574* that that must be wrong.)

[2] Spitzbarth 76, D-P 117, Lattimore *tr* (*ex silentio*). Bodensteiner 731 puts a question mark, and Richter 155, Deckinger 34 n. I consider keeping Clytemnestra on but think better of it. Some have forgotten the stage direction, notably Wilamowitz *ed maj*, Smyth, Lloyd-Jones *tr* (though they mark her later re-entry).

is made relevant to the song (e.g. *Pers* 628ff., *Eum* 307ff.), or there is a dramatic consideration which keeps him on (e.g. Danaus, Prometheus). But there is no such justification for the presence of Clytemnestra. And while there are many places where the stage is not cleared of actors during an act-dividing song, there are many fewer where there is no exit before one. In fact, there are only two straightforward examples from over 100 possible places: *Pers* 622* and *Prom* 525 (see 436*). We should require a really good reason for keeping Clytemnestra here before admitting her as the third unqualified example.

D–P supply no such reason. In *Silences* 89–92 I considered and rejected their argument from dramatic effect: during this song Clytemnestra would either have to remain totally unnoticed or be a distracting irrelevance. I shall argue on 503a* that D–P are also mistaken to keep her on in order to announce the Herald at 489ff. Even if their attribution were right, it would be preferable to send Clytemnestra off here and to bring her back on at 489 (see p. 296 below).

Assuming, then, that Clytemnestra went off here, it only remains to explain why I suspect that she went soon after her last line (350) rather than waiting until 354, which is where the stage instruction has always been put. First consider the function of 351–4. The first line is a reply to the Queen, but the next three, although they refer to her in the second person, are rather a transition to the following song, which also has an anapaestic prelude characteristic of early tragedy (355–66, see Kranz *Forma* 48f., *Stas* 135, 166). For a speech transition to such anapaests cf. *Pers* 619–22 (spoken by an actor), *Eum* 303–6. With ἐγὼ δέ in 352 the chorus turns, in effect, from Clytemnestra to the impending song (cf. p. 137 above). So if Clytemnestra did not wait patiently through these four lines, it cannot be claimed that she rudely turned her back on the chorus.

Note next the irregularity of a departure without speaking the last word on exit: see p. 205 above. For Clytemnestra to wait in silence for the chorus might suggest some modesty or submissiveness on her part, which is hardly appropriate. Besides, elsewhere the silent actor always waits during the lines of another actor or of actor and chorus combined, and never, so far as I can recall, during the words of chorus alone (on the apparent exception at *Hik* 966–76 see *Hik* 974a*). On the other hand, it is common for

chorus to cast lines at a departing back, see *Hik* 951*, and I
ggest that this device would account satisfactorily for the
cond-person verb and pronoun.

Clytemnestra's last three lines (348–50) form a coda to her
appearance. In 348 τοιαῦτα and κλύεις are both regular 'formulas'
for summing up; for the combination cf. *Ag* 580 and 680 (see
Fraenkel ii 178 and 305f.). The next line is a wish, and prayers
or wishes are very common on exit; see p. 306 below. And the
last line (350) is an explanation of the prayer introduced by γάρ,
also a common exit formula (cf. A. *Seven* 77, S. *OC* 1446,
E. *Hipp* 120, *IT* 1087). All three of these constructions are also
found at the end of rheses, and so they are not necessarily a sign
that Clytemnestra goes: the point is that in a context where an
exit is due they show that the end of the speech is meant to be
accompanied by the exit.

The upshot of these points is that all the signs suggest that
Clytemnestra was meant to turn to go after 350, and that 351–4,
or at least 351, were said to her back. Of course we cannot say
exactly when she turned, nor precisely when she went out of
sight; and such things are not important to a commentator as
they are to a producer. But still it may be worth the trouble to
follow the evidence of the text and to put the stage direction by
350 (or 351) rather than at 354, as has been done by every editor
who has bothered to add any stage direction at all.

489 (the chorus remains)

the semblance of continuity of time

Verrall's fantastical conjuring of sub-intrigues from beneath the
seeming surface of *Ag* took as its starting-point the 'fact' (noted
by the scholiast on 503) that the Herald and Agamemnon close
after him arrive within an hour or so of the beacons, although
they have had to cross the Aegean, weather a terrible storm, and
so on. In order to meet this 'fact' Blomfield's old theory, that
the passage of several days at this juncture of the play was marked
by the departure and fresh re-entry of the chorus, has been
revived.[1] But there is no explicit sign of this in the text, and it
would be quite unlike those genuine places where the chorus
goes off and returns: see *Eum* 231*, 244a*. Verrall's theory and

---

[1] See A. E. A. W. Smyth *introd* to Headlam *ed* 9, Campbell 88, Murray 213,
tr 55.

this false reply to it are both based on a failure to realize that real time as shown by the clock has no relation to the progress of a play which is entirely under the control of the playwright (provided he is a good one).

The strict application of neo-Aristotelian canons of the unity of time and place, and the consequent discomfort at their in-applicability, have now been long abandoned.[1] But in their place there seems to be no accepted notion of just how time and place are handled in Greek tragedy, although these are basic aspects of dramatic technique. I have discussed the handling of place on *Pers* 598c*, and shall digress here briefly on the handling of time.

The continuous presence of the chorus and the lack of vacant-stage act-divisions do not allow specific lapses of time during the course of a Greek tragedy; or even if they do not forbid them, they do not occur (I note that at Arph. *Lys* 705/6 there is an explicit lapse of time although the chorus does not leave the stage). In post-classical tragedy when the chorus had no integral part in the play, then lapses of time could occur between acts (see p. 49 n. 2); but in the whole of surviving tragedy the only explicit time lapse is at A. *Eum* 234/5 after the Erinyes leave Delphi and before Orestes arrives at Athens. The intervening time is left vague—see *Eum* 235*. There may, of course, be a passage of time between the plays of a trilogy; but within the plays 'the continuity of performance gave a *semblance* of continuity also to the action', as Flickinger (255) well puts it.[2]

The reason why Flickinger says 'semblance' is that it would be quite wrong to suppose that, because a tragedy takes, say, two hours to perform, the duration of its action is therefore to be taken to be two hours. Dramatists do not deal in 'clock time' but in 'dramatic time'. In the hands of a good dramatist 'clock

---

[1] For a brief survey of the history of the 'Aristotelian unities' see Gudeman Arle. *Poet ed* 155–8.

[2] Flickinger's whole discussion (250–68) is valuable, cf. also Goodell *Athenian Tragedy* (New Haven 1920) 89ff. I have found little of value in Felsch *Quibus artificiis . . . tragici Graeci unitates . . . observaverunt* (diss. Wroclaw 1906). (The dissertations on similar topics by Nilsson (Lund 1884) and Wolf (?1911) have not been available to me.) De Romilly *Time in Greek Tragedy* (Cornell 1968) is using tragedy as a source for the history of ideas, and does not descend to the actual treatment of time in the theatre. The handling of time in Shakespeare is a much more complex matter because of his multiplicity of scenes. E. Jones *Scenic Form in Shakespeare* 41ff. seems particularly enlightening.

time' can be compressed or expanded as required, and the audience is obliged to acquiesce in this. To facilitate their fluid treatment of time the Greek tragedians make sparing references to the time of day and its passing. There may be references to dawn or evening, 'just now' or 'soon' or 'today'; but never in such a way as to invite the audience to consider precisely how long has elapsed between one part of the play and another. Occasionally some point is made of the enclosure of the tragic events within a single day, but the temporal framework is never made more rigid than that.[1] In general, while there is always the sense that the crucial series of events is taking place in a brief span of time, indeed in a continuous sequence, the passage of time in the literal sense is suppressed in the service of the dramatic use of time.

Anyone who has been an involved spectator of the performance of a play will have had his sense of time manipulated by a dramatist, whether he realizes it or not. The minute hand on his wrist moves at quite a different speed, faster or slower, from the time within the play. The most striking example I know is in the last scene of Marlowe's *Dr. Faustus*, when Faustus is left alone to his damnation. The clock strikes eleven—'Ah, Faustus, / Now hast thou but one bare hour to live'; thirty lines later the clock strikes the half-hour, and a mere twenty lines later it strikes midnight. Yet in the audience's mind the scene lasts not one minute more or less than one whole hour. It was astoundingly bold of Marlowe actually to play off the clock against dramatic time; and Greek tragedy is never so reckless as this. But in the Cassandra scene in A. *Ag*, aided by the scene's visionary perspective which moves freely in time, the dramatic time is, so to speak, suspended for more than 200 lines: see p. 322 below. A remarkable, though different, compression of time is contrived in *Seven* (cf. p. 140 above). The enemy is already advancing during the first song (78ff.) and the battle is joined during the second (288ff.); yet Eteocles does not go to his death until 719. Throughout the great central scene (369–676) the dramatic movement goes forward so relentlessly and exclusively that the battle outside, in a way, stops.

[1] See e.g. S. *Aj* 753–7, E. *Hipp* 21f. This is more of a commonplace in New Comedy, see Austin Men. *Aspis ed* ii 40; none the less Daos quotes the reversals of a single day at *Aspis* 417f. as a typically tragic sentiment.

These are examples of a kind of dramatic foreshortening: but the opposite effect is more common. The compression of time occurs particularly in messenger contexts. Seldom if ever is there enough time, literally speaking, in between the departure of the main characters to a catastrophic event and the arrival of the messenger to report it for the things which he reports to have happened. But the tension of such situations is enough to bridge the gap in terms of dramatic time.[1] This place in *Agam* is simply an extreme example of such dramatic compression of time. Comparably in *Pers* Xerxes follows 'too soon' after the advance runner. But there is no problem in performance. There is no question of days elapsing at some particular point; simply the intervening dramatic time is enough to preserve a semblance of continuity of action.

It is often said that longer or shorter stretches of time elapse, or may be supposed to have elapsed, during the choral songs (this notion is fully developed by Kent in *TAPA* 37 (1906) 39ff.). This seems to me a misconceived doctrine which allows too much weight to calculations of extra-dramatic time. We are nowhere told before or after any particular choral song that a given time is passed over during it; and, if the audience is given no indication, then how is it to know which songs are supposed to have bridged some gap and how long, and which songs simply intervene in a continuous action? None the less there is a germ of truth in this misconception, since choral songs help the dramatist to control his dramatic time. The songs tend to move away from the temporal world of the action into a more abstract and timeless world of lyric, and this helps to divert attention away from any unhelpful preoccupation with 'clock time'. Thus, to give a random example, the song at S. *OC* 1044–95, which leaves Colonus and invokes the battle through lyric presentiment, makes dramatic time for the events off-stage.

Aeschylus' technique in this particular place in *Agam* is authoritatively treated by Fraenkel ii 254–6. Yet D–P do not

---

[1] Cf. Winnington-Ingram *Arethusa* 2 (1969) 131f. It is possible that in E. *Andr* we are to suppose that at 1008 Orestes leaves Phthia for Delphi and at 1070 the messenger arrives from Delphi to tell of his deeds there. Those who wish may, however, avoid this particularly drastic compression of time, see Stevens E. *Andr* ed 211–13. In comedy a particularly rapid slide of time—so rapid as to be perhaps deliberately fantastical—occurs in Arph. *Acharn*: the supernatural Amphitheus is dispatched to Sparta at l. 132, and returns, mission accomplished, at 176.

seem to have understood Fraenkel fully, since they still speak of
'an extreme example of an indifference to chronological probability characteristic of tragedy'. It is not a matter of indifference
or of probability, since the impression of continuous time is preserved. In fact Aeschylus takes positive care to ensure that in
performance nothing seems chronologically improbable.

On the theory that Clytemnestra re-entered at this point see
p. 296 below.

503 enter Agamemnon's Herald

(a) the attribution of the announcement 489–502

I have briefly treated this problem in *Silences* 91, but since it is
a hotly disputed issue, I shall discuss it more fully here. The
manuscripts (F and Tr) attribute 489–500 to Clytemnestra and
501–2 to the chorus. The very first point to clear up is that these
attributions can be allowed no authority whatsoever. Recently
published Ptolemaic papyri of E. *Erechtheus* and Men. *Sik* confirm the conclusions of Andrieu and Lowe that our textual tradition has been through a stage when there was little or no
attribution of parts, that is to say that all or most attributions in
our manuscripts are pure conjecture.[1] Even without the conclusive evidence of early papyri, a glance at the apparatus of
Ag shows how unreliable the manuscript attributions can be
(note attributions to ἄγγελος φύλαξ at 258, 264, 269, 271, etc.,
and to Clytemnestra at 622, 626, 630, 634). On the other hand
the actual paragraphoi must be allowed some textual authority
through continuous transmission, though they are easily corrupted.[2] So, since an ordinary entrance announcement is never,

---

[1] Andrieu *passim* esp. 258ff., Lowe *BICS* 9 (1962) 27ff. (on Aristophanes) cf.
Handley Men. *Dysc ed* 44–9, West *Textual Criticism* etc. (Stuttgart 1973) 55.
Andrieu 268 tellingly illustrates wrong attributions in the papyri. I have noted
an interesting example of scribal conjecture over the attribution of parts in the
papyrus of E. *Hypsipyle*: at fr. 64 l. 69 (p. 47 Bond) the papyrus has in the margin
οἱ Ὑψιπ(ύλης) υἱοί which implies that the two lines of farewell which begin
εὐδαιμονοίης should be spoken one by each twin. But Dale *JHS* 84 (1964) 167
points out that Hypsipyle herself must thank Amphiaraus (and note also that only
one of the twins can be a speaking actor in this part of the play): so one line
should go to Hypsipyle, the other to one of the two sons. On the strength of the
'twin' openings of the two lines a scribe has conjectured a false attribution.

[2] Johansen A. *Hik ed* 23 reports that out of 172 changes of speaker in *Hik* M
has marked only 72 even by a new paragraphos.

so far as can be told, split among members of the chorus (*contra* Wilamowitz 168f. and others), the attribution of 489–502 to the chorus would involve emending away the paragraphos before line 501. But Fraenkel ii 253f. gives several examples of places where the closing lines of a speech have been wrongly cut off and attributed to another speaker.

I contend that the prima facie case here favours attribution to the chorus, and the onus of proof is on those who favour Clytemnestra. First, entrance announcements are usually made by the chorus. This is by no means invariable in later tragedy,[1] but the only proper announcement in Aeschylus which is made by an actor once the chorus is on the scene is *Prom* 941–3 (see 944*). Secondly there is no explicit sign that Clytemnestra is present between 355 and 585, and there is no hindrance to her exit and re-entry, so the presumption is that she is off-stage unless some good reason to the contrary is produced. I have already argued on 350* that she did exit then, and I shall consider below whether there is any reason to bring her back before 587.

Besides the manuscript attribution there are three points which are usually put forward by those who favour Clytemnestra.[2] The first is the transmitted reading of 496 ὡς οὔτ᾽ ἄναυδος οὔτε coι δαίων φλόγα . . . cημανεῖ. If the lines are spoken by the chorus and the Queen is not there, then no sense can be made of coι. Nevertheless, even if Clytemnestra speaks the lines, it would still be rather obtrusive: it 'specializes awkwardly and unnecessarily' (Maas *apud* D–P 118). So there is a case for emendation, whoever speaks the lines. Wilamowitz's ἄναυδος οὗτος, οὐ δαίων has been widely accepted; but simpler and preferable are οὔτε τον (Hermann) or οὔτε μοι (Butler, Kirchhoff)—the first-person ethic dative is much more acceptable. Secondly it is argued that the asyndeton at 501 demands a change of speaker; but it is doubtful whether such an asyndeton is impossible for Aeschylus (see Fraenkel ii 253). On the other side, there is no comparable spoken entry announcement which is shared between more than one speaker, whether members of the chorus or actor and chorus (a comparison with the nearest analogies, S. *El* 1429ff., E. *Or*

---

[1] Hourmouziades 139 calculates that in Euripides there are 36 announcements by actors and 49 by the chorus.

[2] They include Dindorf, Conington, Wilamowitz *Analecta* 201 (only), Karsten 39, 185f., Prickard *CR* 14 (1900) 434ff., D–P 116f., Dale *Papers* 215, Lloyd-Jones *tr* 43.

456ff., *El* 962ff., makes the point). This objection to a change
of speaker at 501 applies whether the main part is attributed to
Clytemnestra or to the chorus; and so if the asyndeton is considered intolerable without a change of speaker, then perhaps a
simple emendation is called for.[1]

So, the case for attributing 489ff. to Clytemnestra is far weaker
than the case against it.[2] Above all it is not enough to justify
her presence throughout 355ff. nor through 503–84, where she
has no place. A final word is needed on some attempts to miti-
gate her prolonged irrelevance. It has been suggested by Karsten
(39, 185f.) and recently by Lloyd-Jones (*tr* 43) that she was
indeed off-stage during the choral song, but re-entered at 489.
There are some places, though most of them are debatable,
where a character enters from the skene to meet a new arrival,
and where it may be supposed he has been looking out for the
newcomer: the clearest examples are at S. *Trach* 971, E. *Her* 701
(more dubious are E. *Med* 1116, *Hkld* 784, *Hel* 1512, *Ba* 434,
and *Rh* 264). But here, supposedly, Clytemnestra enters not to
meet the Herald but to announce him. The only comparable
place I can think of is S. *Aj* 1223 where Teucer rushes on because
he has seen the approach of Agamemnon (cf. also Arph. *Lys*
829): but the situation in *Aj* is perfectly clear, and it contrasts
significantly with this long announcement in *Ag* which gives the
impression that the Herald has only just been sighted at this
moment. Another point against the theory is that 489ff. take up
the preoccupations of the preceding epode (475ff.), a technique
of binding act to song which is discussed by Deckinger 54f.,
Kranz 166. Compare particularly the close connection made by
τάχ' εἰσόμεσθα (489) with the use of the same phrase at S. *Ant*
631, *OT* 84, and a similar one at A. *Pers* 246. It would seem
therefore that the announcement should be made by someone
who was present during the epode.

Finally it has also been suggested that Clytemnestra might go

[1] e.g. χώςτιϲ τάδ' Wilamowitz; see Wecklein *Appendix* for other suggestions e.g.
ὥϲτ' εἴ τιϲ Hense, ὅϲτιϲ γὰρ Margoliouth.

[2] I hope to have dealt sufficiently with other minor arguments for Clytemnestra
in *Silences* 91–2. These are that the lines are in character for Clytemnestra and
out of character for the chorus, that the speech is too highly wrought (but cf.
Eum 244ff.) or too long for the chorus (but see p. 208 and 503b* below). I have
also criticized there D–P's claim that Clytemnestra has to be on-stage during
503–86 in order to know that Agamemnon has landed.

off at line 537 to return at 587.¹ But this unnoticed flitting to and fro is unlike the open technique of Greek tragedy—and the arguments adduced for sending her off at 537 are even worse than the arguments for having her on during 503ff.²

(b) long announcements and suspense

Fourteen lines make a long entry announcement. While extended announcements are not uncommon in tragedy, they are usually adapted into the form of a dialogue. It was suggested on *Hik* 234a* that long announcements may have been more frequent before the skene was introduced when the illusion of seeing someone in the far distance was easier to sustain; and this announcement might be a vestigial trace of earlier techniques. But in surviving tragedy the factor which produces a long entry announcement is not date of performance, nor the identity of the entrant and his social standing, nor the ceremoniousness of the entry: it is the dramatic tension of his arrival. Always the arrival is very welcome or unwelcome or in some way of particular emotional significance. By prolonging the introduction the playwright increases apprehension and expectancy about the entry. At S. *Phil* 201–18, for example, what will Philoctetes be like? At *OC* 310–23 there is the emotion of reunion; at E. *El* 962–87 the approach of Clytemnestra brings Orestes' conflict to a crisis (cf. S. *El* 1429–42); at E. *Or* 456–69 how will Tyndareus react?³ The lines in *Ag* contain several of the most common devices for building up tension through an entrance announcement. They anticipate the resolution of ignorance (cf. e.g. A. *Pers* 245, S. *OT* 84, E. *Med* 1116ff.), and they anticipate news (see p. 147). They also speculate on the possible alternative significances of the approach (cf. e.g. A. *Hik* 184ff., *Cho* 10ff.,

¹ Attributed to D. S. Robertson by D–P 117 who consider the idea 'attractive'. Prickard op. cit. 435 suggests that she might have gone off at 502: that means that she announces the Herald with eager anticipation and then does not wait to hear his news!

² 'She should set all her secret machinery in motion at once; in particular she must tell the news to Aegisthus without delay' D–P 117. They speak as though off-stage everything was going on in reality, and as though all that the audience sees and hears is merely what happens to occur outside the front door.

³ Cf. also E. *Her* 514ff., 1153ff., *Ion* 392ff., *Hel* 857ff. (see Kannicht 230), *Or* 1311ff. For other examples see Bodensteiner 711ff. (Incidentally extended entrance announcements often contain questions: this helps to explain τί δὲ σημαίνει κα.[in l. 17 of the new fragment of E. *Phrixos* in *POxy* 2685, cf. e.g. E. *Tro* 233 and the use of τί ποτε at S. *Ant* 381, E. *Hik* 987, *El* 1233 etc.)

S. *Trach* 968ff., E. *Alc* 136ff.), describe the person approaching
(cf. e.g. A. *Hik* 180ff., 715ff., S. *Ant* 528ff., *OC* 310ff., E. *El*
107ff., *Phoen* 1332f.), and imply that he is approaching at speed
(see again p. 147).

In what way, then, is the entry of the Herald a matter of
suspense? His entry fits easily into the form of the play, in that
he has been prepared for 'situationally'. Jens (250f.) has discussed
Aeschylus' structural use of a situation of uncertainty followed
by the resolution of that uncertainty. There is uncertainty: the
Herald is required to resolve it.[1] *Pers* is distinctly similar (cf.
pp. 80–1 above), except that there the breaking of the uncertainty comes much earlier. The important difference in *Ag* is
that Clytemnestra's virtuoso account of the beacons has the
immediate effect of dissolving all uncertainty. This confidence
then has to be undermined so that we are once again in a state
of anxiety which the Herald can settle. This is, I think, the
dramatic purpose of the much-discussed epode 475ff., and
sufficient justification of it. The train of thought of the song has
been carefully led from confidence to misgiving about the meaning of the sack of Troy, and this leads easily into doubts about
the very fact of the sack. The justification for the contradictory
doubts lies primarily in the dramatic technique, as some scholars
have come to acknowledge.[2] The chorus—and the audience—
do not have Clytemnestra's confidence; for them the situation
is fraught with difficulty and paradox. The doubts of the epode
are then taken up in the entry announcement (see above), so
that by the time the Herald enters we, like the Old Men, are in
doubt once more about what the Herald is going to report.

We are kept in suspense by the announcement, and then the
Herald is so overcome with emotion that he does not make his
news clear until 522 on Agamemnon and 525 on Troy. Even a
messenger who has a κῆρυξ function (see *Pers* 249a*) would

[1] I suppose that if Agamemnon himself had entered at this juncture it could
be said that he had been prepared for situationally (as well as personally); but
I see no justification for Dawe's account of this moment (51), 'then a herald
when we are expecting the King'.

[2] Fraenkel ii 246ff. sees this, but also tries to give the epode some autonomous
psychological grounds. D–P 113f. avoid this mistake, but then castigate Aeschylus'
technique severely: this is because they criticize from the point of view of a reader
not of an audience. The sequence is understandable as a train of thought (cf.
Dover *JHS* 1973 p. 68); but its purpose is to prepare the ground for the Herald;
cf. Dawe 43ff., Lloyd-Jones *tr* 42.

normally unburden his news immediately; contrast *Pers* 255.
Instead the Herald opens with a moving address to his native
land. Fraenkel (ii 256f.) has illustrated from tragedy and comedy
how the first words of those returning from abroad are often of
this sort.[1] It is worth comparing and contrasting Agamemnon's
opening words on his entry (810ff.). The Herald in his first rush
of emotion recaptures some of the joy of the Watchman when he
first sees the beacon: but like the Watchman his unalloyed glad-
ness cannot be sustained. By the time that Agamemnon returns
the light which shines at the end of ten years of night, which we
have glimpsed earlier, has become overclouded (see 783a*): so
Agamemnon's return is cold.[2]

587 re-enter Clytemnestra

Clytemnestra's control of the threshold

If my arguments on 350* and 503a* are not completely awry it
will follow that Clytemnestra re-enters just before her rhesis at
587ff. There remains a small question of just when she enters.
After the Herald's speech (551–82), the chorus passes a couplet
of comment, and then adds (585f.) δόμοις δὲ ταῦτα καὶ Κλυται-
μήςτραι μέλειν / εἰκὸς μάλιστα, cὺν δὲ πλουτίζειν ἐμέ. The next line
is the first of Clytemnestra's speech. Is this couplet, as is usually
supposed,[3] said in accompaniment to Clytemnestra's entry, or is
it said before her entry and independently of it? If after 584 the
doors open and all attention is turned to Clytemnestra, and the
couplet is thus delivered as a kind of introduction, then it is
rather a strange arrangement. For the lines are not the usual
kind of announcement which points out the fact of the approach;
they would be, rather, a kind of polite but oblique introduction
of the parties and a modest withdrawal on the part of the chorus.
I suggest that the situation is clearer and dramatically more
effective if the lines are spoken before there is any sign that
Clytemnestra is about to enter.[4] In that case the couplet is, in
effect, a recommendation to the Herald that he should go indoors

---

[1] Cf. Steidle 19 n. 38. To Fraenkel's list may be added Eur. fr. 817 (*Phoinix*),
Men. fr. 287 (*Naukleros*), and probably *Aspis* 491; cf. also Austin on Men.
Sam 101.
[2] On the Herald scene as a whole see especially Reinhardt 80ff., Fraenkel ii 293.
[3] Thus e.g. Hense 68, Wecklein 72, Headlam *ed* 89, Sidgwick 35, Fraenkel ii 292.
[4] Cf. Deckinger 33, 55, approved by Groeneboom 219 n. 7.

and give his news to the Queen.[1] There would then be a kind of 'talk of the devil' entry (cf. *Seven* 39*). The Herald would be about to go inside and all attention would move towards the doors. At that very moment Clytemnestra, almost as though she knew that all thoughts were turned to her, appears at the door. So the intended exit of the Herald into the palace is prevented or postponed by a new entry, that of Clytemnestra.[2] This introduces a scenic and dramatic factor which will become more important and obvious as the play progresses: Clytemnestra controls the doorway. She is the watchdog (cf. 607), and the threshold may only be crossed under her eye. When the Herald is about to go in, she stands in his way. See further 855*, 1372a* for this theatrical theme.

The impression that Clytemnestra is in complete control and knows everything that needs to be known was built up in the previous act, and is now sustained both by the timing of her entry and by the ensuing scene. She knows who the Herald is (588 by implication) and how doubts about the beacons have been raised and settled (591ff.). She did not need to be present to have this superiority, which is typical of her role. Her abrupt, incisive entry without any introductory formalities, and again her abrupt, confident exit at 614 all contribute to this picture.[3]

614 exit Clytemnestra

entrance and exit without dialogue

There can be little doubt that Clytemnestra goes; the case against keeping her on is much the same as before.[4] She should

---

[1] It is possible that after 582 the Herald had made some move as if to go away. His last three lines are very conclusive: for l. 580 cf. p. 290 above; for πάντ' ἔχεις λόγον see Fraenkel ii 291 and *Phoen* 52 n. 1, and add Men. *Aspis* 82 and Austin ad loc. But these concluding phrases seem to mark the end of the speech only and not a frustrated exit.

[2] For exits postponed by a new entry in Sophocles and Euripides cf. e.g. S. *El* 1326, *OC* 887, E. *Andr* 1070, *IT* 1435, *IA* 414, 855.

[3] I should add a point to forestall a possible argument that Clytemnestra did not enter here, but was already on. Her opening words ἀνωλόλυξα μὲν πάλαι might seem at first glance like those of the Queen at *Pers* 290 σιγῶ πάλαι, and hence to imply that Clytemnestra has been similarly present in silence. But the sense and the tense of the verb make a vital difference: in *Pers* 'I have long remained silent', in *Ag* 'I raised my cry long ago'.

[4] Only D–P and Lattimore *tr* 53 keep her on; Kitto *Greek Tragedy*[3] (London 1961) 108 n. 1 and Lloyd-Jones *tr* 62 hesitate. Thomson[2] ii 64 supposes that Clytemnestra goes off here, but then brings her back on at νυμφόκλαυτος Ἐρινύς

614   ENTRANCE/EXIT WITHOUT DIALOGUE   301

go after her last words, namely 613f.[1] Clearly she went immediately after her last line. She may well have delivered her entire
speech from the threshold, and so have had very little way to go.

Assuming that Clytemnestra entered at 587 and went off at
614, then it is noteworthy, though it has never been noted, that
her entire appearance is taken up with her single speech and no
one else speaks while she is on. In performance the unusual
technique of this abrupt appearance would, I suggest, have made
a distinct impression. There are other very brief appearances in
Aeschylus, e.g. *Seven* 792–819 or *Cho* 838–54 (see *Cho* 854*), but
they include some dialogue. Places where there is no dialogue
at all in between the entry and departure of a character are
positively few. Solo prologues (πρόcωπα προτακτικά) and divine
speeches *ex machina* are special cases; and, once these are left
out of account, there are, so far as I know, only two other such
places. One is the Scout in the threatening military situation of
Seven 39–68: see *Seven* 39*. The other is Ajax at S. *Aj* 646–92,
the *Trugrede*. No one else speaks during the entire act which
comes between two act-dividing choral songs. However we are
to interpret the speech, its structural position, which frames it
boldly without any dialogue, throws it into prominent relief,
and shows that its significance within the tragedy must be
crucial. Comparably, though less central and significant, the
isolation of Clytemnestra's rhesis here has dramatic point. She is
aloof and in complete control; she seems almost omniscient. Her
speech is bold and incisive; it wastes no words, it says the right
things, and yet it has a second meaning quite other than its

749. Even if the dramatic technique were not utterly abnormal, the stage directions
of Greek tragedy do not work in this allusive, devious way. Murray 216 speaks as
though Clytemnestra were present during 810ff., and Arnott 38f. seems to think
that she is the first to speak on Agamemnon's return. For the case against her
staying see *Silences* 92–3. Her silent presence throughout the intervening scenes
before 854 is highly undesirable, and her entry at 855 is essential (see 855*).

[1] The manuscripts are said to attribute the couplet to the Herald (though
Page *OCT* does not report this); but Fraenkel ii 305f. shows conclusively that it
is the last two lines of Clytemnestra's speech. One contributory point is that 611f.
would be insufficiently final, and so unsatisfactory as exit lines, while 613f. are
quite appropriate. With 617–19, the chorus turns to the Herald again and brings
up the topic of Menelaus. For cὺ δέ marking a change of subject after an exit,
cf. on p. 137 and n. 1. It is hard to make any sense of the intervening couplet 615f.,
which Page *OCT* obelizes; it was presumably some comment on Clytemnestra's
contribution. One of the main troubles is μανθάνοντί coι: it does not seem right that
the coι should refer to the Herald when he is going to be turned to with cὺ δέ in 617.

surface. Aeschylus conveys her aloofness, efficiency, and ruth-
lessness by framing this speech starkly with an abrupt entry and
exit. Wilamowitz 171 comments on this scene 'die Technik ist in
der Tat recht kunstlos': but the unsoftened spareness shows the
art of a great master.

680 exit Herald

modest exit

The Herald goes presumably down an eisodos. Those with sharp
memories will remember that Clytemnestra gave him a message
to take to Agamemnon (cf. 604); but this has been overlaid and
is irrelevant to his exit. Contrast the dispatch of the herald
Lichas at S. *Trach* 616ff.: there his mission is important. The
Herald simply goes without ceremony after his last line, which
is an exemplary exit line (cf. p. 290 above).

783 enter Agamemnon and Cassandra

(a) preparation and greeting: the light obscured

Agamemnon is made around the return of Agamemnon; and the
first part of the play has been leading up to this. On *Pers* 909b*
I considered the pattern of 'νόϲτοϲ-plays' and some similarities
in this respect between the preparation for Xerxes and that for
Agamemnon, e.g. the relevance of the departure, the advance
messenger (cf. Nestle in 'Droysen' *tr* 184). But while in *Pers*
everything is directed towards Xerxes, even the recollection of
Darius and of the past glory of Persia, in *Ag* the part of Clytemnestra and the choral treatment of the past of the royal house and
of Troy look both to Agamemnon and beyond. Thus, for example,
the first song of *Pers* treats the Persian departure as the vision of
a spectacular host which will contrast with the shabby remnants
on return: the first song of *Ag* is largely taken up with Aulis.

I noted on 503b* how, while in *Pers* the uncertainty is quickly
disposed of by the Messenger, in *Ag* the anxiety is dispelled by
Clytemnestra only to gather again before the Herald. But he
clearly prepares for the imminent return of the King, most
explicitly by ἥκει in a stressed position in 522 and again in 531.
And Clytemnestra will hear all the news from Agamemnon
himself (599), she must strive to receive him in the best way
(600f.), she will open the doors to him (601ff.), and finally at
the end of her message she dwells on his return (605ff.).

Agamemnon has been primarily prepared for as the triumphant victor over Troy (e.g. 264ff., 355ff., 524ff., 575ff.), as the light out of the darkness (e.g. 25ff., 264ff., 522). And it is this aspect which is taken up in the choral greeting at 783ff. But the picture is already clouded: the sacrifice of Iphigenia, the dreadful war all for one woman, the loss of Menelaus, the resentment of the people, the threat of Clytemnestra. The light is by this stage obscured, though it is not yet extinguished.

There is a similar tension between triumph and foreboding when Agamemnon actually arrives. Our uncertainty over the precise timing of the entry makes it difficult, however, to gauge the tone and undertone with any confidence. The progress of Agamemnon's chariot is greeted at length in anapaests by the chorus (783–809, and probably a lacuna between 794 and 795). It was seen on *Pers* 155a* and 155b* that chariot-borne entries were probably quite common in early tragedy and that they are usually accompanied by choral anapaests of this sort. But the greeting in *Ag* is far longer than any other. Is there any significance in the length? It may be that earlier tragedy included many greetings of similar or greater length; on the other hand this is a particularly triumphal entry—Agamemnon is, after all, the sacker of Troy (783). And then again the greeting does not consist only of ceremonial trivialities.

The precise timing of this entry poses an important but difficult point. It is doubtful whether it was practicable that Agamemnon should first become visible to the audience at precisely the moment that the second antistrophe ended and the anapaests began; and yet there is no announcement to cover the entry. Assuming that nothing has been lost from the text,[1] then this means that either the chorus began to address Agamemnon before the audience could see him, which seems undesirable, or he may have become first visible shortly before the end of the second antistrophe of the song, or, least likely, there may have been a short pause while the chorus waited for Agamemnon to

---

[1] Chariot-borne entries usually have an announcement as well as a greeting (see *Pers* 155a* and pp. 277f. above); for exceptions we have to go to *Rh* 380ff., and to the pair of greetings at *IA* 590–606 (on which see p. 77 n. 1). The entry of Agamemnon is strangely abrupt, and provokes the conjecture that a brief announcement, like *Pers* 150–4, may have been lost from before 783 (possibly cut out because it was inconsistent with a lavish spectacle—see 783b* below?). But there is no firm evidence of this.

appear. The previous song on the perils of excessive wealth and
its associated evils is not inapplicable to Agamemnon. If he
entered after the end of the song, then the connection is left
inexplicit: 'we must allow the theme of unholy wealth and the
visible figure of the king to coexist in our reception of the scene'
(Jones 89, cf. Alexanderson *Eranos* 67 (1969) 12f.). But if he was
visible before the strophic song was finished, then we are obliged
to dwell on its possible application. Unfortunately we cannot
know, so far as I can see, whether Aeschylus intended Agamemnon to be in sight or out of sight during the last words of the
song. But even if he was not visible, the ominous shadows of its
themes are still bound to be cast over his entry. Even in the fair-
sounding words of the honorific anapaests the fall of Troy and the
vulnerability of the royal house cannot be masked (cf. Lebeck 50).

(b) chariots, spoils, Cassandra

Agamemnon is on a chariot (906), and so is Cassandra (1039,
1054, 1070). It is unclear whether they are on the same vehicle
or separate ones; but since Cassandra is *with* Agamemnon (see
below) it would be more pointed if she was in the same chariot.
In the text there is no sign of more than one chariot, nor is there
any sign of people to make up a procession. Agamemnon was presumably accompanied by some attendants, just as all important
figures were (see *Pers* 155c*). But no special attention is paid
to them; and at the end of the scene they would presumably
have quietly gone off down an eisodos.[1]

What then of the hypothesis: Ἀγαμέμνων δ' ἐπὶ ἀπήνης ἔρχεται,
εἵπετο δ' αὐτῶι ἑτέρα ἀπήνη ἔνθα ἦν τὰ λάφυρα καὶ ἡ Κασάνδρα?
Using this as a starting-point many commentators (and producers) have turned this entry into a huge procession.[2] But why
accept the authority of a hypothesis which is full of other mis-

---

[1] Some, including Wilamowitz 171f., try to eliminate these attendants on the
ground that they would interfere with the plot (so they have been drowned in the
storm, Wilamowitz claims!). But any attendants are easily discarded when they
are not wanted. Ortkemper 21–6, on the other hand, makes a great deal of them.
He claims that a significant visual contrast is set up between the warlike attendants
of Agamemnon and the domesticated maidservants of Clytemnestra. While this
may well contribute something to the over-all impression of the scene, too much
should not be made of the 'spear-carriers' when absolutely no explicit reference is
made to them.

[2] e.g. Verrall livf., Murray 215, *tr* 67 (the most lavish), Thomson² i 26.

information; and why then exaggerate still further this spectacle which has no justification in the text? The procession was long ago dismissed by Hermann (*ed* 651f.). The reason why his effective attack has been so often disregarded must be that commentators have seized any opportunity to introduce gratuitous spectacle into Aeschylus (see §4). On the other hand the writer of the hypothesis, or his source, was probably not simply guessing,[1] since there is reason to think that this sort of detail may have been derived from a later, perhaps Hellenistic, production. I have argued on *Pers* 155b* that lavish processions of spoils brought back from war were popular in the fourth century, and no doubt later also. The only fifth-century precedent to survive is E. *Tro* 568ff. where Andromache is brought on in a chariot which also holds the spoils and trophies of Troy. The difference from *Ag* is significant, for in *Tro* the spoils are integral and are especially pointed out, since Andromache is merely one item in Neoptolemus' booty. If Aeschylus had meant that there should be a significantly extravagant show of Agamemnon's booty, then there would surely be some indication of it in the words. The entry is triumphal and certainly not mean; but there is no sign of a conspicuous show of wealth. The notion of wealth and the wasting of it is to come later.

There has been no preparation for the arrival of Cassandra. Aeschylus could have included something about her in the Herald scene, but he deliberately has not. Even after she has entered no attention is paid to her for more than 160 lines; and even when she has been pointed out (950ff.), and even when she is directly addressed (1035ff.), she still remains silent (see 1330a*). I have discussed the effect of her entry in *Silences* 77, where I conclude that the audience is bound to be curious about her, and yet to pay her no close attention.[2] This is admittedly unusual dramatic technique, since attention is normally drawn to an entry and some indication made towards its interpretation; but Aeschylus has a special purpose in making Cassandra at first a silent and enigmatic figure (see 1330b*).

[1] As argued by Fraenkel ii 370 and n. 3, cf. Wilamowitz 171, 175 n. 1, Dover Arph. *Clouds ed* xc n. 2.

[2] In *Silences* 77 n. 60 I reject the over-ingenious suggestion that Cassandra was totally masked up until l. 950 (see e.g. Murray 219, Fraenkel ii 370, Arnott 39). Arnott says it would be 'an effective grouping'; but even if practicable it would only be a clever and meaningless stage trick.

It is worth noting that Cassandra enters *with* Agamemnon, probably on the same chariot. Simultaneous entries are not common in Greek tragedy, especially not in early tragedy (see *Seven* 374b*, *Prom* 1a*). Characters cannot be brought on in groups in such a way that we ask no questions about the individual members who are simply 'in the company'. It is possible that in other tragedies before *Ag* kings had entered with women whom they had won in war. This would not only have provided some explanation of Cassandra's presence, but might also have provided some precedent for her silence: note that Iole in S. *Trach* and Alcestis at E. *Alc* 1008ff., where she is offered as a prize of war, are both mute. The audience is meant to notice Cassandra, and to notice that she is with Agamemnon. She is not explained, but she becomes yet one more element wrong in the homecoming, a disquieting presence seen out of the corner of the eye.

855 enter Clytemnestra

victory deserts Agamemnon

Agamemnon ends his rhesis on his return (810–54) with the four lines

> νῦν δ' ἐc μέλαθρα καὶ δόμουc ἐφεcτίουc[1]
> ἐλθὼν θεοῖcι πρῶτα δεξιώcομαι,
> οἵπερ πρόcω πέμψαντεc ἤγαγον πάλιν.
> νίκη δ', ἐπείπερ ἕcπετ', ἐμπέδωc μένοι.

Clearly he intends to go now into the palace. Not only is his intention expressly declared in the first three lines, but the final prayer for victory is a common exit sentiment. (The line is curiously similar to that with which Menander ends several comedies: Νίκη μεθ' ἡμῶν εὐμενὴc ἔποιτ' ἀεί—for a complete list see Austin on *Sam* 736f.) In tragedy other prayers are found on exit in various contexts.[2] So the situation is clear: Agamemnon

---

[1] Page *OCT* accepts Karsten's emendation ἐφέcτιοc. But even without the protection of *Seven* 73 (which Page, following Dawe, brackets) the phrase seems easy to understand in the context.

[2] For some examples in Aeschylus alone see *Hik* 523, 951, *Ag* 349, 972f., *Eum* 776f. Cf. Deckinger 64f., 155, Schadewaldt *Monolog* 101ff.; for Euripides see Langholf *Die Gebete bei Euripides* etc. (Göttingen 1971) 75f. (I cannot resist quoting Puff in Sheridan's *The Critic* Act II scene ii 'You could not go off kneeling, could you? . . . It would have a good effect, i'faith, if you could exeunt praying.')

is about to go into the palace when he is stopped by the entry and the words of Clytemnestra.[1] It might fairly have been inferred that Agamemnon actually left his chariot, were it not that he is still in it at 905f. (so Smyth *tr* 71 'he descends from his chariot' must be wrong). It is still possible that he began to make some movement, but all that we can be sure of is his intention and the resultant dramatic situation. Yet very few commentators have even recognized the situation;[2] and even then, with the exception of Reinhardt, they do not go on to consider its significance for the play.

Aeschylus must have a purpose in framing Agamemnon's last four lines in such a way that they are immediately thwarted by Clytemnestra. The King is about to go into his house and greet the gods who sent him on his way and have brought him back. Attention moves to the house, and the lord's position in his house. Before he is able to move towards the doorway Clytemnestra is standing in it. She blocks the way, she occupies the threshold: Clytemnestra controls the way into the house, and Agamemnon can only leave his temporary transport and enter the house on her conditions. All this, which is contained and embodied in the stage situation, is put by Reinhardt 93–4 with characteristic stylishness. He sees what an audience sees, and rightly stresses its importance.

I have suggested that this situation has already been foreshadowed at 587, and I shall argue that it recurs at 1372 (587*, 1372a*). It is likely that only Clytemnestra has used the door so far. Agamemnon and Aegisthus use the palace door under Clytemnestra's supervision. In this play only Cassandra uses it independently—see further 1330a*. Once we recognize the visual significance of the situation at 855, then Agamemnon's last line (854), which is spoken just before Clytemnestra enters, or perhaps as she enters, takes on a special meaning and irony

[1] I am taking it for granted that Clytemnestra entered at this point (with her maids, since 908ff. does not look like a summons). For her exit at 614 see p. 300 n. 4 above. A further point is that Agamemnon can hardly have been meant to be going in after 854 without even acknowledging her presence (cf. *Silences* 93).

[2] Some exceptions are Verrall 100 (though he pointlessly brings on Clytemnestra at 844), Groeneboom 256, Fraenkel *Kl B* 342 (though not in the commentary), Reinhardt 93f., Roux in *Hommages à M. Delcourt* (Bruxelles 1970) 70. Wilamowitz *ed maj* 212 *actio* actually supposes a movement 'cum Agamemno de curru descendere coepit, obviam venit e regia Clytemnestra . . .'; cf. Campbell 30. Andrieu 200 speaks rather loosely of a 'fausse sortie'.

(see Neustadt 262). Agamemnon has entered Troy and conquered. He is prepared for and greeted as the victor (see 783a*):
yet as soon as he wants to do something in his own house, he is
prevented. At the very moment he prays for victory to stay with
him, he is confronted with the victor over him. This is the
moment that νίκη deserts him. He enters a conqueror, and goes
off himself conquered: see further 974b*.

972 exit Agamemnon

974 exit Clytemnestra

(a) the stage action

We come now to a crucial scene in the greatest of Greek tragedies.
It is also highly controversial. This is, I shall suggest, not surprising, since Aeschylus has deliberately made its significance
both complex and enigmatic.

Anyone who has read the play must have the sense that
Agamemnon's exit over the purple cloth is in some way loaded
with meaning; anyone who has seen it is even more sure of it.
Aeschylus forces us to this sense not only by the impressive visual
picture which makes us want to interpret the action, but also
by the way that it is led up to. From the moment that Clytemnestra turns from her oblique self-defence to direct attack (νῦν
δέ . . . 905) up to the moment when Agamemnon puts his foot
on the purple the central object of attention is the question of
how he will go into the palace. He is bound to go in, but in what
way? It seems that the maids spread out the cloth at 908ff., so
that for all the rest of the scene it is lying there, waiting to be
trodden on. Agamemnon gives in at 944, but we still have to
wait while his sandals are taken off and while he gives instructions about Cassandra, before he finally says (956f.)

> ἐπεὶ δ᾽ ἀκούειν σοῦ κατέστραμμαι τάδε,
> εἶμ᾽ ἐς δόμων μέλαθρα πορφύρας πατῶν.

The dispute over whether the action should take place at all
directs attention and speculation on to the action itself. This
preparation alone belies the kind of insensitivity which is
epitomized by Verrall (xlv n. 2): 'the tapestry is a mere detail,
introduced chiefly for spectacular effect'.

It is important to work out, so far as is possible, what is happening in terms of stage action in the minutes which lead up to Agamemnon's exit. It is clear that he leaves his chariot and sets foot on the cloth during or immediately after 956f.[1] But it is not absolutely clear just when he disappears inside the palace, nor what are his exact actions in between. The traditional stage direction is probably right: he walks slowly over the cloth while Clytemnestra says lines 958–72, and he is gone in by the time she says her final couplet 973–4. He is surely still on stage during 958–72.[2] He is addressed in 961 (there is no good reason to emend the unobjectionable ἄναξ, see Fraenkel ii 435), and coῦ μολόντος in 968 is particularly appropriate if he is at that moment walking towards the house, and 971–2 has extra point if he is entering the house as the words are said. The asyndeton between 972 and 973, the separate tone, and the scarcely concealed significance of the prayer in 973–4 are clear indications that Agamemnon has by then gone inside.

So, although it cannot be proved, I accept the traditional stage direction (interestingly restated by Fraenkel iii 813 n. 1), that Agamemnon is slowly moving the length of the cloth all the time that Clytemnestra speaks 958–72.[3] He would have to move very slowly; and the actor would have to rehearse carefully so that he passed inside at the right moment before 973.[4] It is worth comparing Iphigenia's speech at E. *IT* 1222–32 during which Orestes and Pylades move from the door off down the eisodos in the slow silent procession of sacrificial victims. But Agamemnon has even less distance to cover. He was probably followed by the maids who took up the cloth behind Agamemnon as he went; and Clytemnestra will have followed behind them.

It is worth noting that Agamemnon remains silent during his

[1] Sidgwick 49 says that Agamemnon's sandals were taken off during 958ff. But that must be a mistake, since it was done at 944ff.

[2] So G. Müller S. *Ant comm* 40 is wrong to associate this passage with his few examples of 'lines to a departing back' (on which see *Hik* 951*). It is a pointless question to ask whether this technique might have been taken from early Sophocles.

[3] Vellacott *tr* 196 claims 'dramatically, this is lamentable—to us at least'. This is because he supposes (contrary to Greek tragic technique) that the stage movement should take place in total silence. On the contrary it seems to me much more effective that this disquieting action should be simultaneous with these disquieting and cryptic words.

[4] Fraenkel ii 440 is surely wrong to say that the door closes behind Agamemnon, since Clytemnestra and the maids have to follow him in. (He attributes this to Wilamowitz, but I cannot find the source.)

long exit. A character of high status will normally have the last word when he goes off (see p. 205 above); and if two important characters go together, then the dramatically dominant tends to speak last. I suggest that in the Greek theatre Agamemnon's silence on exit would be noticed: Clytemnestra has the initiative. Compare for example E. *Hec* 1019–22 (Hecuba and Polymestor) or S. *El* 1503–7 (Aegisthus and Orestes); compare also *Cho* 930* contrasted with *Cho* 718*. Another point of dramatic technique is that Clytemnestra speaks 973–4 after Agamemnon has gone, and then follows him. This foreruns a device which becomes common later: the avenger lures the victim inside, and then after he has gone stays on for a few lines of prayer and vengeful gloating.[1] Since the device required the use of the skene, this is an illustration of how remarkably quickly and effectively Aeschylus adapted himself to the innovation (cf. pp. 458f.).[2]

(b) *the significance of the act:* δεῖμα προcτατήριον καρδίαc τεραcκόπου

The significance of the stage action has, of course, been the subject of much discussion.[3] While one can scarcely hope to lay the controversy in such a matter, there are two almost universally accepted assumptions which I would begin by questioning. First, it is assumed that the full significance was immediately clear to Aeschylus' audience: 'scholars disagree over the meaning of the walking on the purple, though presumably it was easily understood by the Greek audience' (Easterling 10). This is

---

[1] For some examples see *Silences* 94 n. 113. For the sake of completeness I should add E. *Hec* 1022 and *Antiope* fr. xlviii 46f. (Kambitsis); there is also a good parody at Plaut. *Mil Gl* 1378ff., cf. 1388–93. Spitzbarth 55 regards this kind of device as exclusively Euripidean; but she neglects this place in *Ag* and S. *El* 1376ff. I hope I do not need to argue *contra* D–P 117 that Clytemnestra does follow Agamemnon in: cf. *Silences* 93–4. (Lloyd-Jones *tr* 68f. omits the crucial stage instructions at 972–4.)

[2] A final practical point: most editors since Wilamowitz have taken Cassandra's words at 1236f. (ὡc δ' ἐπωλολύξατο) to refer specifically to 973f.—see e.g. Fraenkel iii 572f. But I doubt whether they should be taken literally; they refer to Clytemnestra's general tone rather than to the delivery of any actual cry. Editors who interpolate a cry at this point are being too melodramatic (e.g. Murray 219, Thomson² i 28 n. 1, Campbell 35, Vellacott *tr* 75: see *contra* Fraenkel iii 572 n. 3, Zeitlin *TAPA* 97 (1966) 652). Campbell and Vellacott (195f.) actually move the entire speech 958–72 elsewhere; but their arguments are not worth repeating.

[3] The discussions which I have found most useful, and to which I shall sometimes refer to by name without page numbers, are Neustadt 243ff. esp. 261ff., Reinhardt 96f., Goheen 113ff., Jones 79ff., Dawe 48–50, Lebeck 74–9, Easterling 10–19.

usually a fair assumption with a Greek tragedy; but we are here involved in an exceptional trilogy which is full of enigmas and obscurities which are only later solved and clarified (an aspect well brought out by Lebeck). And for this scene there is an explicit sign that it is meant to be to some extent difficult to interpret: the following choral song 975ff. Secondly there is a tendency to assume that the action has only one significance, or at least one dominant significance. This again is usually true of the stage actions of Greek tragedy, but here it is hard to deny that several themes and preoccupations are in the air, and no one to the exclusion of others. The first task is to disentangle these various significances singly before considering their collective effect. I shall take them in a convenient but arbitrary order.

Let us consider first the two aspects of the scene which have received most attention, even though one may easily be over-stressed, and the other, at least in its traditional statement, is not of primary importance. First, then, the religious (or 'hybristic') meaning of the cloth. Agamemnon suspects that treading on rich fabrics is an awful deed, liable to divine resentment (922–5, 946–9); and that it might also invite popular disfavour (937f.). As his shoes are removed Agamemnon prays (946f.) καὶ τοῖσδέ μ' ἐμβαίνονθ' ἀλουργέϲιν θεῶν | μή τιϲ πρόϲωθεν ὄμματοϲ βάλοι φθόνοϲ. And yet who is to say that his prayer is not answered? It is open to doubt whether this is in fact an impious deed in itself, and it is certainly not for this trivial offence that Agamemnon dies. Above all, as Dawe 48 n. 2 stresses, this possibility is given no further direct attention in the play. Lloyd-Jones (tr 67) says 'one must beware of overrating the significance of this scene'. It seems to me, on the contrary, that it is hardly possible to overrate its significance; but it is quite true that we should not overrate its literal religious importance.

Yet, although treading on the rich cloth is not in itself a great guilt, it is important in that it signifies or symbolizes the guilts of Agamemnon. Other much greater acts, especially the sacrifice of Iphigenia and the sack of Troy, have, like this, been ambi-valent deeds liable to incur divine disfavour. And what connects this stage action with the past—and later with the future—is the theme and imagery of impious trampling underfoot, which has already been established in the choral song 367ff., and is con-tinued throughout the trilogy. This is well shown by Lebeck 74–9.

It is perhaps hyperbolic to claim (76) 'we see Agamemnon committing an act which subsumes the particular wrongs of his past and stands as a symbol for all impiety'; but it is fair to say that the vivid, though marginal, sin which we witness stands for or epitomizes Agamemnon's ambivalent past.

Secondly it is claimed that the scene is there in order to reveal the psychology of Agamemnon, and, it is usually added, to show him as a fatally flawed personality who invites his doom. Indeed the characterization of Agamemnon is the only interpretation properly discussed by Fraenkel and D–P (though in private conversation Fraenkel retracted his discussion). But a Bradleian view of Greek tragedy has now gone out of favour, and rightly so: see p. 93 above. On this particular aspect the discussions of Jones and Dawe have been particularly effective. It may be that the new orthodoxy has gone too far and would try to deny even that we may 'believe in' the characters of Greek tragedy (as Easterling rather vaguely puts it). I would not myself wish to deny that Agamemnon has his ἦθος, that he is the kind of man who might do the things he has done and the kind of man who may be vulnerable to ἄτη. Of his own free will he treads on the cloth, just as of his own free will at Aulis ἀνάγκας ἔδυ λέπαδνον.[1] The scene shows a credible person; but the revelation of psychology is only incidental to its primary dramatic purposes.[2]

These two aspects by no means exhaust the significances of the scene. They do not do justice, for instance, to a meaning which is most explicitly brought out by the words: the defeat of Agamemnon and the victory of Clytemnestra.[3] Agamemnon entered the triumphant victor, and remained so until faced with Clytemnestra (see 855*). After that the dispute over how he is to make his exit is put in terms of a battle, of victory and defeat (see 940–3, 956). This is how Cassandra will later view the scene: ὥσπερ ἐν μάχης τροπῆι (1237). Clytemnestra will put her whole plot against Agamemnon in these terms also at 1374ff.[4]

[1] Dover *JHS* 93 (1963) 65, while excellent on ἀνάγκη, seems unjustified in denying any volition to δῦναι when it is used transitively.

[2] For a more sophisticated and circumspect account of Agamemnon's bad *ethos* see Peradotto *Phoenix* 23 (1969) 237ff. esp. 256–7. With reference to this scene, however, Peradotto wishes to stress the revelation of *ethos* to the neglect of other more pressing significances.

[3] Cf. especially Neustadt 262f., Winnington-Ingram 133f., Reinhardt, Dawe.

[4] Clytemnestra will also see her reckoning with Orestes in battle terms: εἰδῶμεν εἰ νικῶμεν ἢ νικώμεθα (*Cho* 890). On νίκη in *Cho* see Schadewaldt *HuH²* i 282f.

Troy is conquered by Agamemnon who is conquered by Clytemnestra. Aeschylus' theatrical masterstroke is to put the battlefield in visible spatial terms before the spectators' eyes: the
threshold and the purple cloth stretched before it. Agamemnon
is enslaved, yoked, and yet not by force. He says of Cassandra
(953) ἑκὼν γὰρ οὐδεὶς δουλίωι χρῆται ζυγῶι: yet at that very
moment he is doing this himself (see Winnington-Ingram 134,
and see p. 321 below). And just as the battlefield is soft and
luxurious, so the weapon with which Clytemnestra conquers is
not of metal but of words: πειθώ (cf. Goheen 126ff., Lebeck
40f.)—the power which overcame Troy (*Ag* 385ff.), will aid
Orestes (*Cho* 726ff.), and finally to good effect will overbear the
Erinyes (see *Eum* 777c*). Clytemnestra's battle will be actually
won with the murder itself, but the turning-point is, as Cassandra
says, this scene.

There is still another significance which is made clear in the
words: when he walks on the cloth Agamemnon is wasting the
wealth of the house. This aspect has been particularly stressed by
Jones, though to the exclusion of all others. The fabric is delicate,
finely woven and embroidered (909, 923 etc.); it seems that even
to tread on it with bare feet will spoil it and render it unusable.[1]
Further, the cloth comes from the palace treasuries and is part
of the family's wealth. These two points are brought together by
Agamemnon in 948f.,

πολλὴ γὰρ αἰδὼς δωματοφθορεῖν[2] ποσὶν
φθείροντα πλοῦτον ἀργυρωνήτους θ' ὑφάς.

And this supplies the overt starting-point for Clytemnestra's
sinister reassurance in 958ff., where words for 'house' occur
seven times in eleven lines.[3] So the scene puts in vivid and visible

---

[1] Cf. Beazley in Fraenkel iii 832 (repr. 1962). The cloths are not *carpets*, since
the point of a carpet, however precious or sacred, is that it is tough enough to
be trodden on. If Fraenkel's interpretation of 926 is right—' "doormats" and
"embroideries" have a very different sound'—then Agamemnon says as much
himself. Although this makes good sense, D–P's linguistic objections (149f.) are
considerable. Lebeck 191 n. 23 is surely wrong to argue that the cloth is really a
carpet and that the more delicate words used of it are purely metaphorical, since
carpets are not damaged by bare feet.
[2] Schütz's convincing emendation of ςωματοφθορεῖν. Neustadt's 245 n. 1 makes
a vain attempt to defend the transmitted reading.
[3] D–P 155 point this out, only to remark 'note the indifference to repetition':
the repetition could hardly be more obviously deliberate. (When D–P xv deny

terms the theme of the dangers of excessive wealth which is
prominent throughout *Ag* (though not so much in *Cho* and *Eum*);
and it shows how members of the family set about damaging
their own house, the 'self wounding of the house' which, as
Jones shows, runs through the trilogy.

The significances observed so far are explicitly evoked by the
words used during the scene; though it may be that none of
them is predominant and that all are somewhat obscure and
ambivalent (see further below). But I am convinced that there
are other more inexplicit suggestions in this scene. It may be no
accident, for example, that the exact nature and function of the
cloth are unclear. It is woven (ὑφάς 949) and decorated (ποικίλα
923, 926, 936); but it is not clear whether it is like a tapestry-
coverlet (πέτασμα 909) or a garment (εἵματα 921, 960, 963).
Lebeck (85f. and *GRBS* 5 (1964) 39f.) has argued for a reminiscence of Iphigenia's robe at *Ag* 231ff. Whatever the precise
interpretation of that difficult passage,[1] the robe falls in a sinister
and bloody context, and βαφάς (239) recurs at 960. Yet this
connection seems remote, one of scores of echoes which reverber-
ate through the *Oresteia*: there is a much more relevant robe or
cloth later in the play.

The robe in which Clytemnestra entangles Agamemnon,
which is seen after the murder (see p. 325) and again in *Cho*
(see *Cho* 973b*), is also a sinister and bloody stuff, and its exact
fabric is even more difficult to define. It is like a net of some
sort (*Ag* 1381ff., *Cho* 997ff.), or a spider's ὕφασμα (*Ag* 1492);
but it is also a φᾶρος (*Cho* 1011) or πέπλοι (*Ag* 1126, 1580, *Cho*
1000, *Eum* 635). Even more tellingly Clytemnestra talks of a
πλοῦτον εἵματος κακόν (*Ag* 1383), and Orestes remarks φόνου δὲ
κηκὶς ξὺν χρόνωι ξυμβάλλεται / πολλὰς βαφὰς φθείρουσα τοῦ
ποικίλματος (*Cho* 1012f.). There is little doubt that the indefiniteness of the nature of the purple cloth allows it to be recalled
directly by the later cloth trap.[2] Agamemnon walks over the
rich tapestry-garment and into an inextricable richness of

Aeschylus any profundity of thought they do at least allow that he is 'first and
foremost a great poet'!)

[1] See especially Lloyd-Jones *CR* n.s. 2 (1952) 132ff., Lebeck 82ff.
[2] See especially Neustadt 263f., Lebeck 68, 85f., Dingel 165ff. (cf. *Bauformen*
363). But Dingel insists on talking of 'magic': although Clytemnestra has more
than masculine, almost supernatural, power, there is no suggestion that she uses
magic. Also see now Macleod *Maia* 27 (1975) 201f.

garment-net. The association of ideas, though retrospective, is clear. It is even possible that one and the same stage-property was used for both cloths, though there is no positive evidence for this.[1] The sustained imagery of the net, one of the most conspicuous in the *Oresteia*, has been established in the song at 355ff. by the inescapable net thrown over Troy (also cf. 866ff.): on the metaphor of the net see further p. 381 below. So it may be that an enigmatic, half-formed association along these lines emerged during the scene.

There is another disquieting aspect of the cloth whose significance is as yet enigmatic and submerged but will later become clear: its colour. While the dye porphyra shows above all the expensiveness of the cloth, it is also inescapably reminiscent of blood. The association was made by Neustadt (264), and was cogently developed by Goheen (esp. 115–26).[2] So a blood-coloured pathway stretches from Agamemnon's chariot to the door. This might simply conjure up vague trains of thought of Agamemnon's bloody past or of blood running from the house;[3] but these possibilities are not developed by Aeschylus. Much more important is the picture of blood irrevocably spilt on the ground, an image which recurs throughout the trilogy, especially in *Cho* and *Eum* (see Goheen, Lebeck 8off., and p. 381 below). Lebeck once more traces this back to Aulis, but the image is first clearly formed in the last antistrophe of the next choral song at 1018ff. This is one of the few clear notions which the chorus can disentangle from the confusion and obscurity which oppress it after the scene of the purple cloth. The idea, then, of blood spilt on the ground and its associations with the endless course of a blood-feud, while it cannot be explicitly formulated during the scene itself, is soon brought into the open. A disquieting hint becomes in retrospect the embodiment of a central theme.

The upshot of this discussion is that the scene has several

---

[1] The suggestion is implied by Vermeule *AJA* 70 (1966) 21. The 'garment' in which Agamemnon is trapped on the Boston Oresteia krater (on which see pp. 329–30 with n. 3 below) may be quite like that used by Aeschylus. It is like a net, yet it is made of a delicate translucent fabric and is decorated by dots of colour and has a decorated hem. But this will not do at all for the earlier scene: it is not purple and it is not big enough.

[2] Cf. also Hiltbrunner *Wiederholungs- u. Motivtechnik bei A.* (Bern 1950) 62, K. Schneider in *RE* xxiii col. 2010f.

[3] See e.g. Lebeck 86, Easterling 18f., Roux (cited above, p. 307 n. 2) 77f.

meanings, all interconnected in various ways. Some are explicit, some implicit, some are clear at the time, others emerge clearly only later in the trilogy. None is dominant, and none, I suggest, is completely self-explanatory and unequivocal. The scene raises unanswered questions, begins uncompleted trains of thought, sets unsolved enigmas. This is a very strange and bold technique, and unlike anything else in Greek tragedy we know of. But the confirmation that the scene is meant to be puzzling[1] is the following choral song at 975ff. The chorus, which has earlier in the play found some light in the darkness of its distress and disquiet, is now plunged back into terrifying ἀπορία. The scene has opened obscure and alarming prospects which it cannot interpret. So too for the audience. Agamemnon's scene has led us into a tangle of dark questions.

If this is right then it goes some way to explaining why the Cassandra scene, much longer than Agamemnon's own scene, intervenes between Agamemnon's defeat on the cloth and his actual death. Cassandra will painfully lead the chorus and the audience out of their bewilderment towards some kind of insight and understanding: see 1330b*. She solves many of the enigmas set by the first thousand lines of the play. When Agamemnon treads on the cloth we know we are seeing him for the last time alive; he is as good as dead. But it is not clear at all why he is to die: several reasons are hinted at, but none is made clear. When nearly 400 lines later we hear his death cries, then, thanks to Cassandra, their meaning is much clearer.

1035 re-enter Clytemnestra

Clytemnestra's first failure

It is often said that at this point the audience expects to hear the death cries. It is certainly true that we have witnessed in the previous act an event as close to Agamemnon's death as may be without the blow itself; it is also true that in later tragedy, as in

---

[1] I pick this word because of Easterling p. 15: 'although great dramatists are often ambiguous they are not puzzling. To be puzzling is to run the risk of distracting or boring the audience; and every great dramatist knows that they must be gripped.' Of course no good dramatist should be confusing in a random, pointless way: but Aeschylus shows that a great dramatist may set puzzles to grip his audience. In a different way the 'deception speech' in S. *Aj* illustrates the same point, as I hope to argue elsewhere.

Cho, when a victim has been lured inside, then the cries almost invariably follow either during the ensuing song or at the end of it.[1] But if at the time of *Ag* the skene was still new, then we cannot say that the conventional sequence was already established; in fact it was probably not. The audience would certainly feel suspense and anxiety, heightened by the foreboding song and by the presence of Cassandra, but they would not know what to expect next. When they see Clytemnestra yet again standing coolly and imperiously at the door, they would feel again her dominating presence. While all else is disquiet and uncertainty, she moves with a sure purpose.

Clytemnestra remains domineering; yet, although she contrives to make her intervention seem to be another of her brief incisive appearances (see 614*), this time she is worsted. Her control in this play is almost complete. The only two times that she gives way are to Cassandra here, and to some degree to the chorus in the great scene at 1372–1576 (see 1577a*). Her retreat here at 1068 is more of significance for what it conveys about Cassandra (see p. 318 below). So far as it concerns our view of Clytemnestra herself, Aeschylus handles the scene very carefully. Although she fails to make any impression on Cassandra, she is still forceful and practical: she remains a person competent to do what she is going to do.

1068 exit Clytemnestra

1330 exit Cassandra

(*a*) θεηλάτου βοὸς δίκην πρὸς βωμόν

The only way to set Cassandra's exit in its place is to survey her entire part looking at the way that her eventual exit is foreseen and approached. She can be little more than a strange, unexplained presence (see 783b*) up until lines 950–5 where Agamemnon gives his instructions for her and explains her status. She is then disregarded again for the rest of the scene and for the choral song 975–1034. The presence of actors during act-dividing songs in Aeschylus is discussed on *Pers* 622*. Here

---

[1] An extraordinary exception is the end of S. *El* where the play ends before the murder of Aegisthus. Perhaps Sophocles means to suggest that the murder has no aftermath. It may be that at E. *Med* 1080 Medea followed her children inside; but more probably she stayed on.

Cassandra can hardly be totally neglected (she is not 'lediglich Statistin' as Aichele 20 n. 1 presumes); yet the audience cannot know what to make of her. She is one of the many elements in the situation at this stage which are problematic and disquieting (see p. 305 above).

Suddenly, after this long neglect, with Clytemnestra's entry at 1035 attention is centred on Cassandra as the Queen repeatedly tells her to get down off the chariot and to go inside; and the chorus echoes her. Her first words are εἴcω κομίζου καὶ cύ, and the injunctions follow in quick succession (1039, 1049, 1053f., 1059, 1070f.). But Cassandra does not move or speak, and Clytemnestra goes back in without her (1035*). Aeschylus goes to these lengths, it seems, in order to make certain preparatory points about Cassandra. The incident drives home what we first found out about her back at 950ff.: she must go inside. And her unmoved silence in the face of Clytemnestra gives her new stature. Cassandra is not to be ordered around; although she is a foreigner, a woman, and a slave, she will be her own mistress. Her silence is, if any is in the surviving plays, a true Aeschylean silence—see *Silences* 77. It is the centre of dramatic attention, and it has real point. Further, it makes Cassandra even more puzzling; it is not even certain she can speak Greek. But the audience is guided towards pity and sympathy for her by the attitude of the Old Men who show a gentle compassion, in contrast to Clytemnestra's imperiousness. This is especially brought out on the exit of Clytemnestra by line 1069. This relationship between Cassandra and the chorus, and hence the audience, is essential for the following scene.

When Cassandra suddenly breaks her silence, her speech is yet more obscure and bewildering, at first, than her silence. A pattern of sense begins to emerge during the masterly lyric dialogue 1072–1177, which, while based on an epirrhematic structure, departs from it to bring out the relative emotional states of Cassandra and the chorus (see, above all, Fraenkel *Kl B* 344f., 375ff.). Unfortunately we can tell little about the stage movements which accompanied Cassandra's lyrics, but we can say with some confidence that she stepped down from the chariot at the beginning (i.e. about 1072): she should be free to move and dance in accompaniment to her lyric (cf. Hermann 652 *contra* Fraenkel iii 492). Moreover the question that she puts to Apollo in 1087—ᾆ, ποῖ ποτ' ἤγαγές με; πρὸς ποίαν στέγην;—makes much more sense if her dance since 1072 has been moving in the direction of the house. This is confirmed by the title she gives Apollo in 1080 = 1085: ἀγυιάτης. Most Greek houses would have a cult stone or altar of Apollo Agyieus before the door, and there is clear evidence that this stone was represented on the tragic (and comic) stage.[1]

So it seems that Cassandra was going to go off into the palace in quiet obedience at 1072ff., then on her way she stops at the altar of Apollo at 1080ff. During the second strophic pair she becomes more aware of the house which she has been moving towards; and in the third (1090ff.) her horrific visions of what has happened and is to happen are set in the physical framework of the palace itself. So Cassandra's intended movement inside is halted by the sights which the palace inspires in her: the house which she was about to enter is filled with the butchery of the past and of the near future, and to enter it would be to walk into death. Her murder-filled visions so possess her once they have begun that it is not until 1136ff. that she returns with gradually encroaching speech-metres to her own place in this slaughterhouse. ποῖ δή με δεῦρο τὴν τάλαιναν ἤγαγες; / οὐδέν ποτ' εἰ μὴ ξυνθανουμένην· τί γάρ; (1138–9).[2] The last two strophic pairs (1136–77) are filled with Cassandra's realization that her death is near. She knows that when she goes in she will die a violent death, yet she will still go. Piece by piece the house is daubed with blood, peopled with corpses, ghosts, and demons. Yet Cassandra will still enter it. The awareness of this hangs over all the rest of the scene.

Before she goes Cassandra must disclose her insights, and the rest of the scene consists of three speeches each followed by a stichomythia. With the change from lyric to speech there is a move from the oracular towards more clarity, as is marked by Cassandra's own proem (1178ff.). Throughout the speeches her

---

[1] See Fraenkel iii 491f., and for New Comedy Handley Men. *Dysc ed* 246 (add *Sam* 309, 444, 474). In most cases the text suits a rectangular ἀγυιεὺς βωμός rather than a conical κίων, see Pearson on Soph. fr. 370 l. 1 and MacDowell *Arph. Wasps ed* 247f. (Arnott 45ff. may be right to argue that the permanent altar of Dionysus was taken as the altar of Apollo when needed; but he relies too much on a dubious entry in Pollux. The altar needs to be near the doors.)

[2] Cf. Lebeck 55. D–P 173 are right to defend ποῖ against emendation to τί: E. *IT* 77 may even be inspired directly by this place. On the other hand I prefer Fraenkel's punctuation.

own situation is never far from the surface, and we are reminded
now and then that she will go inside, and that there she will die.
The house is always there in front of her, and, as during the lyric
scene, it is again and again the physical setting of her visions
(see 1186ff., 1191ff., 1217 etc.). She moves from the distant past
to the near past and then to the near future; and then finally
in the third speech (1256ff.) she comes to herself. When she has
seen that vengeance is due to Agamemnon for the sack of Troy,
and she has foreseen that Orestes will avenge her, then at the
end of the rhesis she prepares to go inside at last. She addresses
the door which she has approached—Ἅιδου πύλας δὲ τάςδ' ἐγὼ
προσεννέπω (1291). She makes a final prayer (1292–4). But she
does not go yet; her departure is painfully long drawn out.

Just as Cassandra approached the palace and then stopped at
the beginning of the scene (see above), so again she approaches
the doors at 1294. It seems to be the chorus' question (1295–8)
which stops her: how can she bear to go in full knowledge of her
own death, as though she were a sacred animal?[1] She replies
that there is no escape; and with the brief lament of l. 1305
she evidently means to go again. The ensuing action is made
clear by the following lines 1306–9: it is not fear or apprehension
which turns her back, but the *smell* which she detects about the
house. That is, the action of turning back occurs after 1305 and
precedes her vocal reaction (φεῦ φεῦ 1307).[2] This gruesome
touch adds the dimension of a further sense to her perception
of the situation.[3] But, although the slaughterhouse arouses such
revulsion, Cassandra again prepares herself to go in, and once
more utters what are meant to be her exit lines: 1313f.

---

[1] For this comparison see Burkert *Homo Necans* (Berlin 1972) 10f.

[2] See Hense 139. D–P 189 (on 1305) are wrong to refer the action described
in 1306 back to 1305; it happens after that line. The scholion on 1307 (παλ. in
Tr.) is rather confusing. It starts ἀπολοφυρομένη λέγει τοῦτο ἐν τῶι εἰσιέναι, which
Hermann and most editors have rightly taken to refer not to φεῦ φεῦ in 1307 but
to 1305. But it then goes on ὀκνεῖ γὰρ εἰσελθεῖν ὥς τι δεινὸν ὁρῶσα, which appears
to be based on 1306 and misses the point about the smell.

[3] There is a curiously similar sequence of action, but in a highly comic context,
at Plaut. *Mil Glor* 1249–59. Acroteleutium pretends to be mad with love for the
Gloriosus, while he looks on imagining his presence to be secret. She is about to
beat down the doors when at 1254 she stops. Why? Because she knows he is not
indoors. How? She smells that he is not indoors. 'Hariolatur' comments Palaestrio
to Pyrgopolynices. The way that she approaches the door and turns back because
of her sense of smell is so similar to Cassandra as to suggest there may possibly be
direct influence (on the model of this part of *Mil Glor*).

ἀλλ' εἶμι κἂν δόμοιcι κωκύcουc' ἐμὴν
Ἀγαμέμνονόc τε μοῖραν· ἀρκείτω βίοc.

(on ἀλλ' εἶμι see Fraenkel *Phoen* 29f.). But again she stops. She explains to the chorus that she turns, not out of fear, but to call on them as witness of the deed which is to be done against her and is eventually to be punished.

She has now begun to go and turned back three times. Possibly Wilamowitz 174 n. 1 is right to claim that she stops once more at 1320 before her final speech. Whether or not she turns back this fourth time, after her final invocation of the sun and her poignant lines on βρότεια πράγματα, with an expression of pity for all mankind, she is gone. She is dead. The quiet pathos of Cassandra's exit is perhaps unsurpassed in Greek tragedy. And the repeatedly delayed exits help to make us more aware of what is involved.

(b) *Cassandra's journey in its dramatic context*

Once he envisaged the Cassandra scene as a piece of theatre Reinhardt (97–105 esp. 102–4) made a simple and crucial observation which eludes those who treat the text as a disembodied poem. He saw that Cassandra has to make exactly the same brief journey as Agamemnon, one on a rich cloth, the other on the ground: they both make the steps from the chariot across the orchestra and in through the palace door to certain death. Once this basic parallelism is seen, then a set of important contrasts and dissimilarities comes to light. Agamemnon is the victorious king returning to his own home, yet he goes into it under Clytemnestra's control, defeated, enslaved, having put on the yoke of necessity. Cassandra is a woman, a slave, arriving at a foreign palace, yet she refuses the yoke. She will go inside in her own time and under her own control (cf. Winnington-Ingram 134). The contrasts go deeper. Agamemnon is deceived, he enters his palace in ignorance, he does not know what he is doing. Cassandra is not only not deceived by Clytemnestra, she not only knows clearly what is happening and what she is doing, she knows *more* than anyone else. Agamemnon's scene was a journey into obscurity and ignorance: Cassandra's is a journey into knowledge and insight.

It is a brilliant Aeschylean touch that the character who is most mysterious and unforthcoming should turn out to be the very one who has most to contribute. Neglected nearly 200 lines, unexplained and alone for 80 more, then stubbornly silent, even when she does utter sounds it is to sing disjointed phrases and riddles. Yet as her scene progresses she tells with a terrible, though often oracular, clarity of Troy and Argos, the past, the present, and future, the human and divine. Many of the enigmas, obscurities, and half-truths of the play are now made only too clear.

And this brave pilgrimage into knowledge seems almost removed from the passage of time (cf. p. 292, Knox 114). All is ready and waiting indoors when Clytemnestra goes back in (see 1055ff.); and when Cassandra goes in, it happens. The relentless forward momentum of her revelations carries us through her scene in such a way that Agamemnon's death follows closely on his departure over the purple cloth. Perhaps this makes more sense of my suggestion in 974b* that the Agamemnon scene is deliberately enigmatic, complicated, and incomplete. His scene takes us into the obscure foreboding which we must share with the chorus during the song at 975ff. It is Cassandra's place to lead the chorus, and us, out of confusion and perplexity towards insight and perspective. Then Agamemnon can die.

1372 enter Clytemnestra; the corpses are revealed

(a) *the transition 1331–1371*

One act ends with the departure of Cassandra at 1330 and a new one begins with the appearance of Clytemnestra and the corpses at 1372. This change of acts is also a major articulation in the play, since 1372 to the end is all aftermath, and is in some ways a transition to the following plays (cf. p. 328 below). And yet the transition is not effected by means of the usual strophic choral ode (stasimon): what stands there 'in place of a stasimon' is curious in several ways.

First there are the anapaests 1331–42, which, although they contain matter and imagery typical of a strophic act-dividing song and indeed comment more clearly and authoritatively than 975ff., are brief and astrophic. I have observed on *Hik* 974a* how anapaests in Aeschylus (and in Euripides astrophic dochmiacs) can come between acts at junctures of heightened tension. Particularly relevant here are the anapaests at *Cho* 855–68 which come in between Aegisthus' exit and his death cries.

There follow Agamemnon's death cries and the chorus's response in five lines of trochaic tetrameters (1343–7). In later tragedy such death cries come sometimes, as here, at the end of the lyric, sometimes during it, but nearly always in the form of complete lines of speech.[1] Outside the *Oresteia* there are no instances in Aeschylus of words heard from off-stage, and, assuming that the skene was still new, it is quite likely that this was one of the very first uses of the device. Philostratus *Vit Apoll* 6.11 includes, as it happens, among Aeschylus' innovations that τὸ ὑπὸ cκηνῆc ἀποθνήcκειν ἐπενόηcεν ὡc μὴ ἐν φανερῶι cφάττοι, but, since most of the other claims in this stretch of Philostratus are suspect, we can count it as no more than luck if he is right in this case.[2]

But the strangest part of the transition is the twelve pairs of iambic trimeters 1348–71. Clearly each pair is meant to be said by an individual choreut, though that does not necessarily mean that the chorus numbered twelve at the time of this production.[3] What is the point of these lines, which may seem at first sight laboured and even embarrassing or comic? First and foremost Aeschylus does not want the old men to stand idly by, and yet he cannot have them interfere or leave the stage. But this motive

[1] Seidensticker *Bauformen* 194 makes a category of 'Mord-Stichomythie' (they are in a sense dialogues, although only one party can hear the other). He illustrates with S. *El* 1398ff., E. *Hipp* 776ff., *Hec* 1035ff., *El* 747ff., *Or* 1296ff.; another good example is *Antiope* fr. xlviii 51ff. (Kambitsis), and cf. paratragic at *Cycl* 663.
[2] Flickinger *TAPA* 40 (1909) 109–15 is too keen to show Philostratus and the hypothesis to *Ag* to be right at any cost.
[3] It is my suspicion that the tragic chorus always numbered 15 (against 50 see p. 203 n. 2). It is usually alleged that there was an increase from 12 to 15 in the decades following *Oresteia*, but such a small change seems pointless. It should be borne in mind that the late evidence (*Life* of Soph., *Suda* etc.) that Sophocles increased the number from 12 may be based solely on this very passage of *Ag*. But these twelve couplets do not prove twelve choreuts, since Aeschylus may have given lines to only 12 out of 15 (thus the 'old' scholion on 1343 cf. Weissmann *Anweisungen* 10f.), or, more likely, the three trochaic lines 1344, 1346, 1347 may have accounted for the other three (cf. e.g. Hammond 419 n. 58). (Incidentally the relevant part of the Σ on Arph. *Kn* 589 is of no authority, see Fraenkel iii 831 addendum to 634.) In p. 393 n. 1 I argue that *Eum* 585–608 was also distributed among the members of the chorus, but that it is not clear evidence for their number. The idea that the tragic chorus was always 15 is not helped, I should add, by the new Basle krater (Inv. BS 415, for a picture see Simon *Plate* 2) which shows six choreutai dancing. This may be, as Simon 16 suggests, a hemichorus. On the other hand it may be two out of five files of three members each. On this important painting see *CR* N.s. 25 (1975) 59.

hardly by itself makes the device admirable,[1] since Aeschylus
did not have to labour it so. In later tragedy some sort of abortive
move towards the palace becomes conventional at murder scenes ;[2]
but nowhere is it so prolonged or so dilatory as this. Some scholars
(first K. O. Müller), who are embarrassed by the lines, try to
hide them beneath a rush of violent action.[3] For example
Wilamowitz *ed maj* 230 *actio* has 'denique strictis gladiis in
portam irrumpunt'. But there is no sign of such action in the
words (cf. Fraenkel iii 642): on the contrary the words are an
alternative to action. The second couplet (1350f.) suggests that
they should break in, but the rest recede from actually doing
anything. The couplets come to nothing, they are the negation
of action—a point well made in different ways by Winnington-
Ingram *CQ* n.s. 4 (1954) 23ff. and Wills *HSCP* 67 (1963) 255ff.
The chorus would not intervene even if it were technically
possible.

This observation leads to an important, though not often
recognized, function of these unique lines (cf. Dawe 45f.). The
chorus consists of men and many of them (at least twelve), and
yet all they can do is dither in a confused and ineffective discussion. They know that the palace is where they should take
action (see 1350, 1363), and all they do is to stay outside arguing.
So once more when attention is on the doors, the woman,
Clytemnestra, appears, still confident and dominant (at first).
The many in confusion prepare by contrast for the one who is
firm and unashamed. So in a sense 1348–71 lead up to the entry
of Clytemnestra, thus adding an extra point and complexity to
the transition.

A final simple point: in most tragedies where an atrocity or
murder is committed inside, a narrative intervenes between the
cries of the victim and the revelation of the dreadful scene (cf.
Dingel 104–12). Aeschylus has made an *exangelos* doubly unnecessary here by the prevision of Cassandra and by the vivid
boasting of Clytemnestra (1377ff.). It is not to deny the efficacy
of the traditional messenger speech to say that Aeschylus' alternatives here are much more powerful.

[1] As is claimed by e.g. Stephenson 44f., Flickinger 158f.; cf. Fraenkel iii 643.
[2] e.g. E. *Hipp* 776ff., *Med* 1271ff., see further Flickinger 158f., Hourmouziades
88f.
[3] Murray *Euripides and his Age* (2nd ed. London 1946) 157f. would interpolate
similar violent action at E. *Med* 1271ff.

(b) the murder tableau

The audience is presented with a scene of carnage. The tableau is given no over-all introduction or description; instead its details are highlighted one by one. Clytemnestra, perhaps spattered with blood (cf. 1389ff.), stands by the corpses of Agamemnon and Cassandra (Reinhardt's 'Gesinde' (105) is superfluous). Also to be seen are the net cloth which trapped Agamemnon (1492 = 1516, 1580) and the fatal bath (1538ff. cf. 1494 = 1518). It seems clear, moreover, that the corpse of Agamemnon is still actually enwrapped by the cloth and still lying in the tub. This might seem grotesque at first sight: but the whole point is, as the chorus repeatedly stresses in the ephymnia, that Agamemnon's death is degrading and unworthy.

There has been controversy over how this macabre tableau was staged. Most scholars since K. O. Müller have supposed that the wheeled platform, ekkyklema, was used. I have come across three other suggestions: that the constituents of the scene were carried out by mute scene-shifters,[1] that the doors were simply opened to reveal a tableau set up inside,[2] or, thirdly, that we are to imagine that the chorus has actually broken into the palace, in which case the scene may then be revealed by any of the other methods.[3] This last suggestion may be ruled out first, since the chorus's discussions lead away from action not towards it (see opposite). Nor is it possible to show the scene in the open doorway. Given the size of the theatre, the size of the doorway and the shadows thrown across it, it simply would not be visible; and it would block the way in and out.[4]

The use of the ekkyklema is discussed on pp. 442–3. In several ways this would seem to be an archetypal opportunity for the contrivance: the chorus remains outside and a tableau including corpses and props is revealed, supposed evidently to be still

---

[1] Thus Neckel Das Ekkyklema (Progr. Friedland 1890) 9ff. esp. 10–11, Reisch in D–R 240 and RE v 2205, Hammond 445. (The Σ on Arph. Lys 611 tends to be quoted in this context; but it refers to a funerary custom, not to a theatrical convention.)

[2] Including Bethe RhM N.F. 83 (1934) 21ff., P-C TDA 106, Spitzbarth 43, D–P 195f., Joerden Bauformen 411.

[3] e.g. Wilamowitz 175f., Stephenson 44f., Murray 227.

[4] These objections were implied by Bodensteiner 660, and have been made more clearly since by Hourmouziades 93f., Barrett E. Hipp ed 317f.; but they do not seem to have got through to all scholars.

inside to judge from Clytemnestra's line 1379 ἔστηκα δ' ἔνθ'
ἔπαιϲ' ἐπ' ἐξειργαϲμένοιϲ, and from the fact that Agamemnon is
apparently still in the bath. On the other hand there are no
lines of introduction or explanation such as are normally found
in later tragedy ('now you can see within' etc.)—in fact there is
no signal beyond the fully integrated line 1379. But if some sort
of 'notice' is given in later tragedy, then surely it is to be expected
here, when the skene was still new and the conventional machinery
still a curious novelty. The audience may have been used to the
convention of interior scenes from the pre-skene theatre (see p.
454), but one would expect some clearer signal of an entirely
new adaptation of this convention.[1] An even more serious problem
arises from the corresponding scene in *Cho* (see *Cho* 973a*,
973b*). There can be no doubt that the two scenes were staged
in the same way. Yet in *Cho* there is no introduction or any other
explanatory indication that the scene is on the ekkyklema; and,
in contrast to *Ag*, there is no indication that the tableau is supposed to be indoors. Indeed after twelve lines Orestes is calling
on the sun as witness (985f.), so that by then the scene is thought
of as outside (cf. Reinhardt 163 n. 1). This does not rule out the
ekkyklema, since the indoor–outdoor distinction is always flimsy;[2]
none the less *Cho* certainly does not weigh in favour of the new
mechanism.

What, then, of the scene-shifters? While not out of the question, it would undeniably be very awkward to carry out this
tableau and set it down. The bath particularly would tend to be
awkward. And Clytemnestra's line 1379 would lose much of its
force, even supposing that the audience would still accept the
interior-scene convention and take it literally as well as figuratively. None the less in the early days of the skene a need must
have been established for indoor scenes before the ekkyklema
was invented, and this might be one such instance. I am undecided between these two alternatives, both of which have
points against them; but in the absence of the kind of textual

[1] Was it, perhaps, a misunderstanding of this convention and not of Cassandra
which led the atrocious writer of the hypothesis to *Ag* to say that Agamemnon was
killed in view of the audience? (Even this gross error has found a friend in Verrall
lvif.)

[2] E. *Her* 1028ff. is one of the best-established uses of the ekkyklema, yet as soon
as he wakes at 1088 Heracles notices the air and the sun (cf. Lesky *Gnomon* 38
(1966) 745).

signals which are found in later tragedy I incline towards the
view that mute attendants were employed.

1577 enter Aegisthus (and bodyguard)

(a) insight approached and then lost

This is late in the play, a play already much longer than any
other we have by Aeschylus, for the first entry of a new character.
It is a surprise entry. Aegisthus has not been brought into the
play much so far, and then only obliquely; we have never been
led to think that he will enter. We may read him into Clytemnestra's protestations of fidelity at 606ff. and 855ff. (esp. 889–94),
but his presence is not explicit. He is there in Cassandra's vision
as the 'housekeeping lion' (1223ff.) and the 'wolf' (1259), but he
is not acknowledged by name until 1435–7 when Clytemnestra
suddenly produces him as her shield. But he is not then invoked
again, and his arrival is a deliberately unexpected turn of events.
No other character in Aeschylus enters when an act is anything
like so far progressed from the previous act-dividing song.[1] In
fact the scene 1372–1576 has been allowed to work itself towards
some sort of conclusion before Aegisthus ever arrives, so that he
is a late addition to something approaching a self-sufficient unit
(cf. the discussion of 'false endings' on *Seven* 1005a*, esp. p. 184).
This extraordinary technique and its dramatic significance have
not been given the attention they deserve.

First one has to consider 1372–1576.[2] Both Clytemnestra and
the chorus start from absolute positions, and they move towards
not so much compromise as insight. The chorus start from total
abhorrence and condemnation, but as the scene progresses they
admit the hand of Zeus (1481ff.), and the help of the ἀλάϲτωρ
as ϲυλλήπτωρ (1505ff.), and finally they are reduced to a moral
dilemma (1560ff.): δύϲμαχα δ' ἐϲτὶ κρῖναι. Clytemnestra starts by
glorying in her sole responsibility. But she introduces the δαίμων

---

[1] It is 234 lines after 1331–42. The next latest is Orestes at *Cho* 212, 129 lines
into the act (on the Herald in *Seven* (158?) see *Seven* 1005a*). For an entry as far
into the act as Aegisthus we have to turn to *late* Sophocles and Euripides e.g.
S. *El* 1326 (228), E. *IT* 725 (258). (It is interesting to note that a new entry with
a new tone near the end of an act is a recurrent Menandrean technique—see
Handley in *Entr. Hardt* xvi (1969) 11ff.)

[2] For a particularly good account see Dodds *Progress* 60; also useful Deckinger
29f., Lesky *Ges Schr* 102, *WSt Beiheft* 5 (*Festschr. für W. Kraus*, Vienna 1972) 218ff.,
Reinhardt 106ff., Lebeck 56–8.

γέννης τῆςδε as a source of the deed (1475ff.), and then claims she is somehow the manifestation of the ἀλάστωρ (1497ff.). Finally, faced with the truth that, since it was θέςμιον for Agamemnon to be a case of παθεῖν τὸν ἔρξαντα (1564), the same must be true for her, she proposes (1567ff.) a bargain with the *daimon*, by which she will exchange most of her goods in return for immunity from retribution. The reason why these shifting positions ring true, why they deserve to be regarded as *insights*, is that they accord with so much of the thematic material explored earlier in the play in the great choral songs and, even more, in the insights of Cassandra. Aeschylus leads us to believe that Clytemnestra and the chorus are somehow getting at the truth of the matter, and are searching for a way out of the tangle. So in *Eum* he will convince us that there are ways out. I offer tentatively two ways in which this scene in *Ag* foreshadows *Eum*. First, it is permeated with judicial language (e.g. 1412, 1421, 1429f., 1505ff., 1560): it is as though it were a trial, but without a legal framework and without an independent arbitrator. Secondly the scene moves from irreconcilable implacability towards a more amenable insight. This happens in a much more important way in the great final scene of *Eum*; but there the movement is successfully and triumphantly concluded.[1]

If the great scene 1372–1576 foreshadows the trial and solution of *Eum*, then the final philistine contribution of Aegisthus foreshadows *Cho*. His first, main speech leads up to the moment of his revenge-return: τραφέντα δ' αὖθις ἡ Δίκη κατήγαγεν (1607). And it is not long before the chorus is wishing that Orestes will do the same (1646–8, 1667; see *Cho* 1a*). On the insight that was being approached Aegisthus reimposes the blind monotony of the blood feud, and his small-minded assertion of right leads to alienation and almost to brute force. He still talks of guilt and justice, but in a very different way (and contrast his intentions on the wealth of Agamemnon at 1638f. with the insight of Clytemnestra at 1567ff. Aegisthus supplies a new and destructive momentum to the final scene just as it appeared to be moving

[1] Note the complex structure of the section 1407–1576: see Kranz *Studien* 272ff., Peretti 181ff., Fraenkel iii 66of. Basically an epirrhematic structure in which Clytemnestra contributes iambics moves on to one where she contributes anapaests. This same shift within an epirrhematic framework is to be found between Athena's contributions to *Eum* 778–891 and 916–1020. The technical resemblance is slight, but perhaps not negligible.

towards understanding. His crude assertiveness sets the scene for
the further vengeance and tragedy of Orestes.

(b) Aegisthus as outsider

Aegisthus' delayed intervention not only breaks the movement
towards insight and thus leads into *Cho*, it also gives dramatic
stress to the role played in the murder by the male, and hence,
more importantly, by Clytemnestra. She achieved the deception
of Agamemnon and his murder entirely by herself without any
direct help from Aegisthus. Although he boasts that he laid hold
of Agamemnon by his plotting (1608–9 cf. 1223–5), he also has
to admit that he took no active part—he was 'out of the house':
καὶ τοῦδε τἀνδρὸς ἡψάμην θυραῖος ὤν . . . (1608). So it is important
to observe that he will have come on, not from the house, but
from a side entrance: he is an outsider to the scene. This also
adds significance to his final exit into the palace (see 1673a*).
It is also worth noting that he has armed henchmen with him;
in contrast to Clytemnestra whose main weapons were the purple
cloth and the net-robe.[1]

The late entry of Aegisthus from outside militates strongly
against the suggestion that the calyx-crater by the Dokimasia
painter in Boston is inspired by Aeschylus.[2] In this painting
Aegisthus strikes the first, and second, blow, while Clytemnestra
merely backs him up with her axe. In Aeschylus great stress is
laid on the fact that Clytemnestra *alone* does the deed and that
Aegisthus only turns up after it. Of course a pottery painter will
feel no obligation to follow a literary inspiration precisely: but
it is only by means of significant correspondences that such
an influence can be upheld.[3] The single-handed mastery of

---

[1] The henchmen, like most 'spear-carriers' (see *Pers* 155c*), probably entered
with their master, rather than on summons at 1649ff. On their exit at the end see
p. 331. Only a few are needed, though Hermann (652) may be too extreme when
he says 'Hastati . . . non sunt plures quam duo ministri'.

[2] This was argued by E. Vermeule on first publication in *AJA* 70 (1966) 1ff.;
against it see Davies *BCH* 93 (1969) 214ff. esp. 258–60. For further bibliography
see Davies *Ant K* 16 (1973) 62 n. 13.

[3] I simply list here other divergences between Aeschylus and the painting. In
Aeschylus (i) no one else is present at the murder; (ii) Cassandra did not run away
(on the contrary she meets death face to face); (iii) Clytemnestra's weapon is
left deliberately inexplicit (see Fraenkel iii 806ff., but also Lesky *WSt* N.F. 1
(1967) 20f.); (iv) Agamemnon is killed *in* the bath. It is also worth noting here
that there are several telling divergences in the 'Choephoroi' painting. In

Clytemnestra, and hence the passive role of Aegisthus, are crucial
to Aeschylus, and are probably departures from earlier versions.

1673 exeunt omnes

(a) Clytemnestra and Aegisthus

Although Aegisthus does all the blustering, it is Clytemnestra
who makes the only two positive and effective contributions
(1654–61, 1672–3). She speaks the last two lines of the play.
Unfortunately the text of this last couplet is not certain. However,
the paraphrase in the scholion (παλ.) gives just the sense required:
ἐγώ, φηςί, καὶ cὺ κρατοῦντεс τῶνδε τῶν δωμάτων διαθηcόμεθα τὰ
καθ᾽ αὑτοὺс καλῶc.¹ Like the scholion the last line of the text has
τῶνδε δωμάτων, and Fraenkel's attack on τῶνδε (iii 802f.),
accepted by D–P (223) though not by Page *OCT*, seems to me
completely empty. In the context of the final departure into the
house a deictic reference to the building itself, the object and
setting of all the events of the tragedy, is entirely in place (see
Wilamowitz *Kl Schr* vi 221, though he is wrong to suppose
Aegisthus is reluctant). This deictic helps to bring out the
significance of this final action for the play and for the trilogy.
Aegisthus entered from outside, see 1577b*: yet at the end he is
taken into the house, as having joint authority. When we see
him go inside with Clytemnestra, we see him drawn inextricably
into the evils of the house. The action has obvious visual meaning;

Aeschylus (i) Aegisthus has only just arrived home, and so would not be sitting
in his palace; (ii) there is nothing about his kithara; (iii) Clytemnestra is *not*
present at the murder; (iv) she calls for an axe but never receives it; (v) there is
no sign that Electra is present at the murder; (vi) Pylades, on the other hand,
should be there; (vii) Orestes is disguised as a traveller and therefore should not
be in arms. These differences far outweigh the similarities, which should be
attributed to an earlier version, presumably Stesichorus.

¹ The text of 1672: out of the scholion and into the text we want to supply,
if possible, equivalents to ἐγώ, καλῶс, and τὰ καθ᾽ αὑτούс; yet we have only four
syllables to spare. So far as I can see the only way to get all three elements into the
text is to emend ὑλαγμάτων in 1672. Fraenkel shows that the genitive would be
idiomatic, but the accusative would still be Greek. We can then read either e.g.
ὕλαγμα ⟨πάντ᾽ ἐγώ⟩ (Musgrave) . . . ⟨καλῶс⟩; or ὑλάγματ᾽ ⟨εὖ δ᾽ ἐγώ⟩ (Hense)
and supply an object at the end of 1673 e.g. τὸ πᾶν, βίον, πόλιν. But before going
to such lengths to supply an object to θήсομεν, it must be admitted that the scholiast's
vague τὰ καθ᾽ αὑτοὺс looks as though he himself had no object in his text and
supplied it out of τῶνδε δωμάτων. If this is possible after all (cf. *Med* 926), then the
traditional restoration ⟨ἐγώ⟩ . . . ⟨καλῶс⟩ could stand. But I am attracted by ⟨εὖ
δ᾽ ἐγώ⟩ and a noun as the last word.

and the deictic points to it. The simultaneous exit (see p. 91 above) links Clytemnestra and Aegisthus together. Together (κρατοῦντε) they will take over the power and wealth of Agamemnon (cf. 1638ff.), and together they are trapped in the history of the house. Their exit is the abandonment of Clytemnestra's bold offer (1568ff.) to give up most of the wealth in return for salvation. This meaning might be reinforced if the armed henchmen follow Clytemnestra and Aegisthus inside: the forces of brute power go into the palace on their side.[1]

(b) the chorus

At 1657 Clytemnestra told the chorus to go home (this much emerges from the textual corruption); and at the end it seems that they steal away in silence. This is unusual and demands explanation. Four of Aeschylus' plays (*Pers, Seven, Hik, Eum*) end with a proper procession, and so do several of Sophocles' and Euripides'. *Cho* ends with an anapaestic tailpiece, and so do nearly all of the later tragedies.[2] At the end of *Prom* the chorus does not have the last word; but the chorus is singularly negligible in that play, and the end is altogether extraordinary (see *Prom* 1093a*, 1093b*). The final exit of a chorus, if it was managed in the usual way, would take time. Indeed in the fifth century the word ἔξοδος referred to the song which the chorus sang as it went off (see pp. 472–3). The silent departure at the end of *Ag* was surely meant to be unusual, and to be noticed. It might be taken to show the chorus' dejected yet hostile subordination: Clytemnestra and Aegisthus have won, and the citizens, represented by the chorus, must be subject to them. Although this ending would have a certain effectiveness, we must admit that

[1] We cannot say whether the corpses were withdrawn, or carried off, before or after the exit of Clytemnestra and Aegisthus. (I do not think much of Bodensteiner's idea (732) that Clytemnestra and the bodies were taken in between 1611 and 1642, and that she re-emerged at 1654. 1654 is an intervention from someone present, not an entry.)

[2] The authenticity of many of these anapaestic tailpieces in Euripides has been attacked by Barrett E. *Hipp ed* 417f. But he should hardly refer without qualification to *Ag* as an instance of a silent final exit, as there are obviously special circumstances. If Barrett is right then did these conventional tailpieces replace genuine ones? (cf. Pearson on the trochaics at the end of S. *OT*, 'periit, ut opinor, anapaestorum clausula'). But Barrett's case as a whole is far from conclusive. Mayerhofer *Über der Schlüsse* etc. (diss. Erlangen 1908) 2–7 defends the end of *Ag* as it is.

some final anapaests may be lost. But, assuming that the ending is sound, then the silent exit of the chorus reinforces the meaning of the exit of the rulers into the palace (see 1673a*): Aegisthus and Clytemnestra are, for the moment, victorious.[1]

[1] It is regrettable that many scholars, including Headlam, Verrall, Thomson, Campbell, and Lloyd-Jones, omit the final stage instructions of *Ag* altogether.

VII. CHOEPHOROI

1 enter Orestes and Pylades (without attendants, see 653*)

(a) Orestes' return

THE return of Orestes has been foreseen in *Ag.* When Clytemnestra explains his absence at 877–86 it is only his absence which
is in question; but Cassandra's premonition of Orestes and his
return at 1280–5 is unmistakable and clear, even though she does
not name him: ἥξει . . . κάτεισιν . . . ἄξειν νιν ὑπτίασμα κειμένου
πατρός. Then in the final scene the forward-looking references
are explicit. At 1646–8 the chorus hopes that Orestes is alive
and will come back (κατελθὼν δεῦρο) and slaughter the pair; and
again at 1667 they trust that a daimon will bring Orestes back
(δεῦρο). Also Aegisthus' own account of his return and revenge
(1603ff.) is obviously applicable in its turn to Orestes, and there
is a positive ironic foreshadowing in its wording, especially at
line 1607.

So the first action of the play, the entry of Orestes, is already
imbued in advance with dramatic meaning. It is no mere
stepping-on to get the play started, it is the return of the avenger.[1]
The significance of the action may have been brought out still
further by the words, but it is underlined to some extent even
in the snippets we have, in particular by line 3: ἥκω γὰρ ἐς
γῆν τήνδε καὶ κατέρχομαι.[2] As Aristophanes' Aeschylus quite
rightly says (*Frogs* 1163–5), Orestes both arrives and returns;
the single stage action has a double meaning. Rather as the
necessary entry of the chorus at the beginning of *Hik* (1a*) turns
out to be a vital element in the play as a whole (see *Hik* 1073*),
so this action in *Cho*, since it is the first of the play, can only be

---

[1] It is misleading of Wilamowitz 57 to include this scene along with 'cancelled'
entries, since the point of them is that the first entry does *not* represent a positive
action within the play (see *Seven* 1b*).

[2] Aristophanes leaves us uncertain whether this was the end of the sentence,
and whether it was immediately followed by l. 4.

seen in its full significance near the end, when it takes its place in the larger dramatic form—see further *Cho* 1063*.

(b) Pylades

It is possible but most unlikely that Pylades spoke during the lost portions of the prologue; and, if he did not, then the only place that he speaks is at 900–2, see further 892b*. Probably the audience will have quickly inferred that Pylades is to be a κωφὸν πρόϲωπον, since he is the lesser member of a fixed pair of characters.[1] Not many such pairs occur in the surviving tragedies, e.g. Kratos and Bia in *Prom* (see p. 240 n. 1), Acamas with Demophon at E. *Hkld* 118ff., and the Dioscuri at the end of E. *El* and *Hel*; but there seem to be many pairs of brothers in the lost plays e.g. A. *Aitnaiai*, *Phineus*, E. *Melanippe Desm*, *Hyps*; and it seems likely that of some of these pairs, only one spoke. Pylades will have been assumed to be one such κωφὸν πρόϲωπον, as he is, indeed, in S. *El*. In other *Orestes* plays (E. *El*, *IT*, *Or*), although he has a considerable speaking part, Pylades tends to retain vestigial traces of his role as the lesser member of a pair. He seldom comes and goes apart from Orestes, and is sometimes silent for a long time in a way that would not be normal for a fully independent character, particularly at E. *IT* 793–900, *Or* 1018–69 (see further Kaffenberger 13–20).

21 Orestes and Pylades go into hiding

the techniques of hiding-scenes

It looks as though Orestes first saw the approach of the chorus at the very point that M resumes (10, Dindorf's extralinear ⟨ἔα⟩ might be right). For six lines he speculates on the significance of the procession (10–15), then he concludes on its purpose and identifies Electra (16–18); then a prayer to Zeus (18–19), before he suggests to Pylades that they should step aside to learn for sure what is going on (20–1). We have here a compact of three devices of dramatic technique, all of which have a long history in Greek drama.

First, someone is seen at a distance so that there is time before the entry to react in some detail to the approach.[2] This has

---

[1] See Spitzbarth 57, Hourmouziades *Hellenika* 21 (1968) 286f.

[2] Lebeck 97f. argues that Orestes' worry over the black-garbed chorus in 12–13 foreshadows his vision of the approach of the Erinyes at the end of the play. But

already been encountered and discussed at *Hik* 176ff. (see 234a*)
and *Ag* 489ff. (see 503b*). Secondly, Orestes and Pylades go
because someone else is approaching. This is also true of Danaus
at the approach of the Egyptians in *Hik*, but there the connection
of the two actions is deliberately played down (see *Hik* 775*).
The device, which allows a close and tense transition, continues
through tragedy and comedy; in later tragedy, see e.g. S. *El*
1428ff., E. *El* 962ff., *Phaethon* 216ff.[1] But it is particularly common
during prologues, see e.g. S. *El* 77ff., E. *Hipp* 51ff., *Hec* 51ff.,
Ion 77ff. (cf. Wilson *GRBS* 8 (1967) 206); and it also recurs on
the approach of the chorus, as here, in S. *OC* 111ff., E. *Phoen*
193ff., *Phaethon* 54ff., *Alope* fr. 105 N². This becomes almost
formulaic in Menandrean comedy; see Handley Men. *Dysc ed*
171f. (and add *Aspis* 245ff.).

   The third point is that Orestes and Pylades do not go away
(as at S. *El* 77ff.), they stay in hiding in order to overhear what
ensues. This recurs also on the approach of the chorus in E. *El*
and S. *OC*; and the device may be traced throughout ancient
comedy.[2] But this useful, if contrived, technique never became
common in Greek tragedy, and there are very few examples of
any other kinds of eavesdropping. It is possible that the procedure was taken over by comedy, as is suggested with knocking
at the door on pp. 340–1 below. Although this may be an early
use of these techniques, Aeschylus handles them with a sure
touch.

   Finally we may wonder where Orestes and Pylades went.
σταθῶμεν ἐκποδών (20) suggests that they simply retreated into
the background. It is possible that there was some scenery where
they could hide; but more likely, since the skene does not at this

no such significance can be read *back* into this place. In any case the πῆμα νέον
(13) is put as an alternative which is then rejected. Lebeck (194 n. 5) also favours
Verrall's far-fetched idea that at 1048ff. Orestes sees the chorus as the Erinyes.
Apart from its pointlessness, this rests on the reading δμωαί in 1048, which is
probably rightly emended by Lobel (accepted by Page *OCT*) to δμοιαί (alternatively ποῖαι Hermann).

   [1] For some examples from Old and New Comedy see Bennett *Motivation of
Exits* etc. (diss. Ann Arbor 1932) 19–21.
   [2] See Fraenkel *Beobachtungen zu Aristophanes* (Rome 1962) 22–6 cf. Lesky *Ges
Schr* 140 n. 10. For Plautus and Terence I note the existence of Hiatt *Eavesdropping
in Roman Comedy* (diss. Chicago 1946); but his note (p. 2 n. 2) on earlier drama
bodes ill for the rest of the work. It is possible that the famous Würzburg 'Skeno-
graphie' fragment (= *Illustrations* iii. 3, 43) shows an eavesdropping scene; but it
is uncertain whether the play in question is a fifth-century tragedy.

stage of the play represent the palace (see 584*), they hid in the doorway (like Oedipus and Antigone in S. *OC*?). We cannot tell; but probably we can reject the one alternative which some commentators, who have passed an opinion, have favoured: that they went away down an eisodos.[1] When Orestes intervenes at 212 he breaks in suddenly ('prosilit' Wilamowitz *ed maj* 254 *actio*), and he makes it clear that he has heard what preceded. It is not plausible to suppose that he came all the way up an eisodos before this line.

22 enter chorus and Electra

staging

The opening words of the chorus ἰαλτὸς ἐκ δόμων ἔβαν seem at first glance to be evidence that they entered directly from the doors of the skene. On the other hand, Orestes gives no indication of this, as might have been expected, and the long announcement of their approach and the way that Orestes can pick out Electra all strongly suggest an entry from the side.[2] The case for entry from an eisodos is stronger, and fits with other indications that the skene did not at this stage represent the palace (see 584*). We cannot know at precisely what moment Electra and the chorus were first seen by the audience; but the stage direction should not go by line 10,[3] since that is when Orestes sees them in the distance. I suspect that they entered as they began their song at 22, like nearly all other choruses (cf. p. 64).[4]

Hermann (*ed* 653; cf. Bodensteiner 733 but *contra* Richter 215) argued that Electra did not enter with the chorus, but first came on after the song at 84. This is refuted by the inclusion of Electra in the announcement at 16–18. Further προπομποῦσα[5]

---

[1] Thus e.g. Bodensteiner 692, Wilamowitz *comm* 53, *ed maj* 248 *actio*, Groeneboom 9.

[2] For entry from the skene see e.g. Hermann 613, Capps 10, Bodensteiner 678, Harmon 12, Webster *GTP* 7. For entry from an eisodos see e.g. Blass 20, Wilamowitz *comm* 53, *ed maj* 248 *actio*, Bolle 14, Groeneboom 105, Reinhardt 125, Dale *Papers* 267.

[3] As e.g. Bodensteiner 733, Lattimore *tr* 93 cf. P-C *DFA*² 244. Lloyd-Jones *tr* 10f. duplicates the stage instruction.

[4] It is instructive that at *Clouds* 534f. Aristophanes does not accurately recall the motive of the entry of Electra and the chorus (cf. Newiger *Hermes* 89 (1961) 422ff., Dover *Clouds ed* p. 168): but he does remember the lock (*Clouds* 536), and the setting at the tomb (*Frogs* 1139).

[5] Lobel's emendation of προπομπός—my point is not affected.

in 23 (cf. πομποί 86) suggests that the chorus accompanies Electra. It seems that Hermann did not like the idea that Electra stood idly by during the whole song. But this is similar to Danaus in *Hik* (see 1b*) and is not at all awkward provided one does not think in realistic terms.[1]

212 Orestes and Pylades come out of hiding

text

The re-entry of Orestes is held back until Electra has clearly shown her loyalty and has been brought to a high emotional pitch by the lock of hair. Then Orestes intervenes abruptly, and the anagnorisis follows quickly. Orestes' first words εὔχου τὰ λοιπά κτλ. (212f.) seem to take up what precedes. And yet they follow very strangely on 205–11, in fact they do not follow at all. Fraenkel (*Ag ed* Appendix D (815ff.)) for this and other reasons revived Schütz's resort of deleting 205–11. As Fraenkel 819 stresses, Orestes' opening line follows extremely well on 201–4, even to the echo of τυχεῖν (203) in τυγχάνειν (213). Lloyd-Jones (*CQ* n.s. 11 (1961) 171ff.) has since strongly contested Fraenkel's arguments and the deletions in E. *El* which Fraenkel claimed go with them. But, while he makes many telling points, he gives (on pp. 175f.) no good reply to the fact that 212f. follows from 204 and not 211. His claim that 'the words of the prayer will still have been fresh in the minds of the audience' is special pleading: at the highly dramatic moment when Orestes suddenly steps out of hiding it would be disastrous to pick up some words which have been followed and obliterated by a startling new discovery. On the other hand, Lloyd-Jones (176) effectively revives Wilamowitz's defence of the dramatic relevance of the footprints, and this has been reinforced by Solmsen.[2]

I rather favour Weil's transposition of the prayer 201–4 to

[1] What did the chorus do with their χοαί when they began to dance? We might be tempted, despite the title, to suppose that only Electra carried a pot, as is claimed by Cunningham *RhM* N.F. 105 (1962) 190, who points to 23, 86, 149f. But this is confuted by lines 14f. (which also look like the source of the title). It is quite likely, in fact, that the χοαί were exploited as an element in the choreography, for the first song at least (cf. A. *Hydrophoroi* and Electra's aria at E. *El* 112ff.).

[2] Solmsen *MKNAW* 30. 2 (1967) 31ff. esp. 35–7. However, Solmsen's positive praise of the present order of lines as a profound piece of female psychology is specious: one could justify any mixed-up order of lines on such elusive grounds.

follow after 211. It has been objected (Blass 100) that 201 does not follow well after 211: but it does not follow ill. The storms referred to in 202 are the tormented confusions of 211.[1] The couplet 207–8 (rejected by Rossbach) is still suspect. Pylades is a marginal figure and should hardly be brought to the fore at such a vital moment (cf. Fraenkel 820f.); or if he must be mentioned then there should be more explanation (which is why many editors have supposed a lacuna after 206 or 208). Also καὶ γάρ in 207, while it can be defended in a dogged way (see Lloyd-Jones 173), is uncomfortable. And 209 follows well on 206. So, while I do not finally deny the Aeschylean authorship of 205–6, 209–11, I doubt that they are in the right place in the text. Orestes' intervention should follow line 204. It is impossible to account for this disruption palaeographically; it may be the result of deliberate alteration.

584 exeunt Orestes, Pylades, and Electra

the move from tomb to palace

Cho is in two distinct parts, divided by the song 585–651 (cf. Wilamowitz 177 etc.). All the play from the end of the first song up to this song forms one huge act, dominated by the monumental kommos, which is at once a θρῆνος for Agamemnon and an invocation of his ghostly aid. The transition from this great invocation to Clytemnestra's dream and thence to the plan of action is effected by the chorus's four lines at 510–13. Orestes lays his plans tersely and efficiently in the final speech (554–84), and after it the stage is cleared of actors.[2]

One of the factors which lead us to talk of the two parts of *Cho* is the way that the first part of the play is set at the tomb of Agamemnon and the second at the palace. This has been a controversial topic, but most commentators now agree that in

---

[1] The ominous ambiguities which Lebeck 108f. detects in Electra's mental turmoil, especially in 211, are not seriously weakened if 211 is transferred to before 201. Rather the juxtaposition of desperation with apotropaic optimism, which pervades Orestes' role, is introduced here.

[2] It seems that Lloyd-Jones (*tr* 46, cf. Andrieu 200) supposes that Orestes stays on during the song, since his only stage instruction is 'Orestes goes up to the gateway' at 653. But Orestes' plan at 560ff. (see esp. ἥξω 561) strongly suggests that he should go off and re-enter. His re-entry at 653 also adds extra point to the last antistrophe of the song; see Kranz *Stas* 165.

the middle of *Cho* the scene changes or 'refocuses': cf. *Pers* 598c*.[1]
Thus here the shift happens not at one particular moment, but
between 584 when Orestes leaves the grave and 653 when he
arrives at the door; and so those who have supposed that some
bits of scenery were actually removed or brought on have only
confused the issue.[2] The chorus does not leave the stage, as in
Eum and S. *Aj*, and the shift is not explicit.

In the first half of the play all attention is on the tomb (cf. esp.
Reinhardt 110f.). The chorus comes on from the side (see 22*)
and ἐκ δόμων (22) is no more a sign that the palace is on stage
than δόμους at *Pers* 159. Lines 264ff. are a sign that the scene is
set away from the palace rather than just outside; and when
Orestes says that Electra must go inside (554, 579) this need not
imply they are outside. Moreover, neither of Orestes' references
to the ἕρκειοι πύλαι (561, 571) has any deictic reference, whereas,
when he re-enters at 653, he goes straight up to them and knocks,
naming them in the first line (653), and so indicating that he has
now arrived at the place formerly referred to verbally.[3] On the
other hand, in the second half of the play it is the tomb which
is neglected. The only reference is in the anapaests at 721ff.,
where there is no deictic indication. At the same time Aeschylus
may here be exploiting some indefiniteness in the dichotomy of
the scenes.

Most editors have supposed that, since Electra has been given
a task inside the palace (554ff., 579ff.), she goes off through the
skene door; and it might be argued that this facilitates the change

[1] For substantial discussions in favour of the change of scene see Wilamowitz
comm 44f., Verrall xxxf., Bethe 95 n. 14, Blass 19f., Tucker xlf., De Falco[2] 9ff. (at
great length), Dale *Papers* 267. Against see e.g. D–R 250f., P-C *TDA* 43, Harmon
TAPA 63 (1932) 11f., Winnington-Ingram *Arethusa* 2 (1969) 131 and n. 31.
Winnington-Ingram's claim that E. *Hel* 1165f. is a dig at *Cho* seems far-fetched,
since in the context it would be pointless (cf. Kannicht 308f.).

[2] See e.g. Wilamowitz 177, Tucker xli, Blass 20, Webster *Chorus* 127 (Webster,
as usual, drags in the ekkyklema).

[3] It is unclear from the text alone what is the reference of τούτωι in 583 at
the end of the scene. Many, including Wilamowitz, take it to be Apollo, represented by the ἀγυιεὺς βωμός before the door (see p. 319 and n. 1 above). But,
apart from the shift of scene, an allusion to Agamemnon would fit the context
much better. Wilamowitz (*comm* 210) says that ἐποπτεύω can only be used of
a god; but the very word is used of Agamemnon at 489, and he is, like Darius
in *Pers*, invoked in cultic terms. Garvie *BICS* 17 (1970) 85, following Tucker,
makes a case for a reference to Hermes; but at the conclusion of the first part of
the play a reference to Agamemnon, the object of the entire kommos, seems
more in place.

of scene by making the skene represent the palace (cf. Wilamowitz 177, but *contra* Bolle 14f.). But if, as has been argued above,
the scene is brought back into focus at line 653, then it would
only be confusing if Electra went off through the door. It is
better if she departs with the others, as though towards the
palace. We do not see Electra again (she does not, of course,
say 691ff.); she is not even mentioned. She is entirely excluded
from the rest of the trilogy, just as she was excluded from *Ag*.
This uncompromising abandonment of a named character is
remarkable. While we are familiar with this sort of technique in
Euripides, this is the only clear instance in Aeschylus, at least
outside *Prom*. She has played her part and so she is dispensed
with.

653 re-enter Orestes and Pylades

the deceitful approach to the palace

Orestes' return to the palace is quite unlike his father's. He is on
foot, carrying his own baggage. Like any ordinary traveller he
must knock at the door and first satisfy the servant who keeps it.
While Clytemnestra's deceit of Agamemnon took a startling,
exotic form, Orestes' deceit of her is achieved through modest,
apparently innocuous, ordinariness.

Orestes goes straight to the door and knocks, and calls out to
a servant (653–6). Again, shortly after the introduction of the
skene, we have the prototype of a theatrical technique with a
long history. But, while common in comedy, knocking at the
door is hardly used again in surviving tragedy despite this precedent. The possible instances are few enough to be surveyed.[1]
E. *IT* 1308 apparently refers to the action of the Messenger at
1304ff., but it seems he has been shaking the door rather than
knocking formally as in *Cho*.[2] Although it has often been assumed,
there is no sign in the text that Menelaus knocked at E. *Hel*
435f., nor the Messenger at *Phoen* 1067ff. Lastly it is accepted
that the sons of Hypsipyle knocked at the door just before E.
Hyps fr. Ii (p. 25 Bond). But this is not definite, for if the woman

---

[1] See also Mooney *The House-door* etc. (diss. Baltimore 1914) 19f., Spitzbarth
49, Petersman *WSt* N.F. 5 (1971) 91ff. esp. 91 n. 3; cf. Burnett 81.

[2] Murray's emendation of E. *IT* 1302 and his interpretation of ἑρμηνεύς as a
ῥόπτρον are highly dubious.

who speaks line 4[1] comes to the door because of this knocking, then why does she not address the young men straight away? It may be that knocking at the door quickly acquired comic or mundane associations, or had them all along, and that is why the device was discarded by the tragedians. It is noticeable that the language of *Cho* 654 and 657 is distinctly colloquial.

The text leaves us uncertain whether the servant who replies in 657 comes outside. Since he speaks only one line it is probably best if he is only heard from inside and the door is not opened until Clytemnestra comes out at 668. Moreover, since 658–67 are all addressed to the doorkeeper, and there is no time for him to fetch Clytemnestra at 667/8, this is another indication that he did not come out: otherwise his presence would be awkward at 668 when Clytemnestra enters without his having fetched her.

According to most commentators Orestes and Pylades are attended by a train of servants and attendants. So far as I can see this is based exclusively on Clytemnestra's instruction in 712–13: M reads ἄγ᾽ αὐτὸν εἰς ἀνδρῶνας εὐξένους δόμων / ὀπισθόπους δὲ τούςδε καὶ ξυνεμπόρους. This plurality is unwelcome. Orestes has returned to his vengeance by stealth and guile, and he should not be encumbered by a camp-following. There is no other trace of these followers in the text which elsewhere indicates that his only companion is Pylades. In the prologue Orestes refers only to Pylades (20); and throughout the kommos no one else is referred to. In 207–8 (if genuine—see pp. 211–2 above) Electra sees just one other set of prints belonging to ϲυνεμπόρου τινός. No other accomplices are brought into the plan at 561ff.: note ἄμφω in 563. And, above all, when Orestes tells his false story in 674ff. he is αὐτόφορτον οἰκείαι ϲαγῆι.

All this evidence conspires to support Pauw's simple emendation of 713 to ὀπισθόπουν τε τοῦδε καὶ ξυνέμπορον,[2] which is then just a periphrasis for Pylades. This extremely attractive emendation implies an interesting consequence. The change of three

---

[1] This woman is always taken to be Hypsipyle herself, but the hypothesis in *POxy* 2455 fr. 14 ll. 193–4 (also in Bond, p. 21) suggests that she may be, rather, the queen Eurydice. The supplement πύλα]ϲ in fr. Ii l. 4 which is taken as evidence of knocking is not certain; χέρα]ϲ is possible, for example.

[2] This is accepted by Hermann, Wecklein, Sidgwick, Thomson[2], Page *OCT*. Pauw still read δὲ, but Stanley had already suggested τε and Hermann combined the two. Either τοῦδε or τόνδε would be possible.

singulars to plurals, including the dubious treatment of ὀπιςθόπους as a plural, can hardly be a scribal error; it is surely a deliberate alteration. Only one motive seems likely: that a later producer wanted to introduce extra mute stage-figures. A group of travellers, all equipped with hats and packs, would provide a picturesque and crowded spectacle. In fact Verrall (184–7) in the spirit of the adaptation ingeniously defends this crowding and advocates 'twenty or fifty' fellow travellers for Orestes.[1] To introduce them no interpolation is necessary, only a slight change to three words (though I would not rule out the possibility that the line is interpolated). If this train of argument is right, then this is an intriguing and instructive glimpse of the work of later producers. Aeschylus was too bare for their taste; and they took any easy opportunity to introduce more colour and spectacle. On the whole question of spectacle in Aeschylus see §4.

668 enter Clytemnestra (with attendants)

the reversal of Agamemnon

This entry can hardly be regarded as prepared for or expected. Of course we have to see Clytemnestra at some stage, but we do not expect her here. When Orestes lays his plans and envisages the outcome at 554–84 he predicts that he will go in through the gate, find Aegisthus on the throne, and spit him on the spot; there is no mention of Clytemnestra.[2] So the excitement of anticipation is developed, but not in the way that it will turn out (further on false preparation see pp. 94–6 above). The intervening song 585–651 takes Clytemnestra as its theme, especially at 623ff., and thus turns attention towards her punishment; but the song also has a complex reference to the other murders in the trilogy (see Lebeck *CPh* 62 (1967) 182ff., cf. Winnington-Ingram 138 n. 76). When after the song Orestes re-enters the emphasis is again on the man (656, 664ff.); but it is the woman who enters.

This approach to the first confrontation of Orestes and Clytemnestra should be borne in mind when we notice how it

[1] Professor Lloyd-Jones sends me this apposite anecdote: Cecil B. de Mille making a film of Christ once said "Who are those guys?" "The Twelve Apostles". "Make 'em fifty!"

[2] Cf. Winnington-Ingram 138f., Reinhardt 129f., Dawe 55f. Note that the plot of Orestes, as well as being misleading in several details, does not include the essential element of Orestes' 'false death'.

corresponds to the meeting of Clytemnestra and Agamemnon at
Ag 855 (cf. Murray 180, Lesky *Ges Schr* 103f.).[1] The first meeting
at the palace door is delayed in *Cho* to a point comparably as
late in the play as was that in *Ag*. Again the rightful lord of the
house is met by Clytemnestra, who again will dictate the terms of
his entry into the house. The male has come from afar after a
long absence, and once again he has to gain entry to the doorway
of his heritage. But in *Cho* the situation is crucially reversed: this
time it is the new arrival, Orestes, who is the deceiver, and
Clytemnestra who is the deceived. Agamemnon was in a chariot
and at a public occasion: Orestes has to knock like an everyday
traveller. But while Agamemnon was met with deceitful ambiguity and dangerous persuasion, Orestes is met by ordinary
civility. For, although Clytemnestra still supervises his entry into
the palace, she is no longer in total command of the situation.

718 exeunt Orestes and Pylades, exit Clytemnestra

the threshold crossed by deceit

It may be that Orestes and Pylades are taken in by servants
when Clytemnestra completes her instructions at 715. But it is
more likely that they stay until 718, since Clytemnestra evidently
says 716–18 for their benefit and not to herself. She is apparently
still in control: she organizes everyone, and she dictates the
moves. Notice how Orestes goes in silence without the last word
on departure, which should indicate that Clytemnestra has the
upper hand; cf. p. 310 above on Agamemnon's silent exit.
Clytemnestra does not really have the upper hand; but the later
reversal of their standing helps to add to the dramatic point (see
930*). At this stage Orestes, in his deceit, has to pretend his sub-
mission: later, when the truth is out, he can assert his superiority.
It is probable, moreover, that Clytemnestra follows the strangers
in through the door (see below), and the audience might be
reminded of the way that she followed Agamemnon in at *Ag* 974.
This would add further irony to the situation, for, while in *Ag*
Clytemnestra ushered in the deceived Agamemnon, here it is she
who is deceived. The victim takes the sacrificer into the house.
    There is a controversy over how many doors there are in the

---

[1] The construction of a minutely detailed parallelism between *Ag* and *Cho* by
Stoessl *Die Trilogie des Aischylos* (Vienna 1937) 29ff. is based on such arbitrary
correspondences that it is of no value, and I shall not refer to it again.

skene in *Cho*. In preparation for the discussion on *Cho* 885*, all
I shall do here is to survey the use of the door(s) up to this point.
The double reference to ἕρκειοι πύλαι in 561 and 571 prepares
for the actual arrival at them in 653, where the first line firmly
resets the scene—see 584* above. It is the main outside gates
into the courtyard that Orestes stands before (cf. αὔλειοι πύλαι
at S. *Ant* 18, E. *Hel* 438). He knocks at them, the servant answers
from them, and at 668 Clytemnestra enters from them. Some
(e.g. Wilamowitz *ed maj* 270 *actio*) have had her come out of a
small side door; and Reinhardt (130) argues that this is yet
another surprise turn contrary to the preparation at 571ff. But
it is enough that it is Clytemnestra and not Aegisthus who enters,
and there is little point to an extra by-play with the doors.
Besides if the scene is set at the outer gates then there should be
no other doors, since all subsidiary doorways should be inside
the court. Of course the scene does not have to be realistic, but
the incongruity here would be intrusive and unnecessary. So
even supposing that there was more than one door available
there seems to be no good reason to bring Clytemnestra out of
any other than the main central one. And, above all, there is
Clytemnestra's role as doorkeeper which continues from *Ag* to
Cho. In *Ag* she guarded the door and everyone except Cassandra
used it under her control; so it is the same doorway which she
should use and be the first to use in *Cho* also. The point is that
in this play she is to lose control of it.

At 718 there is a clear distinction of destination: Orestes and
Pylades are to be taken to the ἀνδρῶνες (712), while Clytemnestra
will consult her advisers. Several editors have supposed that these
two directions were marked by the use of two separate doors.
But the various parts of the house are all in through the main
door. Compare E. *Alc*, where the various parts of the house,
including the guests' quarters, are all in through the main gates
(cf. Hourmouziades 116).

732 enter Kilissa, the nurse

(a) *the anapaests 719–729*

These lines are one of the instances of a few anapaests standing
in an act-dividing position: see *Hik* 974a*.[1] It is a clue to

[1] This structural division is simply suppressed by Aichele *Bauformen* 51, 67.
Lebeck 193 n. 2 is mistaken in calling 720–9 'an anapaestic prelude to the second

Aeschylus' conception of the pace of the play that he chose to
have a few anapaests at this juncture rather than a strophic
song. Between the Nurse and the arrival of Aegisthus he has a
strophic song (783–837), though it is in short sharp strophes and
keeps close to events in hand; and after Aegisthus has gone in
there are only a few anapaests again (855–68) before the next
act. So Aeschylus quickens the pace once Orestes has successfully tricked his way into the house; but he holds it up again
with a strophic song before the climactic rush of activity begun
by the arrival of Aegisthus—see further 892a*.

During these anapaests there is great suspense over what will
happen next. Are we to suppose that Orestes is actually tricking
and threatening Clytemnestra already? Or, as Reinhardt (131)
supposes, are we waiting for Aegisthus' death cry? It is true that
we do not know yet that he is not at home; indeed Clytemnestra's
references to him (672f., 716–18) have fostered the impression
that he is. But the convention of death cries from within was
probably not established yet, so that the audience could not
expect them as a later one would (cf. *Ag* 1035*). Also we expect
to see Aegisthus before he is killed, since we have seen him at his
hour of triumph in *Ag*. Aeschylus meant his audience, I think,
to be in complete suspense over what would happen next.
Something must happen, the anapaests impress on us that it
must happen soon, and yet we have no idea what it will be. Not
even the most astute student of Stesichorus and Pindar would
have been likely to guess the event.

(b) the introduction 730–733

The introduction of Kilissa is unusual, as befits her unusual
contribution. The two lines of announcement 730–1 are strangely
informal, because the announcement proper (731) follows on a
more general observation (730), instead of the other way round.
Also the juxtaposition of ἀνὴρ ὁ ξένος with Ὀρέστου suggests that
the chorus is positively relishing the conspiracy. Wilamowitz
(*comm* 221, *ed maj* 273 *actio*) supposed that 730 is the reaction to
a cry inside before Kilissa is seen at 731; but in that case the cry

stasimon': it is an independent astrophic act-dividing song. However, she has a
point when she calls the anapaests at 855–68 'parallel' to these, in that they are
also driven along by the excitement of imminent action—note the repeated νῦν
in 725, 726, and 859; see further pp. 346–7 below.

should be in the text or at least indicated by the words. After
this couplet the chorus then addresses another two lines to the
Nurse before she speaks. In most cases an 'address' is anapaestic
and betokens either respect or deep emotion (see *Pers* 155a*);
but here the two lines are a familiar, almost homely, question
about where Kilissa is going.[1] While there are quite a few places
where one actor speaks a few lines to another on entry before his
first line, the only other place where the *chorus* does this is at S.
Aj 1316f.[2] There the purpose is quite different: the chorus turns
abruptly to Odysseus as the only possible resolution of the deadlock, and so establishes the complete change of attitude to
Odysseus from earlier in the play. In *Cho* the couplet establishes
a tone of confidentiality and domesticity which is essential for
the following scene.

782 exit Kilissa

838 enter Aegisthus, alone

854 exit Aegisthus

why is Aegisthus so quickly dispatched?

Aegisthus hurries eagerly to his end. He is on stage for only 17
lines, by far the shortest appearance in Aeschylus for a character
of standing; in fact the only speaking character who is briefer is
the servant a little later at ?875–?889 (see 875*). In all surviving
tragedy there are very few comparably short appearances, and
some of those are under the influence of *Cho*, as I shall argue on
892a*.

No one seems even to have commented on the brevity of this
appearance of Aegisthus. Yet it is not only its brevity which is
remarkable, but also the way that his short scene is divided off
as a separate act. It follows on an act-dividing song (783–837)
and is followed by some astrophic anapaests (855–68) and a
snatch of dochmiacs (869–71) which include Aegisthus' death

---

[1] Kilissa is the only slave in tragedy to be named. She is moreover a foreign
slave with a slave's name (the contrast with Stesichorus and Pindar is noted by
the scholiast). Slaves are, of course, regularly named in comedy; see Graeber
36f., Leo *Plautinische Forschungen*[2] (Berlin 1912) 107ff.

[2] *Eum* 574f. is not another example: see *Eum* 574*. E. *Telephos* fr. 699 = Arph.
Lys 706 (and 707?) would be another example, if it was in the same context in
the tragedy as in the comedy, which is very doubtful.

cries. Then follows the new act which brings the second confrontation of Clytemnestra and Orestes. It does not matter
whether the Aegisthus scene is called a separate act or the first
part of a long act, as long as the divisive function of the intervening anapaests is appreciated.[1] Because they are followed by
an entry and preceded by an exit and the stage is vacant during
them, their structural function is quite different from the anapaests at, for example, *Cho* 306ff. which introduce a lyric
dialogue, or from *Ag* 783ff., a greeting on entry (*contra* Lloyd-
Jones *tr* 50). They should also be distinguished from brief
snatches of astrophic lyric such as *Cho* 152ff. or *Prom* 687ff.
Aeschylus uses them here because, when the pace is quickening,
he does not want a strophic choral song, however brief, but he
does want to separate the Aegisthus act off from what follows.
So 838–54 becomes a separate little act bounded by the entry
and exit of one character. This is also the case with the rather
longer Kilissa act 730–82.

So we have an interesting, roughly symmetrical, structure:
two short one-character acts come on either side of the song 783–
837; before and after they are separated by act-dividing anapaests from the first and second confrontations of Clytemnestra
and Orestes. There is a purpose to this construction: the two
short acts reflect significantly backward and forward on the two
confrontations, in that both undermine Clytemnestra's position
as mother—Kilissa by showing a genuinely devoted response to
the news of the son's death,[2] Aegisthus by reminding us of the
adultery and of the political side to the murder of Agamemnon.
The two acts which come between the crucial confrontations
with Clytemnestra show by their thematic links how the apparently human and civil aspect of her first appearance is a hollow
compromise. By the time she faces Orestes again we remember
and understand why she must die.

It is the chorus who urge Aegisthus inside to his death (848–
50). Sometimes in later tragedy it is an accomplice rather than
the assassin himself who herds the victim inside (cf. E. *Her*, *El*,

---

[1] Most commentators agree to call 855ff. a 'stasimon' or 'in place of a stasimon',
but some, e.g. Goodell 95, Aichele *Bauformen* 51, 67, regard 838–934 as a single
'epeisodion'; cf. Groeneboom 13, Thomson[2] i 41.
[2] On the larger significance of the Nurse see esp. Reinhardt 131ff., Goheen
132ff.

Or, see further p. 310 above), though not the chorus. Aegisthus hardly needs any encouragement; usually in later tragedy the deceit is more complex and more long drawn out. But the plot against Aegisthus must not be given too much scope: it is the murder of Clytemnestra that everything is leading up to.

875 enter Servant (?)

preparation for the final confrontation

The Servant is a dramatic pawn. Once Aeschylus made the formative decision to keep the two murders separate, he had to find a way of bringing Clytemnestra on after the murder of Aegisthus; and the servant serves this purpose. Also his frenzied activity adds an extra element to the excitement and to the rapidity of the action—see further 892a*. But his subsidiary function does have the effect of making his exact stage movements unclear. One would suppose, other things being equal, that he entered at 875, but that is put in doubt by the problems surrounding the staging of Clytemnestra's entry: see 885*. Again one would suppose that he went off at 889 in response to Clytemnestra's cry for an axe, but the question of the number of actors and of Pylades' entry puts that in doubt also: see 892b*.

It is worth noting the handling of the chorus in this scene. When they hear the death cry of Aegisthus the coryphaeus (presumably) suggests that they should stand aside (ἀποσταθῶμεν 872) to keep clear of trouble. They did not go right off-stage and out of sight, as some editors think,[1] since it is clear at 931ff. that they have witnessed the preceding scene. An exit means a proper departure and it is very rare for the chorus to go right off during the play (see *Eum* 231*). All they do is to stand aside, perhaps in the eisodos, and thus leave clear the centre of the scene, i.e. most of the orchestra. This is an unusual procedure, but its purpose is clear. Aeschylus wants all attention to be on Clytemnestra and Orestes without any distraction whatsoever. His handling of the chorus here is, in fact, simpler and more effective than the self-conscious excuses sometimes encountered in later tragedy; he does not send it off, and yet he has the

[1] Notably Verrall 124, Wilamowitz *ed maj* 279 *actio*. Others leave it unclear whether they think the chorus went right off, e.g. Hermann 654, Bodensteiner 734, Richter 216, Reinhardt 134.

advantages of its absence.[1] At the end of this intense scene, lines
931–4 unobtrusively cover the time required for the chorus to
reassemble (cf. Wilamowitz *ed maj* 281 *actio*).

885 enter Clytemnestra

Clytemnestra and the central door

The servant frantically calls for ten lines before Clytemnestra
enters. But the panic is to no avail. Although Clytemnestra
quick-wittedly calls for an axe (889), there is no time for it to
be brought before Orestes enters at 892. The speed and tension
of this sequence, which is quite extraordinary, are discussed
below on 892a*.

The problem of the number of doors used here was opened
on 718*. Only Reinhardt 129ff. has tried to elicit some positive
significance from the use of more than one door, which is, he
claims, all part of the 'false' preparation. It has been widely
held that *Cho* shows evidence for more than one door, but usually
this view has been based on the rather loose observation that at
712 the ἀνδρῶνες are mentioned and at 878 the γυναικεῖοι πύλαι.[2]
But recently a tighter and more detailed case has been made by
Dover (*Skene* 7f.). If a second door is once accepted there may
be other places where it might be used, but the decisive issue is
Clytemnestra's entry here. Reduced to essentials Dover's case is
this: (i) the Servant calls for the γυναικεῖοι πύλαι to be opened
in 877–9—ἀλλ' ἀνοίξατε / ὅπως τάχιστα, καὶ γυναικείους πύλας /
μοχλοῖς χαλᾶτε: (ii) Clytemnestra comes out of these 'women's
doors': (iii) the Servant cannot have come out of them: therefore
(iv) there must be more than one door. The flaw is in stage (ii)
which assumes that the 'women's doors' must have been in the
front of the skene in view of the audience. This assumption rests
on the analogy of later practice. There are several places in
Euripides where someone stands outside the doors and calls for
them to be opened; and there is little doubt that the doors in

---

[1] This point is well made by Stephenson 41–3, cf. Groeneboom 247f. Note also
how the chorus of *Ag* makes no contribution during *Ag* 810–974. In comedy the
chorus sometimes stands aside in a similar way, see e.g. Arph. *Acharn* 239, *Wasps*
1516; cf. D–R 192f.

[2] See e.g. Bodensteiner 654, D–R 204, Bethe 123 n. 26, Noack 30ff., Flickinger
(4th ed.) 346.

question are directly visible in the skene.[1] But because this was conventional in later tragedy, that does not mean it must have been the same in *Cho* (when the skene was still new). The doors which the servant calls to be opened may be out of sight.

How then can the scene be managed with only one door? Two suggestions have been offered, both of which seem possible. Pickard-Cambridge (*TDA* 43), who opted for two doors, admitted that 'the γυναικεῖοι πύλαι *might* conceivably be within the palace'. Dale (*Papers* 269) argues that this is perfectly acceptable: the slave is calling back through the gates into the courtyard; Aeschylus is obliged by his theatre to set the scene outside the gates, although it might more realistically take place within the court.[2] An alternative is put forward by J. Roux (*REG* 74 (1961) 36f.), who suggests that the servant shouts 875–80 while still within the skene, i.e. within the court, and that he only enters at 881. This would be more exceptional than Roux acknowledges, since it would mean that from 871 to 881 all attention is on the doors but there is no stage movement at all, only frantic off-stage shouting. This would, in fact, be unique in surviving tragedy, but could be quite effective, if rather crude.[3] Both these theories seem possible, though Dale's simpler alternative is much more likely.

I conclude that the text of *Cho* is by itself inconclusive. Two doors could be used if available, but the case for them is not conclusive and there are acceptable alternatives. If this is right, then the issue is settled in favour of one door only by a consideration of the rest of Greek tragedy and comedy, as I argue on pp. 438–40 below.

But why, if there was no second door in *Cho*, does Aeschylus confuse the issue by dragging in a reference to the 'women's doors'? There is a good reason, a much better one than a petty detail of staging. The whole point of the Servant is to lead up to the entry of Clytemnestra. His shouting moves stage by stage

---

[1] See e.g. E. *Med* 1314, *Hipp* 808, *IT* 1304, *Hel* 1180. In several cases the verb χαλᾶν (cf. *Cho* 879) occurs, and phrases like ἀνοιγέτω τις (cf. *Cho* 877f.) also are common; cf. Petersman *WSt* N.F. 5 (1971) 107 n. 41.

[2] Dale is followed by Webster *GTP* 9f., Arnott 42. This paper was an earlier version of that in *WSt* 1956 = *Papers* 119ff. In the later one she spoils her case (p. 120) by entertaining the idea that the servant enters from the side. This flaw was pounced on by Di Benedetto *SCO* 10 (1961) 153 n. 126, E. *Or ed* 256, Dover *Skene* 7f.

[3] For something similar in comedy see *Knights* 234 and Dover *Ar Com* 94.

from a general alarm (875–7), through a call which brings to
mind Clytemnestra (878–82), and so finally to a call to Clytemnestra in particular (882–4). The γυναικεῖοι πύλαι are an essential
link, since they bring attention to focus on Clytemnestra. The
mention is to bring her to mind, not to place her precisely on
the floor-plan of the house.

889 exit Servant (? see 892b*)

892 enter Orestes and Pylades

(a) *the pace of the movements*

Orestes enters just seven lines after Clytemnestra. She entered
ten lines or less after the servant. The three entries make a
sequence of unparalleled rapidity for Greek tragedy. Commentators do not seem to have realized that Greek tragedy does
not normally run at this pace. Further, the sequence is divided
by only a few anapaests from the extraordinarily brief appearance of Aegisthus, see 854*. And the movement of this part of
the play has also been led up to by the short acts before the song
at 783ff. Orestes was on stage for 65 lines and Clytemnestra for
47; and they were divided by a few anapaests from the nurse
whose act lasted only 52 lines. All this movement to and fro is
in clear and calculated contrast to the first, longer, half of the
play which contains very few exits and entrances and is dominated by the monumental set-piece of the kommos. And yet both
halves in their different ways lead up to the scene we have now
arrived at: 892–930. This too is very short: the action involved
is short and sharp. Yet round this short and momentous action,
the matricide, revolves most of *Cho*, which has led up to it, and
much of *Eum* which follows. This brief but intense act should be
contrasted with the ease and triviality of the quick dispatch of
Aegisthus.

  Perhaps the reason why commentators have failed to pay due
attention to the unique rapidity of all this movement is that in
more recent drama with its many actors and smaller theatre it
would not be so unusual. But a search for similar scenes elsewhere in fifth-century tragedy shows up the unusual techniques.
There are occasionally comparably brief appearances but not
many; for some examples see *GRBS* 12 (1971) 37. There are

occasionally some rapidly consecutive entries, though only two and never three are found in such close sequence as here (e.g. S. *Aj* 1223ff., E. *Ion* 1250ff., *IA* 303ff.). Perhaps the scene which is technically most comparable for rapid succession of movements and for short appearances is *Rh* 565–691, itself an extraordinary and unique *mélange* of novel and exciting dramatic techniques.[1] This is, however, a far cry from *Cho*. I suspect that it is no coincidence that the sequences most reminiscent of *Cho* in Sophocles and Euripides, and among their most rapid, are in two of the 'Orestes' plays: S. *El* 1398–1510 and E. *Or* 1311–69, 1503–67. In the Sophocles the similarities of situation—death cries, trick, pushing inside to murder—combined with the unusual pace of the sequence suggests that this is one of the less obvious ways in which Sophocles has been influenced by *Cho*. While the sequences in E. *Or* are very different from *Cho*, the rapid trick, the frantic slave, and the hurried movements in general may well owe something to Aeschylus.

It is worth noting that the pace of the sequence in *Cho*, never surpassed in what we know of the next fifty years of Attic tragedy, would have been impossible without the use of the third actor, although he was still a recent innovation (cf. *Seven* 1005b*). Though it is just possible that the actor of the Servant changes to Pylades (see 892b* below), it would be impossible for him to have changed to Clytemnestra or Orestes. The third actor is essential for the succession of entries. When considering Aeschylus' use of the third actor scholars tend to look only at his use in dialogue and so fail to observe this skilful and inventive use in the action (cf. Knox 108f.).

The dramatic power of the second part of *Cho* is obvious, and it is enhanced by the entirely different kind of strength of the first half. The play is, as Reinhardt (110) says, 'one of the most effective pieces of theatre even in the modern theatre' (cf. e.g. Murray 180, Seidensticker *Bauformen* 199).[2] A study of the

[1] One need only consider the way that Athena supervises the departure of Odysseus and Diomedes on the approach of Alexandros, and the re-entry of the chorus in hot pursuit of Odysseus.

[2] I cannot understand what Norwood can be talking about when he says that *Cho* is 'statuesque' and remarks how Aeschylus 'carefully retards his speed' (*Greek Tragedy* (London 1920) 108f.). Those, e.g. Arnott 115, who wish to argue, perhaps rather superficially, that Euripides is fast-moving compared with Aeschylus should not neglect the second half of *Cho* and first half of *Eum*.

theatrical technique is a good way to discover how it is that
Cho is dramatically effective. A comparison of the pace of the
second half with all of Sophocles and Euripides (excepting *Rh*)
quickly and clearly brings out one aspect of Aeschylus' mastery.

(b) Pylades

The precise handling of Pylades' entry is involved with the
question of the number of speaking actors. I have just touched
on Aeschylus' use of the third actor; but here it may be that he
employed a fourth. Most scholars agree that he could not have,
and so their chief concern is to make time between the exit of
the servant and the entry of Pylades, so that the actor can complete a quick change.[1] They conclude that the servant must go
after his last line at 886, and that, although 889 would supply a
motivation of his exit, the line need not be addressed to him or
to anyone in particular. Secondly it is agreed that Pylades need
not enter with Orestes; and most bring him on immediately
before the line where Orestes turns to him, i.e. at 899. This leaves
some twelve lines for the actor to change. While this would
probably be the quickest change in surviving tragedy, one has
got to be the quickest.[2] This is the orthodox account of the stage
management here, and it derives from the scholion on 899 which
says simply μετεσκεύασται ὁ ἐξάγγελος εἰς Πυλάδην, ἵνα μὴ δ'
λέγωσιν.

It is my suspicion, however, that concern for a petty detail of
stage management, encouraged, as only too often, by a piece of
ancient scholarship, has led to a neglect of the larger dramatic
considerations and of the tragedy as a play to be performed. The
servant is not important, and we may have no qualms about
sending him off without waiting for Clytemnestra's response to
his riddle; but were it not for the matter of the number of actors
we should surely keep him on until 889. But, more important,
Pylades should be with Orestes. He is the silent member of a
pair (cf. 1b*), and should accompany his partner and not tag
along a few lines later. Orestes turns to him at 899 precisely
because he is always without fail at his side. Knox says 'he turns

---

[1] See e.g. Haigh *AT*[3] 232, Bolle 15, Kaffenberger 17–19 (the best discussion),
Flickinger 178f., P-C *DFA*[2] 140, Groeneboom 252 n. 4, Knox 109.

[2] There are no grounds for slowing down the action by stage business, as e.g.
Tucker 6, 200: on the contrary the pace is quick. (The travesty in Rose *PBA* 37
(1936–7) 202 is best neglected.)

to the silent figure who has followed him step by step throughout the play'; and yet at this very moment Knox himself ceases
to have Pylades follow step by step. It is precisely because
Pylades has so long accompanied Orestes in silence that his three
lines of speech are so effective. Moreover, he should have witnessed the confrontation up to the point where he is consulted
(892–8): it would be strange if he were turned to as a final
authority when he did not know what the position was. And
his entry at 899 would be a disruptive distraction. According to
the orthodox account the stage is clear of everyone except
Clytemnestra and Orestes—and then Pylades ambles on. Entries
on the Greek stage are proper events, not mere apparitions. The
questions that this entry would invite in the mind of the spectator
—why has he entered now? why was he not with Orestes?—
are pointless and irrelevant. It might be claimed that Pylades
would add yet another entry to the extraordinary sequence (see
892a* above), the fourth in twenty-five lines. But the others
(Servant, Clytemnestra, Orestes) build up in a sequence; and
Pylades, essential and awesome though his contribution is, is not
more important than Orestes. It is undeniable, I conclude, that
were it not for the scholion and the three-actor 'rule', no one
would have supposed for a moment that Pylades entered later
than Orestes.[1]

Since everything else points to Pylades' entry at 892, should
we allow the 'rule' to override these dramatic and aesthetic
considerations? I think not. A highly unusual dramatic device
sanctions an unusual piece of stage management. The rule over
the number of actors had recently been altered, and it is by no
means impossible that Aeschylus was allowed a fourth actor
with just three lines of speech. Alternatively, bearing in mind the
use of masks and the size of the theatre, it is possible that some
sleight of sound was used; for example, that the third actor
spoke Pylades' lines from off-stage.[2]

[1] Cf. Richter 217, Rees *CPh* 2 (1907) 387 n. 1, *The so-called Rule of Three Actors*
etc. (Chicago 1908) 43. I note that nearly all the translators have Pylades enter
with Orestes.

[2] Pollux gives two terms to do with the fourth actor (iv. 109–10)—παρασκήνιον
instanced in *Ag*, and παραχορήγημα instanced ἐν Μέμνονι Αἰσχύλου (Ἀγαμέμνονι
in MS. A). If we accept the reading of A and take *Ag* to refer to the whole trilogy,
then we might have a reference to Pylades. But then who believes Pollux? What
is perhaps of interest is that both terms concerning a fourth actor are illustrated
from Aeschylus. Hammond 445f. tries to emend the passage by cutting out the

(c) the corpse of Aegisthus revealed?

Most commentators have supposed that the corpse of Aegisthus was seen at this earlier stage as well as in the full tableau at 973 (see 973a*).[1] This rests simply on the fact that the corpse of Aegisthus is repeatedly referred to 'as if it were present' (Dale *Papers* 269). In Orestes' first line there is τῶιδε, and then Clytemnestra apostrophizes him in 893. In 904 Orestes says πρὸς αὐτὸν τόνδε cὲ cφάξαι θέλω; in 906 Aegisthus is τούτωι and in 907 τὸν ἄνδρα τοῦτον. Lastly in 917 the shame which Orestes alludes to with τοῦτο is presumably Clytemnestra's adultery with Aegisthus. Is it possible that he could be referred to in this way and yet not be actually visible? The deictic pronouns do not of themselves show that he is: see *Seven* 371c*. If the corpse was as a matter of fact not there, the references would still make perfectly good sense: Aegisthus is just inside the house, the vision of his corpse is vivid in the minds of Orestes and Clytemnestra (and of the audience). It would still be 'as if it were present'. And there are positive reasons why the corpse should not be visible. It will be seen in the great scene at 973ff., and it would detract from the effect and significance of the revelation there if half of it has already been seen. Secondly Orestes is going to take Clytemnestra inside to kill her by the side of Aegisthus; he makes this point twice at 894f. and 904-7. This would be more vivid if the dead man is left to the imagination; he is there, just inside. When Clytemnestra is taken through the door, she too is dead (see further 930*).

There are also practical considerations. If the ekkyklema was used, as is usually assumed, then there are none of the signals of its use which we might expect (see p. 443). And does Orestes enter on the trolley at 892, and are the actors trundled inside on it at 930? (Pylades would have to clamber over it if he entered at 899.) Some commentators, embarrassed by these difficulties, have claimed that Aegisthus was simply seen through the doorway;[2] but this would be impracticable, see p. 325 above.

---

most discreditable parts as interpolation; but Pollux's authority is not so easily salvaged.

[1] There are exceptions, e.g. Blass *ed* 179, Andrieu 201 ; *ex silentio* Bodensteiner, Verrall, Mazon.

[2] e.g. Wecklein 221, Wilamowitz *ed maj* 280 *actio*, Groeneboom 251, P-C *TDA* 107.

These practical points and the more important dramatic factors all indicate that Aegisthus was not seen at this stage.

930 exeunt Clytemnestra, Orestes (and Pylades)
death inside the door

Aegisthus is inside and Orestes means to kill Clytemnestra by him: so to go inside means death for Clytemnestra. At 904 Orestes actually says ἕπου, and maybe the stage grouping reinforced the idea that it is the action of going in which will mean Clytemnestra's death. At 930 they go in together (ἕπου may mean simply 'accompany').[1]

This scene in *Cho* corresponds in some significant ways with the 'purple' scene in *Ag*, but with an ironic reversal in the role of Clytemnestra. Winnington-Ingram 140 notices this in general terms, but otherwise the parallelism has scarcely been remarked. Yet the correspondences of subject-matter and dramatic technique are such, I suggest, that an alert audience would be alive to the repetition and to its possible meanings. A man and a woman dispute over going into the house. It is a matter of victory and defeat, life and death. The dispute takes the form of an actor–actor stichomythia as in *Ag*.[2] Though regular in later tragedy, this dialogue form is rare in Aeschylus outside *Prom* (see pp. 462f. below). In the *Oresteia* there is none in *Eum*, and only one in *Ag*, namely 931ff. In *Cho* there are two brief dialogues between Orestes and Electra in the first part of the play (212–24, 489–96). The technique is sufficiently rare to help the reminiscence. Furthermore at the end of the scene there is a simultaneous exit, as in *Ag*. These were not common in the early theatre either (see p. 91). And since two actors go together, only one can have the last word. At *Cho* 930 Orestes' having the last word

[1] Lloyd-Jones *tr* 63 has the strange stage direction 'exit Orestes dragging Clytemnestra's body', as though he may have killed her on-stage; and in the note on 930 he adds 'the killing probably took place off-stage'. But there is absolutely no reason in the text or outside it to doubt that the killing took place off-stage. Nor does the text justify 'dragging', which is also in Tucker 207, Rose 210.

[2] After Pylades' intervention the stichomythia is regular 1/1 until the very end. Page's attribution (*OCT*) of 929 to Clytemnestra, thus giving her 928f. as a couplet, is attractive, though I still prefer Wellauer's conjecture (followed by Wecklein and Wilamowitz) that a line has fallen out between 929 and 930. Without it there is a complex train of thought implied between 929 and 930. Colin Macleod suggests that 928 may be an interpolated gloss on 929, and that 930 can then be a continuation of 927 rather than a reply to 929.

makes the point that he is finally victorious, and reverses the
dominance of Clytemnestra both in *Ag* (see p. 310) and earlier
at *Cho* 718 (see p. 343).

The primary significance of the correspondence is obvious:
the blood feud is repeating itself. Different people, a new generation; but still the same deed, vengeance taken on kindred. This
will be even more strongly brought home later, see 973a* and
b*. But in the long run the differences are no less important.
Clytemnestra knows what is at stake, while Agamemnon did not.
And Orestes, though vigorous, does not indulge in his superiority
as Clytemnestra did (notice he goes in *with* the victim). Orestes
begins to see before the murder the ambivalence of the deed,
especially in his last line at 930. He understands that both father
and mother have hounds of vengeance (see 924–5): in *Ag*
Clytemnestra realized the equivalent ambiguity too late (see
1577a*). These differences begin to pose the question whether
this third murder will really put an end to the succession of the
blood feud, as has been hopefully assumed at e.g. *Ag* 1283, *Cho*
805, 830. This question and this hope will now grow to an
overwhelming importance (see further 1063* below).

973 enter Orestes; the corpses are revealed

(*a*) *stage management*

This tableau scene must have been presented in the same way as
that in *Ag*. The assumption of the use of the ekkyklema in *Cho*
goes back to a scholiast—ἀνοίγεται ἡ σκηνὴ καὶ ἐπὶ ἐκκυκλήματος
ὁρᾶται τὰ σώματα—but we cannot allow a scholiast any special
authority in such a matter (see pp. 435–8). The objections raised
on *Ag* 1372b* to the ekkyklema apply here, but with even more
weight. Above all there is no indication that the scene is set
indoors, as at *Ag* 1379; in fact Orestes calls on the sun to witness
the scene (984ff.). It is implausible to suppose that Aeschylus
used a new and artificial convention without any explanation,
and then undermined the convention a few lines later. So again
I incline to the theory that the bodies and stage properties were
brought on by mute extras, no doubt the same attendants as
those who hold out the cloth at 983ff.[1]

Several commentators also bring on a crowd of Argive citizens

---

[1] This time Neckel (cited above, p. 325 n. 1) 11f. and Reisch (D–R 241) are
followed by Verrall 139, Tucker 215, Hammond 438.

for this final scene.[1] Wilamowitz (*comm* 48) elaborates: '. . . the people of Argos arrive with torches and swords, men and women, and attendants of course. They fill up the stage.'[2] I can see no trace of this in the text: rather they have been interpolated from the Wagnerian opera-house in order to supply Aeschylus with some of the vacuous spectacle which later scholarship has foisted on him. It might, I suppose, be claimed that the chorus of slave women is not a suitable audience for Orestes' defence; that they do not qualify as the ἐπήκοοι of 980. But in performance this would not matter. One could imagine, if necessary, an invisible audience of citizens, but there is no need to bring them actually on stage (cf. Groeneboom 264). The chorus does in any case represent the house of Agamemnon, and even the city to some extent (cf. e.g. 55ff., 942ff., 962ff.).

(*b*) ἴδεcθε δ' αὖτε τὸ μηχάνημα

The visual correspondence of this scene to that at *Ag* 1372ff. has been recognized at least since Weil 109 (in 1860).[3] The tableau shows the murderer, blood on his hands, standing by the two corpses, one a man, one a woman (thus fulfilling the prediction of Cassandra at *Ag* 1318f.). There is also once more the cloth in which Agamemnon was caught: Orestes has it held up for all to view and to ponder. When he draws attention to it at 980 he actually begins ἴδεcθε δ' αὖτε. This αὖτε is not merely a resumption of line 973, it harks back to the scene in *Ag*. Of course it is the audience, and not Orestes or the chorus, who see the robe again; but in its absorbing context this technical chink in the dramatic illusion is not to be noticed. Again the killer faces the world openly without remorse, acknowledges the deed, and attempts to vindicate it. Obviously the parallel is too close for comfort. 'παθεῖν τὸν ἔρξαντα. θέcμιον γάρ.' It is this which accounts for the chorus's unquiet response (1007-9, 1018-20), a response which clearly applies no less to Orestes than to the previous generation. The mirror scene suggests first and foremost that the blood feud has repeated itself and is extended to yet another generation.

  [1] Including Verrall xxxii, 139, Wilamowitz 178, Reinhardt 137, Lloyd-Jones *tr* 65.

  [2] In his commentary (46-8) Wilamowitz stressed the evening-time setting of the second half of *Cho*, hence these torches. But he neglected the sun at 984ff., and in *Interpretationen* 178 he is, instead, patronizing about Aeschylus' 'Inkonstanz'.

  [3] See especially Lesky *Ges Schr* 105, Reinhardt 135ff., Dodds *Progress* 61, Dingel 168-70.

But the similarities also accentuate the differences. Orestes, while he stands by what he has done, has none of the fierce assertiveness of Clytemnestra; and he soon acknowledges the ambivalence of his situation:

> ἀλγῶ μὲν ἔργα καὶ πάθος γένος τε πᾶν,
> ἄζηλα νίκης τῆϲδ' ἔχων μιάϲματα.   (1016f.)

Unlike Clytemnestra, Orestes is prepared immediately to abandon the kingdom and to look elsewhere for salvation. He is already in a state of enlightenment similar to that which Clytemnestra reached only after long dispute, and then only to have it over-ridden by the arrival of Aegisthus—see *Ag* 1577a*.[1] Orestes is, perhaps, approaching that state of enlightenment and fear which will be established as a feature of the just city in *Eum* (cf. Macleod 287). And Orestes, unlike Clytemnestra, is coerced by the direct threats of Apollo (see esp. *Cho* 269ff., 900–2); and he is able to reveal that Apollo has given him some assurance of security (1031f.).

Conspicuous among the visual components of the tableau there is a pair of differences from *Ag* which embody both the ambivalence of Orestes' victory, and the crucial difference between him and Clytemnestra. In *Ag* there is no sign of a weapon, but Orestes probably holds a bloody sword in his hand (see *Eum* 42): in the other hand he holds a suppliant's branch and wreath (1034f.).[2] With these he will go to Delphi. Clytemnestra, once Aegisthus has arrived, regards her victory as the end of her troubles: Orestes has more foresight and more insight.

1063 exit Orestes

return into exile

During most of *Cho* there is a vagueness, deliberate on Aeschylus' part, over how it will all end. There is an optimistic neglect of the consequences of the murder, and a recurrent suggestion that Orestes will live at home happily ever after (esp. 262f., 343f., 479ff., the entire song 783–837). The question of pollution remains

---

[1] Jens 252 briefly remarks that the Erinyes in *Cho* have an equivalent place in the dramatic structure of *Cho* to Aegisthus in *Ag*; but the correspondence is at most very faint.

[2] The wreath is on the branch not on his head—see *Eum* 44f. and Hermann *ed* 654.

latent.[1] So it is that Orestes can override the two threats of his
mother at 912 and 924; and so in the last antistrophe of the song
after the murder (965–71) the chorus can still sing vaguely and
optimistically of the cleansing of pollution. Despite the lesson of
Ag the righteous optimism of the avengers carries us through and
leaves no room for destructive thoughts about the consequences.

But once the deed is done the pollution cannot be disregarded,
the consequences must be faced. Even before Orestes shows
signs of distraction and sees the Erinyes,[2] the chorus is aware,
even if only indirectly, that he must suffer: μίμνοντι δὲ καὶ πάθος
ἀνθεῖ 1009 = μόχθος δ' ὁ μὲν αὐτίχ', ὁ δ' ἥξει 1020 (cf. 973b*).
Suddenly at 1021ff. Orestes reveals that he is losing his wits and
explains at 1034ff. that he will go to Delphi as a suppliant. Then
he sees the irresistible Erinyes (1048–50), and again at his exit,
when the chorus has agreed that Apollo is his hope of purification
(1059f.), Orestes makes it clear that he has no alternative
ἐλαύνομαι δὲ κοὐκέτ' ἂν μείναιμ' ἐγώ (1062 cf. 1050).

It cannot be claimed, I think, that the play has been leading
predictably up to this: the turn of events is sudden and unexpected. Up until 912 at least, even perhaps up to 973, we have
been lulled into a false security and are led to believe that all
will be well. But when at the end the play takes this sudden and
alarming turn, we can see that this fits in a larger pattern of
affairs. Orestes' exit at the end complements his entry at the
very beginning (1a*, cf. Steidle 84): his return to revenge and
his flight from the consequences frame the entire play, which is
the chronicle of his brief tenure of his home. At *Ag* 1280ff.
Cassandra foresaw that an avenger would come, an ἀλήτης
τῆςδε γῆς ἀπόξενος: at *Cho* 1042 Orestes sees himself as ἀλήτης
τῆςδε γῆς ἀπόξενος. At the opening of *Cho* he comes out of a
homeless wandering, and at the end he returns to it. And so we
see with a sudden shock of understanding that Orestes' victory,
the murders, are not the end of his trials, but only the beginning.

---

[1] Lebeck reads foreboding and foreshadowing of the end of the play into several
places in the first half of the play (see pp. 98, 108, 117, 119, 200f.). I find none of
these convincing, since in each case the explicit sense of the text is so powerful
and the alleged undertone so tortuous or slight that there is no justification in
reading back what is to come later. The literal reading of the *topos* in l. 438
(Lebeck 200f.) is especially far-fetched.

[2] I am assuming that the disjointedness of the speech 973–1006 is not supposed
to show the onset of Orestes' distraction, but is due to other causes, largely textual.

This sudden and unmistakable vision of the larger pattern leads on towards the next play in the trilogy. And in a sense Orestes' exit is the first move of *Eum*. Orestes flees pursued by the Erinyes, and the pursuit crosses over between the two plays. At *Eum* 209 Apollo asks the Erinyes what is their function, and the reply is τοὺϲ μητραλοίαϲ ἐκ δόμων ἐλαύνομεν. The first part of *Eum* is much concerned with the pursuit and with Orestes' sufferings, which are vividly conveyed by the action as well as the words (see further *Eum* 231*, 244a*, b*). Here in *Cho* we see the beginning of the long toilsome chase which will end at Athens. Here, of course, the Erinyes are invisible to all but Orestes;[1] but in the next play we too see them.

Orestes' exit is followed by a couplet of good wishes from the chorus (1063f.). On *Hik* 951* I have discussed 'lines cast at a departing back'; and I illustrate there how good wishes are rare in tragedy, though common in comedy, especially in anapaests. But here the plain couplet, the last spoken lines of the play, is coloured by the tragic overclouding of the context. ἀλλ' εὐτυχοίηϲ is a solemn formula for good wishes, and is usually found in the context of an exit (cf. S. *OT* 1478f., E. *Alc* 1153, *IA* 716, Men. *Sik* 380 with Kassel's note).

The rapidity with which the play draws to a close after the murder, contrasting with *Ag*, conveys with a horrible vividness the speed and sureness of the Erinyes' work. Once Orestes has gone, the chorus quickly disperses (down an eisodos, not into the palace) with a few anapaestic lines of shocked response. The play ends with a question, literally; everything, far from being finished, is still unresolved.

1076 exit chorus

---

[1] See 1051f., 1056, 1061 cf. E. *IT* 281ff., *Or* 251ff. Müller (*Eum ed* 73f.), who thought they were visible in *Cho*, was refuted by Hermann *Opusc* vi. 2. 130ff.

VIII. EUMENIDES

1 enter Pythia

33 exit Pythia

34 re-enter Pythia

the priestess reduced to hands and knees

At 33 the Pythia goes inside and out of sight to take up her seat (29), and she calls on those who wish to consult her to follow. There is then a complete break before she re-enters (πάλιν . . . ἐκ δόμων 35). As the scholiast sees παρ᾽ ὀλίγον ἔρημος ἡ σκηνὴ γίνεται: between her exit and re-entry there is a hiatus—nothing happens. This is unique in surviving Greek tragedy, which generally abhors a vacuum, and nearly always preserves continuity. As the scholion goes on to remark, this hiatus can only happen because the chorus is not there. In other prologues there is a break between an exit and an entrance with no connection at all between the two, in fact this happens twice in this very prologue (see 139*); but nowhere else is it the same person on both sides of the break. This technique is hard to parallel from anywhere in Greek drama, even in comedy: I note Men. *Dysc* 908/9. The purpose of this unique device is to break the opening part of the play into two contrasting halves (1–33, 34–63). The break is accentuated because both halves are delivered by the same character without the intervention of anyone else.[1] The first half shows a pious routine which is the outcome of a peaceful Delphic tradition:[2] the second vividly conveys the abhorrent and

---

[1] Many critics note that the prologue of *Ag* is comparably split at 25: but in *Ag* the two halves are not so violently contrasted, and the first looks forward to the second. It is sometimes claimed that the prologue of *Cho* was similarly constructed; but even the fragments show that it was not significantly similar.

[2] On possible hints of the future settlement see Lebeck 142–4. However she does not allow due weight to the fact that it is Athens and Athena, not Delphi and Apollo, who have the necessary understanding to bring peace.

incomprehensible disruption which the Erinyes have brought into this orderly Delphic world. The juxtaposition effectively makes the point.

The sight within reduces the old woman to a state no better than a child (38). The previous line—37 τρέχω δὲ χερcίν, οὐ ποδωκείαι cκελῶν—seems to say that she is on all fours (cf. the scholiast ἔξειcι τεταραγμένη τετραποδηδόν). Scholars have searched for ways to obviate this indignity. Most have supposed that she has to rest her hands on the doorposts or elsewhere in order to keep her balance. Others reckon that she was on all fours inside, but upright by the time she appears. Lloyd-Jones *tr* 14 thinks τρέχω may mean 'tremble'. But the wording seems to be un-equivocally explicit: she is on her hands as opposed to only her legs (cκελῶν), and so is like a crawling child (ἀντίπαιc).[1] Clearly Aeschylus meant her to be on all fours. Bethe 325f. rightly acknowledges this (though he refers to 'krass realistischen Züge', which he considers archaic). The only other entry of this kind to survive is the blind Polymestor at E. *Hec* 1056ff. (see 1058f.), which is also often wrongly explained away. It is admittedly a violent, undignified device (though hardly realistic); and it contrasts strongly with the Pythia's quiet dignity before her exit. Aeschylus wants to make as much as possible at this stage of the horror and foulness of the Erinyes (see further 140*). Not even the Pythia's body can cope with this new horror, let alone her mind.

63 exit Pythia

64 enter Apollo and Orestes

entry in mid-dialogue?

There is a complete break between the exit of the Pythia and the new entry, although her last words (60–3) prepare indirectly for Apollo. This kind of break is only possible when the chorus is not present: see 139*.

Apollo's first words are οὔτοι προδώcω. The conjunction implies that some off-stage words have preceded and that this is the reply to them. It is true that a similar phrasing occurs at the beginning of a speech at *Cho* 269, but that does not open a scene,

---

[1] For a comparison with the old men in *Ag* see Lebeck 17–19.

it resumes a train of thought. So it seems that Apollo enters 'in mid-dialogue' (Wilamowitz 178f. cf. Flickinger *CJ* 34 (1939) 356f.). Special pleading, for example that Apollo gestures at the Erinyes (Deckinger 41 n. 1), or that he replies to Orestes' suppliant posture, do not really make the technique any less peculiar. For this naturalistic device is more strange than Wilamowitz allows. It is hardly found in fifth-century tragedy or comedy; and it is only in New Comedy that it becomes common. The few examples that there are in tragedy are in late plays and in contexts of extreme dramatic tension (E. *Hipp* 601ff., *IA* 303ff., S. *Phil* 1222ff.).[1] But such instances, which begin an excited naturalistic scene, are not comparable to *Eum*, because their context and purpose is quite different. In *Eum* it is hard to see any point to the abrupt, mid-air effect produced by this opening; and the text must be suspected.

This is, I take it, why some critics (including Burges, Kirchhoff, Blass *ed* 77) transpose Orestes' three lines 85–7 to the beginning of the scene. Certainly this produces a more formal and serious opening, and it provides a context for line 64; but it leaves line 88 very isolated. So Maas's suggestion (*apud* Murray *OCT*[2]) that 88 should also be transposed, and so become the first line of Apollo's first speech, is worth consideration, especially as 89 would follow well on 84.[2] It is no serious objection that Orestes would speak before Apollo and thus disturb the 'etiquette': Orestes is alarmed and needs Apollo's reassurance, so in his urgency he speaks first.

Nearly all editors bring on Hermes as well at line 64;[3] and they send him off with Orestes. This is on the strength of 89ff., where Apollo calls on his brother to look after Orestes. But the lines do not necessarily imply Hermes' presence: surely one god

[1] See *GRBS* 12 (1971) 40. E. *Hik* 838 is probably corrupt, see Page 68f. (*Hik* 381ff. is, however, simply an address to a herald, see p. 393 n. 3 below). At E. *Andr* 147ff., 154 is probably interpolated, see Hunger *RhM* 95 (1952) 369f., Stevens E. *Andr ed* 114f.

[2] Maas's conjecture provides no context for μέμνηςο (88); unless perhaps μὴ . . . φρένας can be treated as in parenthesis, and μέμνηςο taken with οὗτοι προδώςω. But some emendation along these lines is plausible (cf. Dawe *Collation* etc. (Cambridge 1964) 187). If the lines were once displaced in a MS. (before the time of the scholiast), they could easily have been put back in the wrong place. In p. 383 n. 3 below I give an airing to a wild speculation that there is a long lacuna between 63 and 64.

[3] Wilamowitz *ed maj* 294 *actio* (cf. Groeneboom 105, Dirksen 8) brings him on at 89.

can call on another when the latter is not actually present, just as humans pray to a god who is not present. There are reasons for not bringing Hermes on. His role would be silent and secondary and he would not even be noticed for 25 lines; while this is acceptable for Bia, Hermes is perhaps too notable to be used in this way. And if Hermes is actually *seen* going off with Orestes, this would imprint his role very clearly in the minds of the spectators, and would make his absence later in the play conspicuous. So I agree with those who prefer to think that Hermes was not actually represented on stage (e.g. Verrall 19, Lloyd-Jones *tr* 17).

The staging of this entry is tied up with the controversial question of the entry of the chorus. So I refer to 140* to justify the assertion that Apollo and Orestes simply entered from the door on foot.

93 exit Apollo, exit Orestes

Orestes leaves Apollo's ground

Orestes goes off in silence by an eisodos. It seems that he must wander far on his way to Athens (75ff., cf. 244b*). Apollo on the other hand simply goes back in through the door.[1] Orestes entered under the protection of Apollo, but he must go off separately. It seems to be important for Aeschylus that Orestes must make his way from Delphi to Athens independently, even though Hermes may protect him. Perhaps some light is thrown on this simultaneous yet separate exit by a word in Apollo's last line (93)—βροτοῖϲιν: Apollo must relinquish Orestes up to the human world. Mortals must judge him, and mortals must accept or reject him. (Perhaps also mortals must purify him—see 244b*.)

94 a dream of Clytemnestra appears (?)

staging

Clytemnestra appears to the Erinyes as a dream (116 ὄναρ cf. 155 ἐξ ὀνειράτων).[2] The dream is visible to the Furies in their

---

[1] Wilamowitz *ed maj* 294 *actio* says 'Apollo non discedit sed ἀφανὴϲ γίγνεται': but what can this mean in practice? (see further, pp. 403–4).

[2] It is hard to make good sense of 104–5 in the context; 105 at least is probably interpolated. The reference of φροιμίου in 142 is obscure, but it seems to refer to the dream.

sleep, since she shows her wounds (103); yet their dream-vision cannot be concentrated solely on her, since it seems that they are also dreaming of the pursuit of Orestes (131).

It is hard to see, given our evidence, how this strange scene, unique in surviving tragedy, was originally played. Again this problem depends on the staging of the entry of the chorus. I shall consider it first on the assumption that the chorus is not seen at all until 140ff., which is what I argue below on 140*. This would mean that although Clytemnestra's words are all directed at the Erinyes, they are none the less out of sight, and their responses (117ff.) are therefore heard from within. In that case the actor of Clytemnestra must either face in through the open doorway, or must abandon all pretence at 'natural' dialogue, and not even face in their direction. On this staging her entry could hardly be made from the doorway; for why should she come out when her audience lies within? She could either enter up an eisodos (cf. Bodensteiner 676, Richter 264), or, if there was the means to do so she could come up from the ground (see p. 447). But in contrast to Darius in *Pers* (681b*) there is nothing in the words to indicate that Clytemnestra comes straight from Hades or returns there: indeed ἀλῶμαι (98) suggests that she does not; compare the ghost of Polydorus at E. *Hec* 1ff. While any of these ways of presenting the scene is possible (cf. Hermann *Opusc* vi. 2. 163f.), they all seem somewhat unsatisfactory, because there is no reason why Clytemnestra should appear in front of the skene when those she is appearing to are still inside.

Flickinger (*CJ* 34 (1939) 357–9) suggested that Clytemnestra was only a voice, and was not seen by the audience. This would mean that from 94 until 139 the stage would be empty, and the audience would only hear Clytemnestra and the dreaming Erinyes within. This would be without parallel in surviving tragedy:[1] Flickinger is mistaken to compare E. *Med* 96ff., *Hipp*

---

[1] It is sometimes supposed that Athena was invisible during the prologue of S. *Aj*, although that would be inconvenient and pointless. This is based on what is, in my view, a misinterpretation of κἂν ἄποπτος ἦιϲ in l. 15, see p. 116 n. 1 above. However it *is* possible that Athena was a disembodied voice in *Rh* 595–674, a scene which I take to be modelled on the prologue of S. *Aj* (cf. Nock *CR* 44 (1930) 173f.). The device (proposed by Vater, but rejected by Ritchie 128) would facilitate the distribution between three actors, help the trick on Paris, account for Athena's inconclusive last line (674), and make more sense of Odysseus' aural

776ff., since in those places there are other actors on the stage who hear the noises from within. But the theory should not be rejected too hastily: the whole scene is unique, and may have been handled in a unique way. With the tradition of Senecan dream-ghosts behind us we tend to assume that both the ghost and the sleeper must be visible. But the empty scene and eerie noises might be rather effective, and could lead on through a growing sense of horror and strangeness to the climax of the entry of the Erinyes (see 140*). It is also worth noting that Clytemnestra's last line (139) has no hint of a departure about it: it forms a climax to her harangue, but it is not final or conclusive. This would suit a disembodied voice better than a visible ghost, which would have to go away without waiting to see whether she had had any effect.

However, besides the lack of parallel, Flickinger's theory is liable to other objections. If at 103 Clytemnestra calls on the Erinyes to look at her wounds, this visual effect would lose some of its potential impact if the audience could not see it also. Nevertheless the line could be only heard and its representation left to the imagination.[1] Secondly Clytemnestra only names herself at the end (116). If a voice is heard off-stage, then the audience must be helped to identify it; but it is not until 98 or even 100 that it is clear the words must be Clytemnestra's. On the other hand, her part in the previous two plays has been the most impressive; and an exceptional actor, as he must have been, might well have given her a voice which would be immediately and unmistakably recognized. In the face of these points, the presentation must remain open to serious doubt: for myself I would not rule out Flickinger's theory.

If, on the other hand, the Erinyes were already visible before the scene with Clytemnestra, as has been generally supposed (see 140*), then the theory that she was an incorporeal voice is distinctly implausible. She could in that case simply step up on to the ekkyklema from inside, or she could enter by an eisodos (cf. D–R 248 e.g.), or she might still enter from beneath the ground.

response at 608ff. But whatever the case in *Rh*, it hardly supplies an analogy for *Eum*.

[1] ὅρα δὲ πληγὰς τάσδε καρδίαι σέθεν. Clytemnestra's wounds or the Erinyes'? καρδία seems to suggest metaphorical rather than literal wounds.

139 the dream of Clytemnestra goes (?)

the construction of the 'prologue'

The structure of the part of *Eum* up to the first song (1–139) is
one of the boldest of its kind in surviving tragedy.[1] It is made
up of four separate parts. I have already commented on the
break at 33/4. Then there is a break without any external connection at 63/4, and another at 93/4. There is yet another
break here with the 'exit' of Clytemnestra, though in this case
Clytemnestra's speech does lead up to the transition and supply
a continuity. Breaks of this kind are also found in Euripides'
prologues, though not in Sophocles nor elsewhere in Aeschylus.
The most complex are *IT*, where there is a complete break
before and after the scene with Orestes and Pylades (67–122),
and *Phoen*, where there is a break at 87/8 and another at 201/2,
which is, however, bridged by the preparation in 193ff. The
prologue of *Hyps* must also have been of this kind.[2] These comparisons from late tragedy serve to stress how very unusual the
construction of *Eum* is.

What, then, is the purpose of this extraordinary series of
externally disconnected scenes? Part of the answer is already in
the interesting scholion on l. 1;[3] it ends οἰκονομικῶc δὲ οὐκ ἐν
ἀρχῆι διώκεται Ὀρέcτηc, ἀλλὰ τοῦτο ἐν μέcωι τοῦ δράματοc
κατατάττει, ταμιευόμενοc τὰ ἀκμαιότατα ἐν μέcωι. Not until the
trial are all the elements of the play brought together; up till
then they are interwoven yet kept apart. The Pythia gives a
neutral view, first of the peaceful Delphic routine, then of the
repulsive disruption which is beyond her understanding (see
34*). Then we see one side, that of Orestes and Apollo: then,
starkly juxtaposed and without a link, we hear and then see the
other side, Clytemnestra and the Erinyes (94–177). After the
clash of Apollo and the Furies, there is another piece of bold and

---

[1] Cf. Wilamowitz 58 'die grösste Kühnheit . . .', Goodell 82ff., Nestle 83f.

[2] Hypsipyle must go before her sons arrive. If the woman in fr. I i (p. 25 Bond)
was Eurydice (see p. 341 n. 1 above), then there must have been another vacant
stage before the re-entry of Hypsipyle.

[3] This scholion, which seems to come from an aesthetic commentary, is at the
bottom of the first page of the play in M, i.e. after l. 48. In T it has become attached
with a lemma to l. 30. However, Vitelli (in Wecklein *ed* 1885) and Thomson[2] i 262
see that it belongs to the whole prologue, and hence should be printed as if on l. 1.
Dindorf's edition (Oxford 1851) is a source of error, since the scholion is not only
printed as on l. 47, but a lemma is fabricated for it. Many commentators, including
Wilamowitz 179, have been misled.

unusual dramatic technique (see 276*), which allows Aeschylus to show Orestes alone (235ff.). Only at 254ff. do the Erinyes and Orestes first meet face to face; and even then they do not communicate. The confrontation is long postponed.

Greek tragedy with its long scenes, few movements, and fixed chorus does not allow much scope for abrupt juxtapositions (in extreme contrast to the Shakespearean theatre). But in the first parts of *Eum* Aeschylus contrives, by means of several infringements of the usual structural techniques, a series of juxtaposed scenes which show one by one different aspects of the same situation.

140 (and after) enter chorus

when and how do the Furies appear?

Both the timing and the staging, and hence the whole dramatic impact, of the first appearance of the Erinyes have been much discussed; already in 1896 it was a 'viel besprochene Frage' (Bethe 110f.). It may seem rather surprising that there has been so much discussion, since the scholia, most handbooks, and nearly every commentary and translation have all agreed that the chorus, or at least some of it, was revealed on the ekkyklema at line 64, at the same time as Orestes and Apollo. Since I do not believe this, I shall have to discuss the matter once more.[1]

The usual view takes as its starting-point and foundation the scholion in M on 64: ... καὶ δευτέρα δὲ γίνεται φαντασία· στραφέντα γὰρ μηχανήματα ἔνδηλα ποιεῖ τὰ κατὰ τὸ μαντεῖον ὡς ἔχει. καὶ γίνεται ὄψις τραγική ... But why should we believe this? It is clear that the scholia and other ancient scholarship often tended to be anachronistic on matters of staging, and simply to describe the way that the scene was or might be played in the later theatre (see p. 407). Thus στραφέντα in this scholion is suspicious, since it suggests a revolving stage rather than the wheeled trolley which was evidently the early form of the ekkyklema, as is clearly argued by Hourmouziades 93ff. esp. 96f. Moreover the scholiast seems to suppose that the entire chorus was carried on

---

[1] I have found the most helpful discussions those of Hermann *Opusc* vi 2 pp. 162ff., Neckel (cited above, on p. 325 n. 1) 12–14, Bodensteiner 663f., D–R 243f., Bethe 111ff., Dale *Papers* 123f.

the contraption, yet it is accepted even by the disciples of this note that the fifth-century ekkyklema could not have been large enough or strong enough for this. And δευτέρα φαντασία is suspicious. Does the scholiast imagine that Apollo appeared on the mechane?[1] I do not wish to claim that the scholiast must be wrong, but simply that his account is only the opinion of a scholar and of no final authority; we do not know that this particular ancient scholar was better equipped to say how Aeschylus produced the scene than we are. As it happens, we know that someone in antiquity entertained a quite different way of staging the entry (*Life* §9, see further below). So for the moment let us leave the scholiast out of account, and assess the other evidence without prejudice.

First, I shall consider the points in favour of an entry at 140, and then in favour of 64. There are arguments for both, but I have little doubt that those for the later entry are decisively stronger. The first, and perhaps most substantial, point to take into account is that the chorus of a Greek tragedy normally enters *to* the first song, not *before* it (cf. p. 225 above). There is only one surviving tragedy where the chorus is on-stage before its 'parodos': in E. *Hik* the chorus of suppliants is on-stage in silence for the first 41 lines of the play (cf. p. 193). It has been alleged for several other plays, but wrongly. Pickard-Cambridge[2] thought that the suppliants at the start of S. *OT* might have become the chorus: but at 144 Oedipus calls for the chorus to be fetched, and at 147ff. the priest takes the suppliants off. It has also been argued[3] that in S. *Phil* the chorus is on-stage from the start because in the first song it knows things which it could not otherwise have found out. But this is too meticulous: the audience would not ask how they got the information. Lastly it is sometimes supposed that the chorus of E. *Ba* was on during the prologue;[4] but there is no indication of this, on the contrary Dionysus calls them on in 55ff. (see Dodds E. *Ba* ed[2] 70). It may be that the chorus was occasionally seen just a few lines before it first

---

[1] Arnott 81f., who does not see that the first φαντασία is the epiphany of Apollo, saddles the scholiast with still more implausible theories.

[2] *DFA*[1] 248 n. 5, *DFA*[2] 243 n. 3, rightly attacked by Calder *Phoenix* 13 (1959) 123f.

[3] e.g. Capps 24f., Bodensteiner 709, Webster S. *Phil ed* 66.

[4] e.g. Bodensteiner 709, Bethe 193 n. 14, P-C *DFA*[1] 249 (retracted by *DFA*[2] 244), Zwierlein 72.

sang (see e.g. *Prom* 128a*): but that is not what is alleged in
Eum. The chorus should, unless there is a very good reason
otherwise, enter for the first song.

There is also considerable dramatic and theatrical advantage
to the later entry at 140. The longer the revelation is held back,
the more the suspense of waiting, and the greater the impact
when it is finally made. This simple but important point was well
made by Hermann,[1] yet few have raised it since. Aeschylus wants
in this part of the play, as opposed to later, to make the Erinyes
as horrible and alarming as possible: it is surely obvious that,
other things being equal, this purpose is better served by a later
entry than an earlier one.

Let us consider the play in sequence as it would be performed.
This should bring out the gradually mounting, threatening terror
and horror. First in *Cho* the Erinyes are present but not seen; we
have only Orestes' few but gruesome words (1048–50, 1057f.).
Yet their speed and efficiency are vividly conveyed, and this
bridges the gap to the next play (cf. *Cho* 1063*). Then we see
the devastating effect that the mere sight of them has on the
Pythia (see 34*), and we hear her detailed description (46–59).[2]
With this picture still vivid it is surely best *not* to reveal its
embodiment immediately after at 64, particularly not a mere
sample (Dale *Papers* 270 actually talks of 'the rather sketchy
selection'). Attention can then be devoted to Orestes and Apollo.
During the scene of Clytemnestra we would then only hear the
Erinyes at 117–30.[3] These bloodcurdling noises issuing from
horrors yet unseen would be very effective, more effective,

---

[1] Hermann *Opusc* vi 2 pp. 163f., *ed* 655: the severe philologist, ironically, shows
more dramatic sense than Müller with his '⸱ .w broad approach'. However,
Hermann argues for a revelation at 94, a compromise which loses more than it
gains.

[2] It is hard to make out the intriguing distinction in the scholion on the prologue
(see p. 368 n. 3 above): the Pythia speaks οὐχ ὡς διηγουμένη τὰ ὑπὸ τὴν cκηνήν
(τοῦτο γὰρ νεωτερικὸν ⟨καὶ⟩ Εὐριπίδειον), ὑπὸ δὲ τῆς ἐκπλήξεως τὰ θορυβήcαντα
αὐτὴν καταμηνύουca φιλοτέχνως. If the distinction is that between an impersonal
messenger speech after the event and a personally involved account of something
which is still going on, then this could be significant for the history of the messenger
speech (and run counter to di Gregorio's kind of thesis, see p. 85 above).

[3] On παρεπιγραφαί (the word is used by the scholion on 117) see p. 15 n. 1.
We might have expected Aeschylus to have supplied the actual noises (μῦ, μῦ,
ὦ, ὦ etc.) rather than the mere abbreviations μυγμός and ὠγμός (inferrable from
118 and 124 respectively). They may be substitutes added by a scribe for the
purposes of brevity or of calligraphy.

surely, than if we had already glimpsed the Erinyes. Noises or words from off-stage are a good way to build up towards an entry whose significance is the object of tension and uncertainty (cf. Medea, Ajax, Philoctetes). All these reactions, descriptions, and noises make a highly dramatic preparation of various and increasing anticipation for the long-delayed revelation itself.

After this the actual entry at 140ff. would have to be well handled in order to live up to the preparation for it. Of course, masks and costumes will have been the basis of the theatrical impact; but choreography and music will also have made a vital contribution. It was noted by the scholiast (on 140 cf. Hermann *Opusc* ii 128ff.) how the Erinyes wake each other one by one, and how the first strophic pair of the song (143–54) is made up of short syntactical units which respond to some extent, and which could well have been distributed among individual choreutai or parts of the chorus.[1] This suggests that the chorus did not enter in the usual ordered formation, but was brought on cποράδην, cf. *Seven* 78*. It is easy to imagine that this would have been more effective in the choreography and the music. The sense of inexorable pursuit would be much more vividly conveyed by the stream of entries (see further 244a*). The conclusion that the entry at 140 was made in this way might, I hope, have been reached without the prompting of the *Life* §9: τινὲς δέ φαϲιν ἐν τῆι ἐπιδείξει τῶν Εὐμενίδων cποράδην εἰcαγαγόντα τὸν χορὸν τοcοῦτον ἐκπλῆξαι τὸν δῆμον ὡc τὰ μὲν νήπια ἐκψῦξαι, τὰ δὲ ἔμβρυα ἐξαμβλωθῆναι. The play itself, not the anecdote, is what matters.[2]

What then, to oppose such a strong case for the later entry, are the arguments in favour of a revelation earlier (always

---

[1] Cf. scholion on 144 κομματικῶc ἕκαϲτον κατ᾽ ἰδίαν προενεκτέον. αἱ γὰρ διακοπαὶ πρόϲφοροι τοῖc πάθεϲιν (incidentally we need not associate κομματικῶc with κομμόc, see *LSJ*). Kaimio 117f. points out that the text does not prove this distribution, and claims that it is 'not really necessary'. But what forces us to exclude the division of the chorus unless there is utterly conclusive evidence *for* it? Page *OCT* 252 is also against the division (a change of mind since *CQ* 31 (1937) 94).

[2] On anecdotes like this and the similar one at Pollux 4. 110 see p. 438 n. 2. It must be the actual entry of the chorus which is in question and not just the waking up (*contra* Weissmann *Anweisungen* 28), as is shown by εἰcαγαγόντα; and it must be the first entry and not the re-entry (epiparodos), as pleaded by Detscheff 23, De Falco² 25, Groeneboom 130 etc., since that is the whole point of the anecdote.

leaving the scholion out of account)? Clearly the Erinyes are not visible during any part of the Pythia's scene (even though a few since K. O. Müller 101f., who imagined a curtain, have thought so). She says that she has come out again (35), and 'she describes the scene so fully that it is clear that the spectators do not see it for themselves' (Pickard-Cambridge *TDA* 107). And in the scene with Apollo and Orestes there is no explicit indication that they are still in the inmost sanctum rather than outside. Once again, as in *Ag* (1372b*) and *Cho* (973a*), there are none of the telltale signs that the new mechanism of the ekkyklema has been used. There is just one line which suggests that the Erinyes are present and visible: 67 καὶ νῦν ἁλούσας τάσδε τὰς μάργους ὁρᾶις. The deictic τάσδε need not mean that they are literally visible— see *Seven* 374c*; compare τοῦδε used by the Pythia of Orestes at 46. It is ὁρᾶις which needs to be explained. It is possible that they look in through the door, and we are to imagine that they see the Furies inside. But it is much better to take the line as an illustration of the protection which Apollo has been promising in 64–6 (on καὶ νῦν see Fraenkel *Ag ed* ii 9), and then ὁρᾶις may be taken in the sense of 'understand' (*LSJ* IId) rather than of literal seeing. If, as a matter of practical fact, the Erinyes were not visible, then the line would still, I suggest, make good sense: 'and so you can understand how it is that . . .'

I have discussed the stage management of the Clytemnestra scene on 94*. While the scene admittedly favours an early revelation of the chorus, it must be weighed against the very considerable points in favour of an entry at 140ff.

One final point is made in favour of the ekkyklema at 64. When Apollo upbraids the Erinyes at 179ff., he begins ἔξω, κελεύω, τῶνδε δωμάτων τάχος / χωρεῖτ', ἀπαλλάσσεσθε μαντικῶν μυχῶν . . . This seems to imply that they are still inside his temple, i.e. either inside the skene or on the special machinery which conventionally showed internal scenes. δωμάτων could mean the whole sacred precinct including the area before the door;[1] but μυχῶν seems to be more specific (cf. 39). However the word could perhaps be extended by association to cover the entire Delphic precinct; the same extension of sense seems to be

---

[1] A good parallel has turned up at *Theoroi or Isthmiastai* fr. 17 ll. 79f. ἀλλ' οὔποτ' ἔξειμ' ἐ[γὼ / τοῦ ἱεροῦ . . . This clearly refers to the whole sanctuary which includes the orchestra, and not just the temple represented by the skene (see l. 83).

invoked in 170 also.[1] The line need not mean, that is, that the Erinyes are actually in the μυχός itself when it is spoken. Any other explanation runs into even greater difficulties. It is out of the question, surely, that the entire parodos was sung from inside the skene, or that it was sung and danced on the small ekkyklema.[2] The song is eminently suitable for dancing and would lose much of its power without it; and in any case choral songs are danced in the orchestra. Rather than lose this, we should suppose that the entire orchestra as well as the ekkyklema is to be imagined as inside the sanctum; but there is no indication of this until 180, when it is too late. A final alternative, widely favoured, is that Apollo drives a last two or three Erinyes out of the skene at 179. But this is a poor compromise, like that of bringing on two or three at 64. The whole chorus should be there for the first song no less than the others; and all are wanted for an effective entry at 140ff. So I prefer to take the μυχός, the core, to stand for the whole.

It should be clear that I prefer the later entry at 140ff.[3] By holding the entry back, giving gruesome descriptions, and letting their beastly noises be heard from inside, Aeschylus prevents the Erinyes from causing visual distractions from the important prologue scenes; and yet he builds up to a highly dramatic moment when they are released into the orchestra. Any staging which previews a representative two or three Furies at 64 dilutes all these effects and salvages nothing in return except the reputation of a scholiast and a more literal meaning for a couple of lines. If this is right, to conclude, the Erinyes are still inside at 64ff., their menace as yet invisible. They are not seen during the Clytemnestra scene either, though they are heard. Finally they are both seen and heard with the full impact of their first entry as they awaken one another and flit singly into the orchestra to join the bestial choreography of the song.[4]

---

[1] Cf. e.g. Hermann *Opusc* vi 2 pp. 164ff., Verrall 33, Rose 243, Kaimio 118.

[2] As e.g. Wilamowitz 179f., Stephenson 37f., Flickinger 151, P-C *TDA* 44, 107, Kaimio 118.

[3] I am not alone in this, though in motley company: I note Hermann op. cit., Bodensteiner 663f., Pickard 208, Neckel (op. cit.) 13f., Richter 219f., D–R 243f., Verrall liif., Rose 229, 248, Dingel 88.

[4] Had Aeschylus wanted the Erinyes to have wings or to resemble bats he would have said so, *contra* Maxwell Stuart *G and R* 20 (1973) 81ff. They are like grotesque snake-infested old women.

179 enter Apollo

231 exit chorus

the departure of the chorus in mid-play

The Erinyes are doubly motivated to depart: they have to pursue Orestes, as they were urged by Clytemnestra (133–9), and also Apollo threatens violence to drive them from his sanctuary (179ff.). Yet there is quite a long dispute before they finally set about departure at 225ff. When it comes their exit is abrupt and unelaborated. So far as we can tell, they began to go at 230 and are on their way before 232.[1] They may still be going off during 233–5, but Apollo's ἐγὼ δέ, picking up theirs in 230, takes attention away from them. All we can say about the stage management of the exit is that it must have been quick and direct, quite likely at a run. Notice how the final couplet uses the image of the Erinyes as hunters following the trail of a mother's blood: see p. 381 below.

It is not usual, of course, for the chorus to leave the scene in the course of a tragedy. Dale (E. *Alc ed* 108) says 'it does not commonly happen, but any dramatist could adopt this expedient when his plot required it' (however, 'required' is the word that needs qualification). It is perhaps misleading that Pollux (4. 108) supplies us with the two terms μετάϲταϲιϲ and ἐπιπάροδοϲ, and that the latter is a favourite word of jargon for Tzetzes; for it is likely that the terms arose in application to post-classical tragedy where it was common for the chorus to go off, perhaps several times, during the course of a tragedy (see p. 49 n. 2, and see in general Zwierlein 80–7). There are four other instances in surviving fifth-century tragedy: each is in various ways different from the others, and is similar to and different from *Eum.* I catalogue them here, and as I come to each point of dramatic technique, I shall note the variations:[2] (i) S. *Aj* 814–66, (ii) E. *Alc* 746–861, (iii) E. *Hel* 385–515, (iv) *Rh* 564–674. Other

---

[1] In 231 J. U. Powell's emendation to κἀκκυνηγέϲω seems pretty sure: Powell (*CQ* 11 (1917) 141f.) was the first to see the relevance of the new forms at S. *Ichn* 44, 75. (However Page *OCT* relegates the conjecture to the apparatus and obelizes.)

[2] There is a laborious and sterile discussion of the ancient terminology and surviving examples, with very full bibliography, in De Falco² 1–55. There are reasonable short discussions in A. Müller 212, P-C *DFA*² 240, Ritchie 118–20.

examples have been posited among the lost plays, but only two deserve serious consideration. One is the Aeschylean play (presumably *Aitnaiai*) which is the subject of the hypothesis in *POxy* 2257 fr. 1, where *Eum* is given as a parallel for repeated changes of scene. This seems to imply that the chorus repeatedly left the scene and returned to it: but see pp. 416f. Since we know nothing concrete about the way this was done, there is no more to be said in this context. Secondly it has been supposed that the chorus went off and re-entered in E. *Phaethon* (226–70).[1] But there is no sign in the chorus's own words that it has been away; and so it is best to suppose that it simply retreated into the background during 226–70 (cf. Webster *The Tragedies of Euripides* (London 1967) 227, followed by Diggle *ed* 150).

How, then, does the removal of the chorus in *Eum* compare with the other four instances? S. *Aj* is somewhat similar: the chorus sets out on the search for someone, and it goes quickly and quietly—indeed the exit is apparently made with the couplet 813f., though it may have started earlier. It seems that they split into hemichoruses and go in opposite directions. Both E. *Alc* and *Hel* are notably different, however, in that the chorus closely accompanies an actor (like Euripidean secondary choruses, see p. 236 above). In *Alc* the procession leaves with a brief set of anapaests (741–6); but in *Hel* there is an extended lyric scene between the decision to go inside and the actual departure (330–85), and it seems that the chorus went off in silence during the last part (362ff.) which is sung by Helen alone. At *Rh* 523–6 Hector tells the chorus to keep a look-out and to meet Dolon. Instead it sings a strophic lyric, interspersed with anapaestic dialogue among its members, about changing the watch (527–64); and at the end they go off to rouse the Lycians. This is the only departure of the chorus which follows on a kind of act-dividing song, since 527–64 divides Hector and Rhesus from Odysseus and Diomedes. Elsewhere, as in *Eum*, the scenes on either side of the exit of the chorus are directly juxtaposed.

---

[1] See e.g. Volmer (E. *Phaethon ed*, Münster 1930), Zwierlein 83, Ritchie 118f. But this depends on the unwarranted assumption that the maids commanded by Clymene in 221 and 216 are the chorus itself and not simply her personal attendants (it is true that the chorus was identified as δμωαί at 55, cf. δμωίδες in 221, but that was long before). Moreover, this theory produces an impossible situation at 269–70, where Merops must rush into the palace and the chorus rush out of it simultaneously.

234 exit Apollo

235 re-enter Orestes

change of scene and lapse of time

The break between the exit of Apollo and the entry of Orestes is complete: there is a totally vacant stage, a change of place, and a lapse of time. There can be no act-dividing song because the chorus is not there to sing it. Yet the break is as heavy as the break between acts, if not heavier; in some ways it is more like the break between the separate plays of a trilogy (see further 276*). The inadequate and artificial terminology in [Aristotle] *Poetics* ch. 12 (see Appendix E) is not able to accommodate the structural technique of a place like this; but this should not make us neglect or underestimate it. To say something like 'the change of scene . . . occurs *in the course* of an episode' (Weissinger 27, W.'s italics) is to be a slave to the terminology, and shut off from the play itself. The same structural point is true of the other four places where the chorus goes off within the play; though in *Eum* the break is perhaps the most heavily marked.[1]

The change of scene has been prepared for by Apollo's instructions at 78ff. where he tells Orestes to go to Athens and to clasp the παλαιὸν βρέτας; and he refers to Athena again just before the break at 224. Immediately on his re-entry Orestes addresses Athena, explains how he has come on Apollo's instructions (235f., 241), and claims that his pollution is 'worn away' (see further 244b*); he ends (242f.) πρόσειμι δῶμα καὶ βρέτας τὸ cόν, θεά. / αὐτοῦ φυλάccων ἀναμένω τέλος δίκης. So the scene change is made absolutely clear in the words. Whether this was reinforced scenically, and if so how, has been the subject of inconclusive speculation.[2] No doubt the statue was represented on stage, but whether it was there from the start or whether it was brought on or revealed at this juncture, we cannot say.[3] When I have spoken elsewhere of the shifting or refocusing of the scene, I have taken it that there was no visual change (see *Pers* 598c*). But the

---

[1] It is worth noting that this point would not be true of the alleged departure of the chorus in E. *Phaethon* (see p. 376). There Clymene sees Merops and the wedding-chorus approaching (216ff.), and it is because of their approach that she hurries off: this provides a positive link across the break at 226/7.

[2] See e.g. Allen *UCCP* 7 (1919) 76, P-C *TDA* 44, Arnott 69.

[3] The Pythia addressed Παλλὰς προναία in 21, but there is no sign that her image was present. On the stage position of the statue see p. 386 n. 1.

scene change here is of a different kind: it is explicit, it takes place at a given moment, and the chorus leaves one place and re-enters to another. This kind of scene change, which is more like that in the more recent theatre, was very rare in the fifth century, though it may have been common later (see p. 49 n. 2).[1] The only other example to survive is in S. *Aj.* Ajax says he is going to the bathing places by the shore (654ff.), and Tecmessa sends the chorus along the shores (805f.). When Ajax comes on alone, he gives no further indication of the place, but in the context it is completely clear that there has been a change of place to a lonely place by the shore. Again there are disputes about the scenic management (see e.g. Allen op. cit. 75 n. 159); but in any case, although it is not so precise or so far distant as in *Eum*, there clearly is an explicit change of place. But this was probably a rare device; when the commentator on *Aitnaiai* wanted to give examples, he cited *Eum* for one and S. *Achilleos Erastai* as another.[2] In *Alc* and *Hel*, on the other hand, the scene explicitly remains before the doors of the palace; and in *Rh* it remains by the εὐναί of Hector (the objective of Odysseus and Diomedes, see 574ff.).

The explicit lapse of time is unique in surviving tragedy. I have discussed on *Ag* 489* the flexibility of the handling of time in Greek drama, and have illustrated how time may be 'compressed': but the situation here in *Eum* is quite different, and it contrasts with the other places where the chorus leaves the stage.[3] Not only does Aeschylus not put in enough material to cover the illusion of a journey from Delphi to Athens (140 lines for Orestes, but only 14 for the Erinyes), but he goes out of his way to make it clear that Orestes did not go directly or without stopping. Orestes wandered far over land and sea. Apollo first predicts this at 75–9 (note μακρᾶς, πλανοςτιβῆ); and Orestes takes up the motif on arrival in 235–41 (esp. 239).[4] The Erinyes corroborate

---

[1] Lloyd-Jones *tr* 25 cannot be right to say 'changes of scene do not occur in any tragedy known to us later than Aeschylus'. Even if post-classical tragedy is left out of account, there is still S. *Aj.*

[2] See p. 376 above. The information about scene changes in *Eum* is introduced by κ(ατὰ) μ(ὲν) γ(ὰρ) in l. 8; and Lobel most ingeniously supplemented ll. 6f. εἰς Ἀ]θήνας ἐκ Δελφῶν μ(ε)τ[αβι]βάζεται. He warns (*POxy* xx p. 66) 'I cannot verify this'; but the restoration is overwhelmingly apt.

[3] Cf. Duchemin *Dioniso* 41 (1967) 208–11. E. *Stheneboia*, even if it contained a lapse of time, would be quite different; see Zühlke *Philol* 105 (1961) 9ff. esp. 13f.

[4] ἀλάστορα in l. 236 is peculiar, since Orestes goes on to claim he is free from

Orestes at 248–51. Orestes reiterates the extent of his wandering before calling on Athena (276–85 esp. 284f.; cf. also 451f.). We are made to think by 235ff. that Orestes has been wandering for weeks or even months rather than hours or days, and this impression is confirmed later. I have not seen this long lapse of time between Delphi and Athens fully explained; I consider it further, but inconclusively, on 244b* below.

244ff. re-enter chorus

(a) the stage picture: the hounds in full cry

First there are ten lines of trimeters (244–53), probably spoken by the coryphaeus only, then an astrophic dochmiac–iambic lyric (254–75). The Erinyes are hunting Orestes by following the trail of blood (244–7, 252f., cf. 230); they are searching around for where he is cowering (252, 254–60)—it seems he is first actually detected at 258. The astrophic lyric could well be split into parts and distributed among individuals or parts of the chorus.[1] And it may well be, as many have supposed, that the chorus again entered *cποράδην* (see 140*). At any rate the text does not contain anything to discourage the idea.

It is worth noting that in two of the four other plays, S. *Aj* and *Rh*, the 'epiparodos' is not a completely regular entry in formation.[2] In *Aj* the chorus re-enters in two parts from either side, and before the strophic lyric at 879ff. there is an astrophic dialogue of trimeters and isolated iambic metra.[3] The chorus is searching

pollution. Dirksen 20–5 makes much of this in an interesting discussion, though his conclusions in terms of Orestes' psychology are unacceptable. Some, e.g. Wecklein *ed* 19 n. 1, try to connect the word with *ἀλάομαι*, but this is not supported by tragic usage elsewhere (see Fraenkel A. *Ag ed* iii 711f.). In a footnote to a footnote I offer the emendation *ἀλήτορα*. The word is only attested in Hesych. who glosses it *ἱερεύς*, but its root meaning is presumably 'wanderer'. The corruption from a rare word to a favourite tragic one would be easy.

[1] The various theories are enumerated by de Falco[2] 25–30. This cannot be the entry referred to by the *Life* (see p. 372 n. 2 above); and de Falco's discussion (19–25) whether 140ff. or 244ff. is the 'real parodos' is meaningless. Kaimio 135f. perversely tries to eliminate any division of parts and to exclude any seeking from the stage action: but an orderly entry in formation would hardly suit the context.

[2] In *Alc* and *Hel* the chorus simply returns from its mission along with the actor it went with. In *Alc* the chorus is secondary to Admetus in the re-entry lyric (861–934); in *Hel* it sings a short astrophic song (515–27) before Helen's rhesis (cf. Kannicht E. *Hel ed* 146).

[3] But Rattenbury *PCPhS* 160 (1935) 9 thought this should be emended into responding strophes.

desperately for Ajax and may not have been in any formation. There are in fact verbal similarities to *Eum*: they have searched every τόπος (*Aj* 869 cf. *Eum* 249), it has brought them πόνος (*Aj* 866 cf. *Eum* 127, 133,[1] and μόχθοις in 248). Secondly, one of the several ways in which *Rh* is different from the others is that the chorus re-enters on a different mission from that on which it set out. They rush on at 674ff. in the act of capturing Odysseus (and Diomedes?), and before the scene settles into the trochaic tetrameters during which Odysseus escapes (683ff.) there is an astrophic sequence (the metre is hard to pin down, see Ritchie 294). The lines could well be divided among the chorus members, and this remarkably lively and realistic entry was very probably made σποράδην: in the excitement and confusion any entry in formation would be out of place. It may well be that these two unconventional choral re-entries are influenced by the precedent of *Eum*; and the same may be true of the structural technique, see 276*.[2]

If it is right that the entries both here and at 140ff. were made σποράδην then this would be a striking visual 'mirror' scene. For a second time the hounds would stream into view, yet still in pursuit of the same quarry. The qualification should be made that the first entry would be from the skene and the second from an eisodos,[3] and so the correspondence would not be precise; but it would still be very obvious. Even if they were not, in fact, both σποράδην we would still have a remarkable repetition at a very short interval of the event of the entry of the chorus. Why then did Aeschylus employ these uncommon techniques (for he need not have done)? The repeated entry of the chorus brings out the relentlessness of the Erinyes' pursuit. They never give up, they are always at Orestes' heels. Their persistent hunt is not only talked about, we see it with our own eyes. It is a mean over-simplification to say, as even good scholars tend to do, that

[1] In 132 Dawe (*apud* Page *OCT*) may be right to regard πόνου as corrupt under the influence of 133. But in that case φόνου is little more likely than a word with no palaeographic similarity e.g. νεβροῦ, ἄγρας.

[2] The only choral entries comparable to these three to be found elsewhere in tragedy are in E. *Hkld* (73ff.) and S. *OC* (117ff.), neither astrophic. It is unlikely that E. *Telephos* contained anything comparable to *Rh* (*contra* Ritchie 129f., see *Telephos ed* Handley–Rea 36).

[3] Cf. Joerden 119. Webster *CR* N.S. 13 (1963) 33 recognized the parallelism, and yet went on to draw the palpably wrong conclusion that the second entry might have been made on the ekkyklema.

Aeschylus sends the chorus off during the play 'in order to' change the scene.[1] So too with S. *Aj*: the chorus leaves, not so that the scene may change, but so that Ajax may be alone.

The stage action also embodies and brings to a head two of the most persistent complexes of imagery in the trilogy. One is the imagery of hunting, which is in turn connected through the hunting net to that of the net and net-cloth (cf. pp. 314–5).[2] The Erinyes are the μητρὸς ἔγκοτοι κύνες (*Cho* 924, repeated at *Cho* 1054). Clytemnestra revives the image which merges with the literal at *Eum* 111–13, 131f. And the chorus refers to itself in the same terms at 147, 230f., and again on re-entry at 244ff. (ὡς κύων νεβρὸν in 246 echoes 111). Secondly the recurrent picture of 'blood on the ground' now becomes near-literal. The motif is first made explicit at *Ag* 1019ff. (but see p. 315 above), and is particularly persistent in the first half of *Cho*.[3] It is the trail of blood left by Orestes which the Furies follow (230, 244–7); then soon at 261ff. the image is taken up again in the resonantly familiar terms: αἷμα . . . χαμαὶ δυσαγκόμιστον κτλ. Thus the image is made literal and yet retains all its metaphorical power at the same time. The visual and choreographic picture of the Erinyes hunting by following a trail of blood evokes the entire framework of murder and revenge.

(b) pollution and blood

These rather rough observations raise a complex of problems which have not been much discussed;[4] it may be some help simply to pose the problems, although I can offer no real solution. Two questions lie behind them: is Orestes purified? why does Orestes have to wander?

Orestes is very insistent that he is no longer polluted. Three times he addresses Athena, first her statue at 235–43, then calling her from afar (276–98), and finally in her presence (443–69): each

---

[1] See recently e.g. Ritchie 119, Kannicht E. *Hel ed* 121.

[2] Hunting imagery in the *Oresteia* is traced perceptively by Lebeck 66–7, 132 and Vidal-Naquet *Mythe et tragédie* (Paris 1972) 135ff. (V-N claims not to be 'banalement littéraire', a phrase which verges on a contradiction in terms).

[3] See *Cho* 46ff., 66ff., 400ff., 519ff. It will recur at *Eum* 647ff., and finally be resolved in the apotropaic benediction at 976ff.; cf. Goheen 115ff., Lebeck 90f. Lebeck 87ff. also points to the incurable poison which the Erinyes threaten to pour on the soil of Athens.

[4] See Verrall xvif., Dodds *Progress* 50f., Jones 103–9, Dirksen 83f.

time he explains first how he is pure, as a preface and justification of his action. So there are three explanations of his
purity: 237–42, 276–87, 443–53. At 473–5 Athena accepts this.
Yet how can he be pure when he still trails his mother's blood?
Immediately after the murder Orestes has blood on his hands (see
esp. *Cho* 1055f., 1059f.); when the Pythia sees Orestes the blood
is still dripping (*Eum* 41f.); and, of course, the Erinyes follow
the blood. Certainly they regard him as still polluted as they
make clear at 316–20, 378, and in general by the δέϲμιοϲ ὕμνοϲ.

But if we are to accept Athena's judgement at 473–5 and suppose that Orestes was purified, at least according to the notions
of the newer generation of gods, then when and where was he
purified? Apparently at Delphi: that is why he goes there (*Cho*
1038f., 1059f.), Apollo is καθάρϲιοϲ (*Eum* 63), and he had told
Orestes προϲτραπέϲθαι τούϲδε δόμουϲ (205 cf. 234). Orestes does
not make this point in each of his three speeches, but he does
evidently say at 282f. that he was purified at Delphi, and Apollo
confirms this at 577–8. If we are *not* meant to suppose that Orestes
was purified at Delphi then all this is positively misleading.[1]
And yet there is no trace whatsoever in the words that Orestes
was purified on-stage during this play. So do we presume that
he was purified at some unspecified time before the play began,
or at least before line 64?

But in that case what is the significance of Orestes' wanderings?
These are emphasized in the text (see pp. 378f. above) and reinforced by the action (see 244a* above); and they cannot be
simply dismissed as residual traces of an epic version (cf. Dirksen
20f.), nor as an allusion to other versions of the purification of
Orestes.[2] Orestes was an ἀλήτηϲ before *Cho* began and leaves as
one at the end (see *Cho* 1063*). Apollo may protect Orestes, but
he cannot save him from wanderings, which he admits will be
arduous and toilsome (74–9). The Erinyes themselves are

---

[1] Dyer *JHS* 89 (1969) 38ff. (cf. Hammond 442f.) argues that besides *Eum*
there is no good reason to think that Apollo ever purified at Delphi. So he tries
to explain away the evidence of each passage, esp. 282–3; but in their contexts
in the play as a whole they clearly imply that Orestes was purified at Delphi. If
Dyer were willing to expunge 282–3 and 578 (which were apparently known in
Southern Italy by the mid fourth century, see Dyer 51), then his case might be
tenable. Amandry *RA* 6ᵐᵉ Sér. xi (1938) 19ff., argued that 282–3 might refer to
Eleusis rather than Delphi.

[2] Though there were many, see Frazer on Paus. ii. 31. 8, Lesky *RE* xviii 988ff.,
Dyer op. cit.

exhausted by them (248ff.). Each of the three times that Orestes assures Athena of his purity he refers to the cleansing and attritive effect of his wanderings. At 238f. he is ἀμβλὺν ἤδη προςτετριμμένον τε πρὸς / ἄλλοιςιν οἴκοιc καὶ πορεύμαςιν βροτῶν. At 276f. he says that he has learned by his troubles πολλοὺς καθαρμούς.[1] At 284–5 he has been with many people ἀβλαβεῖ ξυνουςίαι, and he explains this by adding χρόνος καθαίρει πάντα γηράςκων ὁμοῦ.[2] And finally and most strikingly he says at 448–52 that he knows it is νόμος that he should be purified πρὸς ἀνδρὸς καθαρςίου, and indeed πάλαι πρὸς ἄλλοιc ταῦτ᾿ ἀφιερώμεθα / οἴκοιcι. This can hardly be a reference to Delphi (note ἀνδρός cf. βροτῶν in 239, βροτοῖcιν 93). It seems that Orestes' wanderings have worn away his pollution, and by repeated purifications duplicated or made doubly sure his Delphic purification.

Aeschylus seems to be deliberately complicated and unclear on the matter of purification. Orestes is purified at Delphi and yet also on his wanderings. The Pythia sees blood on his hands; it is worn and washed from them and yet the Erinyes still track him by it. Perhaps there is a simple explanation which reconciles these features; but it seems more likely that they are meant to co-exist without this kind of close scrutiny.[3] Aeschylus wants the supplication at Delphi, but he also wants the salutary suffering of Orestes' wanderings. The chief point which I wish to make is that all these factors, whatever their relationship and significance, are there embodied in the stage action of the entry of Orestes and of the Furies. We see the last paces of the exhausting and harrowing travels, and we see the Erinyes tracking the blood.

[1] In view of the way that this is taken up by καὶ νῦν in 287ff. καθαρμούς should not be emended as it often is (obelized by Page *OCT*). Part of the process of καθαρμός is to speak and keep silent at the right times.

[2] When the line is seen in this context and the transmitted accent καθαιρεῖ altered, the line seems to make good sense and even important sense. Most editors have rejected it.

[3] A full discussion would have to consider, if only to reject as irrelevant, the association, esp. in epic, of pollution with exile and wandering, stories of Orestes' wanderings and of his arrival at Athens, and evidence of gradual purification or purification by time.

Dyer (op. cit.) 39 n. 5 raises and rejects the theory that there is a lacuna before l. 64. There are traces of some textual disruption at that point, see 64*. I merely point out as a wild speculation that *if* in a lacuna Apollo told Orestes (i) his purification at Delphi was only the first of many, (ii) he would have to wander to many houses for further rites, and (iii) that the Erinyes would follow him none the less (cf. 75–7), then this would clear up the factors I have been worrying over.

Orestes' three addresses to Athena and the Erinyes' two songs
(254ff., 307ff.) further bring out and ramify the issues and
conflicts contained in the visible action.

276 (no entry)

the structural technique of 235–397

The procedure of taking the chorus off in mid-play is unusual
and disruptive, and it inevitably brings with it unusual structural techniques because of the temporary absence of the chorus.
In each of the five surviving instances the structural disturbance
is handled in more or less different ways.

In *Eum*, firstly, Orestes enters at 235 to a kind of second
prologue, which is very short. The Erinyes, hot on his heels,
then re-enter for the second parodos or 'epiparodos' (choreo-
graphically this is a parodos since the chorus is coming in). The
song is, however, unlike a proper parodos in that it is preceded
by nine trimeters, it is short and astrophic, and also there is no
exit at the end of the 'epiprologos' nor entry following the
end of the 'epiparodos' (cf. on *Prom* 88*). Instead, at the end of
the song there is simply Orestes' speech (276–97), which makes
the vital transition from his claim to purity (see 244b*) to his
summoning of Athena (see 397a*). The Erinyes try to start a
dispute (299ff.), but when they are met with silence (see *HSCP*
76 (1972) 79) they embark on the anapaestic prelude to their
next song, the binding-song. So once more there is no exit at
the end of the spoken section and before the choral song. The
structural technique has analogies with that at *Pers* 598–681 and
Hik 600–709, see *Pers* 622*: in all three cases all that comes
between two blocks of choral song is a short actor's speech,
which makes an important transition and leads on to the next
choral song without an intervening exit. In *Eum* the entry of
Athena at the end of the song (397) clearly inaugurates a new
part of the play. Aeschylus has, in my view, definite dramatic
purposes in this unusual structural technique; and I shall return
to them, when I have considered the other plays where the
chorus goes off.

In S. *Aj* the exit of the chorus is also followed by a solo rhesis,
though Ajax's death speech (815–65) is much longer and much
more central than Orestes' little 'epiprologue'. Ajax's speech is

both a prologue to the second part of the play and the conclusion of the first. Unlike that in *Eum*, the re-entry of the chorus is preceded by the equivalent of an exit when Ajax falls finally on his sword, thus marking off his speech as an entirely separate unit. The equivalent in *Aj* to Athena's new beginning at *Eum* 397 is Teucros' entry at 974ff. In between that point and the re-entry of the chorus there is, as in *Eum*, an unusual structural sequence, but it is quite different and highly original (particularly bold if the play is early, as is generally supposed). After the first disordered entry (866–78, see pp. 379f. above), there is a large epirrhematic structure of one strophic pair (879–974) during which Tecmessa enters.[1] *Alc* is more like *Eum*. Between the exit and re-entry of the chorus there is the Servant's complaint (747ff.) and his dialogue with Heracles (773ff.), which ends with his exit at 860;[2] but on the return of the chorus there are two songs and an actor's rhesis without any exit or entry, before the return of Heracles with Alcestis at 1006. The first song (861–934), unlike that in *Eum*, is a lyric dialogue, but Admetus' speech (935–61) is brief yet crucial, and then there is no exit before the following choral song (962–1005). By holding back the return of Heracles and leaving Admetus without relief Euripides draws out and savours his despair before he resolves it. Menelaus' arrival in E. *Hel* after the departure of the chorus is very clearly an 'epiprologue' (see Kannicht E. *Hel ed* 122f.). After his confrontation with the woman at the door, there is a kind of exit at 514 before the chorus' return, as Menelaus retreats into the background. The return, however, simply marks the beginning of the long central act without any structural complication beyond a brief astrophic 'epiparodos' (515–27). In *Rh*, finally, there is a very strange and exotic series of scenes while

---

[1] Each strophic pair includes a choral part, then a lyric dialogue, and each is followed by a speech of Tecmessa (915ff. = 961ff.). Each speech consists of two five-line elements, and in my view Schoell was probably right to regard 971–3 as a three-line interpolation which disturbs the epirrhematic structure (defended by Pearson *CQ* 16 (1922) 124ff.). There are other textual possibilities, notably the deletion of 918–19 and of 966–70; but in any case the two speeches should respond (*contra* Jebb S. *Aj ed* 233). Tecmessa enters between the choral and the dialogue part of the first strophe, which is most unusual, and effectively integrates her re-entry in the lyric structure before Teucros' arrival.

[2] It worries stage historians that Heracles and the chorus should meet at 860/1 (e.g. Flickinger 234f., Hourmouziades 133 n. 2). Probably Heracles simply went off on the 'wrong' side; and probably no one in the audience noticed the incongruity.

the chorus is off (565–674, cf. p. 352), all linked together by Athena. Alexandros goes and Athena goes (or fades out, see p. 366 n. 1) just before the chorus re-enters; but Athena provides a link to the return of the chorus by warning the Greeks that they are pursued. After the chaotic scene in which Odysseus escapes (674–91) there is a choral song (692ff.), similarly constructed to that on departure (527ff.), which is followed in the usual way by a new entry (728ff.). To sum up, then, in relation to *Eum. Eum* has by far the shortest scene while the chorus is off; and only in *Aj* is there also just one character involved in the intervening stage; in all the others there is an exit, or something like an exit, before the re-entry of the chorus, while in *Eum* there is nothing. In all except *Hel* there is then a rather complex structural sequence, but in *Aj* and *Rh* it is unique and quite unlike *Eum*; in *Alc*, however, there is a similar sequence of song–rhesis–song without any entrance or exit.

In *Eum* Aeschylus conveys by means of his structure both the relentless menace of the Erinyes and Orestes' incapacity for any independent resistance or escape. Aeschylus has contrived to keep the two parties separate throughout the earlier scenes of the play (see 139*). But then Orestes scarcely has time to clasp Athena's image (242, cf. 259f., 409) before the Erinyes catch him up; and as soon as they have found him they turn on him all their blood-curdling menace in the astrophic song. Orestes can in no way meet this, and in his speech puts all his hope in Athena, as Apollo advised him; all the time he clings unmoving to her image. Then the Erinyes embark on the ὕμνος δέσμιος which is the culmination of all the imagery of destructive binding, and which shows them at their most effective and most terrifying.[1] Of all the choral songs during which an actor stays

---

[1] Cf. Lebeck 67. Lebeck 147–9, 150ff. points out, and perhaps overstresses, that the binding song in some ways already foreshadows the change of aspect in the Erinyes which will become so important later in the play. Incidentally the Erinyes surely dance *round* Orestes, as may be implied by χορὸν ἅψωμεν (307). This is evidence, though of necessity inconclusive, that the statue was somewhere in the orchestra. The possibility or probability that the dance was *circular* by itself outweighs, in my opinion, all the late evidence that dramatic dances were always based on a rectangular formation; cf. P-C *DFA*² 239, Ferri *Dioniso* 3 (1931–2) 336ff. (Webster *Chorus* 112 claims that these testimonia refer only to the entrance-song formation; but regrettably this is not so.) Rose p. 251 makes the sober observation 'the Chorus has now arranged itself in a semi-circle facing the stage. In *real life* they would probably surround the object of the incantation' (my italics)!

on stage (see *Pers* 622*) there is none where the actor is so directly bound up in the song: it is sung 'over' him (ἐπὶ τῶι τεθυμένωι 328 = 341). So the song demands that there should be no exit before it.[1] Orestes has to wait, isolated and pinned down (compare the prolonged isolation of Admetus in *Alc*), while the chorus relentlessly torments him. So the structural technique with its lack of any exits or entrances shows Orestes inescapably tied to his refuge; all he can do is to call on Athena and to wait. The choral songs do not divide acts in the usual way: they are the action, and Orestes' little speeches mere intervals in their infernal spell-binding.

397 enter Athena

(a) preparation

The main part of *Eum* takes on the form of a 'suppliant play'— see *Hik* 1a*. As usual the suppliant arrives at the beginning, though in this case it is a kind of second start to the play (235). The hostile pursuers arrive almost immediately. More often, as in *Hik*, the protector-host has arrived, made his decision, and gone again before the pursuers ever arrive; but in *Eum* they are firmly entrenched when Athena first comes. It is true that in E. *Hkld* Demophon arrives after the pursuer; but there is no hesitation or doubt in his case (and he is urged on by the chorus, which was the first rescuer to arrive). But Athena has to face her dilemma in the presence of both parties (*Eum* 470ff.; compare 480–1 with A. *Hik* 442, cf. 379f., 407ff.). Moreover Athena has a special problem because the rejection of the pursuers is not merely a matter of brute force in battle. By having the rescuer arrive after the pursuers Aeschylus gives a complexity to the problem which means that its solution cannot be simple or one-sided.

In the earlier preparation for the trial at Athens, it is not completely clear that Athena will take part in the play in person (see 79–83, 224); and when Orestes first arrives at her temple he says simply that he will await judgement (243, cf. the chorus

---

[1] I cannot understand why Graeber 48 says that Orestes stays on because the Erinyes stop him from going into the temple.

at 260¹). So it is something of a new development when at 287ff., after his preamble about purity, Orestes actually calls on Athena to come in person. In the other suppliant plays, there is a βοή—see *Hik* 911*; this is because the call for aid is directed to the local citizens or ruler who are hoped to be within earshot. But Athena might be anywhere. So Orestes addresses her in a sort of prayer, which acts as a summons; and his invocation contains elements taken from cult practice (cf. Kranz 186f., and *Pers* 681a* on the summoning of Darius). Orestes touches on the benefits he has to offer (289–91), he enumerates the range of places where Athena might be (292–6), and he uses the characteristic kletic verbs (μολεῖν 289, ἔλθοι 297). This is, so far as I can see, the only place in surviving tragedy, surprisingly enough, where a god actually appears in person in direct answer to a summons or prayer (though cf. E. *Ba* 582ff.). But given the epic precedent it seems a perfectly acceptable procedure. It also seems acceptable that a god should be able to hear at a distance (cf. *Iliad* 16. 515f.); though Aeschylus does, in fact, add a parenthetic apology in 297, and Athena also takes this up with her opening words (397).

(b) staging

Athena has come all the way from Scamander in a short time, and, although we may easily accept that gods can travel fast, Aeschylus chooses to dwell on the way she has made the journey. Unfortunately the lines in question are textually suspect, and leave it uncertain how her entry was staged. The controversial lines (403–5) read, as transmitted:

> ἔνθεν διώκουc᾽ ἦλθον ἄτρυτον πόδα
> πτερῶν ἄτερ ῥοιβδοῦca κόλπον αἰγίδοc
> πώλοιc ἀκμαίοιc τόνδ᾽ ἐπιζεύξαc᾽ ὄχον.

At first glance, the first line seems to say that she came on foot, the second that she flew (without wings), and the third that she rode in a chariot. To judge from the scholia, two of these three

---

¹ 260 ὑπόδικοc θέλει γενέcθαι χερῶν. This is the only occurrence of the technical term ὑπόδικοc in tragedy. The MSS. read χερῶν but the scholion, and it seems Hesych., had the variant χρεῶν which most editors (but not Page *OCT*) prefer. But χερῶν, 'the deed done by his hands', is a much more vivid reading. Paley complains that Aeschylus would have used φόνου to say that: but it is Orestes' *hands* which have become the issue (see 244b*).

ways of taking the lines were current in antiquity;[1] and modern scholars have among them advocated all three.[2] Any of the three ways can be upheld if one is willing to put a very strained interpretation on the other two lines. Thus 403 need not mean she literally moved her foot, but may only be a poetic periphrasis for speed (cf. A. *Seven* 371, E. *Or* 1344; for exotic tragic periphrases with πόδα see Rau 117). 404 does not say she came through the air; her aegis may have whirred as she ran or as she rode her chariot. And in 405, if Athena made it clear that τόνδ' ὄχον was her aegis (cf. Arph. *Clouds* 602) then the πῶλοι might be taken figuratively of the winds.[3] So all three lines might, if the Greek is sufficiently twisted, be kept in the text, and any of the three methods of transport still be upheld. But this is hardly plausible.

Paley (*ed* 1879) and Wilamowitz (1886) rightly insisted that 404 and 405 are incompatible, and that one of the two lines was added in order to change the method of staging. All those who have followed this have taken the chariot in 405 to be the interpolated line, except Arnott who excludes 404. So far as stage history is concerned Arnott has a case: chariot entries were a feature of the early theatre (see *Pers* 155b*), while it is doubtful whether the mechane was yet invented (see p. 446). If the interpolation was made later in the fifth century when chariots were out of fashion and the mechane still a novelty, then Arnott's theory fits well. If on the other hand it was made in the fourth century, as is usually assumed, then the position is reversed: chariot entries may have been back in vogue (see *Pers* 155b*), while epiphanies on the mechane had lost their novelty. Thus, so far as theatre history is concerned, a case can be made either way: but when we turn to the text, then the issue is very different. Lines 403–4 without 405 make a good text. But if we cut 404 then 405 follows very awkwardly on 403; for, while 403 may be a poetic periphrasis, it still strongly implies physical effort on

---

[1] The scholion on 397 says ἐπὶ ὀχήματος ἔρχεται, and that on 404 ὡς ἁρμένωι χρωμένη τῆι αἰγίδι (though ῥοιβδοῦσα is a verb of noise and would fit the use of the aegis as wings no less than as a sail).

[2] For Athena on foot see e.g. Bethe 154, Richter 265, Bolle 17, P-C *TDA* 44f.; through the air e.g. Hermann *Opusc* vi 2 pp. 175f., Wilamowitz *Einleitung* 154 n. 63, *Interpretationen* 181, Weissmann *Aufführung* 15, Robert 569f., Groeneboom 153 n. 7; on a chariot e.g. K. O. Müller 112, Arnott 74f., Hammond 440 n. 97.

[3] πνόοις ἀκμαίοις (Weil) is worth consideration, but the epithet would be strange. κώλοις (Wakefield) was accepted by Hermann, but it seems grotesque.

Athena's part (cf. Paley *ed* 620), and there is an impossible incongruity if she immediately says that steeds have brought her in a chariot. In fact while 405 may be an interpolation, 404 cannot be; and it is inaccurate of editors to speak of a 'dittographia'. So it is best to excise 405;[1] but it is an addition to 404, not an alternative. The lines will date from a production where an entry on a chariot was preferred to one merely on foot or on the overworked mechane.

Even so, I do not concede to Wilamowitz and those who follow him that the original entry in Aeschylus' production was made through the air on the mechane. Line 403 implies that Athena came on foot, and 404 does not say that she flew but that she came without wings: πτερῶν ἄτερ simply explains how she came miraculously over the sea, exactly as the Erinyes explained at 250 that they came over the sea ἀπτέροις ποτήμασιν. Over land Athena travelled at superhuman speed on foot, as she says in 403. All the way she whirred her aegis. I conclude, then, that Athena probably entered on foot.

489 exit Athena

566 re-enter Athena, with Herald and Jurors

(a) *the change of scene and the change in the chorus*

The scene from 235 is set near the παλαιὸν βρέτας of Athena. For the Athenian audience its whereabouts needed no explanation: it was inside a temple in the Acropolis, near or on the spot where the Erechtheum was later built.[2] The trial, on the other hand, is not set on the Acropolis, let alone inside Athena's temple, it is on the Areopagus and in the open air. This is not clear, or at least it is not explicit, immediately at 566ff.; but it is unequivocal in Athena's 'charter' at 681ff., esp. 685–90. Not only are there deictic pronouns (685, 688), but the whole aetiological procedure involves the setting. Yet there has been

---

[1] Though not all of Wilamowitz's arguments are sound, see Dingel 65 n. 5.

[2] Cf. *HSCP* 76 (1972) 68. There has been great controversy over the 'Old Temple of Athena', the 'Hekatompedon', 'Opisthodomos', etc.; but there is no doubt that the ancient image, made of olive wood, was housed in that part of the Acropolis. The Erechtheum was built to house it: see further G. P. Stevens and others *The Erechtheum* (Cambridge Mass. 1927) 433ff., I. T. Hill *The Ancient City of Athens* (London 1953) 137f., 176 and notes.

fierce controversy over this, and even large-scale textual corruption has been preferred to a change of scene.[1] But if it is once accepted that in Aeschylus the scene could refocus without having overtly changed at any particular moment (see *Pers* 598c*), then the difficulty dissolves. It is impossible to pin down a particular point where the scene refocuses; perhaps it is clear immediately from the procedure at 566ff. Possibly the statue was taken off during the song, and at some point benches, voting urns, etc. were brought on; but these stage details are not a prerequisite of the change of scene.[2]

Where is Orestes during the song 490–565? Most of those who have accepted the scene change have had Orestes go off (e.g. Verrall, Pickard-Cambridge, Rose 263, Lloyd-Jones *tr* 40). But there is no sign of this in the text (he can hardly fetch Apollo in obedience to 485f.); and the deictic τοῦδε is used of him in 492. Those who, like Wecklein, oppose the scene-change point to the scholion on 490—ὁ δὲ Ὀρέcτηc ἱκετεύων μένει—and claim that his continuous presence shows that the scene is the same before and after the song.[3] It is true that in the other instances of a refocusing of scene there is a choral song with no actors on stage; but if we accept the convention, then there is no reason why an actor should not stay on as well as the chorus.

There is, perhaps, a dramatic gain if Orestes stays on. The central song is crucial, because it prepares the way for the shift in emphasis away from the individual towards the city and mankind, and away from the Erinyes as blood-curdling monsters towards the Eumenides as powerful figures of awe and respect.[4]

[1] Some of the main discussions: for the change, Hermann *Opusc* vi 2 pp. 170–3, Verrall *ed* 183–8, P-C *TDA* 45; against, K. O. Müller 107f., Wecklein *Schauplatz*, Richter 236f., Wilamowitz 181–3, Ridgway *CR* 21 (1907) 163ff. (for a fatal flaw in this forceful article see Thomson[2] ii 199). Wecklein excluded the entire speech 681ff. as interpolation; see further pp. 399f. below.

[2] Verrall 185f. took the chorus off at 565 and brought it on again for the trial. There is no trace of this in the text and it is unnecessary.

[3] Wecklein *Schauplatz* 66 claims that Athena's intention to return (ἥξω 488) shows she must come back to the same place; but the situation is left deliberately vague. Note how the βρέταc is not mentioned after 409—not until 1024 in a different kind of context.

[4] See e.g. Wilamowitz 181, Kranz 172, Lloyd-Jones *Zeus* 92f., Lebeck 160f. Lebeck 145ff. argues that elements of the less narrow and more awe-inspiring aspects of the Erinyes emerge earlier in the play, especially in the binding song. While there is some truth in this (cf. 269ff., 333ff., 389ff.), her overemphasis detracts from the full impact of the new insights revealed by the later song 490ff.

The previous song was bound round Orestes, see 276*: but this later song takes Orestes only as the starting-point in the first strophe (492), and then moves away from him on to the whole issue of the individual, the City, and Dike. Righteous sentiments are couched in terms which have their ramifications woven through the trilogy: 'wisdom through suffering', hybris and the begetting of evil, the altar of Dike, the overloaded ship of prosperity, and so on. Many of these themes are confirmed in Athena's founding speech (681ff.). This is no blood-thirsty spell. The Erinyes have begun, in the eyes of the audience, a change of aspect which will alter them almost, but not quite, beyond recognition.[1] Perhaps the transitional function of this song would be reinforced if Orestes were on stage, no longer the victim, but the inspiration of much larger issues.

(b) the Court

Athena returns, in fulfilment of her undertaking in 487f., with ἀcτῶν τὰ βέλτατα. Unfortunately we cannot tell how many jurors there were; and there is a venerable controversy over whether they were an odd or even number.[2] It is plausible, though not certain, that there is a couplet to each voter in the dialogue 711–33 (i.e. 11);[3] however I argue on p. 399 below that there may originally have been at least two more couplets. If, on the

---

[1] Kaimio 94f. is, I think, right to hold (against e.g. Kranz 172f., Groeneboom 171, Lebeck 132) that the use of the second person (529, 538) and of the first-person λέγω (532, 538, 553) does not mean that the audience is being directly addressed by the poet, as though in a parabasis (cf. *Seven* 1a*). The devices are paraenetic, and remain within the context of the play.

I am highly suspicious, I should add, of any attempt to read *specific* political content into this song, even when it is done as circumspectly as by Dover *JHS* 77. 2 (1957) 230–3. If we once allow cryptic contemporary references beneath words which have a fully meaningful dramatic context within the play, then there is no end to the game. On the more fundamental way in which *Eum* is political I am unable to improve significantly on the masterly essay by Colin Macleod in *Maia* 25 (1973) 267ff.

[2] See K. O. Müller 161, *Anhang* 40ff., Hermann *Opusc* vi 2 pp. 188–99; for a summary see Thomson[2] ii 220f. Hermann wins.

[3] Kitto *Form and Meaning* (London 1956) 65f., *Poiesis* (Berkeley 1966) 19f. makes too much of the eleven couplets: it would be different if they were addressed to each juror, but they are a dialogue between Apollo and the Erinyes. The scholion in the margin of M at the top of the page says ὁ ἀριθμὸc τῶν Ἀρεοπαγιτῶν λ´ καὶ εἷc. But why believe this? The καὶ εἷc may suggest that the controversy over odd and even numbers was current in antiquity; but more likely, as Professor Dover points out, it is influenced by the ἐφέται who were known as the πεντήκοντα καὶ εἷc.

other hand, we accept Hermann's plausible theory that the jurors became the supplementary chorus of *Propompoi* (see 1047a*), then that suggests, though it does not entail, that the jurors were the same number as the chorus, which was 15 or 12.[1] Out of all this uncertainty we can say with some security that the jurors were unlikely to have numbered less than ten or more than fifteen. This is a fair number of extras; but then they are to become (in my view) a supplementary chorus.

Immediately on entry Athena addresses a Herald—κήρυσσε, κῆρυξ, καὶ στρατὸν κατειργαθοῦ . . . Yet since it is not in the text the audience did not presumably hear any κήρυγμα. Perhaps Athena did not mean a verbal proclamation, since she immediately goes on to tell him to sound a trumpet. This will keep the people quiet (570f.); though it is unclear whether it is also meant to summon them. Presumably this trumpet was heard in the theatre (after 569? or 573?), though it is strange that there is no παρεπιγραφή at what would seem to be exactly the right sort of context.[2] It is likely, then, that the herald-trumpeter is on stage. A comparable entry comes to mind: a Herald enters with Merops and Phaethon at E. *Phaethon* 102ff. However, that Herald does make an opening proclamation: in his dactyls ended by two trimeters (109–18) he calls out the people to hear the king's announcement, and ends ἀλλὰ σῖγ' ἔστω λεώς. This makes an impressive formal opening, and Aeschylus' scene (which has all three actors occupied) is by comparison ragged and unclear (though there may be textual trouble—see 574*).[3]

[1] See p. 323 n. 3 above. In my view there is probably another dialogue in *Oresteia* besides *Ag* 1346ff. which should be distributed among individual choreuts: *Eum* 585–608. The wording of 585f. strongly implies this, and the device would supply variety, while bringing out the way that each Erinys is a member of the pack. (The obscure scholion on 585 may be a relic of a controversy over the distribution of these lines.) Weil and Blass, among others, distributed this dialogue among the chorus members, but this plausible theory has been out of favour since the magisterial rejection by Wilamowitz 183 (cf. Fraenkel iii 634 n. 1). Blass took this as further evidence of twelve choreuts. But the lines might be distributed between anything from 9 to 13 individuals, depending on the attribution of 585–7 and 608–9; and Aeschylus may not have given every member a contribution.

[2] But off-stage noises are not always included in the text; cf. e.g. the approach of Philoctetes at S. *Phil* 201ff., the lyre in S. *Ichn* (it should sound at 124, 136, and 197 in my opinion), the thunder at S. *OC* 1456ff. It may be this place (and this place only) which leads to the inclusion of trumpets among the list of spectacular stage effects in the *Life* §14. At E. *Tro* 1266 Talthybius announces that a trumpet will sound, but it is not clear whether this is heard during the play (at 1325?).

[3] A herald is addressed in an unknown context in A. fr. 633; cf. also Aristarchus

We have, then, a crowded stage movement; yet nearly all editors also bring on a stage crowd of Athenian citizens ('a very large number of supernumeraries, as many as there was room for', Verrall 100). This rests chiefly on the evidence of 566–73 (στρατὸν ... στρατῶι ... πληρουμένου ... βουλευτηρίου) but these references may be to the Jurors rather than to an extra crowd. If they were more than ten and they had to enter and to arrange themselves on benches (brought with them?), then the lines may serve to cover this stage movement. Throughout the second half of the play the Jurors are addressed and referred to as the people of Athens (see 638, 681 (see below), 775, 807, 854, 911f., 927, 948, 997, 1010f.—cf. 1047a*). They are the pick of the citizen body (487), and hence in some ways the founding fathers of the Areopagus and of Athenian justice; and so they stand for the city as a whole. So rather than bring on a large and marginal crowd of citizens who have no function beyond adding to the spectacle, I take the στρατός to be the Jurors who are an essential element.

Other later places which might be taken as evidence of an extra crowd are similarly explicable. Above all there is the opening of Athena's 'charter' at 681: κλύοιτ' ἂν ἤδη θεσμόν, Ἀττικὸς λεώς ... That this is addressed to the Jurors is shown beyond contradiction, so far as I can see, by the next line ... πρώτας δίκας κρίνοντες αἵματος χυτοῦ. Yet it is widely supposed that this is addressed not only to a stage crowd of citizens, but to the entire audience—that is to say that Athena would turn to the audience with a gesture when she says Ἀττικὸς λεώς.[1] On Seven 1a* I have argued that there is not a single place in surviving tragedy where the world of the play expressly acknowledged the world of the audience or where it acknowledges that it is a play. Eum 681ff. is perhaps the best candidate of all for audience address since the audience is the Ἀττικὸς λεώς, and it is in a

TrGF 14 F 1a (with Snell's apparatus). At E. Hik 381 Theseus addresses a herald immediately on entry, though he does not give a clear vocative like Athena in Eum; but this is still clear from the context, and there is no need to suspect corruption as most editors have (nor with Murray to compare such vexed and corrupt places as E. Hik 837, Andr 147; see p. 364 n. 1 above).

[1] First in K. O. Müller 107, disputed by Hermann Opusc vi 2 pp. 167–70. Audience address here is reasserted in e.g. Paley 631, Wilamowitz Arist. u. Athen (Berlin 1893) ii 330, Groeneboom 195, Rose on Seven 1, Lesky TDH² 76, Greek Tragedy (transl. London 1965) 85f.

sense 'present' at the judgement of Orestes: but 682 shows that Aeschylus did not intend a direct gesture to the audience, and did not intend to step out of the world of the play. Athena is addressing the Jurors, who represent Athens at the formative era of the aetiologies in *Eum.* Of course, her words are meant for the ears of the audience, the posterity of 683, 708, 911, etc.: but then *all* the words of every tragedy are meant for the ears of the audience. In the same way, all the addresses and references to the citizens of Athens later in the play apply to the Jurors, who are being treated as representative of the whole citizen body.

574 (?) enter Apollo
textual disruption of the trial scene?

The entry of Apollo for the trial is a big problem. If we could be clear how it was handled, then we might be in a position to gauge its significance; but it is obscurely managed, at least it is so according to a text which is corrupted on a smaller or larger scale. In our text he is addressed in 574–5 and he definitely speaks 576–81; so at least it is sure that he must have entered by 574. Apollo is the only witness at the trial. At the end of the previous act Athena had told Orestes and the Erinyes ὑμεῖς δὲ μαρτύριά τε καὶ τεκμήρια / καλεῖcθε (485f.). This is strangely explicit since there is only to be one witness and he cannot be 'called' in the usual sense, and only one τεκμήριον will be cited—Athena herself (see 662ff.). Lines 485f. come in a textual context where there is some corruption, possibly on a large scale;[1] but I shall assume that nothing relevant to the arrival of Apollo is missing, and shall approach the problems of the text as we have it.

In our text Apollo is never called or summoned; instead he is abruptly addressed in 574f., and that is the first we know of his presence. The entire textual state of these lines will have to be

---

[1] Not only is 489 found after 488 in M and after 485 in other MSS., and makes good sense in neither place, but it is also difficult to extract any good train of sense out of lines 482, 483, 484, as they are transmitted. Most editors suppose that some lines have dropped out between 482 and 485 and that they included 484 and 489; others prefer to patch with petty emendation. But there is a suspicion that we may have lost here several important lines about the procedure of Athena's new court. These lines may also have clarified 485f., and hence have clarified the arrival of Apollo.

considered later, and so I give them here. After Athena has told
the Herald to sound the trumpet, the transmitted text, as it is
accepted by e.g. Page *OCT*, goes on (570–5):

> *Αθ. πληρουμένου γὰρ τοῦδε βουλευτηρίου*
> *cιγᾶν ἀρήγει καὶ μαθεῖν θεcμοὺς ἐμοὺς*
> *πόλιν τε πᾶcαν εἰc τὸν αἰανῆ χρόνον*
> *καὶ τοῦcδ', ὅπωc ἂν εὖ καταγνωcθῆι δίκη.*
> *Χο. ἄναξ Ἄπολλον, ὧν ἔχειc αὐτὸc κράτει.*
> *τί τοῦδε coὶ μέτεcτι πράγματοc λέγε.*

The first point to establish is that 574–5 are wrongly attributed
to the chorus. Athena has just called for silence, and it is out of
place for the Erinyes to intervene out of nothing better than
suspicious irritability. It is Athena's place to ask Apollo what is
his part in the proceedings; and his reply in 576ff. is the respect-
ful and formal reply due to Athena. At 583f. Athena invites the
prosecution to begin in a way that does not suggest that it has
already intervened; and in 585ff. the Erinyes make a formal
opening to their case. Wieseler took the obvious and easy step
of attributing 574–5 to Athena, thus making it a continuation
of her opening speech.[1]

The editors of this century have accepted the text of 570–5,
and apart from some small alterations they register no serious
textual suspicion. Since I suspect large-scale textual tampering,
and since my gloomy diagnosis is based partly on the entry of
Apollo, I had best consider first that question, given the text as
we have it. There are three possibilities: he may enter at the
beginning of the act at 566, or at the moment he is first addressed
at 574, or somewhere in between.[2] I must not tire of insisting
that entries (and exits) in Greek tragedy are not minor and
negligible formalities: when a major character arrives this makes
an impact on the play, and the event is clearly marked. Apollo
is a god, and his arrival is something to be noticed. This rules out

[1] This involves the slight emendation of excising a paragraphos; but the
attribution in the manuscripts is of no authority (see p. 294 above). Only a few
editors have followed Wieseler; they include Sauppe, Wilamowitz *Arist. u. Athen*
(Berlin 1893) ii 330 n. 2, *ed maj* etc., Rose 268, Dirksen 48. Wakefield attributed
the couplet to the Herald (fourth actor?).
[2] For 566 see e.g. Sidgwick 37, Deckinger 44, Rose 267, Lloyd-Jones *tr* 44; for
574 e.g. K. O. Müller 35, Paley 632, Wilamowitz *ed maj* 313 etc., Mazon 254,
Groeneboom 178, Spitzbarth 46, Winnington-Ingram 141 n. 95, Lattimore *tr* 154,
Hammond 441; for somewhere in between see e.g. Verrall 102f., Dingel 223.

an entry at 566, whether with Athena or separately, because his
arrival would then be unexplained and unnoticed. In effect, he
would be hustled on under cover of the new and lively stage
movement: this simply is not the way Aeschylus works. The
same objection goes for an entry at some point between 566 and
573. It might be claimed that Apollo enters in response to the
trumpet (thus e.g. Verrall 101); but the trumpet is not given
this function. Once again it would mean in practice an attempt
to slip Apollo on-stage by sleight of hand.

So the only alternative is that Apollo entered at 574, and that
574f. are in direct response to his arrival. It is known for one
actor (though rare for the chorus, see *Cho* 732b*) to address
another on entry before he speaks, particularly if the speaking
actor is of superior status, as Athena is here (cf. e.g. S. *Ant* 530,
632, *Trach* 227, E. *IT* 1157 cf. *Hel* 1184, *Or* 1321). On the other
hand, whatever the procedure for calling witnesses, this would
be a strange and disruptive juncture for Apollo to make his
entry. Athena has just called for silence, and is apparently about
to deliver her θεϲμούϲ (571); but then she is interrupted. This
peculiar dislocation calls for some positive explanation. It is not
enough simply to say that Apollo's entry is 'sudden' (Wilamowitz) or 'dramatic' (Winnington-Ingram), or even 'miraculous'
(Spitzbarth). Why does Aeschylus have the solemn preparation
in 566–73 only to throw it away? Why should Apollo's entry
come at this surprising and inappropriate moment, rather than
standing by itself at some less disruptive point? Verrall (cf.
Dirksen 48) at least makes an attempt to explain it: 'to enhance
the effect of his unexpected appearance, it is permitted to divert
the course of proceeding and to precipitate the hearing of the
cause' (p. xxiv); 'in fact, from a theatrical point of view, Athena's
speech is commenced here only in order that it may be interrupted, and that the advent of Apollo may produce, so far as
possible, an effect adequate to his dignity and importance' (102).
This ingenuity has a perverse attraction; but really Verrall's
explanation is insufficient and far-fetched; and it also presupposes an anachronistic naturalism of stage production (his
stage instruction on p. 103 'astonishment and great sensation'
is reminiscent of the trial scenes of the late-nineteenth-century
theatre). Yet at least Verrall recognizes the extraordinarily
abrupt and disruptive effect of Apollo's entry at 574 and attempts

to explain it, however inadequately. Without some such explanation, we have no alternative, so far as I can see, but to conclude
that Aeschylus simply could not find some better, smoother way
of introducing Apollo: an admission of grave incompetence.

Anyone who shares my uneasiness over the handling of the
entry of Apollo in the text as we have it will go on to consider
whether the text is sound. Before looking at 570–5 in detail
I shall scrutinize the larger handling of the trial. There are, I
suggest, three suspicious omissions which, whatever the external
evidence for the procedure of the Areopagus, are clearly
pointed to by the text itself; procedures which are alluded to as
though they had been given more attention than they receive
in our text.[1] First, there is the calling and registration of witnesses. This is prepared for by the couplet at 485f. (see p. 395
above). But its only outcome is the arrival of Apollo which is, as
our text stands, undeniably abrupt and informal. What should
be a formal element of procedure is handled hurriedly and
unclearly. Secondly there is the jurors' oath. This is referred to in
483 and 489 (both lines suffer from corruption, but this much is
clear). But it is never sworn on-stage nor is there any direct
allusion to a swearing ceremony off-stage. Yet the oath will be
referred to again at 680 and 710. It is surprising that we never
hear the terms of the oath, and that there is no explanation of
when, where, or how it was sworn. It is an essential feature
of the court, yet its existence is left to incidental allusions. ⌊

The third and by far the most conspicuous omission is that of
any opening speech to establish the court in the first place. At
484 Athena says that she will institute the court (θεςμόν . . .
θήςω); and at 570–3 she seems about to do so (quoted above).
Instead Apollo arrives and the trial begins without any inaugural
θεςμοί. Yet at 614f. Apollo refers to the court as τόνδ᾽ Ἀθηναίας
μέγαν θεςμόν. Then, most strange of all, we do finally at 681–710
hear the inauguration which was to be expected right back at
the beginning: κλύοιτ᾽ ἂν ἤδη θεςμόν . . . Why, when it eventually
comes, it should come in between the end of the speeches and the
final casting of the votes is beyond me; and I have never seen

<hr>

[1] Colin Macleod is probably right to protest that I overstate the case: as an
antidote I cite Wilamowitz *Arist. u. Athen* ii 329ff. esp. 333, who insists that the
trial is supposed to be archetypal in attitude and tone rather than in precise
procedure.

any attempt at a positive explanation.[1] Lines 674–80 lead up to the voting, and 711ff. accompany the voting: in between comes Athena's inaugural speech. Why? Rose 274f. explains that 'Athena feels it proper to explain to them [the jury], on this their first meeting, exactly what their functions are'. But she should do this at the beginning, not at the end.

So I have considerable respect for Kirchhoff's conjecture that the whole speech 681–710 is out of place where it stands, and that it originally belonged after 573.[2] There are several substantial gains besides the proper placing of the 'charter' at the beginning. The correspondence of Athena's speech with the themes of the song 490–565 will be made clearer. The speech can be removed without trace from its present place; and in that event the two couplets 676f., 679f. can begin the series in 711–33. And then Athena's couplet 674f. can be taken properly as a command instead of being twisted into a question;[3] it then begins the voting. However, this admirable conjecture cannot fall back on a simple palaeographic explanation of the displacement (e.g. a column out of order), because the speech has been tailored to fit its present context by the final four lines, 707–10. In these the 'charter' is tied to instructions about voting which cannot possibly belong to the beginning of the trial; and what is more the links are made in mid-line in 708 and 710.[4] So if we

[1] Colin Macleod writes 'The precepts are relevant to how the jurors *vote now* (see 704–6); i.e. in their voting they must set the normative example for all future Areopagites.' This is, I think, the best that can be said for the speech in its present position.

[2] Kirchhoff was supported by Wecklein in his earlier edition (1885), but other- wise has found no followers. In *Schauplatz* 69ff. and in his edition of 1888 Wecklein followed Dindorf in condemning the entire speech 681–710 as unauthentic, and took the genuine speech after 673 to be entirely lost. This is not warranted by the speech itself: on the contrary it is distinctly Aeschylean.

[3] Editors are forced by 678 to take 674f. as a question. But 678 is a suspect line: both the questions in it are unsuited to the context and 679f. is not a reply to it. Wecklein was probably right to exclude it. The couplets 676f. and 679f. were both attributed by the MSS. to the chorus. Winnington-Ingram argued in *CR* 49 (1935) 7–8 that (contrary to all editors since Karsten) the former belongs to Apollo, the latter to the chorus; his cogent case has been accepted by Thomson, Groeneboom, Dirksen (53), Page *OCT*. My only reservation is that *if* 711f. should follow on 679f. then we should have to suppose that at least one couplet (from Apollo) has been lost between 680 and 711. (If there is any textual disruption of the sort suggested here, then, of course, the number of couplets cannot be used safely as evidence for the number of jurors—see p. 392 n. 3.)

[4] If we cut out ὀρθοῦϲθαι . . . ὅρκον we are left with the sound line ἀϲτοῖϲιν ἐϲ τὸ λοιπόν. εἴρηται λόγος. Unfortunately this seems to be precluded by the μέν in 707.

want to transpose the rest, we have to suppose that 707–10 are the work of a *Bearbeiter*, who either composed them or put them together out of genuine lines from different contexts. It is this further step which has, I suspect, deterred editors from following Kirchhoff (see e.g., early on, Weil *REG* 1 (1888) 13). But I wish to argue that the failings of the text as we have it justify serious consideration of even such an elaborate corruption.

If a considerable number of lines, including 681–706, originally stood in the text somewhere between 571 and 575, then we should look there for scars. Apart from the abrupt intervention of Apollo into Athena's speech, there are one or two small signs of some disruption. If the second word of l. 573 is left as τῶνδε, then there is nothing for πόλιν τε πᾶcαν to be paired with. Any small emendation produces a peculiar shape of sentence;[1] and many editors have had recourse to a lacuna (of one line) either after 571 (Hermann, Wilamowitz) or after 572 (Weil, Lloyd-Jones). The other odd phrase is ὧν ἔχειc αὐτὸc κράτει in 574 (which, I suspect, explains why most editors resist Wieseler's attribution to Athena, see p. 396). Wilamowitz (cited above, p. 396 n. 1) 330 regards it as 'highly polite' ('sehr höflich') : but Dirksen (48) is nearer the mark with 'offensive' ('beleidigend'). It is tragic diction for 'mind your own business', and the two closest verbal analogies in tragedy are from heated and abusive scenes (S. *Aj* 1107, *OC* 839). This snappish phrase seems inappropriate; but if the text has been disrupted, then either it may have been inserted to replace something else, or, more likely, the antecedent of ὧν may have been lost.

My thesis is, then, that Aeschylus' text of the trial in *Eum* has been considerably disrupted and cut, and is corrupt on a scale which has not been seriously entertained since the heady days of Kirchhoff and Wecklein. While 566–71, 575–677, and 711–77 are substantially as Aeschylus left them,[2] lines 678–710 have been displaced and altered, and lines 572–4 are the corrupted edges of a large lacuna. This lacuna, perhaps 40 lines, will have contained Athena's inaugural speech, much of it preserved in

---

[1] If we read τόνδε, then the Erinyes are unjustifiably excluded; τούcδε (Hermann) lumps both sides together (admittedly not impossible, cf. 485); τώδε (Bothe) is strange when one of the pair is plural.

[2] 667–73 are not above suspicion (secl. Weil, Wecklein). On the text at the end of the scene see 777b*.

681–706, and it will have included the arrival of Apollo. It may also have contained the oath of the jurors, the summoning of witnesses, and perhaps a formal announcement by the Herald (if he went before Apollo arrived, this could be managed with three actors). Of course, I have no explanation of the corruption. One might speculate that the whole scene was too static and formal for later tastes, or that it had implied political content which was disagreeable, or possibly that it reflected badly on Apollo. But the detection of a motive is a contributory, not an essential, argument for deliberate textual alteration.

I confess that I find it hard to believe whole-heartedly in this hypothesis, which is unfashionable in the present age of textual conservatism. But I would point out two unargued and basically subjective assumptions which must underlie any out-of-hand rejection of it. One is that Aeschylus was, or was sometimes, a crude and undeveloped craftsman. Because he is our earliest tragedian, he is expected to have 'early' and rough techniques. But, while he may be large, bold, and relatively unsophisticated in his techniques, the surviving plays do not confirm him as rough or incompetent. On the contrary, he shows a sure and controlled hand in shaping an art form already developed from its (putative) crude origins, as I hope to have shown. Secondly we assume that our transmitted text is reasonably close to Aeschylus' original, and has not been tampered with in a large way. But the end of *Seven* is a warning (cf. also *Hik* 974a*, 974b*); and, while we should normally continue in this belief, we should not turn a blind eye to signs of possible alteration. In any case, I think this extension of Kirchhoff's conjecture is worth airing because it raises questions and problems which we should face and try to explain.

If, finally, my theory is right, or partially right, then we cannot say anything about the arrival of Apollo, as Aeschylus managed it. If, on the other hand, we accept our text as substantially sound, as we have it, then we can say that the arrival of Apollo is disruptive, hurried, and informal. There is no apparent reason for its timing, and it unaccountably diverts the entire course of the proceedings. I have no explanation for this except incompetence, an explanation which a serious critic should be reluctant to accept when the incompetence could so easily have been avoided.

777 exit Orestes, exit Apollo (?)

(a) Orestes

As soon as the verdict is given, Orestes makes his farewell speech (754–77) and goes. His part is played: the '*Oresteia*' is over. There is one more mention of him in Athena's first speech of the final part (799); but from 778 onwards the play is not about Orestes or Argos or the Atreidai—it is about Athena, Athens, and the Erinyes. The exit of Orestes thus marks an important watershed—see 777c* below.

None the less, the question of the relationship of the Erinyes to Athens has been interwoven far back into the play, and conversely the personal importance of Orestes has been played down. Athena, faced with her original dilemma, recognized that, if they lose, the Erinyes will drip their venom on the soil of Athens (476–9). The song at 490ff. turns away from Orestes in particular towards civic justice in general (see 566a*). Then in the trial, after his initial inquisition (588–613), Orestes himself is silent for the rest of the proceedings; and as it draws to a close, attention is not drawn to his particular fate, except in his own lines (744, 746). The Erinyes remind the Jurors, on the other hand, that they can harm Athens (711f., 719f.). When Apollo (rashly) scorns their venom, they reply that they will await the verdict ὡς ἀμφίβουλος οὖσα θυμοῦσθαι πόλει (733). In this way the issue of the Erinyes and Athens is kept active, while the fate of Orestes is subdued; and so the totally new concentration of attention at 778ff. is not unprepared for. The bearing of the trial on Orestes and Argos is all quickly summed up in his farewell speech, and then it is left behind.

Orestes leaves, a free and repatriated man: he is going straight home to take up his heritage (754ff., 764). We have seen the homeless wanderer of *Cho* driven from his home almost at once (*Cho* 1063*), and we have seen his long flight vividly translated into stage action (see *Eum* 244a*). Now we see him depart finally for home (cf. Dirksen 82–4). We have seen Orestes helpless and powerless (cf. 276*): now he guarantees a pact between Argos and Athens, and he even promises his help as a hero after death (762–74). Even though Orestes is quickly and completely dismissed from the play, the secure strength and confident elation of his final speech and departure, contrasted with his dogged flight earlier, manage to sum up his saga without seeming hurried or negligent.[1] The stage action of his exit, free and independent, will have helped to give a sense of completion to this turning-point.

(b) Apollo

Having made such heavy weather on 574* of the problem of the entry of Apollo, it is with some embarrassment that I have to point out that his exit is hardly less problematical. Although it is given little attention in the commentaries, it is obvious that it is very peculiar and demands explanation.

In our text there is no sign of Apollo's exit; he simply drops out without trace. Not even minor characters often disappear without any indication of exit;[2] and Apollo, whatever one thinks of his role in *Eum*, remains a god. Of course there are places where the timing or event of an entry or exit is open to controversy, e.g. Clytemnestra in *Ag*, but it should be obvious that such problems are quite a different matter from sheer disappearance. So *if* Aeschylus meant to take Apollo off without any indication whatsoever beyond the physical fact, then he was doing something extraordinary, and notable as such.

When did Apollo go? He must stay for the verdict (and Winnington-Ingram's attribution of 676f. (see p. 399 n. 3) puts as much into direct statement). His last certain speech is 729f.; he may say 748–51, but that is far from certain.[3] In any case the earliest moment that Apollo may go is at the end of line 753. It is out of the question that he is on for the final act, and so the latest he can have gone is with Orestes at 777; or he may go at some point between 753 and 777.[4] Before going on to consider

[1] Burnett 72 exaggerates when she says that Orestes in *Eum* 'left the stage almost unnoticed'. None the less her suggestion that E. *IT* is in some way a reaction against *Eum* in vindication of Apollo deserves serious consideration.

[2] Cf. p. 8. Apollo's 'disappearance' would be quite different from the exit of a minor character after his last speech (cf. *Pers* 514*, *Seven* 652*) or of a major character who goes off 'under cover' of another e.g. Electra at *Cho* 584* or Orestes at *Cho* 718*. It is not easy to find an example of mere dropping out even in comedy. I note that the girl of Arph. *Ekkles* 884ff. drops out without trace after 1049.

[3] The four lines (751 is suspect) are not attributed in the MSS., but most editors since Victorius have given them all to Apollo. But alternatively Orestes may say them, or the chorus may say 748 and 750 and Orestes 749 and 751 (for other combinations see Wecklein's Appendix). The attribution to Apollo rests, I suspect, on a not impartial view of his respectability in the trial, and a desire to give him something to say nearer his exit.

[4] For an exit at 753 see e.g. Bodensteiner 736, Verrall 136f., Weissmann

these alternatives, a word on the possibilities for staging a sudden exit. There is a tendency to speak as though Apollo vanishes instantaneously, as he might in epic.[1] But in the fifth-century Greek theatre there were no tricks of artificial light, smoke effects, trap-doors, etc. The only device of this sort was the mechane, and Apollo cannot have used that: he is on the ground, and he must walk. Even to go into the skene he has to cover some ground; he cannot vanish into thin air.

What, first, is involved in an exit at 753? On practical matters Verrall was scrupulous: 'the announcement of the result would be followed by a "sensation" . . . During this Apollo (as I conceive) retires; the attention of the audience being fixed on others, and especially on Orestes and the Erinyes, his exit would be imperceptible, and would have the effect of a disappearance' (pp. 136f.). Even Verrall, I imagine, would have admitted that slipping a character off in this way during a confused and absorbing scene would be without any parallel whatsoever in surviving tragedy (a comparison with the escape of Odysseus at *Rh* 690 makes the point). It is a kind of sleight of hand which runs totally counter to the measured pace and clear scenic technique of Greek tragedy. Even supposing Verrall's version were true, there are two contrary ways in which Aeschylus may have meant his audience to interpret the extraordinary device. The one favoured by Verrall is that the audience would regard his disappearance as a divine sign of Apollo's dignity and power. I suspect, however, that it would not have the desired effect on an audience accustomed to stage movements which were open and clearly accounted for: there is a danger that they would, rather, wonder where Apollo had got to, and puzzle over why he did not make a proper exit. The alternative explanation, less favourable to Apollo, is that, once his part is played and his responsibility to Orestes fulfilled, he is disposed of as quickly and inconspicuously as possible. The audience is not to notice that he has gone, it is

Aufführung 16, Smyth 345, Groeneboom 206, Werner *tr* 237, Dirksen 78; for 776 see e.g. Hermann *ed* 631, Sidgwick 47, Wecklein *ed* 306, Deckinger 44, Rose 280, Lattimore *tr* 103; for in between see e.g. Wilamowitz *ed maj* 320 *actio*, *tr* 287, Mazon 161. It is hardly surprising that several translators have forgotten to send off Apollo at all; e.g. K. O. Müller, Headlam, Thomson[1], Murray, Lloyd-Jones.

[1] He 'disappears' (Smyth), 'verschwindet' (Werner *tr*), 'a déjà disparu' (Mazon). Wilamowitz (*Kl Schr* i 356 n. 1, cf. *tr* 248) goes so far as to suggest that Apollo's miraculous movements in *Eum* display his divinity.

to forget about him altogether. This view is encouraged by the positive lack of due attention to Apollo in Orestes' last speech (see below); and in the reference to his oracle at 797–9 the stress is on Zeus.[1]

If this is at all along the right lines and Aeschylus did mean the exit of Apollo to go by unnoticed, then this would be of some importance for the interpretation of the place of Apollo in *Eum*. It would suggest that he is to be seen as a secondary figure who is not to be taken too solemnly. It might even suggest that his arguments in the trial are to be distrusted, a view of Apollo which has been advocated, notably, by Winnington-Ingram in *CR* 47 (1933) 97ff., cf. Reinhardt 144ff., Dirksen 52ff., 64ff. Yet, against this, Orestes does not lose; Apollo, who has conducted most of the trial on his behalf, does not fail to carry out his responsibilities. Can he be so easily discarded, like a worn-out puppet? Apollo is not treated earlier in the play so subversively that he can be disposed of in this way at the end of the trial. If Aeschylus did mean his exit to be a way of having him rejected and forgotten, then it is very precarious dramatic technique. I am reluctant to believe this, though perhaps it is a less unsatisfactory explanation than the alternatives.

There seems to be no gain in sending Apollo off with Orestes at 777, which would mean that he must stand silent by during Orestes' final speech. Apollo could scarcely receive less attention than he does in this speech. After effusive thanks to Athena (754–7) Orestes puts into the mouth of Ἑλλήνων τιc that he lives in his heritage Παλλάδοc καὶ Λοξίου ἕκατι (758f.), and caps these two with Zeus Soter who is given three lines. There is no more reference to Apollo; and yet at the end of this we are to suppose that he simply tags along with his protégé without any acknowledgement to Athena, the Athenians, or the Erinyes. Deckinger 66, who recognizes that this exit would be 'besonders auffallend', appeals to Aeschylus' τερατολογία: but it is tame rather than portentous. Of course, when two characters go together one must be silent (see p. 310 above); but it is usually the minor character who is silent, unless there is some special dramatic point (as e.g. with the Trojan girls at E. *Hec* 432ff., *Tro* 424ff.). Here it may be that Orestes is of more dramatic interest than

---

[1] ὁ χρήcαc in 798 is an emendation of M (the only MS. at this point). ὁ φήcαc (see scholion) or, better, ὁ πείcαc (Fritzsche, Hermann) are also possibilities.

Apollo, but Apollo's tame silence seems disproportionate. To keep him on throughout this speech only in order to send him off without any attention whatsoever is to court either ridicule or outrage, neither of which seems appropriate. Whether the disappearance of Apollo is meant to be godlike and astonishing or to be mean and inconspicuous, it would be better put before the speech rather than after it. (Wilamowitz's compromise of an exit during the speech seems to have all the disadvantages of both alternatives.)

I am reluctant to accept a disappearance at 753, if only because the significance of such an extraordinary piece of dramatic technique would tend to confusion rather than dramatic meaning. Usually irregular dramatic and theatrical technique has an overt significance: that is why it is such a valuable aid to literary criticism. Here it would obscure rather than clarify. We should at least consider the possibility of textual corruption. The only obvious possibility is that a short self-contained speech of farewell by Apollo has fallen out of the text, either from between 753 and 754 or 777 and 778.[1] The former is very unlikely since Orestes' elated thanks follow well immediately after the verdict. If Apollo originally made a brief final speech after 777, then we still have the difficulty that Orestes scarcely pays attention to him in his speech; but that is perhaps less awkward if Apollo then has a speech. If this theory of a lacuna after 777 is right,[2] then we can hardly judge the tone of Apollo's departure. I would guess, however, that he continued to carp at the Erinyes, and even after victory he did not change the rough and partial attitude which he has shown towards them throughout. I base this guess on the correspondence of the opening words of the Erinyes' song at 778ff. with their line at 731 which is in reply to a taunt from Apollo.[3]

---

[1] I once considered that Orestes might exit after 774, and 775-7 be attributed to Apollo. But the prayer-like sentiment is more fitted to a mortal, and the phrase καὶ χαῖρε (775) is particularly common just before the end of a farewell speech, see Bond E. *Hyps ed* 126.

[2] I am surprised no one has made the suggestion before; this is, I suppose, because of the reluctance to accept textual corruption on any but linguistic grounds. 778-807 are omitted in EFG Tr, but this is not relevant, as the omission is simple haplography of the two identical strophes 778ff. = 808ff.

[3] The young καθιππάζονται the old in *Eum* 150, 731, 778f. = 809f. These are the only four occurrences of the verb in surviving tragedy. For links with other images of trampling under foot see Lebeck 78.

I am by no means confident in the conjecture of a lacuna after 777, since it has left no clear trace in the text and since Apollo is neglected in 754ff. However, I hope to have made clearer some of the issues at stake in the acceptance of any of the alternatives.

(c) the chorus stays

Orestes goes: the Erinyes stay. This is a remarkable twist and reversal of the usual pattern of the suppliant play (see 397a*). For usually, as in A. *Hik,* the pursuer has to be rebuffed and sent packing out of the country, while the suppliant stays in the safe custody of the protecting city. Here there is the opposite of the usual dispensation. Of course it is true that in no other suppliant play are the pursuers the chorus; and the chorus has to stay until the end of the play. But it would be a mistake (one which scholars are prone to embrace) to regard the technical expedient as a sufficient explanation of what happens: a playwright who is tyrannized by theatrical mechanics is a poor one— the good one uses the mechanics for his own ends. Here the point is that the chorus does not stay in Athens only till the end of the play: it stays for good.

In fact Aeschylus puts the issue of the Erinyes' attitude to Athens in terms of whether or not they will stay. During the trial they imply that, if the verdict goes against them, they will prolong their visit just long enough to blast and poison the land (711f., 719f., 732f.). After Orestes has gone, however, their departure means that they will have poisoned the land: their remaining means reconciliation. This decision is gradually made explicit by Athena. First she offers a place in Athens (804–7) and invites them to be a ξυνοικήτωρ (833). Then she tells them how they will regret it if they leave (851ff.), while they will have many benefits if they stay (854–7, 867–9).[1] So in her final speech (881–91) she can put the situation entirely in terms of staying or leaving. The Erinyes will not be able to say that

---

[1] Lines 858–66 fit extremely badly in their context, as has been stressed by Dodds *Progress* 51f. Clearly τοιαῦτα in 867 should follow on 857; and the content of the intrusion is appropriate to the stage *after* the Erinyes have asked what is required of them, i.e. after 902. Dodds argues that Aeschylus himself interpolated the lines because he detects the master's hand behind the mixed metaphors. I have the no less subjective feeling that the lines are overelaborate bombast in the Aeschylean vein, but are not the genuine article ('hoc loco alieni', cf. Wecklein *Schauplatz* 76ff.).

because of Athena and Athens they ἄτιμος ἔρρειν τοῦδ᾽ ἀπόξενος
πέδου (884).[1] The Erinyes have taken over from Orestes the
role of the disinherited, homeless wanderer. But if they respect
Πειθώ they will stay (885–7); and if they do not want to stay,
they should not poison the land, because they are offered a share
in it (887–91). So the stage movement, departing or staying,
will sum up the whole momentous decision. At this point there is
the decisive transitional stichomythia (892–902); and with the
opening words of the second lyric structure, the Erinyes accept.
δέξομαι Παλλάδος ξυνοικίαν . . . (916ff.) : they will stay on stage,
they will stay in Athens for ever.[2]

The place of the watershed at 777 may be made clearer if it is
considered in terms of structural technique. With the exit of
Orestes (and Apollo) and the change to an epirrhematic structure a new part of the play (μέρος, act, episode, or whatever)
begins.[3] There is undeniably a division of acts at 777/8, marked
by the complete change of subject-matter and emphasis, the
change to a lyric structure, and the preceding exit; but there is
no act-dividing song, 'stasimon', or its equivalent. Whether or not
Aeschylus or his audience would see the transition as marking
a new μέρος, they would recognize the formal shaping effect
within the play in dramatic terms, even if not in technical terms.

---

[1] ἀπόξενος as in Ag 1282 and Cho 1041, cf. p. 360 above. The only other occurrence of the word is with a different meaning at S. OT 196.

[2] It is a grave distortion to imply that it is the threat of Zeus' thunderbolt in
827–8 which is the determining factor in the Erinyes' decision (Lloyd-Jones tr 62f.
virtually recants his extreme statement in JHS 76 (1956) 64). Athena immediately
rejects force (would it destroy the Erinyes' venom?) in favour of persuasion.
Peitho, which has served destruction and death earlier in the trilogy (see Ag
385ff., 943, Cho 726ff.; cf. p. 313 above), now wins the day to beneficial effect
(see 885, 900, 970–2, cf. Goheen 130, Dirksen 91ff.). The reason why the thunderbolt is alluded to is that, if Athena is to impress the Erinyes and show that she
can give them τιμή, she must show them that she too is powerful and wise, and
that this is because of Zeus. This is brought out by the openings of her second and
third speeches: at 826ff. she too has power (κἀγὼ πέποιθα Ζηνί . . .), and at 850ff.
she too is wise (φρονεῖν δὲ κἀμοὶ Ζεὺς ἔδωκεν . . .).

It should be noted that, although the Erinyes are in danger of losing ground
to the younger gods, they never challenge or question the status of Zeus. They
revile Apollo, they defy Athena before but not after her arrival (contrast 299 with
435); they respect Zeus. It is Apollo's interpretation of Zeus, not Zeus himself,
they criticize (229, 435, 622, 640, 717f.). And in the final songs they exalt Zeus.
Contrast Prom—see Appendix D p. 498.

[3] According to Poetics ch. 12 (see Appendix E) Eum 566–1047 is all one structural
unit, the ἔξοδος: Aichele Bauformen 60, 68 blindly follows this absurdity, though
Kremer ibid. 119, 127 has more sense.

The lyric structure 778–891 cannot be regarded as a vague kind of act-dividing song (*contra* Detscheff 57) nor can 916ff. (*contra* Goodell 92, Groeneboom 11), because there is no entry or any kind of change of subject, and because they are all part of the great final act (see further below). This is unusual structural technique; indeed it is unique in surviving tragedy. But it is not without similarity to the other three plays of Aeschylus which end with large lyric structures—*Pers, Seven,* and *Hik.* The difference in the others is that as well as the penultimate exit, equivalent to that of Orestes in *Eum,* there is an act-dividing song (only anapaests in *Hik,* see 974a*), and there is a new entry which begins the final act. The analogy of *Eum* with these lyric last acts may be seen if one turns to *Cho* and *Prom.* In both cases the penultimate exit (Orestes, Hermes) comes shortly before the end: it is the beginning of the end, not, as Orestes' exit is in *Eum,* the beginning of a new beginning.

The reason for this unique structure rests in the larger dramatic context. The chorus of *Eum* is an active participant, more so even than in *Hik* where the chorus is more a passive than active centre of the drama. They are the prosecution in the trial, and when they do not win it they are enraged and outraged. This is no time for a detached stasimon: they have a score to settle with Athens. And there is no new element to be introduced into the trilogy by means of that entry which normally begins a new act: what remains is matter between the Erinyes and Athena on behalf of Athens. So the role of the chorus, as Aeschylus boldly conceived it, precludes the normal act-dividing function at this juncture. The structural form yields to the larger conception of the dramatic situation: and it reflects it also.[1]

The final act 778–1047, which is in fact longer than the trial itself, is a structural unit (cf. Peretti 193ff.). It is built around the two great epirrhematic structures 778–891 and 916–1020. These balance and contrast with each other. In the first the fury and destructive malevolence of the Erinyes are rigidly repeated in the strophe and antistrophe of each pair, while in between come Athena's four reasoned and placatory speeches. In the

---

[1] We can say so little about the role of the chorus in earlier tragedy that we cannot tell whether this kind of dramatic problem had often been encountered before; but I guess not. For some observations on the chorus in early tragedy see *Hik* 503b*.

second structure the wonderful incantations of the Eumenides
are confirmed by shorter anapaestic contributions from Athena.[1]
The first scene leads into the crucial transitional bargaining
(892–915), and the second leads on to the arrangement of the
final procession (see below). The whole act holds together in
structure, and in the forward direction of its content. In this
great single final movement of the trilogy all the evil, distortion,
blight, and blood are turned to good, to peace, and fecundity.
The growth, winds, marriages, music, ritual, everything which
has been so perverted and obscured earlier in the trilogy, are
here set right and made clear. And for the audience, out of all
the suffering comes an irresistible sense of enlightenment.[2]

1047 exeunt omnes: Athena, chorus, Jurors, and attendants

(a) the προπομποί and the Jurors

The two short strophic pairs which sing the Eumenides off at the
end (1032–47) are without doubt sung by a supplementary
chorus (though Verrall 178 simply supposes that everyone on-
stage joins in—and he has dozens). The scholion on 1032 and
many editors since Müller have taken this chorus to consist of
women. But there is no particular evidence for this. No doubt
editors have been influenced by the female πρόσπολοι of 1024,
but there is no reason to equate these with the escort of 1005
(see below). The first thing to consider is the entry of this second
chorus. They are given no sort of formal introduction or
announcement, and the first we hear of them is in Athena's
anapaests at 1005f.—πρὸς φῶς ἱερὸν / τῶνδε προπομπῶν. So most
commentators have brought them on at 1005 or shortly before.
But we might expect that a group of extras which is actually
going to sing would be given a clearer introduction than a
passing deictic pronoun. I have discussed on Hik 974b* the topic
of the introduction of supplementary choruses; and the upshot
was that they are usually given a proper introduction and identification, with the exception of the handmaidens in Hik, who,

---

[1] On p. 328 I have suggested that there may be some resemblance between
this act and the scene in Ag where Clytemnestra faces the chorus after the murder.
If Aeschylus did contrive any detectable echo, e.g. in the music, then this will
have served to bring out the enlightenment and finality of Eum.

[2] On the final scene as a whole and its relationship to the rest of the trilogy
see Reinhardt 154ff., Macleod passim; also cf. Peradotto AJP 85 (1964) 378ff.

I argue, are suspect. But whatever the truth about *Hik*, *if* the second chorus in *Eum* entered towards the end of the play then 1005f. must mark its entry.

I can see only one alternative. No one seems to have followed Hermann's suggestion (*ed* 657f.) that the Jurors of the Areopagus became the Escort at the end (though Webster *Chorus* 129 recently made the same suggestion without argument).[1] In the Jurors we already have on-stage a group of extras of about the right size (see 566b*); and at 1005 Athena simply has to gesture to them to make it clear that by τῶνδε προπομπῶν she means 'of these men, acting as escort'. The references to the Jurors since the trial confirm this. They are the chosen representatives of the citizenry (see pp. 394–5 above); and so it is they who are referred to in 775, 807, 883, 912, 927 cf. 991, 949, and 997. When Athena goes on after 1005f. ὑμεῖς δ' ἡγεῖcθε, πολιccοῦχοι / παῖδεc Κραναοῦ (1010f.) she is referring to the same men as were called πολιccοῦχοι in 775 and 883, and not to some new citizens who have only just entered five lines before. These seem to be the only places where the epithet πολιccοῦχοc (or πολιοῦχοc) is used of men rather than gods or heroes. The Jurors, through their part in these momentous events, have become something more than ordinary men: they are the fathers of Athenian justice (cf. 911–12). Not only are they ready available (a help for rehearsals and the choregus' purse), but they have gathered such stature through the play that they are especially qualified for the honour of singing the final lyrics. So, though one cannot be confident about such things, I approve of Hermann's suggestion.

(b) other elements of the procession

The final procession of *Eum* was undoubtedly a grand and impressive stage event. Nearly all scholars accept the traditional picture of a super-spectacular Aeschylus, and have brought on here a great many extras and props, men and women, young and old, sacred and profane:[2] only Hermann (*ed* 657) seems to stand up for the more austere view, put forward in §4, which

---

[1] Hermann's other suggestion that 12 of the 15 Erinyes went off and changed into Athenian women is not acceptable. But that does not affect his theory about the jurors.

[2] For some eminent elaborations see K. O. Müller *Anhang* 27f., Verrall 173f., Wilamowitz 185, Reinhardt 143f.

calls for a comparatively simple spectacle. How many extras and how much extravagance in other stage effects are needed to achieve such an event will in the last resort depend on how lavish or how spare one supposes that Aeschylus' theatre normally was. But it is worth looking at the text to see what it indicates.

I have argued in 566b* that there are during the trial no citizens on stage besides the Jurors. At 856 Athena offers honours παρ' ἀνδρῶν καὶ γυναικείων στόλων, but there is no reason to think, as some have, that these were brought on-stage at the end of the play, any more than were the first-fruits offered at 834. Nearer the end, however, after designating the *Propompoi*, Athena goes on in 1007ff. ἴτε καὶ σφαγίων τῶνδ' ὑπὸ σεμνῶν . . . This does seem to indicate that sacrificial victims were brought on stage (two would do), and presumably there were attendants to lead them.[1] But the chief evidence is in Athena's very last speech (1021–31) which is unfortunately full of difficulties of text and interpretation. Clearly she is instituting the sacred procession, but it is not clear whether she is talking about what can be seen on stage. The text may suggest that the πρόσπολοι of 1024 were on stage; but there is no deictic to confirm this, and, if as a matter of fact they were not, then the words may easily be taken to mean that they would join the procession on its journey (presumably at the temple of Athena). As for the children, women, and old women, they are the victims of a corrupt text. Like Verrall (177), I would obelize ἐξίκοιτ' ἄν in 1026 and I do not see how the text can be used for or against bringing all these extras on stage.

An intriguing detail of the procession, which is involved in this same textual crux, is the red robes of 1028. The difficulties are well known: the string of datives without a preposition cannot describe the women of 1027; on the other hand they go well with τιμᾶτε in 1029, but then there is no accusative to say who is being honoured in this way. Most scholars since Hermann have posited a lacuna between 1027 and 1028.[2] If this is right, and it

---

[1] Hermann was incredulous, and I sympathize; the text even implies that the sacrifices were carried out on-stage, but that is surely out of the question. Of the attempts to emend σφαγίων the best is probably φεγγῶν (Schoemann, Wecklein), which I am tempted to accept.

[2] Most editors have taken this to be a long lacuna. However, I doubt whether Hermann and others are right to suppose that during it Athena bestowed the title of Εὐμενίδες. The scholarship in Harpocration and in the hypothesis to *Eum* is

seems unavoidable, then we cannot say who is to wear the red
robes; and it is not even certain that they are seen on stage,
since Athena may be telling what will happen when the procession reaches its destination (cf. Hense *RhM* N.F. 59 (1904)
170ff.), or she may be supplying an aetiology for something in
the future. Assuming, however, that they are donned on stage
(which will require one or two more extras), then there seem to
be two main theories about their possible significance.[1] One
is the connection of red cloth with cult and with sacrificial
processions; in that case it is more likely the attendants who
wear them.[2] The other is that red was worn by metics at the
Panathenaic procession and other ceremonial occasions (cf. P-C
DFA[2] 61); in which case it should be the metic Eumenides who
wear the red.[3] It is, indeed, an attractive idea that the Erinyes'
change of attitude should be reinforced by a visual change in
appearance; but the text is far from clear. I note two small
qualifying points. If the Eumenides put on the red, it is not a
change of costume since they do not take off their black: ἐνδυτός
has the sense of additional ornament (cf. Hermann *ed* 645).
Secondly there is no question of a change of masks by the chorus,
which would be an unparalleled and probably impracticable
procedure; and Athena's words in 990f. are positive and conclusive evidence to the contrary.[4]

There are torches. It is reiterated that the final procession is
to move by their flaming light (1005, 1022, 1029, 1041; on
1006 see p. 412 n. 1). We have no reason to doubt that the
torches were actually alight and were brought on stage; though
it should be remembered it was not yet the end of the day
(see P-C *DFA*[2] 64-6). These may have been carried by yet
more attendants, or by the *Propompoi* themselves. Torches are

very poor (see Verrall xxxvif.), and it may simply be carelessly derived from the
title of the play. Colin Macleod does not approve my prevarications over the text.
He has now published his views on this passage in *Maia* 27 (1975) 201. He may
well be right, but I have left my text as it stands to promote the debate.

[1] The approach to this red cloth through sustained imagery is explored by
Goheen 122–6, who suggests that it is a transformation of the red cloth in *Ag* and
of the blood throughout the trilogy. See now Macleod op. cit. 201–2.

[2] See e.g. Eitrem *Beiträge zur gr. Religionsgeschichte* iii (Kristiana 1920) 99–101,
Mazon 170 n. 6, Rose 293.

[3] For this view see Headlam *JHS* 26 (1906) 268ff., Thomson[2] ii 221–3. Recent
acceptances include Dingel 51, Lebeck 15, Lloyd-Jones *tr* 72f.

[4] See Hense op. cit., in the right against Robert *Hermes* 38 (1903) 635–7.

occasionally brought on in Greek tragedy for various purposes
(see Arnott 120 f., Dingel 74, *Bauformen* 354 n. 119); for a torch-
lit procession at the end of a play cf. Arph. *Frogs*. The sacred
torches in *Eum* seem simply to add solemnity and detail, though
they may have a more precise cultic significance.[1] It is becoming
a commonplace that the torches at the end of *Eum* 'pick up' or
'resolve' the beacon at the beginning of *Ag*;[2] but this is so vague
and the connection so remote that it means nothing in real
dramatic terms. Fortunately Peradotto (*AJP* 85 (1964) 388–93)
has traced the 'light in darkness' motif through the trilogy, and,
instead of merely linking the end of *Eum* with the beginning of
Ag, he follows through the entire chain of distorted images to
their solemn and pure conclusion.

(c) ὑπ᾽ εὔφρονι πομπᾶι

Like *Pers*, *Seven*, and *Hik*, the play ends with a processional
clearance of the scene. As in the other three, one group escorts
another off the stage to a predetermined destination.[3] In the two
suppliant plays, *Hik* and *Eum*, it is the chorus itself which is
escorted from the stage to its new, safe home—but in *Eum* the
chorus is not the suppliant but the formerly hostile pursuer (see
777c*). They are escorted by Athena (πέμψω 1022), and by the
other members of the procession, above all the secondary chorus
which consists (I have argued in 1047a*) of the Jurors, the
founders of Athenian justice. As usual there is little we can say
about the precise staging. We may guess that the *Propompoi*
followed after the Eumenides (cf. Arph. *Plut* 1208f.); and that
the Eumenides themselves were out of sight by the time the last
line was sung. Athena too is part of the procession. She would
probably go first, and she seems to say as much in 1003ff.[4]

[1] Cf. Eitrem op. cit. Torches seem to have become associated with the Erinyes
in tragedy; see e.g. schol. on Arph. *Plut* 423. But it is doubtful whether this has
any connection with this scene.
[2] See e.g. Hiltbrunner *Wiederholungs- und Motivtechnik bei A.* (Bern 1950) 74;
Aylen *Greek Tragedy and the Modern World* (London 1964) 59f., Garvie 76f.
[3] (προ)πέμπειν recurs in these contexts, see e.g. *Pers* 1077 (cf. 530), *Seven* 916,
1059, 1069. The Argive bodyguard which escorts the Danaids may well have
also been a supplementary chorus—see *Hik* 974b*. It is frustrating to know that
Aeschylus wrote a tragedy called *Propompoi* (and that it offered sufficient histrionic
opportunities to be mentioned by Alciphron—fr. 352b).
[4] The participation of Athena in the procession was useful for those who first
proved that there was little or no raised stage in the fifth century (see p. 441)

The final procession is no mere technical resort to finish off the play: it is a significant movement within the drama. It puts into visible and concrete terms the reconciliation between Athens and the Erinyes, and it embodies their reception into the land as inhabitants. The pure and proper ὀλολυγμός puts an end to its distorted use throughout the trilogy.[1] And in other similar ways the words underline and explain the far-reaching significance of the movement. As the *Propompoi* sing, the Eumenides are going to their home, they will have high honours, they will be favourable to the land, and their pact will be binding for ever. This is what the procession means. And the permanence and security of the ratification gain depth and conviction from the part played by the chorus earlier. They were for ever on the move, driving Orestes by long, exhausting stages from Argos. We actually saw them driven out of Delphi, and we saw them hot in pursuit (see 244a*): now we see them finally accepted at Athens (cf. Reinhardt 144, 156f., Joerden 122f.). Apollo told them that the cave of a bloodthirsty lion was the only fit place for them (193f.), and that by pursuit they would only incur more pain (226): but at Athens they find a sacred resting place and an honourable function. Their ruthless blood-led wanderings end in a prosperous and secure home. The solemn and benevolent final procession puts into action the new-found settlement.

e.g. Capps 13f. The text clearly refutes those few who claim that she went separately e.g. Hermann *Opusc* vi 2 p. 121, *ed* 656, Weissmann *Aufführung* 16.

[1] See Goheen 124f., Haldane *JHS* 85 (1965) 37–8, Macleod 284.

APPENDIX A

The Fragments

THIS appendix discusses only those lost plays (including satyr plays) where there is sufficient evidence to make particular observations on the handling of exits or entrances. Lesser references may be found in the *index locorum*. The plays are taken in alphabetical order. As elsewhere, I use Mette's numeration, but I have not followed his arbitrary order. References to Nauck² and to Lloyd-Jones are added where appropriate.

Aitnaiai

(a) 27 (6 N)

This suggests that the return of the Palikoi to the light may have been a focal point for the entire play, or at least for one act (for one act only see Fraenkel *Kl B* 250f.). It seems that they entered from the underworld (cf. p. 447).

(b) 26 (*POxy* 2257 fr. 1 = 287 Ll-J)

This intriguing fragment of a hypothesis is plausibly referred to *Aitnaiai*. The restoration of l. 6 as a reference to *Eum* (see p. 378 n. 2) fits very well, since the hypothesis goes on to tell of four or five scene changes in a single play: it is set in different parts of Sicily, and two scenes are set at Ἀίτνη. The single change of scene in *Eum* is extraordinary enough (see *Eum* 235*): changes on the scale indicated for *Aitnaiai* were unknown before the publication of this fragment (leaving out of account post-classical tragedy—see p. 49 n. 2).

Scholars have accepted this new information with remarkable equanimity. They say calmly that the peculiar circumstances of the first production will have produced peculiarities of scenic technique; and this comfortable explanation has saved them from following through the implications in terms of dramatic technique and of theatrical practice. First, did the chorus consist throughout of women of Etna, as the title implies?[1] If so, then it seems that, like the Erinyes

---

[1] Supposing Wilamowitz (242 n. 1, cf. Fraenkel *Kl B* 249 n. 1) is right that the true title was Αἴτναι (= Ἀίτνη), this would still not help the problems of formal structure raised here.

in *Eum*, they will have left the scene and re-entered between each act, but they will have done this not once but repeatedly. If the changes of scene were as explicit as in *Eum*, then there can have been no alternative. But this will have played havoc with the formal structure, since the chorus will only have been able to sing exit and re-entry songs, and never a proper act-dividing song (stasimon). And were its exits and re-entries simply juxtaposed, or was there some solo scene in between like Orestes at *Eum* 235–43 (cf. *Eum* 276*)? But even if we suppose that the chorus was different in each act, that hardly alleviates the structural disruption; in fact it aggravates it. For in that case one chorus will be leaving the stage and another entering in between each μέρος, and there will still be no 'stasima'. In A. *Eum* and S. *Aj* there is a single change of scene for a special dramatic purpose (see pp. 380–1 above) and it causes considerable structural disruption. *If* the stage was completely cleared of actors and chorus between each act in *Aitnaiai*, then the play will have been so utterly unlike fifth-century tragedy as we know it, that it is hard to believe that Aeschylus would have done it.

The only ways of avoiding these consequences and of making *Aitnaiai* more like a fifth-century tragedy are rather desperate. One possibility is that the chorus should be independent of the actors in the matter of scene setting. Although the scenes being played by the actors may have moved about, the chorus would simply stay in the orchestra throughout and sing act-dividing songs in the usual way (this may have been normal practice in the post-classical theatre with its high stage). But this would tend to hamper communication between the chorus and the actors; and if the chorus became closely involved in the action, it would be awkwardly intrusive that it was being swept about from place to place. An alternative is that the scene changes were less explicit than the hypothesis implies and that they were, in fact, more like the refocusing of place in *Pers*, *Cho*, and *Eum* (see *Pers* 598c*); in other words it would have emerged that each scene was set in a new place, but the actual change was not explicit nor tied to any specific moment. The hypothesis writers were used to giving a single place for the scene setting;[1] and in *Aitnaiai* the shifting of the scene may have been too conspicuous to escape the hypothesis writer (unlike in *Pers*, see *Pers* 598c*), and so made him unable to set the play at a single place in the usual way. But if this is right, then it means that the hypothesis writer was wrong to quote the analogy of the shift from Delphi to Athens in *Eum*, since that is much more explicit and involves sending the chorus off. A final alternative is that the play referred to in

---

[1] This probably goes back to Aristophanes of Byzantium, see Achelis *Philol* 72 (1913) 520–5.

this hypothesis is the Αἰτναῖαι νόθοι listed in the catalogue in M; this may have been post-classical and hence free from the objections I have raised.

(c) 530 (POxy 2256 fr. 9 = 282 Ll-J)

Fraenkel (*Kl B* 249ff.) attributed this fragment to *Aitnaiai*, but the arguments are tenuous and the conclusion, as Fraenkel admits, extremely speculative. I have explained on p. 464 below why I am sceptical about the further speculations which Lloyd-Jones has added to this, when he suggests that *Aitnaiai* was the third play of the Prometheus trilogy. If the play had the extraordinary formal structure which most scholars seem to accept (see above), then this strongly suggests that it was a curiosity meant to stand by itself, rather than as part of a trilogy.

I note simply that this fragment seems to come from near the beginning of an act, soon after the entry of Dike, and that the stichomythia is between actor and chorus, as usual in Aeschylus. The chorus seems to be 'resident', and it was surely on-stage before Dike arrived. *If* the chorus of *Aitnaiai* changed with each change of scene, then it is hard to see how this was managed.

Diktyoulkoi

(a) 464 (PSI 1209 a = 274 Ll-J)

It is generally agreed that this fragment comes from the prologue, even though it includes some stichomythia (cf. *Prom* 1a*). There is dispute over the identity of the two parties; for recent discussion see Ll-J p. 532, M. Werre-de Haas *Aeschylus' Dictyulci* etc. (Leiden 1961) 30–1 (hereafter W-H). W-H's objection to Silenus, that he should enter with the satyrs, is not cogent, since he enters at S. *Ichneutai* 39 before the chorus (58). The pair are trying to haul an object, apparently straight out of the sea; but we cannot say how this was staged. There are similar problems with the hauling scene in Arph. *Peace* 459ff. (see Newiger *RhM* N.F. 108 (1965) 229ff.); but we should not assume that the two scenes were staged in the same way.[1]

The two of them are not strong enough (16f.), and in 17ff. a βοή is raised for help. On the βοή in general see *Hik* 911*. It is very likely

---

[1] Webster *GTP* 18f. (cf. Dale *Papers* 121, 270) has argued that the ekkyklema was used. But even if it was ever used for this kind of purpose, it is unlikely that *Dikt* had a skene background to house it (see App. C). In *Illustrations* 30f. (ii, 3) Webster is probably right that the mid-fifth-century pyxis shows this same story; but Perseus seems too large for the painting to be inspired by Aeschylus' version—and there are no satyrs.

that this call for help, like Apollo's in S. *Ichn*, was answered by the entry of the satyr chorus. Apollo gives a list of the kinds of people who might answer in *Ichn* 33ff.; compare *Dikt* 18ff.

(b) 465 *(POxy* 2256 fr. 72)

This fragment also comes from a βοή calling for the help of local inhabitants. Lobel, noting the possible restoration c]ε[ι]ρᾶc in l. 7, observed that this might come immediately after the *PSI* fragment just discussed. This is possible; but if such calls for help were a recurrent prelude to the entry of the satyr chorus, then this might well come from yet another Aeschylean satyr play.[1] W-H 33f. suggests that the fragment might come from after the chorus's entry song when the net-hauling was in full swing. But this is most unlikely, because the fragment is still calling for help and so should come before the entry of the satyrs.

(c) 474 *(PSI* 2161 = 275 Ll-J)

According to the most plausible reconstruction of the plot, Diktys has to leave in order to fetch help in defence of Danae, and she is temporarily left at the mercy of Silenus and the satyrs.[2] Probably he has already gone before the beginning of our fragment; but it is possible that his departure came in the first few lines (with παντὶ κηρύccω cτρατῶι in 766 cf. Odysseus at S. *Phil* 1257f.).

Left with Danae the satyrs warm to the impending dalliance which they assume that they will share with Silenus, and in 821–32 they prepare to depart to bed. The lines are anapaestic, and may well have been accompanied with choreography which suggested imminent departure; with these lines the play is evidently drawing to a close, a false close. If Diktys is to return with help then he would have to do so very soon after the end of our fragment. The nuptial procession might well have been actually moving off, when he intervenes, so that the satyrs are frustrated on the verge of success, in contrast to the marriage ἔξοδοι of comedy (on 'delayed exit' see *Seven* 719b*). If this is right the play can hardly have been less than 880 lines long; but we have no other evidence on the length of Aeschylean satyr plays. Also there must have been two speaking actors as well as Silenus. Silenus cannot be equated with the coryphaeus of tragedy, since he has much more

---

[1] Steffen *Eos* 55 (1965) 38–43 fully discusses the 'Hilferuf' in satyr plays. He is completely unjustified, however, in his inference that the use of the *boe* was derived from satyr play: its use in tragedy and its tragic associations in comedy etc. are discussed on *Hik* 911*. Steffen in *Studia Aeschylea* (Wroclaw 1958) 28 actually attempts to join the two fragments discussed here. But there is no actual join, and his collocation involves a highly unlikely change of metre to iambic tetrameters.

[2] See Siegmann *Philol* 97 (1948) 73ff., Ll-J pp. 534f., W-H 42f., 72ff.

independence of speech and movement (cf. also S. *Ichn*, E. *Cycl*); on the other hand he is not exactly an ordinary actor.[1]

Note how there is a considerable stretch of lyric at 786–820, most of it probably choral, yet there are no entrances or exits associated with it. This ties in with my observations of the differences between the formal structure of tragedy and of satyr play; see pp. 57f. above.

Theoroi or Isthmiastai

(a) 16 (*POxy* 2250)

The attribution of this fragment to *Isthm* by Snell[2] seems impossibly speculative. It is not even clear that the fragment comes from a satyr play rather than a tragedy. Snell's main point is the supplement γυμ]ναζομ[in l. 8; but other words are possible, particularly if the metre has by now changed from anapaestic to iambic. However, it is clear that this is a greeting to a king on his entry, comparable to A. *Ag* 783ff., whose opening words it shares; see also on *Pers* 155a*. The lack of a paragraphos suggests that the honorific address went on for at least 4 lines.

(b) 17 (*POxy* 2162 = 276 Ll-J)

In the earlier parts of our fragment the satyrs are jubilant about some portraits of themselves which they have been given. It is generally held that the donor speaks 1–2 and then departs. The surviving words hardly certify this conclusion, though it is true that coι in line 3 should probably be addressed to someone independent of the satyrs. If the orthodox theory is right, then line 3 is thanks cast at the departing back (cf. *Hik* 951*); and the astrophic lyric mixture in 4–17, coming after the exit, has analogies with tragic technique.

There is scope for some guesswork on how the portraits fitted into the play. Inventions seem to have been a recurrent motif in satyr plays (fire, the lyre, wine, etc., cf. Kleingünther *Philol* Supp 26 (1933) 91–3). When first confronted with the new discovery the satyrs are terrified; but gradually they are won round to the delights and uses of the new thing, and they end up singing its praises. So in *Isthm* the satyrs may have been appalled at first by their own portraits: this may explain 20–1, where the satyrs assume that anyone who sees the portraits will be terrified (this seems better than the overcomplicated explanation of Snell *Hermes* 84 (1956) 7). Fraenkel's suggestion that the portraits take the form of antefixes is attractive.[3] Alternatively it may be that

[1] Cf. Collinge *PCPhS* N.S. 5 (1959) 29f., P-C *DFA*² 136.
[2] *Hermes* 84 (1956) 10–11, cf. *Gnomon* 25 (1953) 436.
[3] Fraenkel *PBA* 28 (1942) 245. On the other hand, Fraenkel's idea that the

the inventor has discovered satyr masks, such as those which the actors are actually wearing themselves. It seems that theatrical masks were occasionally used as props in Old Comedy: see Cratinus fr. 205 K, Arph. fr. 5; and in Arph. fr. 131 it appears that some masks are hanging up, as in *Isthm.*

It is generally agreed that a new character enters at 23, and that it is Dionysus.[1] So Dionysus enters to pour cold water on the satyrs' excitement, just when it is at its most lively; compare the entry of Cyllene at S. *Ichn* 215.

The last twenty lines of the fragment are full of problems. It is very hard to tell what is going on in the words, let alone in the action. For present purposes the key question is whether or not a new character enters, and, if so, when. The lines in question (78–86 = fr. 2(a) col. ii 6–14 combined with fr. 2(b)) read:

> παρόντα δ' ἐγγὺc οὐχ ὁρᾶιc τὰ [
> ἀλλ' οὔποτ' ἔξειμ' ε[
> 80 τοῦ ἱεροῦ, καὶ τί μοι [
> ταῦτ' ἀπειλεῖc ἔχ[ων
> "Ιcθμιον ἀντε[
> Ποcειδᾶνοc ο[ἶκον
> cὺ δ' ἄλλοιc ταῦτ[α π]έμπε [
> 85 ... [τ]ὰ καινὰ ταῦτα μα[νθά]νειν φιλεῖ[c
> ἐγὼ [φέ]ρω cοι νεοχμὰ [. . .] ἀθύρματα κτλ.[2]

On the usual interpretation[3] Dionysus announces the approach of a new character in line 78; 79–83 are the satyrs' defiance; and finally 84 is a rejection of the new character, who proceeds in 85ff. to ingratiate himself with new gifts. But it is strange that he should be announced in 78 and then stand by silent for several lines while a dispute which does not concern him is completed. While nothing is impossible (especially in a satyr play) this orthodox arrangement, which has attention wildly alternating between the newcomer and Dionysus, is positively obscure. It is simpler if we suppose that 78–84 are all concerned with Dionysus, and that the new entry does not come until 85. Dionysus or an attendant may be carrying something obviously unpleasant for the

satyrs actually climbed up to the roof to fix them is impracticably fanciful (although accepted by the practical Arnott 5, Hammond 444, cf. *contra* Kaimio 138 n. 3). Note how at Arph. *Clouds* 1486ff. a ladder is needed to get up to the roof.

[1] See e.g. Ll-J 544f. I cannot understand why Mette attributes this stage direction to Untersteiner when it is in the *ed pr* p. 14.

[2] The supplement of 81 is due to Kamerbeek, of 83 and 85 to Snell. For the combination νεοχμὸν ἄθυρμα cf. Cratinus fr. 145 K.

[3] See e.g. Ll-J 544f., Snell *Hermes* 84 (1956) 7ff., Mette *Verl* 168f.

satyrs, e.g. shackles; and in 78 what Dionysus may be doing is drawing attention to these: Reinhardt's restoration τὰ [δεϲμά ϲοι would fit
well.[1] In that case it is Dionysus, not the newcomer, who poses the
threat, and 79–84 is the satyrs' response.

This raises the question, finally, of whether there is a new entry at
all. If Dionysus spoke 85ff., and was referring to the chains or whatever, then the lines would still make sense. He refers ironically to the
satyrs' delight in inventions, and he claims that he is no less able than
his rival at inventing new devices. So far as I can see, this alternative,
which does away with the new entry, makes sense as far as l. 92; and
I know of no interpretation which satisfactorily explains the last few
lines.[2]

Hiereiai

118 (87 N)

The dactyls quoted in Arph. *Frogs* 1274 may well be the opening words
of the chorus on entry. The words both identify the chorus and motivate its entry. It looks likely that the temple they approach was
represented by the skene. For similar 'cultic' choral entries cf. E. *Ba*
68ff., *Kretes* fr. 472 N[2] and perhaps *IT* 123ff. (but I have suggested on
p. 194 n. 3 that the opening words should be attributed to the priestess
Iphigenia).

Memnon

197 (127 N)

It is a reasonable inference from Arph. *Frogs* 962f. that in this play
Memnon made a striking chariot-borne entry (see p. 43 and *Pers*
155b*). Moreover it is plausible to attribute this couplet to a preparatory speech before Memnon's entry, probably made by some
servant or rustic who has arrived in advance of him. Similarly in *Rh* a
shepherd arrives at 264ff. to prepare for Rhesus κωδωνοφαλαρόπωλοϲ.
It seems that there was a stock plot-pattern in which a foreign prince
arrived at Troy with high hopes and quickly met his end.

S. *Poimenes* seems to have been another; and there too we have
fragments (502–4 P) which also seem to come from the preparatory
speech of a Trojan rustic.[3] Cycnus, who is paired with Memnon in
Frogs, was no doubt another; though it would not be safe to conclude

---

[1] *Hermes* 85 (1957) 10 = *Tradition und Geist* (Göttingen 1960) 177.
[2] Ll-J, following Lobel, thinks that 93 must refer to sailing in a boat; but for
an alternative see Reinhardt op. cit.
[3] Ritchie 81 may be right to deny direct influence on *Rh*, *contra* Wilamowitz
Kl Schr iv 411–13.

that Aeschylus wrote a *Kyknos*, nor even necessarily that he made
a spectacular entry in a play by Aeschylus rather than by a contemporary or follower.[1]

Myrmidones

I speculated at length on the reconstruction of this play in *HSCP* 76
(1972) 62–75. The vulnerability of such speculation was immediately
shown up by Herington's exemplary publication of the scholia to
Prom. On pp. 64–5 I quoted Dindorf's inaccurate report of a scholion
on *Prom* 436 (= fr. 212a M); this note which is only in the 'minority
scholia' is properly transcribed by Herington as 437a on p. 139. After
alluding to the silence of Niobe it goes on καὶ ἄλλως, οἷον δι' ὀργὴν
βασιλέως φοβοῦμαι καὶ ϲιγῶ· καὶ οἷον τὸ τοῦ Ἀχιλλέως. ὅταν ἐϲτάληϲαν
πρὸϲ ἐκεῖνον ὁ Ταλθύβιοϲ καὶ Εὐρυβάτηϲ καλοῦντεϲ εἰϲ μάχην, ἐϲίγηϲαν.
Herington followed up the implications of this in *RhM* N.F. 115 (1972)
199–203: the late scholiast is referring not to Aeschylus at all but to
Iliad I. It is amazing that anyone could make so elementary a mistake
about the mission of the heralds in *Iliad* I, but Herington shows that
this is the only reasonable explanation. The consequences of this for
the reconstruction are not very great, and do not affect my argument
as a whole. On p. 70 §3 and probably §4 must be excised. It is still,
however, quite possible that some other Greek, e.g. Ajax or Patroclus,
may have pleaded with the silent Achilles before the scene with
Odysseus (§5). Even without that I think I have demonstrated the
length and centrality of Achilles' silence in *Myrm.*

Mysoi

412 (143 N)

Strabo says that the line came κατὰ τὴν εἰϲβολὴν τοῦ προλόγου and its
use by the scholiast on Hephaestion to illustrate some elementary
metrics confirms that this was the first line of the play. Further, it is
clearly the arrival line of a character who has only just set foot in
Mysia (for entry greetings to a place see p. 299 above). The only
reason for doubting that the character was Telephus himself is that
Arle. Poet 1460a32 criticizes ἐν Μυϲοῖϲ ὁ ἄφωνοϲ ἐκ Τεγέαϲ εἰϲ τὴν Μυϲίαν
ἥκων, and there seem to be references to this in Alexis fr. 178 K and
Amphis fr. 30. If these allude to Aeschylus' Telephus then this suggests

[1] Mette *Verl* 99ff. has obligingly composed an Aeschylean *Kyknos* for us. Achaeus
did compose one, see *TrGF* 20 F 24–5. Mette's attribution of 194–6 (328–9, adesp.
162 N) to *Memnon* does not seem justified: we have no other evidence that an
Aethiopian woman appeared in this play. Fr. 195 looks to me like a line from
a satyr play.

that for the first parts of the play Telephus was silent because he was polluted (cf. *HSCP* 1972 p. 76 n. 59). In that case he could not, it seems, have spoken the first line of the play; unless, perhaps, it was in monologue and he was then silent as soon as others entered the stage. (Fraenkel A. *Ag ed* ii 256 supposes that this line was spoken by a servant because of δεϲπόταϲ in fr. 413 (144 N): but that means surely the masters of Mysia and not necessarily of the speaker.)

Niobe

273 (*PSI* 1208 = 277 Ll-J)

I have briefly discussed this fragment, its bearing on the opening of the play, and on Niobe's silence, in *HSCP* 1972 pp. 60–2. I attribute it to a nurse, or possibly Antiope, and place it in the first scene soon after the choral prologue-parodos.[1]

We already knew from book fragments (278 (158 N)) that Tantalus appeared later in the play. This is confirmed by l. 10 of the papyrus:] μὲν ἥξει δεῦρο Ταντάλου βία. For a prediction of future arrival by ἥξει cf. e.g. A. *Ag* 1280, E. *Hec* 141, *Phoen* 170; cf. A. *Ag* 522, 531, S. *Ant* 33f., *OC* 396f., etc.

Prometheus Lyomenos

(a) 322–3 (190–2 N)

There is not much room for doubt that these anapaests by the chorus of Titans opened the play; this is to say, it began with a choral prologue-parodos which opened with marching anapaests and then turned to lyric—see on *Pers* 1a*. Procopius, though we do not know how he acquired the knowledge, says unequivocally that τέρμονα Φάϲιν was used by Aeschylus εὐθὺς ἀρχόμενος τῆς τραγωιδίας.[2] The chorus gives its motive for arrival straight away (ἥκομεν . . . ἐπ-οψόμενοι), and goes on to give a geographical account of its journey. This kind of elaboration of arrival motifs, which became common in Euripides, is discussed on *Prom* 128a*.[3] Furthermore, there seems to be

[1] The case for attribution to Niobe herself rests exclusively on the MS. reading ἐποιμώζουϲα in l. 7. To keep this involves great difficulties with the main verb; see Ll-J pp. 558f. If it is once granted that this word is corrupt, then the case for Niobe is lost. The evidence of vase painting is reviewed by Trendall (*RA* 1972 pp. 309ff.), who favours a nurse rather than Antiope.

[2] This rules out Schmid's otherwise alluring idea (*GGL* i 3 p. 284 n. 7) that the play began like *Prom Desm* with a Hephaestus scene.

[3] ἥκω with a participle was a conventional entry formula in Euripides, and was characteristic enough to be picked on for Aristophanic parody (see Rau 197 on *Birds* 992). This fragment and S. *Phil* 1413f. should be added to the list in Bond E. *Hyps ed* p. 110 of instances of ἥκω plus participle outside Euripides.

a direct comic exploitation of this choral entry in the fragments of Cratinus' *Ploutoi* (*PSI* 1212 = fr. 73 Austin) : the Ploutoi call themselves Titans (11) and say they have come to visit their aged brother (24ff.) ; they make an elaborate business of explaining their presence (9ff.), and may even say that there will be a second instalment of it (27f.).

Prometheus must have been on-stage already at the start. The problem of how this was stage managed is tied up with the problem of a Prometheus trilogy. If *Prom Lyom* was independent of *Prom Desm* (as suggested in Appendix D pp. 463f.), then either Prometheus was brought on and bound, and then the entry was cancelled (cf. E. *Andromeda*?, see p. 136 n. 1), or some sort of machine like the ekkyklema was used (thus e.g. Reinhardt 77). If, on the other hand, we accept the usual assumption that *Prom Lyom* followed immediately on *Prom Desm* the situation is rather different. If machinery was used at the end of *Prom Desm* (see 1093b*), then this will have been used again; but it is perhaps more likely that the actor would simply have stayed in position ready for the second play (thus e.g. Bethe 178ff.).

However it was staged, and whether the scene-setting was realistic or unrealistic, the setting of the two plays must surely have been visually very similar; and this will have raised the presumption in the audience that *Prom Lyom* was set at the same rock in the same remote place. But, wherever *Prom Desm* was set, it was *not*, as the hypothesis writer noted, the traditional setting of the Caucasus, because that is somewhere on Io's travels (see Bolton *Aristeas* (Oxford 1962) 46ff.) : *Prom Lyom*, however, evidently was set in the Caucasus. Not only does Cicero mention this in the introduction to his translation (fr. 324), it figures at l. 28 of the translation itself; this is confirmed by Strabo (fr. 326), who is expressly discussing geography; and Hyginus also talks of Caucasus in two passages which are thought to be drawing on this play (fr. 321b and c). So the two plays are not set at the same place. If they were performed consecutively, then Prometheus and his rock must be supposed to have been buried and then disinterred at another place. Though not inconceivable, this is awkward and does not count in favour of the orthodox trilogy.

(b) 324 (193 N)

This speech very probably comes from Prometheus' reply immediately after the opening parodos-prologue.[1] This would mean that, as in *Prom Desm*, there was no entry after the first song; though the situation

---

[1] It seems quite possible that fr. 323a (*PHeid* 185) came from this context, as Siegmann suggested, and that 1–13 are the end of the song and 14ff. the beginning of Prometheus' speech. But this is far from sure; see Lloyd-Jones *Gnomon* 29 (1957) 426, Reinhardt *Hermes* 85 (1957) 12–17.

in *Prom Lyom* would be more like that in *Hik*, because there has been no spoken prologue (see on *Prom* 88*). It is possible that Ge entered later in this act without the intervention of another choral song, which would be similar to the structural handling of Oceanus. There is, however, no reason to think that there were any comparable difficulties over the movements of the chorus (see *Prom* 128b*), or to doubt that the Titans addressed Ge, unlike the Oceanids and their father.

(*c*) 326-30 (195-9 N)

It is clear that Prometheus gave Heracles detailed geographical instructions for his journeys, as he does for Io in *Prom Desm*. When Heracles made his final exit, he made it, no doubt, as one about to embark on a great journey (a point rather lost with Io). Note all the verbs of travel even in the surviving fragments (ἥξεις 326, ἕρπε . . . ἥξεις 327, ἥξεις 329).[1]

Prometheus was loosed, and so, surely, walked freely off-stage towards the end of the play, possibly at the very end in the company of his brother Titans. Not only is this suggested by the Alexandrian subtitle, but by the whole subject of the freeing by Heracles and the presumed reconciliation with Zeus. This was surely put into visible dramatic terms by having the immovable Prometheus (note the stress on immovability in fr. 324) moving freely about and leaving the place of his torture: any consideration which contradicts this (e.g. the 'dummy' theory, see *Prom* 1b*) should not be willingly entertained.

Prometheus Pyrkaeus

343-50 (*POxy* 2245 = 278 Ll-J)

These fragments evidently come from a satyr play in which Prometheus first alarms and then delights the satyrs with his new gift of fire (for this sequence see p. 420 above). A satyr play on this subject inspired a whole series of vase-paintings later in the century (see Beazley *AJA* 43 (1939) 618ff.), and the *Prometheus* which Aeschylus produced in 472 B.C. (hypothesis *Pers*) fits perfectly (cf. Fraenkel *PBA* 28 (1942) 246f.). Pollux both gives us the subtitle *Pyrkaeus* (fr. 454) and

---

[1] We cannot tell how the scene with the eagle and Heracles' arrow was managed (though Dingel 32 is surely wrong to think in illusionist terms). An interesting fourth-century Apulean calyx-crater, published by Trendall in *JBerlMus* 12 (1970) 168ff. (= *Illustrations* iii, 1. 27) shows the eagle falling with the arrow in its breast. Although the painting is without doubt inspired by Aeschylus, it does not pretend to be a painting of a production. In *JHS* 95 (1975) 185 n. 3 I discuss the aetiology of the στέφανος (fr. 334) and of the flower προμήθειον in this play, and argue that they do not suit the traditional trilogy. It is true that the aetiology of the Areopagus in *Eum* is the only straightforward analogy, but one would not expect aetiologies in mid-trilogy.

a line (fr. 457) which shows that *Pyrkaeus* was a satyr play (see Wilamo-witz 129). So it is very likely that these fragments come from *Prom Pyrkaeus*.[1] Mette *Verl* 27ff. follows Terzaghi's insupportable idea that they come from a tragedy, and arbitrarily includes fr. 379 N as lines 31–2 of fr. 343. The couplet appears to be instructions to a chorus shortly before they sing (cf. *Hik* 505ff.); but their solemn tone is completely unsuited to the vivacious lyrics in fr. 343 which seem unmistakably satyric.

The lack of correlation between choral songs and exits and entrances in satyr plays (see pp. 57f. above) does not oblige or allow us to relate the lyrics in fr. 343 to actors' movements. Satyrs' lyrics also tend to be astrophic, and this would not prevent their still having ephymnia, so it is probably a mistake to look for strophic responsion in this fragment (cf. Lloyd-Jones pp. 564f.).

Semele or Hydrophoroi

(*a*) 355 (*POxy* 2164 = 279 Ll-J)

Lobel attributed these fragments to *Xantriai* because fr. 1 lines 16ff. are attributed to that play by Asclepiades, cited by the scholion on Arph. *Frogs* 1344. While they might possibly be fitted into a reconstruction of *Xantriai*, they would go much better in *Semele*, as was authoritatively shown by Latte.[2] And since Asclepiades claims that the phrase νύμφαι ὀρεσσίγονοι in the vocative in a parody of a Euripidean monody was derived from νύμφαι ναμερτεῖς in the nominative in a play by *Aeschylus*, it is credulous to trust his attribution (especially to plays in the same trilogy, if they were).

Lines 1–15 are choral lyric, apparently in short stanzas; at 16 Hera enters disguised as a begging priestess. It is an abrupt and striking entry, made without announcement or formality. While it is structur-ally normal, in that it follows an act-dividing song, it is most unusual in that Hera chants or sings in lyric hexameters, which go on for at least fifteen lines in fr. 1 and, it seems, for at least nine lines more in frr. 2 and 3. This 'monody' entry (see *Prom* 561*) is altogether extraordinary, and is presumably connected with Hera's disguise.[3]

[1] Assuming that *POxy* 2242 comes from *Prom Pyrkaeus*, then we have only one very unhelpful line from *Prom Pyrphoros* (fr. 351). It is sometimes suggested that *Pyrphoros* was the same play as *Pyrkaeus*, but that contradicts the whole point of the subtitles: see *JHS* 95 (1975) 185.

[2] *Philol* 97 (1948) 47ff. = *Kl Schr* (Munich 1968) 477ff. The only serious doubter has been Dodds E. *Ba ed*[2] xxxf.

[3] Perhaps the dactylic χρησμολόγος at Arph. *Birds* 959ff. supplies some analogy? Do the dactyls give Hera an air of solemnity, or rather of an itinerant fortune-teller?

Aeschylus must have had some special dramatic purpose for this highly unusual technique.

Appearances in disguise occur now and then in Greek tragedy; though this one is rather exceptional because Hera is not disguised but 'changed' (ἠλλοιωμένην Plato, μεταμορφωθεῖcαν 'Diogenes').[1] Since the metamorphosis is complete and since it involves Hera herself, it is very probable that it was prepared for explicitly in advance. It is hard to see how this could be done except by Hera herself in a prologue, before the chorus (friendly to Semele) enters; cf. Dionysus in E. *Ba*. There is some sort of indirect preparation, perhaps with dramatic irony, in the preceding song (see οὐ πλέον "Ηρας 3); and there is some thematic linking between the song and the Hera scene, as she takes up the topics of marriage and propagation.

(b) 356 (*POxy* 2249)

Mette's attribution of this fragment to the same play as fr. 355 is quite possible. All these *POxy* fragments seem to have been written by the same scribe, and so presumably come from the same collection. The occurrence of the four words ἐμφανη[, "Ηρα, ἥκει, and εὐνάς at the beginnings of four successive lines (16–19) does make a prima facie case for attribution to *Semele*. It seems that one character (coryphaeus?) earnestly advises another (Semele?) to change her attitude in the light of Hera's epiphany.

(c) 358

The scholion implies that Semele was seen on-stage pregnant. It is possible that she was in labour actually during the play (cf. New Comedy e.g. Pl. *Aul*, Ter. *Ad, Andr, Hec*); but the birth was finally precipitated by the thunderbolt. The chorus evidently consisted of the midwife's attendants, and the water they carry is presumably ready for washing the baby (cf. Dodds E. *Ba ed*[2] xxixf.). It is hard to tell whether ἐφαπτομένας τῆς γαcτρός should be taken any more literally than this. It is even harder to imagine what is implied by the information that both Semele and the chorus were ἐνθεαζομένας. But clearly this was a most remarkable play.

Sisyphos Drapetes, Sisyphos Petrokylistes

380 (227 N), 385 (233 N)

The Alexandrian subtitles point to two separate plays (*contra* e.g. Smyth 458). However, not one fragment is attributed specifically to *Sis Drap* and only two to *Sis Petr* (385 and 386). So we cannot know

---

[1] This is reminiscent of Odysseus in E. *Philoktetes* who was transformed by Athena: see Dio Chrys. *Or* 52. 5 and 59. 3.

which of the two the other fragments came. from: Mette is most misleading to attribute to *Sis Drap* all but the two which are cited from the other.

It has been inferred from the subtitles that *Sis Drap* was set on earth, and *Petr* in Hades (with a reference, of course, to Arle. *Poet* 1456a3) ; but I shall offer a chain of speculation which suggests that *Sis Petr* was set on the surface of the earth rather than below it. I start from fr. 385 : Αἰτναῖος ἐστι κάνθαρος βίαι πόνων. A giant dung beetle is obviously an apposite comparison to Sisyphus and his stone; but Αἰτναῖοι κάνθαροι are also a recurrent joke in fifth-century satyr play and comedy—see Pearson *CR* 28 (1914) 223f. Besides Arph. *Peace* 73 there is Epicharmus fr. 76 (Kaibel), Plato fr. 37 K, and S. *Ichn* 300. In *Ichn* this is the climax of a series of guesses by the satyrs (and a giant horned beetle is not a bad guess for the unfamiliar lyre!). This is a clue to the context of yet another beetle in S. *Daidalos* fr. 162 P: ἀλλ’ οὐδὲ μὲν δὴ κάνθαρος / τῶν Αἰτναίων ⟨γε⟩ πάντως (⟨γε⟩ add. Pearson, who translates ‘well it certainly isn’t a beetle—not one from Aetna anyhow’). A stock motif of satyr play seems to have been a series of comic speculations about a person or object which cannot be identified because it is somehow unfamiliar or hard to make out; and I suggest that the κάνθαρος in S. *Daidalos*, like that in *Ichn*, was one of these guesses. A likely Aeschylean example of this stock situation is *Diktyoulkoi* fr. 464 ll. 8–15, where Diktys makes a series of guesses about what it is he and his colleague are pulling out of the sea. But the clearest Aeschylean instance is *Sisyphos* fr. 380: ἀλλ’ ἀρουραῖός τίς ἐστι cμίνθος ὧδ’ ὑπερφυής; (on this fragment and underground entries see p. 449). My suggestion is, then, that both frr. 380 and 385 came from the same scene, in which Sisyphus comes up from the underworld and the satyrs speculate in a series of absurd guesses what on earth this may be emerging from the ground (the change of metre is compatible with a satyr play). In that case the scene must be from *Sis Petr*, since 385 is attributed; and this means that Sisyphus must have pushed his stone all the way up to the world above. This speculation leaves us in total ignorance of the contents of *Sis Drap*, since we cannot tell which fragments, if any, come from it.

Philoktetes

(a) 404 (249 N)

Leo’s notion that this line opened the play is not acceptable. It would be different if it were set in Malis, since it could then be the entry line of a returning traveller (cf. p. 299) ; but since it is set on Lemnos the line may have come at any point where Philoctetes called on his fatherland. But this does not necessarily mean we must infer from Accius that the play began with a choral prologue-parodos (thus most recently Calder *GRBS* 11 (1970) 173f.). Even if true this would be no guide to the play's date, see *Pers* 1a* (*contra* Calder op. cit. 179). Calder further argues (174) that the conjecture is reinforced by ὁ δ' Αἰcχύλος ἁπλῶc εἰcήγαγε τὸν χορόν in Dio Chrys. *Or* 52. 7; but Dio is talking about the *motivation* of the chorus (see p. 70 above). Aeschylus, unlike Euripides, did not labour unlikely excuses for the Lemnians' prolonged neglect of Philoctetes; he simply brought them on.

(*b*) 395

The scene in which Philoctetes was attacked by a fit of pain from his wound was evidently important in Aeschylus and Euripides as well as in Sophocles;[1] compare also Theodectes *TrGF* 72 F 5b. The verb εἰcήγαγεν in the commentary on Aristotle may suggest that, as at S. *Phil* 730ff., Philoctetes' attack came on him as he entered; but the verb can be used in a general way for introducing or including a feature.

Phryges or Hektoros Lytra

I briefly considered this play in *HSCP* 76 (1972) 75–6, where I paid particular attention to Achilles' veiled silence and to the way that this corresponded to his even longer silence in *Myrm*. Here I shall merely catalogue the evidence bearing on entrances and exits.[2] The prologue included a brief dialogue between Hermes and Achilles, cf. p. 242 above. We are fortunate that the evidence of the *Life* (= 243a) corrects the oversimplified schol. on Arph. *Frogs* 911 (= 212a[1]). After this Priam entered with the chorus: the Phrygians' opening dance displayed memorable choreography—see fr. 246. Achilles sat silent throughout this extravagant song, and then, probably, through a scene of considerable length in which Priam pleaded with him. Eventually, and, so far as we know, without any outside intervention, he spoke to Priam.

It seems clear from fr. 254 that there was a scene in which the corpse of Hector was weighed against gold. On the other hand 247 (267 N) is not evidence that Andromache accompanied Priam to Achilles' camp. If the woman referred to was on stage then it is more likely that it was Briseis and that the scholiast has made a mistake.

---

[1] The introduction of Neoptolemus was surely an innovation by Sophocles; and so we should look for a restoration of the fragment of hypothesis mentioning Neoptolemus which gives a reference to Sophocles' *Phil* and not to Aeschylus' (fr. 392 = *POxy* 2256 fr. 5, cf. Calder 171f.).

[2] For full discussions of the play see Schadewaldt *HuH*[2] i 345ff., Döhle 93–5, 136–9.

Psychostasia

205 (p. 88 N)

It is astonishing how much of the standard picture of Aeschylus'
stagecraft is built on conjectures about this lost tragedy. Yet we have
only two, or perhaps three, *words* from it (206–8 = 279–80 N).
Further, the entry in Mette is swelled out by five extracts of Homeric
scholarship (205b¹, b², c, d, e) which all say the same thing: that
Aeschylus wrongly (it is claimed) equated ψυχή with κήρ—and furthermore this observation seems to be based only on the *title* of the play, not
on its text. We are thus left with just two sources which account for
all the attention paid to the play: a passage in Plutarch (205a) and
two consecutive entries in Pollux's list of theatrical terms (205f).

Plutarch (*Mor* 16f–17a), explaining how a poet may take a μυθο-
ποίημα καὶ πλάσμα too literally, quotes *Iliad* 22. 210ff. where Zeus puts
the κῆρε θανάτοιο of Achilles and Hector into his scales and the fatal
day of Hector goes down and departs to Hades; and then he goes on
τραγωιδίαν δ' Αἰσχύλος ὅλην τῶι μύθωι περιέθηκεν, ἐπιγράψας Ψυχο-
cτασίαν καὶ παραστήσας ταῖς πλάστιγξι τοῦ Διὸς ἔνθεν μὲν τὴν Θέτιν,
ἔνθεν δὲ τὴν Ἠῶ, δεομένας ὑπὲρ τῶν υἱέων μαχομένων. Now is it true
that Aeschylus made his play round the passage in the *Iliad*? And does
it follow that Zeus held the scales? There are at least nine vase
paintings dating from before Aeschylus' time down to about 450
which show the *psychostasia* of Achilles and Memnon (not, note, of
Achilles and Hector).¹ In one Zeus holds the scales, in all the others
Hermes. It is generally accepted that the iconography draws on the
epic *Aithiopis*; and many scholars hold that the *psychostasia* was an
important or even central incident in the *Aithiopis* (and some claim
that the *Iliad* passages are adapted from it). It was, then, surely the
case that Aeschylus modelled his play on the *Aithiopis* and not on the
Iliad; and it is likely that in the model Hermes held the scales.²

So, seeing that Plutarch is probably wrong about Aeschylus' source,
might he also be wrong to imply that Zeus was a *dramatis persona* and
that he held the scales? So far as I can see, Zeus did not take part as
a character in any (other) Greek tragedy (cf. Kranz 53).³ If so, then

¹ For the information here I depend on Beazley in Caskey–Beazley *Attic Vase
Paintings in Boston* iii (Boston 1963) 44–6.
² There is a huge literature on the various aspects of Psychostasia. Besides the
bibliography in Wust *RE* xxiii 2 1439–48 and Beazley op. cit. 45 n. 1, I have noted
Schadewaldt *Von Homers Welt und Werk* (Leipzig 1944) 164, Dietrich *RhM*
N.F. 107 (1964) 97ff. esp. 112–13, K. Friis Johansen *The Iliad in Early Greek Art*
(Copenhagen 1967) 26of., Stähler *Grab und Psyche des Patroklos* (Münster 1967) 34.
³ It has been inferred (even by Lobel *POxy* xxiii p. 59) that Zeus appeared in
the guise of an Egyptian in S. *Inachos*, which was almost certainly a satyr play.
But the scholion on Arph. *Plut* 807 (fr. 275P) should be taken figuratively. Webster's

this suggests that there was some sort of inhibition against impersonating Zeus himself on the tragic stage; and this is a consideration against reconstructing *Psychostasia* with Zeus holding his scales on stage. Moreover, the weighing scene would (presumably) have to be set on Olympus, while the rest was (presumably) set at Troy; and the weighing scene would seem to need three speaking actors (cf. Wilamowitz 58f., 246), an innovation of Aeschylus' last years (see *Seven* 1005b*). *Psychostasia* is an unusual title (see Haigh *TDG* 396), and it is possible that the weighing itself did not actually take place on stage (just as the Seven against Thebes did not appear on stage). I conclude that not too much should be built on the Plutarch passage. It is unlikely that he had read the play, and he may have misrepresented his source (or his source may itself have been distorted).

Pollux (4. 130) lists the θεολογεῖον and γέρανος in the company of odd pieces of theatrical equipment which are generally agreed to be post-classical. He writes ἀπὸ δὲ τοῦ θεολογείου ὄντος ὑπὲρ τὴν σκηνὴν ἐν ὕψει ἐπιφαίνονται θεοί, ὡς ὁ Ζεὺς καὶ οἱ περὶ αὐτὸν ἐμ Ψυχοστασίαι. ἡ δὲ γέρανος μηχάνημά ἐστιν ἐκ μετεώρου καταφερόμενον ἐφ᾽ ἁρπαγῆι σώματος, ὧι κέχρηται Ἠὼς ἁρπάζουσα τὸ σῶμα τὸ Μέμνονος. Despite the disrepute which has fallen on many entries in this section in Pollux, which are taken to be drawn from the Hellenistic or later theatre, these two entries have been almost universally accepted; and theatre historians have without qualms done their best to accommodate Aeschylus to them.[1] But are they above suspicion?

First the θεολογεῖον. A preliminary point is that Pollux does not name Aeschylus; so he may possibly be talking about a later play based on Aeschylus. I have expressed doubts above as to whether Zeus ever appeared in tragedy, in the fifth century at least. And who are οἱ περὶ αὐτόν? Are they the other Olympians or just the mothers or what? As well as them, most scholars also rest the fulcrum of some giant scales on the θεολογεῖον. To carry all this it must have been a substantial structure: and yet it was, it seems, a platform still higher than the skene roof (see e.g. Hourmouziades 33f.). If we reckon that the skene itself was an innovation late in Aeschylus' life (see Appendix C), then can we so easily acquiesce in a platform above the skene roof, substantial enough to carry several actors and a giant pair of scales?

Pollux does not actually say that Eos used the γέρανος in the same play as Zeus and his colleagues used the θεολογεῖον; but it is a fair

idea (*The Tragedies of Euripides* (London 1967) 93, cf. *Illustrations* p. 76) that Zeus spoke the prologue of E. *Alkmene* is even more speculative.

[1] Among discussions which accept Pollux without demur I note D–R 218f. Robert 569–71, Wilamowitz 58f., 246, P-C *TDA* 46, 127–8 etc., Murray 38, 45, Reinhardt 11f., Mette *Verl* 112, Hourmouziades 33f., Arnott 4f., Dingel 67f., Hammond 444f.

inference that in a play where she pleaded for her son's life she should also intervene for his corpse—compare the Muse in *Rh.*[1] We may well believe that Eos pleaded for her son in Aeschylus' play, but can we really believe that he used a piece of machinery whose sole purpose was 'for picking up corpses'? And even if we equate the γέρανος with the μηχανή, it is very doubtful whether that was invented during Aeschylus' lifetime either—see p. 446 below.

It is extraordinary that Wilamowitz (58) should have referred to the evidence of Pollux as 'unzweideutig': he was, rather, as Wilamowitz's teachers' teacher, Hermann, put it (*Opusc* vi. 2. 133f.) 'a highly unreliable encyclopaedist, who has collected together his information from all sorts of written sources without any acquaintance with the things themselves'. We have every justification in doubting whether he is talking about the way that Aeschylus produced his *Psychostasia*, and should follow Bethe (153) in rejecting him outright. Pollux (his source, rather) may be talking about a late extravaganza modelled on Aeschylus, or about a late reproduction of Aeschylus which added spectacular effects (cf. Webster *Staging* 499). This fits with my recurrent suggestion (cf. §4) that later producers added huge spectacular effects to enliven their productions of Aeschylus, who was too plain and wordy for later tastes. Ancient scholars of the theatre seldom distinguished between the way that the dramatist himself had produced his play and the way it was reproduced in their own day (see p. 437 below).

[1] For this motif see Ritchie 8of. Compare also the beautiful cup painted by Douris *c.* 490 B.C. (*ARV*[2] i p. 434 no. 74).

APPENDIX B

The Stage Resources of the Fifth-Century Theatre

WHILE problems of stage management have been secondary to my main concerns, they have been recurrent and inevitable. Although so much has been written about the original staging of Greek tragedy, there is still uncertainty and disagreement both on general facilities and on the production of individual scenes. In this appendix I shall first set out what I take to be the right way to approach these problems, and particularly what I take to be the value of ancient scholarship as evidence. I shall then go on to apply these principles to the well-known problems of the various places where entrances and exits might be made—the precise subject, in fact, of Bodensteiner's still valuable prize essay of 1893.[1] Thus I consider the familiar controversies of the door or doors (1), roof (2), raised stage (3), ekkyklema (4), and mechane (5); and the two more dubious possibilities of an underground entry (6) and of a mound at the edge of the orchestra (7). Last (8), but not least, I discuss the side ramps where, in fact, the majority of entrances and exits in Aeschylus were made. The stage building itself (skene) presents particularly complex and important problems, and I shall postpone discussion to a separate Appendix (C).

First and foremost, it can hardly be insisted on too often that the plays themselves are the paramount evidence for their own staging. Not only should any reconstruction base itself on the texts but any conclusion must on no account be incompatible with the texts. No other evidence available to us can be allowed to count against the evidence of the plays themselves.

The most important corroborative and supplementary evidence is certainly that of Old Comedy. An allusion to tragic staging, however great the comic distortion, must in some way allude to something recognizable. Thus, for example, Aristophanes proves for us that

---

[1] Bodensteiner's sensible and thorough work has not been properly appreciated. The standard work on the subject in English is P-C *TDA*, though on many points there is a more interesting discussion in Hourmouziades. Further bibliography on individual points.

Euripides used the ekkyklema on occasion, and that he used the mechane in, at least, *Bellerophon* and *Andromeda*.

Archaeology provides useful but less definite positive evidence and a considerable amount of negative evidence. The remains of the Theatre of Dionysus itself can provide little but negative evidence since the traces of the fifth century are so disturbed and overlain. Vase paintings are always difficult to assess as evidence for staging, since the painter may have represented what in the original was purely verbal (e.g. messenger speeches), and may have conflated separate versions, and may have elaborated and altered on his own account. Few fifth-century paintings can be claimed with confidence as under theatrical influence; though it may well be time for a revaluation of this topic.[1] The later South Italian paintings, whose theatrical inspiration is clear and direct, are not only subject to the same reservations, but may be influenced by later theatrical conventions and productions.[2] The later the painting the more liable it is to include anachronistic theatrical features.

There remains a large body of evidence on which scholars are not so obviously obliged to use their critical faculties: explicit statements about the theatre in ancient authors. A few of these date from within a century of the original production of the play in question, and must be allowed weight accordingly; but nearly all are Alexandrian and later. Even those that derive from the great age of Alexandrian scholarship come down to us in abridged and possibly distorted form, since they are mainly to be found in the scholia on tragedy, Aristophanes, and on non-dramatic authors. Many are also to be found in scholarly compilations, most notably in Pollux's *Onomasticon*,[3] but also in other collections, including several Byzantine treatises. Material of the same

[1] The last twenty years have added several new fifth-century vase paintings which allude to the theatre, mostly painted by mannerist painters of the second quarter of the century; and we may hope for more. Moreover it may be that there are iconographic motifs in vase painting and other arts which are indebted to the tragic theatre, though it is very difficult to detect them (there are some vague but optimistic ideas in Ortkemper 26–31). I am persuaded, for example, that the tableau in A. *Myrmidones* of Achilles sitting with his head covered, which is attested by Arph. *Frogs*, is also reflected in a series of vase paintings from about 490 onwards: see Döhle 63ff., *HSCP* 76 (1972) 62ff. esp. 70f.

[2] This is the case, for example, with the 'prothyron' or 'aedicula'; see P-C *TDA* 75–99. The dragons which draw Medea's chariot are not in Euripides, yet are usual in the later tradition (see Page E. *Med ed* xxvii, who unjustifiably supposes the dragons were in Euripides' original production): they are already in vase paintings from about 400 B.C. onwards (see Page lviiff., *Illustrations* iii 3, 34), and may derive from a later production.

[3] iv §§95–154 are devoted to theatrical and related terms. For a discussion of Pollux's sources, especially on costumes and masks, see P-C *DFA*² 177–8 and literature cited there (I have also seen references to J. Niejahr *De Pollucis loco qui ad rem scaenicam spectat* (Progr. Greifwald 1885)).

sort is also to be found in, for example, Athenaeus, Plutarch,[1] Philostratus, Lucian (not to mention Horace). It comprises in all a huge
mass of testimonia on a wide range of theatrical topics, some of it
purporting to be about the theatre of the fifth century B.C. My
acquaintance with this body of evidence, though limited, has been
enough to persuade me that not one single item of it should be
trusted without question. So much of it definitely or probably is not
true of the fifth century, that none of it, I contend, should be allowed
any particular authority—no more, in fact, than the independent
suggestion of a respectable modern scholar. Much too much respect
has been paid to this kind of evidence, which can at best only corroborate the considerations outlined above, and should never be allowed
any contrary weight. This point may best be made by a brief account
of the history of the place of such evidence in scholarship on the fifth-
century theatre.

The nineteenth century, despite the warnings of some wise men (in
this field most notably Hermann), tended to regard any information
written in ancient Greek (or Latin) as above criticism; and scholars
tended to see their task as one of ironing out the many contradictions
and inconsistencies in the evidence. For theatre history this approach
reached an acme in Albert Müller's monumental edifice of painstaking
scholarship (1886). Yet large parts of Müller's monument had been
exploded within a single decade, and more and more of it has been
pulled down ever since. The attack came from two directions at once.
Several scholars worked from the plays and concluded that many
features repeatedly attested by the later testimonia were directly and
incurably incompatible with the plays themselves. A few examples are
the high stage, the ἄνω πάροδοι, the periaktoi, high-soled kothornoi,
the separation of the orchestra as exclusive to the chorus and the stage
as exclusive to the actors.[2] At the same time the kind of evidence which
had been collected by Müller was also shown to be largely inapplicable to the fifth century by the excavations in Athens by Dörpfeld.[3]
These showed that the fifth-century theatre could not have been the
monumental and elaborate construction indicated by many of the
testimonia. There was no question of a twelve-foot stone stage but

---

[1] See R. Flickinger *Plutarch as a Source of Information on the Greek Theater* (Chicago
1904). The conclusion of his painstaking survey is unequivocal: (p. 60) 'the
conclusion is irresistible that in theatrical matters it was invariably his [Pl.'s]
habit to modernize'.

[2] The most important contributions were, perhaps, those of Capps (1891),
Bodensteiner (1893), and Reisch (1896); though seminal to this approach through
the plays was Wilamowitz's article in *Hermes* for 1886 (= *Kl Schr* i 148ff.).

[3] Published in D–R (1896); but the first hints of Dörpfeld's findings were, as it
happens, made public in the *Nachträge* to Müller (415–16).

rather whether there was even a low wooden stage, no question of seven or five doors but whether there was more than one, no question of ekkyklemata on the second storey but whether there was even one on the ground. The third edition of Haigh's *AT* (1908) represented a kind of last-ditch reaction on behalf of the scholarship of late antiquity against the textual and archaeological tide.[1] But the principle had been incontrovertibly established that the plays themselves, supplemented by the largely negative evidence of archaeology, are the final criterion for their own staging.

A large proportion of the late evidence collected by Müller can now be seen to have nothing to do with the fifth-century theatre. It seems to me only sound method to hold that, if much of this evidence is discredited, then *all* of it should be treated with suspicion. Some of it may well be right, some of it may even go back to a creditable contemporary or near-contemporary source: but not one item may be taken on trust, and none of it can be treated as self-sufficient evidence for staging, but only as possibly unreliable corroboration. Yet scholars still have a way of treating the scholia and late testimonia as unquestionably right, unless they are positively contradicted by the text of the play or by archaeology. Often a sentence from a late source is quoted as gospel when the surrounding sentences are known to be unreliable. Hammond (389) has recently protested that our late sources 'were not inventing their own theories but were drawing on the best authorities they could find'; and he argues that their sources were fifth- and fourth-century writers. But when so much of their material is clearly anachronistic and inappropriate we cannot suppose that the sources they regarded as 'the best authorities' were necessarily the oldest or most venerable: rather, it seems, they were the most copious and most attractive, that is third- and second-century biographers and encyclopedists (cf. P-C *DFA*[2] 178).

I note two factors which contribute to the unreliability of the later testimonia on theatrical matters. One is that they show an insufficient sense of theatre history. That is to say that they do not seem aware of how much the externals of the theatre changed with time. So there is always a danger that they may give an account of how a scene was or might have been produced in their own day as though it were the way that the playwright himself produced it. I have given some Aeschylean examples on p. 47 above.[2] Secondly, the sources of some of our late

[1] Pickard-Cambridge was largely responsible for Haigh *AT*[3]; and *TDA* shows how much his views changed. Arnott's first chapter is an extraordinary relapse into dependence on late and untrustworthy evidence.

[2] Other examples are probably the scholia which assume that Euripides used the mechane for his gods 'ἀπὸ μηχανῆϲ' (cf. pp. 444f. below). Even Aristophanes of Byzantium could claim that the ekkyklema was used at E. *Hipp* 171 (see Σ), which

scholarship were given to straightforward fiction when they had insufficient material to fill out their discussions and biographies of the famous poets.[1] They were also liable to elaborate internal hints and to take literally the jokes of Old Comedy. For example, among the πρῶτα εὑρήματα attributed to the three great tragedians many are palpable falsehoods, and others are attributed to more than one of them. And if this is so even in our meagre sources, then we may suppose that had we more there would be even more such guesswork.[2] In conclusion, sources which show some signs of anachronistic information or of having been drawn from sources which resorted to elaboration or guesswork should be treated with sceptical caution: they should never be used as a basis or starting-point for the history of the theatre in the fifth century.

In the light of this methodological discussion I shall now turn to the actual resources of the fifth-century tragic theatre.

(1) From *Oresteia* onwards almost every tragedy makes use of a *door* in the skene as a means of entry and exit (for possible exceptions see p. 455 below). The door was presumably central, and must have been quite large, large enough for the operation of the ekkyklema. Webster

is surely wrong. Wilamowitz may be right to suppose that Aristophanes took this from later theatrical practice. Webster *The Tragedies of Euripides* (London 1967) 49 says 'we have no reason to distrust Aristophanes': but do we have any reason to trust him? It is instructive to see that Σ on E. *Or* 1366 implies that on the strength of ll. 1371f. some actors of the Phrygian had jumped down from the skene roof. Dale (*Papers* 126f., 268f.) argues, convincingly to my mind, that Euripides did not intend this staging, and that the scholiast's suspicion of 1366-8 is unjustified on these grounds (but see Reeve *GRBS* 13 (1972) 263-4).

[1] To be fair, quite a few scholia admit that they are only guessing, see e.g. Σ on S. *OC* 163, 1044, 1437, E. *Med* 903, *Hec* 1056; see further Weissmann *Anweisungen* 12ff. esp. 17f., 20f.

[2] A catalogue of πρῶτα εὑρήματα was a *topos* of ancient literary biography (for bibliography see Nisbet–Hubbard on Hor. *Od* i 3. 12). Several well-known controversies on such subjects may well be the result of mere biographical guesswork, e.g. the development of σκηνογραφία, the introduction of the third actor, of the high-soled boot. Ancient biography did not have the same standards as we should expect from a historical biographer: see e.g. recently Russell *Plutarch* (London 1972) ch. vi, Fairweather *AncSoc* 5 (1974) 231ff. Later peripatetic biographers of the great poets (e.g. Chamaeleon on Aeschylus, see fr. 40a, b, 41 Wehrli) seem to have been particularly free in inventing material to fill up the required *topoi* e.g. childhood experiences, sex life, interesting death. When not simply fabricating they seem to have drawn uncritically on the poet's own works and on distorted contemporary sources like Aristophanes. One such *topos* is the alienation of the poet from his society and, if possible, his exile, which should preferably be connected with some spectacular anecdotes. For Aeschylus, as well as the entry of the fifty furies (see p. 372 above and *GGL* i 2 p. 164 n. 1), there was the collapse of the ἴκρια, his defeat by Sophocles, and his revelation of the mysteries. For scepticism about similar anecdotes on Euripides' unpopularity see Stevens *JHS* 76 (1956) 87ff. esp. 88-90.

(GTP 8) has estimated that it was about four metres wide, which seems a reasonable maximum.[1]

There is still a controversy over whether more than one door was used in the Greek theatre.[2] The dispute is bound in the last resort to be inconclusive since 'strictly speaking, drama does not *need* anything except people' (Dover *Ar Com* 23). None the less there are arguments for both sides, and in my view there was more probably one door only for all or nearly all of the fifth century (after the innovation of the skene). The dispute has centred on Aristophanes; but there has been one especially disputed tragedy, and that is, as it happens, A. *Cho*. I argue on *Cho* 718* and 885* that, while a second door might be used if available, the play can be staged without confusion with only one; and I conclude that any decision must rest on the evidence of the rest of surviving tragedy.

In the good old days when one relied on late sources, it was taken for granted that there were at least three doors (see e.g. Müller 119–21). But once the tragedies themselves are appealed to it is very striking that almost every one calls for one door and positively one door only. They could not use a second door even if there were one available. And yet we might have expected that some tragedies would have used a second door had it been there (e.g. both the house of Medea and the palace of Creon might have been on-stage in E. *Med*); we might have expected that we would have at least one tragedy which made positive use of the dramatic possibilities of two dwellings on stage—yet there is none. Hourmouziades 21–5 collects five places in Euripides where a second door might be used; but none of them is at all compelling, except perhaps *IA* 855ff., which, if not post-Euripidean, dates from very late in the century.

The situation in Aristophanes is not so clear. But Dover makes as incisive and well-argued a case as may be made for more than one door in *Acharn*, *Clouds*, and *Peace*, and yet, as he himself admits, these plays may be staged with only one.[3] On the other hand for *Ekkles*

[1] Webster based his calculations on the measurements of the stone foundation slab T, which belongs to the same construction as the wall H–H. But I argue in p. 452 n. 3 below that this is probably a fourth-century edifice. If, as argued there, the fifth-century skene was fitted inside the arc of the old terrace wall, then it may have been as little as 16 metres long, in which case a four metre doorway seems disproportionately wide.

[2] The chief antagonists have been Dale *Papers* 107–18, 120, 269 and Dover *Skene* 1ff. and *Ar Com* 23f., 83f., 106–8, 135, 197f.; cf. also J. Roux *REG* 74 (1961) 32ff.

[3] One particular objection: Dover always speaks as though the two doors would be symmetrical, yet surely there was always a larger central door. In *Acharn* the central door must be used for the ekkyklema scene, and yet it must also surely represent Dicaeopolis' country house (*contra* Dover *Ar Com* 83), which is central to much of the play. The symmetry of the final parts of the comedy is not at all

Dover makes a strong case (*Skene* 14–17, *Ar Com* 197–8) for *three* doors. This is suggestive since *Ekkles* is a late play (*c.* 392): suggestive, because New Comedy makes a conspicuous contrast with the fifth century in this respect. Among those plays of Menander where we have enough evidence and among those of Plautus and Terence the majority clearly indicate two doors, several call for three, and hardly any can be limited to one.[1] Not only are the two or three doors clearly signalled in the text and the action, but many New Comedies are entirely constructed around the neighbourhood of two households (e.g. Men. *Sam*, *Phasma*, Ter. *Hec*, Plaut. *Mil Glor*). The availability of two doors is often essential for the entire dramatic conception.

It will not do to imply that dramatic conceptions are determined or inspired by the number of available doors—that would be to put the cart before the horse. None the less, the use of two or more doors in New Comedy, and the non-use, or at best the incidental possibility, of a second door in the fifth century make a remarkably consistent contrast. So the clear evidence of the plays themselves is that from the introduction of the skene down until some time in the fourth century, perhaps early in the century, there was as a rule just one wide central door.

(2) It seems that the *roof* of the wooden skene was substantial enough to carry at least two or three actors. It is likely that most divine epiphanies were made on the roof (see p. 445 below), and there was perhaps an Aeschylean precedent in *Edonoi* (fr. 76) where Dionysus' epiphany may have been above the palace. There are very few, surprisingly few, places where mortals appear on the roof.[2] The clearest are Euadne at E. *Hik* 980ff. (a cliff), Antigone and the Old Man at E. *Phoen* 88ff. on a διῆρες ἔσχατον, and Orestes and his confederates at E. *Or* 1567ff. In Aeschylus it is probable, though admittedly not certain, that the Watchman should be on the roof (see *Ag* 1*); and it is possible but unlikely that it was used for the dream of Clytemnestra (see *Eum* 94*). I do not believe, as many do, that the chorus of Oceanids entered on to the skene roof in *Prom* (see 128b*): quite apart from the problem of structural engineering, there is no good reason to think that the scene was staged in that way. Nor do I believe Pollux (4. 130) that Zeus and his associates were on top of the

---

enhanced if Dicaeopolis' door is the large central one while Lamachus' is a little side one, or vice versa. Rather all the properties should come from the central door. (There is, by the way, some rather dubious fourth-century South Italian evidence for two 'practicable' doors and a third one which remains a 'dummy'; Simon 35–7 takes this rather too seriously.)

[1] According to Duckworth *The Nature of Roman Comedy* (Princeton 1952) 83 only *Amph* and *Capt* are one-door plays.

[2] See further A. Müller 140–2, Bodensteiner 664–72, Hourmouziades 29ff. etc.

APPENDIX B   441

skene in *Psychostasia*, not in Aeschylus' version at any rate—see
p. 432.

Late sources babble of all sorts of higher levels and all sorts of
heavy machinery on them (see A. Müller 152–5). These have nothing
to do with the fifth century. The one most bandied about by modern
scholars is the θεολογεῖον, attested by Pollux in the entry cited above.
But the only place in surviving tragedy which may call for such a
higher platform is the final scene of E. *Or*; and it remains doubtful
whether there was any such thing in the late fifth century, let alone in
Aeschylus' time.

(3) The raised *stage*, if there was one, was not strictly a place of
entry, but as a problem it goes along with the others discussed here.
The question has assumed such a prominent place for scholars because
it became a kind of test case in the battle for the late testimonia against
the plays and archaeology. Systematic studies of the plays in the 1890s
successfully demolished the high stage, and they were confirmed by
Dörpfeld's excavations.[1]

But although the high stage of the later theatre and of the later
sources was conclusively banished from the classical period, we cannot
rule out a low stage made of wood and, say, one metre high, though
even one metre would need several low steps to be ascended. At the
moment some such low stage is widely accepted, and is approaching
an orthodoxy. The most influential exponent has been Arnott (1–42),
who argues in a lively way, but leans heavily on late sources which
were long ago discredited. His arguments from the plays, when not
misinterpretations, are not conclusive: the case is much better put by
Hourmouziades 58–74. He shows that in Euripides the actors are
normally near the front of the skene, while the chorus is normally
away from the skene. Still, he can produce no single scene in Euripides
which does not make sense without a raised platform; and even the
ledge of rock at S. *OC* 192ff., which is perhaps the strongest evidence in
tragedy (cf. Arnott 35), need not have been literally represented.
There are more places in Aristophanes than in tragedy which could
positively use a raised stage, most notably *Wasps* 1341;[2] but even these

[1] The military history is tediously traced by Joerden diss. 1–20, but he gives a
good assessment of the problem in *Bauformen* 407–9. As well as Bodensteiner,
Capps and Pickard are still of value. The case against any raised stage is well
put by Flickinger 78–103. (A certain J. Höpken *De Theatro Attico Saeculi a. Chr.
Quinti* (Diss. Bonn 1884) was the first to suggest that the actors and chorus were
on the same level; but his arguments are sparse and weak, and he has received
more credit than he deserves (a complaint already being made by Bodensteiner
in *JAW* (*Bursian*) 1896 iii p. 51, but seldom heeded).)

[2] Philocleon calls the girl a χρυϲομηλολόνθιον: these beetles would fly spectacu-
larly when attached to a string, see *Clouds* 763. He is inviting her to fly on his
string, i.e. his phallus. So ἀνάβαινε may mean 'take off'; and it may be Philocleon

places could be staged on the level. Hourmouziades' best argument of all remains the simple point that a platform would make the actors more conspicuous, and would distinguish them from the chorus during the acts.

What it is most important to recognize is that, if there was a raised platform, there was still free communication, both physically and vocally, between the actors and chorus, the stage and the orchestra. The chorus could use the skene, and the actors could move among the chorus in the orchestra. Some scenes in Aeschylus where it is important to see that there is no spatial barrier between actor and chorus are *Pers* 909ff. (see 1077*), *Hik* 825ff., *Cho* 22ff., *Eum* 1003ff. (see 1047c*).

The 'stage question' is likely to remain an open one, so it is fortunate that it is not a very important issue. Needless to say, when I have used indispensable idiomatic phrases like 'on-stage' and 'off-stage' these are not to be taken literally.

(4) Although the noun ἐκκύκλημα is not recorded until late, the verb ἐκκυκλεῖν comes several times in Aristophanes, and there is no point in using any other name for the wheeled trolley device which could be rolled out of the skene.[1] Pickard-Cambridge[2] did not believe in its existence for the fifth century: but, although there is much room for dispute over the range and frequency of its use and over its exact mechanics, the allusions in paratragic contexts in Arph. *Acharn* and *Thesm* can leave in no doubt its existence and its basic function (they also give a *terminus a. q.* of 425 B.C.). These scenes show that basically it was used in order to reveal to the audience a tableau, usually of objects as well as people, which was supposed to be *indoors*. This is well put by the scholion on Arph. *Acharn* 408: τὰ δοκοῦντα ἔνδον ὡς ἐν οἰκίαι πράττεcθαι καὶ τοῖς ἔξω ἐδείκνυε (λέγω δὴ τοῖς θεαταῖc). Although the distinction between indoors and outdoors may be broken down and later in the scene the characters may all behave as if they were outdoors, we do not have sound evidence of the use of the ekkyklema except for the revelation of interior scenes.

It is an extraordinarily contrived device, but, once established, it was no doubt readily accepted. If I am right that early pre-skene

who is to be mounted rather than the stage. (For the *double entendre* Professor Lloyd-Jones points to Men. *Perik* 484.)

[1] I have found the most useful discussions in Neckel *Das Ekkyklema* (Progr. Friedland 1890), Bodensteiner 659ff., Bethe 122ff. (retracted in *RhM* 83 (1934) 21ff.), Hourmouziades 93ff., Dale *Papers* 119ff., 264ff., 284ff. Another term τὰ ἔξωcτρα (fem. sing. in some other sources), occurs in an inscription of 274 B.C. from Delos (see Sifakis *Hellenistic Drama* (London 1967) 46, 51). But Snell is surely wrong to attribute the word ἐξώcτρα to the *tragedian* Phrynichus (*TrGF* 3 F 21a?). The word is glossed in Photius and Hesychius, and the Phrynichus referred to must be the Atticist or some other.

[2] *TDA* 100ff., cf. D–R 234f. and recently Joerden *Bauformen* 410–12.

tragedies were sometimes given interior settings (see p. 454 below) then this will have been a considerable help in establishing the new convention and in encouraging its invention. None the less we should expect the audience to be given some sort of sign when the ekkyklema was about to be used, and we do indeed seem to have this in the introductory lines which accompany most of the more probable instances of its use. The lines are usually to the effect 'the doors are open: now you can see inside'; see e.g. S. *Aj* 344, *El* 1458ff., E. *Hipp* 808, *Her* 1028ff. (cf. Bethe 107ff.). It seems that conventional lines of this sort were already well enough established in 431 to be invoked and then not fulfilled at E. *Med* 1314–16 (cf. *Or* 1561).

As to the possible use of the ekkyklema in Aeschylus, I hesitantly conclude that it was not invented during his lifetime. After the introduction of the skene a need would have to be established for the device. There is indeed a case for its use at *Ag* 1372 (see 1372b*); but I conclude there that the lack of any clear explanation or signal of the new device and the even more notable lack of any identification in the parallel scene in *Cho* (973a*) press us to favour some alternative presentation. I also more confidently reject the use of the ekkyklema at *Cho* 892 (see 892c*) and at *Eum* 64 (see 140*). As for the various scenes in plays other than *Oresteia* where its use has now and then been alleged, not only do they presuppose the presence of a skene, they also assume that the function of the ekkyklema was merely 'to extrude or withdraw heavy or immobile objects'.[1] But if the mechanism was particularly associated with the carefully prepared revelation or discovery of internal scenes, then it is an unwarranted and confusing extension of its conventional function to use it incidentally on all sorts of other occasions.

(5) Presumably the word μηχανή could have been applied to anything in the theatre which was the business of the μηχανοποιός; but in all probability it had before the end of the fifth century become particularly applied to the crane from which flying characters could hang suspended by a rope. The comic nickname κράδη was also already current in the fifth century (see below), and other names are encountered in later sources.[2] We do not know how the device worked, but it presumably needed a firm foundation, a pivoted yard-arm, and a system of pulleys. It should be remembered that it could not be hung

---

[1] Dale *Papers* 121; cf. other references to her in p. 442 n. 1 above, and the places cited in p. 455 n. 1 where Webster argues for the ekkyklema. My very limited use of the ekkyklema would be analogous to the limited use of the 'discovery-space' at the Globe which R. Hosely (*Shakespeare Survey* 12 (1959) 35ff.) argues was only used for striking disclosures.

[2] It is apparently this same device which is called γέρανος (e.g. Pollux 4. 130, Bekker *Anecd* i p. 232), and ἐ-(or αἰ-)ώρημα (Σ on Arph. *Peace* 80, *Suda*).

from above as in an indoor theatre, and that it is most unlikely to have
been invented before the skene was there to hide the machinery.[1]

It is once again Aristophanes who proves the existence of the device
in the fifth century, who defines its basic use, and who supplies a
terminus a. q. of 425 (E. *Bellerophon* is referred to at *Acharn* 427f.). The
mechane is exploited in paratragic contexts in *Birds, Peace,* and *Thesm,*
and is also probably used, though with not particularly tragic associations, for Socrates in *Clouds*. The parodies in *Peace* and *Thesm* show
that it was used to present Pegasus with Bellerophon in E. *Bellerophon*
and *Stheneboia* and with Perseus in *Andromeda*.[2] These are the only three
sure instances from fifth-century tragedy, though no doubt there were
others. It should be noted that in three of the four Aristophanic scenes
the notion of flying through the air is essential, and that there are
lines which accompany the operation of the machinery (*Birds* 1184ff.,
Peace 82ff., *Thesm* 1098ff.).[3]

But the mechane is, of course, best known from the phrase θεὸς
ἀπὸ μηχανῆς (and translations of it), and this refers to the divine
epiphanies which occur soon before the ends of tragedies, and are
amply illustrated in surviving Euripides.[4] However, it is open to
dispute whether such epiphanies were made on the crane in Euripides'
own productions. The device was not, so far as we know, ever used by
Aeschylus, and so I shall attempt to put the matter on one side as
briefly as possible.

First, let it be clear that the mechane was conventionally used for
these epiphanies in the fourth century, and it soon became proverbial.[5]
The question is whether this was already the case in the fifth century.
It is notable that none of the Aristophanic uses is a parody of the
'θ.α.μ.' But the most important consideration is internal. Barrett *Hipp
ed* p. 395 lists ten instances from the surviving plays of Euripides
(*Andr, Hik, Her, Ion, El, IT, Hel, Or, Hipp, Med*) and one from Sophocles
(*Phil*). To these may be added *Rh* 595 (Athena) and 890 (Muse);
both have analogies with and differences from the Euripidean uses,

[1] In the Renaissance theatre machines were, it seems, lowered from above or
from the 'heavens'. See G. Wickham *Early English Stages* ii 2 (London 1972) 197f.
[2] The use in *Stheneboia* is confirmed by the deictic τοῦδε in fr. 665a (Snell *Supp*
to N²). Bellerophon and Perseus are the very two examples of the employment of
the mechane given by Pollux 4. 128 and Σ on Clem. Alex. *Protr* ii 12.
[3] Socrates in his basket in *Clouds* is treading air (225) and keeping clear of earthy
influences. His entry, unlike the others, is not meant to be noticed: Strepsiades
first spots him at l. 218.
[4] I have found Hourmouziades 146–69 the most useful discussion. Also of value
are Bodensteiner 664ff., D–R 215ff., Flickinger 289ff., Arnott 72ff., Barrett E.
Hipp ed 395f.
[5] See e.g. Plato *Clit* 407a, *Crat* 425d, Antiphanes fr. 191. 13ff., Alexis fr. 126.
15ff., Menander *Theoph* fr. 5 (p. 148 Sandbach), frr. 243, 951. 12f. (p. 336 Sandbach).

but the latter is clearly meant to be like a '*θ.α.μ.*' From papyri
besides E. *Antiope* (fr. xlviii l. 67 Kambitsis) add Erechtheus fr. 65. 55
(Austin).[1]

This makes a total of fourteen. All of them except two (*Andr, El*)
are fairly urgent interventions in order to prevent some undesirable
course of action; most of them are distinctly sudden, and two (*Hel,
Antiope*) prevent a murder at the last minute. Only five of the instances
(*Andr, El, Her, Ion, Rh* 890) allow time for an announcement, and only
two (*Andr, El*) positively suggest flying. This makes a striking contrast
with Aristophanes, where all refer clearly to flying and where in three
out of four cases there are lines which cover the operation of the
machinery. More comparable to the Euripidean epiphanies is the
abrupt intervention of Penia at Arph. *Plut* 415ff. where there is paratragic language and the right type of situation (not in Rau). We
cannot tell how quickly and unobtrusively the mechane could be
operated, but Aristophanes suggests that it was a bit of a business, and
it must be doubtful whether it could have been effectively employed
for the more sudden of the Euripidean interventions. These epiphanies
could be made more abruptly on the roof than on the flying machine.
It is, then, worth noting that all but one of the five announcements
(viz. *Rh* 885–9, cf. 890ff.) might be regarded as interpolations to suit
later stage practice, as is mooted by Barrett p. 396 n. 1. So the evidence of the plays themselves, especially when compared with
Aristophanes, leaves it far from sure that in the fifth century the θεὸc
ἀπὸ μηχανῆc was in fact ἀπὸ μηχανῆc.

A new papyrus might have added considerably to our knowledge
of the mechane were it not sadly damaged and the parts we have of
it obscure. *POxy* 2742, published by Lobel in 1968, is fragments of
a very full scholarly commentary on an Old Comedy.[2] This note
evidently illustrates a joke which either exploits the term κράδη or the
μηχανοποιός (cf. Arph. *Peace* 174, fr. 188) or both. Four new uses of the
mechane from Old (or Middle) Comedy are welcome, and they confirm that the crane was in quite common use, and suggest that its use
in tragedy can hardly have been confined to heroes riding on Pegasus.

---

[1] I omit *Hyps* (the papyrus is so damaged at the epiphany of Dionysus at fr.
64 col. iii (p. 19 Bond) that nothing can be said about it); also *Ba* (lacuna).

[2] Cratinus fr. 74 Austin. Lobel guessed with uncharacteristic rashness that the
comedy was Cratinus *Seriphioi*. But the lemmata do not indicate that Perseus
was actually a character in the play, as Lobel himself admits. And Cratinus fr.
207 K does not show, or even imply, that the mechane was used in *Seriphioi*.
Luppe *Gnomon* 43 (1971) 120 n. 4 may be right to argue that the corrupt part in
12–13 (which may have been illegible in the exemplar) should read καὶ νεβρῶν
δοραῖc (though his attempt at a palaeographical explanation is mere trifling).
Luppe also supplements 3ff. from Pollux 4. 128, but this is unjustified since it
begs the question of Pollux's authority.

But they do not show that the mechane could be used without a positive notion of flying, or that it was used for 'ἀπὸ μηχανῆϲ' epiphanies. Moreover all the plays are of quite late date, possibly none of them before the end of the fifth century.[1] The new fragments do show for once and for all that κράδη was a comic name for the mechane, based on some joke about a dried fig (ἰϲχάϲ), as was rightly conjectured by Crusius (*Philol* 48 (1889) 697ff.). This means the recorrection of the 'corrected' entry in *LSJ Supp.* κράδη III. Further the fragments tell us that the mechanic could be told 'καθελέτω' someone on the machine, and that he could περιάγειν it (though that might mean 'swivel in its socket' or 'turn the handle'). But the rest is confusion, apparently beyond restoration.

To return finally to the possible use of the mechane in Aeschylus. If I am right about the innovation of the skene (Appendix C), and the mechane presupposes the masking of the skene, then we should only look for its use in the *Oresteia*. There is a possible use for the entry of Athena in *Eum* (397b*); but I argue there that lines 403–4 can mean, and are best taken to mean, that she entered on foot. Otherwise, no fewer than three uses of the mechane have been alleged in *Prom*. The chorus is indeed supposed to be flying on its entry (128b*), but it is very hard to believe, I argue, that they did in fact all fly on, singly or together. Some have held that Hermes flew on (see 944*), but there is no indication of this in the text. There is also Oceanus. Undeniably, he is supposed to fly on his 'four-legged bird' (cf. Pegasus), and his opening anapaests (284ff.) will cover the operation of the machinery: he supplies by far the closest comparison not only from Aeschylus but from all surviving tragedy to the mechane scenes in Aristophanes. On *Prom* 284* I discuss the question further, and consider what bearing it may have on interpretation and authenticity.[2]

[1] Arph. *Gerytades* parodied S. *El* (see Σ on 289); *Phoinissai*, whether of Aristophanes or Strattis, was presumably later than E. *Phoen* and than *Hypsipyle* also; Strattis' *Atalanta* was 'much later' than Arph. *Frogs* (see Σ on 146). Cratinus' *Seriphioi*, *if* that is the subject of the commentary, was probably produced before the death of Cleon (see Σ on Luc. *Tim* 30, p. 116 Rabe—not in Kock).

[2] Some scholars have detected the employment of the mechane in Aeschylus' lost plays. Wilamowitz (*Perser* 390 n. 2; cf. Murray 45f.) offered no fewer than four occasions. But we are totally ignorant about the staging of Perseus in *Phorkides* and the Boreads in *Phineus*, and we have no reason to think that Aeschylus had the corpse of Sarpedon flown on in *Kares or Europe*. The Apulian bell-crater by the Sarpedon Painter (*Illustrations* iii 1, 17), even if it is inspired by Aeschylus' play, can tell us nothing about its original staging. The play was set in Lycia, and presumably, as in the *Iliad*, Sarpedon's body was brought back to Lycia for burial, and presumably it was lamented on stage. This does not mean, however, that it was flown on by means of a machine. Fourthly the only use which is positively attested is in *Psychostasia* (not *Memnon*, as Wilamowitz says): Pollux (4. 130) says that the γέρανοϲ was used for Eos to seize up the corpse of Memnon. I discuss

I sympathize with those (notably Bodensteiner and Flickinger) who try to eliminate the flying machine altogether from the theatre of Aeschylus. One would expect that this complicated and quite bulky apparatus would be a later accession. But Oceanus is difficult to explain away. In the long run this issue is all part of the larger question whether the Greek theatre moved from plain to spectacular or vice versa.

(6) Among the many entries in Pollux which were rejected during the 1890s were the χαρώνιοι κλίμακες (4. 132).[1] While stone subterranean steps have been found in a few theatres, notably in the fourth-century theatres at Eretria and Sicyon (also apparently at Magnesia, Tralles, Segesta, and Philippi), no trace of any such monumental construction has been found at Athens, and all the chief authorities have rejected this method of entry (or exit).[2] But unlike most of the scenic features from late testimonia which were discredited by Dörpfeld the subterranean steps are not totally without support from the plays.[3] Above all it is clear that the ghost of Darius is to be imagined as emerging upwards at A. Pers 681 (see 681b*), and departing down again at 842. The stage directions for the dream of Clytemnestra in Eum are not clear, but she might have used the steps if any were available (see 94*). In A. Psychagogoi the chorus helped Odysseus call up the shades as in the Nekyia (see fr. 475b),[4] and in Aitnaiai the Palikoi are so called πάλιν γὰρ ἵκους' ἐκ σκότου τόδ' εἰς φάος (fr. 27). In S. Polyxena the ghost of Achilles appeared, probably in the prologue, and it seems that, like Darius, he came up from below.[5] And in E. Protesilaos, the hero may have been represented actually returning to Hades, see fr. 646a (Snell Supp to N²). Finally, a recurrent motif in vase painting may suggest that it was quite common in satyr plays for characters to enter from the underworld. Buschor collected several satyr paintings which show a figure half in and half out of the ground, this fully on pp. 432–3, and I strongly doubt whether this has anything to do with Aeschylus' own production.

[1] They are glossed as κατὰ τὰς ἐκ τῶν ἐδωλίων καθόδους κείμεναι, τὰ εἴδωλα ἀπ' αὐτῶν ἀναπέμπουσιν. (The next entry on ἀναπιέςματα—for rivers and furies!—is obscure, and bears marks of belonging to the later theatre with a high stage.)

[2] Including D-R 57f., 248f., Fiechter i 52f., P-C TDA 50f., 146.

[3] Cf. A. Müller 149f., Bodensteiner 672–7, Bethe 84ff. Bethe admittedly has a point when he says that, if there was such an entrance way, it is used remarkably rarely.

[4] Fr. 476 very likely comes from near the beginning of the parodos, where the chorus explains itself. It seems that the chorus comes from the area where the play is set (the Ἄορνος λίμνη? cf. Snell Szenen 110f.).

[5] See fr. 523 P combined with [Longinus] 15. 7 . . . προφαινομένου . . . ὑπὲρ τοῦ τάφου. Calder GRBS 7 (1966) 32 and 44–5 denies (following Welcker) that Achilles appeared above his tomb, but 'Longinus' could hardly have put it more clearly. The sacrifice of Polyxena must have somehow been off-stage.

and traced their inspiration to at least three satyr plays, one of which
may have been S. *Pandora or Sphyrokopoi*.[1] One of Aeschylus' *Sisyphos*
plays apparently had a scene in which Sisyphus emerged from below
(see p. 429); and our fragments may suggest several other such
scenes.[2]

All this speculation about lost plays does not, taken together,
amount to anything as solid as the single surviving scene in *Pers*; but
this evidence might lead to a reconsideration of the archaeology.
While there were certainly no stone-built tunnel or steps as at Eretria,
it seems that the remains do not rule out some sort of crude covered
trench; and archaeologists have now and then favoured some such
arrangement.[3] Polacco has recently argued that there is positive
evidence for a kind of 'fossa scenica' simply covered with wooden
boards (useful for stamping and banging as e.g. S. *Ichn* 211ff., 321ff.).
I am not competent to assess the technical archaeological arguments;
but, if it is a possibility, then a subterranean entry could come in
useful for the staging of a few plays, particularly, it seems, earlier in
the fifth century.

(7) Often in Aeschylus, particularly in the four plays other than
the *Oresteia*, there are references to a mound (πάγος) or some similar
raised area. It has long been disputed whether this was represented
on-stage, and, if so, how this was done.[4] Recently, in the course of an
unconventional contribution on the early theatre and on the staging of
Aeschylus, Hammond has offered an ingenious new theory about this.
On the east side of the orchestra, at V in Dörpfeld's *plan* III (but
neglected in Fiechter and P-C *TDA*), there was once an outcrop of
rock about 5 metres by 5 metres, which Dörpfeld and Dinsmoor
assumed was levelled when the first orchestra was made, since it

[1] Buschor *SBAW* 1937 1ff. ('Feldmäuse') cf. Jobst 112ff., *Illustrations* 33–6.
[2] In S. *Satyrs at Tainaron* Heracles probably went down to Hades and returned
with Cerberus, while the satyrs waited at the mouth of the cave. (I suggest that
this play supplies a possible setting for *PColon* inv. 263, published as a *Wartetext*
by Merkelbach in *ZPE* 1 (1967) 110.) In S. *Ichn* Cyllene's cave is apparently
underground, and she might have entered vertically (cf. Robert *Hermes* 47 (1912)
537ff.). Then in S. fr. 748 P there is the suggestive *Ἄορνος λίμνη*; and similarly in
that strangest of satyr plays—Python's *Agen* (*TrGF* 91 F 1)—Pythionike the dead
hetaira of Harpalus was apparently conjured up from the dead in a *Nekyia*-like
setting (see Snell *Szenen* 110–12). A subterranean entry might also be useful in
the staging of the hauling scene in Arph. *Peace*; and it is also worth recalling that
some Old Comedies centred on figures who returned from the underworld, e.g.
Cratinus' *Archilochoi*, *Ploutoi*, Eupolis *Demoi*, Pherecrates *Krapataloi*, Arph. *Gerytades*.
[3] e.g. Robert 543ff., *Hermes* 47 (1912) 537ff., Noack 7f., 19f., Frickenhaus 61f.,
82f., Buschor (cited above in note 1) 32–4, Schleif *AA* 52 (1937) 35–6, Anti-
Polacco *Nuove ricerche* etc. (Padua 1969) 130ff. esp. 145 (see *plan* 77), Jobst 147.
[4] I have found the most useful previous discussions Capps 70f., Bethe *Hermes*
59 (1924) 109f., Lesky *Ges Schr* 142f., P-C *TDA* 33, Murray 53ff.

would have been partly inside the circle. But Hammond 409ff. argues that this outcrop of rock was in fact left standing in the Aeschylean theatre and was an integral element in its staging. This would certainly be extremely useful for the staging of certain scenes in *Seven*, *Hik*, and *Prom* (see Hammond 416ff.; I have doubts about the tomb of Darius on *Pers* 681*). For these plays I find Hammond's theory distinctly attractive. I am not, however, convinced that the rock was still there for the *Oresteia* (see Hammond 434ff.) since its only use would be for the Areopagus in *Eum*, and it seems implausible that the whole Areopagus should be represented by a small outcrop rather than left entirely to the imagination. It seems better to suppose that the rock was levelled at the same time as the orchestra was reduced and room made for the skene (see p. 457 below), that is shortly before the *Oresteia*.

(8) Finally I come to the side entrances, the most used, though fortunately not the most controversial, place for exits and entrances. Before the introduction of the skene (see appendix C) the only ways of entry and exit for both actors and chorus would probably have been the broad ramps which led up to either side of the orchestra.¹ The usual term for these side entrances is πάροδος: but this term is ambiguous. It first occurs as a part of the theatre in the third century in *IG* xii 9. 207 l. 55 and Semos of Delos (*apud* Athen. 622). It is first used of the entry song of the chorus in comedy at Arle. *EN* 1123a23 (see Sifakis *AJP* 92 (1971) 410ff. esp. 414–16), and of tragedy in the (suspect) twelfth chapter of *Poetics* (see Appendix E, esp. p. 473). Since we have the perfectly good fifth-century term εἴσοδος used of these side ramps in Arph. *Clouds* 326, *Birds* 296, fr. 388, I have thought it best to abandon the traditional but confusing ambiguity, and to use 'eisodos' of the part of the theatre, reserving 'parodos' for the choral entrance song.

Later sources speak of ἄνω πάροδοι which were evidently used exclusively by actors.² Clearly these separate entries belong to the days of the high stage which was inaccessible from the orchestra. It was not, however, archaeology which first gave these the lie, but work on the plays which showed that they are incompatible with the texts themselves. The conclusive discussion was by Bodensteiner (703–24), and

¹ It is conceivable that the terrace wall between the back of the orchestra and the sanctuary of Dionysus below was occasionally exploited, though I doubt it; see *Pers* 681b*, *Prom* 1093b*. (The side ramps apparently had an uphill slope, incidentally. The fact, invoked by Arnott 29, that they led downhill in some other theatres has no bearing at all on the staging of plays intended for the Theatre of Dionysus at Athens.)

² e.g. Plutarch *Vit Demetr* 34, cf. Σ on Arph. *Lys* 321, *Kn* 148. For late terminology connected with the eisodoi see A. Müller 58–60.

since then it has been generally accepted that actors and chorus alike used the same eisodoi.[1]

It has been argued, though only so far as I know by Noack and Flickinger,[2] that the early theatre, i.e. the theatre of Aeschylus, had only one eisodos. This is claimed both on the evidence of archaeology and of the plays themselves. Nothing much can be based on the meagre and controversial archaeological remains, but both Dinsmoor (313) and Hammond (408) accept that Dörpfeld found evidence of both eisodoi in the earliest theatre. As for the plays, what in a play could show that there were one, two or ten eisodoi? Nevertheless most Greek tragedies could make good use of two, if both were available, to signify two separate directions. I shall argue below that two of the earliest tragedies, *Pers* and *Hik*, appear to make use of two eisodoi: they would certainly be impoverished if there were only one.

Assuming, then, that there were always two eisodoi, the most interesting question is whether they represented two directions, and whether those directions were precisely fixed by convention. Pollux (4. 126–7), in a sentence often still quoted as though it were gospel, says that the right entrance led from the country and harbour, while the left led from the city.[3] While some arrangement along these lines probably became established in the later theatre, it is quite clear that no such rigid convention existed in the fifth century. K. Rees in *AJP* 32 (1911) 377ff. showed by the patient accumulation of counter-examples that no fixed division of any kind can be imposed on fifth-century tragedy as a whole.[4] But this need not mean that either eisodos was used at random. In each particular play the dramatist may set up two separate areas of interest off-stage (besides the

---

[1] A futile last-ditch stand was made in Haigh *AT*[3] 191ff. But it was already clear in his unappreciative review of Bodensteiner in *CR* 8 (1894) 176ff. that Haigh was fighting a losing battle, as was made clear by Capps later in the same volume (ibid. 318ff.).

[2] Noack 33ff., Flickinger *TAPA* 61 (1930) 88ff., cf. *Theater* 4th ed. 346–7. Flickinger was effectively but unedifyingly castigated by Allen *UCCA* 1/6 (1937) 169ff.

[3] Cf. Vitruvius 5. 6. 8. Discussions in e.g. A. Müller 158ff., Beare *CQ* 32 (1938) 205ff. The text of Pollux is disputed: see further Rees *AJP* 32 (1911) 378–85, Hourmouziades 128, Joerden 32f.

[4] An earlier attempt along the same lines was made by Niejahr *Commentatio Scaenica* (Halle 1888). M. Bieber *Entrances* 278ff. (a disappointing article) not only foists Pollux's convention on fifth-century tragedy, but even interprets the inscription ΑΣΤΥ[, found in the western eisodos of the theatre (*IG* ii² 3775) as a substantiation of this view. (Obviously it read Ἀcτυ[δάμαc, cf. *TrGF* 60 T 8b.) What on earth would such a thing be cut on stone for, in Bieber's view? As a signpost to actors who had forgotten which eisodos was which? Joerden *Bauformen* 409–10 cf. 379 tries to argue that stage right leads to distant parts and stage left to nearby parts: but this does not work any better than Pollux.

building), and so may establish two different and precise directions for the eisodoi. Their particular topographical significance is thus confined to one play, and has to be established afresh for each individual tragedy. That this is, in fact, the case is one of the chief burdens of Joerden's laborious dissertation (esp. 29ff.). The same is demonstrated more incisively for Euripides by Hourmouziades (128–36).

In A. *Pers*, for instance, it would be helpful if one eisodos led in the direction of 'home', while the other pointed 'abroad', that is to Greece (cf. Dale *Papers* 260, Joerden *Bauformen* 371). There is even more point to two directions in *Hik*: one side represents the dangers of the sea and of the cousins, while the other represents the security of the city of Argos (cf. Joerden *Bauformen* 372f.).[1] The entire conflict of the play is thus given a concrete shape in the two directions of the eisodoi: see *Hik* 1073*. In *Seven* it is likely that the symmetrical entries of Eteocles and the Scout (see 374b*) were from opposite eisodoi, even though there is no clear separation in their spheres of activity off-stage (which is in itself evidence against a fixed conventional significance for the eisodoi). And whoever composed the final anapaests evidently envisaged that the two corpses and the two hemichoruses should move off in opposite directions: see *Seven* 1078*.

So while the precise direction of either eisodos remains flexible and must be established in each play separately, the two ways can in their context take on considerable significance. This is typical of the way that Greek tragedy uses the theatre for dramatic ends.

---

[1] A suppliant play (see *Hik* 1a*) will always tend to have one direction leading from danger and pursuit while the other leads to safety and security. For this in S. *OC* see Fitton-Brown *Greek Plays as First Productions* (Leicester 1970) 13.

APPENDIX C

The Skene in Aeschylus

THERE was a building more or less at a tangent with the orchestra circle[1] on the far side from the audience. This is referred to at Arph. *Peace* 731 as αἱ cκηναί (for some reason not in *LSJ*) and thereafter as ἡ cκηνή.[2] This building served a dual purpose: during the course of a play the outside was part of the world of the play—in tragedy a palace, temple, cave, etc.; in 'real life' it served as a changing room and storehouse for the actors.

In the Theatre of Dionysus at Athens the skene was, it seems, given conglomerate stone (breccia) foundations, perhaps as early as the Peace of Nicias, but more probably in the fourth century.[3] Presumably it was up until then constructed entirely of wood (on the ways in which it may have been temporary or permanent see Hourmouziades 1ff.). The question which concerns me here is whether there always was a skene in the Theatre of Dionysus; or more precisely whether all the surviving plays of Aeschylus were performed before a background building. This is an opportunity to put into practice the principle that the plays themselves should be the first and final criterion on any such issue.

[1] The word ὀρχήcτρα used of the theatre does not occur before [Arle.] *Probl* 901b30 (also anon. comic poet *ap.* Photius s.v. ὀρχήcτρα). It is possible that it belongs to the days when the acting areas of chorus and actors were becoming separated. But we have no other word.

[2] In Plato, Xenophon, Heniochus (fr. 5 K) etc. By the fourth century the word was already used in phrases which had lost their literal sense, notably ἀπὸ cκηνῆc and ἐπὶ cκηνῆc. (The various technical terms which accrued around the skene, e.g. προcκήνιον, ὑποcκήνιον, ἐπιcκήνιον, πρόθυρον, are in all probability irrelevant to the fifth century.)

[3] The date was brought down to the Peace of Nicias by Dinsmoor 318ff. But now Kalligas (*ΑΔ* 18 (1963) *Χρον.* 12ff.) has redated the breccia walls of the later temple to the mid fourth century at the earliest; cf. Travlos *Pictorial Dictionary of Athens* (London 1971) 537, Simon 12 and n. 14 (and my review at *CR* N.S. 25 (1975) 59), Froning *Gnomon* 45 (1973) 79f. However Kalligas also found some even later pottery in the 'foundation trench', and it is far from certain that the sherds he found do provide a *terminus post quem*. Travlos further argues that the long wall (H–H) is nothing to do with the theatre, and that stone foundations for the skene were first laid down about the end of the fourth century (see p. 538 and Plate IV). On Travlos Plan II there is room for a skene front of a maximum of some 20 metres. But see now Newiger *WSt* N.S. 10 (1976) 8off.

Wilamowitz was the first to consider the skene in Aeschylus in this way (*Kl Schr* i 148ff. (1886); cf. *Interpr* 10). As soon as this method was applied, he inevitably made the obvious observation that, while the skene is clearly and repeatedly used in the *Oresteia*, there is no evident trace of its existence in the other four tragedies. He therefore concluded that the background skene was an innovation made in the years between the latest of the other four plays (which he took to be the *Seven* of 467) and the *Oresteia*. One should have thought that Wilamowitz's case was either right or wrong, yet since then there has been no general consensus and little argued controversy: some scholars have simply assumed that there was always a skene, others that there was not.[1] Since I hold that on our present evidence Wilamowitz's case is clearly right and should be accepted, I shall as briefly as may be reconsider the whole matter, taking into account any new evidence. Above all the late dating of *Hik* must be assimilated (see *Hik* 1c*). If, as is now agreed, *Hik* was performed in a year between 466 and 459 (inclusive) then the skene must have been introduced less than ten years before the *Oresteia*. Todt had not thought ten years was long enough, and now Arnott regards the new dating of *Hik* as proof that Wilamowitz was wrong.[2] But why could the innovation not have been made in the late 460s?

So the first task is to scour the four plays for any indication of the presence or absence of a background building. *Prom* is clear: if there was any skene, it must definitely not have represented anything habitable. In *Hik* there is no sign of a building; the scene is set at an open holy place between the shore and the city (see P-C *TDA* 34 on l. 146). Similarly *Seven* is set at an open holy place within the city. The play concerns a royal house, yet there is positively no suggestion of the palace in view.[3] Finally *Pers* too concerns a royal house, yet does not seem to be set before the palace. On the contrary the entry of the Queen

---

[1] It seems that there is at present a swing against Wilamowitz and in favour of a skene for early tragedy; the leaders are Webster and Arnott (cf. e.g. Garvie 161, Jobst 18). However, Hammond, who does not seem to know Wilamowitz's essay, has recently argued the case against a skene in the early theatre.

[2] Todt *Philol* 48 (1889) 534f., Arnott p. 4; also less confidently Joerden 9–12 (in *Bauformen* 373 Joerden changes to the view that the skene was introduced between *Seven* and *Hik*—but there is no trace of it in *Hik*).

[3] P-C *TDA* 36f. thought that the palace formed the background of *Seven*, but his arguments have no substance. The opening is, as he says, like S. *OT*; but that does not mean they were staged identically. At 675 Eteocles calls for his greaves, but that does not indicate that the palace armoury is near at hand; more likely an attendant is carrying them (on the problems of this armour see *Seven* 719a*). P-C thinks that at 861ff. the sisters should enter from the palace; but the long announcement does not refer to it, and the very length argues the contrary. There are in any case reasons to doubt whether the sisters are Aeschylean, see *Seven* 871a*.

at 155 on a chariot is a positive indication that the palace is to be thought of as at a distance.[1] There is one final relevant passage in *Pers* which has been the subject of much discussion, and which, in my view, is another consideration against a background building. At 140ff. we have ἀλλ' ἄγε, Πέρcαι, τόδ' ἐνεζόμενοι / cτέγοc ἀρχαῖον κτλ. I have argued at *HSCP* 76 (1972) 67–8 that this means that the Persian elders are to be thought of as *inside* the council chamber, and that such interior scenes were not uncommon in the earlier theatre.[2] It is incomprehensible that Dale, who saw that this is the significance of the words, nevertheless supposed that they sat down on the steps in front of the council chamber. If they are inside then this is a good reason for supposing that there was no skene, for it would be merely confusing if they are to be thought of as inside a building when they are obviously just outside the front of that building. Similarly the council seats in Phrynichus' *'Persians'* play (see p. 63 n. 2) suggest that there was no background building to that play. Webster (*GTP* 8) says that the seats 'seem to imply a stage-building': but surely they imply the contrary.

There is no sign, then, of the skene representing a building in the four plays outside the *Oresteia*; indeed there are indications to the contrary. This does not rule out the possibility that the actors' changing and property booth was in sight of the audience, and that it was nevertheless not used within the play as a building nor its door as an entrance way. Bethe (83ff. cf. *Hermes* 59 (1924) 114f.), for instance, supposed that the booth was used in the early plays as a feature of the setting—the tomb of Darius, the rock of Prometheus, and so forth: at the same time he admitted that it was not used to represent a building

---

[1] A. Müller (113–16) had assumed that all Greek tragedies were played before a skene; but he made an exception of *Pers* when he saw this point (*Philol* Supp. v (1891) 16 n. 1. Yet several translators have supposed that a skene background represented the palace in *Pers*, e.g. Headlam *tr* 41, Werner 261 (cf. 297, 313, 327), Vellacott 122, Benardete 49. Broadhead xliv n. 3 is quite wrong to say that Wilamowitz held this view. On the rather more sophisticated defence of a palace background by Korzeniewski see p. 107. It has also been held that Xerxes should make his final exit into the palace (e.g. Werner, Murray *tr* 70, cf. Capps 10); but everything points there to a slow procession down one of the side eisodoi, see *Pers* 1077*.

[2] I add some points not included in the article. I omitted to discuss the obvious objection that the Queen's first entry is on a chariot, which does not suit an interior setting. But I think it is sufficient reply that, as with the later ekkyklema, the indoor/outdoor distinction is fluid. The idea that ἐνεζόμενοι could mean 'sitting on the steps in front of' seems to go back to Wilamowitz *Perser* 383. *LSJ* gloss the word here as 'having one's seat or abode in', which does not seem to make sense in the context. Apparently Tucker's translation suggests 'let us go sit within this venerable hall'. This is ingenious, but it would mean that their intention was never fulfilled, and also that the skene although available was never actually used.

with a doorway. While this remains a possibility, it is unlikely that the skene was being used in other ways and yet not as a palace or temple.[1]

It could always be claimed that it is coincidental that none of the four plays calls for the skene or its door. But a quick survey of the surviving plays of Sophocles and Euripides does not encourage this resort. Almost every play positively uses the skene as a palace, temple, house, hovel, cave, or military tent, and almost every one has entrances and exits through the door. S. *OC* and the last part of *Aj* are not set before habitations, but in both cases it looks as though the skene was used to represent a grove or thicket.[2] E. *Hik* does not use the doorway, yet the setting still seems to be before temple doors (l. 104), and it is also likely that the roof was used for the staging of the Euadne scene (980ff., see p. 440). It is, lastly, more than possible that in *Rh* the sleeping place of Hector was not represented by the skene, as is usually supposed, but was in the open or under some rudimentary cover.[3] If the skene was not used in *Rh* this might be the exception which proves the rule, since it would be in keeping with the many realistic ways in which the illusion is built up of a war play set in the open field. Set against the contrast of the use of the skene by Sophocles and Euripides and by Aeschylus himself in *Oresteia* the absence of the background building in Aeschylus' other four plays can hardly be dismissed as coincidental.

A quick survey of the fragments is necessary if this case is to be made cogent. For it has sometimes been claimed that quite a few of the lost plays were performed before a background building;[4] and if the skene was an innovation of the last ten years or less of Aeschylus' life then this should not be true. Among the book fragments that which most strongly suggests a skene is fr. 118 (M) from *Hiereiai*, where it probably represented the temple of Artemis of which the chorus is priestly custodian. Fr. 76 from *Edonoi* suggests, though it does not prove, that the palace of Lycurgus formed the background. But none of the other alleged instances is as strong. Fragments 461 (*Phorkides*), 618 and 746

---

[1] Webster and others have advocated the occasional use of the ekkyklema in the early plays (see e.g. *Pers* 681b*, *Prom* 1b*, 1093b*). But if there is no sign of a doorway being used as such, then it is most implausible to have recourse to a piece of machinery which depends on the existence of a doorway.

[2] Tecmessa emerges from a νάποc at S. *Aj* 894; and it seems likely that Ajax when he kills himself falls near the door of the skene (somehow the actor must get off and return in another part—under cover of the robe put over the corpse at 915ff. and removed at 1003ff.?). In *OC* when Oedipus and Antigone hide in the sacred ἄλcoc from 117 to 137, they may well have used the skene door.

[3] For this suggestion see Björck *Eranos* 55 (1957) 13f., Lattimore *transl* 7. Hector's sleeping-place is never referred to as a cκηνή, but usually as εὐναί (see 1, 23f., 88, 574, 606, 631, 660, cf. A. *Ag* 559 where the Greek εὐναί are in the open field). At 740 the Charioteer speaks of τὸν ὑπαcπίδιον κοῖτον.

[4] See e.g. D–R 199f., Noack 20ff., P-C *TDA* 37. There is no reason to suppose a skene for *Heliades* (*contra* Diggle E. *Phaethon ed* 30).

(unknown plays) may possibly suggest background buildings, but are far from conclusive.[1] It has usually been held that the opening lines of *Myrmidones* (fr. 213) show that Achilles' κλιcία formed the background building to that play. But I have argued in *HSCP* 76 (1972) 66–9 that Achilles is sitting in the open theatre, and is to be imagined as inside his tent. The reasons for thinking that at the beginning of *Myrm* Achilles was sitting 'on-stage' are, I think, strong; and this militates *against* a background building.[2] Finally, among the papyrus fragments of Aeschylus there is just one which evidently requires a skene background: in *Theoroi or Isthmiastai* fr. 17 the background was the Isthmian temple of Poseidon.[3] This notably sparse collection is by no means incompatible with the late introduction of the skene; rather its sparsity is in favour of the theory. Again a comparison with Sophocles and Euripides brings out the contrast. Among the book fragments there are many clear indications of a background building.[4] The papyrus fragments are hard to compare because we have fewer fragments of Sophocles than of Aeschylus and many more of Euripides; none the less the same pattern seems to be clear. Among the papyrus fragments of Euripides it is hard to find a play where there is *not* a clear indication of a skene background.[5]

Archaeology can add little but more controversy to this issue. It has even been suggested that not a single trace remains of the earlier fifth-century theatre, but that all traces were dislodged by the later reconstructions.[6] Even the majority of scholars who accept the antiquity

---

[1] The nonsense in Pollux 4. 109 about παρασκήνιον is far from evidence of the skene in *Memnon* (cf. p. 354 n. 2); and I maintain on pp. 422–3 that Pollux 4. 130 is not to be trusted on the Aeschylean staging of *Psychostasia*.

[2] This argues against a background building in *Phryges* and probably *Nereides* also, since they too were probably set at the κλιcία of Achilles. Further, there is evidence that the Achilles trilogy was an early work *c.* 490, see p. 62 n. 4.

[3] Near the start it seems that the satyrs somehow fix their new portraits to the temple (see 11ff. esp. 18f.). There is probably a further reference at l. 50, and finally at 79ff. the satyrs say that they will not leave the sanctuary under duress. In 83 Snell's Ποcειδᾶνοc ο[ἶκον is attractive. (However the course of the action is disputed, see pp. 421f.)

[4] For example, from Sophocles (P) frr. 458, 775, 815; from Euripides (N²) frr. 65, 310, 350, 399, 623, 671, 694, 790, 1003; cf. P-C *TDA* 51 n. 2, 52.

[5] The skene background is clear beyond reasonable doubt in E. *Antiope, Hyps, Phaethon, Kretes, Erechtheus, Kresphontes, Alkmaion* (*PSI* 1302), *Phrixos* (*POxy* 2685). From Sophocles, *Eurypylos* does not clearly indicate a background, although the palace of Priam is a likely setting (see esp. fr. 1. 91⁷⁺¹¹ Carden). But *Ichn* has Cyllene's cave, and *Inachos* a palace (fr. 2 Carden).

[6] Thus recently Polacco in Anti-Polacco *Nuove ricerche sui teatri greci arcaici* (Padua 1969) 127ff. esp. 159. (The point should be made, incidentally, that if substantial wooden structures are not disturbed, then careful excavation will find traces of them in post-holes, bedding-trenches, and so on: one would not gather this from Arnott 8–10.)

of those three familiar groups of stones SM1, SM3, and J3[1] are not agreed on their position in a reconstruction of the Aeschylean theatre.[2] However, there is a distinct return (notably by Dinsmoor, Hammond, and Travlos) back to Dörpfeld's original theory that both J3 and SM1 are parts of the supporting wall of the original great orchestra circle (over 25 m across). In that case the early skene would either have to be off out of sight of the audience, or else actually *within* the orchestra circle. Obviously this is unlikely and reinforces the theory advocated here, that there was no background building until a few years before the death of Aeschylus. At that stage we may suppose that a smaller orchestra circle (some 20 m across) was marked out within the huge original circle, and that this left room on the far side from the audience for the erection of a not very large skene.[3] Travlos *plans* I and II (p. 540) illustrate this well. (There will have been this intermediate stage, whether the conglomerate wall H–H belongs to the fifth or fourth century, see p. 452 n. 3 above.)

In conclusion, the case based on the plays themselves stands firm. It is not weakened by the fragments and it is not contradicted by archaeological considerations; in fact both seem to support it. Set against this evidence, we can allow late antiquarian sources no weight whatsoever.[4]

---

[1] These sigla in Fiechter *Tafel* I = P-C *TDA* plan III; Hammond figure 2 has returned to Dörpfeld's sigla R, Q, and D.

[2] Fiechter 39ff., followed notably by P-C *TDA* 5ff., reckoned that all three groups were parts of supporting terrace walls beyond the edge of the orchestra circle. If this is right then there always was a space or track in between the edge of the orchestra and the back supporting wall; and this would be an ideal place for the skene to be accommodated. (Some idea of this reconstruction can be gained from Fiechter III *Abb* 29 = Bieber *Hist*[2] fig. 226, and Noack *Abb* 2 = Flickinger fig. 32a (p. 65) = Bieber *Hist*[2] 230.) But this theory seems since Dinsmoor to have lost favour to that discussed in the text.

[3] This seems preferable to Hammond 411ff. (and fig. 3) who puts the skene of the *Oresteia* inside the original circle, and thus cuts off an appreciable segment of the circle.

[4] Webster *Staging* 493ff. has, for instance, built up an ingenious construct of late sources, using stories about the collapse of the ἴκρια (a likely story!) and about the nearby poplar tree, and comes to the conclusion that the original orchestra of Thespis was set in front of the old Temple of Dionysus, and hence that there was always by tradition a background building to tragedy. But the sources are confused and inconsistent, and Webster distorts them in any case: Hammond 391ff. shows clearly that if they are evidence for anything, it is that sixth-century dramatic performances were put on in the Agora. Similarly the story (Vitruvius vii *praef.*) that 'primum Agatharchus Athenis Aeschylo docente tragoediam scaenam fecit' should be disregarded, particularly as dramatist and painter were probably never contemporary (see Rumpf *JHS* 67 (1947) 13, Webster *GTP* 13f.). σκηνογραφία is, of course, attributed to Sophocles by Arle. *Poet* 1449a18f. along with the third actor. It is, however, suspicious that both 'facts' in this sentence were controversial in antiquity, and it is possible that this jotting may be interpolated, or rather

Wilamowitz's hypothesis was, in effect, that the skene was originally out of sight, and that it was first erected on stage and used as a background building in the years between the *Oresteia* and the latest of the other four plays (the date of *Prom* is, of course, a matter of controversy, see Appendix D p. 465). I conclude that his case, based on the plays themselves, is a sound one, and should in the absence of better evidence be accepted. This is of some interest for the earlier plays, not only for the reconstruction of staging, but also for the interpretation of some aspects of dramatic technique.[1]

But by far the most important consequences are for the *Oresteia*. We may, for instance, detect some residual traces of pre-skene theatrical techniques; e.g. the refocusing of scene in *Cho* (584*) and *Eum* (566a*), the long announcement at *Ag* 489ff. (see 503b*), and the chariot entry at *Ag* 783 (783b*). There are possibly also signs of some experiment with the theatrical effects of having a skene. This may have some bearing, for example, on the lack of clear indication of Clytemnestra's movements in *Ag* (258a* etc.), and the lack of distinction whether scenes are set indoors or out-of-doors (cf. *Ag* 1372b*, *Cho* 885*, *Eum* 94*, 566a*). There are also some scenes which have to be reconsidered in the light of the probability that they were among the first ever to be played before a skene: the audience could not have the expectations which later collected around conventional situations. Examples are the death cries of Agamemnon (see *Ag* 1035*, 1372a*) and the tableaux of the corpses (*Ag* 1372b*, *Cho* 973a*).

But by far the most important reward of this whole argument is the light it throws on Aeschylus' adaptability and inventiveness as a dramatic artist. He uses the skene with masterly assurance and effectiveness in the *Oresteia*, often exploiting, and quite possibly inventing, theatrical techniques which became part of the stock in trade of later dramatists.[2]

---

added from a marginal note. I find that Else Arle. *Poet comm* 166–8, 174–9 brackets the words for a mixture of good and bad reasons, and suggests a later Peripatetic source like Chamaeleon. (The fantasy of O. Broneer *UCCA* 1/12 (1944) 305ff. that the captured tent of Xerxes was used as the skene in the theatre hardly deserves mention; yet it is taken seriously by Jobst 13f.)

[1] It may help, for instance, with the explanation of the chariot entry in *Pers* (155b*) and with the 'panoramic' views in *Hik* (234a*, 710*).

[2] Consider, for example, the avenger following the victim inside (*Ag* 974a*, cf. *Cho* 930*), cries from within (*Ag* 1343ff., *Cho* 869, ?*Eum* 117ff. see p. 371), knocking at the door (*Cho* 653*), the entry of the chorus from the skene (*Eum* 140*), exit and immediate re-entry (*Eum* 33/34*—this was never emulated). Moreover, *Ag*, *Cho*, and the first part of *Eum* could not be the masterpieces they are without the skene. Among the dramatically significant uses of it I discuss the way that Clytemnestra dominates the threshold in *Ag* (587*, 855*, 1372a*), and the way that she draws the outsider Aegisthus within (*Ag* 1577b*, 1673a*); the

But not only is the skene worked into the theatrical and scenic fabric of the *Oresteia*, it is also, as the house, prominently and significantly used in the poetry and imagery of the plays. I cannot give here a full account of this, and shall merely point to some highlights in *Ag* alone. (This appears, strangely, to have been neglected in the specialist studies of recurrent imagery in the *Oresteia*.) The house is introduced as witness of the tragedies by the watchman at 37f. It is the last stage of the beacon chain of fire (310f.), it is the house which Clytemnestra guards (606ff. cf. 154–5, 914, 1225), the house which Agamemnon makes cool (966ff.), and it is built round the sacrificial hearth (1035ff., 1056ff. cf. 1297f.). Cassandra sees the palace as a slaughterhouse (1087, 1096ff., cf. 1309ff.), the choir-stalls of the Erinyes (1187ff.), the seat of the children of Atreus (1217ff.), its door is the gates of Hades (1291). Clytemnestra eventually sees that the palace is the home of the *daimon* of the Pleisthenids; yet in the last line she asserts her authority over it (see 1673a*).

The dramatic and poetic uses of the background building in the *Oresteia*, unsurpassed in Greek tragedy and perhaps in all drama, are there in the plays to be seen and appeciated, whether or not the skene was a recent innovation. But an awareness of the probability that the skene was new may help to direct fresh attention on to its many vital functions within the plays, and on to Aeschylus' imaginative and sure-handed genius in the uses he made of it.

delayed but deliberate exit of Cassandra (*Ag* 1330a*, 1330b*) ; the doubling of the meeting of Clytemnestra and the returning man (*Ag* 855* and *Cho* 668*), of the exit to death (*Ag* 974a*, 974b* and *Cho* 930*), and of the revelation of murderer and corpses (*Ag* 1372b* and *Cho* 973a*, 973b*).

APPENDIX D

The Authenticity of *Prometheus Bound*

THE vast majority of scholars are in no doubt that *Prometheus* is entirely
the work of Aeschylus, though some of them are willing to grant
that the authenticity question is still open. In my chapter on the play I
have shown some reluctance to admit the Aeschylean quality of much
of it; and it seems to me that the case against the authenticity of some
if not all deserves very serious consideration. All I shall do here is to fit
my observations and doubts about authorship into a larger framework.
I shall not myself attempt an all-out attack on authenticity, but shall
only attack some of the main arguments on which the generally
accepted *defence* of the play rests. Reading through the scholarly
literature one can pick out the approaches, assumptions, and excuses
on which the orthodox confidence rests: these I shall subject to a
sceptical scrutiny.

The most cogent and thoroughgoing attack on authenticity was
made in 1929 by Schmid.[1] Some of his points are invalid and most are
overstated, but it remains an impressive case which has, on the whole,
been reviled rather than refuted. Kranz 226–8, while accepting the
rest of the play, attacked the choral songs at 526ff. and 887ff.: the
rejection of his case means the rejection of much else in the masterly
fourth chapter of *Stasimon*. On the play as a whole the brief but
trenchant critique by Nestle (in 'Droysen' *tr* 344–53) is worth reading.[2] I am taking it as read that these authors, supplemented by my
chapter, make a case against the play that needs to be answered. All

---

[1] Schmid added little and lost much in *GGL* i 3 pp. 281ff. He traces in both
works the earlier bibliography of the problem; see also Koerte *NJbA* 45 (1920)
201ff., Kraus *RE* xxiii 667ff.

[2] Nestle has influenced Jens and his pupils in the various chapters of *Bauformen*.
Some telling though rather wild observations are made by Rosenmeyer in *The
Masks of Tragedy* (Texas 1963) 51ff. The defence of *Prom* seems somewhat dis-
arrayed, and has depended more on scornful assertion than on solid argument.
The best replies seem to be the general summaries of Séchan (*Le Mythe de Prométhée*
(Paris 1951) 58–64) and Dodds (*Progress* 34ff.). In the last few years there have
been some more detailed works, but none is anything near the last word: Joerden
(134–42) gives a sober but ineffective appraisal, Unterberger (cited above, p. 254
n. 1) an enthusiastic but highly subjective case, and Herington *Author* argues a
lively but incomplete and sometimes unsound defence.

I shall attempt here is a review of the accepted and assumed defences
against attack; though, of course, some of the grounds of attack will be
raised in the course of the discussion. Some of these defences are, I
shall claim, weak, and none is sufficient to settle the entire question.
(i) *Subjectivity.* Doubts about the authenticity of a work of art start
from intuition. I have myself always been dogged by the sense that
Prom does not feel like Aeschylus, does not sound like him, does not
act like him. It is then the place of scholarship to try to bring out or
to explain away the qualities and peculiarities which arouse such subjective feelings. The case must stand or fall on the objective criteria:
but its subjective background does not in any way invalidate it.
Besides, the argument works both ways. Those who defend the play
also tend to start from intuition: they feel that they recognize the hand
of the master (see ix below). But the strength of these feelings in no
way frees a scholar from the obligation to explain the peculiarities and
to substantiate the characteristically authentic qualities.
(ii) *Lack of comparative material.* This is the most widespread and most
weighty defence. But it is, of necessity, not conclusive. It is true that
we have only six other plays, perhaps one for each fifteen that Aeschylus composed, and that this is not a large enough body of evidence to
say with *certainty* what Aeschylus could or could not do. But what
would be large enough? If we had the entire corpus, the same argument would still apply in a diluted form. To have some comparative
material is better than to have none; and we have to work with what
we have. It is fair enough to say that we are so ignorant of Aeschylus'
total output that we can never *prove* the case against (or for): but it is
not permissible to take the step from 'we have not enough evidence to
be sure' to 'therefore the play is genuine'. This simply does not follow.
If *Prom* were the one and only play we had under Aeschylus' name, it
still might not be genuine (witness the fragments of Thespis!).
(iii) *The 'dictates of the plot'.* The argument that any and every
irregularity and peculiarity is somehow dictated, determined, or
demanded by 'the plot' is easy to invoke and appears to banish many
problems at a stroke. However, its use by classical scholars is often very
careless. The argument should be used with great circumspection,
since it rests largely on two questionable assumptions. First it presupposes that in setting about a new composition the dramatist first
determines in the abstract on a story, and then sets about fitting the
subject to his medium. Whereas it is common sense that, in fact, the
characteristics of the medium and the artist's own particular capa-
bilities and techniques within the medium will be important factors
in his choice of a subject in the first place. Secondly it is often assumed
that many features of the dramatization, which are in truth entirely
in the hands of the dramatist, are dictated by the myth. Location,

462   APPENDIX D

selection of scenes, chorus, and characters, sequences, emphasis, thematic priorities, for example, are not dictated but are chosen by the artist: this point is made more fully on pp. 25–8.

I shall give a few connected examples of the way that this argument has been applied over-confidently to *Prom*. It is claimed that certain peculiar features are determined by the 'given fact' that Prometheus is bound on stage for the entire play. But he need not have been: it would have been quite possible to have him bound half-way through, or at the end (in *Prom Lyom* Prometheus may have departed before the end of the play)—it would indeed have been possible for him to be taken off-stage to be bound. Again it is sometimes asserted that the isolation of the scene dictated the disjointedly episodic form of the play. But the degree of isolation (and indeed of disjointedness) is up to the dramatist. Consider the crowding and isolation of Lemnos in the Philoctetes plays of Euripides and Sophocles (see Dio Chrys. *Or* 52). Next, it is always said that the unimportant part of the chorus in *Prom*, particularly the brevity of its songs, is 'determined' by the continuous presence of the actor; even Schmid succumbs to this claim.[1] But look at the other act-dividing songs in Aeschylus where an actor is present: *Pers* 628–80, *Hik* 1–175, 625–709, *Ag* 975–1034, *Cho* 22–84, *Eum* 307–396, 490–565 (for details see *Pers* 622*). These average over 70 lines in length, while the three 'stasima' of *Prom* average exactly 30 lines. (Were the Titans of *Prom Lyom* content with two-strophe ditties?) There is no reason why the continuous presence of an actor should affect choral technique. It makes no appreciable difference to the handling of the chorus in S. *OC* or E. *Tro*.

There are related features besides the brevity and comparative triviality of the choral odes which have also been unjustifiably explained away on these grounds. There is only one lyric dialogue in the play, the parodos; there is no mid-act lyric dialogue or epirrhematic lyric at all. Contrast this with *Pers* (3), *Seven* (4), *Hik* (4), *Ag* (2, both long), *Cho* (2, one very long), *Eum* (3).[2] It cannot be simply claimed that all this is 'dictated' by the role of the chorus, because the use or disuse of the chorus rests in the hands of the playwright. No more can it explain why in the other plays of Aeschylus stichomythia between actor and chorus is the rule, between actor and actor the exception, while in *Prom* it is the other way round (as in Sophocles and Euripides). Put as proportions of actor–chorus stichomythia to actor–actor the

[1] Schmid 20: 'If you have a hero who is immovably fixed throughout the entire drama, then the extent of the choral lyrics would inevitably have to be abbreviated . . .' Focke 260 is much more careful.

[2] Yet it is an accepted cliché that *Prom* is lyrical. Robert Lowell begins his *Author's Note*: 'Prometheus Bound is probably the most lyrical of the Greek Classical tragedies.'

reckoning is: *Pers* 2–1, *Seven* 3–0[1], *Hik* 5–1, *Ag* 7–1, *Cho* 5–3, *Eum* 5–0, and *Prom* 3–5. Features of dramatic technique of this kind are in no relevant sense predetermined. The subsidiary role of the chorus in *Prom*, like its identity, was determined by the playwright himself.

(iv) *Production in Sicily.* We have evidence, some of it far from respectable, that Aeschylus visited Sicily; and we know that he composed at least one play specifically for a Sicilian occasion.[1] So it is sometimes suggested that *Prom* was composed for a Sicilian production, and that this explains some or most of its problems; indeed this solution is occasionally treated as a kind of panacea. The best exposition of this theory is by Focke (esp. 285ff.),[2] who claims that it accounts particularly for the linguistic simplicity and strange spectacular effects of *Prom*. But there is no good reason to think that *Prom* rather than any other play was produced for the Sicilian market. There is, of course, the description of Typhon and the prediction that he will erupt one day (353–76); but if every description or prophecy of some non-Athenian matter were taken as a sign of production elsewhere then there would be hardly any tragedies left for the theatre at Athens. Nor is there any reason to think that Aeschylus would abandon his characteristic language or choral or theatrical techniques for a Sicilian production. (Are Pindar's odes for Sicilian patrons relevantly distinguishable from his others?) If the greatest artist of the time in a peculiarly Athenian art form were to produce abroad, why should he suddenly produce something radically different? We have plays of Euripides which were probably for production outside Athens (*Ba, IA, Andr*?[3]), and yet this has left, it seems, virtually no trace in subject-matter or dramatic technique.

(v) *Trilogy.* It is assumed that *Prom* was the first play of a connected trilogy; and it is widely held that the other two plays of the trilogy would somehow have resolved many of the problems of our play, particularly the theological problems (see e.g. Dodds *Progress* 40–4). Yet *Seven* and *Hik* are not comparably incomplete if taken by themselves, and the three plays of the *Oresteia*, while closely linked in many ways, stand each as a complete and self-sufficient unity (see Wiesmann cited in p. 196 n. 1). All the same, *if* it is true that *Prom Desm* was part of a connected trilogy with *Prom Lyom* and a third play, then this would be a severe weakness in the case of those who attack its authenticity.

[1] The evidence is conveniently collected by Herington *JHS* 87 (1967) 82–5; for further bibliography see Garvie 49 n. 5.
[2] See also Lloyd-Jones *Zeus* 100f. Herington *Author* 112ff. is interested in highly speculative Sicilian influences rather than in a Sicilian production. There are some possible but not certain peculiarities in *Aitnaiai*, see p. 416f.
[3] See Lesky *TDH*[3] 338, Stevens E. *Andr ed* 15ff.

Not only do they have to argue that an entire spurious trilogy found its way into the Aeschylean corpus, but they have to attack the genuineness of *Prom Lyom*, one of Aeschylus' most famous plays, which was parodied by Cratinus (*Ploutoi PSI* 1212 = fr. 73 Austin), and whose fragments seem to bear Aeschylus' authentic mark (admittedly a subjective assertion). Rather than attempt this, one who suspects the surviving play should attack the assumption of the connected trilogy, and should regard *Prom Lyom* as genuine, and argue that it was used as the model for *Prom Desm* (cf. Schmid 97ff., esp. 102f.). This might account for their well-known similarities. I would even hazard the guess that *Prom Desm* was composed, or put together, after Aeschylus' death specifically to be a companion piece to *Prom Lyom*.

I must excerpt here the arguments used on *Hik* 1c* against the overhasty reconstruction of connected trilogies by Aeschylus. He did not always compose in this way, as is shown by the plays of 472 B.C., and there is no reason, besides the masterly construction of the *Oresteia*, to think that it was even his usual practice. All but four or five of his alleged trilogies are the product of learned speculation. Other tragedians returned to the same group of myths in different years, and Aeschylus may well have done the same.

In *JHS* 95 (1975) 185–6 I have questioned the arguments which are usually adduced in favour of a *Prometheus* trilogy; and also added one positive argument from the titles of the plays which suggests the opposite conclusion, that the *Prometheus* plays belonged to different years. I dare say my arguments will be refuted, but until they are I reiterate my opinion that the traditional trilogy is based more on faith than on the evidence.

I should like, however, to pay more attention to a recent theory which was rather curtly dismissed in that article. Lloyd-Jones (*Zeus* 95–103) suggests that the third play after *Prom Desm* and *Lyom* was *Aitnaiai*, which, he argues, was linked to them by thematic and ethical connections. For all the erudition and ingenuity brought to bear, this is, as Lloyd-Jones admits (97, 102) 'nothing but a speculation'. Not only does it involve guesses about the roles of Dike and of Heracles, it also depends on the guesses of others over the attribution of *POxy* 2256 fr. 9 to *Aitnaiai* (see p. 418) and over the Sicilian production of the trilogy (see iv above). A positive point against this theory is that the connective factors in this trilogy would be unlike those in the *Oresteia* or any other Aeschylean trilogy we know of. In the others all three plays either involve a common central character (Dionysus, Achilles; Danaids, cf. Clytemnestra) or the successive generations of a family (Laius–Oedipus–Eteocles, Agamemnon–Orestes). Lloyd-Jones's theological and moral connections with the tenuous thread of the wanderings of Heracles, seem too abstract for

Aeschylus. When such a network of guesses includes such a weak link it cannot take much strain.[1]

(vi) *Stylometrics.* Much of the dispute over authenticity has been diverted into stylometric controversies, and about half of Herington's recent defence is given up to this aspect. But this is a notoriously dangerous and inconclusive field. Not only are we hampered by a corpus too small for statistical purposes and by a lack of well-established controls, but we find it hard to distinguish conscious stylistic device, which may always be varied by the artist sufficiently to run counter to his general pattern, from unconscious linguistic phenomena which should, in theory, be beyond his control. Reading some recent sophisticated studies on the style of some controversial plays (Ritchie, Garvie, Herington) one has the feeling that, given sufficient allowances and careful use of statistics, a clever scholar could prove any play by any of the three tragedians to be the work of one of the other two.

However, assuming that the method has some validity, what Herington seems to have shown is that, if *Prom* is the work of Aeschylus, then it must have been a very late work, in fact his last. The proposal of a late date goes back to Hermann, and was also the conclusion of Koerte's study in *NJbA* 45 (1920) 201ff. But Koerte's finding was that (204) 'if nothing else stood in the way, we should confidently date *Prometheus* 10 or 20 years later than the *Oresteia*'. This tendency often shows through Herington's figures also; and it is yet clearer in the more impartial chapter of Garvie (28–87). Garvie concludes (86): 'In many respects it [*Prom*] belongs to the group formed by the *Oresteia*, and often it seems to have carried to much greater lengths the development that is discernable between the early plays and the *Oresteia*; to such lengths, in fact, that any attempt to explain the development on purely chronological grounds is manifestly absurd.'

(vii) *Date.* Page (*OCT* 288) may be extreme when he says 'quonam anno acta sit fabula omnino ignoramus'. But it is doubtful whether the widely accepted dating of *Prom* to the very last years of Aeschylus' life does anything to alleviate its problems. Some may be happy to see it with Bergk (*Gr. Literaturgeschichte* iii (Berlin 1884) 312) as 'die reife Frucht dieser letzten Lebensjahre': for me, however, this would only accentuate and aggravate the problem of its authenticity, since then *Prom* must be seen as belonging to the same years as the *Oresteia*. The *Oresteia* is for us Aeschylus' masterpiece. It is outstanding for (among other qualities) the mastery of its poetry and imagery, its social and

[1] If a late date is accepted for *Prom Desm* (see vii below) this is a further blow to Lloyd-Jones' theory since it would be too late for Hieron. And would Hieron have appreciated the obvious anti-tyrant politics of *Prom*? (cf. Herington *Author* 113).

moral wisdom, its handling of the chorus, its use of formal structure, and (as I hope to have indicated in the relevant chapters) its use of dramatic and theatrical techniques. None of the three earlier plays reaches quite the same mastery of these qualities; and *Prom*, for all its impressiveness, suffers most of all by comparison.[1] In the chapter I have concentrated on *Prom*'s shortcomings as a piece of drama, though its comparative shortcomings in these other respects may have been incidentally shown up. If only *Prom* could be regarded as a youthful work, where ideological and argumentative fervour dominate to the detriment of poetry, construction, and theatre, then that might dispel some of the doubt (at least of my doubt) as to its shortcomings. But the evidence of dramatic technique no less than of stylometrics points to a late date, either Aeschylus' last years or after his death.

(viii) *Spectacular effects.* The text of *Prom* indicates some extravagant bouts of theatrical spectacle (see 128b*, 284*, 1093*); and some scholars have contrived to add other grandiose visual effects (see e.g. 1b*, 944*). All this spectacle and stage machinery are usually reckoned to be typical of Aeschylus, and *Prom* is seen, above all by Murray (38ff.) and Reinhardt (76–8, cf. Wilamowitz 157f.), as the outstanding illustration of this aspect of Aeschylus' theatre. I have argued throughout that, while Aeschylus was keenly alive to the visual possibilities of his theatre and used them to great effect, he did not indulge in spectacle for its own sake without any integral dramatic meaning; and I have questioned one by one all the places where there is supposed to have been a visual extravaganza without further significance for the play as a whole. This is hardly possible for *Prom*. We are faced with odd examples of what Nestle called ('Droysen' *tr* p. 352) 'rein Theatercoup ohne wirklichen Sinn'. If *Prom* is genuine then I should probably have to admit some unwelcome counter-examples to my thesis.[2]

(ix) *Grandeur of conception.* It is, above all, the primeval setting and scale of the tragedy and the gigantic defiance of Prometheus which has gained *Prom* its high esteem in the eyes of Europe since the Renaissance, and particularly in the eyes of the Romantic movement and its heritage. It is this grandeur of conception which in the last resort, I suspect, persuades most critics that *Prom* must be the work of the great master himself. '*Prometheus* is authentic Aeschylus. The scenic grandeur, the profundity of thought, and the entire archaic composition are

[1] Rather as Shakespeare's brilliant contemporaries are dimmed when seen by his light. Herington (*Author* 106) aptly quotes Hamlet: 'Look here upon this picture, and on this.'

[2] Bethe (158–85) tried to eliminate all the spectacular events from *Prom* as late-fifth-century interpolations into what was originally an archaic and austere play. I discuss some of his arguments on e.g. *Prom* 128b*, 1093a*.

witness of this', Kranz 226.[1] I do not deny a certain Wagnerian grandeur, though it is not much to my taste.[2] But any such subjective response can only be used as a starting-point for a defence, and it is no proof in itself (see i above).

Primeval grandeur of conception is *per se* no guarantee of the greatness of the author. Any inflated poetaster can have a grandiose conception: most do. In more recent times there have been only too many allegories of basic forces, epics of fundamental symbolism, which are disasters as works of art. It is the *way* in which the vision is translated into the medium which makes a great work of art. Aeschylus did indeed dwell on the times when Zeus' power was new (cf. *Eum*, *Prom Lyom*), and he portrayed stubbornness and courage on a heroic scale (cf. Eteocles, Cassandra, the Achilles trilogy); but so in all likelihood did contemporaries and followers whose less than great works were soon forgotten. It was Aeschylus' genius as a dramatist and poet that turned these conceptions into great tragedies.

And it is precisely on dramatic and poetic grounds that I, for one, have doubts about the authenticity of *Prom*. It is all very well as a romantic vision of defiance against the powers of tyranny and destructiveness, but it is not so good as a *drama*. It is episodic and disjointed, it lacks forward dramatic momentum, and it is on the whole sluggish and wordy. I quote Nestle ('Droysen' *tr* 351f.): 'The two scenes which we would call dramatic come at the beginning and the end, the scenes which depict the clash of Zeus and Prometheus: everything in between is stagnation . . .' It needs close study of dramatic and thematic techniques rather than a romantic sense of the portentous to rebut such a criticism.

(x) *Aeschylus' cosmic development.* In a series of articles, and finally in his monograph, Herington has developed a theory of the development of Aeschylus' cosmic view, which seems to have found wide acceptance. According to this Aeschylus' earlier view, represented by *Pers* and *Seven*, moved from disaster to annihilation, while his later view (Danaid trilogy, *Oresteia*, Prometheus trilogy) had 'rather the complex movement of a lyric triad, turn—counter turn—non-responding epode' (*Author* 79); and in this later scheme the 'epode' finally reconciles opposing cosmic forces.

This is built on thin air. As a single independent play about a recent historical event, *Pers* must be left out of account, leaving the *Seven* trilogy as the sole representative of the earlier world-view. The

[1] Cf. Smyth *Aeschylean Tragedy* (Berkeley 1924) 92ff., Murray *passim*, Reinhardt 27f., 64ff., Herington *Author* 106ff. etc.
[2] Needless to say Wagner was very impressed by *Prom*: 'die tiefsinnigste aller Tragödien'—cf. *GGL* i 3 p. 308.

reconstruction of the Danaid trilogy is pure speculation based solely on the analogy of the *Oresteia*; the alleged Prometheus trilogy is the problem in question: so this leaves the *Oresteia* as the one and only basis for the later view. For all we know, many of Aeschylus' earlier works may have ended with reconciliation; in fact there is some evidence that this was the case with the probably early Achilles trilogy (see *HSCP* 76 (1972) 76). For all we know most of the later works ended with annihilation. Herington asks us to believe in a sublime revolution in Aeschylus' world-picture solely on the evidence of *Seven* and *Oresteia*.[1] The theory is almost as grand and empty as *Prom* itself.

(xi) *The treatment of Zeus*. A final word on this, the most controversial aspect of *Prom*, in this century at least. Lloyd-Jones has recently said (*Zeus* 95) 'the differences in language, style and dramatic technique, appreciable though they are, would not I believe by themselves have caused the play's authenticity to be disputed. Most of the doubts expressed on this score have been occasioned by the play's theology.' So I should make it clear that this aspect plays a minimal part in my own equivocations over authorship, which are based primarily on considerations of dramatic technique (in its widest sense). Lloyd-Jones (*JHS* 76 (1956) 55ff., *Zeus* 84ff.) has argued that Aeschylus is not a profound or original theologian, but that he is a great dramatist and poet. And it is as drama and poetry, not as theology, that I have doubts about *Prom*. I have yet to see it shown that a coherent and consistent theology was high among Aeschylus' priorities. Why should he not have adapted his gods to suit his dramatic and thematic priorities? 'Whatever private worship the poet may have favoured or whatever his personal philosophical interests, when it was a matter of using the gods in his plays Aeschylus was, within the limits of mythology, bound only by the dictates of his dramatic purposes', Rosenmeyer 251 (Rosenmeyer's whole attack (242–60) on viewing Aeschylus as a theologian deserves attention).

Nevertheless, there are objections to Lloyd-Jones's case that Zeus in *Prom* is just the same as elsewhere in Aeschylus, namely (as he claims) the same primitive, harsh, and self-interested superpower as in Hesiod. For Zeus in *Prom* is not presented neutrally as a harsh, inevitable fact: we are positively asked, obliged, to hate Zeus and to side against him. Not only must we side with Prometheus who sided with men, but the manifestations of Zeus' power through his henchmen and through his treatment of Io and Prometheus are shown as repulsive brutality. We are given no chance to view this in a larger perspective, for the play is

---

[1] If the Danaid trilogy was performed in 466 B.C., as is quite possible, then Aeschylus' cosmic revolution will have come precisely during 467–6!

completely partial.[1] However the balance may have been redressed by the rest of the alleged trilogy, *Prom Desm* gives Zeus no positive attributes besides his brutish power. Secondly, Zeus is presented in human political terms: the analogy with the upstart τύραννοϲ is obvious and sustained, both in the way he came to power and in the way he wields it.[2] Although it is set in primeval times and at the desert verge of the world, *Prom* is more blatantly and precisely *political* than any of Aeschylus' other plays. *Prom* is, in some ways, an anti-tyrant tract which merely uses Zeus for political allegory. The religious problem, if there is one, is one of the use of the gods for dramatic purposes, not one of theology.

[1] In defence Herington (*Author* 84f.) offers the interesting analogy of the Erinyes in *Eum* 1–396, where they are still seen as repulsive monsters. But the context and dramaturgy there are much more complex and subtle. First, these are the same Furies which inhabited the palace in *Ag* and which Apollo threatened against Orestes in *Cho* (283ff.). Then the Dream of Clytemnestra and the first song of *Eum* give us some partial, though still obscure, sense of the wrong done to their side of the dispute (see *Eum* 139*). Apollo does not unequivocally win the *agon* in 179–234; the Erinyes, like Orestes, suffer from the relentless pursuit (see 244a*); the deadlock at Athens is two-sided, for the Erinyes are as powerless as Orestes to resolve the situation (see 276*). Although the Erinyes are seen almost exclusively through Apolline eyes, it is clear before Athena arrives that there are two sides to the case. There is no such subtlety in the partiality of *Prom*.

[2] Cf. e.g. *GGL* i 3 p. 299 n. 2, Thomson *ed* 6ff., Séchan (cited above, p. 460 n. 2) 53–5, Méautis *L'Authenticité et la date du Prométhée* etc. (Neuchâtel 1960) 46ff., Podlecki *Political Background* etc. (Ann Arbor 1966) 103ff.

APPENDIX E

[Aristotle] *Poetics*, Chapter 12

IN §5 I asserted that the structural account of Greek tragedy given in *Poetics* 1452b17–27 does not truly reflect the way that the tragedies themselves are put together; and I set about finding a new more faithful analysis. Although the terms and definitions in *Poetics* have in practice fallen into some disuse, they are still often quoted and taken for granted, and the wholesale rejection of them calls for some justification.[1] So in this appendix I put those terms and definitions to the test: of each term I shall ask whether it was in use before Aristotle's time and if so with what meaning; and of each definition I shall ask whether it does in fact accord with the fifth-century tragedies.

In Kassel's Oxford text the chapter reads: Μέρη δὲ τραγωιδίας οἷς μὲν ὡς εἴδεςι δεῖ χρῆςθαι πρότερον εἴπομεν, κατὰ δὲ τὸ ποςὸν καὶ εἰς ἃ διαιρεῖται κεχωριςμένα τάδε ἐςτίν, πρόλογος ἐπειςόδιον ἔξοδος χορικόν, καὶ τούτου τὸ μὲν πάροδος τὸ δὲ στάςιμον, κοινὰ μὲν ἁπάντων ταῦτα, ἴδια δὲ τὰ ἀπὸ τῆς ςκηνῆς καὶ κομμοί. ἔστιν δὲ πρόλογος μὲν μέρος ὅλον τραγωιδίας τὸ πρὸ χοροῦ παρόδου, ἐπειςόδιον δὲ μέρος ὅλον τραγωιδίας τὸ μεταξὺ ὅλων χορικῶν μελῶν, ἔξοδος δὲ μέρος ὅλον τραγωιδίας μεθ' ὃ οὐκ ἔςτι χοροῦ μέλος· χορικοῦ δὲ πάροδος μὲν ἡ πρώτη λέξις ὅλη χοροῦ, στάςιμον δὲ μέλος χοροῦ τὸ ἄνευ ἀναπαίστου καὶ τροχαίου, κομμὸς δὲ θρῆνος κοινὸς χοροῦ καὶ ἀπὸ ςκηνῆς. μέρη δὲ τραγωιδίας οἷς μὲν ⟨ὡς εἴδεςι⟩ δεῖ χρῆςθαι πρότερον εἴπαμεν, κατὰ δὲ τὸ ποςὸν καὶ εἰς ἃ διαιρεῖται κεχωριςμένα ταῦτ' ἐςτίν.

[1] I name a handful of those who have uncritically attempted to make an acceptable structural analysis out of *Poet* ch. 12: Waldaestel *De trag. graec. membris e verbis Aristotelis recte constituendis* (Neubrandenburg 1837), Ascherson *Umrisse der Gliederung des gr. Drama* (*NJbPh* supp. 4. 419ff.), Westphal *Prolegomena zu Aischylos Tragödien* (Leipzig 1869), Oehmichen *De compositione episodorum trag. Graec. externa* (Erlangen 1881), Haigh *TDG* 348ff. Recently Aichele has based on an uncritical acceptance of the *Poetics* analysis a morass of statistics, which, quite apart from the rigid indiscrimination of the method, are of little value because of their arbitrary structural basis. Aichele never defends his analysis, but merely presents it in tables as an accomplished fact. Even those who use the traditional analysis come to very different results: compare the tables at the back of Detscheff with those at the back of Aichele. Of the qualifications and partial rejections of *Poet* ch. 12 the best known is Wilamowitz 1–2; fuller is Detscheff 39ff., cf. also Goodell 71ff., Weissinger.

So far as I know, no other attempt at a complete structural analysis of Greek tragedy is preserved from the scholarship of many centuries after Aristotle. There are some attempts from late antiquity and from Byzantine times; but while they supply some variations, additional terms and illustrations, they are all sufficiently similar to *Poetics* for us to be reasonably sure that they belong to the same tradition, if they are not derived directly from it.

I have noted the following (they are in no particular order):

(i) An interpolation in the hypothesis to A. *Pers.* This classifies the choral elements as παροδικά, cτάcιμα, and κομματικά.

(ii) Marginal scholia in three late MSS. of Arle. *Poetics* ch. 12; see Vahlen *Poet ed* pp. 26f. This is the same as (i).

(iii) Scholion on A. *Prom* 397 in Cod. Neap. (T), published by Smyth in *HSCP* 32 (1921) 31. This is by Triclinius. It is similar to (i), but adds some very strange illustrations.

(iv) Scholion on Arph. *Wasps* 270 (not in R or V); based on (iii) and probably by Triclinius, see Fraenkel A. *Ag ed* iii, 635 n. 1.

(v) Tzetzes περὶ τραγικῆc ποιήcεωc, edited by Kaibel in *CGF* 43ff. This incorporates most of *Poet* ch. 12 in one place or another.

(vi) *Tractatus Coislinianus* §9, in Kaibel *CGF* 52f. This is on comedy, but gives similar definitions to *Poet* ch. 12 for the spoken parts and leaves χορικόν without subdivision.

(vii) Pollux 4. 53. The four choral terms are listed without definition in a huge catalogue of poetic terms. They recur (plus ἐπειcόδιον) in 4. 108, but with different definitions from *Poet* ch. 12.

(viii) Byzantine compilation on tragedy by ?Psellus, edited by Browning (cited above, p. 57 n. 2), §1 and §4. This is fairly close to Ar. *Poet* ch. 12; but it adds extra terms, and gives no definitions (see also Glucker *Byzantion* 38 (1968) 269–71).

(ix) *Life* of Aristophanes §16. On parts of comedy; similar to (vi).

I now take the terms and definitions one by one.

(1) πρόλογοc. This term was indeed current in the fifth century, and it is obviously handy. But it emerges from the discussion of Nestle (6–13) that before Aristotle, and usually after him too, the term was used only of the first expository speech of the play, and not of the entire part up till the entry of the chorus, regardless of how it was constructed. And we may wonder how in terms of structural analysis the *prologos* on the *Poetics* definition is any different from any other non-choral element or act, except that it is the first. When we turn to the plays we find that the *prologos* can be so broken up that it is often not helpful to regard it as a μέροc ὅλον: see e.g. on *Eum* 139*. Moreover, the division point at the end of the *prologos* and the beginning of the next part (*parodos*) is not always as clear-cut as this definition implies; the transition can be complex and gradual, especially in Euripides.

A. *Prom* is a case in point: see *Prom* 88*. Finally there are occasions when the beginning of the *parodos* definitely does not mark the transition, notably in E. *Hel* and *Hyps*, where the strophic lyric structure begins before the chorus enters (see p. 64 above).

So this is a useful term, but the definition given does not do justice to the complexity of fifth-century practice, and probably does not preserve the fifth-century usage.

(2) ἐπεισόδιον. This term and related words do not have the meaning 'act' elsewhere in *Poetics*, elsewhere in Aristotle, or in earlier comedy.[1] Primarily it has, as one might expect from the first prefix, the same kind of associations as the English adjective 'episodic', viz. parenthesis, digression, subplot, interlude. To supply the sense 'act' ἐπεισόδιον, though it could be argued to mean this at *Poet* 1449a28 and 1456a31, probably does not recur until much later (see above). Not only is there no evidence that this was the fifth-century sense, there is even evidence that it meant something quite other.

Turning to the definition the obvious problem is ὅλων χορικῶν μελῶν. Most scholars, including Aichele, forced into circularity by the shortcomings of the chapter, simply equate ὅλον χορικὸν μέλος with *stasimon*. They then have to disregard the inadequate *Poetics* definition of *stasimon*, and simply regard both terms as meaning 'strophic choral song'. But in practice, as already shown in §5, the acts of Greek tragedy cannot be properly defined as 'the parts in between strophic choral songs' (which would make single acts of e.g. S. *Phil* 730–1471, E. *Her* 815–1428, *Hel* 252–1106, *Or* 843–1693). For there are in fact several other ways of dividing acts other than by strophic choral songs (as may be seen at a glance by comparing the table of strophic songs in Kranz *Forma* 26–7 with the table in *Stasimon* 124–5 which contains all lyrics which in Kranz's view divide *epeisodia*).

The upshot of §5 (pp. 51–3) is, in effect, that if an 'episode' or act is to be defined in a helpful and significant way, then it is not necessarily the case that it comes in between ὅλων μελῶν, nor necessarily between χορικῶν μελῶν, nor even on occasion between μελῶν of any kind. In fact the definition of the acts in terms of the act-dividing songs, besides being circular, does not do justice to the actual practice of the playwrights. Even if one wants to preserve the dubious term ἐπεισόδιον, one still has to work out a definition independently of *Poetics* ch. 12.

(3) ἔξοδος. The definition of this is so inane that it betrays the others. In the fifth century the word was evidently used of the music

[1] For Old Comedy see Metagenes fr. 14K, Cratinus fr. 195K; cf. Norwood *CPh* 25 (1930) 217ff., Fraenkel *Beobachtungen zu Aristophanes* (Rome 1962), 164, n. 2. For a discussion of ἐπεισόδιον in general in *Poetics*, see Nickau *MH* 23 (1966) 155ff. On p. 160 he finds no problem over the different sense of the word in ch. 12.

which accompanied the final exit of the chorus: see Arph. *Wasps* 582 (and scholia), Cratinus fr. 276K. Even the late theorists follow this obvious sense, and do not share the useless definition of *Poetics*.[1] If we once apply this definition to the surviving tragedies it brings together a multifarious collection of extracts, sometimes almost half the play, which have nothing significant in common except that they all end in the end of the play. Not only is there the difficulty that acts may be divided in other ways than by a χοροῦ μέλος, but that the last act is indistinguishable in structural terms from any other act.

The scheme behind this definition and the definition of the other non-choral parts is only too clear: the πρόλογος is the μέρος ὅλον *before* the first choral song, ἐπεισόδια are μέρη ὅλα *between* choral songs, and so ἔξοδος is the μέρος ὅλον *after* the last choral song. Facile symmetry of definition overrides all applicability. And not only does this rigid scheme fail to do justice to the complexity of the tragedians' practice, it also throws the whole problem of the isolation of acts on to the definition of the 'choral songs', a definition which is not then provided.

(4) πάροδος. The term is probably used of the entrance song of the chorus in comedy at Arle. *EN* 1123a19ff. (see Sifakis *AJP* 92 (1971) 410ff. esp. 414–16); but otherwise it only recurs in later writers. (On its other meaning as part of the theatre see p. 449.) Why for the purposes of structural analysis should the first choral song be distinguished from the other act-dividing choral songs? It is, in fact, the case that it is more often structurally peculiar than the other songs (see *Prom* 88*), but this is simply because the opening parts of the tragedy lend themselves to more structural fluidity. The only point in distinguishing *parodos* from *stasimon*, as A. M. Dale (*Papers* 34ff.) clearly shows, is not structural but choreographic. She decides (34) 'In the parodos the chorus is "coming on", and has to move on to and across the orchestra to take its place in the middle; in all the stasima . . . its evolutions are performed from that middle position.'

When one applies the definition to the plays themselves there are the usual qualifications. The most obvious are that the entry of the chorus is not always the clear point of act-division, and that the first song is often not purely choral but takes the form of a lyric dialogue (see further *Prom* 88*, and cf. Kranz *RE* xviii 1686ff.).

(5) στάσιμον. The word does not occur before Aristotle and does not recur until much later. The scholiast on Arph. *Frogs* 1281 was quite wrong to think that στάσις μελῶν there has anything to do with it.

The definition in *Poetics* has given scholars a great deal of trouble since it is so broad, and yet so limited in the kinds of choral song it excludes. Dale (*Papers* 35) is probably right that it means to exclude

[1] See e.g. Pollux 4. 108, and the works cited on p. 471 as nos. (iv), (v), (vi), (ix).

recitative metres. But in that case it is no help at all with identifying act-dividing choral songs; above all it does not distinguish them from choral songs, whether strophic (the only example is A. *Hik* 418ff.) or astrophic, nor from lyric dialogues, which occur *within* acts and not between them. Most scholars simply abandon the *Poetics* definition, and arbitrarily equate *stasimon* with strophic choral songs. And whenever they encounter songs which divide *epeisodia* and yet are not strophic or not wholly choral, they say that they 'stand in place of a stasimon' (see p. 52). But since *epeisodion* is defined as the part between strophic choral songs, i.e. on this account 'stasima', the process is obviously circular. Some other structural factor has to be introduced in order to break the circle, and for most scholars this has been intuition: my §5 tries to be more objective.

The explanation of *stasimon* given by Dale (quoted on p. 473 above) is convincing, as is her rejection of the late scholarship, unwisely accepted by Wilamowitz and Kranz, which took the word to mean that the chorus stood still as it sang. So cτάcιμον is not a structural term at all, but a choreographic one, and neither the term nor the definition can be accepted.

(6) κομμόc. Scholars take this word from here and use it to cover any lyric dialogue whatsoever. But in A. *Cho* 423 and throughout antiquity a *kommos* is a certain kind of lyric dialogue, a dirge: this is what the definition in *Poetics* also says—θρῆνοc. The term denotes content and has nothing to do with structural function. It is completely unjustified to extend *kommos* to all lyric dialogues regardless of their contents just because *Poetics* supplies no alternative term. In fact the majority of lyric dialogues are not θρῆνοι (see Cornford *CR* 27 (1913) 41ff., Diehl *RE* xi 1195ff.). The important distinction for structural purposes is between those lyric dialogues which divide acts ('in place of a stasimon'), and those, the great majority, which come within acts. Since *kommos* is a subdivision of lyric dialogues in terms of content, it is necessarily no help with this.

(7) τὰ ἀπὸ τῆc cκηνῆc. This is left without a definition. So it remains unclear whether it is meant to refer only to actors' monodies and duets, or to all lyrics in which actors take a part.[1] Either way the phrase refers to a mode of delivery and is not a structural term.

Now to draw together the main points from these observations. First, the usage: most of the seven terms were current by Aristotle's time with a theatrical sense—πρόλογοc, ἐπεισόδιον, ἔξοδοc, and probably κομμόc. But only *prologos* seems to have carried a sense similar to the one it is given by definition in the chapter.

---

[1] μονωιδία is a perfectly good fifth-century term for solo songs, see Arph. *Peace* 1012, *Thesm* 1077, *Frogs* 849, 944, 1330, fr. 154K.

Turning to the six definitions, the basic scheme underlying them, as in all the late analogies on p. 471, is the distinction between actors' speech and choral song. Both kinds of delivery are given three defined subdivisions. The 'acts' are defined in terms of their relation to the songs: *prologos* before the first, *exodos* after the last, and *epeisodia* in between. Of the three choral parts, on the other hand, *parodos* is apparently distinguished by choreography, *stasimon* by delivery and metre, and *kommos* by delivery and subject-matter. When we turn to the plays we find that this does not give us a satisfactory classification of songs in structural or any other terms. And within the *Poetics* scheme we cannot even begin with the spoken parts without an analysis of the songs, since they are defined in terms of the placing of the songs. In fact, to be blunt, we are no better off than if the *Poetics* chapter had simply said that tragedy consists of a succession of acts coming between choral lyrics. And I hope to have shown that this hardly begins to do justice to the truth. My conclusion is that the chapter must be discarded, and a fresh start made without it.

It is enough for my purposes to have shown that, regardless of the authority of its author, the chapter is totally inapplicable to fifth-century tragedy. But its authorship must be seriously in question. It is often claimed (see e.g. Lucas Arle. *Poet ed* 136) that the chapter might fit late-fourth-century tragedy better, and this might be partly true; but there are things in it which can have fitted no tragedy at all, and which we should be reluctant to attribute to any careful student, let alone to a genius of analysis and classification. I have in mind, for example, the inclusion of τὰ ἀπὸ τῆc cκηνῆc under χορικά, the definition of ἔξοδοc, and the implication that all lyric dialogue is threnetic. Moreover it is generally accepted that the chapter does not belong in its present position in *Poetics*, and that it is hard to fit it in anywhere else. This fact and the way that 1452b25–7 repeats 1452b14–16 and thus makes the chapter a self-contained unit strongly suggest that it has been added. In the nineteenth century it was widely accepted that the chapter is an interpolation, notably by Ritter, Bernays, Gomperz; but more recently this has been upheld only by Else. Else's attack on the chapter (*comm* 359–63) makes several telling points quite apart from those I have raised, and seems to me one of the best things in an uneven book.[1]

One may guess at authorship. It is notable that in the discussion of usage it repeatedly emerged that the terms were not used in the same way as elsewhere in Aristotle, let alone in the fifth century, but that

[1] I am grateful to Professor R. Kassel for letting me quote from his correspondence with Professor Lloyd-Jones on this subject: 'Ich halte die Verdachtmomente gegen das Kapitel [12] für *sehr* stark; auf jeden Fall ist es an seiner jetzigen Stelle, zwischen 11 und 13, ein Fremdkörper.'

they did recur in the same context in the late scholarship listed above. This suggests a common source, as likely as not a late Peripatetic patchwork of learning on tragedy. It is particularly noticeable that Tzetzes' 'poem' ((v) on p. 471) has many details in common with the chapter, and yet quotes as his source Εὐκλείδης τε καὶ λοιποί (3). In 51ff. he gives exactly the same singularly useless definition of *stasima*, and he attributes it not to Eukleides but to ἄλλοι, though he does not apparently mean to exclude Eukleides. The source might be a commentary on Aristotle by one of *Die Schule des Aristoteles*, e.g. Themistius (cf. Glucker *Byzantion* 38 (1968) 271f.) ; or it might be Eukleides.[1]

[1] For the little that can be said of this Eukleides see Cohn in *RE* vi 1003. Tzetzes and the related material have now been edited by Koster in *Scholia in Aristophanem* I. 1A (Groningen 1975). Koster p. xxviii may well be right that Eukleides is pure fiction.

APPENDIX F

Aristotle *Poetics* on ὄψις

IN §2 (p. 25) I maintained that Aristotle's *Poetics* was partly responsible for the neglect of the visual meaning of Greek tragedy. There are really three separate though connected insinuations in *Poet*: that the play is best appreciated when read, that the visual aspects of a play in performance are mere externals put there to satisfy the spectators, and that the visual aspects of the tragedy are the sphere not of the dramatist but of theatre mechanicals.

Thus, first, at *Poet* 1450b18ff. Aristotle remarks ἡ γὰρ τῆς τραγῳδίας δύναμις καὶ ἄνευ ἀγῶνος καὶ ὑποκριτῶν ἔστιν. Similarly at 1453b1ff. it is maintained that tragedy should be able to have its full effect ἄνευ τοῦ ὁρᾶν. This comes out most clearly in his claim for the superiority of tragedy over epic, where Aristotle asserts in 1462a11ff. ἔτι ἡ τραγῳδία καὶ ἄνευ κινήσεως ποιεῖ τὸ αὑτῆς . . . διὰ γὰρ τοῦ ἀναγινώσκειν φανερὰ ὁποία τίς ἐστιν. Now these places are not strictly irreconcilable with an appreciation of the visually significant in a tragedy: by keeping the mind's eye constantly and keenly on the visualization of the play the reader can fairly well appreciate this aspect; cf. Aristotle himself at 1462a17f. καὶ τὸ ἐναργὲς ἔχει καὶ ἐν τῆι ἀναγνώσει καὶ ἐπὶ τῶν ἔργων. (The modern critic can, and must, do this, since performances are few and far between and usually pay little attention to the dramatist's visual intentions.) But elsewhere in *Poet* Aristotle does not reinforce the hope that this is what he means when he says tragedy can have its full effect ἄνευ τοῦ ὁρᾶν and ἄνευ κινήσεως. Rather he suggests that all that performance adds to the text is external embellishment. Even in the much-quoted passage where he insists that the playwright should envisage the performance (1455a22ff.) he has in mind his usual priorities of probability and consistency, and not the potential significance of the visual embodiment of the play.

In *Poet* Aristotle does not say in so many words that the visible presentation of tragedy is mere outward show to please the vulgar, and that the discriminating read the text. But he does say that the theatre-going public and the actors who play up to them have vulgarized and spoiled the tragedies; and in his day this was probably true.[1]

---

[1] Arle. *Poet* 1453a33ff., 1461b29ff., 1462a5ff., *Polit* 1341b15ff., 1342a18, *Rhet* 1403b32ff.; cf. Aristoxenus fr. 124 Wehrli, Plato *Laws* 659bff., 700eff. See P-C

But from saying that the vulgar demand spectacle it is not a long step to saying that some spectacle is put there solely to please the mob, and from there to saying that spectacle in general is merely inessential show. This standpoint has been common among modern critics (though it is seldom put so bluntly); and it has been particularly damaging to an appreciation of Aeschylus' stagecraft (see §4).

There are also two well-known passages where Aristotle asserts that visual presentation is not really the province of the ποιητής. At 1450b16–20 we have ἡ δὲ ὄψις ψυχαγωγικὸν μέν, ἀτεχνότατον δὲ καὶ ἥκιστα οἰκεῖον τῆς ποιητικῆς . . . ἔτι δὲ κυριωτέρα περὶ τὴν ἀπεργασίαν τῶν ὄψεων ἡ τοῦ σκευοποιοῦ τέχνη τῆς τῶν ποιητῶν ἐστιν. And at 1453b 1–8 ἔστιν μὲν οὖν τὸ φοβερὸν καὶ ἐλεεινὸν ἐκ τῆς ὄψεως γίγνεσθαι, ἔστιν δὲ καὶ ἐξ αὐτῆς τῆς ουστάσεως τῶν πραγμάτων, ὅπερ ἐστὶ πρότερον καὶ ποιητοῦ ἀμείνονος . . . τὸ δὲ διὰ τῆς ὄψεως τοῦτο [pity and fear] παρασκευάζειν ἀτεχνότερον καὶ χορηγίας δεόμενόν ἐστιν. Commentators, unwilling to accept that Aristotle should be so high-handed about the entire visual presentation of tragedy, hasten to point out that the references to the σκευοποιός and the χορηγός seem to show that he is only talking about costumes and masks. ὄψις could indeed mean 'mere external trappings'.[1] But elsewhere in *Poet* Aristotle uses the word to mean 'what is seen' i.e. the entire visual aspect of the play in performance. This is most clear where ὄψις is introduced as one of the six elements of tragedy at 1449b31ff.: ἐπεὶ δὲ πράττοντες ποιοῦνται τὴν μίμησιν, πρῶτον μὲν ἐξ ἀνάγκης ἂν εἴη τι μόριον τραγωιδίας ὁ τῆς ὄψεως κόσμος. πρῶτον ἐξ ἀνάγκης shows that ὄψις here must mean 'what is seen' and cannot have a more superficial sense.[2] Aristotle is, it seems, equivocating between two senses of the word, and is exploiting the superficial sense in order to disparage the fuller sense. That he himself may have been aware of this verbal ambiguity is suggested by the recurrence of ἀτεχνότατον, ἀτεχνότερον: for the visual τέχνη of the dramatist lies not, of course, in paying for the costumes or in the carpentry or the mask-making, but in the *use* of what is seen for

---

*DFA*² 277. For the scholia see e.g. Σ on S. *Aj* 346, 815, E. *Phoen* hypoth., cf. Σ on S. *El* 1404 (καὶ τὸ φορτικὸν τῆς ὄψεως ἀπέστη); and see passages in *GGL* i 2 p. 154 n. 6.

[1] A pleasant illustration is Antiphanes fr. 327 (= Alexis fr. 340 = Men. fr. 936!): ψυχὴν ἔχειν δεῖ πλουσίαν· τὰ δὲ χρήματα / ταῦτ' ἐστὶν ὄψις, παραπέτασμα τοῦ βίου.

[2] Faith in Aristotle is so great that some are led to believe that external trappings really were the most important part of visual presentation. An example at random: Rees *G and R* 19 (1972) 10 n. 2 says ὄψις in this passage 'must be understood as referring to the visual aspect of the drama as a whole, which would for a Greek mainly be concerned with the appearance of the chorus and actors'. This virtually comes down to saying that Greek tragedy was a combination of a recitation and a costume display.

dramatic ends. The possibility of such a τέχνη is admitted when Aristotle allows in both passages that ὄψιϲ can move pity and fear. Nowhere else in *Poet* does Aristotle give due attention to all the other aspects of the visual presentation of tragedy besides those which are the contribution of the χορηγόϲ and ϲκευοποιόϲ. We must conclude that he contrives to suppress consideration of the entire visual aspect of the tragedian's work—ὄψιϲ in the full sense—by insinuating that all that the sight contributes is mere external trappings—ὄψιϲ in the superficial sense. This shiftiness is well reflected by the traditional translation 'spectacle'. For, while 'spectacle' might cover the entire dramatic use of the sight of the play in performance, it tends to draw attention to the superficially spectacular. So it is that modern critics when they consider 'visual effects' in Greek tragedy tend to look no further than a few extravagantly spectacular scenes.[1]

[1] Witness, for example, the latest commentator, Lucas, on *Poet* 1449b33, where he is hard pressed to think of four examples of Aristotelian ὄψιϲ.

BIBLIOGRAPHY

This is a bibliography of works which are cited at least three times, except for standard reference works and for commentaries on ancient authors other than Aeschylus. It also serves as a key to the citations by author or short-title, since the works are listed by the abbreviated reference. It is divided into (i) books, articles, etc., (ii) commentaries etc. on Aeschylus, (iii) a brief doxography of the study of theatrical technique.

(i) *Books, articles, etc.*

Aichele (K.)	*Die Epeisodien der griechischen Tragödie* (Diss. Tübingen 1966).
Andrieu (J.)	*Le Dialogue antique: structure et présentation* (Paris 1954. Coll. d'études lat. sér. sci. 29).
Arnott (P.)	*Greek Scenic Conventions in the Fifth Century B.C.* (Oxford 1962).
Bauformen	*Die Bauformen der griechischen Tragödie* herausg. v. W. Jens (Munich 1971. *Poetica* Beiheft 6). (Individual contributors are named in each citation.)
Bethe (E.)	*Prolegomena zur Geschichte des Theaters im Alterthum* (Leipzig 1896).
Bieber (M.) *Entrances*	'The Entrances and Exits of Actors and Chorus in Greek Plays', *AJA* 58 (1954) 277–84.
Bieber (M.) *Hist²*	*The History of the Greek and Roman Theater* (2nd ed. Princeton etc. 1961).
Bodensteiner (E.)	*Szenische Fragen über den Ort des Auftretens und Abgehens von Schauspielern und Chor im griechischen Drama* (*Jb. f. cl. Phil.* Suppbd. 19 (1893) 637ff.).
Bolle (L.)	*Die Bühne des Aeschylus* (Progr. Wismar 1906).
Burnett (A. P.)	*Catastrophe Survived, Euripides' Plays of Mixed Reversal* (Oxford 1971).
Capps (E.)	'The Greek Stage According to the Extant Dramas', *TAPA* 22 (1891) 5–80.
Croiset (M.)	*Éschyle. Études sur l'invention dramatique dans son théâtre* (Paris 1928).

Dale (A. M.) *Papers* *Collected Papers* (Cambridge 1969).

Dawe (R. D.) 'Inconsistency of Plot and Character in Aeschylus', *PCPhS* N.S. 9 (1963) 21–62.

Deckinger (H.) *Die Darstellung der persönlichen Motive bei Aischylos und Sophokles* (Diss. Tübingen, Greifwald 1911).

De Falco (V.) *Studi sul teatro greco* (2nd ed. Naples 1958. Coll. di studi gr. 28).

Detscheff (D.) *De tragoediarum Graecarum conformatione scaenica et dramatica* (Diss. Göttingen, Sofia 1904).

Dignan (F.) *The Idle Actor in Aeschylus* (Chicago 1905).

Di Gregorio (L.) *Le scene d'annuncio nella tragedia greca* (Milan 1967. Pub. Univ. catt. del S. Cuore, sag. e ric. ser. iii, sci. fil. e lett. 6).

Dingel (J.) *Das Requisit in der griechischen Tragödie* (Diss. Tübingen 1967).

Dinsmoor (W. B.) 'The Athenian Theater of the Fifth Century', *Studies Presented to D. M. Robinson* (Saint Louis 1951) i 309–30.

Dirksen (A. J.) *Die aischyleische Gestalt des Orest und ihre Bedeutung für die Interpretation der Eumeniden* (Nuremberg 1965. Erlanger Beitr. zur Spr.- u. Kunstwiss. 22).

Dodds (E. R.) *Progress* *The Ancient Concept of Progress, and Other Essays* (Oxford 1973).

Döhle (B.) 'Die "Achilleis" des Aischylos in ihrer Auswirkung auf die attische Vasenmalerei des 5. Jahrhunderts', *Klio* 49 (1967) 63–149.

Dover (K.) *Ar Com* *Aristophanic Comedy* (London 1972).

Dover (K.) *Skene* 'The Skene in Aristophanes', *PCPhS* N.S. 12 (1966) 2–17.

D–R Dörpfeld (W.) and Reisch (E.) *Das griechische Theater* (Athens 1896).

Duchemin (J.) *L'ΑΓΩΝ dans la tragédie grecque* (2ᵐᵉ éd. Paris 1968).

Easterling (P. E.) 'Presentation of Character in Aeschylus', *G and R* 20 (1973) 3–19.

Erbse (H.) 'Interpretationsprobleme in den Septem des Aischylos', *Hermes* 92 (1964) 1–22.

Fiechter (E.) *Das Dionysos-Theater in Athen* (Stuttgart 1935–50. Antike griechische Theaterbauten 5–9).

Flickinger (R. C.) *The Greak Theater and its Drama* (4th ed. Chicago 1936).

Focke (F.) 'Aischylos' Prometheus', *Hermes* 65 (1930) 259–304.

Fraenkel (E.) *Kl B* *Kleine Beiträge zur klassischen Philologie* (Rome 1964).

Fraenkel (E.) *Phoen* 'Zu den Phoenissen des Euripides', *SBAW* 1963, 1.

482 BIBLIOGRAPHY

Fraenkel (E.) *Schluss*   'Zum Schluss der Sieben gegen Theben', *MH* 21 (1964) 58–64.

Frickenhaus (A.)   *Die altgriechische Bühne* (Strasbourg 1917. Schr. d. Wiss. Ges. in Strassburg Heft 31).

Garvie (A. F.)   *Aeschylus' Supplices, Play and trilogy* (Cambridge 1969).

GGL   Schmid (W.) [and Stählin (O.)] *Geschichte der griechischen Literatur* i (Munich 1929–40. Handb. der Altertumswiss. vii 1).

Goheen (R. F.)   'Aspects of Dramatic Symbolism. Three Studies in the *Oresteia*', *AJP* 76 (1955) 113–37.

Goodell (T. D.)   'Structural Variety in Attic Tragedy', *TAPA* 41 (1910) 71–98.

Graeber (P.)   *De poetarum arte scaenica quaestiones quinque* (Diss. Göttingen 1911).

H.   See section (ii) under *Prom*.

Haigh (A. E.) *AT*[3]   *The Attic Theatre* (3rd ed. rev. Pickard-Cambridge, Oxford 1907).

Haigh (A. E.) *TDG*   *The Tragic Drama of the Greeks* (Oxford 1896).

Hammond (N. G. L.)   'The Conditions of Dramatic Production to the Death of Aeschylus', *GRBS* 13 (1972) 387–450.

Harms (C.)   *De introitu personarum in Euripide et novae comoediae fabulis* (Diss. Göttingen 1914).

Herington (C. J.) *Author*   *The Author of the Prometheus Bound* (Austin, Texas 1970).

Hermann (G.) *Opusc*   *Opuscula* (Leipzig 1827–77).

Hourmouziades (N. C.)   *Production and Imagination in Euripides. Form and Function of the Scenic Space* (Athens 1965. Gk. soc. for hum. stud. publ. ser. 2. v).

Illustrations   Trendall (A. D.) and Webster (T. B. L.) *Illustrations of Greek drama* (London 1971).

Jackson (J.)   *Marginalia scaenica* (Oxford 1955. Oxf. class. and phil. monographs).

Jens (W.)   'Strukturgesetze der frühen griechischen Tragödie', *Studium Generale* 8 (1955) 246–53.

Jobst (W.)   *Die Höhle im griechischen Theater des 5. und 4. Jahrhunderts v. Chr.* (Vienna 1970. Österreich. Akad. der Wiss. phil.-hist. Kl. Sitzungsber. 268. 2).

Joerden (K.)   *Hinterszenischer Raum und ausserszenische Zeit* (Diss. Tübingen 1960).

Jones (J.)   *On Aristotle and Greek Tragedy* (London 1962).

Kaffenberger (H.)   *Das Dreischauspielergesetz in der griechischen Tragödie* (Diss. Giessen 1911).

483

Kaimio (M.)   The Chorus of Greek Drama within the Light of the Person and Number Used (Helsinki 1970. Soc. scient. Fenn. comm. hum. litt. 46).

Kirkwood (G.)   'Eteocles Oiakostrophos', Phoenix 23 (1969) 9–25.

Knox (B. M. W.)   'Aeschylus and the Third Actor', AJP 93 (1972) 104–24.

Korzeniewski (D.)   'Studien zu den Persern des Aischylos', Helikon 6 (1966) 548–93 and 7 (1967) 27–62.

Kranz (W.)   Stasimon: Untersuchungen zu Form und Gehalt der griechischen Tragödie (Berlin 1933).

Kranz (W.) Forma   De forma stasimi (Diss. Berlin 1910).

Kranz (W.) Studien   Studien zur antiken Literatur und ihrem Nachwirken (Heidelberg 1967. Bibl. d. klass. Altertumswiss. N.F. I. 3).

Lebeck (A.)   The Oresteia. A Study in Language and Structure (Washington D.C. 1971).

Leo (F.)   'Der Monolog im Drama: ein Beitrag zur griechisch-römischen Poetik', Abh. Ges. Wiss. Göttingen phil.-hist. Kl. N.F. 10, 5 (Berlin 1908).

Lesky (A.) Ges Schr   Gesammelte Schriften (Bern etc. 1966).

Lesky (A.) TDH², TDH³   Die tragische Dichtung der Hellenen (2nd ed. Göttingen 1964, 3rd ed. 1972. Stud. zur Altertumswiss. 2).

Ll-J   See section (ii) under The Fragments.

Lloyd-Jones (H.) End   'The End of the Seven against Thebes', CQ N.S. 9 (1959) 80–115.

Lloyd-Jones (H.) Supplices   'The Supplices of Aeschylus: the New Date and Old Problems', AC 33 (1964) 356–74.

Lloyd-Jones (H.) Zeus   The Justice of Zeus (Berkeley etc. 1971. Sather Class. Lect. 41).

M   See section (ii) under The Fragments.

Macleod (C. W.)   'L'unità dell'Orestea', Maia 25 (1973) 267–92.

Müller (A.)   Lehrbuch der griechischen Bühnenalterthümer (Freiburg 1886. K. F. Hermann's Lehrb. d. gr. Ant. 3. 2).

Murray (G.)   Aeschylus: the Creator of Tragedy (Oxford 1940).

Nestle (W.)   Die Struktur des Eingangs in der attischen Tragödie (Stuttgart 1930. Tübingen Beitr. z. Altertumswiss. 10).

Neustadt (E.)   'Wort und Geschehen in Aischylos' Agamemnon', Hermes 64 (1929) 243–65.

Noack (F.)   Σκηνὴ τραγική (Tübingen 1915).

Ortkemper (H.)   Szenische Techniken des Euripides. Untersuchungen zur Gebärdensprache im antiken Theater (Diss. Berlin 1969).

Page (D. L.)   *Actors' Interpolations in Greek Tragedy* (Oxford 1934).

P-C *DFA*²   Pickard-Cambridge (A. W.) *The Dramatic Festivals of Athens* (2nd ed. rev. J. Gould and D. M. Lewis, Oxford 1968).

P-C *TDA*   Pickard-Cambridge (A. W.) *The Theatre of Dionysus in Athens* (Oxford 1946).

Peretti (A.)   *Epirrema e tragedia* (Florence 1939. Fac. di lett. e fil. ser. 3 vol. 9).

Pfeiffer (R.)   *History of Classical scholarship, from the Beginnings to the End of the Hellenistic Age* (Oxford 1968).

Pickard (J.)   'The Relative Position of Actors and Chorus in the Greek Theater of the V. Century B.C.', *AJP* 14 (1893) 68–89, 198–215, 273–304.

Pohlenz (M.) *Kl Schr*   *Kleine Schriften* (Hildesheim 1965).

Rau (P.)   *Paratragodia. Untersuchung einer komischen Form des Aristophanes* (Munich 1967. Zetemata 45).

Reinhardt (K.)   *Aischylos als Regisseur und Theologe* (Bern 1949. Samml. Überlieferung u. Auftrag Schr. 6).

Richter (P.)   *Zur Dramaturgie des Äschylus* (Leipzig 1892).

Ritchie (W.)   *The Authenticity of the Rhesus of Euripides* (Cambridge 1964).

Robert (C.)   'Die Scenerie des Aias, der Eirene und des Prometheus', *Hermes* 31 (1896) 530–77.

Rosenmeyer (T. G.)   'Gorgias, Aeschylus and ἀπάτη', *AJP* 76 (1955) 225–60.

Rutherford (W. G.)   *A Chapter in the History of Annotation, being Scholia Aristophanica vol. III* (London 1905).

Schadewaldt (W.) *HuH*²   *Hellas und Hesperien* (2. Ausg. Zürich etc. 1970).

Schadewaldt (W.) *Monolog*   *Monolog und Selbstgespräch. Untersuchungen zur Formgeschichte der griechischen Tragödie* (Berlin 1926. Neue Philol. Untersuch. 2).

Schmid (W.)   *Untersuchungen zum Gefesselten Prometheus* (Stuttgart 1929. Tübingen Beitr. zur Altertumswiss. 9).

Séchan (L.)   *Études sur la tragédie grecque dans ses rapports avec la céramique* (Paris 1926).

Shisler (F. L.)   'The Use of Stage Business to Portray Emotion in Greek Tragedy', *AJP* 66 (1945) 377–97.

Simon (E.)   *Das antike Theater* (Heidelberg 1972. Heidelberger Texte: didaktische Reihe 5).

Snell (B.) *Szenen*   *Szenen aus griechischen Dramen* (Berlin 1971).

Spitzbarth (A.)	*Untersuchungen zur Spieltechnik der griechischen Tragödie* (Zürich 1946).
Steidle (W.)	*Studien zum antiken Drama, unter besonderer Berücksichtigung des Bühnenspiels* (Munich 1968. Studia et testimonia antiqua 4).
Stephenson (R. T.)	*Some Aspects of the Dramatic Art of Aeschylus* (Diss. Stanford 1913).
Strohm (H.)	*Euripides: Interpretationen zur dramatischen Form* (Munich 1957. Zetemata 15).
Von Fritz (K.)	*Antike und moderne Tragödie* (Berlin 1962).
Webster (T. B. L.) *Chorus*	*The Greek Chorus* (London 1970).
Webster (T. B. L.) *GTP*	*Greek Theatre Production* (2nd ed. London 1970).
Webster (T. B. L.) *Preparation*	'Preparation and Motivation in Greek Tragedy', *CR* 47 (1933) 117–23.
Webster (T. B. L.) *Staging*	'Staging and Scenery in the Ancient Greek Theatre', *BRL* 42 (1959–60) 493–509.
Wecklein (N.) *Schauplatz*	'Über den Schauplatz in Aeschylus' Eumeniden und über die sogennante Orchestra in Athen', *SBAW* 1887 62–100.
Weissinger (R. T.)	*A Study of Act Divisions in Classical Drama* (Iowa 1940. Iowa stud. in class. phil. 9).
Weissmann (K.) *Anweisungen*	*Die scenischen Anweisungen in den Scholien zu . . . und ihre Bedeutung für die Bühnenkunde* (Progr. Bamberg 1896).
Weissmann (K.) *Aufführung*	*Die scenische Aufführung der griechischen Dramen des 5. Jahrhunderts* (Diss. Munich 1893).
Wilamowitz (Tycho von)	*Die dramatische Technik des Sophokles* (Berlin 1917. Philol. Untersuch. 22).
Wilamowitz (U. von)	*Aischylos. Interpretationen* (Berlin 1914).
Wilamowitz (U. von) *Analecta*	*Analecta Euripidea* (Berlin 1875).
Wilamowitz (U. von) *Einleitung*	*Einleitung in die griechische Tragödie* (3rd ed. Berlin 1921).
Wilamowitz (U. von) *Kl Schr*	*Kleine Schriften* (Berlin 1935–72).
Wilamowitz (U. von) *Perser*	'Die Perser des Aischylos', *Hermes* 32 (1897) 382–98.
Winnington-Ingram (R. P.)	'Clytemnestra and the Vote of Athena', *JHS* 68 (1948) 130–47.
Zwierlein (O.)	*Die Rezitationsdramen Senecas* (Meisenheim 1966. Beitr. zur klass. Philol. 20).

(ii) *Texts, commentaries, and translations of Aeschylus*

This handlist of works cited more than twice simply gives the place and year of publication.

All or most of the plays

Dindorf (G.)	(Oxford 1851).
'Droysen' (J. G.) *tr*	ed. Nestle (W.) (Stuttgart 1962).
Groeneboom (P.)	*Seven, Prom, Ag, Cho, Eum* (Groningen 1930–53). *Pers* (German transl. Göttingen 1960).
Headlam (W. and C. E. S.) *tr*	(London 1909).
Hermann (G.)	(Leipzig 1852; the essay *De re scenica in Aeschyli Orestea* is quoted from this edition).
Mazon (P.)	I (5me éd.), II (4me éd.) (Paris 1949).
Murray (G.) *OCT*²	(Oxford 1955).
Murray (G.) *tr*	(London 1952).
Page (D. L.) *OCT*	(Oxford 1972).
Paley (F.)	(London 1879).
Rose (H. J.)	(Amsterdam 1957–8).
Sidgwick (A.)	*Pers, Seven, Ag, Cho, Eum* (Oxford 1884–1903).
Smyth (H. W.)	(London etc. 1957).
Untersteiner (M.) *tr*	(Milan 1947).
Vellacott (P.) *tr*	(Harmondsworth 1956–61).
Wecklein (N.)	(Leipzig 1888–1902; *Appendix* quoted from the edition of Berlin 1885).
Weil (H.)	(Giessen 1858–67).
Werner (O.) *tr*	(Munich 1959).
Wilamowitz (U. von) *ed maj*	(Berlin 1914).

Pers

Broadhead (H. D.)	(Cambridge 1960).
Conradt (C.)	revision of ed. Schiller (Berlin 1888).

Seven

Arnott (P.) *tr*	(London etc. 1968).
Dawson (C. M.) *tr*	(Englewood Cliffs N.J. 1970).
Grene (D.) *tr*	(Chicago 1956).
Italie (G.)	(Leiden 1950).
Schadewaldt (W.) *tr*	(Frankfurt 1964).

Tucker (T. G.)	(Cambridge 1908).
Verrall (A. W.)	(London 1887).

Hik

Johansen (H. Friis)	I (Copenhagen 1970. *Class. et Med.* Diss vii).
Tucker (T. G.)	(London 1889).
Vürtheim (J.)	(Paris etc. 1928).

Prom

Grene (D.) *tr*	(Chicago 1956).
H.	Herington C. J. *The older scholia on the Prometheus Bound* (Leiden 1972. *Mnem.* Supp. 21).
Lowell (R.) *tr*	(London etc. 1970; 'derived from Aeschylus').
Sikes (E. E.)–Willson (J. B. W.)	(London 1898).

Oresteia

Lattimore (R.) *tr*	(Chicago 1953).
Lloyd-Jones (H.) *tr*	(Englewood Cliffs N.J. 1970).
Thomson[2] (G.)	(2nd ed. Prague etc. 1966).
Verrall (A. W.)	(London 1893–1908).
Wilamowitz (U. von) *tr*	(8. ed. Berlin 1919. *Griechische Tragödien* ii).

Ag

Campbell (A. Y.)	(Liverpool 1936).
D–P	Denniston (J. D.) and Page (D. L.) (Oxford 1957).
Fraenkel (E.)	(Oxford 1950).
Headlam (W.)	(Cambridge 1910).
Hense (O.)	revision of Schneidewin (W.) with *Anhang* (Berlin 1883).

Cho

Blass (F.)	(Halle 1906).
Tucker (T. G.)	(Cambridge 1901).
Wilamowitz (U. von) *comm*	(Berlin 1896).

Eum

Müller (K. O.)	with *Anhang* (Göttingen 1833).

The Fragments

Ll-J	Lloyd-Jones (H.) *Appendix* in vol. ii of Smyth (see above).

488 BIBLIOGRAPHY

M   Mette (H. J.) *Die Fragmente der Tragödien des Aischylos* (Berlin 1959. Deutsche Akad. zu Berlin Sekt. f. Altertumswiss. 15).

Mette (H. J.) *Verl*   *Der verlorene Aischylos* (Berlin 1963. Deutsche Akad. etc. 35).

(iii) *Doxographical note*

The roots of the study of theatrical technique go well back in nineteenth-century *Altertumswissenschaft*, particularly perhaps to K. O. Müller and G. Hermann who, for all their enmity, shared an appreciation of the fact that Greek tragedy was made to be performed. But it was the pupils of Wilamowitz and Leo who produced the first really valuable fruits from the systematic study of dramatic technique. There was a spate of interesting dissertations in the years before and during the First World War. The most promising of all was Tycho v. Wilamowitz on Sophocles: though he may have gone too far on some points he was leading the way in the right direction (for a critical appreciation see Lloyd-Jones *CQ* n.s. 22 (1972) 214ff.). His manifesto on pp. 39f. is particularly stimulating: note, for instance, '. . . the construction of the play is always arranged with a view to its proper purpose: presentation on the stage'. Between the wars this movement produced several important books (much of this work was assimilated by W. Schmid in *GGL* i 2 and i 3). One might single out Schadewaldt on monologue, Nestle on prologues, and, above all, Kranz on lyric elements. Outside Germany one might note Flickinger, Peretti, and Duchemin. The tradition has been continued by pupils of Schadewaldt and Jens at Tübingen, whose work is collected in *Bauformen* (1971). But in all this work stage action and visual techniques did not receive much direct attention. There was some useful classificatory work on acting, notably by G. Capone (*L'arte scenica degli attori tragici greci*, Padua 1935), Shisler, and Spitzbarth; but this was all done in an antiquarian way without reference to its bearing on the plays as literature.

The first book on Greek tragedy which really took notice of the dramatic significance of the play in performance was Karl Reinhardt's on Aeschylus (1949). None the less his ideas on Aeschylus as theologian have received much more attention than those on Aeschylus as stage craftsman. For nearly twenty years few followed the approach so well pioneered by Reinhardt. There were two interesting contributions by Schadewaldt, *HuH*[2] i 357ff. (1961), where he coins the phrase 'Poesie des Dinglichen', and *HuH*[2] i 483ff. (1966); and mention should be made of Goheen ('imagery of action and imagery of scene'), and of Kitto *Form and Meaning in Drama* (London 1956) who at least acknowledges 'spectacle as an expression of thought', though he notices little of it.

While I have been working on the subject there have been several substantial contributions. The most directly related have been Dingel (diss. 1967) and Steidle (1968) whose subtitle is 'Unter besonderer Berücksichtigung des Bühnenspiels' (there is an acute critique by Zwierlein

GGA 222 (1970) 196ff.). Steidle and to a lesser extent Dingel concentrate on Euripides, and most other recent work on scenic technique has been on Euripides. There are one or two good things in Ortkemper (1969, though many of his points are already in Steidle, and some others are wild); and there are some outstandingly percipient observations in Burnett (1971). Despite Reinhardt's example there has been less on Aeschylus, though the approach is occasionally put to good effect by Lebeck (1971); there has been even less on Sophocles. Yet the dramatic use of scenic techniques is not, so far as I can see, significantly more developed or more plenteous in Euripides than in the other two. All three show a sure grasp in their use of the theatre as a medium.

[*Addendum*. I am sorry I have been able to take no account of two important new books: D. Bain *Actors and Audience* (Oxford 1977) and M. Griffith *The Authenticity of* Prometheus Bound (Cambridge 1977).]

INDEXES

Heavy type signals a special discussion.

(i) *Passages in Greek Tragedy*

Most of the line references in this index refer to that line and a section of lines following. Individual lines within these sections are only singled out if they are the subject of particular discussion.

INDEX

(ii) *Other ancient authors* (*including comedy*)

(iii) *Topics, etc.*

for exits: 9–12, 163–4, 317–21, 360, 402–3, 415, 426
false: **94–6,** 144, 182–3, 342, 344, 349
lack of: 105–6, 183, 267, 305, 327
processions: 47, 72–3, 77, **127–8,** 180–1, 190–1, 234, 239, 304, 411–15
prologue, in general: 52, **62–3,** 139, 242, 246, 335, 362, **368–9,** 371–2, 418, 430
prologos **471–2,** 473–5
props, portable: 5, 15, **36–8,** 77, 99, 127, 243–5, 308, 313–15, 337 n, 358–9, 377, 391, 412–14, 420–2, 426
stage fixtures: 36, 106, 117–19, 319, 325, 377

quick changes: 215, 224, 353

rapid scenes: 227–8, 235, 345–9, **351–3,** 361
reading tragedy: **12–18,** 25, 178, 259, 477
realism: *see* imagination
Reinhardt, M.: 23, 39
reperformance of tragedy: 17, **22–4,** 29, 42, 233 n, 433, 437
ring composition: *see* symmetrical construction
roof (and *theologeion*): 253–4, 256 n, 274 n, 276–7, 420 n, **432,** 437 n, **440–1**

satyr play: 57–8, 132 n, 142 n, 195, 220, 251 n, 420–1, 426–7, 429
scene change: *see* place
scene painting: 32 n, 107, 438 n, **457 n**
scholia etc., on aesthetic matters: **22,** 368, 371 n, 477 n
authority of: 21–2, 47, 244, 254, 256 n, 353, 357, 369–70, 372, 423, **435–8,** 471, 476
separations: *see* exits
Shakespeare, W.: 11 n, 15 n, 20 n, 31 n, 34 n, 36 n, 39 n, 51, 72 n, 103, 133 n, 147 n, 149 n, 159 n, 291 n, 369
Sheridan, R.: 306 n
short acts, single-rhesis acts, etc.: 108–9, 138–9, 167–8, **301–2,** 346–7
silences, insignificant: 87, 116, 179–80, 193 n, 204–6, 214, 242, 265 n, 300 n

significant: 14, 45, 74, 281 n, **284,** 305–6, **318,** 331–2, 384, 423–4, 430
see also entrances, exits
skene (stage building), dramatic use: 71 n, 87, 151, 276–7, 310, **319–20,** 330, 349–50, 422, 455, **458–9**
late introduction of (c. 460 B.C.): 76, 105, 117, 200, 274, 323, 326, 432, 442–3, 446, **452–9**
sounds, death cries: 316–17, **323,** 335, 345, 458
off-stage heard on-stage: 71 n, 278 n, 341, 345–6, **366–7,** 371–4, 393
on-stage heard off-stage: 72, 115, 220, **281,** 335, 366, 397
spectacle (*opsis*), in general: **39–49,** 123, 150, **201–3,** 234, 258 n, 260–2, 271–2, **275,** 305, 411–12, 433, 463, **466, 477–9**
highly significant use (visual meaning): **19–20,** 100, 123–7, 191, 243, 266–7, 307, **308–16,** 321–2, 329–31, 333, 359, 383–4, 402–3, 415, 477–9, **488–9**
see also interpolation of spectacle, stage instructions
sporaden entry: *see* chorus
stage instructions, implicit signalling in text: 8, **28–31,** 37, 41, **75–9,** 135–6, 150, **159,** 235, 243, 251, 278, 280, 297, 300 n, 309, 363, 395–6, 403–7, 458
parepigraphai (explicit in text): 15, 21, 371 n, 393
stage, raised above orchestra?: 128, 414 n, 436–7, **441–2**
stasimon (choral act-dividing song): 52–3, 209 n, 472, **473–4,** 475
stichomythia: 86, 165, 188, 208–9, **242,** 323 n, **356,** 408, 418, **462–3**
story patterns: *see* plot patterns
structural technique, in general: **49–60,** 108–14, 141, 170–2, 175–6, 181, 209–10, **224–7, 245–50, 262–4,** 268, 283–4, 288–9, 301, 322, 344–7, 368–9, 377, 384–7, 408–10, 416–17, 420, **470–6**
act division without lyric: 52, 55, 172, 226–7, 377, 408–10
actor on during choral song: 54, **110–13,** 139–40, 263, 282, 288–9, 317–18, 337–8, 386–7, 391–2, **462**